COLLECTED WORKS OF ERASMUS

VOLUME 36

COLLECTED WORKS OF
ERASMUS

ADAGES

IV iii 1 to V ii 51

translated and annotated by John N. Grant and Betty I. Knott

edited by John N. Grant

University of Toronto Press
Toronto / Buffalo / London

The research and publication costs of the
Collected Works of Erasmus are supported by
University of Toronto Press.

© University of Toronto Press Incorporated 2006
Toronto / Buffalo / London
Printed in Canada

ISBN 0-8020-8832-5

Printed on acid-free paper

Canadian Cataloguing in Publication Data

Erasmus, Desiderius, d. 1536
[Works]
Collected works of Erasmus

Includes bibliographical references and index.
Contents: v. 36. Adages IV iii 1 to v ii 51 /
translated and annotated by John N. Grant and Betty I. Knott;
edited by John N. Grant.
ISBN 0-8020-8832-5 (v. 36)

1. Erasmus, Desiderius, d. 1536 – Collected works. I. Title.

PA8500 1974   199'.492   C74-006326-X rev

University of Toronto Press acknowledges the financial assistance to its
publishing program of the Canada Council and the Ontario Arts Council.

University of Toronto Press acknowledges the financial support
for its publishing activities of the Government of Canada
through the Book Publishing Industry Development Program (BPIDP).

Collected Works of Erasmus

The aim of the Collected Works of Erasmus
is to make available an accurate, readable English text
of Erasmus' correspondence and his
other principal writings. The edition is planned
and directed by an Editorial Board, an Executive Committee,
and an Advisory Committee.

Contents

Preface

The aim of this volume, which completes the translation and annotation of the *Adagia* as left by Erasmus in the final edition published in his lifetime (in 1536), is the same as that of the preceding volumes in this series (CWE 31–5). The primary object of the translators has been to provide an accurate and fluent English version of the original text, with the identification of the many sources upon which Erasmus drew. The translators are indebted to the late Sir Roger Mynors and to the editors of volumes II-7 (R. Hoven and C. Lauvergnat-Gagnière) and II-8 (Ari Wesseling) of the Amsterdam edition of the *Omnia opera* of Erasmus (ASD). Before his death Sir Roger had worked his way through the whole work, and left behind photocopied pages of the Leiden edition of 1703–6 (LB), on which he had identified almost all of the references and marked the expansions and changes that occurred in the eight editions of the *Adagia* that followed the first one in 1508. The annotation in the two volumes of the Amsterdam edition has also been valuable, but this has been abbreviated in some respects and supplemented in others to suit the interests of the translators and the readers for whom this series is intended. Betty Knott wishes to acknowledge the unstinting help and advice given by Olivia F. Robinson, Douglas Professor Emeritus of Roman Law at the University of Glasgow, in the interpretation and translation of the numerous legal texts drawn on by Erasmus in *Adagia* IV viii, IV ix, and V ii.

For this volume the translation and annotation have been shared between John N. Grant (the first five centuries) and Betty I. Knott (the second half, comprising the last 451 adages). No attempt has been made to impose a rigid homogeneity of style, but each contributor has read, commented on, and benefited from the other's work. Because of this the translations in the two sections are more similar in style than they might have been. Annotation has been confined for the most part to the identification of Erasmus' sources and to how adages were expanded in successive editions. Biographical information of persons mentioned by Erasmus is brief, and for information on his sources readers should consult the introductory volume on the *Adagia* (CWE 30).

This volume differs from the five preceding ones in the series in that almost all the adages it contains made their first appearance subsequent to the 1508 edition.[1] Only the first 65 (including IV iii 29A) and another 11, scattered among new adages, were in that first edition. The major expansions occurred in the editions of 1515 and 1533. In the former the expansion starts at IV iii 65 of the adages translated here, and stretches to IV v 9, interrupted occasionally by adages from the 1508 edition. In the edition of 1533 almost 500 adages made their first appearance (IV vi 19; IV vii 59–V ii 46, excluding IV x 65). In the final edition prepared by Erasmus (1536) there are only five new adages (v ii 47–51), and the work ends abruptly without any sense of closure, as had been true of all editions after that of 1526; for that was the last of the editions to end with 'A Dutch ear' (now IV vi 35; see introductory note, 235 below), an adage on his fellow Hollanders that Erasmus concluded with a modest remark, more conventional than sincere, about his own talents.

JNG / BIK

* * * * *

1 For discussion of the growth of the *Adagia* in the editions subsequent to the 1508 edition, see Phillips part I.

ADAGES

IV iii 1 to V ii 51

1 Vita molita
Living on milled fare

Ἀληλεσμένος βίος, Living on milled fare, or to put it another way, Food made of flour. Suidas points out that the proverb is understood in different ways.[1] Some, he says, apply the expression to the life of early man who fed on acorns, perhaps because the eating of meat and fish was still unknown at that period and humans ate only meal made from acorns. Others refer it to those who enjoyed a luxurious life-style free of toil, since the process of making flour was not known for some time after the discovery of wheat. Flour is readily available to whoever wants to eat it, but the earth must be ploughed, the wheat must be sown, harvested, winnowed, ground, and pounded. Others, he adds, apply the proverb to those who lived their lives enjoying a plentiful supply of what they wanted. This would be close in sense to the proverb 'No more thorns' that appears elsewhere in this work.[2]

Caesar in the first book of his *Commentaries* writes, 'They ordered each man to bring for himself from his home a three-month supply of ground wheat.'[3]

* * * * *

1 *Suda* (see n1); also Zenobius (Aldus) column 20; Zenobius 1.21; Diogenianus 1.17; Apostolius 2.15. Tilley A 21 Acorns were good till bread was found. A very brief version of this adage appeared in *1508* as the fifteenth in the third chiliad, entitled *Macerata vita* (see n5). When it was moved here in *1515*, the commentary was considerably expanded into what is now the first paragraph, thus providing a fairly substantial adage to introduce a century, a recurring feature of the *Adagia*. The second paragraph was added in *1526*, and the rest (from 'Aristophanes seems') did not appear until *1533*. Aristophanes was one of the sources on whom Erasmus particularly drew in *1533* (there are 15 citations from the *Knights* in that edition).

1 *Suda* A 1183, the reference being added in *1515*. The *Suda*, which means 'treasure-house' or 'fortress,' came down to us under the title 'Suidas.' Until quite recent times this title was thought to be the name of the author of the work, which is an alphabetical compilation of words, places, and antiquities in general. Erasmus always uses 'Suidas' as the author's name. In the footnotes the title will be given in the form *Suda*. For some of the information given in the first few sentences Erasmus may have drawn on Zenobius (Aldus) column 20 in *1508*.

2 *Adagia* II ix 81

3 Caesar *Bellum Gallicum* 1.5.3

Aristophanes seems to allude to this proverb in the *Knights* when Cleon, trying to win over People, says, 'But I shall give you barley meal, already made.' Another character responds to this by saying, 'I shall give you barley cakes, already baked, and fish, already cooked. Do nothing but eat.'[4] The last part relates to the proverb we have reported before, 'Living softly.'[5] Again, in the same play when Cleon offered barley scones, the other counters, 'I'll give you bread scoops,' meaning bread that had already been softened and moistened with gravy and was therefore ready to be eaten.[6] Then he offers wine, already mixed so that it could be drunk immediately. He says, 'Take this wine, mixed three to two.'[7] In antiquity wine was not drunk unless it had been diluted (not a German custom), and in fact the best dilution was thought to be two parts water to two parts wine.[8] A little later, People declares that he prefers food already prepared. For when Cleon boasted that he had stolen at great personal risk what he was giving and the other character said that he had cooked his offering, People says to Cleon, 'Be off with you. I favour him who has served it up.'[9] He meant that he had to support the one who placed before him food ready to eat.

* * * * *

4 Aristophanes *Knights* 1104–6. At this point in the comedy Paphlagon (who represents Cleon, an Athenian politician) and the Sausage Seller, here not identified as such by Erasmus but referred to as 'the other,' are in a contest to win the support of the character Demos, to whom Erasmus refers here as simply *populus* 'the people,' without making it clear initially that the people are represented by a character in the play. Erasmus' failure to identify Cleon's opponent as a sausage seller (ἀλλαντοπώλης) may arise, as ASD II-7 143 suggests, from a misunderstanding of this character's designation in the text of the early editions (ΑΛΛ). Erasmus may have taken this as an abbreviation for ἄλλος (= *alius* 'other').

5 *Adagia* I viii 63, virtually a doublet of this adage, but much shorter

6 Aristophanes *Knights* 1168. Here Erasmus gives only the Greek without a Latin translation.

7 Aristophanes *Knights* 1187

8 Cf *Adagia* II iii 1 Drink either five or three or anything but four, where the proportions of water to wine are discussed more fully.

9 Aristophanes *Knights* 1205. Erasmus follows the text of the manuscripts for the preceding line. Most modern editions give the whole line to Paphlagon (= Cleon), who thus claims that he had also cooked his offering. But even so, People still gives preference to his opponent.

2 Malum est bonum
A blessing can be a bane

Κακὸν τὸ καλὸν ἤν τι μὴ καιροῦ τύχῃ, A blessing can be a bane if it is not received at the proper time. Nothing that is untimely is pleasing. If given at the proper time, a drug brings recovery; if not, it brings death. In book seven Athenaeus cites this verse from Timon: 'There's a time to love, a time to wed, a time to end all that.'[1]

3 Caricum sepulcrum
A Carian tomb

Καρικὸς τάφος, A Carian monument. Said of a splendid and costly object. Derived from the tomb of Mausolus in Caria.[1] Pliny in book thirty-six, chapter five, says that this was thought of as one of the seven wonders of the world, particularly because of the fame of the artists who worked on it:

> On the north and south side it stretched for sixty-three feet. The facades are not so long, the complete perimeter being four hundred and eleven feet.[2] It rose to a height of twenty-five cubits and was enclosed by forty-six columns. The east side was carved by Scopas, the north by Bryax, the south by Timotheus and the west by Leochares.[3]

* * * * *

2 Apostolius 9.57, resuming a series of adages drawn from this proverb collection (IV ii 80–IV iii 100) and continuing until IV iii 10. The third sentence was added in 1517/18 and the reference to Athenaeus in 1528.
1 Athenaeus 7.281E, citing PPF Timon of Phlius fragment 17

3 Apostolius 9.53. The section on Pliny was added in 1515, and the remainder in 1526.
1 Mausolus was satrap of Caria, who died in 353 BC.
2 Erasmus' figure for the length of the complete perimeter, like that in Pliny's text (440 feet), does not agree with the measurements he has given for the sides. The actual measurements of the sides of the tomb were 127 and 108 feet. In modern texts of Pliny the number of columns is thirty-six, and the name of the sculptor of the north side is Bryaxis.
3 Pliny Naturalis historia 36.30–1. There are three main systems of enumerating the sections and sub-sections of the books of Pliny's Natural History (all

Artemisia died before it was completed.[4] In Latin such monuments are called *mausolea*: so Martial in book one, 'the Mausoleum poised on empty air,' and Propertius in his third book, 'not the sumptuousness of the tomb of Mausolus.'[5]

4 Malum munus
A bad gift is as good as a loss

Κακόν γε δῶρον ἴσον ἐστὶ ζημίᾳ, A gift is evil in proportion to the losses it causes. Those who give a harmful gift do not help, but cause damage; for example, if anyone were to supply a young man with money, or entrust a position of authority to a fool or a priesthood to an uneducated man.

5 Inani spe flagrat
Burning with empty hopes

Κεναῖσιν ἐλπίσι θερμαίνεται, He is ablaze with empty hopes. Of a man who futilely promises himself great things. For hope gives courage to the foolish, even if their aspirations are very far from being realized. Even if he has hopes, the wise person conceals them. It is clearly taken from Sophocles, where Ajax says this: 'I would not buy a foolish man who is spurred on

* * * * *

indicated in the Teubner edition of Ian-Mayhoff). Erasmus' reference here to chapter 5 reflects one of these, a system that is not noted in most editions and is not followed in this volume. The numeration of the sub-sections here agrees with the numeration of the sub-sections in the Loeb edition of Pliny.

4 Artemisia, the wife of Mausolus, died in 353 BC. Erasmus is paraphrasing Pliny in this sentence.

5 Martial *Liber spectaculorum* 1.5 and Propertius 3.2.21

4 Apostolius 9.58, which Erasmus has expanded to create an iambic trimeter. Cf *Adagia* I iii 35 Gifts of enemies are no gifts. The last part of Erasmus' discussion ('or entrust' to the end) was added in *1515*.

5 Apostolius 9.67. 'For hope ... realized' was added in *1517/18*; what follows this was added in *1528*.

by empty hopes.'[1] Aeschines in *Against Timarchus*: 'After filling him with empty hopes.'[2]

6 Volvitur dolium
A barrel rolls easily

Κεκύλισται ὁ πίθος, The barrel is rolled. Said of those who are stirred to do some foolish action, following the example or instigation of others. For a barrel can be rolled to where you want it to go by the slightest push. The wise man, however, is like a cube, always fixed and unmoveable.[1] The proverb clearly originated in the story of how Diogenes rolled a barrel at a time of civic turmoil. Lucian tells this story in *How History Should Be Written*.[2]

7 Ceram auribus obdis
Your ears are stopped with wax

Κηρὸν τοῖς ὠσὶν ἐπαλείφεις, You stop up your ears with wax. Said of those who refuse to listen to anything, good or bad. Its origin is the story in Homer of how Ulysses blocks up his and his companions' ears with wax to counteract the enchanting song of the Sirens.[1]

* * * * *

1 Sophocles *Ajax* 477–8. Erasmus mistranslates the Greek, which means 'I would not buy at any cost a man who burns with empty hopes.' He also changes the metaphor in his Latin translation.
2 Aeschines 1.171

6 Apostolius 9.74. 'For a barrel . . . unmoveable' was added in *1515*; what follows this was added in *1520*.
1 Cf *Adagia* IV viii 35 A four-square man (378 below); v ii 39 To square up (623 below).
2 Lucian *Quomodo historia conscribenda sit* 3. While all the Corinthians were busy preparing for war, Diogenes rolled his barrel up and down a hill so that he would not appear to be idle.

7 Apostolius 9.77
1 Homer *Odyssey* 12.173–7. But in Homer only Odysseus' companions have their ears stopped with wax. The final sentence is an expansion of *1515*. In *1508* it simply read 'it originated with the wax of Ulysses.'

8 Corvi lusciniis honoratiores
Crows are more revered than nightingales

Κόρακες ἀηδόνων αἰδεσιμώτεροι, Crows are more revered than nightingales. Used when ignorance is preferred to erudition, wickedness to honesty, blethering nonsense to eloquence, or when plunderers and thieves are preferred to those who are prudent and are of impeccable character; or when more respect is given to wickedness and shameless behaviour than to erudition and wisdom.

9 Commune naufragium
A shipwreck shared

Κοινὸν ναυάγιον τοῖς πᾶσι παραμύθιον, A shipwreck shared is consolation to all. We bear a misfortune much more easily if it is common to all or shared with many. Why, even today we hear the scholastics say, 'It is poor consolation to have a companion in disaster.'[1]

10 Cyparissi fructus
The fruit of the cypress

Κυπαρίττου καρπός, The fruit of the cypress. Applied to fine-sounding, but useless words. The proverb has come from the nature of the tree, which

* * * * *

8 Apostolius 9.90. Also used by Gregory of Nazianzus in *Epistolae* 12 (PG 37 44C). Expansion occurred in *1515* ('blethering ... eloquence'), in *1517/18* ('or when plunderers ... character'), and *1528* ('or when more' to the end).

9 Apostolius 9.96. The final sentence was added in *1533*.
1 This is a sarcastic jibe against the adherents of scholasticism, who were often criticized by Erasmus and other humanists as being out of date, irrelevant, and unreceptive to the revival of the study of classical texts. In particular many of them rejected the application of the philological methods of the humanists to sacred texts. See J. Farge 'Erasmus, the University of Paris, and the Profession of Theology' ERSY 19 (1999) 78–46, especially 39–44. For a contemporary German proverb see Suringar 42.

10 Apostolius 10.20. Tilley C 945 Like cypress trees that have fair leaves but no fruit

Pliny says in book sixteen 'grows grudgingly, has useless fruit, astringent berries, bitter-tasting leaves, a strong smell, and does not even afford agreeable shade'; so Pliny.[1] Although it has these features, it always
seems to promise some new fruit, because of its great height (which is why
it is called 'cone-bearing' by poets) and its continuous greenness, and especially because of the slowness of its growth.[2] In book one of *Causes of Plants*
Theophrastus writes:

> The seed of the cypress is so tiny that it can scarcely be seen. For its seed
> is not the whole fruit, which looks like a ball, but is what grows in the
> cone, being extremely thin and narrow (very like the seed of a larch tree),
> and when the ball splits open the seed slips out; an expert is needed to
> gather it.[3]

11 Ματτυάζειν
To eat mattya

Athenaeus in book fourteen of the *Doctors at Dinner* tells of a kind of
food that was first discovered by the Thessalians but which was also a
favourite in Athens when the city was under the control of the Macedo-
nians.[1] This food was called ματτύα in their language, from the Greek
word μάττω, meaning 'to pound' or 'to soften.' It was then also called

* * * * *

1 Pliny *Naturalis historia* 16.139
2 The logical connection between the epithet 'cone-bearing' and the tree's height
  is difficult to see. The adjective is rare, being used by Virgil at *Aeneid* 3.680 (see
  Servius' commentary on the passage), Nemesianus *Eclogues* 2.86, and Claudian
  De raptu Proserpinae 1.205.
3 Theophrastus *De causis plantarum* 1.5.4: there is no reference to the seed of
  a larch tree in the original Greek. Erasmus gives only a Latin version of
  Theophrastus here, one based on that of Theodore of Gaza (1400–75). Theodore
  was an important Greek scholar who lived in Italy in the middle of the fifteenth century. His translations of Aristotle and Theophrastus were used in
  the Aldine editions of these authors.

11 This adage first appeared in *1520* with additions in *1528*, the major ones being
  'In support ... means "skin" in Greek' and 'In book four ... ἐπάϊκλα.'
1 Athenaeus 14.662F–663D. Erasmus closely follows Athenaeus down to 'excessively in sex.'

μάζα, and this too gave rise to a proverb: those who lived rather luxuriously were said Ὑπερμαζᾶν 'To eat too much barley-bread.'[2] Later, the
name ματτύα was given to every kind of food that was rich and luxurious, including fowl, fish, vegetables, and stuffings, and those who
enjoyed this very pleasant way of life were said Ματτυάζειν 'To be
mattya-eaters.' In support are cited verses from Alexis: 'Make prepara-
tions, set to the feast, λέπεσθε "husk nuts," and eat *mattya*.'[3] But in Attic Greek λέπεσθαι is a verb used of those who indulge excessively in
sex. This alludes, if I am not mistaken, to the fact that λεπίζω means
deglubo 'peel off,' a word that has acquired an obscene meaning in
Latin also;[4] for λέπος means 'skin' in Greek. Anyone who wishes to discover more about *mattya* should read the end of book fourteen, which
I have just cited. He will have his fill and more of *mattya*, so many
sources does Athenaeus use to explain the meaning. In book four he
also tells us that among the Spartans a dessert was called ματτύη.[5] This
was served at the end of an αἶκλον, a form of banquet, and these were
also called ἐπάικλα. Martial mentions this food in book nine: 'Only *mattya*
delight.'[6]

* * * * *

2 *Adagia* II vi 77, at the end of which there is a reference to Athenaeus and the
  verb ματτυάζειν
3 PCG 2 Alexis fragment 50. Erasmus' translation is quite free. He coins a Latin
  verb *lepari* to translate λέπεσθε. The verb sometimes denoted the idea of 'peel-
  ing' or 'flaying.' It probably had an obscene meaning in the fragment of Alexis.
  See W. Geoffrey Arnott *Alexis: The Fragments. A Commentary* (Cambridge 1996)
  170–71.
4 See Ausonius *Epigrams* 79.7, with the notion of masturbation. Cf Catullus 58.5
  where *glubit* is used to describe Lesbia's sexual activities with a host of men.
  See J.N. Adams *The Latin Sexual Vocabulary* (Baltimore 1990) 168.
5 Athenaeus 4.141D
6 Martial 10.59.4. Erasmus added 'in book nine' in 1520. The error may
  have arisen from the use of an edition in which the beginning of book
  ten was not indicated, as happens in some editions (for example the 1485
  Venice edition of Baptista de Tortis). Or it may be just an error of Erasmus. Modern editions read *mattea* and *iuvat* (singular) for *mattya* and *iu-
  vant* (plural). Erasmus' text is in agreement with that of the Aldine edition
  of 1501.

12 Ματιολοιχός
Matioloechus

Used as a common term of abuse for a gourmand and someone who was very fastidious about even the most trivial of things.[1] Hesychius actually points out that μάτιος means 'insignificant' in Greek.[2] It is said to be a type of food. In the Greek *Collections* I find that μάτιος either means 'very small' or is a type of measurement.[3] Therefore ματιολοιχός fits those who try to save themselves money in even the most trivial things by cheating, being from μάτιος and λοχεῦσαι 'to produce, give birth,'[4] unless you prefer to

* * * * *

12 Apostolius 11.9, drawing very much on *Suda* M 284. Part of the explanation given at the beginning of the essay seems to be Erasmus' own. Both in Apostolius and the *Suda* we are told that the term 'was applied to those who were dishonest about trifling things and gluttonous.' Another series of adages drawn from Apostolius begins here (down to *Adagia* IV iii 18).

1 'Gourmand' is a translation of the very rare word *liguritor*, which literally means 'licker.' Erasmus probably used it to translate λίχνος, meaning 'gluttonous' and related to λείχειν 'to lick.' The verb *ligurire* appears not to have a pejorative meaning (which it must have here) at Terence *Eunuchus* 936, where it is usually taken to mean 'to eat daintily.' In *Adagia* v i 60 Your own slice pie (576 below) Erasmus glosses the verb as *gustare cum voluptate* 'to eat with enjoyment.'

2 Hesychius M 401. This sentence was added in 1520. The Aldine edition of Hesychius appeared in 1514; see CWE 31 11 n35. However, Erasmus did not make extensive use of the lexicon until more than a decade later, for the edition of 1526 and subsequent editions. For example, Hesychius is the sole source for *Adagia* IV v 97, IV v 98, and IV vi 15 (all first appearing in 1526) and for VI vi 44 (first appearing in 1528).

3 Instead of the more usual term *Collectanea*, Erasmus uses here, as elsewhere (see *Adagia* IV iii 57 A river does not always bring axes, 34–5 below), *Commentaria* in the sense 'collections.' Here he is referring to the proverb collections of Apostolius, who gives the two meanings indicated here.

4 Erasmus here confuses the Greek verbs λοχᾶν 'to ambush, try to capture' and λοχεύειν 'to produce, beget,' thinking, as the reference to cheating suggests, that the latter has the meaning of the former. Apostolius and the *Suda* derive ματιολοιχός from λοχᾶν, to which Erasmus gives the meaning 'plot against.' The alternative derivation from λείχειν was added in 1515.

derive the second part from λείχειν 'to lick.' Aristophanes uses the word in the *Clouds* in a list of many epithets that he applies to a scoundrel.[5] The scholiast explains it in several different ways, saying that the word is used of those who give short measure or of those who are mean and miserly, or of those who have silly ideas or who collect worthless objects – a sufficiently clear admission of his ignorance.

13 Post Marathonem pugna
Another battle follows Marathon

Μετὰ τὴν Μαραθῶνα μάχη, Another battle follows Marathon. Used when after one dangerous situation someone encounters another new one. Marathon is a place in Attica, famous for many disasters. A very fierce battle with the Persians took place there. Herodotus tells of it in book six.[1] Similar to this is the proverb Μετὰ πόλεμον ταραχή 'After war there is upheaval.'[2]

14 Ne vities musicam
Don't ruin the music

Μὴ κακούργει τὴν μουσικήν, Don't ruin the music. This means that you should not say discordant words or try new-fangled things. Plutarch relates in his 'Sayings of Spartans' that Emerepes said this when he cut off two of the nine strings on the instrument of Phrynis, a musician, because he thought that seven were sufficient.[1]

* * * * *

5 Aristophanes *Clouds* 451 with the scholion on the passage. This sentence and the next one were added in *1526*.

13 Apostolius 11.30, whose explanation Erasmus follows. Also in *Suda* M 739. 'Marathon is a place ... book six' was added in *1515*.
1 Herodotus 6.102–17
2 This proverb is also mentioned by Apostolius in a slightly different form, 'After war there is upheaval or a treaty.'

14 Apostolius 11.38. Cf Erasmus *Apophthegmata* I 175 (LB IV 115C–D).
1 Plutarch *Moralia* 220c *Apophthegmata Laconica*; cf *Agis* 10.7. Modern editions name the character Ekprepes. The story appeared in *1508*, but Erasmus did not identify its source until *1526*. His original source was Apostolius.

15 Astutior coccyce
As crafty as a cuckoo

Μηχανικώτερος κόκκυκος, Craftier than a cuckoo. Said of those who shrewdly looked after their own interests. Taken from the nature of the bird, which lays its eggs in other birds' nests, especially those of doves. Pliny and Aristotle describe it in great detail.[1]

16 Hesperidum mala
The apples of the Hesperides

Μῆλα Ἑσπερίδων δωρῆσαι, To give the apples of the Hesperides as a gift. Said of someone giving splendid and magnificent presents. The story of the golden apples is well known. Our Maro seems to allude to it in his *Eclogue*: 'I have sent ten golden apples, I shall send you another ten tomorrow.'[1]

17 Solae Lacaenae viros pariunt
Only Spartan women produce men

Μόναι Λάκαιναι ἄνδρας τίκτουσι, Only Spartan women produce men. The strongest men were born in Sparta, where mothers brought up their sons very strictly. The origin of the proverb is an apophthegm of Gorgo, the Spartan wife of Leonidas.[1] When a foreign women said to her, 'Only you Spartan women hold sway over men,' Gorgo replied, 'Yes,

* * * * *

15 Apostolius 11.39. Minor additions were made in *1515* ('which lays ... nests') and *1533* ('especially those of doves').
1 Pliny *Naturalis historia* 10.25–7; Aristotle *Historia animalium* 6.7 (563b–564a) and 9.29 (618a)

16 Apostolius 11.57
1 Virgil *Eclogues* 3.71; the reference to Virgil and the quotation were added in *1515*.

17 Apostolius 11.78. 'The origin' to the end was added in *1526*, the Latin translations of the Greek passages being added, however, in *1528*.
1 Plutarch *Moralia* 227E *Apophthegmata Laconica*; Erasmus *Apophthegmata* I 268 (LB IV 126F)

for only we produce men.' The story is told by Plutarch in his *Life of Lycurgus.*[2]

18 Myrteam coronam ambis
You want a crown of myrtle

Μυρρινοῦν, To want myrtle. Said of some one seeking to be king or magistrate. For in antiquity, if we believe Suidas, leading men of the state were crowned with myrtle wreaths.[1]

19 Praevertit ancorae iactum Deus
God forestalls the dropping of the anchor

Ἀλλ' ἀντέπεσε τὴν ἐπ' ἄγκυραν θεός, But God acts before the anchor is dropped. Said when something happens unexpectedly. It comes from sailing. When sailors are preparing to drop anchor as they are about to put into port, their ships are often driven back by the winds and pulled back into the middle of a storm.

20 Pro Delo Calauria
Calauria for Delos

Ἀντὶ Δήλου τὴν Καλαυρίαν, Calauria for Delos. There is a story that Poseidon made an exchange with Leto: she gave him the island of Calauria and in

* * * * *

2 Plutarch *Lycurgus* 14.4

18 Apostolius 11.86 was Erasmus' original source. In *1508* the adage read Μυρρινῶν ἐπιθυμεῖς 'You want myrtle.' For *1515* and subsequent editions he followed the *Suda* (M 1438) in taking the first word to be the participle of a verb μυρρινοῦν rather than the genitive plural of a noun. In the *Suda* the meaning is explained as 'desiring office.'
1 *Suda* M 1438. The words 'if we believe Suidas' were added in *1515*.

19 Zenobius (Aldus) column 24 (= *Suda* A 1066), from whom the whole explanation of the adage is taken

20 *Collectanea* no 694 (*Calauriam insulam*), but this expression was very briefly explained there.

return took possession of Delos; for giving him Taenaros she received Pytho. Calauria is a small island not far from Crete.[1] In his 'Corinthian Matters' Pausanias tells us that Calauria was once sacred to Apollo, and Delos to Neptune, and that they exchanged these places.[2] Strabo too mentions this in book eight. He says:

> Troezen was sacred to Poseidon (that is, Neptune). Consequently it was once called Posidonia. It occupies an elevated site about fifteen stades from the sea. The town itself is quite important. Near its port, called Pogon, lies Calauria, a small island, thirty stades in circumference. Here there was a sanctuary sacred to Neptune. The story is that this god made exchanges with Latona and Apollo. He received Calauria in return for Delos, and Taenarus for Pytho. Ephorus reports an actual oracle: 'It makes no difference whether you live on Delos or Calauria, or on lofty Pythos or windy Taenarus.'[3]

This was used proverbially whenever 'one hand washed the other' and one service was repaid by another.[4]

21 Antiquior Codro
As old as Codrus

Πρεσβύτερος Κόδρου, Older than Codrus. About things that are ancient and worthy of admiration because of this. Codrus was a very ancient king of Attica whom we have mentioned elsewhere.[1] Those who wished to be thought of as noble traced back their family to him.

* * * * *

1 Calauria is an island situated near Troezen. Erasmus is following Stephanus of Byzantium (sub Καλαύρεια) in locating it near Crete.
2 Pausanias 2.33.2
3 Strabo *Geographica* 8.6.14; the quotation from Ephorus, cited by both Pausanias and Strabo, is *FGrHist* 70 F 150. Erasmus takes the rest of the essay from Strabo, apart from the final sentence. Strabo reads 130 stades, not 30 as in Erasmus' translation.
4 Cf *Adagia* I i 33 One hand rubs another.

21 Zenobius (Aldus) column 145; Apostolius 14.73; *Suda* Π 2258
1 *Adagia* II viii 33 As nobly born as Codrus. He is also mentioned in IV i 46 Since Nannacus, and III iii 1 The Sileni of Alcibiades (CWE 34 269).

22 **Hirundo totos schoenos anteibit**
A swallow will be miles ahead

Πρόσω τις χελιδῶν ὅλους σχοίνους παρεῖται, A swallow will be miles ahead.
Said when anyone wins by a huge margin; for σχοῖνος is a Greek measure that is equivalent to sixty stades, as Herodotus thinks in book two.[1]
Hermogenes also informs us of this in his essay entitled *On the Method of
Cleverness*, pointing out that it is an Egyptian word, just as *parasang* is a
Persian one.[2] Pliny, however, in book twelve, chapter fourteen, attributes
forty stades to the *schoenus*, thus making it a distance of five miles. In book
five, chapter ten, he writes that a *schoenus* is thirty stades in length.[3] The
difference seems to have arisen by a scribal error.

I suspect, however, that in this expression χελιδών 'swallow' should be
understood to be the name of a man, mentioned elsewhere, who probably
was outstanding as a fast runner.[4]

23 **Nihili cocio est**
Haggling brings no money

Plautus in *Comedy of Asses*: 'It's an old saying, haggling is worth nothing.'[1]
It seems to be said about those who make promises for the future and do
not offer ready cash. Gellius tells of Laberius using the very vulgar word

* * * * *

22 Drawn from Zenobius (Aldus) column 146 where the proverb is given in a
   different form (ὁλοσχοίνους, meaning 'rushes,' for ὅλους σχοίνους, which is
   probably an emendation of Erasmus, made without explanation). Zenobius'
   text gives no sense – 'a swallow passes by rushes.' The final sentence was
   added in 1515. 'So Hermogenes ... scribal error' is an addition of 1526.
 1 Herodotus 2.6.3
 2 Spengel 2.427
 3 Pliny *Naturalis historia* 12.53 and 5.53. For the chapter numbers given by Erasmus see on IV iii 3 n3 (5–6 above).
 4 Chelidon is mentioned at *Adagia* IV ii 53 Listen to Chelidon, though there he
   is a prophet.

23 *Collectanea* no 376. Otto 402
 1 Plautus *Asinaria* 203, where modern editions read *coactiost, coactio* meaning
   'collection' (that is, of money). The sense of the Plautine passage would then
   be 'there's no chance of collecting – you know what!'

cocio for what the early Romans called *ariolator* 'haggler.'² In Plautus the expression is spoken by a bawd who declared that her hands had eyes and
that they only believed what they saw. Others read *coactio*, but this is inadmissible metrically unless one elides the vowel [*co'ctio*]. From Festus Pompeius one can pretty well conjecture that *coctio* should be read.³ For he says
that *coctiones* 'hagglers' received their name from *cunctatio* 'delaying' because when they were buying or selling merchandise they were very slow
in finally reaching the proper price. Accordingly, the ancients customarily
spelled the first syllable *cu–* and not *co–*. This is supported, I believe, by
what Seneca writes in book eleven of the *Letters*, arguing that one should
not refrain from helping people because one sometimes encounters an ungrateful person.

> Even after a bad harvest one must sow. Often the rich harvest of one year
> restores all that had been lost through the persistent barrenness of infertile
> soil. It is worthwhile experiencing ungrateful persons to find someone who is
> grateful. No one has such a sure hand that he is not often deceived. Let them
> wander so that they may get stuck sometimes. After shipwrecks, the seas are
> put to the test again. A moneylender does not flee the forum because he sees
> a *coactor* 'debt-collector' there. We shall soon waste away in idle leisure if we
> avoid whatever harms us.⁴

So much for Seneca. I leave it to scholars to decide whether or not
coactor should be read in this place.⁵

From the etymology we should read *cuntio* or *cunctio*, or, with a change
of letter, *contio*, if Festus Pompeius did not point out that *coctio* and *cocio*
are the same.⁶ On the word *arulator* he agrees with Gellius, saying that *cotio*
means the same as *arulator*: '*arulator* is derived from the Greek αἶρε "pick

* * * * *

2 Aulus Gellius *Noctes Atticae* 16.7.12. In Erasmus' discussion there is confusion of *ariolator* – an agent noun related to *(h)ariolari* 'to prophesy' or 'to talk
  nonsense' – and *arulator*, the reading in the 1515 Aldine edition of Gellius, to
  which he refers in the final sentence. Modern editions of Gellius read *arillator*
  'haggler.'
3 Pompeius Festus 44.15–18 Lindsay
4 Seneca *Letters* 81.1-2
5 Most modern editions do not read *coactor*, preferring *coctor* or *decoctor* 'a
  bankrupt, swindler.'
6 Pompeius Festus 19.1–4 Lindsay

up" because he follows merchandise so as to pick up anything of value from whatever is dropped.'

24 Non navigas noctu
You are not sailing at night

Οὐ νυκτὶ πλοεῖς, You are not sailing at night. About a person who is not at all sure what course of action to follow. The reason is that sailors navigate more accurately at night-time, because of the stars, about which I have spoken elsewhere.[1] Chrysippus is said to have removed the negative, saying Νυκτὶ πλοεῖς 'You are sailing at night,' though the sense, in my opinion, remains the same.[2] For why else should it have been mentioned here that Chrysippus had given the proverb without the negative? Surely both expressions are equally valid. And indeed, although the stars guide sailors at night, navigation is much more accurate during the day.

25 Mores hominum regioni respondent
Human character matches habitat

Καὶ τῶν φυτῶν τὰ σπέρματα καὶ τῶν ἀνθρώπων οἱ βίοι ταῖς χώραις συνεξομοιοῦνται, Both the seeds of plants and the lifestyles of humans match their habitat. This is also included in the *Collections* of Greek proverbs.[1]

* * * * *

24 Zenobius (Aldus) column 137 = Zenobius 5.32, whom Erasmus follows down to 'You are sailing at night.' Cf also Apostolius 13.39 and Diogenianus 7.20.
  1 See *Adagia* III v 42 To go by the stars.
  2 Chrysippus was a third-century philosopher who, when head of the Stoa, established much of Stoic orthodoxy. As the final sentence of the essay suggests, the sense that Erasmus ascribes to Chrysippus would be something like 'you are wandering in the dark.' Ἐν νυκτὶ πλοεῖς is to be found in Zenobius (Aldus) column 82, with virtually the same explanation as that given for the negative form of the expression.

25 Zenobius (Aldus) column 54 (= Apostolius 4.96), though with different word order. 'For my part ... in which they live' is an addition of *1517/18*. All that follows this addition first appeared in *1523*.
  1 Erasmus is probably referring to the Aldine edition of Zenobius published in 1505 (see introductory note and n2 of the previous adage).

Otherwise I would not have included it.[2] For my part I think that it originates in an apophthegm that Plutarch mentions.[3] Just as grain degenerates into a different strain in some fields, because of the fault of the soil, so the natural disposition of humans varies according to the region in which they live. Mountain people are generally rough and cruel. Those who live by the sea are usually larcenous and pitiless. Plain-dwellers are gentle and kind. Herodotus, at the end of his final book, quite clearly states that this saying originated in a reply given by Cyrus to the Persians.[4] After they acquired their empire, the Persians asked to be moved from the wild region in which they were then living to a more pleasant and more fruitful one. Cyrus granted their request, but he warned them to prepare after that to be slaves instead of rulers: 'Soft men spring from soft lands. For the same land cannot produce both rich harvests and outstanding warriors.'

26 Cum cane simul et lorum
The leash as well as the dog

Σὺν τῷ κυνὶ καὶ τὸν ἱμάντα, The leash as well as the dog. This is the ending of a dactylic hexameter. Eudemus points out that it is said whenever everything is lost at the same time so that nothing at all remains, not even the hope of recovering what has been lost.[1]

* * * * *

2 This sentence was added in 1515, perhaps in response to some criticism disputing the proverbial nature of the adage.
3 Plutarch *Moralia* 172F *Regum et imperatorum apophthegmata*, where the anecdote in Herodotus (see n4) is also reported. Cf Erasmus *Apophthegmata* v Cyrus Maior 2 LB IV 229E.
4 Herodotus 9.122

26 Apostolius 15.68. Cf *Suda* Σ 1643. The final part 'not even . . . has been lost' is an addition of 1533.
1 Eudemus was the author of a work called *Rhetorical Sayings*, only part of which has been published. See K. Ruprecht *Apostolis, Suidas und Eudem* (*Philologus* Supplementband 15, 1922) 145–60. He is sometimes referred to in the *Suda* and in Apostolius and Arsenius (see the apparatus in CPG 2 on Apostolius 5.26), but there is no mention of him in their interpretation of this proverb. The source of Erasmus' knowledge of Eudemus' comment on this proverb remains a mystery.

27 Te ipsum inspice
Have a good look at yourself

Μὴ τοὐμὸν ἀλλὰ καὶ τὸ σὸν φῦλος σκόπει, Look not just at my family back-ground, but also at your own. In some tragedy when Agamemnon insults Teucer for being a bastard, Teucer throws back this reproach, since Agamemnon was descended from the effeminate Cleisthenes.[1] It is foolish to insult someone with anything that can be hurled back at you. The adage is in Plutarch.[2]

28 Ne mihi vacuam abstergas
Don't level off what is empty

Theocritus in the *Women of Syracuse*:

> Persephone, let there be but one master that we recognize.
> This does not bother me. Watch out you do not level off what is empty.[1]

A proverb seems to be present in the words Μὴ μοι κενεὰν ἀπομάξῃς 'Do not level off what is empty.' We must understand 'jaw,' 'hand,' or something

* * * * *

27 This is based on Apostolius 15.52, whom Erasmus follows closely until the final sentence. Erasmus has replaced φίλος in Apostolius (a vocative, the sense of the Greek being: 'consider not just my family, but also your own, friend') by the non-existent form φῦλος. This is probably a mistake for φῦλον, meaning 'tribe, family.' Erasmus also changed the word order to form an iambic trimeter. The line is similar to Sophocles *Ajax* 1313, spoken by Teucer in response to Agamemnon, who has described him as 'born from a captive slave woman' (1228).
1 The name 'Cleisthenes' is an error of Apostolius, whom Erasmus follows, for Pleisthenes, who was the father of Agamemnon according to Apollodorus *Bibliotheca* 3.2.2. The more common tradition gives Atreus as his father.
2 Plutarch *Moralia* 187B *Regum et imperatorum apophthegmata*, where a similar expression occurs

28 Theocritus (see n1). Most of the essay (the last two paragraphs) was an addition of *1533*.
1 Theocritus *Idylls* 15.94–5, where Praxinoa is retorting to a stranger who has given her an order

similar.[2] It seems to be spoken by someone who threatens or fears a blow or punch. I say this, for the meaning of the passage has not yet been made clear. We leave it therefore for scholars to unravel the meaning more carefully.

The makers of moulds, who smear clay on an object they are replicating, are also said ἀπομάττειν 'to smooth away' the clay. Some people often pretend to perform a service, as when they seem to be wiping away dirt from someone's cheek, but in fact are smearing the cheek with dirt without the other's being aware of it, so that he is like Bacchus as represented on stage, with his face smeared with gypsum and grape juice.

However, the commentator,[3] neither very learned nor attentive, prefers that a measure, perhaps a *choinix*, be understood. Whatever exceeds the measure is levelled off by wiping away the excess with a smooth stick. So the person who does this to a measuring pot that is not yet full, pretending that there is some excess, is being deceitful. The speaker means that she is not the man's serving woman to be rebuked by him. Angry masters cheat their slaves of their daily ration. If I am not mistaken, the woman's meaning is this: 'I am not worried that you level off my pot when it is empty.'[4]

29 Cum sis nanus, cede
Yield, since you are a dwarf

Νάνος ὢν ὕπεικε, Yield since you are a dwarf. Said of very tiny people. For

* * * * *

2 How Erasmus interpreted the Greek with such words being understood is not clear. The Latin verb, translated here as 'to level off,' means literally 'to wipe away.'

3 The commentator referred to is the scholiast on Theocritus 15.94–5.

4 The scholiast is nearer the mark than Erasmus, whose explanations do not persuade. The general sense of the expression is more likely to be 'do not waste your time giving orders to me' (see K.J. Dover *Theocritus: Select Poems* [London 1971] 208). The *choinix* is a dry measure of grain, the daily allowance given to slaves (see Thucydides 4.16). This may be the reason that Erasmus interprets the words to be a denial that the woman is the man's slave. This explanation is in accordance with Erasmus' interpretation of what the woman has just said (line 90), 'Give orders to those you have fed' (*Adagia* IV iv 24 n1, 75 below). See also *Adagia* V i 14 If you want to give orders, you must buy a slave (550 below), where the Theocritean passage is cited.

29 Apostolius 11.97

humans who are smaller than normal and of unbelievable shortness are called *nani*. Juvenal: 'We call a dwarf "Atlas."'[1] The word νάνος in Greek seems to come from μὴ ἄνω 'not upwards' because a dwarf does not grow to any height.[2] Theophrastus is cited as believing that those whose genitals were larger than normal were called *nani*.[3] Probably this can be found to be true of such persons.[4] The expression can be applied aptly to wretched persons who are poor and of low fortune, and, as Horace says, are 'two-footers,' trying to match their superiors in spending.[5]

29A Nocte lucidus, interdiu inutilis
Bright at night, useless in daylight

Ἐν νυκτὶ λαμπρός, ἐν φάει δ' ἀνωφελής, Bright at night, useless in day-time. Said of persons who do the opposite of what they should – those who are full of ideas when there is no need of them, but who doze off when there is. I myself, however, think that the saying is more suited to those who are thought to have some accomplishment in literature when in the company of the ignorant, but who are ignorant in the company of the learned.[1] Or the proverb should be reversed: 'Bright in daylight, use-

* * * * *

1 Juvenal 8.32

2 See *Etymologicum magnum* 597.27–9, but there the word is derived from the negative prefix νη- and ἄνω, the latter strangely being taken as a verb equivalent to αὐξάνω 'increase' rather than the adverb meaning 'above, on high.' The reading of μή in the *Adagia*-text may be an error, either of Erasmus or of the printer, for νη-, since phonetically the latter is closer than μή to νάνος. This sentence was added in 1533.

3 Theophrastus is cited by Apostolius (cf *Suda* N 26), who simply says that according to him a dwarf, as well as being small, had huge genitals. But this ascription to Theophrastus seems to be an error. It is Aristotle who refers to the size of a dwarf's genitals at *Historia animalium* 6.24 (577b): 'Mules, like dwarfs, have huge genitals.'

4 This sentence was added in 1533.

5 Horace *Satires* 2.3.309. The last sentence is an addition of 1515.

29A Apostolius 7.47A. Apostolius says the proverb relates originally to bats. In 1536 this adage has the same number as the preceding one. In LB it is numbered IV iii 30; see introductory notes for the next two adages.

1 This sentence and the next were added in 1515.

less at night.' Taken from a precious stone that we have mentioned elsewhere.[2]

30 E Tantali horto fructus colligis
Gathering fruit from the garden of Tantalus

Ταντάλου κῆπον τρυγᾶς, You are gathering fruit from the garden of Tan-
talus. In other words, you are pursuing what does not exist or what you
cannot enjoy. It will be appropriate to say this of those who are slaves to
worldly pleasures. While they are enjoying such pleasures like drunkards,
they think that they are extremely lucky. As soon as they have come to their
senses, however, they are like those who have awakened and realize that all
these pleasures are only the dreamlike creations of a quite irrational mind.

31 Telenico pauperior
As poor as Telenicus

Τελενίκου πενέστερος, Poorer than Telenicus. His poverty was so notorious
that the people of Seriphos fashioned a word after him; they say τελενικῆσαι
'to do a Telenicos' for 'to empty one's bowels.'

32 Telenicia echo
An echo of Telenicus

Τελενίκιος ἠχώ, An echo of Telenicus. It will be appropriate to describe the
words of a fool in this way. For this is how the sound of empty barrels is
described. The adjective is taken from the same Telenicus about whom we
have just spoken. Plutarch, however, mentions among the witty sayings of
Epaminondas a certain Tellen, a dreadful flute-player, who was very unlike

* * * * *

2 *Adagia* III iv 30 An emerald, dark in the light

30 Apostolius 16.1, whose brief explanation Erasmus expands; *Suda* T 80. This
adage is numbered IV iii 31 in LB.

31 Apostolius 16.23; *Suda* T 257. In LB this adage, like the preceding one, is numbered IV iii 31.

32 Mentioned by Apostolius at 16.23; cf *Suda* T 257.

Antigenidas.¹ Let the reader judge therefore whether he prefers to derive the proverb from this person. And indeed I have spoken elsewhere about Tellen's songs.²

33 Terebintho stultior
As stupid as a turpentine-tree

Τερεβίνθου ἀνοήτερος, More foolish than a terebinth tree. Directed at those who are stupid and very proud of themselves, since this tree spreads its branches far and wide, the characteristic of those who are arrogantly ostentatious. In addition the tree is marked by its black colour, thick foliage, sap that is oily and resinous, and it has a different appearance in different places. It brings forth its fruit at the same time as the vine, but produces a very different kind.¹

34 Moenia Semyramidis
The walls of Semiramis

Τείχη Σεμυράμιδος, The walls of Semiramis. This was said of walls that could not be breached and were extremely well fortified. Ovid in the fourth book of the *Metamorphoses*: 'Where Semiramis is said / To have surrounded her city with walls of brick.'¹

* * * * *

1 Plutarch *Moralia* 193F *Regum et imperatorum apophthegmata*. Cf Erasmus *Apophthegmata* v Epaminondas 21 (LB IV 252C). This sentence and the following ones were added in *1526*. Antigenidas was a famous musician of Thebes.
2 *Adagia* II vi 8 Sing Tellen's songs

33 Apostolius 16.27, who reads, correctly, ἀνοητότερος against ἀνοήτερος in the printed editions of the *Adagia*. This may have been an error of Erasmus rather than of the printer. The correct form is pointed out by Estienne (LB II 1013 n1). In *1508* the adage concluded at 'far and wide.' The rest was added in *1517/18*.
1 Most of this information comes from Pliny *Naturalis historia* 13.54.

34 Apostolius 16.43
1 Ovid *Metamorphoses* 4.57–8. The quotation was mistakenly ascribed to Juvenal until *1517/18*. One may compare the scholion on Juvenal 10.171, which mentions Babylon and its brick fortifications.

35 Manum admovere
To add your hand to

Τὴν χεῖρα ἐπιβάλλειν, To put a hand to. This was said of those who insin-
uated themselves into some important event and thereby shared in it. It is
taken from ritual where it sometimes happened that when people were offering sacrifice someone else came up and put his hand on the victim so
that he himself became part of the ritual.

36 Patris est filius
He is his father's son

Τοῦ πατρός ἐστι τὸ παιδίον, He is his father's son. This is said when anyone
imitates his father's traits; and in general we call anyone at all the son of
a person whom he resembles in his traits, because almost always children
remind one of their parents. Varro gave this title to one of his *Menippeans*,
cited by Nonius Marcellus.[1] Indeed the titles of Varro are usually proverbial.
In his *Aristides* Philostratus mentions that a sophist used this proverb to
impugn Alexander because he was imitating his father's ambition.[2]

37 Parvo emptas carnes
Cheap meat feeds the dogs

Τὸ εὔωνον κρέας οἱ κύνες ἐσθίουσιν, It's the dogs that eat cheap meat. Some
people buy rotting meat to save some money. When no one touches the
meat, it is kept to provide several meals for the dogs. This adage also smacks
of the common herd of our own times.[1]

* * * * *

35 Apostolius 16.46

36 Apostolius 16.79. Tilley F 97 You are your father's son. 'And in general ...
their parents' is an addition of *1515*. What follows was added in *1533*.
1 Nonius Marcellus 14.11, 108.16–17, 544.3 Lindsay. The *Menippeans* refer to
satires composed by Varro.
2 Philostratus *Vitae sophistarum* 2.9 (584)

37 Apostolius 16.83. The last sentence was added in *1517/18*. Cf *Adagia* III iii 50
No hard bargainer eats good meat (CWE 34 297, 416).
1 Suringar 166

38 Qui domi compluitur
Not even God pities the man who is rained upon in his own house

Τὸν οἴκοθεν βρεχόμενον οὐδὲ θεὸς οἰκτείρει, Not even God pities the man who is rained upon in his own home. A common saying among the Greeks.[1] The sense is that those who are so lazy that they cannot be safe from rain even in their own homes completely deserve their misfortune. Unless my nose completely deceives me, the proverb is 'of the same flour' as the previous one.[2]

39 Tragicus Theocrines
A Theocrines, the tragic actor

Τραγικὸς Θεοκρίνης, Theocrines, the tragic actor. Demosthenes used this adage against Aeschines.[1] Theocrines was first of all an actor in tragedies, then a bringer of false accusations and an informer. Accordingly, in his speech *In Defence of Ctesipho* Demosthenes calls Aeschines 'A Theocrines, the tragic actor.' A speech of Demosthenes against this Theocrines survives, although some attribute it to Dinarchus.[2] If I am not mistaken, St Jerome uses this proverb in his *Letter to Furia on Widowhood*: 'Whenever they saw a Christian, they immediately used that expression of the streets: "He's a Theocrines, the tragic actor."'[3] They hurled this insult at Christians on the

* * * * *

38 Apostolius 16.91. Suringar 187; cf Tilley T 767 A house dry overhead is happy. As in the preceding adage the last sentence was added in *1517/18* (see n2).
  1 Erasmus is following Apostolius who says 'and this is δημῶδης "popular,"' implying that the proverb was current in his time. See on *Adagia* III iv 2 Everyone thinks his own fart sweet CWE 35 4 with n3.
  2 Cf *Adagia* III v 44 The same flour as us. In both this and the preceding adage the additions of *1517/18* imply that the adages are unrefined.

39 Apostolius 17.21. In *1508* the discussion of this adage was extremely short. All that was said of Theocrines was that he was an informer. The rest was added in *1515*.
  1 Demosthenes 18.313 (*De corona*, to which Erasmus refers as *In Defence of Ctesipho*)
  2 On the question of authorship Erasmus follows Apostolius. See Pseudo-Demosthenes *Against Theocrines* (no 58 in the corpus of Demosthenes).
  3 Jerome *Letters* 54.5 PL 22 552, CSEL 54 470. The phrase ὁ τραγικὸς Θεοκρίνης 'the

grounds that they feigned piety and censured in lofty terms how others lived.

40 Tragicum malum
A tragic misfortune

Τραγικὸν πάθος, A tragic misfortune. It will be applied to a great misfortune of the kind that is portrayed in tragedies; for these are not found in comedy. Quintilian says that there are two kinds of emotions.[1] Some are rather fierce, and those are loved by tragedy. Some are milder, and comedy uses these. Indeed tragic emotions are called πάθη 'passions,' the emotions in comedy are called ἤθη 'dispositions.' Tragedy always has a sad ending, comedy a happy one. Accordingly, Plautus, as cited by Festus Pompeius, used the word *comoedice* 'in the style of comedy' for *suaviter* 'pleasantly': *Euge, heus astitisti et dulce et comoedice* 'Hey there, bravo! Your posture is pleasant and in the style of comedy.'[2]

* * * * *

tragic actor Theocrines' is actually an emendation of Erasmus for ὁ Γραικός, ὁ ἐπιθέτης 'the Greek imposter.'

40 Apostolius 17.29; cf *Suda* T 892. 'Quintilian ... dispositions' is an addition of 1517/18. The remainder first appeared in 1533.
1 Quintilian 6.2.8, 20
2 Plautus *Miles gloriosus* 213, cited by Pompeius Festus 53.24–5 Lindsay. Erasmus follows in part the text of the line in the 1513 Aldine edition of Festus in reading *astitisti* (2nd person) for *astitit* (3rd person), found in most editions. Erasmus is quite wrong in his explanation of *comoedice* as a synonym for the immediately preceding *dulce* 'pleasantly.' This form, the reading of the manuscripts, is a corruption for *dulice*, a hybrid equivalent of δουλικῶς 'like a slave.' The speaker is comparing his own slave to a comic slave. Giambattista Pio gave a similar interpretation of *comoedice* (= *dulciter*) in his Milan edition of Plautus of 1500, an edition that Erasmus owned. It is no 213 in the so-called mailing list of Erasmus' library; see F. Husner 'Die Bibliothek des Erasmus' in *Gedenkeschrift zum 400. Todestage des Erasmus von Rotterdam* (Basel 1936) 228–59. Erasmus frequently draws on Pio's text and commentary in the *Adagia*, sometimes critically, but without naming his source (*Adagia* IV iv 52; IV ix 19, 95, 98; IV x 30, 39, 41, 42, 91, 92; V i 1, 5, 18, 59, 71). See ASD II-4 217:23–33n; CEBR 3:88.

41 **Caecus auribus ac mente**
Blind in ear and mind

Τυφλὸς τά τ᾿ ὦτα, τόν τε νοῦν τά τ᾿ ὄμματά εἶ, You are blind in ear and mind and eye. This suits a person who is clearly stupid.

42 **Caecum insomnium**
A blind dream

Τυφλὸν ὄνειρον, A blind dream. Said of something trifling and insubstantial; for some dreams prophesy something, some are meaningless. The same goes for lightning bolts that strike blindly.[1]

43 **Asinos non curo**
I have no interest in asses

Τῶν δ᾿ ὄνων οὔ μοι μέλει, I am not interested in asses. This fits a person who is content with his own household possessions and does not seek after what belongs to others; for those who have their own cart do not need the use of hired asses. We have cited the complete line elsewhere.[1]

44 **Plurium calculus vincit**
The vote of the majority prevails

Τῶν πλειόνων ψῆφος νικᾷ, The vote of the majority prevails. Whenever in a council we yield to the majority. In his *Letters* Pliny complains that votes

* * * * *

41 Apostolius 17.37, quoting Sophocles *Oedipus Tyrannus* 371; cf *Suda* T 1215.

42 Apostolius 17.38; cf *Suda* T 1218 and Diogenianus 8.26.
1 Cf Pliny *Naturalis historia* 2.113.

43 Apostolius 17.43. In this proverb Erasmus follows Apostolius in giving a shorter and slightly different version (οὔ μοι for οὐδέν) of an earlier and longer proverb (see n1), of which this is virtually a doublet. In the earlier one Erasmus follows the wording in Zenobius (Aldus) column 41 and the *Suda* A 3450.
1 *Adagia* III vii 7 Use a cart and you don't have to worry about asses

44 Apostolius 17.45

are counted, not weighed, and Livy says, 'The larger party defeated the better.'[1]

45 Ὑπεψηνισμένη
Bitten by the bug

Ὑπεψηνισμένη, Bitten by the bug. This is said of a woman who is just about to give birth. The metaphor is taken from figs that begin to mature after small gall-insects have entered them. We have explained this process in the proverb 'You need artificial fertilization.'[1] It can be applied to someone who by his nature is strongly inclined to engage in some activity or another.

46 Subdititius es
You are counterfeit

Ὑποβολιμαῖος εἶ, You are a supposititious child. Offspring that are not true offspring are called counterfeit or supposititious. On the basis of this the term is applied to a person who is not what he says he is and has been commissioned and suborned by someone for the purposes of deceit. Closely related to κίβδηλος ἄνθρωπος 'a counterfeit man.'[1]

47 Subiugus homo
A man under the yoke

Ὑποζυγιώδης ἄνθρωπος, A man under the yoke. Of a man who does not do anything that he himself wants to do, but only what another person

* * * * *

1 Pliny *Letters* 2.12.5; Livy 21.4.1. Both are quoted in *Adagia* I vi 28 This is sovereign (CWE 32 23).

45 Apostolius 17.57; cf *Suda* Υ 407. The final sentence was added in *1533*.
  1 *Adagia* III ii 66 and notes (CWE 34 249 and 400). The method is described by Theophrastus at *Historia plantarum* 2.6.2 and *De causis plantarum* 2.9.6.

46 Apostolius 17.58; cf *Suda* Υ 458.
  1 This expression is cited and described as 'virtually proverbial' in *Adagia* III ii 6 Of a bad stamp. Cf *Adagia* III iv 5 Adulterated.

47 Apostolius 17.60; cf *Suda* Υ 495. All the text following 'are yoked together' was added in *1526*.

orders. Taken from animals that are yoked together. Pertinent to this are the following proverbial metaphors, *mittere sub iugum* 'to send under the yoke,' as in Horace:

> So Venus decrees; it pleases her in cruel jest
> To send under brazen yoke
> Unequal forms and minds.[1]

Also, *deiicere iugum* 'to cast off the yoke,' which Cicero used in his first *Philippic;*[2] *subducere collum iugo* 'to draw the neck from the yoke,' as in Ovid: 'And draw your neck from the yoke that will hurt.'[3] Also *excutere iugum* 'to shake off the yoke.'[4]

48 Pistillo nudior
As naked as a pestle

Ὑπέρου γυμνότερος, As naked as a pestle. Said of those who are dreadfully poor. Related to Παττάλου γυμνότερος 'As naked as a peg';[1] for the bark is removed from wooden pegs.

49 Pistillo calvior
As bald as a pestle

Ὑπέρου φαλακρότερος, As bald as a pestle. Also a proverbial hyperbole, said of very bald persons; for the bottom part of a pestle seems to resemble a bald man's skull. It can also be applied to those who are in extreme want or those who are ingenuous and incapable of dissimulation.

*　*　*　*　*

1 Horace *Odes* 1.33.10–12
2 Cicero *Philippics* 1.2.6
3 Ovid *Remedium amoris* 90, though the verb used is *subtrahere*, not *subducere*
4 No reference is given by Erasmus for the phrase *excutere iugum,* but cf Seneca *Letters* 51.8 and Tacitus *Agricola* 15.3.

48 Apostolius 17.65; cf *Suda* Υ 392. In *1533* 'for the bark ... wooden pegs' was added.
1 *Adagia* II x 100

49 Apostolius 17.65. 'For the bottom part ... skull' was added in *1515*. The final sentence was added in *1528*.

50 **Aureum subaeratum**
There's copper beneath the gold

Ὑπόχαλκον χρυσίον, Gold mixed with copper. An expression applied to a person who is completely insincere, openly displaying one attitude and concealing another within. Taken from debased coins.

51 **Nihil de vitello**
None of the yolk

Νεοττοῦ οὐδέν μοι δίδως, You have given me none of the yolk. This suits perfectly those who give to others what is less valuable and keep what is more valuable for themselves. Marcus Tullius in book two of *On Divination* tells the following story and it is generally agreed that this proverb was borrowed from it.[1] A certain man had dreamed that he saw an egg hanging from his bed tied to a ribbon. When he reported this dream to an interpreter, the reply was that the dream indicated a treasure. He should immediately dig at the spot where he dreamed he saw the egg. When he did so, he found gold completely covered all round with silver. He sent a little of the silver to the interpreter, concealing the discovery of gold. As the interpreter accepted the silver, he said, 'None of the yolk?'

52 **Queruli in amicitia**
Critics don't make friends

Οἱ φιλομεμφέες εἰς φιλίην οὐκ εὐφυέες, Those who criticize their friends are not suited to friendship. To turn a blind eye to the faults of your friends, 'it's this joins friend to friend and keeps them joined.'[1] The sentiment seems

* * * * *

50 Apostolius 17.66; cf *Suda* Υ 636. The Latin expression is found in Persius 5.106.

51 Apostolius 12.7; cf *Suda* N 214.
  1 Cicero *De divinatione* 2.65.134, of which the following account is a close paraphrase

52 Apostolius 12.43, who assigns it to 'Democrates' (Democritus fragment 109 Diels-Kranz). From 'The sentiment' to the end was added in *1528*.
  1 Horace *Satires* 1.3.54 (quoted also at *Adagia* II ix 53 Flattery wins friends and truth engenders hate)

to have been taken from Herodotus.[2] We would have a trimeter if we read οἱ φιλομεμφεῖς εἰς φιλίην οὐκ εὐφυεῖς, but I do not understand the form φιλομεμφεῖς. If we read φιλομεμφεῖς, we must add a particle and read οἱ δὲ φιλομεμφεῖς. In this way the Greek line will scan: *Qui querulus est amicitiae haud accommodus* 'To criticize a friend ill makes a friend.'[3]

53 Cleomenes superat cubile
Cleomenes is too big for his bed

Ὁ Κλεομένης τῆς κοίτης ὑπερέχει, Cleomenes is too big for his bed.[1] About a person who has a greater abundance of what is unnecessary than of what is necessary. It is obviously derived from someone whose body was too large for the size of his bed. So also Juvenal: 'Codrus had a bed too small for Procula.'[2]

54 Dives promissis
Rich in promises

Ὁ μὲν λόγος θαυμαστός, ὁ δὲ λέγων ἄπιστος, Fine words, but the speaker cannot be believed. Used whenever anyone promises great things that no one thinks he can perform. Plutarch in 'Sayings of Kings and Generals'

* * * * *

2 Nothing similar has been identified in Herodotus.
3 Since it is his practice to render Greek verse into Latin verse, Erasmus ends his essay with a Latin senarius that translates the Greek trimeter he has reconstructed.

53 Apostolius 12.62. From 'It is obviously derived' to the end is an addition of 1515.
1 Nothing seems to be known of this Cleomenes. Presumably he was rich but did not have a bed to sleep properly on.
2 Juvenal 3.203. The speaker is describing the hardships of those who live in the apartments of Rome. Procula must have been a dwarf.

54 Apostolius 12.71. Estienne (in LB II 1015F n1) points out that *Dives promissis* should not be regarded as the title of the adage. If Erasmus had followed his usual procedure, the actual adage would have been *Magnifica quidem oratio, ceterum non habetur fides loquenti*, his translation of the Greek. For his choice of the title he may have had *pollicitis dives* at Ovid *Ars amatoria* 1.444 in mind (this is cited in *Adagia* II viii 74 Wishes make wealthy).

attributes the following words to Eudaemonidas. When he heard that someone (a Stoic, I believe) had said that only the sage was a good general, he
retorted, Ὁ μὲν λόγος θαυμαστός, ὁ δὲ λέγων οὐ περισεσάλπισται 'The words
are wonderful to be sure, but the speaker has never had trumpets sounding around him.'[1] Plutarch gives a fuller version in 'Sayings of Spartans':
'The words are wonderful, but the speaker cannot be believed; for he has
never had trumpets sounding around him.'[2] The adage will also suit theologians who give instruction on heavenly matters but whose mode of life
does not match their words.

55 Uterque ambo
Each is both

Ὁ μὲν Ἑκάτερος ἀμφότερος, ὁ δὲ Ἀμφότερος οὐδέτερος, Each is both and Both
is neither. This is like a riddle; Plutarch mentions it in the *Moralia* and it is
to be found in the Greek epigrams.[1] There were two brothers one of whom
was called Each and the other Both, the former being honest, the latter a
scoundrel. When Philip saw them he is said to have made this joke against
them. The saying will fit two persons when the probity of one balances the
villainy of the other.

56 Os inest orationi
The speech has bones

Ὀστοῦν ἔνεστι τῷ λόγῳ, The speech has bones and muscle. Said of a speech
that is not insubstantial, but has weighty proposals. This saying is attributed

* * * * *

1 Plutarch *Moralia* 192B *Regum et imperatorum apophthegmata*, with the omission of
  ἄπιστος, which appears in the later quotation (see next note). Modern editions
  give the name of the individual as Eudamidas. From 'Plutarch in . . .' to the
  end was added in *1526*.
2 Plutarch *Moralia* 220E *Apophthegmata Laconica*

55 Apostolius 12.72. The riddle is better explained by Apostolius where Each has
  two good qualities that are lacking in Both.
1 Plutarch *Moralia* 177F *Regum et imperatorum apophthegmata*, but not to be found
  in modern editions of the *Greek Anthology*

56 Apostolius 13.4. Two sentences were added in *1528*: 'Said of a speech . . .
  weighty proposals' and 'It seems to have been taken . . . iambic dimeter.'

to Themistocles.[1] It seems to have been taken from some poet, since it is an iambic dimeter. Quintilian also calls the subject matter the 'bones of a speech.'[2] The metaphor is taken from the bodies of living beings. The body is supported by bones, bound together by sinews, and covered with flesh and skin; it coheres with the soul, and moves by propelling itself.

57 Fluvius non semper fert secures
A river does not always bring axes

Οὐκ ἀεὶ ποταμὸς ἀξίνας φέρει, A river does not always bring axes. One should not immediately hope for the same good fortune that has befallen others. This originates in one of Aesop's fables.

A certain man was cutting down a wood when his axe slipped out of his hands. Mercury was invoked and gave him a silver axe. When the man said that this was not his, Mercury gave him a golden one. When he said that this one too did not belong to him, Mercury finally restored the iron axe and gave him the others in addition. Another fellow, hoping for the same outcome, deliberately allowed his axe to slip away from him. After he had lost it and after Mercury had not appeared in answer to his prayers, he complained bitterly to the other man, who responded in this fashion: 'A river does not always bear axes.'[1]

This fable, however, is told differently in other collections, where Mercury did appear, brought forth a silver axe, and asked the man whether

* * * * *

1 An error for Empedocles, to whom Apostolius and Aristotle *Metaphysics* 1.10 (993a17–18) attribute the saying, though the meaning of the expression in Aristotle is different from Erasmus' interpretation.

2 Quintilian 1, preface 24. The technical term for the subject matter is *inventio*.

57 Apostolius 13.67A. This was added by Arsenius to the original collection of Apostolius. In Arsenius' version of the fable Hermes makes no appearance. It is the river itself that offers up first a silver axe, then a golden axe, and finally the original one. Erasmus is therefore drawing to some extent from Aesop in which Hermes does appear, although the actual proverb itself is absent from known versions of Aesop's fable.

1 Aesop 183 Hausrath; 173 Perry. Also in the Aldine edition of 1505 (page 33). The phrase 'and gave him the others in addition' was added in *1515*.

it was his.[2] When he immediately said that it was, Mercury was angered by the man's shamelessness and did not restore even the iron
one.

58 Non est dithyrambus si bibat aquam
There is no dithyramb if he drinks water

Οὐκ ἔστι διθύραμβος ἂν ὕδωρ πίνῃ, There is no dithyramb if he drinks water. There is no joy without wine. Poets' inspiration flags unless it is heated
up by wine. This is why Horace says, 'By his praises of wine Homer is
proved to be fond of wine,' and 'Father Ennius himself leapt forth to sing
of epic battle only when drunk,' and 'No poetry can please for long or
really live if written by drinkers of water.'[1] In fact, as Plutarch relates in
his 'Table-talk,' Aeschylus drank while he composed his tragedies.[2] For the
heat of wine summons up the power of invention (which sometimes lan-
guishes in abstainers), stirs imagination, gives forcefulness, supplies confidence. Plutarch adds that Gorgias was wrong in attributing Aeschylus'
tragedy to Mars, since it ought to be credited more to Bacchus. Dithyrambs
were sung in honour of Bacchus, who himself was called 'Dithyrambos' because he was born twice and, in a manner of speaking, came forth from
two doors.[3]

* * * * *

2 Here Erasmus uses the term *commentarii* in the sense of 'collections' (see *Adagia*
IV iii 12 Matioloechus, 11 above). The version in which Mercury did appear to
the second man is in the extant versions of Aesop. The source of the version
of the fable's ending as given at the end of the preceding paragraph has not
been identified.

58 Apostolius 13.67; Diogenianus 7.39. The verse is quoted more accurately in
Athenaeus 14.628B, where it is attributed to Epicharmus in his play *Philoctetes*
(fragment 132 Kaibel).
1 Horace *Epistles* 1.19.6, 7–8, and 2–3. The first two quotations were added in
1515, the third in *1533*.
2 Plutarch *Moralia* 715E *Quaestiones convivales*
3 *Etymologicum magnum* 274.44. The name 'Dithyrambos' is falsely derived from
Di- 'two' or 'twice' and *thura* 'a door.'

59 Post acerba prudentior
Sadder but wiser

Παρὰ τὰ δεινὰ φρονιμώτερος, After misfortune wiser. Related to this is 'When a thing is done, a fool can see it.'[1] Plato in the *Symposium* writes, 'I say this to you too, Agathon. Do not be deceived by this man, but learn from my misfortune and do not, as the proverb goes, be wise after misfortune, like a foolish man.'[2]

The saying will apply to someone who becomes more cautious because of his misfortune.

60 Pausone mendicior
As poor as Pauson

Παύσωνος πτωχότερος, Poorer than Pauson. Pauson was some painter who was exceptionally poor, like Codrus in Juvenal.[1] Aristophanes impugns him in the *Plutus*. When Poverty exclaimed, 'O city of Argos, heed what he says,' Chremylus replies, 'Invite Pauson to be your guest at table.'[2]

61 Ultra Hyperbolum
Worse than Hyperbolus

Ὑπὲρ τὸν Ὑπέρβολον, He surpasses Hyperbolus. Hyperbolus was some-one who was incredibly litigious. Consequently, the saying fits those who

* * * * *

59 Apostolius 13.90. This is a virtual doublet of I iii 99 Sadder and wiser, a pro-verb that Erasmus acknowledges there that he has taken from Apostolius. The Greek phrase occurs in Plutarch *Moralia* 172F *Regum et imperatorum apophtheg-mata*. The quotation from Plato was added in *1528*, the final sentence in *1517/18*.
1 *Adagia* I i 30
2 Plato *Symposium* 222B

60 Apostolius 14.2; cf *Suda* Π 824.
1 See *Adagia* IV iii 53 n2 (32 above).
2 Aristophanes *Plutus* 601–2. From 'Aristophanes impugns' to the end was added in *1533*.

61 Apostolius 17.68

suffer from the same disease. Plutarch in his *Life of Alcibiades*,[1] Thucydides in book eight of the *Peloponnesian War*,[2] and Aristophanes in the
Knights[3] show that Hyperbolus was a most shameless man in all respects
and that all he was distinguished for and competent in was abusive
language.[4] In addition, Marcus Tullius writes this about Saturninus in his
book *On Famous Orators*: 'A fellow very like Hyperbolus, whose bad character is impugned in the old Attic comedies.'[5] In addition to other remarks
Aristophanes also writes this about Hyperbolus:

> Hyperbolus, a shameless man and a sour-tempered, good-for-nothing
> citizen.[6]

62 Sus in volutabro caeni
A washed pig rolls in muck

Ὗς λουσαμένη εἰς κύλισμα βορβόρου, A pig when washed returns to the mud-
pile. Said when anyone repeats a crime for which he has already paid, as
we have indicated elsewhere.[1] It appears in the *Epistles* of Saint Peter.[2]
Related to this is what is found among the proverbs of Sirach, 'Wash after
touching a corpse and then touch it again, and what have you gained by
washing?'[3]

* * * * *

1 Plutarch *Alcibiades* 13.4. From here to the end was added in 1526, except for
  'and that all he was distinguished for ... abusive language,' which was added
  in 1533.
2 Thucydides 8.73.3
3 See n6 below.
4 Hyperbolus was a popular politician and orator in Athens. He was ostracized
  in 417.
5 Cicero *Brutus* 62.224, though Cicero is here referring to Caius Servilius Glau-
  cia, not Saturninus
6 Aristophanes *Knights* 1304; cf *Knights* 1363.

62 Apostolius 17.75; cf *Collectanea* no 750.
  1 See *Adagia* III v 13 A dog goes back to his vomit. The cross-reference 'as we
    have indicated elsewhere' is an addition of 1515.
  2 2 Peter 2:22
  3 Ecclus 34:30(25). This reference was added in 1528.

63 Ob textoris erratum
Paying for the weaver's mistake

Ὑφάντου πταίσματος ὑπήτης ἐτύφθη, The *hypetes* got a beating for the weaver's mistake. When someone pays for another's mistake. I have not yet discovered in our sources what a *hypetes* is.[1]

64 Mendax atraphaxis
Lying atraphaxis

Ψευδῶν πλέα ἀτράφαξις, Atraphaxis is full of lies. Said of those who are puffed up in pride and are full of wind. *Atraphaxis* is a kind of green vegetable that grows quickly to a great height. Its Latin name is *atriplex*, and it is related, if I am not mistaken, to the genus of the beet family, which also grows quickly, but is tasteless. This is what Theophrastus says in his *History of Plants*, book one, chapter five.[1] The same plant is listed by the same author among those that make a quick appearance, namely on the eight day after being sown.[2] Its stalk is quite large and thick, but it is also soft and fleshy. Suidas tells us that the expression was directed at Cleon, who was falsely accusing the knights in the assembly. When his listeners seemed to be believing him, the following words were said: 'The assembly is full of lying atraphaxis.'[3] They were a rebuke aimed not only at the worthlessness of Cleon's accusations but also at the people's credulity. For it is a characteristic of calumny to elevate the slightest of misdeeds into the greatest tragedy. This is very much what Suidas writes on this saying. The adage was taken from the *Knights* of Aristophanes.[4]

* * * * *

63 Apostolius 17.76. The final sentence was added in *1528*.
1 Erasmus' perplexity is not surprising, since the word is corrupt. The correct reading is ἠπήτης meaning 'mender,' an emendation of P. Leopardus, *Emendationes et miscellanea* (Anvers 1568) 10.5, accepted by Estienne (in LB II 1017 n2).

64 Apostolius 18.49. 'Its Latin name ... Suidas writes on this saying' was added in *1515*. The final sentence was added in *1526*.
1 Theophrastus *Historia plantarum* 1.5.3 (only on the relationship of atraphaxis to the beet family)
2 Theophrastus *Historia plantarum* 7.1.3
3 *Suda* Ψ 45
4 Aristophanes *Knights* 629–30

65 Inflige plagam ab aratro
Land a plough punch

Παῖε τὴν ἐπ᾽ ἀρότρου, Land the plough punch, or, Punch the ploughshare. Spoken when we tell someone to fight with all his strength though he lacks skill.[1] It is said to have sprung from a story like the one told by Pausanias in book two of 'On Elis.'[2] When a certain Glaucus of Carystus was plough-ing his land, the ploughshare happened to fall off. He lifted it up and fitted it onto the plough with his hand instead of with a hammer. After seeing this, his father Demylus entered him in the Olympic games, in the box-ing competition. Glaucus was inexperienced in boxing skills, and was just about worn out from the shower of blows that he was suffering when his father shouted out, 'Land your plough punch.' He was advising his son to attack his opponent in the way he was accustomed to drive his ploughshare into the earth.[3] These words restored the young man's spirits and he won the match. After this he also had two victories at the Pythian games, eight at the Nemean, and eight at the Isthmian. The source is Pausanias.

66 Summis ingredi pedibus
To walk on tiptoe

Those who attempt something secretly or cautiously or *pedetemptim* 'step by step,' as they say, are described as 'Walking on tiptoe.' The Greeks express

* * * * *

65 *Suda* Π 872 and Γ 281. From this point until *Adagia* IV v 9 (144 below) the adages, with a few exceptions, were first introduced in 1515.
1 The last part of this sentence ('though he lacks skill') was added in 1533.
2 Pausanias 6.10.2. The source of the story is first identified as Pausanias in 1526. The last two sentences of the commentary were also added in 1526.
3 This explanation of the father's words does not tally with the earlier incident. They should refer to the force used by Glaucus in re-attaching the ploughshare with his hand instead of with a hammer. From 1515 to 1523 the Latin in this sen-tence can be translated 'He was advising him to punch the ploughshare that he had picked up while ploughing.' In 1526 the text was changed to what is trans-lated here. Better would be 'he was advising him to attack his enemy in the way that he had driven in the ploughshare that he had picked up while ploughing.'

66 Otto 555. Cf *Adagia* II ii 16 To walk on tiptoe (*Summis unguibus ingredi*). The phase *summis pedibus* is not attested in classical literature. The first two sen-

this more pleasingly with a compound adverb ἀκροποδιτί. The following mean the same: *suspenso gradu* 'with pointed step' and *suspensis pedibus* 'on pointed feet.'[1] Drawn from the posture of those who walk in such a way that no one may be aware of the sound of their feet or those who plant their feet cautiously and lightly on the ground beneath them because they do not trust it. Somewhat different is what we find in Plato in *Laches*, 'Not even touching it with the tip of their feet.'[2] This relates to the adages 'To taste with the tip of one's tongue' and 'To touch with the fingertips.'[3]

67 Caelum digito attingere
To touch the heavens with your finger

It is certainly proverbial hyperbole when those who seem to be far above the human condition and to be very close to the gods are said 'To touch the heavens with their finger.' Marcus Tullius in book two of *Letters to Atticus*: 'Our leading men think that they are touching heaven with their finger if in their pools they have bearded mullet that swim right up to their hand.'[1] Related to that expression we have reported elsewhere, 'To be in heaven.'[2] Similarly, Horace:

> But if you place me among the lyric bards,
> The stars I'll strike with lofty head.[3]

Ovid: 'When him you please and touch the stars with head.'[4] And in Theocritus in the *Wayfarers*: 'Since I have won the lamb, you will think I've

* * * * *

tences of the commentary originally appeared in *1508* in the first chiliad (no 888, since the adages were not grouped in centuries in *1508*) in a somewhat different form. 'The following ... cautiously and lightly' was added in *1515*, and the rest in *1528*.
1 The phrase *suspenso pede* is mentioned in *Adagia* IV iv 2 With a limp hand.
2 Plato *Laches* 183B (used also in *Adagia* IV ix 59 Dip the toes, 458 below)
3 *Adagia* I ix 92 and I ix 94

67 Cicero (see n1). Otto 289. The adage and the first part of the commentary (in a somewhat different form) appeared in *1508* in the first chiliad (no 500).
1 Cicero *Ad Atticum* 2.1.7
2 *Adagia* I v 100. This reference was added in *1515*, as was the following quotation from Horace.
3 Horace *Odes* 1.1.35–6
4 Ovid *Ex Ponto* 2.5.57. Added in *1536*

reached the stars.'[5] When Lysimachus had reached Thrace and had occupied only the outermost boundaries of Alexander's kingdom, he said, 'Now the Byzantines come to me since I touch heaven with my spear.' A Byzantian called Pasiades, who happened to be present, reproached this very arrogant remark by saying, 'Let us be off, in case the point of his spear pierces heaven.'[6]

68 Corinthiari
To play the Corinthian

Often the ancients used to say as a joke that those who indulged in whoring and frequented brothels or those whose trade was pimping Κορινθιάζεσθαι 'Played the Corinthian.' Nowadays Venice is the most profitable place for that trade. The expression originated with the courtesans of Corinth, about whom I have spoken at the appropriate place.[1] For they were held in such great honour in that city that, as Athenaeus informs us from his sources, they prostituted themselves in the temple of Venus and in the solemn prayers a request for the gods to increase the number of courtesans was customarily added.[2] Athenaeus actually says that by sacrificing to Venus the courtesans saved the city when it was in extreme danger, since Venus had been appeased. Stephanus mentions this proverb in *About Cities*, adducing the *Cocalus* of Aristophanes.[3]

* * * * *

5 Theocritus *Idylls* 5.143–4. Added in 1526

6 The story from 'When Lysimachus' to the end is based on Plutarch *Moralia* 338A *De Alexandri magni fortuna aut virtute* and was added in 1533. Lysimachus was one of the successors of Alexander and became the most powerful one for a period. The story is meant to illustrate the arrogance of Lysimachus compared with Alexander's character.

68 This adage first appeared in 1515 as I v 75 until being moved to its current position in 1523. 'For they were held ... had been appeased' was added in 1528.

1 *Adagia* I iv 1 It is not given to everyone to land at Corinth; III vii 91 You seem like a Corinthian woman

2 Athenaeus 13.573C. Erasmus misunderstands Athenaeus who says that as many prostitutes as possible were invited to participate in the prayers at Corinth. The other incident relates to the saving of Greece and not just Corinth from the Persians.

3 Stephanus of Byzantium sub Κόρινθος, who is Erasmus' source for the adage, quoting PCG 3.2 Aristophanes fragment 370

69 Si tanti vitrum, quanti margaritum?
If glass is worth that much, what price pearls?

St Jerome in a letter to a young girl called Demetrias says, 'Some wretched parents, Christians but lacking true faith, customarily consign daughters who are ugly and lame to a life of virginity because they cannot find worthy sons-in-law. As the saying goes, "If glass is worth that much, what price pearls?"'[1]

He employs the same proverb in several other places. It is also used by Tertullian in his essay *To the Martyrs*.[2] This saying expressed the greatest possible difference in value that two things could have. Among gems pearls used to be accorded the highest praise, while glass was very cheap, even though to some extent it resembles gems. If you are so devoted in your concern about your physical health, how much attention should be given to the health of your soul? If you do everything to please a mortal Prince, how much more should you strive to please the Divine Prince? If wealth that is procured at the cost of so much sweat will be lost by being spent or stolen, why do we not apply ourselves even more strenuously to heaping up the riches of heaven? The proverb will be appropriate in these and similar circumstances.

70 Haeret in vado
He is stuck in shallow water

In the commentary that he published on the Gospel according to Luke St Ambrose used a rather witty adage to signify that the problem of the genealogy of Christ, which is reported differently by the gospel writers, cannot be resolved.[1] 'In our discussion we have come,' he says, 'to the

* * * * *

69 Jerome (see n1). Otto 1923. Added in *1515*
  1 St Jerome *Letters* 130.6 PL 22 1111, CSEL 56.1 182. He also refers to the proverb at *Letters* 107.8.3 PL 22 874–5, CSEL 55 299.
  2 Tertullian *Ad martyras* 4.9 PL 1 700A. This sentence was added in *1533*.

70 Ambrose (see n1). This adage and the first part of the commentary appeared in *1508* in the first chiliad (no 427). From 'or reefs' to 'jolt' was added in *1515*. See notes for further expansions. Cf *Adagia* I iv 99 You are sticking in the same mud, I iv 100 (= *Collectanea* no 44) He is stuck in the water.
  1 Ambrose *Expositio Euangelii secundum Lucam* 3.44 PL 15 1691B. The problem of Christ's genealogy rests on the contradictions between the accounts in Matt

edge of a precipice. We are stuck in shallow waters.' The metaphor of course is taken from a ship that has run aground on shallows and cannot be turned around and cannot hold the course that was set, as happens to those who encounter sandbanks or reefs. A proverb of this kind is expressed by Cicero in book five of *On the Definitions of Good and Evil*: 'He came to the edge; he is stuck fast on a reef.'[2] Similarly, elsewhere in the same work: 'If he could have done his definitions and divisions, if he had retained the forcefulness of speaking or held to his normal practice, he would never have landed on such *salebrae* "obstacles."' *Salebrae* are obstacles in rivers or on roads, called this from *saltus* 'jolt.' Cicero expressed the same idea with a similar metaphor: 'The water is blocked.'[3] For this is what he writes to his brother Quintus: 'In this case the water is blocked for me,' meaning that no progress has been made in the case.[4] I suspect that this was usually said about a case that was to be continued later. Just as water is not poured into a water-clock until one is about to speak and it is not permitted to speak after the water-clocks are drained, so an orator's speech can only be interrupted and resumed when the remaining water in the clock is preserved. Plautus in *Pseudolus*: 'I'm done for. Now the fellow's wallowing in mud. / He doesn't know the name. This affair is stuck.'[5]

71 In culmo arare
To plough among the stubble

Ἐπὶ καλάμης ἀροῦν, To plough among the stubble. Said of those who never rest from labour and thereby exhaust their mental faculties. Or of those who never stop begging friends to give them something. The metaphor is taken from excessively greedy farmers who never allow their fields to rest but drain all the good out of the soil by continuous cultivation, sowing anew immediately after the harvest. Suidas cites this from Lysias.[1]

* * * * *

1:1–17 and Luke 3:23–38. See NCE 6.319–21.

2 Cicero *De finibus* 5.28.84 and 2.10.30

3 Cicero *De officiis* 3.33.117; cf Otto 142. 'Cicero expressed . . . clock is preserved' was added in *1526*.

4 Cicero *Ad Quintum fratrem* 2.6.2

5 Plautus *Pseudolus* 984–5. This was added in *1533*.

71 *Suda* (see n1). Added in *1515*
1 Lysias fragment 212 Baiter-Sauppe (II 202), cited in *Suda* E 2348

72 **Taciturnior Pythagoreis**
   As silent as Pythagoreans

Σιωπηλώτερος ἔσομαι τῶν Πυθαγόρᾳ τελεσθέντων, I shall be more silent than
those who have consecrated themselves to Pythagoras. It is customarily used
of those who are extremely taciturn. Taken from the school of Pythagoras
in which a five years' silence was imposed on his disciples. This is called
ἐχεμυθία, from the fact that they ἔχειν 'restrain' their μῦθος 'speech.'[1] Suidas
reports it as a proverb, as does Zenodotus in his *Collection*.[2]

73 **Attagenae novilunium**
   A francolin's new moon

Ἀτταγᾶς νουμηνία, A francolin's new moon. The proverb is reported by
Suidas, but is not explained.[1] However, it can be readily conjectured from
the different passages where it occurs that it was directed at a crowd of
worthless and low-born persons.[2] The francolin is a marsh bird, distinctive

* * * * *

72 *Suda* (see n2). Otto 1496. Added in *1515*
   1 The word is found at Plutarch *Numa* 8, Athenaeus 7.308D, and Iamblichus *De
     vita Pythagorica* 6.32.
   2 *Suda* Σ 469. 'Zenodotus' is the usual name used by Erasmus to refer to Zeno-
     bius, which seems to be the correct form of the name (see CWE 31 10 n21).
     This error is based on an arbitrary emendation of Marcus Musurus in a scho-
     lion on Aristophanes *Clouds* 133 (see Bühler 1.102 n52). Erasmus must have
     drawn this proverb from Zenobius (Aldus) column 150, since it is not to be
     found among the proverbs of Zenobius in CPG. The final phrase referring to
     Zenodotus was added in *1526*.

73 *Suda* (see n1). This adage (added in *1515*) was referred to in *Adagia* IV i 5
   Woodcock. The connection between francolins and the new moon is obscure
   and probably fanciful. Numenius (Νουμήνιος) may have been, like Attagas,
   the name of a bird that was applied to a scoundrel, and the similarity with
   νουμηνία may have led to a connection with the new moon. See Mynors' note
   on *Adagia* III ii 4 Attabas and Numenius (CWE 34 390).
   1 *Suda* A 4306
   2 At *Adagia* IV i 5 Woodcock, Erasmus adduces Aristophanes *Birds* 760–1 to
     support the interpretation of the term 'francolin' being applied to a branded
     runaway slave.

because of the multicoloured marks on its plumage. Because of this slaves who were branded and whose backs had different-coloured patches from the weals left by beating were called francolins. The new moon, which the Greeks call the beginning of the month since they do not have a Kalends, was a time when slaves were torn apart as punishment in Athens and when levies of soldiers were held.

74 Ingens intervallum
A long distance

In book six of his *Letters to Atticus* Marcus Tullius refers to the following senarii as if they were proverbial: Πολλὰ δὲ ἐν μεταιχμίῳ / Νότος κυλίνδει κύματ᾽ εὐρείης ἁλός 'Many are the waves that the South wind stirs up / In the middle of the broad sea.'[1] The meaning is that Atticus is far away. One can stretch the use of the expression to mean also that a situation is still far from being dangerous.

75 Vivus vidensque
Though alive and seeing

Marcus Tullius points out that what Terence said in the *Eunuch*, 'Though alive and seeing, I am done for,' was used proverbially. For this is what he writes in his speech *For Sextius*: 'That wretched Cyprian, who has always been our friend and ally and of whom no harsh suspicion has ever reached the senate or our generals, "Alive and seeing," as the saying goes, has had everything confiscated with fare and finery.'[1] St Jerome also uses it in some

* * * * *

74 Here the proverb should be drawn from the quotation given by Cicero (or from his translation) rather than the title given by Erasmus. A more appropriate title would have been something like 'Many are the waves' (*Multae undae*). The unidentified fragment of Greek verse is quoted in *Adagia* v 1 45 Much in between (567 below).
1 Cicero *Ad Atticum* 6.3.1. The reference to book 6 was added in 1520. As often, Erasmus uses the term 'senarii' for what should be more accurately described as iambic trimeters.

75 Terence by way of Cicero (see n1). Otto 1932. Added in 1515
1 Cicero *Pro P. Sestio* 27.59, referring to the text of Terence *Eunuchus* 73. Erasmus gives the title of the speech as *Pro Sextio*.

passages.[2] In fact *cum victu suo ac vestitu* 'with fare and finery' also has the flavour of a proverb.

76 Praestat habere acerbos
Bitter enemies are better

In his dialogue *On Friendship* Marcus Tullius writes, 'For that is a shrewd proverb of Cato's: "Some people are much better served by bitter enemies than by friends who only seem sweet."'[1] I certainly admit that this is a quite splendid sentiment, but I would deny that it is a proverb. First of all, it does not have the appearance of a proverb. Secondly, proverbs are popular sayings, not just peculiar to any particular person. I think, therefore, that we should read *scitum est enim illud Catonis* or *scitum est enim illud verbum Catonis* 'for those are shrewd words of Cato.'[2] We thought, however, that it should be included in case anyone thought we had overlooked it through carelessness.

77 Columnas rumpere
Shattering columns

Aelian tells us that there were once huge animals in Samos (they are called *neades*) that could break open the earth with the sound they made.[1] From

* * * * *

2 The reference is perhaps to Jerome *Letters* 54.2 PL 22 550, CSEL 54 467. Cf *Adagia* III vi 13 To put one's hand in the flame intentionally, where 'intentionally' is a translation of *sciens et videns*, a phrase similar to *vivus vidensque*. Cf also *Adversus Rufinum* 2.32 PL 23 475C (*sciens et prudens*).

76 Cicero (see n1). Added in *1515*
1 Cicero *De amicitia* 24.90
2 The first part of the quotation is given by Erasmus as *scitum est enim illud proverbium Catonis*, where Erasmus is following the text of contemporary editions. The reading in modern editions is *illud Catonis*, without *proverbium*.

77 Juvenal (see n3). Added in *1515*
1 Aelian *De natura animalium* 17.28. Aelian refers to the expression 'to roar more loudly than *neades*' as a proverb. For some reason Erasmus makes no mention of this.

this originated a proverb directed at persons who were very noisy and excessively talkative. They were said to shatter doorposts and columns. Virgil uses it against Philistus, who was always carping and criticizing him.[2] So also Juvenal:

> Fronto's plane trees and tormented statues echo with the sound,
> [And columns are shattered by the never-ending recitations.][3]

78 Leporis vita
A hare's life

Λαγωοῦ βίον ζῆν, To live the life of a hare, is said of those who live their lives in great anxiety and trepidation. For this animal, an easy prey for all others, even sleeps with its eyes open. Demosthenes *Against Aeschines*: 'You lived the life of a hare, fearful and trembling and always expecting to be whipped.'[1] Plutarch used it in his essay 'On Love of Riches,' which we translated into Latin some time ago.[2] Athanasius wrote λαγωῶν δειλότεροι 'more cowardly than hares,' in his first *Apology*.[3] In Strabo too: 'As timid

* * * * *

2 As recorded in the *Life of Virgil* in Donatus Auctus: 'You shatter not only men's ears but also walls with your loquacity'; cf *Georgics* 3.328 and Plutarch *Moralia* 461D *De cohibenda ira*.

3 Juvenal 1.12–13. Line 13, which includes the proverbial expression (*semper et adsiduo ruptae lectore columnae*) is missing from the *Adagia*-text, but ought to have been cited. Perhaps the omission was a printer's error that was never noticed. See E. Courtney *A Commentary on the Satires of Juvenal* (London 1980) 86 for the translation 'tormented statues.'

78 Not to be found in CPG, but cf *Adagia* I x 57 A hare asleep, the point of which is that the hare's eyes remained open when it was asleep. Tilley H 153 A hare sleeps with his eyes open. Added in *1515*

1 Demosthenes 18.263 (*De corona*)

2 Plutarch *Moralia* 525E *De cupiditate divitiarum*. Erasmus translated this in 1514, presumably just before the publication of the second edition of the *Adagia*. 'A hare's life' does not appear in this work, though *Adagia* IV iv 57 A snail's life (101 below) does.

3 Athanasius *Apologia de fuga sua* 10 PG 25 657A. This sentence and what follows it were added in *1528*.

as Phrygian hares,' of which I have spoken elsewhere at the appropriate point.[4]

79 Victi non audent hiscere
The conquered dare not even mutter

Νικώμενοι ἄνδρες τῇ ἀγρυξίᾳ δέδενται, The conquered are bound by silence. In his essay entitled 'How One can Profit from Enemies' Plutarch cites this from Pindar.[1] It is similar to what we have reported elsewhere, 'Losers must expect to suffer.'[2] Ἀγρυξία is a splendid word to use when anyone does not dare to make a sound. From the verb γρύζειν 'to grunt, grumble,' of which I have spoken more than once.[3]

80 Thersitae facies
The look of Thersites

Θερσίτειον βλέμμα, The look of Thersites. Usually spoken of someone unbelievably ugly, because Homer wrote that Thersites had been the most unsightly of all who had come to Troy. He describes the man from head to feet,[1] as they say, so graphically (and not just his physical flaws but also his moral deficiencies) that one can say that in him a very foul character had a worthy home. The passage in Homer *Iliad* book two is too well known to be worth citing here.[2] The proverb will have more appeal if you give

* * * * *

4 *Adagia* II iv 7. Erasmus does not quote the Greek of Strabo (*Geographica* 1.2.30), but gives a Latin translation (*Phrygiis leporibus timidior*). See also 'Timid as a hare' at CWE 31 26 *Introduction* xiii.

79 Pindar by way of Plutarch (see n1). Added in *1515*
1 Plutarch *Moralia* 89B *De capienda ex inimicis utilitate*, citing Pindar fragment 229 Snell
2 *Adagia* II vi 1
3 *Adagia* I viii 3 Not a grunt; II i 82 To grumble

80 Added in *1515*. The second-last sentence beginning 'The proverb will have' was added in *1528*.
1 *A capite usque ad pedes*, very close in wording to *Adagia* I ii 37 From head to heel (*A capite usque ad calcem*)
2 Homer *Iliad* 2.216–19

it a moral application and say of someone who is handsome, but decadent, 'To look at his body, he is Nireus; to look at his character, you will find he surpasses "The look of Thersites."'[3] Suidas mentioned the adage.[4]

81 Picifer
A jay-bearer

Κιττοφόρος, Jay-bearer, seems to be a common term of abuse directed at someone of the lowest rank who is living in the most despicable circumstances. For Demosthenes in his speech *For Ctesipho* says that old women addressed Aeschines by this word as well as by λικνοφόρος 'basket-bearer' because he used to carry jays and winnowing baskets on his head.[1] For jays were used in the Bacchanalian rites since this bird was sacred to Bacchus, and a winnowing basket was used in all mystery rites. Accordingly, Maro writes 'and the mystic basket of Bacchus.'[2]

82 In numerato
Ready cash

'To have ready cash' may have the status of a proverb if applied metaphorically to mental abilities. Octavius Augustus, for example, as Seneca relates, declared of the orator Vinitius that he had wits like ready cash because when he was pleading cases he had the quickest intellect.[1] Whatever would

* * * * *

3 Nireus was the second most handsome warrior of the Greeks (after Achilles) who went to Troy. See Homer *Iliad* 2.673–4, Lycophron 1011–2.
4 *Suda* Θ 257; also Appendix 3.19

81 Demosthenes (see n1). Added in *1515*. Erasmus mistakenly confuses here the Greek words κίττα 'jay' and κιττός 'ivy' (see n1).
1 Demosthenes 18.260 (*De corona*). A λίκνον was a basket used to winnow the grain from the chaff. It was sacred to Dionysus and the god's celebrants carried baskets on their heads as well as wearing ivy wreaths.
2 Virgil *Georgics* 1.166

82 Seneca (see n1). Added in *1515*. Cf Allen Ep 396:132–3. The verb to be understood with the phrase is *habere* 'to have.'
1 Seneca *Controversiae* 2.5.20. Lucius Vinicius was suffect consul in AD 5. Erasmus gives Seneca as the source of the story in *1517/18*.

occur to others only after long thought would strike him the moment he applied his mind to the problem. The phrase was taken from those who liquidated their possessions, that is, changed them to ready cash. Quintilian in his sixth book says, 'Of an orator speaking off the cuff it used to be said that his wits were like ready cash.'² See the proverb 'You talked as easily as 1 2 3.'³

83 Quantum habet
Each is only as good as he's worth

'Everyone is valued according to his possessions.' Horace wrote this in his first satire. 'He says, "I never have enough, because one is only as influential as what one is worth."'¹ So also Juvenal in his third satire: 'A man's word is believed in proportion to the amount of cash he keeps in his strong-box.'² I would not have counted this as a proverb for fear that someone might cry out that I had been gathering maxims, not proverbs. St Augustine, however, specifically cited it as a proverb in his book *On Christian Teaching.*³ He says, 'Whence arose also that proverb: "You will be as influential as what you are worth."' And yet Horace too shows quite clearly that the sentiment was commonly expressed by his words that precede it: 'But a large number of people, deceived by false cupidity.'⁴ Apuleius also uses it in his *Apology*:

* * * * *

2 Quintilian 6.3.111. This sentence and the final one were added in 1533.
3 *Adagia* III vii 58 You talk like 1 2 3. Erasmus inaccurately quotes the proverb as *Numero dixisti* (for *Numero dicis*).

83 The full form of the proverb, as given at the beginning of the discussion, is *quantum habet quisque tanti fit,* which is not found as such. Close to it is Lucilius 1120 Marx (1128 Krenkel) *tantum habeas, tantum ipse sies tantique habearis.* Erasmus might have used a similar Greek expression from Plutarch in *Moralia* 526c *De cupiditate divitiarum*: 'Count yourself worth exactly what you have.' Otto 775. Added in 1515
1 Horace *Satires* 1.1.62. The subject, unexpressed here, is later shown to be *bona pars hominum* 'a good number of people.' Erasmus added 'in his first satire' in 1526.
2 Juvenal 3.143–4. This sentence was added in 1520, apart from 'in his third satire,' which first appeared in 1526.
3 Augustine *De disciplina Christiana* 11 PL 40 676
4 Horace *Satires* 1.1.61. This sentence and those following it were added in 1526.

'You are truly only as great as what you are worth.'[5] It seems to have come into common parlance from Euripides,[6] among whose verses Seneca includes this one: *Vbique tanti quisque, quantum habuit, fuit* 'Everywhere, each was only as influential as what he was worth.'[7]

84 Imis ceris eradere
To scrape away to the lowest level of wax

This means 'to delete completely,' so that not the slightest trace of what was originally written remains. Taken from those who write on wax tablets. Their practice is sometimes to invert their stilus and draw it over the top level of the wax in such a way that some traces of the former writing remain. Sometimes they erase it completely. St Jerome to Chrysogenus: 'You have so completely forgotten our friendship that you have erased that letter said by the Apostle to be written in the hearts of Christians, not changing it to a slight extent but, as the saying goes, erasing it down to the bottom of the wax.'[1] The proverb will be suitable when friends or former circumstances are completely forgotten, or in some similar situation.

85 Macilenta manu pinguem pedem
Thin hand, swollen foot

Λεπτῇ δὲ παχὺν πόδα χειρὶ πιέζοις, Press your swollen foot with a thin hand. This is how in his poem entitled *Works and Days* Hesiod described poverty, in a kind of riddle.[1] For the hands become thin through hunger, while the feet swell up through cold. The poem reads as follows: 'May the hard times of winter not find you resourceless, / And may you not press your swollen

* * * * *

5 Apuleius *Apologia* 23
6 See *TrGF* 2 *Adespota* 461. Only the last five of the twelve verses quoted at this point (in Latin translation only) by Seneca (see next note) are now thought to be the work of Euripides. This line is the fourth of the twelve.
7 Seneca *Letters* 115.14

84 Added in *1515*. Otto 374
1 Jerome *Letters* 9.2 PL 22 342, CSEL 54 34. He is referring to Paul in 2 Cor 3:2.

85 Added in *1515*
1 Hesiod *Works and Days* 496–7

foot with a thin hand.' It will be more attractive if it is used in a more metaphorical sense – to saving money for old age or something similar.

86 Non semper erit aetas
Summer will not last forever

Quite close in sense to this is what is said in the same work, Οὐκ αἰεὶ θέρος ἐσσεῖται, ποιεῖσθε καλιάς 'Summer will not last forever; make your nests.'[1] We shall not always be young and strong. Prepare for your old age. Or, good fortune will not last forever; fortify your mind with the tenets of philosophy so that you shrug off adversity. Cato too advises farmers to think how long winter lasts.[2] There is the well-known fable about the ants that chastized the cicada for having idled away the whole summer doing nothing except singing and for having to beg in winter because of this.[3] The proverb should have been inscribed on young men's caps. For its advice is that for our old age we should acquire not only money but also learning, virtue, and a good reputation, the best means of support when we are old.

* * * * *

86 Hesiod (see n1). Added in 1515
1 Hesiod *Works and Days* 503
2 Cato *De agri cultura* 30. This sentence and all the following ones were added in 1533. This expansion was probably prompted by a small collection of proverbs compiled by Joannes Alexander Brassicanus and published in Vienna in 1529. Brassicanus sent a copy of this collection to Erasmus, who drew on it, without acknowledgment, for the new edition of his *Adagia* in 1533, either to expand the content of existing adages or to insert new adages. In the case of this adage Erasmus' references to Cato and the fable are to be found in Brassicanus no 74 (*Cogitato quam longa sit hyems* 'Think how long winter lasts'). However, it must be stressed that Erasmus does not merely copy Brassicanus. In almost every instance he himself has had recourse to the sources, often amplifying the scope of the quotations. In this volume Brassicanus' influence is to be detected in IV iii 94; IV vi 74; IV vii 43, 65, 69, 88, 89, 92; IV viii 1, 10, 14, 18, 27, 31, 41; IV ix 19, 29, 52, 58, 67, 87; IV x 3, 6, 28, 35, 56, 70; V i 20; V ii 12, 20, 23, 24, 40. See ASD II-8 13–14 with n14; CEBR 1:191–2.
3 Aesop 114 Hausrath; Aesop (Aldine 1505) page 50; Perry 373 (Babrius 140). The words of the ants were, 'You sang in the summer, now you can dance in the winter.'

87 Cum exossis suum rodit pedem
When a polypus gnaws its own foot

Hesiod described poverty in the same work, using a similar metaphor:
"Οτ᾽ ἀνόστεος ὃν πόδα τένδει 'When the boneless one eats its own feet.'[1]
He uses the term *exossis* 'the boneless one' for the sea-polypus because
it has no bones. Some believed that the polypus gnawed its limbs when
it did not have food, for it is very greedy. Pliny, however, thinks that
shellfish do this to it; but he believes that the limbs grew back again, like
lizards' tails, after they had been cut off.[2] Alcaeus, cited in book seven
of Athenaeus: 'I am devouring myself like a polypus.'[3] Accordingly, the
polypus was also called 'self-devourer.' But Athenaeus also rejects this
belief.[4]

88 Centum plaustri trabes
A wagon has a hundred planks

What Hesiod wrote in the same work, entitled *Works and Days*, is as like
a proverb 'As one egg is like another':[1] Ἑκατὸν δέ τε δούραθ᾽ ἁμάξης 'A
hundred planks are needed to make a wagon.'[2] It will be appropriate to
use this to point out that what we are being asked for costs a great deal.
For it is easy for us to use other persons' goods without reckoning how
much they cost the lender. This is what Hesiod's poem says:

> It is easy to say, 'Lend me your oxen and your cart.'
> It is easy to say, 'No. My bulls have much work to do.'

* * * * *

87 Hesiod (see n1). Added in *1515*
1 Hesiod *Works and Days* 524
2 Pliny *Naturalis historia* 9.87. An error, since early and modern editions offer
  congris 'eels' for *conchis* 'shellfish'
3 Alcaeus was a writer of comedies; PCG 2 Alcaeus fragment 30. Cited by
  Athenaeus 7.316C. This sentence and the next two were added in *1528*.
4 Athenaeus 7.316E–F

88 Added in *1515*. The final sentence was added in *1530*.
1 Cf *Adagia* I v 10 As like as one egg to another.
2 Hesiod *Works and Days* 456

The wise man undertakes to build a wagon,
The foolish man does not know that it is built from a hundred planks.[3]

And so whenever someone needs different kinds of help for what he is
undertaking, for example, holding a magistracy, writing a book, composing
a public address, setting up house, travelling abroad in distant lands, it will
be quite appropriate for us to use Hesiod's phrase, 'A wagon has a hundred
planks.'

89 Araneas eiicere
To cast out spiders' webs

What is in the same work by the same author also has the appearance of a
proverb: Ἐκ δ᾽ ἀγγέων ἐλάσειας ἀράχνια 'You should cast out spiders' webs
from your pots.'[1] Even today we indicate poverty and emptiness in this way.[2]
Similarly, Catullus: 'For the purse of your friend Catullus is full of spiders'
webs.'[3] Nowadays, there is no more common expression than this one.
Lucian in *Pseudologista*: 'Stuffed full of rotting matter and spiders' webs.'[4]

90 Muris circumcurrentibus
Surrounding walls

Τῶν τοίχων περιτρεχόντων, Surrounding walls. Plutarch in his 'Table-talk,' in
the seventh decade and fifth problem, says that this was a proverb used by
women to mean something was being kept secret, obviously because walls
keep away witnesses and listeners.[1] He says, however, that the pleasures
and amusements of upright men ought to be such that they have no need

* * * * *

3 Hesiod *Works and Days* 453–6

89 Hesiod (see n1). Added in 1515. The final sentence was added in 1526. Otto
149–50
1 Hesiod *Works and Days* 475
2 Suringar 18
3 Catullus 13.7–8
4 Lucian *Pseudologista* 24

90 Plutarch (see n1). Added in 1515
1 Plutarch *Moralia* 705A *Quaestiones convivales*

of the protection of walls. One may use this expression to mean that some wondrous thing is being devised in secret and that because of this other persons are trying to find out about it.

91 Κερασβόλος
Horn-struck

In the same work, in the second problem, Plutarch tells us that persons who are very stern and fierce and of harsh character are accustomed to be called κερασβόλοι, a word that is not very easily translated into Latin.[1] The metaphor is taken from agriculture when seeds drop on the horns of bulls before falling onto the earth. These seeds are named κερασβόλα, from their striking (βάλλεσθαι) against horns (κέρατα). Such seeds are said to be much harder than all others. Consequently, they are also called ἀτεράμονα 'hard.'[2] The author of the *Etymologicon* says that this word was used only once by Plato and that it was taken from legumes that neither fire nor water could soften. We see some things of this kind, small and black, mingled with legumes. The passage occurs in Plato, book nine of *On the Laws.*[3] In this passage indeed the translator appears not to have known what κερασβόλα are.[4] For he translates the word as 'legumes hardened by being struck with lightning,' as if the word were κεραυνόβολα. Furthermore, Plutarch gives the reason why seeds that strike against the horns of oxen either come to nothing or turn out drier and harder.[5] Those seeds that the earth nurtures immediately after receiving them from a warm hand are helped because of the heat that is good for seeds. But those that are dashed on horns seem to have been scattered rather than planted; they become chilled because they do not immediately enter the soil. Theophrastus doubts whether what the farmers say about *cerasbola* is worth anything.[6]

* * * * *

91 Plutarch (see n1). Added in *1515*

1 Plutarch *Moralia* 700C *Quaestiones convivales*

2 *Etymologicum magnum* 505.19

3 Plato *Laws* 9.853D. This section on Plato, as far as κεραυνόβολα, was added in *1526*.

4 The translator is the famous neo-Platonist philosopher Marsilio Ficino; see *Adagia* IV viii 97 n2 (417 below).

5 Plutarch *Moralia* 701B *Quaestiones convivales*, but according to Plutarch it is the soil's warmth, not the hand's, that promotes growth in seeds planted by hand.

6 Theophrastus *De causis plantarum* 4.12.13. This sentence was added in *1533*.

92 Respublica virum docet
Politics instruct a man

Πόλις ἄνδρα διδάσκει, Politics instruct a man. It means that no one can be equipped to do anything unless he has been trained for it by experience. Plutarch cites it from Simonides, though it is only half of a dactylic hexameter.[1] However long you have lived in the countryside, you will not become suited for administering affairs of the state unless you have spent your life in the forum, in the senate house, in the packed assembly. In Plato Socrates alluded to this when he replied to an invitation to visit beautiful areas in the country; he said that he was eager to learn, but trees do not teach one anything.[2]

93 Faber cum sis
You are a carpenter, stick to your trade

In his 'Civil Precepts' Plutarch cites from Euripides the following senarius, clearly proverbial: Τέκτων γὰρ ὤν, οὐκ ἔπραττες ξυλουργικά 'Although you are a carpenter, you do not work in wood.'[1] This will suit persons who attempt something for which they are unsuited, either through lack of training or inappropriate nature. For example, if someone who is inarticulate and untrained in the arts of persuasion undertakes the role of an ambassador, or if a careless person manages the household expenses, or if an old or weak man joins the army, or if a priest engages in hunting or if a Scotist in rhetoric.[2] Those words of Horace, *tractant fabrilia fabri* 'artisans work

* * * * *

92 Simonides by way of Plutarch (see n1). Cf *Adagia* I x 76 'Tis the place that shows the man. Tilley A 402 Authority (honour, office) shows what a man is. Added in *1515*. Additions were made in *1517/18* ('though it is ... hexameter') and in *1533* ('in the packed assembly' to the end).
1 Plutarch *Moralia* 784B *An seni respublica gerenda sit*, citing Simonides fragment 15 West
2 Plato *Phaedrus* 230D

93 The full Latin form of the adage is *faber cum sis, opera haud facis fabrilia*. Cf *Adagia* I vi 16 Let the cobbler stick to his last. Added in *1515*
1 Plutarch *Moralia* 812E *Praecepta gerendae reipublicae*, citing Euripides fragment 988 Nauck. As often, Erasmus uses the term 'senarius' for 'trimeter.'
2 The Scotists were followers of Duns Scotus. The dry expository style of the

the material for which they are trained,' apparently based on this verse of Euripides, have been proverbial for a long time now.[3]

94 Aquam igni miscere
Mixing fire and water

Πῦρ ὕδατι μιγνύναι, To mix fire with water. This proverb ought also to be included among those indicating what is impossible. In his essay entitled 'On Primordial Cold,' where Plutarch is eager to prove that coldness is a property of water rather than of air, he adduces the evidence of this proverb.[1] Water fights with fire in both its properties; for the hot and the dry fight with the moist and the cold. In the same passage he says that it was a Persian custom for supplicants to go into a river carrying fire and to threaten to hurl the fire into the water if they were not given what they sought. In this way they certainly got what they wanted, but they were punished because they had threatened to do what was contrary to nature. For water is the enemy of fire and always extinguishes it. Among non-Greeks this mode of supplication was thought to carry most weight and one where it would not be proper to refuse the request. Marcus Tullius in the thirteenth *Philippic*: 'Wave and flame will sooner be reconciled.'[2] Again, 'Sooner will wave and flame, as some poet said, sooner will all elements be

* * * * *

Scotists had none of the emotive elements of rhetoric. Scotus is named by Erasmus as one of the commentators who 'simply teach and do not affect people's emotions' (*On the Christian Widow* CWE 66 246).
3 Horace *Epistles* 2.1.116

94 Plutarch (see n1). Otto 131. Tilley w 110 Mix water with fire. In his essay on *Adagia* IV i 1 War is a treat for those that do not know it, Erasmus uses this proverb in a slightly different form, *aquam flammis miscere* 'to mix flames and water' (CWE 35 419). Added in *1515*
1 Plutarch *Moralia* 950F *De primo frigido*
2 Cicero *Philippics* 13.21.49. This sentence and the following one were added in *1533*. Erasmus actually cites part of the same passage twice, the first time inexactly, and the second more accurately. He has probably taken the first part from Brassicanus, in whose collection (see *Adagia* IV iii 86 n2, 52 above) proverb no 118 is 'Wave and flame will sooner be reconciled,' and then given a fuller version of the passage without expunging the first part.

in harmony than the republic will be reconciled with men like Antony or men like Antony with the republic.'

95 Velut e specula
As if from a watch-tower

Ὡς ἀπὸ σκοπιᾶς, As if from a watch-tower. A simile used proverbially when anyone examines something in its entirety from every angle. For it is most advantageous to look at all things from a height, since nothing stands in the way to impede one's view. Plutarch uses it in his essay entitled 'On the Fortune of the Romans.'[1]

96 Velut in cratere
The cup of friendship

Ὥσπερ ἐν κρατῆρι φιλοτησίῳ, As if in a cup of friendship. This simile is also proverbial. By it we shall show that situations once racked by disorder are now settled and calmed down and that previous enemies are reconciled in friendship. The glass that everyone stretches out to each other at banquets is called the cup of friendship, a symbol and pledge of amity. An example is when a man who was betrothing his daughter proffered the cup of friendship to his future son-in-law, after first taking a sip. The Scythians too used to seal friendships, to which they were extremely devoted, by a cup of wine, as Lucian attests in On Friendship.[1] Even Christ himself, Prince of our religion, consecrated the mystery of his love for his followers with a cup.[2]

* * * * *

95 Plutarch (see n1). Added in 1515. Cf Adagia IV x 95 Tamquam de specula, As if from a watch-tower, drawn from Cicero (540 below).
1 Plutarch Moralia 317C De fortuna Romanorum

96 Lucian (see n1). Added in 1515. Cf Adagia IV vii 70 The cup of friendship (Philotesius crater); see 329 below.
1 Lucian Toxaris 25
2 Cf Matt 26:27–9, Mark 14:23–4, Luke 22:17–19. The final sentence was added in 1517/18.

97 Sero venisti
You have come too late

Ὄψ᾽ ἦλθες, You have come too late. This fits those who undertake something after the appropriate time, like someone whose desires have been cooled by old age preparing to marry or someone starting to learn new languages when he is quite old. It originated with the oracle that the Pythian priestess gave to a man who consulted her on whether he ought to enter politics. 'You have come too late in consulting me about high political office and administering the state, and you knock on the door at a time unsuited for war.' Plutarch mentions it in his essay entitled 'Ought an Older Man to Enter Politics?'[1]

98 Prius antidotum quam venenum
Antidote before poison

St Jerome, replying to Rufinus: 'In this way you should censure the prefaces of books unknown to you whose future charges you have foreseen, thus fulfilling the proverb "Antidote before poison."'[1] You need to understand 'take' with the proverb. It can be appropriately used whenever someone clears himself of a charge that has not yet been laid against him. For an antidote is given to combat poison. No one takes it unless he has tasted poison. There are some, however, who fortify themselves in advance through antidotes so that any poison that they may perchance take will not do them any harm. We read that Mithridates did this.[2]

* * * * *

97 Plutarch (see n1). Added in *1515*. Cf *Adagia* II ix 17 You're late; off with you to Colonus.
1 Plutarch *Moralia* 784B *An seni respublica gerenda sit*. Erasmus mistranslates the last part of the quotation, which in the Greek means 'and you knock on the door of the chamber at an inappropriate time.'

98 Jerome (see n1). Otto 118. Added in *1515*
1 Jerome *Adversus Rufinum* 2.34 PL 23 476C
2 See Pliny *Naturalis historia* 23.149, 25.62; see also Aulus Gellius *Noctes Atticae* 17.16.

99 Statua taciturnior
As mute as a statue

Even in our times there is the proverb 'As mute as a statue.' Directed at a person who is extremely tongue-tied and taciturn. Horace used this hyperbole in his *Letter to Julius Florus*: 'He emerges mute as a statue for the most part and makes the people shake with laughter.'[1] Similarly, Juvenal describes a man who is rich but cannot speak publicly and is unlettered as being like a statue of Mercury: 'Very like a limbless Hermes.'[2] There is a similar form of the proverb in St Chrysostom in his sixth book *About Priesthood*, used of someone slow and stupid: 'Then, as we Greeks are wont to say, he will be no different from statues.'[3] We have spoken of this on another occasion as well.[4] Xenophon in his *Symposium*: 'Their voices were more inaudible than those of stone statues.'[5] Statues often have the appearance of wise and eloquent men, but they themselves can say nothing.

100 Hoc noveram priusquam Theognis natus est
I knew this before Theognis was born

In his work entitled 'The Philosopher Ought to Argue with Princes' Plutarch mocks those who would make two kinds of philosophy, one situated in the mind that originated with Mercury *Hegemon*, that is, 'Mercury the Leader,' the other based on utterance that was granted generously by Mercury *Diactoros*, that is, 'Mercury the Messenger.'[1] He says, 'It's worthless and out of date; that saying should be applied to it, Τουτοὶ μὲν ᾔδειν πρὶν Θεόγνιν

* * * * *

99 Horace (see n1). Otto 1689. Tilley s 834, P 490 As mute as a statue, as dumb as a post; Suringar 214. Added in *1515*
  1 Horace *Epistles* 2.2.83–4. The subject is *ingenium* 'intellect,' with reference to a poet who has sequestered himself for years while composing his verse.
  2 Juvenal 8.53. It is not so much the riches of the man that are relevant to Juvenal but his high birth (he was a great grandson of the Emperor Tiberius).
  3 Chrysostom *De sacerdotio* 6.7 PG 48 683
  4 This does not seem to refer to the *Adagia*.
  5 Xenophon *Lacedaemonia Respublica* 3.5 (not the *Symposium*)

100 Plutarch and Aulus Gellius (see nn1, 3). Otto 1776. Added in *1515*
  1 Plutarch *Moralia* 777B *Maxime cum principibus philosopho esse disserendum*, citing PCG 8 *Adespota* 461

γεγονέναι "I knew this before Theognis was born."' He also uses this proverb to refute the same belief in his work entitled 'Why the Pythia No Longer Gives Oracles in Verse,' citing it from some writer of comedy.[2] In his first book of *Attic Nights*, chapter 3, Aulus Gellius cites from Lucilius: 'Cicero says, "Arms ought not to be taken up for a friend against one's country." To be sure, everyone knew this, even, as Lucilius says, "before Theognis was born."'[3] There can be no doubt that this senarius is proverbial, used to indicate something that was trivial and foolish.[4] It apparently refers to Theognis, a writer of tragedies, whose style was extremely frigid, according to Suidas and, if I am not mistaken, Plato.[5] I give this information as there was also another writer of this name whose aphorisms survive.[6]

1 Phocensium desperatio
Phocian desperation

Φωκέων ἀπόνοια, Desperation of the Phocians, or Φωκικὴ ἀπόνοια, Phocian desperation. Stephanus tells us that this was customarily said of stupid and irrational plans.[1] From Plutarch of Chaeronea, however, we can conclude that it was usually said when people resorted to extreme measures in a desperate situation.[2] The expression arose from the following circum-

* * * * *

2 Plutarch *Moralia* 395D *De Pythiae oraculis*. Plutarch here is talking about two kinds of argument rather than two kinds of philosophy.

3 Aulus Gellius *Noctes Atticae* 1.3.19. See Cicero *De amicitia* 11.36; Lucilius 952 Marx (957 Krenkel).

4 This refers to the trimeter cited by Plutarch.

5 *Suda* Θ 137. The reference to Plato is an error, for Aristophanes. Cf Aristophanes *Acharnians* 11, 138–40.

6 Theognis of Megara, whom Erasmus cites just under 50 times; see Phillips 402.

1 Stephanus of Byzantium and Plutarch (see nn1–2). A similar adage *Phocensium amolitio* 'The removal of the Phocians' was present in *1508* (no 556 in the first chiliad). It remained even when IV iv 1 first appeared in *1515* until being dropped in *1528*. The references to Pausanias and Stephanus at the end of the discussion were added in *1526* and *1528* respectively.

1 Stephanus of Byzantium sub Φωκίς

2 Plutarch *Moralia* 244B–D *Mulierum virtutes*, whom Erasmus follows closely for the rest of the paragraph

stances. Between the Thessalians and the Phocians there was fierce hatred and irreconcilable enmity, and, to use Plutarch's words, Ἄσπονδος πόλεμος 'A truceless war.'[3] The Phocians had slaughtered on the same day every single leading man in the cities of Thessalia, while the Thessalians in turn had crucified 250 Phocian hostages.[4] The Thessalians then gathered together all their forces and invaded Phocis by way of Locris, having issued a decree that no mature male was to be spared and that the women and children were to be taken off into slavery. Accordingly, Daiphantus, one of the three leaders of the Phocians, proposed that the Phocian men should go to meet the Thessalians to join battle with them, but that all the women and children in Phocis should be assembled and sequestered in one place under guard. A huge supply of wood should be heaped up around the location and the guards were to be instructed to set fire to it and burn to death the women and children immediately they learned that the Phocians had been defeated in battle. All agreed with this proposal except for one man who rose to his feet and said that this action was not right unless the women voted and approved it as well. If they disapproved, they should not be compelled to follow it. And so when the women learned of the proposal, they themselves met together in council. They praised Daiphantus for having considered the interests of Phocis in the best possible way and said that both the wives and their children agreed with the proposal. When this procedure was over, the Phocians joined battle with the Thessalians and emerged victorious. The Greeks called that decree 'madness of the Phocians.'

The reason was that even though the situation had a happy ending they thought the decree extremely rash and very unwise. This is very much what Plutarch tells us. Pausanias gives a fairly similar account in his 'Phocis.'[5] He also mentions this proverb, which he says is applied, because of this event, to 'all ruthless proposals.' Stephanus also mentions it, pointing out that it was customarily said of 'those who make ruthless proposals.'[6]

* * * * *

3 *Adagia* III iii 84

4 According to Plutarch the Thessalians did not crucify their hostages but trampled them to death. The verb in modern editions of Plutarch is a form of κατελαύνω 'drive down upon.' Erasmus has either misconstrued the verb or had a variant in his text. Pausanias (see next note) says that 300 men were trampled by the Thessalian cavalry.

5 Pausanias 10.1.6–7

6 Stephanus of Byzantium sub Φωκίς

2 Suspensa manu
With a limp hand

Pliny in book six of his *Letters* said *Suspensa man* 'With a limp hand' in the sense of 'lightly' or 'very half-heartedly.'[1] He writes, 'You ought not to commend to me with a limp hand those whom you think need to be assisted.' For the expression has more appeal if one transfers the sense from the physical to the mental. In *Declamation* 12 Quintilian uses *levi manu* 'with a light hand' in the same sense as if it were a proverb,[2] while Cicero uses *levi bracchio* 'with a light arm,' about which I have spoken elsewhere.[3] We also say *suspenso pede* 'on tiptoe' in the sense of 'gently and quietly.'[4] Ammianus in book fourteen: 'They threw themselves into the skiffs *suspensis passibus* "quietly."'[5]

3 Extremum occupet scabies
The last one's a scab

In antiquity when children raced each other they often used to shout, 'The last one's a scab,' using these words to encourage every one to run fast and putting a curse on who was last. This became an adage used by those

* * * * *

2 Pliny (see n1). This adage is a good example of the continual expansion in successive editions. In *1515*, where it first appeared, the adage consisted of only the first two sentences. The third sentence was added in *1517/18*, while the references to Quintilian and Cicero (along with Ammianus) first appeared in *1520* and *1528* respectively. Otto 1047

1 Pliny *Letters* 6.12.1

2 Pseudo-Quintilian *Declamations* 12.11

3 *Adagia* I iv 27 With a gentle touch, with a light touch; Cicero *Ad Atticum* 2.1.6; 4.17.3

4 This expression is mentioned (in the plural) in *Adagia* IV iii 66 To walk on tiptoe (40 above).

5 Ammianus Marcellinus 14.2.2. Erasmus appears to take the phrase *suspensis passibus* in a metaphorical sense. It is more probable that Ammianus has compressed two ideas into one: 'They approached the skiffs on tiptoe and threw themselves in.'

3 Horace (see n3). Otto 1598. Tilley D 267 The devil take the hindmost. Added in *1515*

who indicated that they wanted to prevail by any means and would not allow themselves to be among the last. Accordingly, those who increase their
wealth by fair means or foul so that they will not fail to be among the élite,
those who by deceitful practices rise to the position of magistrates, and those
who hunt unscrupulously for highly paid offices in the church can say to
someone who urges them to behave differently, 'The last one's a scab.' And
yet nothing prevents us from applying it differently in a good sense. Whoever strives with all his might not to be surpassed by his contemporaries
in erudition or by a friend in kindnesses and the duties of friendship may
say, 'The last one's a scab.' We credit this proverb, therefore, to children,
as also Τὴν κατὰ σαυτὸν ἔλα 'Seek a wife of your own sort,'[1] and this one
in the Gospel according to Matthew chapter 11, 'We piped for you and you
did not dance.'[2] Horace used it in his *Art of Poetry*: 'The last one's a scab; it
is a disgrace for me to be left behind.'[3] Acron points out the origin.[4]

4 Ἡμερόκοιτος
Daysleeper

It seems to be a common joke for thieves to be called Ἡμερόκοιτοι 'Daysleep-
ers,' because they sleep during the day and are awake in the night. So Hesiod in *Works and Days*: 'Let not him who is a ἡμερόκοιτος "a sleeper by day"
remove your goods.'[1] It will be apt to apply it to a pilferer and a thief. There
is also a fish of the same name, as Suidas points out – a *phoca*, I think.[2]

* * * * *

1 *Adagia* I viii 1
2 Matt 11:17. The specific gospel reference did not appear until 1528 where it
   was given as 'Matth. ii.' It was corrected in 1536.
3 Horace *Ars poetica* 417, where the proverbial expression goes more closely
   with the preceding words 'I fashion wonderful poems.'
4 Pseudo-Acron on Horace *Ars poetica* 417; see also pseudo-Acron on *Epistles*
   1.1.59–60 and Porphyrion on *Epistles* 1.1.62.

4 Hesiod (see n1). Added in 1515. The final sentence was added in 1528.
1 Hesiod *Works and Days* 605
2 *Suda* H 307. This sentence was added in 1528. In Adler's edition of the *Suda*
   the word is explained simply as the equivalent of 'thief,' no fish being mentioned. In the *editio princeps* of 1499, however, the word is defined as 'a fish
   and a thief.' Oppian refers to a fish of this name (*Halieutica* 2.199, 224), its
   major characteristics being laziness and gluttony. Galen mentions a fish φωκίς
   (emended to φυκίς by Helmreich) at *De temperamentis* 1.6 (1.551 Kühn), and

5 In omnia potentes
Powerful over all things

The following words of Hesiod will suit those who have the greatest power to harm or help: Ἐν τοῖς γὰρ τέλος ἐστὶν ὁμῶς ἀγαθῶν τε κακῶν τε 'For in them [Zeus and Poseidon] lies the supreme power of good and evil.'[1] What was said by the poet about the gods we can apply also to a human being who has supreme authority or to something that is of very great importance. For example, to a prince or to something that is very highly-regarded, such as money if we wish to be facetious or literature and virtues if we are serious.

6 Ne uni navi facultates
Do not put all your wealth on one ship

In fact I think what is in the same work, Μὴ δ' ἐπὶ νηυσὶν ἅπαντα βίον κοίλῃσι τίθεσθαι 'Do not entrust all your possessions to curved ships all at once,'[1] should be regarded as a proverb if it is used in a figurative way. Do not attempt anything that will endanger everything. For you must not gamble all that you have on one throw. Sea commerce is dangerous; for a shipwreck carries off everything. It is safer to trade on land. We have reported elsewhere the saying of a Spartan, who said he did not like wealth that depended on the sheets of a ship.[2]

*****

perhaps this lies behind Erasmus' tentative and strange identification of the 'fish' as a *phoca*, the usual meaning of which is 'seal.'

5 Added in 1515. The title of the adage has little of a proverbial ring, and, as the beginning of the commentary suggests, Erasmus is probably thinking of the Hesiodic verse as the actual adage. For quotations being used in the same way as proverbs see the numerous Homeric verses that are given this status of adages at *Adagia* III viii 1–III x 75.
1 Hesiod *Works and Days* 669

6 Hesiod (see n1). Tilley A 209 Venture not all in one bottom. Added in 1515. 'Sea commerce' to the end was added in 1533.
1 Hesiod *Works and Days* 689
2 *Adagia* I ix 72 It hangs by a hair. It hangs by a thread. The story derives from Plutarch *Moralia* 234E–F *Apophthegmata Laconica* and is translated by Erasmus in *Apophthegmata* II 45 (LB IV 139B–C).

7 **Urit absque torre**
You don't need fire to burn someone up

This verse is used now and then in a proverbial sense by Plutarch, Εὕει
ἄτερ δάλοιο καὶ ὠμῷ γήραϊ δῶκεν 'She burns him up without a firebrand and
consigns him to old age.'[1]

This is said of course of a shameless wife who by her behaviour makes
her husband prematurely old. The expression will have charm if one applies
it to avarice, ambition, envy, shameful lust, and similar moral flaws to which
humans are exposed and which torture them and cause them to waste away.

8 **Adhuc caelum volvitur**
The heavens are still revolving

Whenever we mean that there is still hope and that time, which usually
brings an opportunity for better fortune, still remains, those words of Theocritus from the *Graces* will be appropriate: Οὔπω μῆνας ἄγων ἔκαμ᾽ οὐρανὸς
οὐδ᾽ ἐνιαυτούς 'The heavens are not yet weary and have not ceased to roll
round the months and years.'[1]

For what one year denies us the next confers of its own accord.

9 **Multae rotae volventur**
There's many a wheel to turn

What follows next is a proverbial expression and is related in sense: Πολλοὶ
κινήσουσιν ἔτι τροχὸν ἅρματος ἵπποι 'There is many a horse that will move
the wheel and make it turn.'[1]

* * * * *

7 Hesiod by way of Plutarch (see n1). Added in *1515*
1 Plutarch *Moralia* 100E *Consolatio ad Apollonium* and 527A *De cupiditate divitiarum*,
citing Hesiod *Works and Days* 705

8 This and the next sixteen adages (with the exception of 19) are drawn from
Theocritus. Added in *1515*. The final sentence was added in *1533*.
1 Theocritus *Idylls* 16.71

9 Theocritus (see n1). Added in *1515*. 'The interpretation' to the end was added
in *1533*.
1 Theocritus *Idylls* 16.72. Erasmus translates 'the chariot's wheel' of the Greek

In other words, there is still a lot of time remaining and many changes in circumstances will occur. This adage is commonly spoken even today in our own time.[2] The interpretation of some that it relates to the Olympic games is quite unappealing.[3] The poet is not dealing with these in this context, in a pastoral poem.

10 Ne nomen quidem
Not even the name

What is said in the same eclogue, is also proverbial: Βοᾶς δ᾽ ἔτι μηδ᾽ ὄνομ᾽ εἴη 'No longer will there be even the name of war and discord.'[1] Similarly Paul to the Ephesians: 'Let not fornication or indecency of any kind or greed be even named among you.'[2] But why? Is it such a crime to say the words 'greed' or 'lust'? I do not think so, but the Apostle used a proverbial hyperbole to denounce strongly these vices. For both Judas and Pilate are named by the devout.

11 Cervus canes trahit
The stag drags off the hounds

Among the adages that we use to signify a reversal of nature or what is impossible we should count too what appears in Theocritus in the *Thyrsis*: Τοὺς κύνας ὁ ἔλαφος ἕλκει 'The stag drags off the hounds.' For it is a reversal of nature for a stag to hunt hounds. This is how the Theocritean verse runs:

* * * * *

by 'wheel.' The Latin *rota* can refer on its own to the sun (cf Virgil *Aeneid* 6.748), and Erasmus may have understood the Theocritean verse to refer to the passage of time; see Gow in his commentary on Theocritus ad loc.

2 Suringar 122

3 Cf the scholion on Theocritus *Idylls* 16.72: 'There will be many victors in need of poets.'

10 Theocritus (see n1). Added in *1515*. The last sentence was added in *1533*. More aptly it would follow immediately after 'I do not think so.'

1 Theocritus *Idylls* 16.97

2 Eph 5:3

11 Theocritus (see n1). Added in *1515*. The Virgilian reference at the end was added in *1517/18*.

Δάφνις ἐπεὶ θνάσκει, καὶ τὼς κύνας ὤλαφος ἕλκοι 'Now that Daphnis is dying, may the stag drag off the hounds.'[1]

Similarly, Virgil in the *Pharmaceutria*: 'Now may the wolf flee from the sheep.'[2]

12 Bubo canit lusciniae
The owl sings to the nightingale

Also what immediately follows: Κὴξ ὀρέων τοι σκῶπες ἀηδόσι γαρύσαιντο 'And may the mountain owl sing to the nightingales.'[1] When an inarticulate person tries to persuade someone who is eloquent, or an ignorant person tries to instruct someone who is very learned.

13 Ne vidit quidem oleum
He has never even laid eyes upon oil

The eclogue entitled the *Swineherds* is full of proverbial expressions and figures. The first of these is Καὶ πόκα τῆνος ἔλαιον ἐν ὀφθαλμοῖσιν ὀπώπει; 'And when had that fellow ever laid eyes on oil?'[1] This will suit those who are very ignorant of some profession or un-skilled in it. For example, if anyone were to claim knowledge of medicine when he has never learned anything of that art, this verse will be a witty criticism of him.[2] Athletes were smeared with olive-oil so that their limbs would be stronger. Because of this the contest itself is signified by the word 'oil.' The scholia, however, state that some take 'oil' to refer to the tree,

* * * * *

1 Theocritus *Idylls* 1.135. Cf *Iliad* 17.558, 22.335; Euripides *Hercules Furens* 568.
2 Virgil *Eclogues* 8.52

12 Theocritus (see n1). Added in *1515*
1 Theocritus *Idylls* 1.136. The text and interpretation of the Theocritean line is uncertain; see Gow in his commentary ad loc.

13 Theocritus (see n1). Added in *1515*. 'Because of this' to the end was added in *1526*.
1 Theocritus *Idylls* 4.7
2 The Greek verse already cited is now quoted again.

since competitors in the Olympic games were awarded wreaths of olive or oleaster.[3]

14 Et me mater Pollucem vincere dixit
And my mother said I was better than Pollux

Also what follows in the same poem, Κῆμ᾽ ἔφαθ᾽ ἁ μάτηρ Πολυδεύκεος ἦμεν ἀμείνω 'And my mother said that I was better than Pollux.'[1] When anyone is ranked higher than or reckoned equal to those with whom he in no way ought to be compared. For mothers are blinded by love for their sons and think that they are extremely handsome when they are ugly, and extremely brave when they are very cowardly. Pollux is believed to have been the best boxer, as Horace attests: 'Castor takes delight in horses, the other one born from the same egg takes delight in boxing.'[2]

15 Suade lupis ut insaniant
Persuade wolves to go mad

Again in the same poem: Πεῖσαι τοι Μίλων καὶ τὼς λύκως αὐτίκα λυσσῆν 'Milo, next persuade even wolves to go mad.'[1] When someone turns his mind to doing something very foolish, which he would not attempt unless he were mad. For wolves are mad by their very nature. It is as if someone were to goad on a tyrant to be cruel when he has the natural dis-

* * * * *

3 The scholia on Theocritus *Idylls* 4.7

14 Theocritus (see n1). Added in *1515*. The final part of the commentary, from 'as Horace' to the end, was added in *1533*.
1 Theocritus *Idylls* 4.9
2 Horace *Satires* 2.1.26–7. Castor and Pollux, were known as the Dioscuri, the 'sons of Zeus.' In most versions of the myth Pollux is the immortal son of Zeus, Castor is the mortal son of Tyndareus, the husband of Leda, who was seduced by Zeus in the form of a swan.

15 Theocritus (see n1). Added in *1515*
1 Theocritus *Idylls* 4.11. Erasmus misunderstood the Greek. A more literal translation is 'Milo may as well persuade wolves to go mad on the spot.'

position for excessive violence. Rabies is a characteristic of dogs. Accordingly, the scholiast of Theocritus thinks that these words are offered as a reversal of nature. But dogs are mad only sometimes, wolves are always rabid.

16 Rore pascitur
Feeding on dew

What is said of a skinny calf in the same *Idyll* will suit perfectly a person who is extremely thin: Μὴ πρώκας σιτίζεται ὥσπερ ὁ τέττιξ 'Does it live on dew like the cicada?'[1]

For in Doric the word for dew is πρώξ because it falls πρωΐ 'in the morning.'[2] In addition Pliny attests, in book eleven, chapter twenty-six, that cicadas feed on dew: 'They do not have a mouth, but on their breast, which is porous, they have a sharp needle like our tongues. They lick up the dew with this. When they are disturbed and fly off, they give off moisture, the only proof that they feed on dew. For they have no orifice to excrete the body's waste.'[3]

So also Virgil: 'As long as the bees will feed on thyme and the cicadas on dew.'[4] The proverb will be more wittily used if applied to intellect or to a style of writing that is very spare and dry, or in irony to a person who is excessively fat.

17 Tuam ipsius terram calca
Walk on your own land

When we tell someone to confine himself to his own place and not to come into ours, the words from the same author's the *Wayfarers* will be very fitting: Τὰν σαυτοῦ πατέων ἔχε τὰς δρύας 'Why don't you walk on your own

* * * * *

16 Theocritus (see n1). Added in 1515. 'For in Doric' to the end of the Virgilian quotation was added in 1526. Suringar 235
1 Theocritus *Idylls* 4.16
2 For the etymology Erasmus is following a scholion on Theocritus *Idylls* 4.16.
3 Pliny *Naturalis historia* 11.93–4. The passage is abbreviated by Erasmus. For Erasmus' chapter-number see *Adagia* IV iii 3 n3 (5–6 above).
4 Virgil *Eclogues* 5.77

17 Theocritus (see n1). Added in 1515

land and keep to your own oak trees?'[1] It will be suitable when we do not trust someone very much and do not want to allow him to frequent our house.

18 Nihil simile
In no way similar

To signify a comparison of things that are in no way equal the words from the same poem will be effective: 'It is foolish to compare a *kynosbatos* or an anemone / With roses.'[1] *Kynosbatos* means 'dog's-bramble' in Greek. It is a kind of bush, but produces a rose that is extremely unattractive and has a most unpleasant smell.[2] Dioscorides seems to make the anemone a kind of poppy.[3]

19 Ne fascines
To avoid the evil eye

Ἵνα μὴ βασκαίνῃς με, So that you may not cast the evil eye on me. Customarily said when someone has received something pleasant and shares

* * * * *

1 Theocritus *Idylls* 5.61

18 Theocritus (see n1). Added in *1515*. The form of the adage looks like an error, since *nihil simile* hardly seems proverbial, and one would expect the Latin form of the proverb to be a translation of the Greek verse. This is virtually a doublet of II vi 41 You match a rose with an anemone, which is clearly derived ultimately from the same source.
1 Theocritus *Idylls* 5.92–3: Ἀλλ᾽ οὐ σύμβλητ᾽ ἐστὶ κυνόσβατος οὐδ᾽ ἀνεμώνη / Πρὸς ῥόδα.
2 The source of this information is not clear. The Theocritean scholia (ad loc) say that the anemone has no smell and that dog's-bramble excites dogs. Erasmus may have put these two items together. Aristotle (*Historia animalium* 5.552b) says that blister beetles come out of the caterpillars that infest dog-thorn (κυνακάνθη), which is described as 'evil-smelling stuff.' This too may have played a part in what Erasmus says.
3 Dioscorides *De materia medica* 2.176; 4.63

19 Aristotle (see n1). Added in *1528* to replace a doublet of *Adagia* I viii 72 Jay strives with nightingale. This doublet had itself been added in *1515*.

part of it with those present to avoid annoying others by enjoying it alone. Aristotle explains this in item 34 of *Problem* 20.[1] When someone was taking something from the common table for himself alone, he would share it with anyone who saw him, saying, 'So that you may not cast the evil eye on me.' In addition, before eating they would eat rue to protect them against the evil eye. For at that time people used to fear its harmful power whenever they ate too greedily, or when they were gripped with fearful anticipation of some misfortune, or when they were suspicious of the food they were eating. As a result of this they were always extremely anxious when they ate or drank, and gulped in air at the same time. If this was expelled, food came out with it; if the air was retained, it caused colic. Therefore rue was eaten first and this warmed[2] the stomach and the rest of the body so that the trapped air could be dispersed and be got rid of. Because of this, 'there's need of rue' has also a proverbial ring about it, signifying that there is danger of some harm, as we have said elsewhere about hazelwort and celery.[3]

20 Non omnis fert omnia tellus
All fields do not produce all things

Just as the words of Virgil, 'All fields do not produce all things,' will be a proverb if it is used metaphorically of different talents or to mean that we

* * * * *

1 Aristotle *Problemata* 20.34 (926b20). When this adage first appeared in *1528* the reference ('item 34') was correct. In *1533* and *1536* the *Adagia*-text offered *vigesimo quarto* (24) for *trigesimo quarto* (34). What follows, down to 'got rid of,' is drawn from Aristotle.

2 In the Greek original the verb used means literally 'rarefied.'

3 *Adagia* II x 85 It's celery he needs. But there is no mention in that adage of hazelwort (*baccar*). Cf Servius on Virgil *Eclogues* 4.19: 'Hazelwort is a plant that drives away the evil eye.'

20 Virgil (see n1). If Erasmus had followed his usual practice in this section, he would have given the Latin translation of the Theocritean verse (*illa quidem producit hyems, illa educat aestas*) as the actual adage, but the heading is rather the Virgilian phrase, with which he compares the Greek verse. There are really two adages here. Added in *1515*. The final sentence was added in *1528*. Otto 1290.

should not seek just anything from just anyone,[1] so the words of Theocritus in the *Cyclops*, 'Some flowers bloom in summer, some in winter grow,' will have the force of a proverb when we want to say that a young man and an old man should engage in different activities, and that we should not behave in the same way at different times.[2] Virgil beautifully describes in the *Georgics* what is produced by each kind of soil,[3] as does Hermippus, quoted in Athenaeus book one.[4]

21 Dum virent genua
While our knees are fresh

What is in the same poet's *Thyonichus* also has the appearance of a proverb: Ποιεῖν τι δεῖ οἷς γόνυ χλωρόν 'We should be active while our knees are fresh.'[1] We ought to study literature when our minds are still sharp. We should take a wife, but do so when we are young. Similarly, Horace:

And while our knees are fresh
And while it is appropriate, let us smooth out the furrowed brow of old age.[2]

And yet the figure *genu viret* 'green-kneed' is itself proverbial whenever we use it to mean 'youthful.'

* * * * *

1 Erasmus has conflated Virgil *Eclogues* 4.39, which lacks a negative, with a similar expression at *Georgics* 2.109.
2 Theocritus *Idylls* 11.58: Ἀλλὰ τὰ μὲν θέρεος, τὰ δὲ γίγνεται ἐν χειμῶνι, cited also in *Adagia* I vii 70 Wasp buzzing against cricket
3 Virgil *Georgics* 2.109–35
4 Athenaeus 1.27E–G, citing PCG 5 Hermippus fragment 63

21 Theocritus and Horace (see nn1–2). Added in *1515*
1 Theocritus *Idylls* 14.70. Both in Greek and Latin the expressions translated as 'fresh' mean literally 'green' and metaphorically 'young, strong.' This is the point of the final sentence; the expression is proverbial even when it refers to youthfulness because of the metaphorical use of the verb *virere* 'to be green.'
2 Horace *Epodes* 13.4–5. Most commentators take *senectus*, translated here as 'old age,' to have the sense 'moroseness.' Erasmus seems to have taken the word literally and may have thought that the line meant, 'Let us [who are not old] not think now of old age and its furrowed brow,' a possible interpretation.

22 Neque pessimus neque primus
Neither worst nor first

We can indicate average quality in this way: Οὔτε κάκιστος / οὔτε πρᾶτος 'Neither worst nor first.'[1] It will be quite witty if used to praise someone's abilities. For in Theocritus in *Thyonichus* it is said of a soldier who speaks of himself in modest terms.[2]

23 Scit quomodo Juppiter duxerit Junonem
He knows how Jupiter married Juno

Those words from the *Women of Syracuse* will suit those who are inquisitive and try to find out what everyone is doing in his own home: Πάντα γυναῖκες ἴσασι καὶ ὡς Ζεὺς ἠγάγεθ᾽ Ἥρην 'Women know everything, even how Jupiter once married Juno.'[1] The scholiast of Theocritus thinks that this is a reference to the secret marriage of Jupiter and Juno, as described by Homer: 'They went to bed without the knowledge of either parent.'[2]

He adds the story told by someone called Aristotle in a work that he wrote about the temple of Hermione.[3] When Jupiter was plotting against his sister's virginity and saw by chance that she had been separated from the other gods (for it is not safe even for young female goddesses to stroll about on their own),[4] he turned himself into a cuckoo and took up position on a mountain, now called Coccyx, but previously

* * * * *

22 Theocritus (see n1). Added in 1515. In 1526 'in *Thyonichus*' was added; 'who speaks of himself in modest terms' was added in 1533.
1 Theocritus *Idylls* 14.55–6
2 In the poem the expression refers to a soldier's way of life when compared with that of others. It has nothing to do, as Erasmus implies, with a soldier who talks with modesty in contrast to the stock figure of the braggart warrior.

23 Theocritus (see n1). Added in 1515. 'The scholiast of Theocritus ... old wife's tale' was added in 1533. The final sentence was added in 1526. Otto 880.
1 Theocritus *Idylls* 15.64
2 Homer *Iliad* 14.296
3 Aristotle is the name given in the manuscripts. This was emended to 'Aristocles,' now generally accepted.
4 The parentheses here and later in the paragraph are Erasmus' own comments on what the scholiast writes.

Thronax.⁵ On that day Jupiter stirred up a great storm. And so it happened
that Juno, who was all on her own, came to the mountain and sat down in
that very spot where there is now the temple of Juno Telia (that is, Juno All-
powerful). The cuckoo, unkempt and shivering because of the storm, flew
down and perched on Juno's knees. Juno took pity on it and covered it with
her clothes. Thereupon the King of the Gods suddenly abandoned the form
of the cuckoo and became himself again and embraced Juno. When she refused to have intercourse out of fear of her mother, Jupiter promised that
he would marry her.

This is thought to be the origin of the proverb. The scholiast adds that
a statue of Juno had been placed in the temple, depicting her as sitting on
a throne, holding in her right hand a sceptre, on the tip of which sat a
cuckoo. For my part, I can scarcely believe that this story is to be found in
the ancient writers. Rather, I suspect that it has been concocted by some idle
schoolteacher, so much does it smack of an old wife's tale. What Plautus
writes in the *Three-shilling Day* is very similar to this:

> They knew what the king of the gods whispered to the queen,
> They know what Juno said to Jupiter;
> What won't happen or hasn't happened – they still know it.⁶

24 Ubi paveris impera
Give orders to those you have fed

In the same eclogue, Πασσάμενος ἐπίτασσε 'Give orders to those you have
fed.'¹ The women say these words in reply to someone who upbraids them

* * * * *

5 'Thronax' is the reading of the scholion, emended to 'Thornax' by Hemster-
huys.
6 Plautus *Trinummus* 207–9

24 Theocritus (see n1). Added in *1515*
1 Theocritus *Idylls* 15.90. Erasmus interprets πασσάμενος as the aorist participle of πατέομαι 'drink, eat, partake of,' when in fact it is from *πάομαι 'possess, acquire.' The meaning of the passage in Theocritus, with the reading
πασσάμενος, is 'give orders to those you own.' Estienne (LB II 1029 n1) points
out Erasmus' error and compares Plautus *Trinummus* 1061 *emere melius est cui
imperes* 'it is better to buy the person you want to give orders to,' and Plautus *Persa* 273 *emere oportet quem tibi oboedire velis* 'you should buy the person

for being too talkative and tells them to be silent. The proverb will suit an occasion when someone keeps issuing orders to those whom he has no right to treat in such a way.

25 **Gallus in suo sterquilinio plurimum potest**
A cock has most power on its own dunghill

What is written in Seneca's humorous bagatelle has the appearance of a proverb.[1] 'He realized,' he says, 'that no one had been his equal in Rome but that he did not have the same popularity there. A cock has most power on its own dunghill.'[2] Seneca is referring to the emperor Claudius, born in Lyon. Today it is commonly said of a dog that 'it dares the most on its own dunghill.'[3] We are all somewhat timid in someone else's domain; all of us are fiercer and braver in our own.

26 **Isthmum perfodere**
To dig through the Isthmus

Those who worked at something with great but futile effort were said to be digging through the Isthmus. Taken from the Isthmus of Corinth, the

* * * * *

whose obedience you want.' Cf *Adagia* v i 14 If you want to give orders, you must buy a slave (550 below).

25 Seneca (see n1). Otto 752. Tilley c 486 Every cock is proud on his own dunghill. Cf *Adagia* IV viii 75 As aggressive as a cock in his own backyard (403 below). Added in *1515*.
   1 Seneca *Ludus de morte Claudi* 7.3
   2 There is a play on *gallus* 'a cock' and *Gallus* 'a Gaul.' Claudius, the subject of the first sentence, was born in Gaul, as Erasmus tells us in the next sentence.
   3 Suringar 83; see Allen Ep 2130:22–3 where a Dutch proverb is quoted.

26 Cf *Adagia* II x 59 To visit the Isthmian games, where Erasmus refers to his discussion of this adage here. The proverb was perhaps taken over from Polydore Virgil, who included a similar adage (*Isthmum fodis* 'you dig through the isthmus') in his *Proverbiorum libellus* (Venice 1498). Added in *1515*. The references to Suetonius and Herodotus were added in *1517/18*; the final sentence first appeared in *1526*.

existence of which forced ships to circumnavigate the peninsula, close to the shore, in a long and dangerous voyage. Because of this several persons undertook to dig across it at its narrowest point: 'King Demetrius, the dictator Caesar, the emperor Gaius, Domitius Nero – an ill-omened enterprise, as is clear from how all of them died.'[1] The source is Pliny chapter four of book four.[2] Tranquillus informs us that the same deed was attempted by Caligula.[3] Philostratus in the *Life of Apollonius* says that it was not the difficulty of the enterprise that forced Nero to give it up, but rather the fear that bringing the sea onto the Isthmus might portend the destruction of Aegina or the beginning of revolution in the Roman empire.[4] For Egyptian prophets had foretold this. In fact, the very early writer Herodotus also tells us in the first book of his *History* that the Cnidians began to dig through their isthmus at its narrowest point, five stades in length, to create an island. When the rocks were struck, however, the fragments leapt back into the eyes of the diggers. The Delphic Apollo was consulted and gave the following reply in trimeters:

> Gird not the Isthmus with walls nor through it dig.
> For in the brine would Jove have placed it if that was his desire.[5]

Finally, Nicanor Seleucus began work on the isthmus that separates the Black and Caspian Seas, but did not complete the project, because of his death at the hands of Ptolemy Ceraunus.[6]

* * * * *

1 They were all assassinated.

2 Pliny *Naturalis historia* 4.10. For Erasmus' reference to 'chapter 4' see *Adagia* IV iii 3 n3 (5–6 above).

3 Suetonius *Caligula* 21. This sentence was added in *1520*. But the reference to Caligula is redundant since Pliny includes Caligula (= Gaius) among those who had attempted to excavate a channel through the Isthmus.

4 Philostratus *Life of Apollonius* 4.24, whom Erasmus follows closely, down to 'had foretold this'

5 Herodotus 1.174.3–5

6 Nicanor Seleucus is Seleucus I. Erasmus is following Pliny *Naturalis historia* 6.31. 'Nicanor' is a variant reading for 'Nicator.' The ancients underestimated the distance of the land mass separating the Black and Caspian Seas, but even so it could hardly be called an isthmus.

27 Lingere salem
To lick salt

In antiquity persons of humble means used salt as relish, just as nowadays some use vinegar. This custom also resulted in a proverb even if it is not quite clear what the proverb was. But it may be better to append the words of Pliny himself on this subject, from book thirty-one, chapter seven. 'Varro,' he says, 'is our source for telling us that the ancients used salt as a relish. For they were accustomed to eat salt with bread and cheese, as is apparent in a proverb.'[1] Persius in his fifth *Satire*:

> Swear falsely. 'But Jupiter will hear.' Alas,
> Varus, if you want to live in accordance with Jupiter's wishes, you'll go on,
> As now, content to scrape out the salt cellar with your finger,
> Even when you have already licked it again and again.[2]

In other words, you will live a life of great poverty.

28 Sellisare
To act like Sellus

A humorous proverb was directed at persons who were boastful and excessively swollen with pride; they were said Σελλίζειν 'To act like Sellus.' Suidas tells us that it was taken from the habits of someone called Sellus who strove to be thought of as rich although he was of very poor means.[1] It can be applied also to those who boast of their learning and use their reputation to promote themselves even though they are strangers to literature. Hesychius points out that in Greek σελλίζεσθαι means the same as

* * * * *

27 Added in *1515*. Otto 1569
  1 Pliny *Naturalis historia* 31.89. On Erasmus' reference to chapter 7 see on *Adagia* IV iii 3 n3 (5–6 above). See also IV v 87 To eat salt and cheese (201 below).
  2 Persius 5.137–9. Erasmus reads *Vare* (the vocative of the name 'Varus') for *baro* 'blockhead' in modern editions.

28 *Suda* (see n1). Added in *1515*. This proverb had already been mentioned and explained in Erasmus' discussion of *Adagia* II ix 6 Theagenes' wealth.
  1 *Suda* Σ 210

ψελλίζεσθαι 'to stutter.'[2] Plato uses this word once or twice in the *Gor-gias*.[3] And a person who pronounces 's' indistinctly is called a ψέλλος. We touched on this to some extent in the proverb Ἡ ψελλὴ οὐ πιττεύει 'The girl who stammers doesn't b-b-believe.'[4] Hesychius adds that some-times σελλινίζειν is the same as ἀλαζονεύειν 'to boast,' clearly agreeing with Suidas.

29 Cecidis et Buphoniorum
Cecides and tbe Buphonia

Τὰ Κηκείδου καὶ Βουφονίων, Like Cecides and the Buphonia. Of something extremely ancient that, because of its antiquity, has long since fallen into disuse and been cast aside. Aristophanes in the *Clouds*: 'These are ancient things, to be sure, and hoary, and filled with cicadas, with things like Ce-cides and the Buphonia.'[1] For Cecides was a very early dithyrambic poet, whose writings smelled of mould, so to speak; because of this, his po-etry became the butt of popular humour.[2] So today we laugh with justifi-cation at those who have an excessive and inappropriate fondness for ar-chaisms and use diction from the Twelve Tables, Ennius and Lucilius, 'as if they are speaking with Evander's mother.'[3] They think nothing is ele-gant unless it is far removed from popular and contemporary use. Simi-larly, the Buphonia, given this name because of the slaughter of an ox, was an Athenian festival that had been neglected and abandoned because of

* * * * *

2 Hesychius Σ 392. From here to the end was added in 1526.
3 Plato *Gorgias* 485B–C
4 *Adagia* I vi 51

29 Aristophanes (see n1). Added in 1515
1 Aristophanes *Clouds* 984–5. Already cited in *Adagia* III iii 95 Full of grass-hoppers
2 Cecides is the name in the manuscripts and the early editions. The name was emended to Cedides by Nauck. For the content of this sentence Erasmus follows the scholion on Aristophanes *Clouds* 985.
3 Erasmus closely echoes what Favorinus is reported to have said to a young man who was very fond of using archaisms; see Aulus Gellius *Noctes Atticae* 1.10.2. For the reference to Evander's mother cf *Adagia* IV i 46 Since Nannacus. See Otto 612 and Otto *Nachträge* 25.

its antiquity.[4] We see that such festivals still endure in Italy, especially in Rome, called Bull-games, even now still clearly bearing the traces of ancient madness.

The adage can be used in a humorous way to point out that something is neglected just because it is thought to be extremely ancient. For example, some popes, bishops and priests regard as old-fashioned what the gospels teach us about poverty, about the need to accept injury without retaliation, and about the insignificance of this earthly life; or they have the same attitude to what the early popes decreed about simony, about bribery having no place in choosing bishops, and about the removal from office of wicked men. If you want to impugn such persons, you will be able to say, 'Such teaching and decrees are treated by them like Cecides and the Buphonia!'

30 Serenitate nubem inducit
Bringing clouds to a clear sky

What Plutarch says in 'On Distinguishing a Flatterer from a Friend' has the appearance of a proverb as much as an egg is an egg:[1] Εὐδίᾳ γὰρ ἐπάγει νέφος 'He brings clouds to a clear sky.'[2] About the person who in the midst of merriment and gaiety dispenses poison that spoils the happy atmosphere and prompts others to frown and scowl. In the same way Horace in book three, ode fifteen, says of an ugly old woman who joined a group of young girls, that 'she casts a cloud over shining stars.'[3]

31 Μονόγραμμοι
Mere outlines

In antiquity a humorous proverb was applied to persons who were extremely thin, feeble, and pallid: Μονόγραμμοι 'Mere outlines.' Lucilius: 'A

* * * * *

4 The Buphonia is a compound of βοῦς 'ox' and φόνος 'slaughter.'

30 Plutarch (see n2). Added in 1515
1 Cf Adagia I v 10 As like as one egg to another.
2 Plutarch Moralia 68C–D Quomodo adulator ab amico internoscatur
3 Horace Odes 3.15.6. Only in 1528 was 'in book three, ode fifteen' added.

31 Lucilius (see n1). Added in 1515

man scarcely alive and a mere outline.' Again the same poet elsewhere: 'Such is the piety of a mere outline.'[1] Nonius Marcellus says that it was taken from a picture that is fashioned from a shadow before it is filled in with colours. Marcellus is certainly not wrong, but the adage will have more charm if we think of ancient painting. All agree that this initially started with the tracing round of a person's shadow, a process called delineation. When painters began to use one colour, such paintings were called μονοχρώματοι 'one-colour paintings.' Soon the art developed and the use of light and shade was discovered, so that some things seemed to stand out, while others were hidden and concealed through the difference in colours. Then brightness was added, by which is meant something other than light, but something midway between light and shade. This is why they call this *tonos* 'contrast.' For to the joining together and gradations of colours they give the name ἁρμογή 'attunement.' Such for the most part is what Pliny says in book thirty-five, chapter five.[2] The expression will suit, then, an unsightly person whose face either has no colour at all or is all the same colour, like the representations of the ancients. Marcus Tullius in book two of *On the Nature of the Gods*:

> For they [the gods] are not held together by veins and sinews and bones. Nor do they feed on food or drink so as to contract too sharp or too sluggish a condition of the humours. Nor do they have bodies such as to make them fear either a fall or blow or make them frightened of illness because of physical exhaustion. It was through fear of such dangers that Epicurus invented the notion of the gods as being insubstantial (*monogrammoi*) and inactive. They are endowed, however, with the most beautiful form, and live in the purest region of the heavens, moving around and controlling their courses in such a way that they seem to have conspired to save and preserve everything.[3]

Cicero calls those who have no form and no appearance *monogrammoi*.

* * * * *

1 Lucilius 59 and 725 Marx (68 and 728 Krenkel), cited by Nonius Marcellus 53.12–14 Lindsay
2 Pliny *Naturalis historia* 35.15, but this is a correct reference only for the first part of what is given. 'Soon the art ... "attunement"' is based on Pliny *Naturalis historia* 35.29. For Erasmus' reference to 'chapter 5' see *Adagia* IV iii n3 (5–6 above).
3 Cicero *De natura deorum* 2.23.59–60

32 Aliorum medicus
A doctor to others

Ἄλλων ἰατρός, αὐτὸς ἕλκεσι βρύων, He is a doctor to others, but covered in sores himself. These words of some poet, reported by Plutarch in his essay 'On Distinguishing a Flatterer from a Friend' remain very popular even in our times.[1] He also uses it in the essay entitled 'Against Colotes.' It will suit those who are wise in other persons' affairs, but not in their own, who are observant and careful for others, but not for themselves. They know how to console others, but they themselves do not bear their own misfortunes with equanimity. Christ used it in the same sense in the Gospel according to Luke. When the Jews marvelled at his deeds and words and said, 'Is not this the son of Joseph?' he replied in this way: 'Doubtless you will quote to me this proverb, "Physician, heal yourself."' 'What we have heard you did in Capernaum, do here also in your own country.'[2]

33 Lapsana vivere
To live on charlock

It will be witty to say that those who live very frugally and poorly 'Live on charlock.' The soldiers of Caesar took turns in taunting him in verse that they had lived on charlock at Dyrrachium, and it is generally agreed that this jest gave rise to a popular expression. *Lapsana* is a vegetable that grows wild and is very common, growing everywhere. It has three leaves, and is of the cabbage family, if I am not mistaken. If anyone, however, wants the words of Pliny, this is what he says in book nineteen, chapter eight: 'There is also a kind of wild cabbage, three-leaved, well-known because of the verses directed at the deified Julius, especially in the soldiers' jests. For they took

* * * * *

32 Euripides by way of Plutarch (see n1). This is a doublet of *Adagia* II v 38 You physic others, full of sores yourself, but the commentary is different. Tilley P 267 Physician heal thyself. Added in *1515*
1 Plutarch *Moralia* 71F *Quomodo adulator ab amico internoscatur*, citing Euripides fragment 1086 Nauck. The second reference is to Plutarch *Moralia* 1110E *Adversus Colotem*. Suringar 7
2 Luke 4:22–3

33 Pliny (see n1). Added in *1515*. The final two sentences were added in *1528* as was the earlier phrase 'and is very common, growing everywhere.'

turns in taunting him in verse about how they had lived on charlock at Dyrrachium, complaining in jest about his meanness in rewarding them. For charlock is a wild cabbage.'[1]

So says Pliny. In book twenty the same writer says that *cyma* 'wild cabbage' is unwholesome and difficult to digest.[2] He explains [elsewhere], however, that *cyma* is the name given to a more delicate and more tender sprout growing on cabbages and that this goes well with burdock and asparagus.[3] Dioscorides says that *lapsana* is also called *napium* by the Romans and that its stalk is boiled and eaten as well as its leaves.[4] He thinks that this is more wholesome than sorrel, which Horace mentions when he talks about a frugal dinner: 'Or the sorrel that loves the meadows and mallows that are good for a sick body.'[5]

34 Haud contra ianuam
Not against the door

Οὐ κατὰ θύρας, Not against the door, meaning something that is inappropriate to a subject and unsuited to what is being discussed. This was used, certainly in a proverbial sense, by Aristotle in book four of his *Physics*: οὗτοι μὲν οὖν οὐ κατὰ θύρας πρὸς τὸ πρόβλημα ἀπαντῶσιν 'these do not confront the question against the door.'[1] Argiropolo[2] translates οὐ κατὰ θύρας as *non recte* 'not directly,' and quite correctly (*neque non recte*) at

* * * * *

1 Pliny *Naturalis historia* 19.144. Erasmus follows the text of the early editions in reading *trium foliorum* 'three-leaved' for *triumpho* of modern editions: 'at the triumph of the deified Julius ...' For the chapter number given by Erasmus see *Adagia* iv iii 3 n3 (5–6 above).

2 Pliny *Naturalis historia* 20.90

3 Pliny *Naturalis historia* 19.137, though burdock (*lappa*) is not mentioned here or elsewhere in Pliny, so it seems, in association with *cyma* or asparagus. This sentence was added in 1526.

4 Dioscorides *De materia medica* 2.116

5 Horace *Epodes* 2.57–8

34 Aristotle (see n1). Added in 1515

1 Aristotle *Physics* 4.6 (213b2–3)

2 Giovanni Argiropolo of Constantinople taught in Florence in the second half of the fifteenth century. He was responsible for new Latin translations of many of Aristotle's works: see *Adagia* iv viii 6 n2 (355 below).

that! It has the same meaning as *ad scopum* 'on target.' Consider, reader, whether this adage is related to Tίς ἂν θύρας ἁμάρτοι 'Who could miss the gate?'[3]

35 Climacides
Little stairs

Those who are prepared to perform any task for the rich, even the most sordid one, can humorously be called Κλιμακίδες 'Little stairs.' This was the name given as a common insult to certain Cyprian women, flatterers living in Syria, who allowed kings' wives to board their chariots by using them as stairs. Plutarch mentions it in his essay 'On Distinguishing the Flatterer from a Friend.'[1] Athenaeus too in book six of *Doctors at Dinner*.[2] Also Valerius Maximus in book nine, chapter one.[3]

36 Valeat amicus cum inimico
Away with friend as well as foe

Ἐρρέτω φίλος σὺν ἐχθρῷ, Away with friend as well as foe. This suits those who are completely engrossed in themselves and think no more of a friend than an enemy. Timon the famous misanthrope is said to have been such a person. Plutarch in the essay that we have just cited: 'If that saying "Away with friend as well as foe" does not please us in any way.'[1] The Greek

* * * * *

3 *Adagia* i vi 36. Erasmus' comment here might suggest that he had abandoned his suggested emendation of that adage (θῆρας for θύρας), giving the sense 'Who would miss the target?'

35 Plutarch (see n1). Added in *1515*. The reference to Athenaeus was added in *1517/18*, the one to Valerius Maximus in *1528*.
1 Plutarch *Moralia* 50D *Quomodo adulator ab amico internoscatur*
2 Athenaeus 6.256D
3 Valerius Maximus 9.1 ext 7

36 Plutarch (see n1). Added in *1515*. The final sentence was added in *1517/18*. Cf *Adagia* iv v 100 May my friends perish (208 below). Otto 94
1 Plutarch *Moralia* 50F *Quomodo adulator ab amico internoscatur*; *Iambica adespota* fragment 30 Diehl (*Anthologia lyrica Graeca* fasc 3 page 79)

expression is the hemistich of a trochaic verse.[2]

37 Manica
Worthy of a Manes

Μανικά, Worthy of a Manes, a Phrygian proverb applied to great and out-standing achievements. It derives from a certain Manes, an early king of theirs who they say was extremely powerful and wonderfully brave. The source is Plutarch in his essay 'On Osiris.'[1] In fact in Latin too something that is out of the ordinary is described as 'mad': 'It pleases me to be mad,'[2] and 'it pleases me to indulge a mad labour.'[3]

38 Ruta caesa
Minerals and timber excluded

'Not even with minerals and timber excluded.' This was without doubt said in a proverbial sense by Cicero in book two of the *Making of an Orator* in the sense of 'not even anything': 'But he will say that when you were selling your house, you did not hold back any of your father's estate, not even minerals and timber being excluded.'[1] At this point I must point out in passing that in the printed editions of Tullius *reliquisse* 'to have left' is read for *recepisse* 'to have excluded,' wrongly, as can be clearly seen from Nonius Marcellus, who adduces this very passage from Cicero when discussing the word *receptitius*.[2] For here *recipere* has the same sense as *excipere* 'to exclude.'

* * * * *

2 It would form the first half of a trochaic tetrameter catalectic. But as the pre-ceding note shows it could be viewed as part of an iambic verse, in particular an iambic tetrameter catalectic.

37 Plutarch (see n1). Added in *1515*. The last sentence was added in *1533*.
1 Plutarch *Moralia* 360B *De Iside et Osiride*
2 Virgil *Eclogues* 3.36
3 Virgil *Aeneid* 6.135

38 Cicero (see n1). Added in *1515*. The last sentence was added in *1517/18*, the second-last in *1533*.
1 Cicero *De oratore* 2.55.226
2 Nonius Marcellus 77.17–19 Lindsay; cf 241.6–8 Lindsay.

In addition the meaning of *ruta caesa* is abundantly clear from book nineteen
of the *Pandects* (the words are peculiar to the legal writers) in law 18. Ulpian
says:

> If minerals and timber are excluded in a sale, in law minerals constitute those
> that have been quarried, like sand and similar materials, and the timber con-
> stitutes trees that have already been cut and charcoal and similar things. Gal-
> lus Aquilius, whose opinion Mela reports, is right in saying that exclusions
> about minerals and timber in the law of sale are pointless, because if they are
> not specifically for sale negotiations for including them can still take place.
> A seller should be less concerned about cut timber, quarried stones, or sand
> than about all the other things that are more valuable.[3]

Marcus Cicero also mentions minerals and timber in his *Topica*: 'For, to
avoid passing over anything that might pertain to producing arguments of
every kind I have included perhaps more than you needed. I have done what
generous vendors often are wont to do. When they have sold their house
or farms, minerals and timber excluded, they nevertheless give the buyer
something that seems to be an appropriate adornment.'[4] He also mentions
it in his *Parts of a Speech*.[5]

And when we want to mean that everything is removed quite ruth-
lessly and that nothing at all is left, it will be witty to say, in lawyers' terms,
'not even minerals and timbers excluded.'

39 Aetna, Athon
An Etna, an Athos

'An Etna, an Athos.' These mountains were used to express proverbially
the idea of troublesomeness or weariness, as is attested by Lucilius, cited
in book sixteen, chapter nine, of Aulus Gellius, even if the passage is thought

* * * * *

3 *Digest (Pandects)* 19.1.17.2. See *Adagia* IV ix 1n (419 below).
4 Cicero *Topica* 26.100
5 Cicero *De partitionibus* 31.107. This sentence was added in *1533*.

39 Lucilius by way of Aulus Gellius (see n1). Added in *1515*. The final sentence
    was added in *1528*.

to be corrupt.[1] The verses of Lucilius that he adduces are the following:

> All this was sport to us, to us it was all one.
> It was all one, I say, all sport and play.
> Hard toil it was when Setia's land we neared.
> Henceforward, as they say, mountains, all Etnas, rough Athoses.[2]

This was said of Etna, a mountain in Sicily, because according to the poets it covers a giant with its great mass,[3] or because its frequent fires once posed serious and deadly danger to the inhabitants. Because of this Marcus Tullius also says in his *Cato the Elder* 'a weight heavier than Etna.'[4] About Athos we have spoken elsewhere, that because of its vast height the shade it casts is a nuisance; its shadow is three hundred stades in length extending right as far as Lemnos.[5] Pomponius Mela tells us that its peak is too high for rain to fall upon it.[6] The basis for this conjecture is that 'ashes are not washed away from the altars that it has on its summit but remain in the pile in which they were left.' It is also a barrier to sailors since it protrudes from the mainland far into the sea with its long ridge. Because of this Xerxes dug a channel through it. Athenaeus in book ten mentions a certain Erysichthon who had an insatiable appetite and was commonly called βορᾶς Ἄθωνα 'an Athos of gluttony.'[7]

* * * * *

1 Aulus Gellius *Noctes Atticae* 16.9.6, citing Lucilius 110–13 Marx (108–11 Krenkel). The translation follows closely that of J.C. Rolfe in the Loeb edition of Aulus Gellius.

2 For what is translated as 'henceforward' Erasmus prints ἐπὶ τὸ λοιπόν 'for the rest,' the reading in the 1515 Aldine edition of Gellius. The readings in the manuscripts of Gellius point to αἰγίλιποι 'steep, destitute even of goats.'

3 As, for example in Horace *Odes* 3.4.73–6 and Pseudo-Virgil *Aetna* 71–3

4 Cicero *De senectute* 2.4

5 *Adagia* III ii 90 Athos darkens the flanks of the Lemnian cow

6 Pomponius Mela 2.2.31–2, whom Erasmus follows closely as far as 'a channel through it'

7 Athenaeus 10.416B, but the passage has nothing to do with Mt Athos. Erasmus gives the wrong reading and misunderstands the syntax. What is said there is that a man of insatiable appetite (ἄπληστος βορᾶς) was given the nickname *Aithon* 'Fiery.'

40 Immunem venire
To come empty-handed

A person whom the Greeks call ἀσύμβολος is called *immunis* in Latin, meaning someone who contributes nothing to a banquet. Horace in the Odes:

> A small onyx-box of nard will elicit a jar ...
> I do not intend ... like a rich man in a full house
> To steep you, who are empty-handed, in my cups.[1]

But it will be more attractive if it refers metaphorically to mental activities, for example, scholarship, poetry, or some such thing. Aulus Gellius in book six, chapter thirteen, shows that this word had become a common proverb: 'So that we might not come completely empty-handed, as the saying goes, and without a contribution, we brought to the meal, not dainty foods, but clever topics of conversation.'[2] Terence in his *Phormio*: 'Oh, that you should come from the baths, washed and anointed, without a contribution!'[3] According to Athenaeus Ephippus wittily said 'a non-contributing hand': 'When you go in, learn how to eat someone else's food and how to stretch out a non-contributing hand to the meal.'[4]

41 Soterichi lecti
Couches of Soterichus

It is clear that the 'Couches of Soterichus' was an expression commonly used to make fun of anything that was cheap, old, crudely made, and in no way attractive. For this is what Seneca says when mocking some verses of Ennius about Cethegus: 'Those who love verses of this kind would admire the couches of Soterichus too.' Aulus Gellius (for these words are re-

* * * * *

40 Aulus Gellius (see n2). Added in *1515*. The last part, referring to Athenaeus, was added in *1528*.
 1 Horace *Odes* 4.12, 17, 22–4
 2 Aulus Gellius *Noctes Atticae* 7.13.2 (not book 6)
 3 Terence *Phormio* 339
 4 Athenaeus 13.572C; PCG 5 Ephippus fragment 20

41 Seneca by way of Aulus Gellius (see n1). Otto 1678. Added in *1515*

ported by him in book twelve, chapter two): 'Seneca would surely appear worthy of being read and studied by the young when he has compared the dignity and beauty of early Latin with the couches of Soterichus, the latter being very unattractive and obsolete and despised!'[1] One can conjecture that Soterichus was some artisan whose works displayed primitive and crude simplicity. For Pliny attests, in book thirty-three, chapter eleven, that in later times at Rome the rich had silver couches.[2] Horace points out in his *Satires* that among painters Fulvius, Rutuba, and Placidianus were like Soterichus:

> Or when, madman, you swoon over a painting of Pausias,
> How are you less in error than I when, with knee bent stiff,
> I wonder at the battles of Fulvius, Rutuba, or Placideianus,
> Painted in red chalk or charcoal?[3]

42 Peribis si non feceris
Dead if you don't

When someone has been reduced to such a state that he cannot undertake some action without incurring great harm, but cannot safely shrink from it, then this common expression, originally an oracle, is often used: 'I'll be dead if I don't, thrashed if I do.' It is reported by Aulus Gellius in the third book of his *Nights*, chapter three, from the comedy of Plautus entitled *Fretum*. These are the verses of Plautus:

* * * * *

1 This is a fragment of the lost book 22 of Seneca's *Letters*, cited by Aulus Gellius *Noctes Atticae* 12.2.11–12. Erasmus added 'in book twelve, chapter two' in 1526.
2 Pliny *Naturalis historia* 33.144. For the chapter number given by Erasmus see *Adagia* IV iii 3 n3 (5–6 above).
3 Horace *Satires* 2.7.95–8. The three individuals named as painters were actually gladiators. Erasmus makes the same mistake at *Adagia* IV v 1 (see n17, 134 below). The implication in Horace is that their battles were depicted by an incompetent artist. The name 'Placideianus,' which is the reading in the Aldine edition of 1502, has been emended to 'Pacideianus' in modern editions.

42 Plautus by way of Aulus Gellius (see n1). Added in 1515. 'The verses are iambic' to the end was added in 1517/18. Otto 626. Cf the English saying 'Damned if you do, damned if you don't.'

Now here we have the oracular response of Arietinus at the great games:
I'll be dead if I don't, thrashed if I do.[1]

Gellius himself attests that the story behind the oracle was not clear to him
and that he had copied out these verses of Plautus with the intention of
investigating it. The verses are iambic tetrameters catalectic. Because of this
we have removed the word *dicitur* (for in the printed editions the text is
magnis ludis dicitur), which was added in my opinion by a scholiast.[2]

43 Ex se fingit velut araneus
Spinning tales like a spider

The comparison of a spider weaving its web from its own body and of a
person making up lies also seems to be proverbial. For this is what Plutarch
says in his essay entitled 'On Osiris': 'Poets and orators are like οἱ ἀράχναι
γεννῶντες ἀφ᾽ ἑαυτῶν "the spiders who create material that is their very
own" and is not supplied by others, and start to weave their webs and then
expand them.'[1] Pliny reports that the larger spiders stretch their webs on
the ground over the small openings of their holes, and that the smallest
spiders do not weave webs, and that a third type is distinguished by the
adroitness of its workmanship. He says, 'The spider begins with the warp-
threads and its belly supplies the material for such a great enterprise, either
bowel-matter that decays at a fixed time, as Democritus holds, or from some
internal organ for producing thread. Employing its own weight and with
a careful use of its claw the spider draws out smooth and even threads of

* * * * *

1 Aulus Gellius *Noctes Atticae* 3.3.8: *Nunc illud est quod Arietini responsum magnis
ludis: / Peribo, si non fecero; si faxo, vapulabo.* This is the only surviving fragment
from this play of Plautus. The text and the meaning are unclear. Erasmus
follows the text of the 1515 Aldine edition of Gellius in offering *Arietinus.*
The better manuscripts read *Arretinus.* This has been taken, as by Gellius,
to refer to the oracle of Jupiter Ammonius, or to the town of Arretium (the
modern Arezzo), or to a person.

2 In their editions of Plautus Leo and Lindsay retain *dicitur* and read *responsum
Arreti,* thereby scanning the first line as an iambic octonarius, the second as
an iambic septenarius (another name for an iambic tetrameter catalectic).

43 Plutarch (see n1). Added in *1515*
1 Plutarch *Moralia* 358F *De Iside et Osiride*

finely controlled thickness. Then it begins from the centre with the creation of the weft, attaching it to the warp to make circles, at gradually increasing intervals, though each circle is equidistant from the preceding one. The mesh, though very fine, is tied together by an indissoluble knot.'[2]

This agrees with what Aristotle relates in the *Nature of Animals*, book nine.[3] Aristotle adds that spiders produce thread as soon as they have been born, not from inside their bodies, like waste material, as Democritus thinks, but from the body's surface, like the bark of a tree, or like a porcupine that shoots spines from its skin. Only the females spin webs or hunt. The male shares in the spoils, not in the labour.

44 Bove venari leporem
To hunt a hare with an ox

Τῷ βοῒ τὸν λαγὼ κυνηγετεῖν, Hunting the hare with the ox. This is said of those who undertake something that is ridiculous, foolish, and absurd. For example, if anyone in the Curia at Rome were to seek election as a bishop without having any money. Plutarch in his essay 'On Tranquillity of Mind':

> For it is not a question of ill luck if someone wishes to shoot arrows with a plough and hunt a hare with an ox. Nor is it a question of divine malevolence if someone does not catch deer with fishing nets. Rather, it is foolishness or perversity in undertaking what cannot be done.[1]

There is not a single thing that is suited for all circumstances. For example, whoever entrusts the conduct of a war or the government of the state to a person who is naturally disposed to learning and a life of peace 'is hunting a hare with an ox.' Or if someone were to entrust court judgments to a fool or a dullard. In the same essay Plutarch cites these verses, of Pindar if am not mistaken:

* * * * *

2 Pliny *Naturalis historia* 11.80–1. Pliny is actually writing here specifically about wolf-spiders.

3 Aristotle *Historia animalium* 9.39 (623a30–3) and (for the last two sentences) 623a24–30

44 Plutarch (see n1). Added in *1515*

1 Plutarch *Moralia* 471D *De tranquillitate animi*, used in *1515* in *Adagia* II vii 45 You shoot with a plough

Horses for chariot, ox to the plough,
A dolphin can swim as fast as any ship.
For a wild boar bent on slaughter a hound of great courage must be found.[2]

I quote these lines, since they too have a proverbial look about them.

45 Ab uno diagrammate
In one key

Plutarch in his essay 'On the Difference between a Flatterer and a Friend':
'A flatterer always sings in one key (ἀφ᾽ ἑνὸς διαγράμματος) whatever is
pleasing and agreeable; he does not know how to object to any action or
how to say anything hurtful. All he can do is agree with what the other
person wishes, always being in accord and harmony with him.'[1]
        Ἀφ᾽ ἑνὸς διαγράμματος 'In one key.' This obviously has the appearance
of a proverb. A *diagramma* is also a diagram or illustration used by philosophers to show something in visual terms. It means, then, the same as if one
were to say *de eadem formula* 'by the same formula.'

46 Non filius Achillis
You are not the son of Achilles

I think that the following can be included in the verses of famous poets
that are used by the learned in a proverbial way: Οὐ παῖς Ἀχιλλέως, ἀλλ᾽
Ἀχιλλεὺς αὐτὸς εἶ 'You are not the son of Achilles, but Achilles himself.'
        It seems to have been taken from some tragedy or comedy since the
verse is an iambic trimeter. It is used by Plutarch in the same essay, entitled 'How to Distinguish a Flatterer from a Friend.'[1] For he says that

* * * * *

2 Pindar fragment 234 Snell, cited in Plutarch *Moralia* 472C *De tranquillitate animi*.
  In modern editions the Greek of the last line has been emended to give the
  sense 'for the man bent on slaughtering a wild boar ...' Erasmus also cites
  the fragment in *Adagia* II ii 82 Each man had best employ what skill he has.

45 Plutarch (see n1). Added in *1515*
 1 Plutarch *Moralia* 55D *Quomodo adulator ab amico internoscatur*

46 A verse of Greek tragedy by way of Plutarch (see n1). Added in *1515*
 1 Plutarch *Moralia* 51C *Quomodo adulator ab amico internoscatur*, quoting *TrGF* 2
   Adespota 363

a flatterer acts the part of a friend in every way so that one can say of him, 'You are not the son of Achilles, etc.' Similarly Terence's Parmeno, speaking of Gnatho, who slavishly goes along with whatever Thraso says, remarks, 'Heavens, one could say this fellow is born from this other one.'[2]

47 Ulysses pannos exuit
Ulysses has stripped off his rags

In the same essay that I have just mentioned Plutarch uses this verse of Homer, from *Odyssey* 22, which has the appearance of a proverb: Αὐτὰρ ὁ γυμνώθη ῥακέων πολύμητις Ὀδυσσεύς 'Then Ulysses stripped off his cheap rags.'[1]

One can apply this to those who experience a sudden change in their circumstances, becoming rich instead of poor, elegant instead of filthy, happy instead of sad. For as soon as Ulysses stripped off the rags that he wore when pretending to be a beggar among the suitors and was decked out with magnificent clothes, he suddenly seemed a different person. Plutarch applies this to a flatterer, who, like a cuttlefish, adapts himself to everyone's pursuits. While living with a friend devoted to philosophy, he wears a long beard and cloak and is completely immersed in his books, prattling on about Plato's numbers, rectangles, triangles, and nothing else.[2] A short time later, if by chance he falls in with a friend who is a voluptuary, his appearance suddenly changes as if he has been transformed by Circe, and he becomes a Sardanapalus.[3]

* * * * *

2 Terence *Eunuchus* 460. Erasmus quotes the verse with a different text from that found in modern editions, the translation of which would be, 'There's the other fellow. Would you say he has a human being for a father?' Gnatho is a fawning parasite of the soldier Thraso. Both characters were probably drawn by Terence from Menander's *Kolax* 'Flatterer.'

47 Homer by way of Plutarch (see n1). Added in *1515*. To the text as it appeared in *1515* there were two minor additions in *1526*: 'from *Odyssey* 22' and 'when pretending to be a beggar among the suitors.'
1 Plutarch *Moralia* 52C *Quomodo adulator ab amico internoscatur*, citing *Odyssey* 22.1. The Greek verse was not printed in the text of the *Adagia* until *1526*.
2 Cf *Adagia* III vi 32 As obscure as Plato's maths.
3 Sardanapalus, a Persian prince, was renowned for his dissolute way of life. See *Adagia* III vii 27 A Sardanapalus.

48 **Subito alius**
Suddenly another person

Similarly, Plutarch also applies the words of Homer, from book sixteen of
the *Odyssey*, to a person who suddenly changes and seems to have become
someone else: Ἀλλοῖός μοι ξεῖν' ἐφάνης νέον ἠὲ πάροιθεν 'Friend, you appear
to be someone different from who you were a little while ago.'[1]
    Similar to this are the words of Theocritus: 'Surely the gods have not
turned me into someone else?'[2]

49 **In durum et implacabilem**
Unyielding and implacable

It will be appropriate to apply to a person who is excessively rigid and
implacable those words of Homer, from book ten of the *Odyssey*: Σοὶ δέ τις
ἐν στήθεσι ἀκήλητος νόος ἐστί 'You have a heart in your breast that cannot
be enchanted.'[1]
    In his essay 'On Distinguishing a Flatterer from a Friend' Plutarch
says that Antony's entourage often used this verse to rebuke him, because
his love for Cleopatra did not match her consuming passion for him.[2]

50 **Asinus balneatoris**
A bath-keeper's mule

῎Ωσπερ ὄνος βαλανέως, Like a bath-keeper's mule. This was said of those
who enjoyed no fruit from their labour. Plutarch in his essay 'On Desire

* * * * *

48 Homer by way of Plutarch (see n1). Added in *1515*. The final sentence and
   'from book sixteen of the *Odyssey*' were added in *1526*.
 1 Plutarch *Moralia* 53B *Quomodo adulator ab amico internoscatur*, citing Homer
   Odyssey 16.181
 2 Theocritus *Idylls* 20.20

49 The adage here should properly be the Homeric line. Instead, the context in
   which the verse should be used is given as the actual proverb ('about someone
   unyielding and implacable'). Added in *1515*
 1 Homer *Odyssey* 10.329
 2 Plutarch *Moralia* 61B *Quomodo adulator ab amico internoscatur*

50 Plutarch (see n1). Added in *1515*

for Riches': 'Deriving no benefit, like a bath-keeper's mule that carries logs and wood, always smothered in smoke and ash, but never enjoying a bath, warmth or cleanliness.'[1] He is speaking about a rich man who is mean and niggardly; although he is laden with riches, he never enjoys them.

51 Lychnobii
Livers-by-lamplight

Λυχνόβιοι, Livers-by-lamplight. This is obviously a proverbial expression humorously describing those who spend their lives in lamplight. It can be applied, therefore, to a nocturnal drinker, to an excessively studious person, since, as was said of Demosthenes,[1] such a person uses more oil than wine, or to mean and niggardly persons, because they were thought to subsist on lamp-oil. Seneca in book twenty-two of his *Letters*, letter 122, points out that this was said of someone who shunned daylight and who lived in a topsy-turvy way, doing at night whatever ordinary people usually do in daytime.[2] He would rise at nightfall and go to bed at dawn. Varus, a very witty raconteur, made a joke against such a person, saying that he lived extremely frugally, since the only thing he spent was night.[3] And when some people said that such a man was mean and miserly, he said, 'You should call him a *lychnobius* "a liver-by-lamplight."' There is, however, some ambiguity in the joke. You can understand it to mean that this person was so far from being miserly that he actually used up all his lamps or that he was so tight-fisted that he lived by lamplight. But the allusion was really to a person's topsy-turvy way of life like that of a certain Atilius Buta described in the same letter.[4]

* * * * *

1 Plutarch *Moralia* 525E *De cupiditate divitiarum*

51 Seneca (see n2). Added in *1515*
 1 Cf Jerome *Adversus Rufinum* 1.17 PL 23 430A.
 2 Seneca *Letters* 122.16. In modern editions this letter is not in book 22, but is the fifth letter of book 20, the last book of the collection that has survived. In the manuscript tradition and in the early printed editions the book division, when marked, is not consistent. Seneca is our sole authority for the existence of *lychnobius*.
 3 Erasmus misidentifies the speaker. In the letter it is Pedo Albinovanus who makes the joke against the *lychnobius*.
 4 Seneca *Letters* 122.10

52 Quasi Sutrium eant
As if going to Sutrium

Sutrium is a very old town in Etruria. At one time the Sutrians had revolted from the Romans, with whom they had formed an alliance. Camillus was chosen by the senate to force them to keep faith.[1] So that little time would be wasted in procuring supplies and so that the Sutrians would be caught out by his quickness in getting there, he ordered each soldier to bring with him a three-day supply of food. This then ['As if going to Sutrium'] became proverbial, customarily being used whenever someone worked for others at his own expense.[2] For this is how Festus Pompeius interprets it in some fragments that are to be found in Rome.[3] I think this is the same story as the one that Titus Livius tells, somewhat differently, in book six of *From the Founding of the City*.[4] Plautus in *Cassina*: 'Then also see to it that they come as if they are going to Sutrium.'[5] Alcesimus is ordering him [Lysidamus] to send his servants to his house, but they are to be equipped with their

* * * * *

52 Pompeius Festus (see n3). Added in 1515. The reference to Livy was added in 1526. Otto 1725

1 Camillus was an important figure of early Roman history. His accomplishments at the time of the Gallic invasion at the beginning of the fourth century led to his being thought of as the second founder of Rome

2 See *Adagia* II viii 90 Three days' rations.

3 Pompeius Festus 406.30–408.4 Lindsay. The fragments to which Erasmus is referring are either the codex Farnesianus (now Naples IV.A.3), discovered in the 1470s and the sole independent manuscript containing part of Pompeius Festus rather than the epitome of Festus by Paul the Deacon, or to copies made of it in the later fifteenth century after its discovery. Erasmus did not find this proverb in the Aldine edition of Festus of 1513 (along with Perotti's *Cornucopiae* and Nonius Marcellus) which jumps (col 1207) from *placato* (402.34 Lindsay) to *suopte* (408.4 Lindsay). The source of Erasmus' information is unclear and perhaps at second-hand.

4 Livy 6.3. In fact Livy's account differs significantly from that in Pompeius Festus.

5 Plautus *Casina* 524, cited in Pompeius Festus. The spelling 'Cassina' as the title of the play, used here, was current in Erasmus' time. There is confusion here in Erasmus' account. The speaker is actually Lysidamus (not named by Erasmus) and Alcesimus is the addressee. Erasmus follows the text of the 1500 Milan edition of Giambattista Pio in reading *tum quoque* 'then also' for a corrupt part of the text. For Pio see *Adagia* IV iii 40 n2 (27 above).

own food. The poem of Catullus in which he invites Fabullus to dinner, but only if he brings with him all that is needed for an elegant meal, is well known.[6]

53 Αὐτολήκυθοι
Those who carry their own oil-flask

Those who cultivated friends not out of true feeling for them but for the sake of their bellies were called Αὐτολήκυθοι 'Those who carry their own oil-flask,' a popular word coined because such persons travelled to and fro of their own accord with an oil-flask and attended banquets, though uninvited. In his essay entitled 'How One can Distinguish between a Flatterer and a Friend' Plutarch attests that these same persons were called 'frying-pan friends and post-prandial pals' by Eupolis and were also termed τραπεζεῖς 'table-men': 'But are we not to think, as ordinary people do, that those so-called *autolecythoi* and 'table-men' who are to be heard, as someone said, only after the call of "water for hands" are flatterers?'[1] Demosthenes used this word in his speech *Against Conon*.[2] Commentators explain it in different ways, as describing either those who are prepared to put up with anything at all, or poor people who possess only a cheap bowl, or those who are quick to take money, because some people are in the habit of keeping their money in such bowls, and in other ways as well, none of which agrees with Plutarch's view.[3]

In Athenaeus, book four, those who take pleasure 'in living at other men's tables'[4] are called ἀλλοτριοφάγοι 'those who eat other persons' food.'[5]

* * * * *

6 Catullus 13

53 *Suda* A 4505; Plutarch *Moralia* 50C *Quomodo adulator ab amico internoscatur*. Added in *1515*. The second-last paragraph on Athenaeus was added in *1528*. Contrast with this proverb *Adagia* v i 60 Your own slice of pie (576 below).

1 Plutarch *Moralia* 54B *Quomodo adulator ab amico internoscatur*; see PCG 5 Eupolis fragment 374. Erasmus wrenches the second quotation (Plutarch *Moralia* 50C) from its syntactical context. A more literal translation of Erasmus' rendering would begin 'but let us not think, as ...' The passage is also referred to in *Adagia* I v 23 Cupboard love.

2 Demosthenes 54.14

3 See *Suda* A 4505.

4 Erasmus quotes Juvenal 5.2 (*aliena vivere quadra*).

5 Athenaeus 4.164A, quoting *TrGF* 4 Sophocles fragment 329

In the same book he relates a story that is not without wit.[6] A dispute
arose about which water was the best. Some preferred the water of Lerna,
others the water from Pirene, others had different choices. Then Carneus
said, adopting an expression of Philoxenus, 'The sweetest water is "water
poured over your hands."'[7] For when the host bids the guests wash, this
shows that the meal is ready.

This proverb is similar to what has been said elsewhere: *Fervet olla,
vivit amicitia* 'When the pot boils, friendship thrives.'[8]

54 Melitaeus catulus
A Maltese lapdog

Μελιταῖον κυνίδιον, A Maltese lapdog. This was applied to someone whose
services were of no use for any serious purpose but who was kept only
for amusement. There is no small number of such persons in the house-
holds of the rich. Different dogs serve different purposes. Some are entrusted with guarding the house, so that they keep watch at night against
thieves. These are called οἰκουροί 'watchdogs.' There are some whom we
use for hunting, called θηρευτικοί 'hunting dogs.' Some serve no useful
purpose except to amuse idle, spoiled women and even today it is surprising how popular such pets are. These are called 'Maltese' from the island of Malta situated between Corcyra Nigra and Illyricum. The source
is Pliny, book three, in the final chapter.[1] Also Strabo and Stephanus.[2]

* * * * *

6 Athenaeus 4.156E. The humour of the story lies in the circumstances of the
   dispute – the meal for the guests was very slow in being served.
7 PMG fragment 836 (only for the expression 'water poured over hands'). Erasmus implies, wrongly, that Philoxenus said that this water was the best.
8 This is cited as a proverb in *Adagia* I v 23 Cupboard love. The Greek form of
   the proverb is Ζεῖ χύτρα, ζεῖ φιλία; see Zenobius 4.12, Diogenianus 4.96, and
   Suda Z 48.

54 *Suda* M 519; Apostolius 11.24. This is a doublet of *Adagia* III iii 71 (also translated as 'A Maltese lapdog,' though the Latin is not quite the same), but the essay and classical sources are different. The adage was considerably expanded
   from the form it took when it first appeared in 1515 (see accompanying notes).
   Cf *Adagia* II vi 13 A lapdog takes after its mistress.
1 Pliny *Naturalis historia* 3.152; 'in the final chapter' was added in 1528.
2 Strabo 6.2.11 and Stephanus of Byzantium sub Μελίτη, both added in 1536

Aristotle mentions these in problem fourteen of book ten, pointing out their whole bodies were very tiny and thin.[3] They are attractive because of this, in the same way that some cannot live without having dwarfs and pigmies. In Lucian in the *Lapiths* the jokester calls Alcidamas, the Cynic philosopher, 'A Maltese lapdog.'[4] In his twelfth book Athenaeus writes that Maltese dogs were very special favourites of the Sybarites.[5] Among dogs these seem to be the equivalent of dwarfs and pigmies among humans.[6] Masinissa is deservedly praised for preferring to rear children instead of monkeys and puppies and he did so until they were three, only then giving them back to their parents.[7] It is more intolerable, however, that in Britain many persons keep groups of dancing bears, a dangerous animal that has a voracious appetite. Monkeys too are like these, although less voracious. Is it not shameful for Christians to have such playthings when so many poor persons go hungry? Yet why do we deplore this when some people follow a custom that began in Italy and stroll about parading a young boy or girl who has been taught to act in a silly way, and when the dreadful plight of one girl occupies the leisure time of four or five sturdy wastrels?[8] Christians, however, look at such idle sport without blinking an eye.

55 Ilico hiems erit
Suddenly it will be winter

In his *Problems* in section 13 Aristotle gives this verse without citing the author but as if it were a common saying: Εἰ δ᾿ ὁ Νότος Βορέαν προκαλέσσεται,

* * * * *

3 Aristotle *Problemata* 10.12 (not 14) (892a21). Added in *1528*

4 Lucian *Convivium* 19. The *Lapiths* was an alternative title.

5 Athenaeus 12.519B; added in *1526*

6 This sentence was added in *1528*.

7 See Athenaeus 12.518F–519A. Masinissa, king of Mauretania, was asked by Sybarites if he had any monkeys or puppies for them. He rebuked them for wanting these animals instead of children by asking if they had not women to bear children. He took care of his grandchildren on his own, only giving them to their parents when they were three.

8 What Erasmus means by 'dreadful plight' (literally 'tragedy') is not specified. It probably refers to the sexual treatment of the girl by the men.

55 Aristotle (see n1). Added in *1515*

αὐτίκα χειμών 'It is suddenly winter once the south wind calls forth the north wind.'[1]

He gives this reason, that by its very nature the south wind gathers clouds and rain in abundance. Therefore, if the north wind gets up at such a time, everything freezes because of this wind's coldness, and so suddenly there is winter. In the same problem he adds another verse expressing much the same: Εἰ Βορρᾶς πηλὸν καταλήψεται, αὐτίκα χειμών 'If the North wind comes upon mud, immediately there is winter.'

Even if it is clear that this is a simple and common saying, nevertheless we can apply it to mean that a great danger threatens us if one misfortune is followed by another. For example, if someone who is excessively tortured by the labours of study also falls in love, or if someone not well liked by his ruler also incurs the hatred of the common people, or if a very lenient and easy-going king is succeeded by one who is extremely strict, or vice versa. For such sudden changes usually stir up the greatest unrest.

56 Eundem calceum omni pedi inducere
Putting the same shoe on every foot

Galen in book nine of his *Medical Treatment*: 'To be sure, these neither search out nor have knowledge. In fact, as the proverb says, Ἐνὶ καλαπόδι πάντας ὑποδέουσιν "They fit the same shoe on everyone."'[1] He is speaking about some inexperienced doctors who lack knowledge of diseases and apply the same remedies to all ailments, although different illnesses need different treatment. It is very similar to what we have said elsewhere: 'You know how to paint a cypress tree.'[2] Related to this expression is what Jerome adduces at the beginning of his preface of the commentary that he wrote on the Epistle to the Ephesians: 'And not to wish, like an inexperienced doctor, to treat the eyes of all with the same salve.'[3]

* * * * *

1 Aristotle *Problemata* 26.46 (not section 13) (945a37–b3), which Erasmus follows as far as 'Even if it is clear'

56 Galen (see n1). Added in *1515*. Tilley s 364 Every shoe fits not every foot
1 Galen *Therapeutike* 9.16 = 10.653.9–11 Kühn
2 *Adagia* I v 19 To paint a cypress; Otto 409
3 Jerome *Commentaria in Epistolam ad Ephesos, prologus* PL 26 441A. Cf *Adagia* IV viii 21 One salve for all sores (367 below).

57 Cochleae vita
A snail's life

Κοχλίου βίος, A snail's life. Said of those who live frugally and on little, or
have withdrawn from business and are aloof from the activities of commer-
cial daily life. The creature from whom the metaphor has been taken is well
known. Plutarch in his essay 'On Love of Wealth': 'You are beset by many
troubles, you torture and upset yourself when you live a snail's life because
of your stinginess.'[1] We have quoted elsewhere from the *Two Captives* of
Plautus about how snails 'live on their own juice . . . when it is hot weather.'[2]

58 Bello parta
Spoils of war

Ἐκ πολεμίας, From enemy land. Used when anyone spends extravagantly.
For we are accustomed to squander quickly and rashly whatever has been
plundered from enemies. Even today we have heard this adage being commonly said everywhere of gluttons and spendthrifts.[1] Plutarch in his essay
that he entitled 'Advice about Good Health': 'They fill themselves with expensive food at another's table and enjoy it, ladening themselves with food
as if it were booty from an enemy.'[2] He also uses this in the sixth problem of the seventh decade of the 'Table-talk.'[3] In book four of Athenaeus
Satyrus describes such persons in these words: 'Trampling on their land,
plundering their household, selling their possessions as if they were λα-
φαροπωλοῦντες "selling the spoils of war."'[4] For λαφαροπωλεῖν means 'to
put up for sale booty that has been seized from the enemy.' Because of

* * * * *

57 Plutarch (see n1), not in the *Suda* or CPG. Added in 1515. The last sentence was
   added in 1533.
1 Plutarch *Moralia* 525D–E *De cupiditate divitiarum*
2 Plautus *Captivi* 78–83, quoted in *Adagia* II viii 80 They live on their own juice.
   Erasmus' version of the title of Plautus' play is common in early editions.

58 Plutarch (see nn2–3). Added in 1515. The second paragraph was added in 1528.
1 Suringar 28
2 Plutarch *Moralia* 125E *De tuenda sanitate praecepta*
3 Plutarch *Moralia* 708E *Quaestiones convivales*
4 Athenaeus 4.168C quoting Satyrus fragment 20 (FHG 3.164). Satyrus was a
   Greek historian of the third century BC.

this, those who dissipate their assets in luxurious living are called λαφύκται in Greek, as Athenaeus points out in book eleven.⁵ Suidas points out that such squandering is called λαφυγμός and that λαφύσσειν means 'to plunder,' or 'to squander extravagantly' or 'to consume completely.'⁶ For λάφυρα means spoils taken from living enemies, while the spoils taken from dead enemies are σκῦλα 'armour.'

59 Panis lapidosus
Gritty bread

If anyone denies that 'Gritty bread,' mentioned by Seneca in book two of *On Kindnesses*, is a proverb, I shall certainly not fight to the death with him.¹ But it certainly deserves to be included in the company of adages because of how frequently it is used. For this is what Fabius Verrucosus called a kindness that a hard-hearted man pitilessly gives to someone who in his hunger has no choice but to accept it. Such a kindness, he says, is cruel and harsh. Some people spoil a kindness by giving it with a scowl² or a truculent expression, or by speaking sharply or by flaunting it in an annoying way. The result is that if any one can do without the kindness he will not accept it.

60 E Patroclis domo venit
He comes from the house of Patrocles

Ἐκ Πατροκλέους, From the house of Patrocles. Of mean persons, taken from the character of a certain Patrocles, an Athenian, who was certainly very

* * * * *

5 Athenaeus 11.485A
6 *Suda* Λ 156, 158

59 Seneca (see n1). Horace also uses the adjective *lapidosus* of bread in *Satires* 1.5.91. Added in *1515*
1 Seneca *De beneficiis* 2.7.1. 'Fabius Verrucosus ... cruel and harsh' closely follows Seneca.
2 ASD (II-7 214) here reads *contatione* (= *cunctatione* 'with hesitation'), while LB (II 1038F) offers *contactione*, which does not make much sense. The correct reading should probably be *contractione* 'furrowing of the brows,' as reflected in the translation.

60 *Suda* and a scholiast on Aristophanes (see n2). Added in *1515*

rich but also parsimonious and miserly in spending money. Old Comedy depicts him very much as Plautus depicts Euclio.[1] The evidence comes from a scholiast on Aristophanes whose words are reported by Suidas as well, who also regards this as a proverb. It is in the *Plutus* of Aristophanes.[2] Since Wealth was grubby, dishevelled, and covered in dirt, he was asked from where he had come: 'Tell me where you are coming from since you are so dirty and unkempt?' And he replied, 'From the house of Patrocles, who has never washed from the day he was born.'

61 Tam in proclivi quam imber
As easy as rain can fall

The following words of Plautus in his play entitled *Two Captives* have the appearance of a proverb: 'This is as easy for you as it is for raindrops to fall when there are showers.'[1] For *proclive* properly describes what hangs downwards.[2] And indeed it is difficult to push heavy objects up a hill, but they roll down it of their own accord.

62 Et post malam segetem serendum est
Even after a bad harvest we must sow

I would not argue very strongly that the *epiphonema* of Seneca in book eleven of his *Letters*, 'Even after a bad harvest we must sow,' is a proverb although it is very similar to one.[1] It may be used whenever something has not turned out at all as we thought, meaning that we must not give up trying. Seneca,

* * * * *

1 Euclio, a miser, is a character in Plautus' *Aulularia*.
2 Aristophanes *Plutus* 83–5; see scholiast on *Plutus* 84 and *Suda* Π 795.

61 Plautus (see n1). Otto 850. Added in *1515*
1 Plautus *Captivi* 336. Erasmus gives the play a title that is found in the early editions.
2 The reason for this comment may be that the adjective *proclivis* can mean 'difficult' as well as 'easy' depending on whether it denotes an uphill or a downhill slope.

62 Seneca (see n1). Otto 1619. Added in *1515*
1 Seneca *Letters* 81.1–2. An *epiphonema* is a term in rhetoric for an ornamental flourish that rounds off an argument or section, without adding anything new. See Demetrius *On Style* 106; Quintilian 8.5.11. Here the *epiphonema* follows

however, is talking about those who shrink from doing a kindness to any one because they have once encountered ingratitude. What Seneca adds in the same passage, *post naufragium maria tentantur* 'after shipwreck sailors try the seas again,' is of the same kind.

63 Spes servat afflictos
Hope preserves the afflicted

In his essay 'How to Keep Well' Plutarch points out that there was a common proverb about hope, although he does not reveal what it was: 'Using a proverb to defend their weakness and intemperance, most people are led by hope to take to their customary way of life the moment they leave their beds.'[1] On the identification of the proverb that people use to excuse their intemperance he makes it clear in what follows: 'As if they will cast off and dispel wine with wine, drunkenness with drunkenness.' It is obvious from this that Plutarch was alluding to the proverb 'To drive out one nail by another.'[2] Even today this is an equally common expression among fellow imbibers.[3] They add a joke about 'the hair of a rabid dog' and put into practice a witticism that can prove fatal to many.

There is a passing allusion to this proverb ['Hope saves the afflicted'] in the sayings that have been culled, so it appears, from comedies: ἀνὴρ ἀτυχῶν σώζεται ταῖς ἐλπίσι 'good hope saves a man in adversity.'[4] These

* * * * *

Seneca's statement that it is better to confer benefits and get no return than never to confer any.

63 Plutarch (see n1). Erasmus changed his mind about the proverb to which Plutarch was referring. Originally (in *1515*) he thought it was the one that is the title of the adage. In *1526*, however, he changed his mind and added 'On the identification of this proverb ... fatal to many' and then a transitional passage 'There is a passing allusion to' in order to return to what he had originally written in *1515*. Tilley H 603 Hope is the poor man's bread
1 Plutarch *Moralia* 127F *De tuenda sanitate praecepta*
2 *Adagia* I ii 4
3 Suringar 212
4 Very similar to Menander *Sententiae* 30; cf Menander fragment 636 Körte-Thierfelder. Erasmus' version was taken from the Aldine edition of Theocritus (*1495*), which also includes a section containing Greek sayings, cited anonymously.

words of Naso are well known: 'Good hope gives strength, good hope strengthens the mind as well. I have seen a person on the point of death living through hope.'[5] Then those words of Pindar almost became proverbial among the learned: Ἐλπὶς γηροτρόφος 'Hope the nourisher of old age.'[6] For so Plutarch in his essay 'On Tranquillity of Mind': 'And a more pleasant and stable memory than that hope of Pindar's, the nourisher of old age.'[7] And indeed Plato recalls this Pindaric passage in book one of the *Republic*: 'Because to him who has lived an upright and pious life hope is a friend, hope that is sweet and gladdens the heart, hope that nourishes old age, hope that especially guides the resilient minds of mortals.'[8]

64 Tria saluberrima
The most wholesome three

This too, in the same work,[1] appears to have been spoken as a proverb, since he reports it without naming its source. But it is better to give his actual words: 'Accordingly, it is a splendid saying, that the most wholesome things are to stop eating before one is full, never to shrink from toil, to preserve the seed of nature.'

65 Admoto capite
With head brought near

In his work entitled 'How One Should Distinguish between Friend and Flatterer' Plutarch uses this verse (which occurs frequently in Homer) as if

* * * * *

5 Only 'Good hope gives strength' is from Naso (Ovid *Heroides* 11.61). The whole couplet, however, is attested from mediaeval times; see H. Walther *Proverbia sententiaeque Latinitatis medii aevi* (Göttingen 1963–7) nos 30180, 34005.
6 Pindar fragment 214 Snell
7 Plutarch *Moralia* 477B *De tranquillitate animi*
8 Plato *Republic* 1.331A

64 Hardly a proverb. The title is invented by Erasmus. Added in *1515*
1 Plutarch's 'How to Keep Well,' mentioned at the beginning of the commentary of the immediately preceding adage. The passage cited here is from *Moralia* 129F *De tuenda sanitate praecepta*.

65 Homer by way of Plutarch (see n1). Added in *1515*

it were proverbial: Ἀγχὶ σχὼν κεφαλήν, ἵνα μὴ πευθοίατ' οἱ ἄλλοι 'With head brought near, so that the rest might not be able to hear.'[1]

In this passage Plutarch is advising that if a friend deserves a rebuke this should be done, first of all, at the appropriate time, secondly, in a friendly and affable manner, and finally, privately with no witnesses present: 'And so, this is what is best, "With head brought nearer."' Instead of this expression, Livy used *conferre capita* in book ten of *From the Founding of the City*: 'The consuls *capita conferunt* "put together their heads" as if in deliberation.'[2]

66 Cur cessatum est?
Why have we stopped?

In the same essay Plutarch also makes use of this verse of Homer from *Iliad*, book eleven: Τυδείδη, τί παθόντε λελάσμεθα θούριδος ἀλκῆς; 'Son of Tydeus, what has happened that we have forgotten our martial valour?'[1] We may use it whenever we recognize a fault that we share with a friend and thereby indicate that it was wrong to have stopped in some action.

67 Abiiciendum procul
It must be cast far away

Whenever we advise that some vice or something harmful in other respects ought to be cast far away, this verse (of Homer, if I am not mistaken) will be appropriate: Εἰς ὄρος ἢ εἰς κῦμα πολυφλοίσβοιο θαλάσσης 'On to a mountain

* * * * *

1 Plutarch *Moralia* 71B *Quomodo adulator ab amico internoscatur* 'How One Should Distinguish between Friend and Flatterer,' citing Homer *Odyssey* 1.157. The whole line occurs frequently in Homer; see, for example, *Odyssey* 4.70, 17.592.
2 Livy 2.45.7 (not book 10). This sentence was added in *1528*.

66 The title given for this adage is Erasmus' interpretation of the quotation, from Homer, not the 'proverb' itself. Added in *1515*
1 Plutarch *Moralia* 71F *Quomodo adulator ab amico internoscatur* (mentioned in the previous adage), quoting Homer *Iliad* 11.313. The identification of the source 'from *Iliad*, book eleven' was added in *1526*.

67 Again the title is not the proverb itself, but is an explanation of the Homeric verse. For a similar adage compare *Adagia* IV x 67 To the ends of the earth (522–3 below). Added in *1515*

or into the swollen waves of the roaring sea.'[1] So too Horace in his *Odes*,
book three, ode fourteen:

> Let us cast into the Capitol,
> Where clamour calls and the supporters throng,
> Or into the nearest sea
> Our gems and our rare stones and useless gold,
> Of deepest wrong the occasion and the means,
> If we are truly sorry for our crimes.[2]

Theognis, however, bids us throw into the mighty sea not wealth, but
poverty itself.[3] Similarly, we say that an extremely dangerous person ought
to be deported to the remotest of islands.

68 Testudinem equus insequitur
The steed is in pursuit of the tortoise

Plutarch in the essay that he wrote 'Against the Stoics':

> It is a much more shameful belief and one going against all reason that nothing
> can catch up with anything, μηδ᾿ εἰ χελώνην ... μετόπισθε διώκοι Ἀδράστου
> ταχὺς ἵππος 'not even if the swift steed of Adrastus were in pursuit of a
> tortoise,' as the proverb says.[1]

An appropriate use will be when we mean that something is being
done in a quite absurd and unnatural way. It is related to what we have
said elsewhere: 'You match a tortoise against Pegasus' and 'Sooner will the
tortoise outrun the hare.'[2]

* * * * *

1 Homer *Iliad* 6.347
2 Horace *Odes* 3.24.45–50 (ode 24 not 14). Lines 47–50 are quoted in *Adagia* II i
   97 Throw him in the river; the translation there is adopted here. The reference
   'book three, ode fourteen' was added in *1528*.
3 Theognis 1.175–6: εἰς μεγακήτεα πόντον / Ῥίπτειν 'throw into the mighty sea'

68 Plutarch (see n1). Added in *1515*
1 Plutarch *Moralia* 1082E *De communibus notitiis adversus Stoicos*. Plutarch is dealing with locomotion. What follows is a reference to the Epicurean view that
   all atoms move with equal velocity.
2 *Adagia* I viii 76, I viii 84

69 Stultior Melitide
As stupid as Melitides

Μωρότερος Μελιτίδου, More stupid than Melitides. Melitides was one of those lucky fools whom Homer made famous in his poetry. He is said to have come to help Priam when Troy had already been destroyed, as Eustathius mentions in his commentary on book ten of the *Odyssey*.[1] Lucian in his *Love Affairs*: 'For heaven's sake, do you think that I am Melitides or Coroebus?'[2] The proverb is cited by Zenodotus, who informs us that this fellow was a target for the abuse of the comic writers because of his stupidity: he could not count beyond five and he never laid a finger on a new bride when he married her for fear that she would lay accusations against him to her mother.[3] In the same place he mentions another extremely stupid man who did not know which parent gave him birth. We have mentioned Coroebus, the friend of Melitides, elsewhere.[4] Pausanias said that Aristophanes counted this man along with Butalio and Melitides as a fool.[5] Suidas says the same, quoting these verses from Aristophanes: 'Up to now the most abject of men, idly gaping / They sit, like a Mamakuthes or a Melitides.'[6]

* * * * *

69 *Suda* Γ 118; cf Apostolius 5.27 and Diogenianus 5.12. Otto 1087. This adage appeared in *1508* (no 924 of the second chiliad) but the title was different: Γελοιότερον Μελιτίδου 'As ridiculous as Melitides.' The accompanying essay was also changed and expanded in *1515*. Further additions were made in *1526* ('The proverb is cited by Zenodotus') and *1528* ('Pausanias recalls' to the end).
1 Eustathius 1669.51 on *Odyssey* 10.552, but he does not give the information recounted by Erasmus. This story is also mentioned in *Adagia* III i 17 To bring up the artillery when the war is over.
2 Lucian *Amores* 53
3 This does not appear in the collection of Zenobius in CPG, but is to be found in Zenobius (Aldus) column 59. The name of the other stupid man who did not know whether his mother or father gave him birth was Amphisteides. On Erasmus' use of the name Zenodotus (for Zenobius) see *Adagia* IV iii 72 n2 (44 above).
4 *Adagia* II ix 64 As foolish as Coroebus
5 The reference to Pausanias has not been identified. Perhaps Erasmus was thinking of Pausanias the Atticist, who is sometimes cited in the *Suda* (note the reference to 'Suidas' in the next sentence). There is nothing of this nature, however, in Erbse's edition of the fragments of Pausanias (see *Adagia* IV vi 17 n2, 221 below).
6 *Suda* B 468, quoting Aristophanes *Frogs* 989–91

70 Non pluit nocte qua sus foetum aedit agrestis
It stops raining the night the wild sow farrows

Plutarch in his 'Natural Causes' gives this verse as a proverb among the ancients: Μηκέτι νυκτὸς ὕει, ἦ κεν τέκῃ ἀγροτέρα σῦς 'The rain stops on the night that the wild sow farrows.'[1]

He is enquiring into why domesticated sows farrow fairly often and at different times of the year, while wild sows do so only once and almost on the same day each year. This occurs at the beginning of summer, the season of the year that has least rain, especially in Greece. I do not see any use for the proverb other than to indicate that there will be fair weather, once spring or autumn is over. But if you want to apply it in a more metaphorical way, it will be possible to use it humorously to indicate that there will be an end of troubles for us when something or other that will happen soon has come to pass.

71 Electro lucidior
As clear as amber

Ἠλέκτρου διαφεγγέστερος, Clearer than amber. Of something extremely translucent or about an object that is exceptionally bright, since amber shines in a marvellous way. Accordingly, Virgil calls it *liquidus* 'clear': *liquidove potest electro.*[1] Lucian in his *Love Affairs*: 'More translucent than amber, as the saying goes, or than Sidonian glass.'[2] He describes glass as 'Sidonian' because Sidon was once famous for the manufacturing of glass.

* * * * *

70 Plutarch (see n1). Erasmus abbreviates the adage to *Non pluit, etc.* The full form has been taken from the Latin translation in the body of the commentary (see n1). This adage is a doublet of *Adagia* II v 43 The wild sow's farrow will bring a fine morrow. The explanation is similar but not exactly the same. Added in *1515*

  1 Plutarch *Moralia* 917B *Quaestiones naturales.* Erasmus' Latin translation of the Greek verse runs *iam non nocte pluit qua sus foetum aedit agrestis* (a dactylic hexameter).

71 Lucian (see n2). Added in *1515*

  1 Virgil *Aeneid* 8.402. This is an incomplete quotation of the verse, and the phrase on its own does not make any sense. Erasmus took the full line to mean 'All that can be made from iron or from clear amber.' However, in this verse *electro* refers not to amber, but to a metal alloy, and *liquido* means 'molten,' not 'clear.'

  2 Lucian *Amores* 26

72 Tam perit quam extrema faba
As precarious as a bean on the edge

Festus Pompeius points out that a frequently spoken proverb was 'As precarious as a bean on the edge,' the reason for the proverb being 'that beans growing on the edge [of a plot] are generally either trampled on or picked by passers-by.'[1] It will suit, then, an individual or a thing that is exposed to all kinds of harm from everyone. For example, if one were to say that theology is as precarious as a bean on the edge because there is no place where the most ignorant men do not engage in it and defile it.

73 Tyria maria
Tyrian seas

'Tyrian seas' was said proverbially about a situation that was very turbulent and fraught with danger. Festus Pompeius says that the adage arose because 'the Carthaginians, who originated in Tyre, had great control of the sea. Accordingly, a voyage that would take one through them was dangerous for all.'[1] And he cites Afranius, since he said of some individual 'that he was stirring up Tyrian seas,' in other words, that he was stirring up great troubles.

74 Altera manu fert aquam, etc
He carries water in one hand, etc

Τῇ μὲν ὕδωρ φορεῖ, τῇ δὲ ἑτέρῃ τὸ πῦρ,[1] He is carrying water in one hand and fire in the other. One can apply this figuratively to someone who flatters a

* * * * *

72 Pompeius Festus (see n1). Otto 619. Added in *1515*
1 Pompeius Festus 496.28–30 Lindsay

73 Pompeius Festus (see n1). Otto 1808. Added in *1515*
1 Pompeius Festus 484.21–5 Lindsay, citing CRF Afranius 112. The individual is referred to as *Sirrius* in Festus, though the 1513 Aldine edition of Festus identifies him simply as a slave (*servus*).

74 Plutarch (see n3). Tilley F 267 He bears fire in one hand and water in the other. Added in *1515*. The last sentence was added in *1517/18*.
1 Archilochus fragment 184 West

man to his face but privately does him harm. Or to someone who speaks with two tongues, sometimes praising, sometimes reviling, or to someone whose feelings are quite different from what he says. It is related to those words of Plautus, 'He bears a stone in one hand and offers a loaf in the other.'[2] It is reported by Plutarch in 'The Principle of Cold': 'Deceitfully she brought water in one hand, and fire in the other.'[3] He is talking about a woman whose intentions are quite different from and contradictory to what she professes. It is surprising, however, that the same saying, in almost the same words, is commonly on our lips today.[4]

75 Vapula Papiria
You be hanged, Papiria

'You be flogged, Papiria.' Sisinius Capito writes that this was a proverb frequently used whenever persons wanted to show that they did not pay any attention to someone else's threats. We find this only in the fragments of Festus Pompeius.[1] I suspect that it originated with Papirius Praetextatus, whose mother tried to extract from him what had happened in the senate, in vain, even though she threatened a flogging.[2] Therefore one should read *Papiri*,[3] not *Papiria*, unless one prefers to understand *lege* 'law,' so that the words

* * * * *

2 Plautus *Aulularia* 195 and *Adagia* I viii 29
3 Plutarch *Moralia* 950F *De primo frigido*
4 Suringar 8

75 Pompeius Festus (see n1). Otto 1846. Added in *1515*
1 Pompeius Festus 512.15–19 Lindsay. On the fragments of Festus see *Adagia* IV iv 52 n3 (96 above). The proverb was not preserved in Paul the Deacon's excerpts of Festus. 'Sisinius' (for 'Sinnius') is the reading in Erasmus' immediate source, the 1513 Aldine edition. Sinnius Capito was a grammarian of the late 1st century BC; see Funaioli 457–66.
2 The story is told in Aulus Gellius *Noctes Atticae* 1.23. While still a boy (and thus wearing the *toga praetexta*) the young Papirius was taken to the senate by his father. Because he refused to divulge to his mother what he had heard, he was honoured by being given the nickname 'Praetextatus.' Gellius does not say anything of the mother threatening to flog her son; it is an embellishment of Erasmus.
3 The vocative of *Papirius*. The proverb would then reflect what the mother allegedly said to her son.

are a threat to inflict the punishment of the *lex Papiria*.[4] Unless you prefer to understand it as referring to Papiria, the wife of Paulus Aemilius, who was divorced by her husband although no one could find the reason for it.[5] What can one do? We must engage in conjecture when no sources can help us.

76 Quasi millus cani
Like a hound's collar

According to the same author, another attractive proverb was spoken by Scipio Aemilianus when addressing the people.[1] He said, 'You will be protection for us and the state, as a collar protects a hound.' For *millus* is a collar for hunting dogs, made of leather, in which are embedded iron nails that protrude to repel attacking wolves. By using this proverb, then, we shall indicate a sure and strong means of protection.

77 Non liberat podagra calceus
A sandal does not cure gout

Plutarch in his essay 'On Tranquillity of Mind' cites the following expression, which he says was commonly spoken and which shows its proverbial nature in any case by the trope: Οὔτε ποδάγρας ἀπαλλάττει καλτίκιος, οὔτε δακτύλιος πολυτελὴς παρωνυχίας, οὔτε διάδημα κεφαλαλγίας 'A sandal does not cure gout, nor an expensive ring a hangnail, nor a diadem a headache.'[1]

* * * * *

4 The translation would be 'be flogged under the *lex Papiria*.' The *lex Papiria*, introduced by Caius Papirius Carbo in 131 or 130 BC, extended the use of the secret ballot to legislative assemblies. See T.R.S. Broughton *The Magistrates of the Roman Republic* (New York 1951–2) 1.502.

5 See Plutarch *Aemilius* 5.1–3.

76 Pompeius Festus (see n1). Added in *1515*
1 Pompeius Festus 137.3–6 Lindsay, from whom Erasmus draws most of what he writes here. In the quotation of Scipio Erasmus follows in part the text of the 1513 Aldine. Modern editions read 'he will be protection for you and the state . . .'

77 Plutarch (see n1). Added in *1515*. The last three sentences were added in *1533*, as was 'the Latin for which is *reduvia*.'
1 Plutarch *Moralia* 465A *De tranquillitate animi*. In his translation of the Greek Erasmus uses *unguium vitium* 'a flaw of the nails' to translate παρωνυχία, not

The Greek word for hangnail is παρωνυχία, the Latin for which is *reduvia*. Plutarch uses it to express the idea that if wealth and the other gifts of good fortune do not remove physical illnesses, how much less can they cure flaws of the soul. A ring is the mark of a doctorate, but it does not remove dullness of intellect. A diadem is the symbol of kings, but it does not free a person of stupidity. A red cap is the mark of outstanding piety, but not even this frees one from impious thoughts.

78 Uno digitulo
With one little finger

'With one little finger' describes the ability to do something with the utmost ease. Terence in the *Eunuchus*:

> You who are lucky enough now to open the door with one little finger
> Will often strike it with your feet in vain, I warrant it.[1]

Jerome in the *Dialogue of Luciferianus and Orthodoxus*: 'This spear, then, that you have hurled with all your might, with which you threaten us, I shall parry with one little finger, as the saying goes.'[2] The adage we have spoken of elsewhere, *Minimo provocare*,[3] to indicate that we can prevail even with no effort at all, is also relevant.

79 Muli Mariani
Marian mules

'Marian mules,' a proverb of the army camp, was applied to soldiers suffering from varicose veins who were accustomed to carry their loads on a

* * * * *

reduvia, as one might expect from the following sentence.

78 Terence and Jerome (see nn1–2). Added in *1515*. Otto 545
  1 Terence *Eunuchus* 284–5. This was added in *1526*.
  2 Jerome *Adversus Luciferianos* 13 PL 23 176A
  3 *Adagia* III vi 45 To challenge with the little finger

79 Pompeius Festus (see n1). Otto 1164. Added in *1515*. 'From this the expression ... obeyed orders' was added in *1533*. 'Julius Frontinus ... became a proverb' was added in *1520*. The proverb is mentioned in *Adagia* III v 48 An Egyptian brick-carrier.

board that rested on a fork-shaped yoke, a practice instituted by their leader Caius Marius. Festus Pompeius is also our source for this.[1] But Plutarch in his *Life of Caius Marius* gives two explanations of the adage's origin.[2] When the general Marius was building up his soldiers by making them go on training runs and on different kinds of forced marches, and by making them carry heavy loads, they became accustomed to these activities and put up with them in silence and without rancour. By a camp joke they were called Ἡμίονοι Μαριανοί 'Marian mules.' From this the expression was applied to anyone who readily obeyed orders. Julius Frontinus also mentions the adage in book four of his *Strategies* in this way: 'In order to cut down the baggage with which an army on the move is especially burdened, equipment and the soldiers' provisions were fitted into baskets and placed on fork yokes. The purpose was to make the weight easier to bear and to allow the soldiers to rest more easily. Because of this "Marian mules" became a proverb.'[3]

This was doubtless because of the soldiers' great tolerance of toil, since Homer continually calls mules ταλαεργοί 'toil-enduring.'[4]

Some give a different origin for the adage.[5] For when Scipio was besieging Numantia and decided to inspect not only the soldiers' weapons but also their horses, mules, and chariots to see how each had trained and prepared them, Marius had led out a horse that had been extremely well looked after by him, and in addition a mule that far surpassed all others in its physical condition, obedience, and strength. And so since the general was delighted by Marius' animals and continually referred to them, the outcome was that anyone who was untiring, strong, and

* * * * *

1 Pompeius Festus 134.6–9 Lindsay. Festus says that the soldiers were accustomed to carry their burden *varicosius*. The meaning of the comparative adverb is disputed. It could mean 'with more dilated veins,' or 'with feet spread further apart' (ie to balance the wide load they were carrying), or 'more quickly' (literally, 'with greater strides'). Erasmus has replaced the comparative adverb with the adjective *varicosi* and moved it to a different clause, and this suggests that he took it, wrongly I think, in the sense reflected in the translation.
2 Plutarch *Marius* 13.1
3 Frontinus *Strategemata* 4.1.7
4 Homer *Iliad* 23.654, 662; *Odyssey* 4.636
5 See Plutarch *Marius* 13.2–3.

hard-working in performing his duties was called 'a Marian mule' as a humorous term of praise. This other origin for the proverb is given by Plutarch in his *Life of Marius*, which I have just cited.[6] In his humorous bagatelle directed at the emperor Claudius Seneca describes mules as *perpetuarii* 'non-stop workers.'[7] It will be rather amusing if it is applied to someone completely engrossed in an immense project or in never-ending business.

80 Osculana pugna
An Osculan battle

Festus Pompeius points out that 'An Osculan battle' was a proverb customarily used whenever those who had been defeated were later victorious.[1] It originated when the general Valerius Laevinus was first defeated by Pyrrhus and then a little later crushed the same king. He cites Ticinius who mentioned the adage.[2] However, this passage in Festus, like others, is corrupt and lacunose.[3]

81 Osce loqui
Speaking Oscan

'Speaking Oscan,' an old proverb applied to those who spoke in a disgusting and shameless way. The allusion is taken from the customs of the Oscans; for among them the practice of satisfying foul desires went

* * * * *

6 This sentence was added in 1526.
7 Seneca *Ludus de morte Claudi* 6.1. In the text it is the muleteers who are described as *perpetuarii*.

80 Pompeius Festus (see n1). Otto 1315. Added in *1515*
1 Pompeius Festus 214.26–30 Lindsay, whom Erasmus follows closely down to 'the same king'
2 CRF Titinius 181–2
3 The 1513 Aldine edition of Festus indicates lacunae in this passage. Turnebus emended *Osculana* to *Asculana*.

81 The comic writer Titinius by way of Pompeius Festus (see nn1–2). Added in *1515*. The expression is hardly proverbial.

unpunished. Because of this some think that whatever is disgusting in word or deed is also called obscene (*obscaena*), though Festus Pompeius rejects this.[1] And indeed he cites a certain Ticinius who wrote as follows: 'They speak Oscan and Volscian, because they do not know how to speak Latin.'[2]

82 Sero molunt deorum molae
The gods' mill grinds slow

Plutarch in his essay 'On Those Punished Late by the Gods': "Ὥστε οὐχ ὁρῶ τί χρήσιμον ἔνεστι τοῖς ὀψὲ δὴ τούτοις ἀλεῖν λεγομένοις μύλοις τῶν θεῶν 'I do not see the value in those mills of the gods that are said to grind slow.'[1] But from what precedes in the same passage one can infer that it was frequently said of those who finally, though belatedly, were punished for their misdeeds by an avenging god.

83 In transcursu
On the run

Plutarch in his essay 'On Bringing up Children': 'But they learn this Ἐκ περιδρομῆς "On the run," as if they are just having a taste.'[1] The metaphor clearly has the flavour of a proverb. Instead of this expression Quintilian used *in transitu*.[2] Pliny prefers *in transcursu*; *obiter* means the same.[3]

* * * * *

1 Pompeius Festus 204.24–35 Lindsay, the source of the phrase. Erasmus here follows the spelling *Osce* of the 1513 Aldine edition, although the manuscripts have *obsce*. The connection between 'Oscan' and 'obscene' is fanciful.
2 CRF Titinius (the usual form of the name) 104

82 Plutarch (see n1). Tilley G 270 God's mill grinds slow but sure. Added in *1515*
1 Plutarch *Moralia* 549D *De sera numinis vindicta*

83 Plutarch (see n1). In *1515*, where it first appeared, the essay was even shorter than it is now, ending at 'flavour of a proverb.' The rest was added in *1533*.
1 Plutarch *Moralia* 7C *De liberis educandis*
2 Quintilian 2.20.15
3 Pliny *Naturalis historia* 3.39

84 Tribus verbis
In three words

'In three words' is a proverbial expression for 'in very few words.' St Jerome in the *Dialogue of Luciferianus and Orthodoxus*: 'You have solved that huge problem in three words, as the saying goes.'[1] Similarly Terence's Geta says in the *Phormio* that some persons 'will not exchange three words.'[2] Pindar in the *Nemeans* in hymn twelve: 'Τρία ἔπεα "three words" will suffice.'[3] And yet I am fully aware that on this passage the commentators philosophize quite superstitiously on 'three words.' Marcus Tullius in *For Cluentius*: 'He accused Scamandrus in three words; the poison has been seized . . .'[4] Using the same trope we say 'six hundred' to mean 'many': 'Bring six hundred suits against me then.'[5] In the opposite way a person who explains in a few words is said 'to complete the matter in a word' and the person who says nothing at all is said 'to expend not even a syllable on the matter.' So Galen, speaking against Erasistratus, I think: 'How is it he has no shame? He has made distinctions about problems in digestion, saying that they are many and occur from different causes, but has said not even one word, not even one syllable, about deficiencies in blood-production.'[6]

85 Ne punctum quidem
Not even a point

St Jerome in his *Letters*: 'Let us follow in the footsteps of the Apostolic will and not depart by even a point, as the saying goes, or a nail's breadth

* * * * *

84 Jerome (see n1). Otto 1869; cf *Adagia* III vii 50 In three throws. The commentary on this adage was considerably expanded from its original state in *1515*. 'In the opposite way' to the end was added in *1528* (and see notes).
1 Jerome *Adversus Luciferianos* 21 PL 23 184C
2 Terence *Phormio* 638–9 ('in the *Phormio*' was added in *1528*)
3 Pindar *Nemeans* 7.48 (not ode 12). Most of this sentence was added in *1526* but 'in hymn twelve' was added in *1528*.
4 Cicero *Pro A. Cluentio* 18.50. Added in *1533*
5 Terence *Phormio* 668, a very loose quotation and probably quoted from memory
6 Galen *De naturalibus facultatibus* 2.8 (= 2.108, 10–14 Kühn)

85 Jerome (see n1). Otto 1489. Added in *1515*

from its tenets.'[1] For the mathematicians a point is the smallest unit of measurement. It cannot be divided and if imaginarily extended vertically it produces a line. Again if the line is extended horizontally it makes a plane figure. Similarly Terence in the *Woman of Andros*: 'Moreover, I have only a point of time for this.'[2]

86 Incita equum iuxta nyssam
Ride your horse close to the turning point

Κέντει τὸν πῶλον περὶ τὴν νύσσαν, Spur your horse close to the line or turning point. This was said when a speaker's words were wandering from what had been prescribed. It seems to have its origin in Homer's *Iliad*, book twenty-three.[1] When Nestor is instructing his son Antilochus at great length how he ought to steer his horse, he adds this: 'But let the boundary of the turning post graze the horse on the left.' Taken from a horse race which took place between fixed turning points and boundaries beyond which it was forbidden to go. Undoubtedly Fabius alludes to this in book eleven of his *Principles of Oratory*, when he recalls that Cassius Severus used to demand that a line be drawn to thwart those who crossed over to their opponents' seats, on the grounds that they were transgressing a prescribed boundary.[2] It is related to 'Beyond the olive trees'[3] and also to 'To overleap the pit.'[4] Gregory of Nazianzus uses it in a proverbial way in his speech *On Holy Easter*: 'But at this point perhaps one of those who like festivals and are rather hot-headed may say to us, "Steer your horse close to the turning point and talk about the festival."'[5] He also uses the same proverb in his

* * * * *

1 Jerome *Letters* 120.10.3 PL 22 998, CSEL 55 501
2 Terence *Phormio* (not *Andria*) 184, quoted in *Adagia* II ii 70 A point of time

86 *Suda* K 1331 or Gregory of Nazianzus (see n5). Added in *1515*. In the first sentence 'or turning point' was added in *1528*, as was the final sentence.
1 Homer *Iliad* 23.338. The reference to Homer and the quotation were added in *1526*.
2 Quintilian 11.3.133. Quintilian is talking about how some orators walked about and approached their adversaries while delivering their speech.
3 *Adagia* II ii 10
4 *Adagia* I x 93
5 Gregory of Nazianzus *Orationes* 45.10 (PG 36 636B), 38.10 (PG 36 321B), 27.5 (PG 36 17A). This sentence and the following one were added in *1526*.

speech *On the Birthday of Jesus Christ.* He also varied it somewhat in the speech *Against the Eunomians*: 'Let us not, like excited and unmanageable horses unseating their riders, shake off reason and religious caution that properly restrain us within the bounds; let us not run far from the turning point.'

87 Praestat invidiosum esse quam miserabilem
Better envied than pitied

No expression is more frequent in the vernacular than this one: 'Better envied than pitied.'[1] For envy is generally the companion of good luck, pity of disaster. It is in Herodotus in his *Thalia* where Periander says this to his son: Σὺ δὲ μαθὼν ὅσῳ φθονέεσθαι κρέσσον ἐστὶ ἢ οἰκτείρεσθαι 'You who have learned how better it is to be envied than pitied.'[2] There survives a Greek epigram of Palladas on this idea:

> Pity is worse than envy, says Pindar,
> For those assailed by envy prosper.
> Pity befalls those whose lot is cruel.
> I do not wish for either,
> To be too lucky or to be pitied by any.
> For it's better moderation in all things,
> Since peril sits next to lofty lot
> And he who bears the unbearable is crushed low.[3]

The expression is to be found in Pindar in the *Pythians* hymn one: 'But envy is better than pity. Do not abandon what is good, guide your army with a just rudder.'[4] Again in the *Nemeans*, hymn eight: 'Slander is the food of the envious. It is aimed at those who are upright, it has no concern with the inferior.'[5] Again, in the eleventh hymn of the *Pythians*: 'For prosperity

* * * * *

87 Herodotus (see n2). Added in *1515*
1 Suringar 177; Tilley E 177 Better be envied than pitied
2 Herodotus 3.52.4. Erasmus adds the detail 'where Periander says this to his son' in *1528*.
3 *Anthologia Palatina* 10.51, probably taken from the Aldine edition of the *Greek Anthology* (see *Adagia* IV v 57 n1, 181 below)
4 Pindar *Pythians* 1.85–6
5 Pindar *Nemeans* 8.21–2

incurs much envy. But the roars of a man who is weak and humble go unheard.'[6]

88 E nassa escam petere
To seek food from a fishtrap

Plautus, cited by Festus Pompeius, said, 'I'll never seek food from that trap,' using what is certainly a proverb.[1] Cicero too in *Letters to Atticus* in book fifteen, the final letter: 'I've decided to leave this trap, not that I may flee, but that I may have better hope of death.'[2] A *nassa* is a 'kind of container for fishing, from which a fish cannot escape once it has entered.'[3] Because of this the following are also proverbial: *in nassam incidere* 'to fall into a fishtrap' and *e nassa elapsus* 'having escaped from a fishtrap.'[4]

89 Nec mulieri nec gremio credendum
Trust neither a woman nor your lap

'One should trust neither a woman nor your lap.' Festus also points out that this proverb was in frequent use: 'The reason is that a woman has a wavering and fickle mind, and often what has been placed in the lap is forgotten and falls when one stands up.'[1] In the same way, things placed close to your breast drop to the ground if your garment falls loose. Accordingly, when promising to say nothing, Cicero says, 'It's in my bosom. I shall not be ungirt.'[2]

* * * * *

6 Pindar *Pythians* 11.29–30

88 Pindar by way of Pompeius Festus (see n1). Otto 1196. Added in *1515*
1 Plautus *Miles gloriosus* 581, cited by Pompeius Festus 168.23–4 Lindsay
2 Cicero *Ad Atticum* 15.20.2 (not the final letter in modern editions, however)
3 Pompeius Festus 168.23–4 Lindsay
4 This final sentence is Erasmus' own contribution, not derived from Pompeius Festus.

89 Pompeius Festus (see n1). Otto 1155. Added in *1515*. 'In the same way' to the end was added in *1533*.
1 Pompeius Festus 160.29–32 Lindsay
2 Cicero *Ad Quintum fratrem* 2.12(11).1

90 Una cum templis et aris
Along with temples and altars

In some passages in his 'Table-talk' Plutarch points out that it was the custom in antiquity to offer prayers to all the gods whenever a religious ceremony was being conducted for any one of them.[1] Clearly the purpose was to avoid a repetition of the tragedy of the Calydonian boar.[2] When they were invoking the gods, they would add these words as if they were an established part of the ritual: Ἅμα σὺν ναοῖς καὶ βωμοῖς 'Along with temples and altars.' He does not say explicitly that this is a proverb, but he appears to use it in such way that one can infer these words were customarily spoken in a proverbial way when people wanted to show that nothing at all had been overlooked. Even today common sayings are *una cum vestibus et calciamentis* 'with clothes and shoes,' and *demigrarunt una cum sarcinis et impedimentis* 'they left along with bag and baggage.'[3]

91 Mercurius supervenit
Mercury has now arrived

Ὁ Ἑρμῆς ἐπεισελήλυθεν, Mercury has now arrived. It was the custom to say these words whenever a silence fell over a large gathering. The meaning was that it was not proper to speak when Mercury was present since he was the inventor of speech. Even today it is thought ominous whenever a sudden silence occurs at a meeting or a party.[1] The adage is reported by Plutarch in his essay 'On Garrulity.'[2] Related to this is what is said elsewhere: 'The wolf in the story.'[3]

* * * * *

90 Plutarch (see n1). Added in *1515*
1 Plutarch *Moralia* 708c *Quaestiones convivales*
2 The Calydonian boar was sent by Artemis as a punishment because she was slighted by not being offered a sacrifice.
3 Suringar 240

91 Plutarch (see n2). Added in *1515*
1 Suringar 117
2 Plutarch *Moralia* 502F *De garrulitate*
3 *Adagia* III viii 56; IV v 50 (175 below)

92 Dulce pomum cum abest custos
Sweet is the apple that has no guard

Γλυκεῖ᾽ ὀπώρα φύλακος ἐκλελοιπότος,[1] Sweet is the apple when the guard is away. The verse is proverbial and one may use it to mean that impunity tempts the wicked to sin. The metaphor is taken from children and young persons who cannot restrain themselves from stealing apples if they are aware that the guard is absent. Plutarch uses it in his essay entitled 'On Love' against philosophers who employ the pretext of philosophy to satisfy their own desires:

> And so friendship and virtue are used as excuses. He is befouled with dust, he washes in cold water, he raises his eyebrows and says that he is a philosopher. In public he is sober because of the law, but then secretly at night 'Sweet is the apple when the guard is away.'[2]

It is to be found in the proverbs of the Hebrews: 'Stolen waters are sweeter.'[3] And Pindar in hymn six of the *Isthmians*: 'A most bitter end awaits what is sweet but dishonourable.'[4]

93 Sanior es pisce
You are as healthy as a fish

Undoubtedly Juvenal's words 'You are healthier than a fish' were used proverbially. For people, even today, commonly say, 'You are as healthy as

* * * * *

92 Plutarch (see n1). Also *Suda* Γ 311; Diogenianus 3.95. Tilley F 779 Stolen fruit is sweet; O 75 It is easy to rob an orchard when none keeps it. The adage first appeared in *1515*, the final two sentences being added in *1526*.
1 Listed as a fragment of tragedy by Nauck (*Adespota* 403) and of comedy by Kock (*Comica adespota* 1239). It is omitted however by PCG and *TrGF*.
2 Plutarch *Moralia* 752A *Amatorius*
3 Prov 9:17
4 Pindar *Isthmians* 7.47–8 (not ode 6)

93 Tilley F 301 As whole as a fish; T 536 As sound as a trout. The expression is not in Juvenal. Added in *1515*

a fish.'[1] This arose from the belief that fish did not experience sickness. And yet Aristotle in book eight of the *Nature of Animals* opposes this view and Pliny followed him in book nine.[2] For fisherman infer that fish can be sick because among plump and healthy fish they sometimes find some of the same species that are extremely thin, discoloured, and languid. And yet disease does not attack a whole species of fish, as frequently happens in the case of humans and all other animals, wild as well as tame ones.

94 E Creta raptus
Booty from Crete

Plutarch in his essay 'On the Education of Children': 'The sexual practices of the Thebans and the people of Elis should be shunned as should what is called Ἐκ Κρήτης ἁρπαγμος "Booty from Crete." Those of the Athenians and the Spartans should be imitated.'[1] It is clear that these words indicated secret love-making, because sometimes young girls were brought from there by traders.

95 Euparyphus ex comoedia
Like Euparyphus in comedy

In his 'Table-talk' Plutarch used what is clearly a proverbial expression: Ὥσπερ Εὐπάρυφος ἐκ κωμῳδίας 'Like Euparyphus from comedy.'[1] He is referring to a man wearing luxurious clothes and trailing behind him a huge crowd of slaves. For this is how braggart soldiers are depicted in comedies. Their distinguishing mark is a red cloak, as Donatus points out.[2] So Lucian

* * * * *

1 Suringar 200
2 Aristotle *Historia animalium* 8.19 (602b19) and Pliny *Naturalis historia* 9.156

94 Plutarch (see n1). Added in *1515*
1 Plutarch *Moralia* 11F *De liberis educandis*, but the correct reading in the Plutarch passage is ἐν Κρήτῃ 'in Crete,' not ἐκ Κρήτης 'from Crete.'

95 Plutarch (see n1). Added in *1515*. From 'By contrast, poor and low-born persons' to the end was added in *1533*.
1 Plutarch *Moralia* 615D *Quaestiones convivales*
2 Donatus on Terence *Eunuchus* 771

on a soldier: 'I mean that Euparyphus, that man in the cloak.'[3] Because of
this the Greeks call all rich men who are splendidly garbed εὐπάρυφοι, and
this on its own has something of the characteristics of a proverb. For a
paryphis is a kind of garment, mentioned by Julius Pollux in book seven.[4]
This had a red border on each side, because in Ionic Greek *paryphi* is the
word for red threads woven into a garment. He also tells us that εὐπάρυφος
is a word in New Comedy. By contrast, poor and low-born persons, not
distinguished by any elegant garb, are called *tunicati* 'tunicked.' Cornelius
Tacitus in his *Dialogue on the Orators*: 'As these pass by, very often the inexperienced throng and those tunicked people call them by name and point
to them.'[5] Similarly Horace: 'Selling cheap trash to the tunicked rabble.'[6]
For the *praetexta* was the distinguishing mark of nobles, while the toga was
that of citizens. Marcus Tullius in *Against Rullus*: 'Now what fear there was
of those tunicked men.'[7] Also in *For Marcus Caelius*: 'In times past we were
given a year to keep our arms restrained in our toga and to enjoy exercise
and sport on the Campus clad in tunics.'[8]

96 **Tranquillo quilibet gubernator est**
In a calm sea anyone can be a pilot

Seneca in a letter to Lucilius: 'A storm does not so much impede a pilot's
skill as reveal it. For, as they say, in a calm sea anyone can be a pilot.'[1] What
he is saying there is that misfortune and difficult circumstances, so far from
harming the wise man, allow his virtue, which lies hidden in prosperity and
peace, to reveal itself then especially. It is no great achievement to govern
a state when there is complete concord.

* * * * *

3 Lucian *Dialogi meretricum* 1.1
4 Pollux *Onomasticon* 7.46
5 Tacitus *Dialogus* 7.4
6 Horace *Epistles* 1.7.65
7 Cicero *De lege agraria* 2.34.94
8 Cicero *Pro M. Caelio* 5.11. The relevance of this quotation is doubtful. Cicero
   means that youths were given a year free of the demands that will be made on
   them later. See R.G. Austin ed *Cicero: Pro M. Caelio oratio* (Oxford 1964) ad loc.

96 Seneca (see n1). Otto 772. Tilley s 174 In a calm sea every man may be a pilot.
   Added in *1515*
1 Seneca *Letters* 85.34

97 Neque Lydorum carycas
Neither Lydian black-puddings

Μήτε Λυδῶν κάρυκας, μήτε μαστίγων ψόφους, Neither Lydian black-puddings nor the crack of whips. This will scan as a trochaic tetrameter catalectic if one adds the definite article (μήτε τῶν Λυδῶν) and if we read κάρυκκας, with a double kappa, as in Hesychius[1] and Athenaeus.[2] Hesychius tells us that καρύκκη is a mixture made from blood and different spices. Athenaeus adduces these verses: 'You are wont to mix together honey, flour, and eggs. / For all these are quite different from each other.'[3] Therefore καρυκκάζειν means 'to mix together different kinds of things,' and καρακκεύματα means 'foods with different spices' and καρυκκεία 'a rather exotic sauce.' He shows later, in book twelve, the ingredients of this kind of food and how it is made, saying that it was the invention of Candaulus, who thereby made a great name for himself.[4] Suidas gives the adage, but does not explain it.[5] One can guess that it was customarily said to indicate an average mode of living, one that was both removed from the greatest luxury and free of the worst misfortune. For we read that the Lydians had been extremely corrupted by luxury and pleasures,[6] so much so that they gave their name to ludii 'pantomime actors.'[7] It is certain too that barbarians, perhaps the Lydians but certainly the Etruscans, were accustomed to whip their slaves to the accompaniment of the flute, thus bringing together extreme tender-

* * * * *

97 *Suda* K 437. Also Zenobius (Aldus) column 114 (and Zenobius 5.3). This is virtually a doublet of *Adagia* II vi 97 Lydian black-puddings, but here the commentary is much expanded. Added in *1515*. The final sentence (except for 'if I am not mistaken,' which first appeared in *1526*) was added in *1517/18*, 'The adage will have more charm ... words and figures' in *1526*. There was further expansion in *1528*: 'This will scan ... great name for himself,' 'For we read ... extreme cruelty,' and 'or of those who spice up ... to create a hodge-podge.'

1 Hesychius K 915
2 Athenaeus 12.516C
3 Athenaeus 4.172B, citing Menander fragment 451.7–8 Körte-Thierfelder
4 Athenaeus 12.516D
5 *Suda* K 437
6 Athenaeus 12.515D–516C
7 This seems to come from Isidore 18.16.2, where, however, in modern editions it is said that *ludi* 'games' got their name from the Lydians.

ness and extreme cruelty.[8] The adage will have more charm if it is applied metaphorically to intellectual things, for example, to a speech that is neither completely crude in style nor too carefully polished. Accordingly the term καρακκεύειν 'to make a hodge-podge' can be said not only of those who use different spices with their food, but also of those who spice up their style of speaking with an excessive and meretricious adornment of words and figures, or of those who put together a sermon from contradictory elements that do not cohere well, the custom of certain show-offs. They expound upon the Scripture in a few words, they insert a problem from the Sorbonne, and stitch on something from imperial law, something from canon law, then from Aristotle, and from poets. As a colophon they add[9] an old wife's tale. This is truly καρακκεύειν 'to create a hodge-podge.' But we have mentioned this adage elsewhere, if I am not mistaken.[10]

98 Tamquam de narthecio
As if from the medicine box

Very like a proverb too is that phrase of Cicero in *Definitions of Good and Evil*, book two, *Tamquam de narthecio* 'As if from the medicine box,' meaning what is ready and at hand.[1] For by *narthecium* he means the box from which druggists take out their medicines. Cicero's words are these: 'Now let them take out those Epicurean treatments for pain, as if from the medicine box. If the pain is severe, it will be short, if long, it will be slight.'

99 Quod non opus est, asse carum est
What you do not need to have is dear at a penny

The pronouncements of Cato (oracles, one might say) seem to have become proverbial in antiquity, like those of Apollo: 'Know thyself,' and 'Nothing too much.'[1] From their number the one that Seneca reports in a letter to

* * * * *

8 Athenaeus 12.518B
9 Cf *Adagia* II iii 45 He added the colophon.
10 See *Adagia* II vi 97 Lydian black-puddings.

98 Cicero (see n1). Added in *1515*
1 Cicero *De finibus* 2.7.22

99 Cato the Elder by way of Seneca (see n2). Otto 175. Added in *1515*
1 *Adagia* I vi 95, I vi 96

Lucilius is extremely useful, 'What you do not need to have is dear at a penny.'[2] Cato means that a careful head of the house likes to sell, not to buy, and buys not what he wants, but what is necessary. 'For what you do not need to have,' he says, 'is dear at penny.' He terms as 'necessary' something that one cannot do without, for example, a plough to a ploughman, as 'wanted' something that may be useful if one has it but is such that one can do without it. Whatever you do not need to have is quite superfluous and useless. The adage can be adapted so as to have several meanings. If someone says that some skill can be learned with the minimum of effort – a skill, however, that will bring no profit, a possible response would be, 'What you do not need to have is dear at a penny.'

100 **Nunc tuum ferrum in igni est**
Now your iron is in the fire

It was said of someone who was already working on some enterprise that 'his iron was in the fire.' For iron is first softened by fire before it is worked upon. So Seneca in his humorous bagatelle *On the Death of the Emperor Claudius.*

> For since Hercules saw that his iron was in the fire, he ran now to this one, now to that, saying, 'Don't begrudge me this. It's my case that is at stake. If you want anything after this, I'll return the favour. One hand washes another.'[1]

The point of this is that Hercules too had been a mortal who became a god, something that Claudius was seeking. When Alexander the Great

* * * * *

2 Seneca *Letters* 94.27, citing a fragment of Cato the Elder: *Ad Marcum filium* fragment 10 Jordan (page 79)

100 Seneca (see n1). Otto 657. Tilley I 99 He has many irons in the fire. This adage was mentioned in *Adagia* II viii 83 It's alive, kindle the fire. Added in 1515. The final two sentences, which have no relevance to the proverb itself, were added in 1528.
1 Seneca *Ludus de morte Claudii* 9.6. The context is a debate among the gods to decide whether Claudius should become a god. The incident is referred to in *Adagia* I i 33 One hand rubs another, where Erasmus mentions that the form of the proverb given by Seneca here, 'One hand washes another,' is an alternative version.

was asked how he had taken possession of Greece, he replied, 'By never procrastinating.' This is cited by the scholiast on Homer at *Iliad*, book two.[2]

1 Ne bos quidem pereat
Not even an ox would be lost

In some earlier proverbs we have already shown the great value of having a good neighbour and the troublesomeness of having a bad one.[1] But it is profitable to stress again and again those features that make for a happy life so as to fix them more deeply in our minds. For having a good neighbour is important in almost all aspects of our life, not just when buying property or a farm. This is why Porcius Cato's view about having a good neighbour concerns not only farmers, but also each one of us.[2] Indeed, if anyone of advanced age reviews the whole course of his life, he will come to realize that most of his good fortune and bad has sprung from having good or bad neighbours. Columella quotes a verse of Hesiod as if it were proverbial: 'Not even an ox would be lost if you did not have a wicked neighbour.'[3] But the loss of an ox is slight when compared with those misfortunes that one suffers at the hands of unscrupulous associates, false friends, or disloyal wives and servants. Some have thought that Cato's view is to be rejected since the kind of neighbour we have is not in our control: 'Sometimes death or other circumstances bring us new neighbours.'[4] This is undeniable, but it

* * * * *

2 Scholiast on *Iliad* 2.435–6

1 Hesiod by way of Columella (see nn2–3). This adage first appeared in 1526, being placed here, appropriately for a proverb with an extensive commentary, at the beginning of a century. It thereby interrupted a sequence of adages that had been introduced in 1515. It replaced an adage ('Hail, dear light') that was dropped from the collection rather than being moved. The final paragraph was added in 1528.

1 *Adagia* I i 32 Something bad from a bad neighbour; I x 73 If you live next to a cripple, you will learn to limp; III v 6 Wish for something for the neighbour, but more for the pot

2 Erasmus reports Cato's view as given in Columella *Res rustica* 1.3.5. What follows (down to 'behave like one') is for the most part a free paraphrase of what is in Columella 1.3.1–5.

3 Hesiod *Works and Days* 348

4 An exact quotation from Columella at *Res rustica* 1.3.5

was wise advice of Cato's that a farmer should take care, as far as he could, to have a good neighbour, and not only a good neighbour, but also an obliging one. (For a man who is not obliging can still be good.) Two things in particular will help to achieve this, being very careful when buying land, and being accommodating and helpful to one's neighbour. For we often have a bad neighbour because we ourselves behave like one. As Columella so elegantly says:

> As a wise man bears with fortitude the misfortunes of chance, so a madman creates his own bad fortune. This happens to the man who acquires a good-for-nothing neighbour when he spends his money; and yet, if born from free parents, he may have heard even in earliest childhood, 'Not even an ox would be lost if you did not have a wicked neighbour.' This applies not only to an ox, but to all parts of our estate. Indeed many have chosen to give up their household gods and have fled from their homes because of their neighbours' wrongdoing – unless we think that whole nations abandoned their ancestral lands and made for distant regions for any reason other than that they could not tolerate wicked neighbours. I mean the Achaeans and the Iberians, the Albanians too, as well as the Sicilians, and, to touch on our own beginnings, the Pelasgians, the Aboriginals and the Arcadians. And, to speak not only of calamities that afflicted whole peoples, tradition has handed down the memory of individuals who were hateful neighbours both in the regions of Greece and here in Hesperia itself. Could anyone have tolerated living next to the infamous Autolycus? Did Cacus, who lived on the Aventine hill, bring any joy to his neighbours on the Palatine?[5] I prefer to mention persons of the past rather than those of the present so as not to name my own neighbour, who does not allow a tree of any great size on our land to stand, or any seedbed or any vine stake to remain undisturbed, or even our herds to graze without their being carefully watched. For what my opinion is worth, then, Marcus Porcius was right in thinking that such nuisances were to be avoided and especially in warning the farmer-to-be not to put himself into such a situation of his own accord.[6]

* * * * *

5 The two examples chosen by Columella are apposite. Autolycus was a mythological character renowned as a cattle thief, while Cacus was a monstrous giant who stole the cattle of Geryon from Heracles when he was at the future site of Rome.

6 Columella *Res rustica* 1.3.5–7

So much for Columella, who, with an eloquence that has something of the flavour of a declamation, has both supported Cato and informed us what a pest a bad neighbour is. And yet Cato has views not only on a neighbour's character but also on how well cared for is his property. 'Observe,' he says, 'how prosperous your neighbours look. In a fertile region they should be thriving.'[7] For sometimes healthy crops show that the land is good, but in soil that is not very fertile they reveal the industriousness of the farmer. Moreover, just as a hard-working man stimulates his neighbour's household with the desire to farm well, so neighbours who are lazy and extravagant corrupt it. Similarly, having an over-powerful neighbour weighs hard upon those of little means, while extremely poor neighbours are always paring your resources, either by begging or by stealing. With sour-tempered and dishonest neighbours there are incessant disputes: about boundaries, damages incurred, rainwater from the roof, rights of way, the view from the house, or the blocking of light. But if circumstances have given us such a neighbour and if we cannot move our residence, all that we can do is to change him from a bad neighbour into a good one by being very obliging ourselves and certainly to avoid making him more troublesome by provoking him. The most shameful thing will be to turn a helpful neighbour into a disagreeable one by our own behaviour. Clearly this is the point of Cato's advice, 'Be good to your neighbours.'[8] And in case you may think it sufficient if you yourself refrain from injuring your neighbour, he adds, 'Do not allow your household to err in this way.' Next he points out the advantages of having good neighbours. He says, 'If you are popular with your neighbours, it will be easier for you to sell your products, contract out jobs, hire workmen. If you are building, they will help you with labour, animals, materials. If, heaven forbid, the need ever arises, they will be glad to defend you.'

Now, at one time, those who put up their farm for sale would inform the auctioneer of the features that made the property attractive: healthy climate, convenient location, fertile soil, well-constructed buildings. But when Themistocles, a man of the keenest intellect, was selling his farm, he gave instructions that to attractive features such as these there should be added 'good neighbours.'[9] At first this action met with widespread laughter and

* * * * *

7 Cato *De agri cultura* 1.2
8 Cato *De agri cultura* 4.2, the source also of the following quotations
9 Plutarch *Themistocles* 18.8. The same incident is cited at *Adagia* I i 32 and I x 73 (see above n1).

mockery; later it was realized that to commend land in this way was of especial importance.

And so, to have an agreeable way of life in all its aspects the kind of neighbour each person chooses for himself is of the highest importance, as is also how he treats the neighbour that he happens to acquire. A prince who seeks new territory that he cannot protect without great difficulty and without spending all the resources of his ancestral realm creates bad neighbours for himself. On the contrary, a prince who appoints to his service loyal, intelligent counsellors and magistrates of irreproachable character who are devoted to their country creates good neighbours for himself. It is also of the greatest importance which nations he unites through marriage. If consideration of dowry or rank prompts him to take a wife with a disagreeable character and insolent relatives, he is creating bad neighbours for himself. The prince who makes a treaty of friendship with those who are unscrupulous is actually seeking out bad neighbours. The man whose desire for prestige makes him rush to join a college or a monastery whose members are irreligious or even superstitious is acquiring bad neighbours. The first precaution, then, should be in choosing one's associates, the next in correcting them, the final one in fleeing from those who are incorrigible. But even when one flees there is need of caution. Otherwise, 'if it is not done properly, fleeing from one fault can lead to another vice.'[10] And it often happens that in our loathing for one evil we rush headlong into a different, more serious one. Those who have chosen a friend judiciously rarely have regrets about the friendship. And it is often our fault that a friendship breaks up, because we do not treat our good friends well and also because we do not know how to put up with or correct friends who are unhelpful. No less in the wrong are those who do not know how to extract themselves from harmful friends whom they have encountered, but either cling to those whom they secretly detest or break off the friendship suddenly instead of allowing it to dissolve gradually.

The same thing happens to people in my situation in choosing and keeping patrons and supporters of our studies. We pass over those who offer themselves to us voluntarily, or we embrace those that do not suit us, or, if we have someone suitable, we do not exert ourselves to foster his good will towards us by performing services in return. I made most grievous errors of the first kind when I was young. Indeed if I had responded to the favours of the important men who had begun to embrace me I would

* * * * *

10 Horace *Ars poetica* 31

have made something of myself in literature. But because of an excessive love of independence I wrestled for a long time with treacherous friends and persistent poverty. And this would not have come to an end had it not been for the great William Warham, Archbishop of Canterbury,[11] a man to be revered more for his outstanding virtues, worthy of the highest prelate, than for the dignity of his title and office. I was like a fugitive that he snared and enticed into his friendship. After only a brief taste of his kindness I went off to Italy. When I was lingering there with no thought at all of going back to Britain, of his own accord he invited me back with the offer of a benefice. This too was treated with disdain. But when another wind returned me to England, he put me under such obligation to him that I surrendered to him, unwilling though I was. He achieved this, not so much by his kindness, which was, and still is, unequalled, as by an amiable and pleasant disposition and a wonderful constancy of affection – extremely rare in men of the highest rank. These qualities were the bait with which he enticed me into his service. In this way I was captured, much to my advantage, fortunate simply in his being my Maecenas, but I would have been by far the most fortunate of men if it had happened sooner.[12] I do not know whether he has regrets about me as his protégé, but I have certainly not repaid to my own satisfaction his kindnesses with my services to him, and I do not think that I will ever be able to do so. Accordingly, I must ask all who are devoted to good letters and to religion and who have derived from my works anything that pleased them to give thanks to this most holy prelate instead of to me, and indeed repay him if they can. They will repay him if they will not allow his memory to fade away among the generations to come. It is to his generosity they owe whatever they have drawn from my books – if they have actually drawn anything of value from them.

* * * * *

11 William Warham (1450–1532), who became Archbishop of Canterbury in 1503 and was Lord Chancellor of England from 1504 to 1515, was a generous bene- factor of Erasmus. Erasmus was in England from 1505 to June 1506 and ded- icated his Latin translations of two plays of Euripides, published in 1506, to him. After Erasmus returned from Italy to England in 1509 Warham gave him the living of Aldington (in 1512), later commuted to a pension. On Erasmus' reaction to Warham's death see the letter of dedication below (318 nn4, 6, 7). See CEBR 3:427–31.

12 Maecenas, the close advisor of the emperor Augustus, was a patron of the arts. The poets Virgil and Horace were the most famous of those he supported.

On all sides there is the clamour of complaints from those bewailing that they do not have a Maecenas to foster their studies. And yet Maecenas did not immediately embrace Virgil or Horace, and neither Maevius nor Bavius had a Maecenas.[13] The first thing a young man should do is to provide an outstanding specimen of his work as a pledge that what is given him will not be wasted. Let him not think it sufficient to carry off gifts (or, more accurately, plunder them) by any means at all. Generosity is not to be sought by shameless begging, but by continuously improving one's writings and character. Land that never fails to repay with considerable interest whatever a farmer entrusts to it invites him to sow seed more copiously.[14]

Nor should one continually change patrons, abandoning one whom you have worn out and then seeking another who is fresh and undepleted. Do not shake one oak clean and then gather acorns under another.[15] You should serve only one or two, and do so as if you are always going to rely on them. How many do we see at present who by their behaviour bring odium to literary studies and shame and unpopularity to their patrons! One way to show gratitude is to celebrate a patron's name in what you write and say, but how you praise someone is of great importance. Hollow-sounding praise prompts disbelief even if what is said is true. The result is that instead of thinking more highly of the person praised a reader thinks worse of the person doing the praising. Extravagant praise brings ill-will rather than glory. Those who extol those characteristics that are condemned by good and wise men are actually censuring those whom they are praising.

First of all, the content of your encomium should be true; this should then be handled so as also to seem believable. Away with the hyperbole of certain poets by which they transform at will a mortal into a god! Depict in particular those virtues that win favour and goodwill, such as piety, honesty, purity in thought and deed, humility, generosity, openness and affability. Nothing is more prone to envy than human nature, or more captious in judging others. If, therefore, you have to touch on any of these qualities that the general public admires so much that it envies those who possess them, you must handle this skilfully, so that he who is praised will not have to fear the evil eye of envy. No one envies the rich man who acts not as the owner, but only as the steward of possessions that he has received

* * * * *

13 Virgil refers disparagingly to the poets Maevius and Bavius at *Eclogues* 3.90.
14 This sentence is based on Pliny *Naturalis historia* 2.155.
15 Cf *Adagia* I v 34 Go and shake another oak-tree.

by the kindness of fortune or has acquired honestly. And no one envies a powerful man who uses his power for the good of his country, and who is as self-effacing in humility as he is exalted in rank, winning over even the low-born by his affability. No one envies a handsome man when in addition to his physical appearance he has also propriety and good morals. No one envies those who are healthy or have lived long lives if they use their health or years to benefit many others.

Whoever lacks the talent or skill for treating these things in the appropriate way should abstain from encomia rather than be like a bad painter who turns a beautiful form into an inferior one through his clumsiness. Perhaps Alexander the Great was too fastidious when he would not allow himself to be painted by anyone but Apelles.[16] Yet no handsome person would wish to be painted by a Fulvius or a Rutuba.[17] Let what you bring into public view be such that it promises to be remembered by posterity. Finally, praise must be so tempered that the duty you are performing may not appear to have been prompted by the person you are praising (for no one seeks or even tolerates praise less than those who especially deserve it), but rather by virtue itself, which even against its will has glory in its train,[18] and by the desire to inspire others to similar achievements. In this way not only will it be profitable to praise a man who has deserved it, but the risk of envy and the suspicion of flattery will also be avoided. When praising the dead, however, one should be much less inhibited in unleashing the power of which eloquence is capable, since in these circumstances envy is felt much less keenly and the suspicion of flattery is diminished.

So far I have shown how scholars can commend themselves to their patrons. Now I shall touch briefly on the ways in which they have the power to win universal support for their scholarly activities as well. For in many places the study of languages and of what is called 'good letters' meets burning hostility. This is partly the fault of the older generation,

* * * * *

16 Apelles of Ephesus was a renowned painter of the fourth century BC. Horace refers to an edict of Alexander forbidding anyone other than Apelles to paint him (*Epistles* 2.1.239-40); cf also Pliny *Naturalis historia* 7.125.

17 Fulvius and Rutuba were gladiators, not painters. They are referred to by Horace at *Satires* 2.7.96. Erasmus makes the same mistake at *Adagia* IV iv 41 Couches of Soterichus (89 above).

18 See Otto 764. Cf Seneca *Letters* 79.13 'Glory is virtue's shadow and will accompany it even against its will'; Cicero *Tusculan Disputations* 1.45.109; *Adagia* IV viii 71 Virtue begets glory (401 below).

who think that the acquisition of any of the new learning by the young
detracts from their authority. Content with what they learned as children,
they do not allow anything different to be taught, nor do they bear to learn it
themselves, either because the thought of doing so annoys them or because
they are ashamed of their ignorance. In part too this is the fault of those who
take up[19] these ancient 'new' disciplines. For in this group there are some
who are intolerably arrogant; as soon as they have learned twelve words of
Latin and five of Greek they think that they are a Demosthenes or a Cicero;
they babble on in their writings, which are quite silly and sometimes even
venomous; with incredible contempt they spurn all liberal studies, and rant
and rave in a scurrilous fashion at those who study them as a profession.
And there are also some who use good letters for the worst of ends –
for factious slander and to disturb, damage and destroy the harmony and
tranquillity of Christendom. But in the past those who were learned in such
studies would settle strife among princes with their eloquence, wage war
with the leaders of heretical sects, celebrate the memory of the saints, sing
the praises of Christ in verse and prose, and urge men to despise this earthly
world and to love heavenly things. Such were Basil, Nazianzenus, Ambrose,
Prudentius, and Lactantius, but they are not objects of hostile criticism since
they used their knowledge of languages and classical literature in the service
of their pious works.

Fields of study, however, are customarily judged by the character of
those engaged in them. For example, nowadays, many loathe the Gospel because of the immorality of some who use it for self-promotion. By guarding 'against every appearance of evil,'[20] Paul glorifies his Gospel, 'having
become all things to all men'[21] so as to win all. If those who profess letters were like him and commended their profession by living pure lives
and by using courteous and temperate language, they would reap a much
richer harvest and incur much less hostility. On the opposite side, if the
older generation accepted, with civility and calmness, such studies as old
friends being repatriated instead of as new immigrants, they would realize that their addition brings them considerable enlightenment and profit.
As it is, they are waging a never-ending war with old friends as if they are
fighting with enemies. Those things that are very ancient they call 'new,'
and they term as 'ancient' what is new. The early doctors of the Church had

* * * * *

19 Reading *ineunt* for *invehunt* in the printed editions
20 1 Thess 5:22; for the next phrase, 'Paul glorifies his Gospel,' cf 2 Thess 3:1.
21 1 Cor 9:22

a knowledge of Scripture that was combined with mastery of languages and of secular literature. We see the same thing in ancient philosophy, medicine and law. Where do Aristotle and Hippocrates utter solecisms? Are not Plato and Galen eloquent? How skilled in both languages were the ancient jurists! The purity and majesty of the Latin language is revealed by the very fragments that the boastful Justinian thrust upon us instead of complete works, though even they are full of the most unbelievable textual errors.[22]

What *is* new is cramming children's heads with 'the modes of signification' to teach them grammar, and reading out lists of senseless words that teach them nothing but how to speak improperly.[23] What *is* new is accepting young men into the study of philosophy, law, medicine and theology when they understand nothing in the ancient authors because of their ignorance of the language. What *is* new is to be excluded from the holy shrine of theology unless you have sweated long over Averroes and Aristotle.[24] What *is* new is stuffing young candidates for a degree in philosophy full of sophistic rubbish and imaginary problems. All these do is torture the brain! What *is* new is that in our schools different answers are given according to whether one follows the path of the Thomists or Scotists, Nominalists or Realists.[25] What *is* new is the exclusion there of arguments taken from the founts of divine Scripture, and the acceptance only of those that

* * * * *

22 Justinian, the eastern Roman emperor AD 527–65, organized the consolidation of earlier Roman law into three volumes, the *Codex Justinianus*, the *Institutiones*, and the *Digesta* or *Pandectae*; see *Adagia* IV ix 1n (419 below). Justinian, described as *gloriosus* here, took great pride in his consolidation (see the prefaces to the *Institutiones* and *Digesta*). At *Adagia* I ii 1 Exchange between Diomede and Glaucus, Erasmus describes Justinian as 'too full of self-love and unjustifiably conceited' (CWE 31 146).

23 Like other humanists, Erasmus is here critical of the abstruse philosophical reflections on linguistic terminology of the Modists that were often part of language instruction at the time. For a disparaging remark on Michael Modista in the *Antibarbarus* see CWE 23 34.

24 Averroes was an Islamic philosopher of the twelfth century who wrote commentaries on most of Aristotle's works. These were incorporated into the Latin commentaries on the Aristotelian corpus.

25 Two pairings of opposing philosophical groups. One of the points at issue was the existence of and the nature of universals.

are drawn from Aristotle, papal decretals, schoolmen's tenets, definitions of professors of canon law, and precedents from Roman law, which are usually pointless and distorted. If new things offend us, these are the things that are really new. If we approve of what is old, it is the oldest disciplines that are now being sacrificed – unless perhaps what goes back to the time of Origen is new, and what came into being three hundred years ago and has continuously deteriorated since then is old.

But some persons who are even more hostile to such studies do not shrink from babbling, both privately and publicly, and even while preaching, about how these are the source of all heresies, not noticing that this slander applies to Jerome, Ambrose and Augustine, and many others – the doctors in whom the church takes such pride. When hearing confession they din the ears of young men with such stupid nonsense as 'Beware of the Greeks, lest you become a heretic; avoid Hebraic literature lest you become like the Jews; throw away Cicero lest you be damned along with him.' What grave admonitions! They do not realize that boys will spout such words to all and sundry, for all sensible people to laugh at. They drop similar words into the ears of parents, their aim being to have the children's education entrusted to them. Women and simple ordinary folk are easily taken in by sanctimonious deceit. But you might just as well entrust a sheep to a wolf as entrust children to such *ventres* 'maws'![26] What do I hear? 'Were the Waldensians (the Poor of Lyon) or Wycliff versed in languages and good letters?'[27] Surely it does not follow that Jerome was a heretic because he was pre-eminent in his knowledge of languages and all kinds of literature. If anyone who knew only French wrote heretical views in his own language, would we immediately issue a general admonition that no one should learn French? Recently they have even persuaded the courts of

* * * * *

26 Cf *Adagia* II viii 78 Idle bellies (*Ventres*), applied, according to Erasmus, to 'gross eaters, slaves of their stomachs and digestions.'

27 The Waldensians were an evangelical group, also called 'the Poor of Lyon.' It was started by a rich merchant of that city, named Valdes, who renounced his possessions to live in poverty; see NCE 14:770–1. John Wycliff, circa 1330–84, is associated with the first complete English translation of the Vulgate, and wrote voluminously in Latin. It is doubtful whether he knew Greek. Erasmus seems to be adducing them as examples of pious but simple people in order to make a facetious contrast with the learned St Jerome. Both the Waldensians and Wycliff, however, incurred charges of heresy.

princes that all this turmoil, of Lutheranism and the peasants' revolt, had its source in the study of languages and classical literature.[28] Courts have their Midases and Thrasos, and the more naive the highest princes are and the more they indulge their inclinations the more exposed they are to the tricks of such men.[29] If a person who knows Greek and Hebrew runs the risk of heresy because Luther is not unskilled in these languages, why is such a person not said to be safe because of John, Bishop of Rochester, and Girolamo Aleandro, Archbishop of Brindisi, who are stout defenders of the tottering church?[30] The latter excels in all languages, the former is embracing the study of three languages with extraordinary zeal even though he is in his declining years.

They add another slander as well. When a young man admits his sins in confession, they hear of some licentious behaviour, a defect that belongs particularly to those of such an age. They ask what authors he is reading. When they hear that it is Virgil or Lucian, they blame his studies for what is a vice of their time of life (or of general human weakness), immediately making literature the cause instead of youthfulness, as if they do not hear much worse things from those who have never read even a word of literature. To be sure, while the study of literature does not free us from all vices, it is undeniable that it protects those at a dangerous age from many of them. Yet nothing is so sacred that it cannot be used as a pretext for wrongdoing by someone who is naturally prone to wicked be-

* * * * *

28 The peasants' revolt of 1524–5, which occurred throughout much of what Erasmus describes as Germany, was a protest against serfdom and other constraints. Its outbreak at this time was not unconnected with the aims of the Protestant reformers and, at least initially, Luther was sympathetic to it.

29 King Midas was given ass's ears by Apollo; see *Adagia* I iii 67 Midas has ass's ears, '... properly applied to stupid people' (CWE 31 291). Thraso is the name of a braggart soldier in Terence's *Eunuchus* who is stupid as well as vain.

30 John Fisher (1469–1535), a friend and correspondent of Erasmus, was appointed Bishop of Rochester in 1504. He did not undertake serious study of Greek and Hebrew until his mid- to late-forties. He wrote against Luther and other reformers. See CEBR 2:36–9. Girolamo Aleandro (1480–1542) was renowned for his learning and intellectual powers during his lifetime. He met Erasmus in Venice in 1508 when the latter was preparing the first greatly expanded version of the *Collectanea*, and lent him a manuscript of Apostolius' collection of proverbs. He played an active role in opposing and condemning Luther, and this led to a strained relationship with Erasmus. See CEBR 1:28–32.

haviour. But if we should remove whatever provides the slightest opportunity for immorality, why does the requirement of celibacy receive such
praise?[31] Do they think no one knows what 'A Lerna of troubles' springs
from that?[32]

But, I ask you, what profit will there be if all honourable disciplines
collapse in ruin because those who devote themselves to learning are tear-
ing each other to pieces? We see that this has already happened to a great
extent in some places. Without such disciplines, however, humans no longer
live like humans but like beasts. The only course left for us, then, is that
the study of languages and the study of good letters should return from
exile and, like plants springing up again from the roots, make their way,
with courtesy and civility, into the society of those disciplines that have
ruled now for many centuries in the universities, without attacking anyone's particular subject of study but rather helping all disciplines. Let them
make some concession to a profession's prestige, to long-established practices that have become second-nature, and to the advanced age of many
practitioners, not readily adaptable to change. Let them leave those who
are incurable to follow their own inclination so as not to stir up greater
catastrophes. Let them win over those who are more treatable with timely
and flattering advice. Let them advise, help and correct, as a conscientious
attendant advises, helps, and corrects her mistress. Theology is by rights
the queen of all disciplines, but she will be more distinguished and more
enlightened if she receives into her service such useful attendants with
the appropriate friendliness. Philosophy is a very splendid subject, but it
would win much more esteem by acknowledging old friends. Jurisprudence is a noble mistress, but such elegant servants will bring no little
adornment to her. Medicine is a pre-eminent discipline, but is almost blind
without knowledge of the ancient languages and literature. If the disciplines
share with each other what each possesses, all will become richer and more
splendid.

I would like to advise monarchs not to listen to the kinds of whispering
that I have been talking about. Rather, let them think how much profit and
prestige will accrue to their lands from such disciplines, as it did in the
past. Finally, all will be more prosperous, both publicly and privately, if
each is a good neighbour to his neighbour.

* * * * *

31 For Erasmus' views on celibacy of the priesthood see L-E. Halkin *Erasmus. A
   Critical Biography* (Oxford 1993) 167–8, 179–81.
32 *Adagia* I iii 27

To return to the proverb, it agrees with what has been mentioned elsewhere, 'Something bad from a bad neighbour,'[33] used by Demosthenes in his speech against Callicles: 'Nothing is more harmful, men of Athens, than to acquire a neighbour who is wicked and not content with what he has.'[34]

2 Caput artis decere quod facias
The secret of artistic success is doing what suits you

Quintilian in book eleven of his *Principles of Oratory* seems to adduce a well-known common expression: 'The prime means of attaining artistic success is to do what suits you well.' I shall add his actual words.

> One further point must be made. While what is seemly is the main consideration in delivering a speech, different things often suit different people. For there is some hidden and inexplicable principle underlying this, and while it is a true saying that the prime means of attaining artistic success is to do what suits you, this cannot be achieved without art nor can it be taught in its entirety by art.[1]

So Fabius. We can use this not only of some unseemly action (for example, of an old man singing or playing games, or of a young man walking ahead of or castigating older men), but also to deny that there is anything that suits all persons. We often see that something said or done by one individual happens to please everyone, while no one would tolerate it if someone else tried the same thing, even if he were more learned and more experienced. Although we see this happening every day, it is impossible to explain it.

* * * * *

33 *Adagia* i i 32
34 Demosthenes 55.1. The printed editions of the *Adagia* offer 'Callictes' instead of 'Callicles,' although the correct form is noted in the 1526 edition of the *Adagia* that is now in the Vatican Library (codex Chigianus R.VIII.62) and contains Erasmus' own corrections and annotations. Obviously the correction was overlooked and not implemented in later editions.

2 Quintilian (see n1). Added in *1515*
1 Quintilian 11.3.177

3 Domus recta
A good home

Annaeus Seneca in book sixteen of his *Letters*: 'We shall see what is roughly hewn, poorly constructed, and has nothing of the polish that is now fashionable. When you consider everything as a whole, you will see no useless nooks. Granted there are no different kinds of marble, no complex network of water channels, no 'pauper's room' or anything else that luxury adds when it is not content with simple charm; all the same, in the common phrase, it is a good house.'[1]

So Seneca. If the passage is not free of error, it means that what is commonly called 'a good house' refers to one that does not lack the proper furnishings, not to one that has expensive and ostentatious fittings. In the same way Marcus Tullius compares the Greek language to a pretentious harlot living in a surfeit of luxury, the Latin language to a modest and upright wife who has all that is needed for simple elegance.[2]

4 Non est beatus esse qui se nesciat
He is not happy who does not know it

The same author in the same work adduces this verse from some comic poet, 'He is not happy who does not know it.'[1] It must have been a common expression of everyday speech since he has not given the author's name. The sense is that it is not enough to enjoy good fortune unless you realize you have it. Virgil, alluding to this: 'How blessed are farmers if they

* * * * *

3 Seneca (see n1). Otto 576. Otto says, rightly, that the expression is hardly proverbial. Added in *1515*

1 Seneca *Letters* 100.5–6. Seneca is actually talking metaphorically about literary style.

2 Erasmus appears to be writing from memory. No such comparison has been found in Cicero. But cf *Orator* 23.78–9 and Tacitus *Dialogus* 26.1.

4 Seneca (see n1). Tilley κ 182 He is not happy that knows not himself happy. Added in *1515*

1 Seneca *Letters* 9.21. The author of the verse is not known. Erasmus' quotation is inaccurate since the standard version of the line, going back to the *editio princeps*, is *non est beatus esse se qui non putat.*

know their blessings.'² What Martial mentions as one of the principles of happiness, 'Wish to be what you are,' is similar in nature.³ For what is happier than freedom? And yet we can see many persons bewailing their lot because they find no place in the courts of princes. They think themselves miserable because they cannot be slaves. But just as those who do not think themselves happy are not happy, so twice miserable are those who think themselves fortunate, even though they are unfortunate in respect to their moral weaknesses. To be sure, the man who is healthy but thinks himself sick does not enjoy his good fortune. Similarly, the man who is gripped by disease but does not realize his misfortune is very far removed from good health; so far from being healthy, he is even incurable.

5 Amicus certus in re incerta cernitur
Uncertainty sees a certain friend

Marcus Tullius in his *Laelius* cites this senarius from Ennius as a proverb, 'Uncertainty shows a sure friend.'¹ This means that a friend's loyalty is tested in adversity. For what is linked to danger is termed *dubius* 'doubtful,' for which Ennius wrote *incertus* 'uncertain,' aiming for ἐναντίωσις 'the conjunction of opposites' and προσονομασία 'assonance,' figures that he took particular delight in.² And he was not alone in this; that whole period up to the time of Marcus Tullius did so too. Plautus also asserts that a friend is 'he who helps in times of doubt.'³ The same sentiment is found in the proverbs

* * * * *

2 Virgil *Georgics* 2.458–9
3 Martial 10.47.12

5 Ennius by way of Cicero (see n1). Otto 92. Tilley F 694 A friend is never known till a man have need. Added in *1515*. From 'Plautus also asserts' to the end was added in *1533*.
1 Cicero *De amicitia* 17.64, citing Ennius *Scaenica* 210 Vahlen. Vahlen, following Hartung, assigned it to Ennius' *Hecuba*, as a translation of Euripides *Hecuba* 1226–7. See, however, H.D. Jocelyn *The Tragedies of Ennius* (Cambridge 1969) 306.
2 The first of these Greek terms does not appear to be used in a rhetorical sense, while the second (*prosonomasia*) is probably a mistake for παρονομασία (*paronomasia*). The conjunction of opposites is seen by Erasmus as a stylistic feature of proverbs; see CWE 31 22 *Introduction* xiii.
3 Plautus *Epidicus* 113

of the Hebrews: 'A friend loves at all times and is proved a brother in adversity.'[4]

6 Avarus nisi cum moritur nil recte facit
A miser does nothing right except when he dies

I am aware that almost all the aphorisms of Publius were celebrated as proverbs, and quite rightly too.[1] For nothing wittier or more pleasing can be imagined. We ourselves recently published an emended version of his 'mimes' and were happy to explain them in brief notes. It is not my intention, therefore, to take all of them over into this collection, except for one or two that appeal to me more than others. One of these is 'A miser does nothing right except when he dies.' Certainly the man who has bound himself over to the pursuit of money does no one a good turn while he lives. Death alone brings pleasure and profit to his heir.

7 Bona nemini hora est
Time is good for no one

This one too appealed to me: *Bona nemini hora est quin alicui sit mala* 'Time is good for no one without being bad for someone else.'[1]

Fortune has so tempered human affairs that what brings joy to one produces pain for another, what profits one person brings loss to another. No one becomes rich except at the expense of someone else. No one conquers

* * * * *

4 Prov 17:17

6 Publilius Syrus (see n1). Otto 230. Tilley M 85 A covetous man does nothing good until he dies. Added in *1515*

1 In Erasmus' time Publius was thought to be the first name of Publilius Syrus, who lived in the first century BC, at the end of the Roman republic. He was a writer of theatrical productions called mimes, though in fact the actors spoke in these. Later a large number of aphorisms were drawn from his work. These were edited by Erasmus in 1514 with other items in his *Opuscula aliquot*. The adage given here is line 23 in the Loeb edition (*Minor Latin Poets*).

7 Publilius Syrus (see n1). Tilley M 337 No man loses (wins) but another wins (loses). Added in *1515*

1 A senarius of Publilius Syrus (no 62 in the Loeb edition of *Minor Latin Poets*)

in war without another's death. Unless you prefer to read *alicubi* 'somewhere' instead of *alicui* 'someone.'[2]

8 Spontanea molestia
Trouble of one's own making

An especially fine and elegant trimeter is well known among the Greeks: Αὐθαίρετος λύπη 'στὶν ἡ τέκνων σπορά 'Having children is self-inflicted pain.'[1]
    It is impossible to say what a great and troublesome task it is to bring up children, especially when there are so few who are capable of fulfilling the duties of a parent. But there is no one else parents can blame for this trouble since one can choose to be a bachelor. It can be applied less literally to those who seek out danger and trouble for themselves of their own accord. Having children and writing books are very similar activities. We must protect and correct what we have written, but there is no one to complain to, since we are free to sleep instead of writing.

9 Sapiens sua bona secum fert
The wise man carries his resources with him

Ὁ σοφὸς ἐν αὐτῷ περιφέρει τὴν οὐσίαν, The wise man always has his resources with him.[1] In origin this is an apophthegm of Bias, if I am not mistaken. When he was asked why he was not removing any of his possessions when his native city was ablaze, he said, 'I carry all my goods with me.'[2] He

* * * * *

2 The sense would then be 'Time is good for no one without its being bad on some other occasion.'

8 Menander (see n1). Added in *1515*
1 Menander *Sententiae* 70 Jaekel. This is to be found in the 1495 Aldine edition of Theocritus (see *Adagia* IV iv 63 n4, 104 above).

9 Menander (see n1). Otto 1293. Tilley M 207 A learned man carries his treasures with him. This was the penultimate adage in *1515*, which ended with 'A Dutch ear' (later *Adagia* IV vi 35, 235 below).
1 Menander *Sententiae* 569 Jaekel. Also in the 1495 Aldine edition of Theocritus; see note to the preceding adage. Erasmus' Latin translation is somewhat expanded to accommodate the metre in which it is given.
2 Bias lived in Priene in the sixth century and was respected for his eloquence and legal knowledge. The story is recounted in Cicero *Paradoxa Stoicorum* 1.8. Erasmus also refers to Bias' sayings at *Adagia* III iv 62 He is wearing all his wealth.

meant that those things that are truly ours, such as learning and virtue, lie within us. Similarly, one cannot escape those things of ours that are really bad, no matter how often you change your abode.

10 Citius Telegorae donarim
I would sooner give it to Telegoras

Telegoras was an extremely rich and powerful man in Naxos. Because he received many gifts every day it became the custom in everyday speech for traders to say to those who offered too little for their wares, Μᾶλλον προέλοιμι τῷ Τελεγόρᾳ δοῦναι 'I would rather give it to Telegoras.' It is cited from Aristotle in Athenaeus, in book eight of his *Doctors at Dinner*.[1] We have pursued the topic at greater length in the proverb 'No bad big fish.'[2] I do not see how we may use the proverb except to point out that it is better to perform a service for upright and important persons at no charge than one for worthless scoundrels at a price.

11 Hecatae cena
A Hecate dinner

The ancients called a very frugal and cheap meal 'A Hecate dinner,' because according to the religious views expressed in the poets those in the underworld have a very tenuous existence and live on a very small amount of food (and the cheapest at that). The ordinary shades live on mallow and leek, while sprats and *triglides* 'tiny red mullet,' fish that we think little of, are Hecate's favourites since they are sacred to her. Because of this there was a place in Athens called Trigla, where there was a statue of Hecate Triglantina. Others think that Trigla was sacred to her since its name was

* * * * *

10 Aristotle by way of Athenaeus (see n1). This adage marks the beginning of the modest expansion in *1517/18* (only nine new adages, most of which were drawn from Athenaeus, an Aldine edition of which appeared in 1514).
1 Athenaeus 8.348B, citing Aristotle fragment 558 Rose. Erasmus follows the text of the 1514 Aldine edition of Athenaeus in giving the name as Telegoras. Modern editions have Telestagoras. In the *Adagia*-text the particle ἄν, which should stand before προέλοιμι is omitted.
2 *Adagia* II iii 92, where it is suggested that 'I would sooner give it to Telegoras' may be proverbial

11 Athenaeus (see n1). Added in *1517/18*. 'But a learned reader' to the end was added in *1526*.

explained as deriving from the number three and Hecate too is of triple
form. This is found in book seven of Athenaeus.[1] He also mentions it in
book eight. So also does Lucian somewhere.[2] But a learned reader should
consider whether the proverb can be taken to refer to the dinner placed by
the rich each month at the crossroads, which were sacred to Hecate, and
plundered by the poor. Aristophanes also mentions this in the *Plutus*:

> This you can learn from Hecate, if you wish,
> Whether 'tis better to be rich or poor,
> Since she says that those with wealth
> Offer a generous dinner a month,
> But the poor steal it almost before they serve it up.[3]

At this point the commentator[4] says of these words: 'Formerly Hecate
was worshipped where three roads met because she is called by three
names: Moon, Artemis, and Hecate. At the new moon the rich used to
send a meal in the evening as an offering for Hecate at such crossroads. In
their hunger, however, the poor snatched up what had been set down and
ate it, saying that Hecate had eaten it.' And so the proverb will be appropriate when something is seized violently.

12 Mens videt, mens audit
The mind sees, the mind hears

Νοῦς ὁρᾳ καὶ νοῦς ἀκούει, The mind sees, the mind hears. It seems to be the
first half of a trochaic verse, a tetrameter catalectic. It is cited by Aristotle

* * * * *

1 Athenaeus 7.325A–D and 8.358F. 'He also mentions it in book eight' was added
  in *1528*. See also on *Adagia* II ix 39 The triplets that exist among the dead.
2 Lucian *Dialogus mortuorum* 1
3 Aristophanes *Plutus* 594–7
4 An Aldine edition of Aristophanes and the accompanying Greek scholia appeared in 1498, edited by Marcus Musurus. He is named in *Adagia* II i 1
  ('Make haste slowly') as one of those who helped Erasmus to prepare the 1508
  edition of the *Adages* in Venice. See CEBR 2:472–3. There is no need to think
  that Erasmus is not referring to the author of the ancient scholia (ASD II-7
  249:382n suggests he is thinking of Musurus himself). Erasmus gives only a
  Latin version of the original Greek.

12 This adage first appeared in *1528*, disrupting the series of new ones that

as a common saying in problem 33 of section 11, where the question under
discussion is 'Why do we hear more keenly at night than during the day?'[1]
Among other reasons, he gives this one too, that during the day the mind has
to focus on different tasks. For if the mind were not so focused, the bodily
senses would not perform their functions. Indeed, if the mind is distracted
we sometimes do not feel any physical pain. (I myself have experienced
this when suffering the excruciating pain of toothache or of the stone, that
one is much less aware of the pain if one can direct the mind into thinking
of something quite different.) 'As the saying goes,' Aristotle says, 'the mind
sees and the mind hears.' At night, however, our eyes are resting and our
minds are more tranquil, but access to our ears is as unimpeded as during
the day, and they are no less receptive of sounds. The ears can communicate
these sounds to the mind more easily, since the mind is at rest and is not
distracted by sight sensations, as happens in the day. The result is that our
hearing is more acute. The adage can be used when we tell someone to
be attentive, just as we say, 'Are you with me?' or 'I am with you.' I have
spoken elsewhere about a wandering mind.[2]

13 Thymbra victitans
Living on savory

Θυμβροφάγοι, Those who live on savory. Said of those who lived their lives
in safety and freedom, or of those who had an unpleasant disposition, or of
those who lived happy lives free of worries since they were content with
a little. Savory, also called *cunila*, is a kind of plant that Pliny does not

* * * * *

was first introduced in *1517/18*. It replaced an adage that was dropped
completely and not simply moved (see ASD II-7 249 critical apparatus on
line 387). Erasmus' source here was probably Aristotle, but the proverb
appears in CPG (Apostolius 12.13). It is attributed to Epicharmus (fragment 249 Kaibel) by Plutarch *Moralia* 336B *De Alexandri magni fortuna aut
virtute*.

1 Aristotle *Problemata* 11.33 (1903a20)
2 *Adagia* III vi 47 A mind elsewhere

13 The Greek word is found at Aristophanes *Acharnians* 254, but Erasmus prob-
    ably drew it from the *Suda* (Θ 553) and Hesychius Θ 871, to whom he refers
    and to whom he is indebted for the interpretations given at the beginning of
    his commentary. The expression is mentioned at the end of *Adagia* II v 47 Do
    not make a Mercury out of any and every wood. Added in *1517/18*

distinguish from *satureia*,[1] although Columella seems to differentiate them, since he says, 'And *satureia*, recalling the taste of thyme and savory.'[2] It has a rather bitter taste, and grows everywhere in the fields. The meadow savory has much better medicinal power than the garden variety, according to Dioscorides, and likes rocky ground.[3] The garden variety is more suitable for eating. Suidas listed the proverb, as did Hesychius. Epaminondas is said to have lived an unbelievably frugal life, and said the following about a very light and scanty lunch: 'Such a lunch does not promote betrayal.'[4] These words have two meanings, either that no one engages in treachery if he is of modest means or that those who are content to live modestly are not easily bribed to betray their country. Amphis in book ten of Athenaeus: 'A cheap dinner does not lead to drunken behaviour.'[5] The Greek verse seems to be a trimeter that has been corrupted by the exchange of two words. The metre will be restored if one reads Δεῖπνον γὰρ εὐτελές.[6] Drawing on Alexis, Athenaeus tells us that at first very lengthy parties produce scurrilous jokes, which generally give more offence than pleasure. Then these give way to curses that are thrown back at the speaker; then words lead to blows. Not so for those who live on savory.

14 Doryphorematis ritu
Like a bodyguard

The Greeks give the name δορυφόρημα 'bodyguard' to escorts hired from the dregs of the barbarians. In antiquity tyrants used these as protection;

* * * * *

1 Pliny *Naturalis historia* 19.165
2 Columella *Res rustica* 10.233
3 Dioscorides *De re medica* 3.37
4 Cf Plutarch *Lycurgus* 13.6.
5 Athenaeus 10.421A, citing PCG 2 Amphis fragment 29 (Εὐτελὲς γὰρ δεῖπνον οὐ ποιεῖ παροινίαν) and PCG 2 Alexis fragment 160. From here to the end was added in *1528*. Other additions to the adage as it first appeared in *1517/18* are 'as did Hesychius ... betray their country' (*1526*) and (in *1528*) 'also called *cunila*,' 'medicinal,' and 'The garden variety is more suitable for eating.'
6 In suggesting the change in word-order Erasmus anticipated an emendation of Kock, although the correct reading is ἀτελές, not εὐτελές.

14 Athenaeus (see n2). Added in *1517/18*

now kings have them in their household more for show. And not just kings
but even the highest prelates![1] In tragedies kings were given an escort
who simply stood beside them, saying not even a word. Because of this,
those who sit beside you in silence are said to attend you Δορυφόρηματος
τρόπου 'Like a bodyguard.' So Athenaeus in book five: 'When Peisistratus
interposes a word, one should not be present like a bodyguard,'[2] in other
words, being silent and contributing nothing to the conversation. It is used
by Lucian in his essay *On Writing History* in these words: 'So, friend, that I
might not be the only mute at such a talkative time and, like a bodyguard
in comedy, wander around in silence with mouth agape ...'[3]

15 Musicam docet amor
Desire is a teacher of the arts

Plutarch adduces this proverb too, expressed in a trochaic verse: Μουσικὴν
ἔρως διδάσκει, κἄν τις ἄμουσος ᾖ τὸ πρίν 'Love teaches the arts, even in someone who is uncultured.'[1] The meaning is that love stirs the mind to industry
and that it is the best teacher of the arts and of everything that is elegant.
Socrates in the *Banquet* of Plato thinks that the soul, immersed in the body,
is, so to speak, awakened by the goads of love and is first impelled by it to

* * * * *

1 A reference to the Swiss guards of the Pope, who were established by Julius
   II in 1506
2 Athenaeus 5.190E
3 Lucian *Quomodo historia conscribenda sit* 4

15 A fragment of Euripides by way of Plutarch (see n1). After appearing in 1508
   this adage was dropped in 1515 before being reinstated in this position in
   1517/18. 'Socrates ... has shaken off its lethargy' is an addition of 1517/18 to
   what originally was in 1508. There were other additions in 1533: 'Bion alluded
   ... applies to all' and the final two sentences.
1 Plutarch *Moralia* 622C *Quaestiones convivales* quoting Euripides fragment 663
   Nauck (from *Stheneboea*). But the metre is iambic if there is a verse break
   before ἔρως and if τις is omitted, as in Nauck. A more correct version of the
   quotation is given at Plutarch *Moralia* 405F *De Pythiae oraculis*, where ποιητὴν
   δ᾽ ἄρα is read instead of μουσικήν. Part of the fragment is also quoted at Plato
   Symposium 196E.

pursue what is good.[2] It is as if the soul has shaken off its lethargy. This is
the reason that Plato also describes this god, Eros, as παντὸς ἐπιχειρήτης 'he
who attempts all things,' because there is nothing he does not put his hand
to.[3] For he turns someone who is taciturn into a chatterer, someone who
is shy or doltish into one who is friendly and charming, someone who is
careless into one who is conscientious. There is a rather charming story, of
Boccaccio I think, about Cimon that relates to this expression. Touched by
love for a young girl, he became polished in every kind of literature and
in his manners so that she could not despise him as being uncultured.[4] I
say this for in this verse *musice* means literature, which the ancients dedicated to the nine Muses. Bion alluded to the proverb in the *Bucolics*.[5] After
expounding in many verses that the Muses are always the companions of
love, he adds, 'I myself am a witness that this saying applies to all.'

The proverb can be used in a less immodest context if one says that
love of one's teacher is a giant step towards learning. It can also be applied
to a devout person by saying that love of one's fellow beings is the teacher
of all virtues. For if you do not have that love, nothing you do will be
righteous.

16 Sicyon arrodens, uxor, lacernam texe
Gnaw on your gourd, wife, and weave the cloak

In book three of the *Doctors at Dinner* Athenaeus adduces this hexameter
line as proverbial: Τὸν σικυὸν τρώγουσα, γύναι, τὴν χλαῖναν ὕφαινε 'Gnaw
at your gourd, wife, and weave the cloak.'[1] These are obviously the words

* * * * *

2 As for example at Plato *Symposium* 210B–E, but Erasmus does not seem to be
referring here to a specific passage in the dialogue.
3 Plato *Timaeus* 69D. The two immediately preceding sentences (added in
1517/18) break the logical connection of this one with 'The meaning ... of
everything that is elegant.'
4 Boccacio *Decameron* 5.1
5 Bion 9.7 (the reference is to the OCT edition of *Bucolici Graeci*)

16 Athenaeus (see n1). The first part of this adage (down to the quotation from
Athenaeus) appeared in 1508 and 1515 in different positions. The rest was
added in 1517/18, when the adage took up its final position.
1 Athenaeus 3.73D

of a husband, telling his wife to be content with very modest fare and to complete her work. For *sicyon* or *sicyos* is a kind of gourd or melon. Some think it is a kind of cucumber. This expression suits quite well the princes of our times, who spend eagerly and extravagantly what their starving people have accumulated for them with the greatest labour. And they think it is their right, like drones, to enjoy what is earned by the sweat of others.

Ermolao Barbaro in chapter 366 of his *Corollaria* on Dioscorides seems to interpret it differently.[2] Following Aristotle he writes that most weaver-women are promiscuous. Whether the *sicyos* reduces sexual desire I do not know!

17 Tetigit lapidem a cane morsum
He has touched a stone that a dog has bitten

In his discussion of a rabid dog's poison in book twenty-nine chapter five, Pliny says, 'The poison is so strong that it is harmful even to step in the urine of a rabid dog, especially if one has open sores. The cure is a poultice of horse manure to which vinegar has been added and which has been placed and heated in wine. This will occasion less surprise to anyone who remembers that "A stone that a dog has bitten" has become a proverb for quarrelsomeness.'[1] So Pliny. We can infer from his words that it was a common belief that whoever touched or stepped on a stone that had been bitten by a dog became more irritable and was inclined to quarrelsomeness.[2] Perhaps it was said of a person who ranted and raved and was

* * * * *

2 H. Barbarus *Corollarii libri quinque* book two, chapter 366, sub *cucumis*. Erasmus' reference (366) is not erroneous, *pace* ASD II-7 253:471–3n.

17 Pliny (see n1). Otto 322. Added in *1517/18*
1 Pliny *Naturalis historia* 29.102. For Erasmus' reference to chapter 5 see on *Adagia* IV iii 3 n3 (5–6 above). For 'in wine' Pliny's text reads 'in a fig.'
2 Erasmus' interpretation of the proverb mentioned by Pliny is not persuasive. The point may have been simply that a dog is so ill-tempered that it will bite even a stone. Another interpretation is that 'a stone bitten by a dog' refers to an innocent victim. When a dog is hit by a stone, it often attacks the stone rather than the person who threw it (see *Adagia* IV ii 22 A dog getting angry with the stone).

always ready for a fight, 'This fellow has stepped on a stone that a dog has bitten.'

18 Erecti
To one's full height

Athenaeus in book five of his *Doctors at Dinner*:

> And what is marvellous, although we were low in spirit and suffering from heads that were heavy from drinking, whenever we saw any of these things being brought in, we all pulled ourselves together, ὀρθοὶ . . . ἀνιστάμενοι 'raising ourselves to our full height,' as the saying goes.[1]

The expression will be suitable for describing someone who is wholeheartedly set upon some enterprise. Those who are rather eager to listen to or see something raise themselves to their full height and sometimes stand on tiptoe.

19 E clibano boves
Pot-roast oxen

What Aristophanes writes in the *Acharnians* has the flavour of a proverb: 'Then he welcomed us and set before us whole Ἐκ κριβάνου βοῦς "Oxen pot-roast."'[1] It will be used to indicate the sumptuousness of a banquet or excessive greed. 'Hecatomb' was a term used with the same figure of speech, as appears somewhat later in Athenaeus in a citation from the same poet: καὶ πολυπόδων ἑκατόμβη 'and a hecatomb of octopuses.'[2]

* * * * *

18 Athenaeus (see n1). Added in *1517/18*

1 Athenaeus 4.130B (not book 5). The correct reference (book 4) was erroneously changed in *1528* and was not corrected thereafter.

19 Aristophanes by way of Athenaeus (see n1). A doublet of *Adagia* III i 9 Whole pot-roast oxen. Added in *1517/18*

1 Aristophanes *Acharnians* 855–6, cited from Athenaeus 4.130F, Erasmus' immediate source

2 Not the same poet, but Anaxandrides (PCG 2 Anaxandrides fragment 42.29), cited in Athenaeus 4.131C

20 Sequitur perca sepiam
A perch follows a cuttle-fish

In book seven Athenaeus reports this proverb, without naming a source: "Ἕπεται πέρκη μελανούρῳ 'A cuttle-fish brings along a perch as a companion.'[1] In book ten he adduces it from Aristophanes, but he does not add in what sense it is customarily used.[2] I conjecture, however, that it was said of a gang of scoundrels. A little later in the same author these verses of Numenius, who wrote about fish, are adduced: 'Wrasse and labrus and scorpion fish red in its skin / Or a cuttle-fish, the guide to perch.'[3]

21 Feri puer
Shoot, child

In book fifteen of his *Doctors at Dinner* Athenaeus points out that in antiquity approbation was shown by the proverb ἴη παιών, which indicated that someone had completed his task – much the same as we are accustomed to say, 'Bravo, well done,' when congratulating someone for an act of consummate bravery.[1] He says, for example, that when someone left a banquet quite drunk and very sleepy all the others called out to him ἴη παιών. He adds that this adage is mentioned by Clearchus in *On Proverbs*, who says that it originated in the following event.[2] When Latona was taking Apollo and Diana from Chalcis to Delphi, they came to the cave of Python. The serpent, disturbed, rushed out at them. Latona, who was carrying her daughter

* * * * *

20 Antiphanes by way of Athenaeus (see n2). Added in *1517/18*
  1 Athenaeus 7.319C
  2 Not Aristophanes, but Antiphanes (PCG 2 Antiphanes fragment 192.4), cited by Athenaeus at 10.450C
  3 *Supplementum Hellenisticum* ed H. Lloyd-Jones and Peter Parsons (Berlin and New York 1983) fragment 577, cited by Athenaeus at 7.320E. Numenius was a didactic poet of the third century BC.

21 Athenaeus (see n1). See *Adagia* II iv 28 Io Paean, which contains much of what is here. Added in *1517/18*
  1 Athenaeus 15.701C, whom Erasmus follows quite closely down to 'the verse will be iambic'
  2 Clearchus fragment 64 Wehrli

in her arms, begged Apollo for help and called out Ἴε παῖ 'Shoot, son,' since by good luck he happened to be carrying a bow, ἴε παῖ meaning much the same as ἄφιε παῖ, that is, 'Shoot and strike, son.' Then some people varied the expression somewhat, saying ἴε παιών.[3] This is customarily used in a proverbial way whenever we beg for help in danger. Others think that those who have successfully performed their duty and have achieved their aim are acclaimed in this way. However, in light of how they are commonly used, the words that are solemnly spoken in the rites of Apollo, ἴη παιάν, ἴη παιάν, ἴη παιάν,[4] do not seem to be proverbial.

It is thought that the iambic trimeter, which by its nature expresses forcefulness and speed, sprang from these words. If you pronounce the first syllable in ἴη as a long vowel, the verse will be a dactylic hexameter; if you pronounce it as short, the verse will be iambic.[5] The fact that in the text of Athenaeus ἴε and ἴη sometimes have a rough breathing, sometimes a smooth one, probably results from the carelessness of scribes.

Ovid in his *Art of Love* appears to use it as a shout of approbation, one that congratulates a victor or someone whose aspirations have been fulfilled: 'Say "io Paean," repeat "io Paean"; / The booty I sought has fallen into my nets.'[6]

22 Pulchre fallit vulpem
It's a fine thing to deceive a fox

Παλεύει καλῶς τὴν ἀλώπεκα, It's a fine thing if he deceives a fox. Suidas only lists this, without explanation.[1] It appears to have been said of someone who tried to get the better of a clever person by deceit but set his trap

* * * * *

3 The meaning is 'shoot, striking!' Erasmus now connects the expression with the Greek verb παίω 'strike.'

4 The phrase ἴη παιάν is a cry of thankful invocation to the god Apollo, one of whose titles was *Paian* or *Paion*. The word has nothing to do with the Greek word παῖς 'child' or παίω 'strike.'

5 This sentence and the next one were added in 1528.

6 Ovid *Ars amatoria* 2.1–2

22 *Suda* (see n1). Here begins a series of twenty adages (22–42, excluding 25) that first appeared in 1520.

1 *Suda* Π 75

in vain. For παλεύειν means to allure by artifice. This is why παλεύτριαι is the name given to doves that fowlers blind and place in a net. As they flutter around they will deceive other doves and lure them in. In addition, those who stretch out nets for wild beasts are called παλευταί.[2] It is difficult, however, to get the better of a fox by deceit.

23 Aut piscem olet aut florem
Smelling of fish or flower

Ambrose in *Hexaemeron* 5.2: 'Smelling of fish or *timallus*.' He attests that the saying is directed at someone smelling nicely, since *timallus* is the name of a fish with a most pleasing aroma, and the flower of the same name is equally fragrant. But it may be better to give Ambrose's words:

> I shall not send you away unhonoured in my inquiry, timallus, on whom the name of a flower has been engrafted; whether nourished by the waters of the river Ticinus or of the beautiful Atesis, you are a flower. A more powerful witness is a saying that has been wittily applied to a person who gives off the aroma of a pleasing and sweet fragrance, 'Smelling of fish or flower.' The smell of the fish is said to be the same as that of a flower. What can be more pleasing than your appearance, more enjoyable than your sweetness, more fragrant than your aroma? You breathe the fragrance of honey from your body.[1]

I rather think, however, that instead of *timallus* one should read *tithymallus*, various kinds of which are listed by Pliny in book twenty-six chapter eight,[2] and which Dioscorides repeatedly mentions in different passages.[3]

* * * * *

2 This sentence was added in 1526 and breaks the original sequence of thought between the preceding and following sentences.

23 Ambrose (see n1). Otto 1782. There is confusion here of *thymallos*, the name of an unidentified fish (perhaps a grayling), and *tithymallos*, the plant euphorbia. The form *timallos* (*timallus* in Latin) does not exist. Added in 1520
1 Ambrose *Hexaemeron* 5.2.6 PL 14 222
2 Pliny *Naturalis historia* 26.62–71. For Erasmus' reference to 'chapter 8' see on *Adagia* IV iii 3 n3 (5–6 above).
3 Dioscorides *De materia medica* 4.164

24 Equi dentes inspicere donati
Looking a gift horse in the mouth

There are some common sayings even of our own day that deserve to be included among ancient adages.[1] An example is 'One should not look at the teeth of a gift horse,' when we mean that one should look well upon and be pleased with whatever is given for nothing and not purchased. For the purchaser of a horse looks at its teeth, the surest indicators of its age, to avoid being cheated. But it would be impolite to do the same to a horse that you are being given for nothing. St Jerome used the proverb in the preface to commentaries which he wrote on Paul's Epistle to the Ephesians. He says:

> I am not very eloquent. What is that to you? Read someone who is more stylish. If I do not translate the Greek into Latin in a proper way, then either read the Greek authors yourself if you know the language or if you know only Latin do not make judgments on a service freely given or, as the common proverb says, do not look a gift horse in the mouth.[2]

So Jerome. Recently, however, we ourselves experienced, not to say were astounded by, the impoliteness of the kind of people with whom Jerome finds fault. We published the New Testament, correcting and explaining countless passages, and doing so after an incalculable number of hours of study.[3] The clamour of protests that came from certain theologians and a crowd of monks who were helped most by this labour of mine was beyond belief. These ungrateful men were as offensive in their protests as they were deficient in my industriousness. Such persons almost worship a fellow who gives them so sumptuous a meal that they leave the table stuffed full and tipsy. On the man who gives them such useful material for nothing and at the cost of much sweat they actually heap abuse.

* * * * *

24 Jerome (see n2). Otto 607. Added in *1520*
1 Suringar 68; cf Tilley H 678 Look not a given horse in the mouth.
2 St Jerome *Prologus commentariorum in Epistolam ad Ephesios* PL 26 469A
3 Erasmus published his edition of the New Testament (under the title *Novum Instrumentum*) in 1516. The title became *Novum Testamentum* in 1519 when the second edition appeared.

25 Grata brevitas
Brevity has charm

Χάρις βαιοῖσιν ὀπηδεῖ, Small things are attractive. This is the second half of a
dactylic hexameter, and certainly has the look of a proverb. For even today
there is no expression more common than this one.[1] Some things please by
their mass and greatness. There are others that are attractive because they
are very small, for example, some gems and carvings. The same is true
of letters and books. If brief, these are often more appealing, especially
to those who are fastidious and busy. Dwarfs too are the delight of some
persons simply because of their unusual lack of height.

26 Amicitias immortales esse oportet
Friendships should last for ever

In his tenth book on the Macedonian and Asian wars, part of which we owe
to 'golden' Mainz,[1] Titus Livius writes as following: 'Because of its truth
that common saying, "Friendships should live for ever, enmities should
die," has become proverbial.'[2] The context itself suggests that we should

* * * * *

25 The Greek phrase occurs in what is now known as *Anthologia Palatina* 9.784,
   though in Erasmus' time it was the Planudean anthology that had been printed
   (organized in seven books) and was in circulation (see on *Adagia* IV v 57, 181
   below). This adage first appeared in *1515* and was moved, unchanged, to this
   position in *1526*. It replaced what later became IV vi 12 A cautious man's
   mother sheds no tears (216 below).
 1 Suringar 84

26 Livy (see n2). Otto 84. Added in *1520*. 'In the second book of his *Rhetoric*' to
   the end was added in *1533*.
 1 The epithet 'golden' was attached to Mainz when it became the centre of a
   league of Rhenish towns in the mid-thirteenth century.
 2 Livy 40.46.12 (the tenth book of the fourth decade, which was entitled 'The
   Macedonian War' in the manuscripts). The reference to Mainz is to a manuscript, now lost and once in the cathedral there, our only source for part of
   book 40 (§§37.3 to the end); see L.D. Reynolds ed *Texts and Transmission: A
   Summary of the Latin Classics* (Oxford 1983) 212.

read it in this way.[3] The proverb does indeed give sound advice, but human behaviour has come to this, that feuds last for ever and friendships are more fragile than glass. Infatuation is more powerful than a hundred Prayers and 'Resentment is the last thing to grow old,'[4] while feelings of friendship disappear at the slightest chance. Even if it is stitched together, 'it does not knit but tears apart again.'[5] The reason, I think, is what we have learned from the philosophers: each person ignores the public weal and serves his own interests. In the second book of his *Rhetoric* Aristotle cites a verse on this sentiment, which, if I am not mistaken, we have reported elsewhere: 'No lover he whose love can ever cease.'[6] He also cites another verse in the same place: 'Nurse not wrath for ever; for you yourself are mortal.'[7]

27 Ad bonam frugem
To good harvests

Those who came to their senses and changed their way of life to engage in better pursuits were said proverbially to take themselves 'To better har-

* * * * *

3 Erasmus has departed from the text of the proverb as transmitted in the Mainz manuscript by adding the word *mortales*, so that the Latin version of what is translated here reads *amicitias immortales, inimicitias <mortales> esse debere*. The Mainz manuscript was first used by Nicolaus Carbachius for his edition of Livy published in Mainz in 1519. In that edition *mortales* is omitted. Since this adage first appeared in 1520, Erasmus should probably be credited with the emendation. The text of the passage in the Froben edition of Livy of 1531 is the same as that of Erasmus.

4 *Adagia* I vii 13, where Erasmus also talks about Infatuation (the Greek Ἄτη), a divine power that causes humans to embark on disastrous actions, and Prayers (Λιταί), also thought of as divine, 'who do their best ... to mend the confusion caused by Infatuation' (CWE 32 73)

5 Horace *Epistles* 1.3.32

6 Aristotle *Rhetoric* 2.21 (1394b16), cited at *Adagia* II iii 76 Friendship is for the steadfast. The verse is Euripides *Troades* 1051.

7 Aristotle *Rhetoric* 2.21 (1394b21), quoting Menander *Sententiae* 5 Jaekel (formerly *Adespota* 79 Nauck)

27 Cicero (see n1). *Collectanea* no 476. Otto 722. Added in 1520. The reference to Plautus *Trinummus* was added in 1526. What follows that, excluding the final sentence, was added in 1533.

vests.' Marcus Tullius uses it in his speech for Marcus Caelius: 'And they
have taken themselves "to good harvests," as is said, and have become
important and famous men.'[1] Also Plautus in the *Three-shilling Day*: 'I am
resolved to apply my mind to fruitfulness.'[2] Lampridius in his *Heliogabalus*: 'The soldiers said they would spare him if he returned "to good
harvests."'[3] Because of this those who do what they are expected to do,
especially servants whom we keep and feed to perform their tasks, are
said to be *frugi* or *bonae frugi*. Ulpian on the *lex Aquilia*, in the chapter
beginning 'Therefore Neratius': 'But if a slave who is *bonae frugi* "virtuous" has been killed within a year after changing his character ...'[4]
Also in the section entitled 'On what matters a case should go before the
same judge,' the chapter beginning 'If anyone makes a slave worse': 'It
seems to be in the interest of the usufructuary that his slave be *bonae
frugi* "upright."'[5] Again in the *Digest* book eleven, in the section entitled 'On corrupt slaves,' the chapter beginning 'As for what the praetor says': 'But is he held liable if he has driven a slave who is *bonae
frugi* "good" to misdeeds?'[6] Plautus in the *Casina*: 'I believe it is so, if
you are *frugi bonae* "honest."'[7] Again in the *Pseudolus*: 'You wish me to
be a scoundrel, but I shall be *frugi bonae* "virtuous."'[8] Plautus contrasted
nequam with *frugi*. For *nequam* means 'good-for-nothing.' And so we say
frugi homo just as we say *nequam homo*, both words being indeclinable.
Columella in *On Agriculture* book one: 'An honest man is better than a
scoundrel when they are equally diligent in their work.'[9] And in the *Declamations* a son who is *frugi* 'upright' is contrasted with one who is *luxu-
riosus* 'extravagant.'[10] Accordingly, the former is also called *frugalis*. The
proverb seems to have been taken from fields; they produce a harvest after
cultivation.

* * * * *

1 Cicero *Pro M. Caelio* 12.28
2 Plautus *Trinummus* 270
3 *Heliogabalus* 15.1 in the *Historia Augusta*. Lampridius is named as the author of
   the life of this emperor.
4 *Digest* 9.2.23.5
5 *Digest* 11.3.9.1
6 *Digest* 11.3.1
7 Plautus *Casina* 327
8 Plautus *Pseudolus* 468
9 Columella *Res rustica* 1.9.5
10 Pseudo-Quintilian *Declamationes minores* 245.6

28 Per manus tradere
To pass down from hand to hand

What comes down from one person to another who follows him in some way or other is said to be passed down from hand to hand. This seems to be a metaphor drawn from men unloading a ship or a wagon. The same procedure frequently occurs in military service, for example, in the first commentary of the *Civil War*. Caesar says, 'Steep crags were blocking the route in many places. Weapons had to be passed down from hand to hand, and then the soldiers completed a large part of their way, unarmed, supporting each other.'[1] Again, in book seven of the *Gallic War*: 'A Gaul in front of the town gate hurled into the fire clods of grease and pitch that reached him by being passed from hand to hand from the region of the tower.'[2] In the same book: 'Some were let down from the walls, being passed from hand to hand.' Also in book eight: 'This was the plan for retreat that they adopted. When they had taken up their position, bundles of straw and faggots, of which there was a great supply in the camp, were passed from hand to hand and then placed in front of the line of battle.'[3] In these passages, however, the expression is meant literally. Whenever it is used figuratively, the expression becomes proverbial and we frequently encounter it in authors. For example, in book twelve of Fabius: 'Know not only those things that are recorded in history or transmitted orally, "passed from hand to hand," as it were, and the things that occur everyday, but do not neglect what has been made up by poets.'[4] Also Livy in book five of *From the Founding of the City*: 'Even if no religious ordinances had been established when the city was founded and then passed down to us "from hand to hand."'[5] The same author in book nine: 'Then the military training that had been "passed down hand to hand" right from the beginning of the city had become a skill based on fixed precepts.' Marcus Tullius in his speech

* * * * *

28 Caesar (see nn1–3). Added in *1520*
1 Caesar *Bellum civile* 1.68
2 Caesar *Bellum Gallicum* 7.25.2 and, in the next sentence, *Bellum Gallicum* 7.47.6
3 Caesar *Bellum Gallicum* 8.15.4
4 Quintilian 12.4.1, added in *1533*
5 Livy 5.51.4, then 9.17.10. The second quotation was added in *1533*, the expansion stretching to 'He is speaking about a letter.'

On the Consular Provinces: 'Is Gaius Julius Caesar, who has been given all these splendid honours by the senate, to pass over this province from his hand to the hand of him whom you least wish to have it?'[6] In fact even the jurists use the expression *per manus* 'handed down' for what 'is passed from hand to hand.' For example, Papinianus in book twenty-nine of the *Pandects*, in the section entitled 'On the law of codicils': 'The rule handed down, that an inheritance cannot be granted in codicils, has this justification ...'[7] Plautus in the *Three-shilling Day*: 'He himself gave it from his hands into mine.'[8] He is speaking about a letter. A more pleasing use is whenever the proverb is applied to intellectual matters, as when we say that some teaching, belief, custom, or discipline has come to us by being passed down from hand to hand.[9]

29 De manu in manum
From hand to hand

Although I do not think that what Cicero writes in book seven of his *Letters to Friends* is the same as the above, it is not completely dissimilar: 'In short, *trado* "I give over" the whole man to you, "from my hand to your hand," as they say, as distinguished for his loyalty as for his victories.'[1] For those who are recommended *traduntur* 'are given over.' Terence: 'She gives this girl into my hand.'[2] Horace too: 'So that I may try to praise him to you and recommend him.'[3] Also: 'If you wished to recommend this fellow.'

* * * * *

6 Cicero *De provinciis consularibus* 16.39
7 *Digest* (*Pandects*) 29.7.10
8 Plautus *Trinummus* 902
9 The second part of this sentence, from 'as when we say,' was added in *1528*.

29 Cicero (see n1). Otto 1039. Added in *1520*
1 Cicero *Ad familiares* 7.5.3
2 Terence *Andria* 297. Donatus ad loc takes the phrase to mean 'she puts her hand in mine.'
3 Horace *Epistles* 1.9.3, then *Satires* 1.9.47. These citations exemplify simply the use of the verb *tradere* in the sense of 'recommend.' The phrase *in manum* is not present.

30 Mira de lente
Wondrous words about a lentil

In book three of his *On Dialectic* Rodolphus Agricola, a man worthy of immortal memory, attests that the Greeks often used the proverb 'Outstanding things about a lentil' whenever something insignificant and trivial was
extolled with magnificent praise, just as if you were to honour a lentil, a
cheap and tiny legume, with a splendid encomium.[1] I think the Greeks expressed it in this way: Δεινὰ περὶ φακῆς.[2]

31 Non una manu capere
Catch with both hands

Οὐ τῇ ἑτέρᾳ ληπτέον, Not to be caught with only one hand. About something
difficult, complex and not easy to grasp. For we usually use both hands
in such cases. Plato used it in the *Sophist*: 'You see then that it is a true
saying, that this beast is resourceful and, as the saying goes, "Not to be
caught with only one hand."'[1] Taken from hunting where some animals
are marvellously adept and slip out of the very hands of the hunters. Plato
thinks that a sophist is like these animals, since he is well equipped with
all kinds of guile to escape.

It can also be applied to a rich benefice that no one can acquire easily,
but must struggle with all his might to get.

* * * * *

30 Rodolphus Agricola (see n1). Added in *1520*
  1 Rodolphus Agricola *De inventione dialectica* 3.14. The alleged proverb, as quoted
    by Agricola, is actually *egregia fabula de mente* 'an outstanding story about a
    lentil.' On Agricola (1444–85), a renowned humanist from Friesland who was
    greatly admired by Erasmus (as in *Adagia* I iv 39 What has a dog to do with
    a bath?), see CEBR 1:15–17. On Erasmus' involvement in the publication of
    Agricola's work in 1515 and his motives see Lisa Jardine *Erasmus, Man of
    Letters* (Princeton 1993) chapters 3 and 4. For the reference to the lentil cf
    Adagia I vii 23 Perfume on lentils.
  2 This Greek version of the Latin expression seems to be Erasmus' invention.

31 Plato (see n1). Added in *1520*
  1 Plato *Sophista* 226A

32 Omnes laqueos effugere
To escape from every snare

In the same dialogue he adduces a very similar metaphor, one that is used proverbially: 'It is difficult to escape from every snare.' This is taken from hunting when all the escape routes are blocked in such a way that an animal must be trapped somewhere. 'For the proverb is right that says Τὰς ἁπάσας μὴ ῥᾴδιον εἶναι διαφεύγειν "It is not easy to escape from every snare."'[1]

33 Hostis domesticus
An enemy within

'An enemy within.' Again, in the same work Plato attests that this expression is frequently used proverbially when misfortune does not have an external source but originates from our own nature; for example, when someone betrays himself, or refutes himself, or destroys himself by his own anger or envy: 'They have no need for others to refute them, but as the proverb says, Οἴκοθεν τὸν πολέμιον ... ἔχοντες "They have an enemy within who will be their adversary."'[1] He is talking of a sophist who talks too much, and therefore often provides the material for his own rebuttal.

34 Capere civitatem
Capturing a city

In the same dialogue Plato points out that the proverb 'Capturing (or storming) a city' was customarily said of someone who had completed a

* * * * *

32 Plato (see n1). Added in *1520*
 1 Plato *Sophista* 231C

33 Plato (see n1). Added in *1520*
 1 Plato *Sophista* 252C. This passage (with proverb) is cited in *Adagia* IV i 39 Eurycles, though it did not appear there until *1533*.

34 Plato (see n1). Added in *1520*. There were additions in *1533*: the phrase 'or storming' at the beginning, 'In the relevant passage ... crucial part of the argument,' and the two final sentences.

very difficult task. For a city is not captured immediately on the first attack. In the relevant passage the stranger is encouraging Theaetetus to continue steadfastly in what he has begun. For the man who gets stuck or
shrinks back in the face of less demanding difficulties will never bring anything to completion in the crucial part of the argument. These are Plato's
words:

> You should have confidence, Theaetetus, that the man who makes some
> progress, even if very little, will always make advances beyond that. For
> if a person gives up in these circumstances, what will he achieve in others,
> when he is making no progress or when he is even being compelled to re-
> treat? Ὁ γε τοιοῦτος ἄν ποτε ἕλοι πόλιν 'Such a man will never capture a city,'
> as the saying goes.[1]

In war it is easy to have some success in making sallies or in burning
villages, but it is extremely difficult to storm fortified cities. This is similar
to 'Faint hearts never set up a trophy.'[2]

35 Divinam excipio sermonem
I except the gods

In book six of the *Republic* Plato points out that Θεῖον ἐξαίρω λόγον 'I except
the gods' was a proverb commonly used, I believe, whenever something
rather boastful was said and, as a good omen, the gods were excluded.[1] For
they are all powerful and no one gives orders to them. I shall give Plato's
words: 'For there is not, there never has been, and there never will be a
character altered and made virtuous by a system not in line with theirs. I
am talking in human terms, my friend. I exclude the gods, as the proverb
says.'

* * * * *

1 Plato *Sophista* 261B. Erasmus misconstrues the first part of the quotation, which
   should be translated as 'The man who makes some progress ... should have
   confidence.'
2 *Adagia* II vi 25

35 Plato (see n1). Added in *1520*
1 Plato *Republic* 6.492E

The expression seems to be part of an iambic verse. Perhaps the sentiment originated in Homer: 'Nevertheless the gods are all powerful.'[2] It can
be applied to the highest dignitaries, the pope, for example, or cardinals –
or monks!

36 Una pertica
By the same pole

'By one pole,' meaning 'in the same manner.' Pliny the Younger in book
eight, letter 2:

> The whole region is praising the novelty of my rebate and the way in which it
> was carried out. And the people, whom I did not measure by the same pole, so
> to speak, but individually and by their different levels, have departed, feeling
> obliged to me in proportion to their moral worth and being satisfied that I
> am not a person in whose mind 'the wicked and the good are held in equal
> honour.'[1]

The expression seems to have been taken from field surveyors. Pliny
used *pertica* in the sense of *decempeda* 'a ten-foot rod.' Servius Sulpicius, as
Festus Pompeius points out, said that the *pertica* was the line that marked
off fields.[2] The verse is from Homer, in book nine of the *Iliad*. We have cited
and explained it elsewhere.[3]

* * * * *

2 Homer *Odyssey* 10.306

36 Pliny (see n1). Otto 1388. Added in 1520. From 'Pliny used *pertica*' to the end
was added in 1526, except for 'in book nine of the *Iliad*' and 'and explained,'
which were added in 1528.
1 Pliny *Letters* 8.2.8. The quotation with which the passage ends is from Homer
Iliad 9.319. Only the Greek was given until 1528, when a Latin translation was
added.
2 Pompeius Festus 262.24–6 Lindsay. Festus is commenting on *postica linea* and
there is no mention of *pertica* in the manuscripts or in modern editions. Erasmus is following the edition of Festus that appeared with Perotti's *Cornucopiae*
in which, by emendation, Servius Sulpicius is supposed to have said that the
pertica was used to mark off fields.
3 *Adagia* III viii 34 No discrimination

37 Sarta tecta
Windproof and watertight

'Windproof and watertight' is an expression describing things that have been completed and well cared for and in which nothing has been over-looked. This was a formal legal term that became proverbial. Plautus in the *Three-shilling Day*:

> I have resolutely refrained from causing you grief.
> I have always kept your precepts 'Windproof and watertight' by my
>   self-control.[1]

Cicero in book thirteen of his *Letters to Friends*: 'Grant me this that you may keep Marcus Curius "Windproof and watertight," as they say, untouched by any trouble, harm, or damage.'[2] Also in the third speech against Verres: 'As for how he behaved with respect to what were "Wind-proof and watertight," what am I to say?'[3] The same author in his speech to the people before he went into exile: 'If therefore you have at any time consulted the interests of those who have abandoned religious piety, you ought to look out for me now, who have kept all that is consecrated to the gods "Windproof and watertight" and safe from every danger.'[4] Also in the same speech against Verres: 'Therefore hear me on the crimes of his prae-torship so that you may ask what this defendant especially deserves with respect to both kinds – his legal judgments and his demands for what is "Windproof and watertight."'[5] In the same speech: 'He asked who ought to hand over the temple of Castor "Windproof and watertight."'[6] And in sev-

* * * * *

37 Plautus, Cicero, and the *Digest* (see nn1–10). Otto 1589. Added in *1520*, where the essay ended with the first quotation from Cicero. The rest was added in *1526*, with the exception of the quotation from Cicero *Verrines* 2.1.40.103, which was added in *1533*. The phrase is mentioned in *Adagia* IV x 30 Clean and clear (at the end, 503 below).
1 Plautus *Trinummus* 316–17
2 Cicero *Ad familiares* 13.50.2
3 Cicero *Verrines* 2.1.49.127
4 Cicero *Oratio pridie quam in exilium iret* 6.14. No longer considered to be by Cicero
5 Cicero *Verrines* 2.1.40.103
6 Cicero *Verrines* 2.1.50.131

eral other places, as in the fifth speech against the same Verres.[7] Ulpian in book one of the *Pandects*, the section entitled 'On the duty of the proconsul and legate,' the chapter beginning 'If in some city': 'He should go around the sacred temples and the public works to inspect them to see whether they are "Windproof and watertight" or need some repair.'[8] Also Celsus in book seven of the *Pandects*, the section entitled 'On usufruct,' the chapter beginning 'So far,' when he is speaking of repairing buildings: 'To this extent he should keep them "Windproof and watertight." If any part collapses through age, neither party is compelled to repair it.'[9] And soon after this: 'How Celsus inquires into how things should be kept "Windproof and watertight."' Again in book forty-eight, the section entitled 'On the law of extortion,' the chapter beginning 'The Julian law': 'That too we should see to, that no one should be credited for carrying out a public work, for giving or providing corn to the general public or for importing it, or for keeping buildings "Windproof and watertight" before everything is completed, approved, and answered for, according to law.'[10]

Festus Pompeius informs us that the ancients 'said *sarte* for *integre*, so that public works that are contracted out to be made *integra tecta* are contracted out to be *sarta tecta*. For *sarcire* means "to make whole."'[11] But I think Festus read *sarte tecta* for *sarta tecta* in the sense of *integre tecta*, unless perhaps we should read *sarta et integra tecta* for *integra tecta* in the preceding phrase.

38 Pulmo prius venissent
A sea-lung would have come more quickly

In ancient times it was said of those who were slow or loiterers, 'A sea-lung would have come more quickly.' The reason, I think, is that although

* * * * *

7 Cf Cicero *Verrines* 2.3.7.16.
8 *Digest* 1.16.7.1. On Erasmus' use of Roman legal texts see *Adagia* IV ix 1n (419 below).
9 *Digest* (*Pandects*) 7.1.7.2
10 *Digest* 48.11.7
11 Pompeius Festus 429.4–6 Lindsay. For the second occurrence of 'are contracted out' the modern text of Festus here reads *vocantur* 'are called,' not *locantur* as in Erasmus' quotation.

38 Plautus (see n1). Added in *1520*

the sea-lung is always in motion, it never moves its position. Plautus in *Epidicus*:

> Heavens above, did I order you to take your shoes off? For a sea-lung
> Would have arrived before you, as the saying goes.[1]

39 Pedem conferre
To put foot to foot

'To put foot to foot' is taken from the military sphere. It is used when one is getting nearer to something. Cicero in his speech for Plancius: 'I cannot put foot to foot more quickly, as they say, or approach more closely.'[1] We have mentioned this elsewhere in passing as coming from Quintilian.[2] It seems to have been taken from Homer in whom the phrase ἐγγὺς ἰόντες 'coming together,' that is, fighting at close quarters, is very common. Vegetius in book three, chapter fourteen, of his *On Warfare*, expressed the same idea in an equally appealing figure of speech: 'The first and second lines of battle bear the brunt of the whole war when it has come down to *spathae* "long swords" and *pila* "spears," as they say.'[3] The name *spathae* was given to longer swords, while *pila* were shorter spears, five-and-a-half feet in length, which were later called *spicula*. Our source is Modestinus.[4] Quintus Curtius describes such a battle in book three:

* * * * *

1 Plautus *Epidicus* 627–8. Erasmus' text, as translated here, reflects that of the early editions and is corrupt. Modern editors offer a quite different text in which a sea-lung makes no appearance.

39 Cicero and Quintilian (see nn1–2). Otto 1401. Added in *1520*. 'It seems to have been taken ... source is Modestinus' was added in *1526*. All that follows this first appeared in *1533*.
1 Cicero *Pro Cn. Plancio* 19.48
2 Quintilian 5.13.11, 8.6.57. The phrase *conferre pedem* is mentioned among the examples of metaphors in proverbs at CWE 31 21 *Introduction* xiii (line 13 of that section), where the phrase is translated as 'to set to.'
3 Vegetius *Epitome rei militaris* 3.14
4 Modestinus is an error for Modestus, the author of *De vocabulis rei militaris*. The passage can be found at sig m iiii[v] in the 1515 Paris edition of Vegetius, Frontinus, Aelianus, and Modestus. See *Adagia* v i 73 n1, 583 below.

Compelled therefore to fight hand to hand they promptly drew their swords. Then indeed was much blood spilt. For the two lines were so close together that arms struck on arms, and they aimed the tips of their swords at each other's faces. This was no time to be timid or cowardly and do nothing. They stood, foot to foot, as if they were each fighting a duel, they stood in the same spot until they could make room for themselves by victory.[5]

And Maro: 'Foot clings fast to foot, men are packed tightly together.'[6]

40 Qui multum obfuit
He who did great harm as an enemy

Just as the same author can be gifted when telling what is false and in telling what is true, so the same person can give great help and inflict great harm. Thucydides in the speech of Alcibiades in book six attests that this was a proverb in antiquity. He writes, 'That saying, used by all: "If I did you serious harm when I was your enemy, I shall also be able to be of great help to you if I should become your friend."'[1]

41 Non vulgari ancora nititur
Depending on no ordinary anchor

Demosthenes in his speech for Ctesipho: Οὐκ ἐπὶ τῆς αὐτῆς ὁρμεῖ τοῖς πολλοῖς 'He does not depend on the same anchor as most people,' meaning that he depends on novel and by no means ordinary help.[1] Suidas tells us that it is a proverb and that 'anchor' is to be understood in the Greek expression.[2]

* * * * *

5 Curtius 3.11.4–5
6 Virgil *Aeneid* 10.361

40 Thucydides (see n1). Added in *1520*
1 Thucydides 6.92.5: εἰ πολέμιός γε ὢν σφόδρα ἔβλαπτον, καὶ ἂν φίλος ὢν ἱκανῶς ὠφελείην.

41 Demosthenes (see n1). Similar in sense to *Adagia* I i 13 Secured by two anchors, in which this adage is also cited; cf also IV viii 72 Safe riding at two anchors (401 below). Added in *1520*
1 Demosthenes 18.281 (*De corona*)
2 *Suda* O 879. In the Greek there is no noun present.

42 Non pluris quam simias
Worth as little as monkeys

The monkey, a ridiculous animal and one that is commonly despised, has prompted many proverbs. Dio of Prusa in his essay 'On the Non-capture of Troy' says, 'I care less for them than for monkeys.'[1]

43 Aspis a vipera
An asp borrows poison from a viper

Tertullian in book three of *Against Marcio* cites as a proverb 'An asp from a viper,' referring to when a despicable person takes some of his evil nature from some other despicable person.[1] He says, 'Let the heretic stop borrowing poison from the Jews, as the asp, so they say, borrows poison from the viper.' It is reported among the apophthegms of Diogenes, who, when he saw two women secretly conversing with each other, produced a verse, taken I believe from some comedy: Ἀσπὶς παρ᾽ ἐχίδνης φάρμακον δανείζεται 'The asp borrows poison from the viper.'[2]

The poison of neither snake can be treated, and is equally harmful, except that a viper's bite brings more excruciating suffering before death, while the asp's bite is so free of pain that it can bring a feeling of well-

* * * * *

42 Dio Chrysostum (see n1). This was the last of the adages that first appeared in *1520*. It was followed by *Adagia* IV vi 35 A Dutch ear (which ended that edition; see 235 below).
1 Dio Chrysostom *Orationes* 11.14. Erasmus does not give the Greek version.

43 Tertullian (see n1) and, later, Diogenes (see n2). Otto 1904. This marks the point where new adages were introduced in *1523*. The addition stretches from here to *Adagia* IV v 82 (195 below), except for 44 (introduced in *1528*) and 49 (moved from I viii 100 in earlier editions). 'The poison of neither snake ... is called ... a spitter' was added in *1528*. The reference to Diogenes and the quotation did not appear until *1533*.
1 Tertullian *Adversus Marcionem* 3.8.1 PL 2 359
2 Diogenes the Cynic fragment 204 (G. Giannantoni ed *Socratis et Socraticorum reliquiae* 2 [Naples 1991] 316). Erasmus probably drew this from *Scriptores aliquot gnomici* (Basel 1521) 175. The authorship of the verse quoted has not been identified.

being, if we believe Pliny.[3] There is a kind of asp that can kill humans with its poison without biting them but simply by spitting on them. And so in Greek it is called πτυάς 'a spitter.'

The proverb will be used whenever anyone who is wicked in himself becomes worse through contact with one of the same kind.

44 Neque intus neque foris
Neither inside nor outside

In book one, chapter nine, Irenaeus reports this proverb, saying that it suits some women who realized that they had been tricked by the followers of Valentinus, but did not surrender themselves to the church in such a way as to repent and to be received into the fellowship that they had left.[1] Instead they lived together, neither adhering to the Valentinians nor being reconciled with the church. A proverb with a similar figure of speech is used today of a person who lived simply for himself and belongs to no group: *Neque caro est neque piscis* 'Neither fish nor flesh.'[2]

45 De toga ad pallium
From the toga to the pallium

What Tertullian says in his work *On the Pallium* certainly has the appearance of a proverb: 'This surely is a mark of shame, to go "From the toga to the pallium."'[1] This can be used in a double way, either when someone undertakes a quite different mode of living or when he moves from a higher

* * * * *

3 Pliny *Naturalis historia* 29.65

44 Irenaeus (see n1). This adage was introduced in *1528*, replacing one that was dropped from the collection. See ASD II-7 267, critical apparatus on line 812.
1 Irenaeus *Contra haireses* 1.13.7 PG 7 591. Valentinus was a gnostic philosopher of the second century whose followers founded a sect in Rome and who were often criticized by the writers on heresies.
2 Suringar 139; Tilley F 319 Neither fish nor flesh nor good red herring

45 Tertullian (see n1). Otto 1791. Added in *1523*. 'The toga is Roman ... garb of philosophers' was added in *1528*. Cf *Adagia* IV viii 9 (357 below).
1 Tertullian *De pallio* 5.1 PL 2 1045

status to a lower one. For example, if a courtier becomes a monk, a prefect becomes a tutor, the highest magistrate becomes a teacher of rhetoric. The toga is Roman, the pallium is Greek. Later the pallium began to be the garb of philosophers. The proverb is similar to 'From horses to asses.'[2]

46 Extrema linea
The finishing line

Since at one time the point at which a race began and ended was marked by the same line, those who repeated something from the beginning were said 'to begin from the starting line' or 'to return to the starting line.' The final part of anything was also called 'the finishing line.' So Phaedria in Terence: 'Finally, it is better than nothing to love "From the finishing line."'[1] And Tertullian in the work he wrote against Hermogenes calls him 'the finishing line' of ignoramuses because he was the last of the heretics.[2] For he was still alive when Tertullian wrote these words.

47 Caecus et claudus non intrabunt templum
The blind and the lame will not enter the temple

It is recounted in book two of Kings, chapter five, that when David had become king of the whole nation of the Israelites by the agreement of all the tribes and had already decided to establish his palace on Mount Sion, which was then the citadel of Jerusalem and was occupied at that time by the Jebusites, the latter told him that he could not enter the city until he got rid of the blind and the lame.[1] When this had been done, a proverb

* * * * *

2 *Adagia* I vii 29

46 Terence and Tertullian (see nn1–2). Otto 956. Added in *1523*
 1 Terence *Eunuchus* 640–1. The sense of the phrase here seems to be 'from a distance.' How *extrema linea* comes to mean that is puzzling; see John Barsby ed *Terence. Eunuchus* (Cambridge 1999) ad loc.
 2 Tertullian *Adversus Hermogenem* 3 PL 2 224B

47 2 Sam (see n1). Added in *1523*
 1 2 Sam 5:6. In the Vulgate there were four books of Kings, of which the first two are now known as the two books of Samuel.

arose: 'The blind and the lame will not enter the temple.' There is no clear unanimity among the commentators on the meaning of 'blind and lame' in this passage. Some think that it was an expression of contempt, meaning 'You will not enter the city until you remove the defenders of the walls, to protect which our blind and lame are sufficient.' The Jewish commentators are in the habit of making up stories to explain the problem in some enquiry. They say that two statues had been placed on the walls of the city, of Isaac and Jacob. Isaac had become blind in old age, the latter limped as a result of his struggle with the angel. The statues had been placed there by the Jebusites in order to be a reminder of the pact that they had once made with Abraham. Chapter twenty-one of the book of Genesis tells of this.[2] And so when these were removed, the citadel was captured and a proverb came into being, the sense of which, however, I do not clearly perceive. For I do not see how what is said in Leviticus about the blind and the lame being kept away from the sacred rites of the temples has anything to do with the story.[3] If one can make a guess, perhaps there used to be small statues on the top of temple roofs, like those that are often placed on the highest points of buildings. These were commonly called the blind and the lame because they could not walk since they were fixed and they could not see. There was no access into the main area except by crossing over the temple pinnacles. Accordingly, as a reward David promised that whoever first happened to get to the water-courses would be commander of his soldiers.[4]

Perhaps there will be an opportunity to use the proverb whenever someone is excluded from an honour on the grounds that he is unworthy of it. For it is right for those who were seen to exclude others to be themselves excluded. And such images are fixed on temple roofs, on the outside, although they are never to be found inside the temple itself.

* * * * *

2 Gen 21:22. The pact was that Abraham would not deal falsely with Abilemech or his descendants, the Jebusites. For what Erasmus reports of Jewish commentators ASD II-7 267:845–9n refers to the commentary of Nicolas of Lyre on 2 Sam 5:6 in *Postillae perpetuae*, notes which accompanied a text of the Bible and were published several times at the end of the fifteenth century.

3 Lev 21:18

4 The sense of this and 2 Sam 5:8, on which it is based, is not clear. The water-courses (*fistulae*) may be the troughs on the temple roof, where the statues would be located.

48 Homini diligenti semper aliquid superest
There is always something for a hard-working man to do

'There is always something for a hard-working man to do.' In his sermon on John chapter 19 Chrysostom says that this was an extremely common proverb in everyday speech.[1] A person who is truly conscientious in whatever he does is never satisfied, and always sees something more that he may do in what he has undertaken. Lazy persons think anything at all they have done to be too much.

49 Fuit et Mandroni ficulna navis
Mandro too had a ship made of fig-wood

Ἐγένετο καὶ Μάνδρωνι συκίνη ναῦς, Mandro too had a ship made of fig-wood.[1] Customarily said of those who have been elevated to good fortune and wealth beyond their deserts and do not remember their former condition. Instead they enjoy their new prosperity too arrogantly. This is generally the way with οἱ νεόπλουτοι, that is, those who come to new riches from the most humble of circumstances. It is taken from a certain Mandro who was transformed from an ordinary sailor into an admiral though he was unworthy of it and did not deserve it. And indeed to show contempt his ship was said to be made of fig-wood.[2] For the Greeks usually describe something that they think is cheap or despicable as being made of fig-wood.[3]

* * * * *

48 Chrysostom (see n1). Added in 1523
1 Chrysostom *Homiliae* 20.1 PG 59 123. The Greek version of the proverb, not given by Erasmus, is Παντὶ τῷ μεριμνῶντι ἔνεστί τι περισσόν.

49 Zenobius 3.44; *Suda* E 49. Erasmus follows these sources for most of what he says. This adage originally appeared in 1508 in the first chiliad (no 700), but was moved here in 1526 to replace 'A Dutch ear' (now *Adagia* IV vi 35).
1 The identity of Mandro is unknown.
2 The translation departs from the Latin text here, which means 'He [Mandro] said (*dixit*) that his ship was made of fig-wood.' This makes little sense. In Zenobius the sense is 'they say (φασί) that he commanded a ship made of fig-wood.' This then would be a comment of others to show their contempt of the upstart Mandro. Erasmus has either mistranslated φασί or *dixit* is a typographical error (perhaps for *dixerunt* 'they said').
3 See *Adagia* I vii 85 Fig-wood.

50 Lupus in fabula
The wolf in the story

Although we carefully explained this proverb in the first edition published
in Paris, somehow or other it seems to have been omitted in all later ones.[1]
It was usually said when the subject of a conversation suddenly appeared
on the scene. Donatus, the commentator on Terence, thinks that it arose from
the belief that a wolf can render a person speechless if it sees him first.[2]
The person loses not only his voice and words but also forgets what he
had previously been thinking about. Some try to give a philosophical reason for this phenomenon or belief, namely that the wolf is a natural enemy of man. It releases certain vapours and directs an innate native power
from its eyes at the person it has seen, suddenly paralysing his strength.
Because of this there is a sudden silence. Donatus thinks that germane to
this is the Theocritean phrase that has been cited by us elsewhere: Λύκον
εἶδες; 'Have you seen a wolf?'[3] Also the Virgilian phrase, 'The wolves have
seen Moeris first,' when the shepherd was complaining that his voice had
been taken away because of his age.[4] Some think it originated with the tales
of nurses who deceive children through their fear of a wolf; they say that
a real wolf has crept from its cave up to the bedroom door. (There is also
a fable about a mother and a wolf. To stop her child crying, she frequently
called to a wolf to carry the child off to be eaten if it did not stop sobbing. Finally the wolf had come in hope of the booty, but after opening its

* * * * *

50 Terence (see n2). *Collectanea* no 517. Otto 988; see also Suringar 117. The title
   of this adage is also given as the title of *Adagia* III viii 56, although there the
   main point of the adage is not this proverb *per se* but a Homeric line that
   might be suitably used when there was a sudden silence. Added in *1523*

1 By 'the first edition published in Paris' Erasmus must mean not just the 1500
  edition of the *Collectanea* but also the expanded edition of 1506/7, since the
  adage appears in both. It did not appear in the *Chiliades* until the edition of
  1523, where what Erasmus says here is appropriate. In later editions Erasmus'
  words became inaccurate, but he did not bother to change the wording in
  these editions.

2 Donatus on Terence *Adelphoe* 537 whom Erasmus follows for most of his discussion down to 'Romulus and Remus were suckled by a wolf'

3 Theocritus *Idylls* 14.22, cited in *Adagia* I viii 86 The wolves have seen him first.
  The adage is also mentioned in IV x 77 You could light a lantern (529 below).

4 Virgil *Eclogues* 9.54

jaws to no purpose had gone off, the wiser only for this, that one should not place any trust in a woman's promises.)[5] This, I think, is what Donatus thought the expression meant. I say this for the passage does not seem to be free of corruption in the printed editions.[6] Donatus rejects a third view according to which the expression originated in the sudden appearance of a wolf during a performance of a play of Naevius that depicted how Romulus and Remus were suckled by a wolf. Silence suddenly fell over the whole performance because such an unexpected spectator had appeared. This was how Terence's Syrus used it in the *Brothers*, signalling to Ctesipho to be silent because Demea, the young man's father, whom he thought to be in the country, had unexpectedly arrived. Plautus used it more humorously in *Stichus*. He says, 'Look, there you have your wolf in the fable, here in person and ravenous.' He is speaking of the glutton Gelasimus who suddenly comes upon the brothers while they are talking about him.[7] The allusion to the fellow's greed makes the proverb more attractive, just as in Theocritus 'Have you seen a wolf?' alludes to the name of the young man being talked about.[8] Marcus Tullius also uses it in book thirteen of his *Letters to Atticus*: 'We were talking of Varro. The wolf in the fable! For he arrived at my house.'[9] It generally happens that we fall silent whenever someone we are discussing suddenly appears. If he was being praised, we are ashamed to say to his face what it is appropriate to say of him in his absence. If he was being bitterly criticized, we are afraid to offend him.

* * * * *

5 What is in the parenthesis does not appear in Donatus. Erasmus has drawn it from a fable ('The wolf and the old woman') ascribed to Aesop (perhaps from the 1505 Aldine edition, D ii).

6 Erasmus is almost certainly responsible for 'from its cave' (*e cavea*), an emendation of the meaningless reading in the manuscripts (*Capua* 'from Capua'; a variant reading is *capna*). This emendation is credited to Westerhovius of the eighteenth century in the Teubner edition of Donatus. Surprisingly, in Erasmus' own edition of Terence (1532) *Capua* is still the reading in this note of Donatus.

7 Plautus *Stichus* 577. Here Erasmus describes Gelasimus as a parasite (*parasitus*), a stock character in New Comedy whose prime concern is to get free meals.

8 Theocritus *Idylls* 14.22. The young man's name is Lycos, meaning 'wolf.'

9 Cicero *Ad Atticum* 13.33.4

51 Prolixius Iliade
As long-winded as the Iliad

Μακρότερα τῆς Ἰλιάδος λαλῶν, Talking at greater length than the *Iliad*. Cited by Julius Pollux in book six of his *Names of Things*[1] adding to what we have already explained, that Τὸ ἐκ Δωδώνης χαλκεῖον 'Dodonean bronze' and Ἀράβιος αὐλός 'An Arabian piper' fit persons who are excessively talkative.[2] This is how it is reported by Pollux. Aeschines also used it against Demosthenes, in a passage already cited by us elsewhere.[3] The expression is not dissimilar to 'An Iliad of troubles.'[4] But since the latter suits great misfortunes, and what we are now reporting fits unbridled loquacity, I thought it best to separate them because of their different use. The *Iliad* is a great work of Homer's, in which he unfolds the story of the capture of Troy in twenty-four books. Virgil, however, fitted into twelve books what he decided to take from both works of Homer.[5]

52 Apud novercam queri
To complain to a stepmother

Those who bewail their bad luck to those who will give no help or who will take greater pleasure in the misfortunes of the complainers are said 'To complain to a stepmother,' because stepmothers are generally ill-disposed to their stepchildren. The pimp Ballio in *Pseudolus* of Plautus:

> For as for your present lamentation, that you have no money,
> You are complaining to a stepmother.[1]

* * * * *

51 Pollux (see n1). Otto 849. Added in 1523. The final words 'what he decided to take' to the end were added in 1526.
 1 Pollux *Onomasticon* 6.120
 2 *Adagia* I i 7 and I vii 32
 3 Aeschines 3.100, cited at *Adagia* I iii 26 An Iliad of troubles
 4 *Adagia* I iii 26
 5 The *Odyssey* as well as the *Iliad*

52 Plautus (see n1). Otto 1240. Added in 1523. 'The pimp has put himself in the role of a stepmother' was added in 1533.
 1 Plautus *Pseudolus* 313–14, spoken to the young man whose slave is Pseudolus

The pimp has put himself in the role of a stepmother. Pseudolus, pretending that he does not understand the expression, says, 'What! Did you ever marry this fellow's father?'

53 Animus habitat in auribus
The mind lives in the ears

The ancients located the mind in the eyes, although most have placed it in the heart. But Herodotus, apparently following a view commonly expressed, tells us in *Polyhymnia* that the mind lives in the ears, since those who have good hearing experience pleasure, while those who do not are irritable.[1] I shall give Herodotus' words: 'And now learn this: Ἐν τοῖσιν ὠσὶ τῶν ἀνθρώπων οἰκέει ὁ θυμός "The minds of mortals live in the ears." When the mind hears good things, it fills the body with pleasure. When it hears the opposite, it causes the body discomfort.'

I think that the sense of the adage is that the mind is especially soothed or irritated by what we hear. For the most direct passageway to the mind is by the ears. A friendly and pleasing word often transforms the fiercest anger into goodwill and rough words provoke the deepest enmity. In fact some people are killed by abuse, just as if by a sword or poison. Therefore the most deadly kind of murderers (and they hold sway particularly in this day and age) are those who carry the poison of asps on their tongue and who achieve the same with their tongue as murderers do with their sword.

54 Inscitia confidentiam parit
Ignorance begets overconfidence

Ἀμαθία μὲν θράσος, λογισμὸς δὲ ὄκνον φέρει, Ignorance begets overconfidence, while prudence begets caution. It can be found in Thucydides in book two of the *Peloponnesian War*.[1] St Jerome quotes it in the following form

* * * * *

53 Herodotus (see n1). Added in 1523
  1 Herodotus 7.39. The books of Herodotus' *Histories* were given the names of the Muses as titles.

54 Thucydides (see n1). Otto 853. Added in 1523
  1 Thucydides 2.46.3

in a letter to Euagrius: *Imperitia confidentiam, eruditio timorem creat* 'Inexperience produces overconfidence, learning produces fear.'[2] Pliny too reports it in the fourth book of his *Letters*: 'Just as ignorance begets overconfidence and careful thought begets caution, so diffidence weakens virtue, while brazen behaviour strengthens vices.'[3] Since Lucian also uses it in his *Nigrinus*, there can be no doubt that this expression was extremely common in antiquity in everyday conversation.[4] Knowledge makes a man more cautious when about to undertake a task. That is why, of course, the young are more bold than the old, and, as Quintilian informs us, those who have less skill speak more vigorously, while an orator who is skilled and understands the risks is initially very nervous.[5] Those who have less knowledge have less shame, while those who have not yet learned what knowledge is claim for themselves knowledge of everything. Finally, those who have never experienced what war is are the most eager to want it.[6] Just as today the world is in terrible turmoil under the rule of young princes.

55 Non statim finis apparet
The end is not immediately in sight

Herodotus in *Polyhymnia* points out that the following was often used proverbially: 'The end of something is not immediately in sight at the beginning.'[1] He says, 'And it is an old adage, in which it was correctly said, Μὴ ἅμα ἀρχῇ τὸ τέλος καταφαίνεσθαι "The end is not immediately in sight at the beginning."' This will suit the unbelievable attitudes of some people who think that the moment they have begun an enterprise they have completed it, although often the outcome does not correspond to initial expectations. There is a popular joke directed at a Dutchman. When he was told to take a draught of medicine, he asked the doctor what it would accomplish.

* * * * *

2 Jerome *Letters* 73.10 PL 22 681, CSEL 55 22–3
3 Pliny *Letters* 4.7.3. Pliny gives the adage in Greek.
4 Lucian *Nigrinus*, prefatory letter
5 Quintilian 2.12.1
6 As Erasmus propounds at length in *Adagia* IV i 1 War is a treat

55 Herodotus (see n1). Added in *1523*
1 Herodotus 7.51

The doctor replied that his bowels would move. He swallowed it down, and then, when the doctor had not yet left, shouted out that he was beginning to shit, no doubt thinking that the end was immediately in sight at the beginning. Another man with the same level of intelligence was sent by his parents to France to learn French. When he had been there for four days, he complained to his associates that he was not yet speaking the language. He thought that the very fact of going to France was alone sufficient for anyone to speak French immediately. There are also some of this type who are amazed that their son does not yet know his letters three days after he has been in elementary school and complain that it has been a waste of effort and money. The saying can be turned to serious matters. We should devote ourselves to virtuous behaviour so that at some time we can reap the best harvest for outstanding labours. We must act honourably in this life; we will have our rewards some time even if we do not get them in this world.

56 Philippide tenuius
As skinny as Philippides

Athenaeus in book twelve of *Doctors at Dinner* reveals that Philippides was a writer of comedies who was so thin that there was even an expression 'to have been Philippidesized' that meant 'to have become skinny.'[1] He cites the proverb from Aristophon: 'In three days I shall make him Ἰσχνότερος Φιλιππίδου "Skinnier than Philippides."'[2] Again from Menander:

> When your hunger gnaws away at this handsome young man,
> It will turn him into a corpse thinner than Philippides.[3]

He also cites this saying from Alexis: 'A cup thinner than Philippides.'[4] It will be witty to apply the saying to a speech that lacks substance or to an argument of pointless subtlety.

* * * * *

56 Athenaeus (see n1). Added in *1523*
  1 Athenaeus 12.552D–E
  2 PCG 3.2 Aristophon fragment 8
  3 Menander fragment 305 Körte-Thierfelder
  4 PCG 2 Alexis fragment 2, cited by Athenaeus at 11.502F–503A

57 **Quae semel ancilla, numquam hera**
   Once a servant, never a mistress

In the first book of Greek epigrams, in a poem ascribed to Palladas, a common saying is reported: Μὴ ποτε δουλεύσασα γυνὴ δέσποινα γένοιτο / Ἐστὶ παροιμιακόν.

> May she who has once been a servant never become a mistress,
> As the proverb says.[1]

The reason for the saying seems to be that those who are elevated from low fortune to high are usually more arrogant than others and more insufferable than those who are born to good fortune.

58 **Exurere mare**
   To burn up the sea

We have suggested that ἀδύνατα 'impossible things' are generally closely related to proverbs.[1] Of such a kind is the one that Virgil uses in book nine of the *Aeneid*: 'Turnus will be able to burn up the seas before he burns sacred pines.'[2]
   Not dissimilar is what Propertius says:

> Sooner will you be able to dry up the waves of the sea
> And draw down the lofty stars with mortal hand.[3]

* * * * *

57 *Anthologia Palatina* (see n1). Added in 1523
   1 This is now *Anthologia Palatina* 10.48.1–2. The epigram appears in book 1 of a collection of epigrams published by the Aldine press in 1521 (*Florilegium diversorum epigrammatum in septem libros* . . .). In Erasmus' lifetime it was the Planudean anthology that was known and published (the *editio princeps* was published in 1494). Palladas was a Greek epigrammatist of the fourth century AD.

58 Virgil (see n2). Added in 1523
   1 CWE 31 22 *Introduction* xiii
   2 Virgil *Aeneid* 9.115–16
   3 Propertius 2.32.49–50

59 Oboedientia felicitatis mater
Obedience is the mother of prosperity

Aeschylus in *Seven against Thebes*:

> For Obedience is the mother of Prosperity,
> The wife of Jupiter the Saviour, as the saying goes.[1]

The poet imagines that Jupiter, through whose kindness we are kept safe, is called Saviour, and that he has a wife called Πειθαρχία (this means 'obedience,' but literally the obedience we show to magistrates and princes). From their union was born a daughter called Εὐπραξία 'Prosperity.' It is the duty of a prince to concern himself with the safety of his citizens; he attempts to do this by good and just laws. It is the duty of the people to obey these if it wishes to be prosperous. I only wish, however, that princes were not Jupiter Ὀλέθριος 'Destroyer,' whose wife is Ἁρπυῖα 'Plunderer' and whose daughter is Δυστυχία 'Misfortune.'

60 Ver ex anno tollere
To remove spring from the year

Ἐκ τοῦ ἐνιαυτοῦ τὸ ἔαρ ἐξαιρεῖν, To remove spring from the year. This was said of anyone who dispensed with the most important part of some task. Herodotus mentions this in his book entitled *Polyhymnia*. The Spartans and the Athenians sent envoys to Sicily and asked Gelon of Syracuse for an alliance and support against Xerxes, who was waging war on Greece. Gelon agreed, provided that they appointed him as commander-in-chief of the navy or of the land forces. When the envoys refused this condition, he told them to leave and to tell the Greeks 'that they themselves had removed spring from the year,'[1] obviously suggesting that his army was the outstanding flower and strength of the Greeks, and that without it they

* * * * *

59 Aeschylus (see n1). Added in 1523
1 Aeschylus *Septem contra Thebas* 224–5: Πειθαρχία γάρ ἐστι τῆς Εὐπραξίας / Μήτηρ, γυνὴ Σωτῆρος, ὧδ᾽ ἔχει λόγος.

60 Herodotus (see n1). Added in 1523
1 Herodotus 7.162

would lack what was essential. For spring is the most important part of the year. In the third book of his *Rhetoric* Aristotle mentions 'spring' as a type of metaphor.[2] Again, in the first book of his *Rhetoric* he points out that this was a saying used by Pericles in the funeral oration. Pericles said:

> The youth of the state have been lost, just as if spring were removed from the year.[3]

The adage can be used in a more oblique way if we say that those who remove the knowledge of languages and literature from the schools are removing spring from the year.

61 Etiam si Cato dicat
Even if Cato were to say it

Plutarch in his *Life of Cato* tells us that Cato commanded so much trust and influence in the minds of the people that there was a proverb about unbelievable things: Τοῦτο μὲν οὐδὲ Κάτωνος λέγοντος πιθανόν ἐστίν 'This cannot be believed, even if Cato were saying it.'[1] And when a certain orator was saying by way of hyperbole that no witness should be believed, he added, 'Not even Cato.'[2] Marcus Tullius in a letter to Atticus, book two: 'What of that Cato of ours, who on his own I think is as good as a hundred thousand?'[3] Among the Athenians Aristides had the same kind of influence, as did Xenocrates, who was the only person granted dispensation from taking an oath, although no other witness was accepted without an oath.[4] Related to this adage is *Nec iurato istuc crediturus sim* 'Even

* * * * *

2 Aristotle *Rhetoric* 3.10 (1411a1–4)
3 Aristotle *Rhetoric* 1.7 (1365a31–3). Both of these citations from Aristotle were added in *1533*; see *Adagia* IV viii 4n (354 below).

61 Plutarch (see n1). Otto 360. Added in *1523*
1 Plutarch *Cato the Younger* 19.4
2 Cf Jerome *Adversus Rufinum* 2.24 4 PL 23 468. This sentence was added in *1533*.
3 Cicero *Ad Atticum* 2.5.1, also added in *1533*
4 See Diogenes Laertius 4.7. The reference to Xenocrates was added in *1533*.

were he on oath I would not believe that.'[5]

62 Decipienti semel
A once-deceiver

I suspect that there was a common saying among the Italians, reported by
Giovanni Campano, a great man of his age and one of remarkable abilities,
in his *On Avoiding Ingratitude*, book two: *Decipienti me semel dii male faxint,
faxintque bene si bis idem deceperit* 'May the gods damn the man who deceives
me once, and bless him if he does it twice.'[1] It may be right to blame the
perfidy of a deceiver if you are tricked on one occasion, but the man who
has experienced this once and then again trusts the same person may seem
to deserve to be tricked. It is closely related to an expression we have noted
elsewhere, 'He wrongly rails at Neptune who suffers shipwreck twice.'[2]
Since Campano was a man of wide and learned reading, it may be that
he came across this saying when it was cited in some work. For with few
changes these words seem to be two senarii: *Decipienti semel me, dii faxint
male / Faxintque bene si bis idem deceperit.*[3]

And Campano himself adduces it as an old proverb, although even
what has come into being in living memory can be termed 'old.'

* * * * *

5 This also appears at the end of *Adagia* I viii 23 A man with whom you could
   play morra in the dark, but is not given the status of an independent adage.
   Cf Plautus *Amphitryo* 437 'I think he'll put less trust in you on oath than on
   me not on oath.'

62 Campano (see n1). Suringar 51. Added in *1523*
 1 Iohannes Campanus *De ingratitudine fugienda ... libri tres* (*Opera*, Rome 1495,
   c iiii[r]). On Campano (1429–77), the famous Italian humanist, see DBI 17:424–9
   and CEBR 1:252.
 2 Not as an independent adage but in Erasmus' discussion of *Adagia* I v 8 To
   stumble twice over the same stone. The line is quoted by Aulus Gellius *Noctes
   Atticae* 17.14.4 in a group of the sayings of Publilius Syrus. This one is no 331
   in the Loeb edition (*Minor Latin Poets*).
 3 Erasmus' point is that if the words were originally in verse (iambic senarii)
   they might go back to antiquity. The only change that Erasmus has made from
   Campano's text is to have exchanged the position of *faxint* and *male* in the first
   line. The second line, however, is a flawed senarius.

63 Qualis hera, tales pedissequae
Like mistress, like maids

'Like father, like son,' a distortion of part of the Athanasian Creed,[1] is
a common saying even today.[2] Very like it is an extremely old adage in
book five, letter eleven of Cicero's *Letters to Atticus*.[3] He says, 'If the saying Ὁποία ἡ δέσποινα, τοῖαι καὶ θεραπαινίδες "Like mistress, like maids," is
true.' And yet this is not far from being a senarius: Δέσποιν᾽ ὁποῖα τοῖαι καὶ
θεραπαινίδες.[4] Plato in book four of the *Republic*: 'Does not always like attract like?'[5]

64 Bibere mandragoram
To drink mandrake

Mandrake has a soporific power so that too large a draught made from it
is even fatal, if we believe Pliny in book twenty-five, chapter eleven, of
his *History of the World*.[1] Dioscorides informs us that the root is boiled in

* * * * *

63 Diogenianus 3.51, where the proverb is given in the form 'As is the mistress,
so is her bitch.' Erasmus follows the fuller form of the proverb as it is to be
found in early editions of Cicero. Modern editions of Cicero give only the first
part of the proverb: 'As the mistress.' Tilley M 1022 Like mistress, like maid.
Added in *1523*

1 Athanasius *Symbolon* PG 28 1582

2 Suringar 182

3 Cicero *Ad Atticum* 5.11.5. Cicero's cites only the first three words of the Greek
quotation. The final three were added in early editions, but are omitted in
modern editions.

4 As often, Erasmus calls the verse a senarius when, more strictly, he means an
iambic trimeter. Again, as often, he seems eager to suggest that the expression
originally appeared in Greek poetry (including drama).

5 Plato *Republic* 4.425C: Ἦ οὐκ ἀεὶ τὸ ὅμοιον ὂν ὅμοιον παρακαλεῖ; Added in *1528*

64 Pliny (see n1). Tilley J 101 To drink the juice of mandrake. Added in *1523*.
'Dioscorides ... lover's potion' was added in *1528*, as was 'Similarly, those
who sleep ... effects of mandrake.'

1 Pliny *Naturalis historia* 25.150. For Erasmus' reference to chapter eleven see
Adagia IV iii 3 n3 (5–6 above). Here, however, 'eleven' may be an error for
'thirteen' even in Erasmus' system of enumeration.

wine, the liquid being reduced down to one-third, and that a draught of
the strained juice is taken for insomnia.[2] It is also given to those undergo-
ing surgery to combat the intolerable pain. In fact if the root is inserted in
the rectum, in a pellet form like an acorn, it produces sleep. Pythagoras described this plant as 'anthropomorphic' because its root resembles a human
form. Because of this Columella calls it 'half human' in a verse:

> Although fertilized by the insane herb of the half-human mandrake
> It produces flowers.[3]

It is also called 'Circean' because it is thought to be useful as a lover's
potion.[4] Because of its effects those who are idle at their task and doze off
are said to have drunk a lot of mandrake. Julian used it in this way in a letter
to Callixenes: 'Do you not think that he has drunk a lot of mandrake?'[5] Demosthenes also uses it in the fourth *Philippic*: 'We seem like those who have
drunk mandrake or another, similar drug.'[6] Similarly, those who fall asleep
while working are said 'to be sleeping under the effect of mandrake.' Lucian in *Timon*: 'Since you are sleeping under the effects of mandrake.'[7] This
is not unlike the proverb that we have given elsewhere, 'Drink hellebore.'[8]

65 Ne pictum quidem vidit
He has not even seen a picture of it

We say of someone who is quite unknown to us, 'I do not know if he has
even been born.' A similar expression is 'He has not seen even a picture of
it.' For we have some knowledge of many cities, objects, and even persons
that we have never seen from pictures. Marcus Tullius in the final book of
Definitions of Good and Evil: 'You say that all the same things are both good

* * * * *

2 Dioscorides *De materia medica* 4.75.3 which Erasmus follows down to 'resembles a human form'
3 Columella *Res rustica* 10.19–20
4 Cf Propertius 2.1.53; from Circe the sorceress in the *Odyssey*.
5 Julian *Letters* 42 (Loeb); *Letters* 81 in the Budé edition by J. Bidez
6 Demosthenes *Philippics* 4.6
7 Lucian *Timon* 2
8 *Adagia* I viii 51

65 Cicero (see n1). Otto 1414. Suringar 148. Added in 1523

and evil. This is said by those who, as the saying goes, have never seen even a picture of a philosopher.'[1] Plautus in the *Comedy of Asses*: 'I have never seen the representation of a pimp acting honourably, either in sculpture or in painting or in poetry.'[2] The adage will be even more attractive if it is used in a less literal sense: 'He has not seen even a picture of Rhetoric, not even a picture of Virtue.' For pictures of these are also made.

66 Scrupulum inicere
To cast a small stone

Scrupuli are small stones that get into one's shoes while one is walking and cause the foot great pain. This is why those who cause someone to worry are said 'To cast a small stone.' And those who remove anxiety 'remove a small stone.' Terence in the *Brothers*: 'He's afraid. I've cast a small stone in the man's mind.'[1] Marcus Tullius in book four of *Definitions of Good and Evil*, at the end of the discussion: 'That's a sharp stone for me when I am leaving, but we shall see.'[2] This expression is quite similar to the one we have given elsewhere, 'To flee after planting the spear.'[3] Also Terence in the *Woman of Andros*: 'But there is still one small stone remaining that troubles me.'[4]

67 In angulo
In a corner

What is done secretly is said to be done Ἐν γωνίᾳ 'In a corner.' This is used in the gospels by the Lord Jesus Christ and can be found in Plato in his *Gorgias*: 'To live the rest of one's life, whispering with three or four

* * * * *

1 Cicero *De finibus* 5.27.80
2 Plautus *Asinaria* 174–5. Added in *1533*

66 Terence (see n1). Added in *1523*
1 Terence *Adelphoe* 227–8
2 Cicero *De finibus* 4.28.80
3 *Adagia* I i 5
4 Terence *Andria* 940

67 Plato (see n1). Added in *1523*

young men in a corner.'[1] Also Lucian in *On the Assembly of the Gods*: 'Do not whisper from now on, gods, and do not resort to corners, breathing words in each other's ear.'[2] Marcus Tullius in book one of the *Making of an Orator*: '[I allow them] to discourse about all these things in every corner so as to use up their leisure time.'[3] So also *Super tectum praedicare* 'To proclaim upon the housetops' was a proverbial expression in the gospels.[4] For we never read of the apostles shouting from the housetops.[5]

68 Calidum mendacium
A hot lie

We have said that Θερμὸν ἔργον 'A hot deed' is said of an act that is bold.[1] By a similar metaphor, *Calidum mendacium* 'A hot lie' was customarily said of a lie that was bold and shameless, as is shown by Plautus in the *Haunted House*: 'I have heard to be sure that a hot lie is the best lie.'[2] If we must lie, then we should do so brazenly. For the man who lies with diffidence is soon caught out: so Aeschinus in Terence, who says, 'I didn't knock at the door – as far as I know.'[3]

69 Muti citius loquentur
Sooner will a dumb man speak

'Sooner will the dumb speak,' in Plautus in the *Persian*, is related to those

* * * * *

1 Matt 6:5 (not quoted) and Plato *Gorgias* 485D–E
2 Lucian *Deorum concilium* 1
3 Cicero *De oratore* 1.13.56
4 Matt 10:27; Luke 12:3
5 In other words, the expression is metaphorical and can therefore be thought to be proverbial.

68 Plautus (see n2). Otto 1092. Tilley L 232 A hot (sudden) lie is the best. Added in *1523*
1 *Adagia* II v 50. Also mentioned in v ii 3 A hot heart in a cold task (599 below)
2 Plautus *Mostellaria* 665
3 Terence *Adelphoe* 641

69 Otto 1189

proverbs that express ἀδύνατα 'impossibilities.'[1] He says:

> It has been strongly enjoined upon me
> Not to say this or entrust this to any man,
> So that sooner will the dumb speak than I.[2]

70 In transennam inducere
To lure into the snare

The person who tricks by deceit 'Lures into a snare.' Plautus in the *Persian*: 'I'll lure this fellow this day into a snare by clever wiles. / The trap is set for him. I'll approach the man.'[1] It was taken from fowlers, who trap birds by scattering food in cages. Because of this even today a person who is caught through trickery is said to be 'in the snare.'[2] 'To lure into the pit and into the net,' which we have mentioned elsewhere, is very like this proverb.[3]

71 Ab transenna cibum petere
To go after food from a snare

A person who is very close to danger is said 'To be going after food from a snare.' Plautus in the *Bacchis Sisters*: 'Now this thrush is going after the worm in the snare.'[1] The words are directed at an old man who is reading a letter that was designed to deceive him. Based on the same metaphor that we have just mentioned.[2]

* * * * *

1 On ἀδύνατα see *Adagia* IV v 58 n1 (181 above).
2 Plautus *Persa* 240–2

70 Plautus (see n1). Otto 1797. Added in 1523
1 Plautus *Persa* 480–1
2 Suringar 98
3 Erasmus gives an inexact rendering of *Adagia* I x 5 To draw into the net. Erasmus may have also been thinking of *Adagia* I i 52 He fell into the pit which he had made.

71 Plautus (see n1). Otto 1797. Added in 1523
1 Plautus *Bacchides* 792
2 That is, in the immediately preceding adage

72 Omnes adhibere machinas
To employ all one's artillery

Marcus Tullius in his book of letters to Brutus: 'To my other tasks this one too has been added, that I should employ all my artillery to hold on to the young man.'[1] Also Plato in book seven of the *Laws*: 'And so we say that Ἅπασαν μηχανητέον μηχανήν "All the artillery should be used."' Again in the same book: 'Applying all the artillery.'[2] It is taken from those who attack a town or citadel with all their might, using every kind of machine and leave nothing untried.

73 Leo cordula vinctus
A lion tied up with a thread

Lucian in his essay *Salaried Posts*: 'Now I walk up and down, Λέων κρόκῃ δεθείς "A lion tied up with a thread," as the saying goes.'[1] As when a great man is bound to a prince for a tiny advantage and is openly displayed at court to show that he is part of the prince's household. For princes think that it redounds to their glory if they compel bishops or scholars to abandon their work and be slaves to the pomp of the court.

74 Sinapi victitare
To live on mustard

Those who are sour-faced and exceptionally crabbed-looking are said 'To live on mustard.' Even today this is a common saying.[1] Plautus in *Truculentus*: 'Heavens, if this fellow were living on mustard, / I don't think he

* * * * *

72 Cicero and Plato (see nn1–2). Otto 1004. Added in *1523*
 1 Cicero *Epistulae ad M. Brutum* 1.18.4
 2 Plato *Laws* 7.798E, then 7.792B

73 Lucian (see n1). Added in *1523*
 1 Lucian *De mercede conductis* 30

74 Plautus (see n2). Otto 1653. Tilley M 1333 He looks at if he lived on Tewksbury mustard. Added in *1523*
 1 Suringar 209

could be so sour-faced.'[2] Aristophanes in the *Knights* used a similar figure
in saying, Ἀκἄβλεψε νᾶπυ "he looked like mustard" and knitted his solemn
brow.'[3] The commentator on Aristophanes tells us that *napy* is a seed from
which mustard is made. It can make one's eyes water, and this is why Ennius, as quoted in Macrobius, describes it as bitter. 'He is not looking for
the bitter mustard or the tearful onion.'[4] We have spoken about onions elsewhere.[5]

75 Pueri senesque
Young boys and old men

At the beginning of the *Chiliades* we suggested that usually all expressions comprising opposites, such as the following, are proverbial: 'Great
and small,' 'Young and old,' 'Gods and men,' 'Sacred and profane,' 'Right
or wrong,' 'Speakable and unspeakable.'[1] Horace: 'Let us hasten, the humble and the great,' since he means that everyone must strive together.[2] Plato
in book seven of the *Laws*: 'Nay, as is often said, every boy and old man,
as best they can . . .'[3]

76 Omni voce
In full voice

What is asserted with the greatest vigour is said 'to be proclaimed with
full voice or with the whole voice.' For intense feeling usually makes us

* * * * *

2 Plautus *Truculentus* 315–16
3 Aristophanes *Knights* 631. The commentator referred to is probably the ancient
   scholiast (see *Adagia* IV v 11 n4, 146 above).
4 Macrobius *Saturnalia* 6.5.5, citing Ennius *Saturae* 12–13 Vahlen
5 *Adagia* III ii 38 To eat, or sniff, onions

75 Plato (see n3). Added in *1523*
1 CWE 31 22–3 *Introduction* xiii
2 Horace *Epistles* 1.3.28
3 Plato *Laws* 7.804D

76 Plato (see n1). Similar to *Adagia* IV vi 57 To use every kind of tone (252 below).
   Added in *1523*

raise our voice. Plato in book ten of the *Laws*: Πᾶσαν δὴ τὸ λεγόμενον φωνὴν ἱέντι 'Releasing the whole voice, as they say.'[1] We speak loudly when we are making strong assertions, and we proclaim in the loudest voice we can muster if we have very deep feelings about something.

It can be adapted to the following use. If anyone uses everything to try and persuade us, such as compliments, rebukes, promises or threats, he can be said to be 'using his whole voice.'

77 Arcus tensus rumpitur
The bow breaks if strung too tight

In his essay entitled 'Whether an Old Man Should Govern the State' Plutarch says, 'As the saying goes, Τόξον . . . ἐπιτεινόμενον ῥήγνυται "A bow, if strung too tight, often breaks." In contrast, the mind breaks when it is too relaxed.'[1] And indeed this is said to have been part of the epitaph of Theophrastus, who was extremely healthy as long as he worked, and died as soon as he relaxed:

> That you are broken once you loosen the taut bow of study
> Were the words of the prophetic bard.
> For constant toil kept Theophrastus well
> And when he ceased, he died, his body weak.[2]

78 Ne Apollo quidem intelligat
Not even Apollo would understand it

It was said of anything extremely obscure or very difficult to understand that 'Not even Apollo could understand it.' Athenaeus in book three of *Doctors at Dinner*: 'What the letter means I do not think Apollo himself understands.'[1] He adduces there also a senarius from Antiphanes: Ταυτὶ

* * * * *

1 Plato *Laws* 10.890D

77 Plutarch (see n1). Otto 159. Cf Tilley B 561 A bow long bent at last waxes weak. Added in *1523*
1 Plutarch *Moralia* 792C *An seni respublica gerenda sit*
2 The epigram is reported by Diogenes Laertius 5.40.

78 Athenaeus (see n1). Added in *1523*
1 Athenaeus 3.98F and 99B, citing PCG 2 Antiphanes fragment 120, more precisely a trimeter and not a senarius, as Erasmus terms it. This is line 15 of

δ᾿ ὅτ᾿ ἐστὶν οὐδ᾿ ἂν Ἀπόλλων μάθοι 'Not even Apollo would understand what this means.'

79 Destitutus ventis remos adhibe
When the winds desert you, use the oars

When something is not going well in the way that we wish, we must resort to other means of assistance, or we must strive all the harder when we experience misfortune. In a Greek letter that is included with Poliziano's letters, Ermolao records an adage: Τοῦ πνεύματος ἁμαρτών, φασίν, ἐπὶ τὰς κώπας χώρει '"When the winds desert you, take to the oars," as they say.'[1]

80 In pace leones
Peace-time lions

Aristophanes in *Plutus*: Ὄντες οἴκοι μὲν λέοντες, ἐν μάχῃ δ᾿ ἀλώπεκες 'Although they are lions at home, in battle they are foxes.' The commentator on Aristophanes points out that the proverb was directed at the Spartans who had been unsuccessful in war in Asia: 'They may be lions at home, but they are foxes in Ephesus.'[1] This was certainly what the comic writer was alluding to. Plutarch in his comparison of Sulla and Lysander cites this expression as a common saying targeted at rulers.[2] For this is

* * * * *

the fragment. As quoted by Erasmus, the beginning of the verse is flawed metrically.

79 Ermolao Barbaro (see n1). Added in 1523
  1 Erasmus is referring to a collection of letters by different authors including Poliziano and Barbaro; perhaps *Angeli Politiani et aliorum virorum illustrium epistolarum libri duodecim* (Basel 1522). In this edition the letter, written in Greek, occurs in book 12 (page 539). It can be found in Ermolao Barbaro *Epistolae, orationes et carmina* ed V. Branca (Florence 1943) 2.93. The letter also appears in the edition of Poliziano's *Opera omnia*, in book 12 of his *Epistolae*.

80 Aristophanes (see n1). Otto 933, 934. Added in 1523
  1 Aristophanes *Peace* (not *Plutus*) 1189–90 with the scholion on the passage: Οἴκοι λέοντες, ἐν Ἐφέσῳ δ᾿ ἀλώπεκες. On 'the commentator' see *Adagia* IV v 11 n4 (146 above).
  2 Plutarch *Sulla* 41.2 (= *Comparatio Sullae* 3.1). This sentence and what follows down to 'but also abroad' were added in 1526.

what he declares about Lysander's thriftiness: 'But if anyone else had escaped the criticism of that common saying, "Lions at home but foxes outside" ...' Perhaps in antiquity this is how powerful men gained promi-
nence; later they became lions (or an even more savage animal, if there
is one) not only at home but also abroad. The expression will suit those
who do the opposite of what they should. They are fierce when there
is no need, cowardly when the situation demands manliness. Or it suits
those who are cruel to their own people, but do not dare to act in the
same way towards their enemies, an accusation levelled by Sallust at Cicero: 'He was abusive of his friends, but he fell prostrate before his enemies.'[3] Or it will suit those who feign a gentle disposition and become
tyrants.[4]

81 Certissima paupertas
The surest poverty

Junius Columella in book twelve, chapter two, of *On Agriculture* gives a
proverbial expression: 'Therefore you should make ready containers and
arrange the articles so that each is in its appropriate place according to its
kind. And some things too should be put in smaller separate groups so that
one can more easily find something when the circumstances demand it. For
there is an old proverb, "The surest poverty of all." This is when you need
something and cannot make use of it because you do not know where it
has been put.'[1]

    So much for Columella. His view, if I am not mistaken, is that if a
person cannot find something he has in his possession when he needs to
use it, he is more needy than if he did not possess it at all. For the man who
does not possess what he needs asks someone to lend it to him. But when
a man possesses something that has to be used immediately and does not
know where it is, we can say that not only does he not possess it but also
that he cannot use someone else's.[2]

* * * * *

3 Pseudo-Sallust *In Ciceronem invectiva* 3.5
4 The final sentence was added in *1526*.

81 Columella (see n1). Otto 1359. Added in *1523*
1 Columella *Res rustica* 12.2.3
2 Because he has not made arrangements ahead of time to borrow it

82 Mercator, naviga et expone
Merchant, just sail in and sell

Strabo in book fourteen of his *Geography* records the following proverb:
Ἔμπορε, κατάπλευσον, ἐξελοῦ, πάντα πέπραται 'Merchant, just sail in, unload,
and everything is as good as sold.'[1] He says that it originated with the
Cilicians, who were once pirates and whose chief profit came from selling
slaves, the location of Cilicia being suitable for easily taking captives and
selling them very quickly. For Delos, which was nearby, had a huge market
with wealthy buyers, and many thousands of slaves could be sold there in
lots for ready cash and shipped off on the same day. An additional reason
was that the Romans had become very rich after conquering Carthage and
Corinth and had begun to use more slaves.

   If the proverb has any relevance beyond its historical context, we can
use it whenever we want to point out that something is so greedily desired
that no supply of it can suffice. This is especially so if what is sought is
bad, as when certain worthless and factious books are desired and excellent
authors are treated with disdain.

83 Nisi crura fracta
Unless his legs are broken

Marcus Tullius in the thirteenth *Philippic* informs us that the following was
directed proverbially at Gaius Plancus: 'He cannot perish unless his legs
are broken.'[1] Plancus had set the senate house on fire, and although he had
been exiled for this crime he later dared to return to the city under arms.
The adage was taken from those who were crucified for their crimes but
whose evil nature was so strong that they could not die even on the cross
unless death was hastened by their legs being broken. Cicero is making a

* * * * *

82 Strabo (see n1). The 1523 edition ends with this adage, which itself first appeared in it.
 1 Strabo *Geographica* 14.5.2, whom Erasmus follows in the first paragraph

83 Cicero (see n1). Otto 470. Here the expansion that occurred in *1526* (down to
   Adagia IV vi 50) begins.
 1 Cicero *Philippics* 13.12.27. The target of the proverb was Titus Plancus (not
   Gaius, as in some manuscripts).

joke that Plancus' legs had been broken when by law he did not have the right to return to the city. And yet he lived and did return. I shall give the words of Marcus Tullius:

> There follow the other tribunicians, with Caius Plancus among the leaders, who would never have set the senate house on fire if he had respected the senate. After being found guilty of this crime, he returned under arms to this city that the law had compelled him to leave. But he has this in common with very many others who are completely different from him. Nevertheless, what is customarily said, as a proverb, of this Plancus, that 'He cannot die unless his legs have been broken,' is true. They *have* been broken and yet he lives. This, however, like many other things, must be put to the credit of the eagle.

So Tullius' words. At the end there is a joke on the word 'eagle,' by which is meant 'armed band.' For the principal standards of the Romans had an eagle on top.[2] He also mentions this in his speech for Roscius Amerinus: 'But if you take pains to prove that a son killed his father and yet cannot say either why or how, and if you can only bark since there is no cause for suspicion, no one will break your legs. But if I know these gentlemen well, they will affix to your head that letter which you hate so much that you hate all letters[3] – and will do it so vigorously that you will be able to bring charges against no one except your ill-luck.'[4]

Some think that the letter theta is meant here. I have spoken about this on the proverb 'To prefix a theta.'[5] It seems to me that he is thinking more of the tau, because it looks like a cross and those who had been fixed to the cross often had their legs broken. This letter was used to acquit

* * * * *

2 The eagle was the standard of the legion. In modern editions the word *aquila* is taken to be a proper noun, referring to Pontius Aquila, tribune of the plebs in 45 BC and one of Caesar's assassins. All that follows this sentence was added in *1533*.

3 The translation of the text as printed in modern editions would be 'that letter which you hate so much that you hate every Kalends.' The letter in question that was branded on the forehead (by the *lex Remmia*) is neither theta nor tau, but 'K,' the first letter of *calumnia*, and of Kalends, the first day of the month, on which debt-payments were usually made.

4 Cicero *Pro S. Roscio Amerino* 20.57

5 *Adagia* I v 56. Cf IV x 85 The sinister letter (533 below).

defendants, but sometime a plaintiff received it as a mark of his calumny and shamelessness for having made accusations of a terrible crime that he could not prove by any arguments.

84 Cuculus
Cuckoo!

In antiquity those who had been caught out in something disreputable were called 'cuckoos,' a common term of reproach. This originated with vine-dressers who had begun to prune their vines too late and had not completed the task before this bird was heard, so that it was as if the cuckoo were reproaching their dilatoriness. Passers-by used to make fun of vine-dressers by imitating its cry. So Pliny in book eighteen, chapter twenty-six:

> In this period of time in the first fifteen days the farmer must quickly complete before the equinox those things that he has not had time to finish. He is aware that such dilatoriness gives rise to foul abuse directed at vine-pruners through the imitation of the cry of the bird that is called a cuckoo, which was seen at this time. For it was thought to be disgraceful and worthy of reproach that this bird should come upon a pruning hook on the vine. Because of this there is great sport in hurling insolent witticisms even at the very beginning of spring. However, it is thought that they should be avoided as bringing bad luck. To such an extent are even the smallest things in farming linked with the hints that nature gives.[1]

Moreover, even in this day and age we can recognize in some countries what Pliny means by the exchange of insolent witticisms. For in the spring months when the *coccyx* is heard (if this is the cuckoo as Gaza thinks)[2] married men have fun exchanging jibes, saying, 'This bird is calling to

* * * * *

84 Pliny (see n1). *Collectanea* no 171. Suringar 48. Added in 1526. 'This is a trochaic verse' was added in 1528. Everything that follows was added in 1533. Cf *Adagia* IV viii 81 Up, ye castrated, and to the fields.
1 Pliny *Naturalis historia* 18.249. For Erasmus' reference to chapter 26 see *Adagia* IV iii 3 n3 (5–6 above).
2 Theodore of Gaza, the translator of Aristotle, whom Erasmus draws on elsewhere for his translations of Theophrastus as well as of Aristotle (see n3 on *Adagia* IV iii 10 The fruit of the cypress (9 above). The Greek *coccyx* means cuckoo.

you.' They mean that the husband has not kept careful enough watch of his wife. In fact Plautus in the *Comedy of Asses* depicts a wife railing at her husband whom she has caught with a girlfriend: 'But even the cuckoo goes to bed! Get up, lover boy, come home.' Then shortly afterwards, 'Your wife is dragging you, a hoary-haired cuckoo, from the brothel.'[3] Horace in book one of his *Conversations*, satire seven:

> Then in answer to the copious streams of wit the man of Praeneste
> Hurls back abuse, the very essence of the vineyard,
> Like a wine-dresser, hard and unconquerable, to whom often
> The traveller has yielded, while shouting at him 'Cuckoo'![4]

This certainly agrees with what Pliny writes, that abuse was directed at vine-dressers if the cuckoo came upon them pruning the vine. Porphyrion explains the Horatian passage in this way: 'For peasants cutting the light (*levia*) bushes beside the road are often called cuckoos by passers-by. The pruners are provoked by this and hurl such a bitter tirade on the travellers that they yield, content to call them cuckoos over and over again.'[5]

Acron gives the following: 'We know this from the very fact that travellers often hurl abuse at vine-dressers as they pass by, and the latter respond in such a way that the travellers call a pruner a cuckoo, meaning that he is lazy, and they call this out to the guards because they are always sitting beside them.'[6] In these words of Porphyrion and Acron I see that some corruption is present.

In agreement with the latter is the Plautine passage 'even the cuckoo goes to bed' since the man who was sitting beside the girl was reluctant to stand up.[7] And indeed I think that in the insult 'cuckoo' there is an allusion to the word *cubare* 'to go to bed.' Therefore, I think that in Porphyrion

* * * * *

3 Plautus *Asinaria* 923, then 934
4 Horace *Satires* 1.7.28–31
5 Porphyrion on Horace Satires 1.29–30
6 Pseudo-Acron on Horace *Satires* 1.29–30. Erasmus follows the vulgate text of the commentary, which differs in several respects from that in modern editions.
7 This seems to pick up the last part of the quotation from Acron where the guards 'sitting beside' the pruners are called cuckoos, perhaps because cuckoos will not abandon the nest they have taken over.

one should perhaps read *lenti* 'sluggish, sleepy' instead of *levia* 'light.'[8] As for creating the form *cucullus*, a garment, from *cuculus*, the bird, as some do, this is not at all necessary since the penultimate syllable is long, as in a trochaic verse of Plautus: *At etiam cubat cuculus, surge amator, i domum* and then a little later: *Cano capite te cuculum uxor ex lustris trahit.*[9] This is a trochaic verse. In *Pseudolus* the word seems to be used as a general term of abuse: 'Why are you crying, you cuckoo? You will live.'[10] But perhaps the speaker calls the lover, who is sobbing and gasping, a cuckoo because he is making the sound of the call of the 'cuckoo' (κοκκύζω).[11] Similarly, in the *Merchant*: 'I shall not entrust these things to a son who obeys his father. / I shall not give them to this man, who is a pure cuckoo.'[12]

Also in the *Persian*: 'Thanks to you, cuckoo. / By heavens I'll have no fear if I cut your tongue out, you piece of dead meat.'[13]

85 Arator nisi incurvus praevaricatur
The ploughman is no ploughman unless he is bent

What Pliny cites in book eighteen, chapter nineteen, 'The ploughman does not do his job properly unless he is bent,' has the appearance of a

* * * * *

8 The meaning of the first part of the Porphyrion passage would then be 'For peasants lazily cutting the bushes . . .'

9 Plautus *Asinaria* 923 and 934, already cited. Erasmus is right in saying that the second *u* in *cuculus* is long. But the point of all this is not clear. *Cucullus* is the word for a cap or hood (the garment mentioned?). He seems either to be talking about the spelling of this word and arguing that it should not have the double *l*, or to be criticizing those who would like to read, for metrical reasons, *cucullum* for *cuculum* at the end of Horace *Satires* 1.7.31. The Aldine Horace reads *cucullum*.

10 Plautus *Pseudolus* 96

11 The Greek verb κοκκύζω occurs at Aristophanes *Frogs* 1380 in this sense of 'to make the call of a cuckoo.'

12 This quotation occurs in an interpolated passage that is not found in modern editions. It appeared in Giambattista Pio's edition of Plautus published (with commentary) in Milan in 1500; see *Adagia* IV iii 40 n2 (27 above).

13 Plautus *Persa* 282–3

85 Pliny (see n1). Otto p 34 note on *arator*. Added in 1526

proverb.[1] Pliny is giving instructions to the ploughman. He says that he should first break up his field in straight furrows from end to end, then afterwards plough it with furrows at an angle to these. This can scarcely be done unless the ploughman applies his whole bodily strength to the toil. Because of this Virgil too calls a ploughman 'bent,' but *praevaricari* really means 'to plough a crooked furrow.'[2] This is why those who help the opposing cause in the courts are also said *praevaricari* 'to plough a crooked furrow.' Clearly, this is what Pliny means in the following: 'Then this charge of prevaricating was transferred metaphorically into public life. One should therefore beware of using the term in its original context.'

It can be transferred to anyone; for example, a pimp who is *not* a perjurer 'ploughs a crooked furrow' and a soldier who is *not* completely unprincipled 'ploughs a crooked furrow.' It will suit a task that cannot be completed without much sweat.

86 Metiri digitis
To count up on one's fingers

A person who weighs up something more carefully than one should is said 'To count up on his fingers'; for example, if someone calculates with his friend as to which of them has performed more services for the other. Marcus Tullius in his third *Paradox*:

> I pay no attention to a poet counting up on his fingers the errors he has made in his trifling poems. Am I to pay attention to a fellow citizen counting up on his fingers the peccadilloes of his daily life? Even if these seem trifling, how can they be thought to be less grave when every kind of transgression, no matter what, is a violation of reason and order?[1]

Cicero was alluding to a custom of poets in checking the feet of their verse with their fingers. So also Horace: 'And we know the proper sound through

* * * * *

1 Pliny *Naturalis historia* 18.179. For Erasmus' reference to chapter 19 see *Adagia* IV iii 3 n3 (5–6 above).
2 The Virgilian reference is to *Eclogues* 3.42.

86 Cicero (see n1). Added in 1526
1 Cicero *Paradoxa* 3.2.26. The text Erasmus gives differs in some respects from that found in modern editions.

our fingers and our ear.'[2] However, I do not think that a poet who does not immediately detect a fault in the verse with his ear is an excellent one.

87 Salem et caseum edere
To eat salt and cheese

Pliny in book twenty-one, chapter seven, refers to a proverb without however citing it. For when he is praising salt, he also says this: 'Varro is also the source for our knowledge that the ancients used salt as a relish. For they ate salt with bread and cheese, as is clear from the proverb.'[1] One can guess that the saying was something like this: 'The feast lacked nothing; we had salt, bread, and cheese'; or 'Do not worry about what supplies you have to entertain me. I shall require nothing other than salt, bread, and cheese.' I have spoken elsewhere about 'Xenocrates' scrap of cheese.'[2]

88 In agro surculario capras
Like goats in a young orchard

Varro in book one, chapter two, of *On Agriculture* adduces this saying as a rule of farming: 'Let not the husbandman pasture goats on a young orchard.'[1] It can be applied metaphorically to persons who corrupt those of tender years by exposing them to harmful things or persons. For example, if someone brings together young nuns and lusty men, or lustful girls and teenage boys, or if someone mixes with his studies pleasures that are inimical to study. For a goat is deadly to all plants, not only through the damage it does with its teeth but also through the poison of its bite. This is especially true for the olive and the vine.[2] That is why a goat is sacrificed to Bacchus as a kind of punishment, while

* * * * *

2 Horace *Ars Poetica* 274

87 Pliny (see n1). Otto 1569 ('salt with bread'). Added in *1526*
 1 Pliny *Naturalis historia* 31.89 (not book 21), used also in *Adagia* IV iv 27 To lick salt (78 above)
 2 *Adagia* III v 33

88 Varro (see n1). Added in *1526*
 1 Varro *Res rusticae* 1.2.17
 2 Varro *Res rusticae* 1.2.18; cf Virgil *Georgics* 2.380.

no goat of any kind is sacrificed to Minerva, the reason being that Bacchus is said to be the inventor of the vine, and the olive is sacred to Minerva.[3]

89 Oportet agrum imbecilliorem esse
The land should be more feeble

Columella in book one, chapter three, attests that among African farmers there was a very common proverb of this kind: 'The land should be weaker than the farmer.'[1] This puzzling statement is explained in the following way by Virgil, in a form no less proverbial: 'Praise large estates, cultivate a small one.'[2] But it is better to append the actual words of Columella.

> One should apply moderation in everything and this should be understood to apply in particular to those about to buy a farm lest someone wish to purchase a larger property than a reckoning of his resources permits. Pertinent to this are the words of our great poet, 'Praise large estates, cultivate a small one,' since by this verse that most learned of men (at least in my opinion) gave added weight to an ancient precept that has come down to us. For it is agreed that the Carthaginians, a very shrewd people, said 'that the land ought to be weaker than the farmer' since in the inevitable struggle with the land the owner is crushed if the farm prevails. And there is no doubt that a huge estate, if not properly cultivated, gives less return than a small farm that is cared for with the greatest diligence.

The proverb will suit those who are eager to extend their dominion when they cannot administer the territory that they actually have, or those who undertake a task that they are incapable of performing. It will be in harmony with what we have cited elsewhere, 'Sparta is your portion, do your best for her.'[3]

* * * * *

3 This last sentence is based on Varro *Res rusticae* 1.2.19.

89 Columella (see n1). Otto 40. Added in *1526*
1 Columella *Res rustica* 1.3.8–9
2 Virgil *Georgics* 2.412–3
3 *Adagia* II v 1

90 Ab ipsa messe
From the actual harvest

It is not my intention to sweep up anything at all that has the appearance of a proverb and include it in this work. It did not seem right, however, to pass over a few sayings that I came upon by chance, especially if I thought that they were rather wittily expressed and were quite useful. Of such a kind is what is found in Seneca in the third book of his *Letters*, letter twenty-two: 'Shall I leave at the very time of the harvest?'[1] For he is talking about those who are constrained by the advantages they enjoy or by the hope of such advantages from extricating themselves from their occupations. It is the same as if they were about to abandon a farm when the harvest was imminent. How many there are in the courts of princes who are disgusted with their kind of life and are tortured by the longing for freedom! At such aspirations, however, their greed calls out in protest, 'Shall I abandon such great hopes? Shall I leave at the very time of the harvest?'

91 Cum sarcinis enatare
To swim to shore with your baggage

No less salutary is what was said in the same letter: 'No one swims to shore with his baggage.'[1] In other words, no one achieves freedom unless he despises the rewards of servitude. For the person who cannot abandon the recompense he receives for his employment cannot give it up. It is consistent with what we have recorded elsewhere from Martial: 'For my cap of freedom I have bartered all that I possess.'[2] Also with the fable that Horace adduces about the fox that feasted itself in a granary.[3]

* * * * *

90 Seneca (see n1). Added in *1526*
  1 Seneca *Letters* 22.9 (in book 4, not 3)

91 Seneca (see n1). Added in *1526*
  1 Seneca *Letters* 22.12
  2 Martial 2.68.4, cited in *Adagia* II i 27 To call one to his cap of liberty
  3 Horace *Epistles* 1.7.29–33. Horace's text has *cumera* 'barrel' for *camera* 'room' here. The latter is probably an inadvertent error of the printer or Erasmus' helper rather than a deliberate deviation from the text, although *camera* is a variant found in early Carolingian manuscripts.

92 Dosones
Shall-givers

Plutarch in his *Life of Aemilius Paulus* reports the story of king Antigonus, the grandson of Demetrius.[1] As a joke people called him Doso, which would be *Dabo* in Latin, because he made generous promises to all, but did not keep them. When people asked him for anything he would customarily say δώσω 'I shall give.' Similar are the χρηστολόγοι 'glib talkers' that we have spoken about elsewhere.[2] Ovid: 'Be lavish with your promises. For what harm can they do? Promises are a currency in which anyone can be rich.'[3]

The courts of princes are full of such 'Shall-givers': 'Tomorrow.' 'Come back soon.'[4]

93 Humeris sustinere
To carry on one's shoulders

Those whose authority and diligence are extremely effective in preventing someone from encountering harm are said 'To carry him on their shoulders.' Marcus Tullius speaking for Lucius Flaccus: 'On the issue of the state I say nothing. In this case you judges, I say, carry all of it on your shoulders.'[1] Ammianus Marcellinus book sixteen: 'He carried on his shoulders, as they say, the weight of the wars that were engulfing him, and was distracted by many cares.'[2] Cicero in *Concerning his House*: 'You said that you would bring me back into the city on your shoulders as guardian of the city.'[3] This metaphor is applied to those who carry the state on their shoulders (which otherwise would collapse) and are called 'Atlases of the state.'

* * * * *

92 Plutarch (see n1). Added in *1526*
  1 Plutarch *Aemilius* 8.2
  2 *Adagia* I x 54 Fair-spoken
  3 Ovid *Ars amatoria* 1.443–4, already cited in *Adagia* II vi 84 Chares and his promises and II viii 74 Wishes make wealthy
  4 Terence *Adelphoe* 204, words ascribed by a pimp to young men who promise to pay what they owe

93 Cicero (see n1). Added in *1526*
  1 Cicero *Pro L. Flacco* 37.94
  2 Ammianus Marcellinus 16.3.3. This sentence was added in *1528*.
  3 Cicero *De domo sua* 15.40

94 Arcem ex cloaca facere
To make a citadel out of a sewer

Those who exalt worthless things or persons with splendid words of praise
are said 'To make a citadel out of a sewer.' Marcus Tullius in *For Gnaeus
Plancius*: 'Now I come to that last point you made, that in extolling Plancius'
services to me I was making a citadel out of a sewer, that I was worshipping
a tombstone as a god. You said that there had been no danger of treachery or
death.'[1] So Cicero. In this passage, *lapis e sepulchro* 'a tombstone,' describing
a completely powerless person, also looks like a proverb.

95 Archimedes non posset melius describere
Archimedes could not describe it better

Archimedes of Syracuse was a very famous geometrician, always engrossed
in geometrical diagrams, so much so that he was killed while drawing one.
This gave rise to what Cicero says in his speech *For Aulus Cluentius* in the
form of a proverb:

> If, as you say, it was to win good favour, what is the point of the extra
> forty thousand sesterces? If, as we say, it was so that forty thousand sesterces
> could be given to each of the sixteen jurors, 'Archimedes could not describe
> it better.'[1]

Geometricians customarily draw mathematical diagrams in the dust.

96 Porta itineris longissima est
Going through the gate is the longest part of a journey

'The gate is the longest part of a journey.' In book one, chapter two, of
On Agriculture Varro implies that this was a popular saying.[1] I think that

* * * * *

94 Cicero (see n1). Otto 174. Added in 1526
 1 Cicero *Pro Cn. Plancio* 40.95

95 Cicero (see n1). Otto 158. Added in 1526. The last sentence was added in 1533.
 1 Cicero *Pro A. Cluentio* 32.87

96 Varro (see n1). Otto 1453. Suringar 174. Added in 1526
 1 Varro *Res rusticae* 1.2.2

it has the same sense as 'He who begins has half performed the deed.'[2]
In fact even today it is said that a man has completed a good part of his
journey once he has passed through the gate. For someone who is preparing
to make a journey can always find something to delay him. Even if there is
no business to delay him, then his feelings for his friends hold him back.
And indeed in our day and age it is thought that a journey will not turn
out well unless some days are given over to eating and drinking with one's
friends. I shall append Varro's words: 'Do you want us then to make use
of that old proverb "The Roman conquers by sitting still,"[3] until the fellow
arrives? And thinking at the same time that the gate is said to be the longest
part of a journey, he leads the way to a bench with us in his train.'

97 Deorum concio
The assembly of the gods

Θεῶν ἀγορά, The assembly (or the senate-house) of the gods. Hesychius
points out that this was customarily applied to those who spoke without restraint and with great authority, just as if they were gods speaking to mortals.[1] He adds that there was a place of this name in Athens. The expression
will suit the rich or very powerful who sometimes wish whatever they have
said to be thought of as an oracle; even though they speak in a most foolish
manner, they place great weight on their wealth and influence. It is related
to what we have recorded elsewhere, 'The springs of silver speak.'[2]

98 Camarine loqui
To speak Camarinian

Quite similar is an expression found in the same author,[1] Καμαρινῶς λέγειν
'To speak Camarinian.' It is used of speaking boldly, briefly, and solemnly.

* * * * *

2 Horace *Epistles* 1.2.40, cited in *Adagia* I ii 39 Well begun is half done
3 *Adagia* I x 29 Rome wins by sitting still

97 Hesychius (see n1). Cf *Adagia* IV i 30 Even in the assembly of the gods. Added
  in *1526*
1 Hesychius Θ 437
2 *Adagia* II iii 13 Springs of silver

98 Hesychius (see n1). Added in *1526*
1 Hesychius K 568

Its origin is not quite clear, though Juvenal lists the Camarini among the families of ancient noble lineage. 'Take care,' he says, 'that you not be a Creticus or a Camarinus.'[2] Hesychius points out that soldiers' belts were called καμάραι.[3] It is possible then that the proverb originated with the fierceness of soldiers. The same author informs us that there were some columns called κάμαροι on which was depicted a map of Asia. Perhaps it was from this display that those who behaved like barbarians were said 'To speak Camarinian.' He also points out that a couch with several canopies is called a καμαρία.

Everyone says whatever he wants to in his own bedroom. I could add more conjectures about its origin if I did not fear that those that I have already given are more than enough for the reader.

99 Glossogastores
Bellytalkers

Those who have a tongue that can be bought and say only what profits their belly were attacked by the wit of the comic poets and were called Γλωσσογάστορες 'Bellytalkers,' a word comically formed from 'tongue' and 'belly.' It will perfectly suit unscrupulous advocates or preachers whose words reek of profit or flatterers. The source is Julius Pollux in the second book of the *Names of Things*.[1] Athenaeus in book three informs us that such men were called κνισοκόλακες and κνισολοιχοί by some poets because they fawn over the smell of the kitchen and suck it in.[2] He also says that the disease was called κνισολοιχία 'fatlickitis.' So Juvenal: 'He thinks that you have been captured by the smell of his kitchen.'[3]

* * * * *

2 Juvenal *Satires* 8.38, but the spelling is different (*Camerinus*). The Camerini were a family of the *gens Sulpicia*. Erasmus' text has *sis* for the correct *sic*, restored by emendation. With *sic*, the meaning of the line is 'see that you are not a Creticus or a Camerinus on these terms' (that is, in name only, and not in character).

3 The following explanations are taken from Hesychius K 563, 569, 567.

99 Pollux (see n1). Added in *1526*

1 Pollux *Onomasticon* 2.108

2 Athenaeus 3.125D–E. From here to the end was added in *1528*. The Greek word *knisa* means 'smell of fat.' The two words mean literally 'flatterers of fat' (parasites) and 'fat-lickers' (gourmands).

3 Juvenal 5.162

100 **Pereant amici ...**
     May my friends perish ...

Marcus Tullius in his speech in defence of king Deiotarus records this verse
as one that was a proverbial: 'May my friends perish, if my enemies perish
along with them.'[1] He says that the same idea was also celebrated in a Greek
verse, but I have not found it yet. Unless perchance it belongs to the verse
a fragment of which we have previously recorded: Ἐρρέτω φίλος σὺν ἐχθρῷ
'Away with friend as well as foe.'[2] I shall append Cicero's words:

> And so when he was told that Domitius had perished at sea and that you
> also were being besieged in a fort, he spoke a Greek verse with reference to
> Domitius that expresses the same idea as the Latin verse that we have, *Amici*
> *dum una inimici intereant* 'May my friends perish if my enemies perish with
> them.' But if he had been your fiercest enemy, he would never have said it.
> For he is a man who is *mansuetus* 'civilized,' and the verse is *inanis* 'pointless.'

It will suit those who spare neither friends nor foes provided that they
satisfy their extravagant desires. But the verse is not only *inanis* 'pointless'
but also *immanis* 'cruel,' since it is a mark of humanity to allow even one's
enemies to go unpunished in order not to harm one's friends. And I would
not hesitate to contend that Cicero wrote *immanis* 'cruel,' which was corrupted by a scribe into *inanis*.[3] For *mansuetus* 'gentle, civilized' does not
contrast well with *inanis* 'pointless,' but with *immanis* 'cruel' and in this
verse there is nothing *inane*, that is, frivolous or vainglorious, but a bestial-
ity that is unworthy of a human being. Although the verse in Cicero does
not quite scan, it will do so if one reads *pereant amici, inimici dum intereant*
simul. The proverb we have recorded elsewhere. 'When I am dead the earth
can burn up,' is similar.[4]

* * * * *

100 Cicero (see n1). Otto 94. Added in 1526
  1 Cicero *Pro Deiotaro* 9.25
  2 *Adagia* IV iv 36 (84 above). This sentence was added in 1533.
  3 This sentence and the next two (down to *intereant simul*) were added by Eras-
     mus in 1528. The suggested emendation *immanis* is in fact the reading of
     the MSS, which also offer *intercidant* (for *intereant*) in the verse that Cicero
     quotes. The recasting of the line by Erasmus for metrical reasons is therefore
     unnecessary.
  4 *Adagia* I iii 80

1 Plenis velis
At full sail

Those who undertake something with all their energy and devotion are said
to be going 'At full sail' and 'with sails spread.'[1] So Marcus Tullius in his
speech to the priests concerning his home:

> When those black and stormy clouds enveloped the state, what if you had
> cast the senate from the helm, tossed the people overboard, and you yourself,
> the arch-pirate, had proceeded at full sail? If you had gone through with
> what you had then promulgated, what you had decided to do, what you had
> promised, what you had sold, which place on earth would have been free of
> the extraordinary power and authority of Clodius?[2]

So Cicero. Philostratus in his *Polemon*: 'After he heard Euphrates of
Tyre, he rushed Πλήρεσιν ἱστίοις "At full sail" to embrace his philosophy.'[3]
I have spoken more than once elsewhere about similar expressions.[4]

2 Pecunia absque peculio
Money without savings

Money without savings is precarious. This seems to have been a proverb
used by farmers in ancient times. It is given in the *Pandects* book thirty-
two, the chapter entitled 'On legacies and bequests,' the section beginning
'If a group ...'

* * * * *

1 Cicero (see n2). Otto 1856. Added in 1526. The reference to Philostratus and
the quotation were added in 1533.
1 For 'with sails spread' (*velis passis*) see Cicero *Tusculan Disputations* 1.49.119.
For the singular form (*velo passo*) see Plautus *Stichus* 369.
2 Cicero *De domo sua* 10.24
3 Philostratus *Vitae sophistarum* 25.536
4 *Adagia* I iv 17 With sail and horse; I iv 18 With oars and sails; I iv 33 To spread
the sails to the winds; II iii 24 To hoist topsails

2 *Digest* (see n1). The statement that this was a proverb taken from farming
seems to be based solely on the reference to 'old men of the countryside' in
the passage quoted from the *Digest*. Added in 1526

The words 'my moveable goods I give and bequeath' mean that money stored there for the purpose of loans is not bequeathed. So Proculus says. But money that has been put aside as a safeguard, as had been done in some of the civil wars, is part of the inheritance. Proculus also said that he had often heard old men of the countryside saying, 'Money without *peculium* is precarious,' meaning by *peculium* money that had been put aside as a safeguard.[1]

We have adduced elsewhere a proverb that warns us not to entrust all our wealth to one ship, in case there is nothing left to make good the loss if the ship goes down.[2] This is why old men often keep a sum of money separate from the rest of their possessions; they will have something left if their property is lost through fire, war, or theft. If you would like to use the proverb metaphorically, it will suit a person who does not share all his plans with his friends or a person who finds complete happiness not in material things, but in the blessings of the mind. When material things are lost by misfortune, he has something to take refuge in and is not in despair. For what properly belongs to us is called *peculium* and those things that are properly ours cannot be snatched away from us by chance events.

3 Rana cum locusta
A frog against a locust

Theocritus used this figure to express an unequal contest in his *First-fruits*: Βάτραχος δέ ποτ' ἀκρίδας ὥς τις ἐρίσδω 'I am like a frog competing against locusts.'[1] The scholiast adds that the Greek word for a frog was βάτραχος (that is, βοάτραχος) because of the rough sound of its voice.[2]

* * * * *

1 Celsus in *Digest* (*Pandects*) 32.79.1. On the legal texts used by Erasmus see *Adagia* IV ix 1n (419 below)
2 *Adagia* IV iv 6 Do not put all your wealth on one ship (65 above)

3 Theocritus (see n1). For other proverbs that describe an unequal contest cf for example *Adagia* I viii 71 Wasp buzzing against cricket; see also I viii 72, 75, and 76. Added in *1526*
1 Theocritus *Idylls* 7.41
2 The scholiast ad loc derives the word from βοή or βοά 'shout' and τραχύς 'rough.'

4 Musarum aves
Birds of the Muses

Μουσῶν ὄρνιθες, Birds of the Muses. This is how poets are described in the same eclogue, because they continuously sing their verses: 'And all the birds of the Muses, the poets who dare with their crowing / To vie with the Chian bard, are toiling in vain.'[1]

5 Ad pedes, ad caput
At my feet, up to my head

These words of Theocritus in the *Herdsmen*, relating to abundant and plentiful possessions, have the appearance of a proverb: 'Their fleeces surround me, up to my head, and at my feet.'[1] The words are those of a shepherd boasting of his wealth, which surrounds him on all sides.

6 Psydracia
Lie pimples

Theocritus in his *Aites*: Ψεύδεα ῥινὸς ὕπερθεν ἀραιᾶς οὐκ ἀναφύσω 'Lies will not grow above my nostrils.'[1]
    The scholiast adds that in Sicily those who had white pustules on their nose, called ψυδράκια or ἴονθοι or ὄνθιοι, were commonly regarded as liars.

* * * * *

4 Theocritus (see n1). Added in 1526. The adage is repeated at *Adagia* IV x 87 (535 below), where the explanation is slightly expanded.
1 Theocritus *Idylls* 7.47–8. The 'Chian bard' is Homer.

5 Theocritus (see n1). Added in 1526. The final phrase ('which surrounds him on all sides') was added in 1533.
1 Theocritus *Idylls* 9.18: Ὧν μοι πρὸς κεφαλῇ, καὶ πὰρ ποσὶ κώεα κεῖνται. Erasmus follows the 1516 edition of Calliergis in reading πάρ for πρός.

6 Theocritus (see n1). Added in 1526. The second half of the commentary (from 'as the same scholiast tells us') was added in 1533, as was 'or ὄνθιοι.' The meaning of the title 'Aites' is uncertain. Most probably it means 'boyfriend,' the younger member of a homosexual relationship.
1 Theocritus *Idylls* 12.24 and the scholia ad loc

In fact even nowadays a common saying is 'Your nose proves that you are lying.'[2] (There is a similar popular joke about the spots on nails.)[3] Indeed the Greek word for the actual pustules on the nose is ψεύσματα, as the same scholiast informs us.[4] In the poem a lover uses these rather puzzling words to mean that he will not tell any lies about his girlfriend. The Ionians give the name of ψύδρακες to several kinds of pustules.[5] The diminutive of this is ψυδράκια. Also called ἐξανθήματα, because they break out on the surface of the skin.[6] The whole idea of this is pure superstition and I think it just chance that I know someone – the most deceitful and shameless liar I have ever known – whose whole face and not just his nose was covered with pustules.[7]

7 Cum sacco adire
To come with a sack

An expression that is taken from Paulus in book forty-six of the *Pandects*, the chapter entitled 'On performances and releases,' the section beginning 'As for our saying,' sounds like a proverb. He writes: 'As for our saying that the heir should immediately pay what is due to the testator's executor before he actually receives the inheritance, some leeway as to time should be understood. For he need not come with a sack when he takes up the inheritance.'[1]

* * * * *

2 Suringar 179. There is a Dutch expression that translates as 'I can tell from your nose.'

3 For the Dutch proverb that translates as 'Spots on the nails, lies in the mouth' see ASD II-8 21:53–4n.

4 This seems to be the only evidence for this meaning of ψεύσματα (literally 'lies'). The scholiast actually says that this word was used in this meaning by the Sicilians.

5 This sentence and the next two were drawn from the *Etymologicum magnum* 819.10.

6 The verb from which the noun is formed means 'to burst out,' often used of flowers.

7 Phillips (153) suggests that Erasmus may be referring here to Ulrich von Hutten, initially a friend of Erasmus but later a bitter enemy. He died in 1523 of syphilis. See CEBR 2:216–20.

7 *Digest* (see n1). Added in 1526. From 'In Greek' to the end was added in 1528.

1 *Digest* (*Pandects*) 46.3.105. Erasmus may have misunderstood the expression 'Come with a sack.' Andrew Watson (*The Digest of Justinian* [Philadelphia 1985]

That is what we read there. There is no doubt that this was an expression commonly said of anyone who demanded that he be given immediately what he sought. (Moreover, for some things, such as olive oil or
wine, there is no need of a sack.)[2] In Greek θυλακίζειν is the verb used to
describe someone who asks for something, bag in hand, as is the way of
beggars, whence the proverb 'Beggar's wallets are always empty.'[3] And indeed θύλακος is the word for a flour sack. Hesychius informs us that this
word [θυλακίζειν = 'to beg'] was peculiar to the people of Tarentum.[4]

8 Officere luminibus
To obstruct someone's light

'To obstruct someone's light' is said of a person who obscures the glory of
another. This figurative use was taken from legal texts in accordance with
which, in order to comply with servitudes placed on estates, no one should
block his neighbour's light by constructing a building of too great a height.
So Paulus in *Pandects* book eight, the chapter entitled 'On urban praedial
servitudes,' section three. He says:

> When a servitude giving a right to light is established, what seems to have
> been acquired is a right that our neighbour should respect the light that we
> enjoy. When, however, a servitude is imposed, to the effect that there should be
> no blockage of light, we seem to have obtained this right, that our neighbour
> is not permitted to raise the height of his buildings against our wishes in such
> a way as to diminish the light that our buildings receive.[1]

* * * * *

4.721) translates the final sentence of the quotation as 'For he does not have
to accept [the inheritance] with an [already full] purse.' According to Watson,
therefore, the phrase means 'to be prosperous.' On the legal texts used by
Erasmus see *Adagia* IV ix 1n (419 below).

2 The point of this sentence seems to be that the expression must be metaphorical, necessary if it is to be regarded as a proverb.

3 *Adagia* II x 11; cf II v 24 A beggar's satchel is never filled.

4 Hesychius Θ 848

8 Cicero (see nn2, 4). Added in 1526. The final quotation from Cicero was added
in 1533.

1 *Digest* (*Pandects*) 8.2.4. On the legal texts used by Erasmus see *Adagia* IV ix 1n
(419 below).

Marcus Tullius very elegantly applied this expression to something else in his *Brutus*: 'For just as Theopompus cast into the shade Philiscus' and Thucydides' pithy though sometimes unclear mode of expression through his lofty and elevated style (and Demosthenes did the same to Lysias), so the lights of Cato were dimmed by the towering style of those who came after him.'[2]

Also in *In Defence of Caius Rabirius Postumus*, speaking of Julius Caesar: 'And he does not allow his modest[3] friend to fall. He does not dull the brilliance of that man's intellect by the splendour of his own name, nor does the loftiness of his fortune and reputation block out the radiance, so to speak, of the other's mind.'[4]

9 **Manu longa et manu brevi tradere**
To give with a long reach and a short reach

In the *Pandects* book forty-six, in the chapter entitled 'On performances,' we read as follows: 'You owe me money or something else. If I should tell you to place it within sight of me, the result is that you are immediately released of it and it becomes mine. The reason is that because no one has physical possession of that object it must be thought to have been acquired by me and to have been delivered "With a long reach," so to speak.'[1]

There is a similar figure in the expression to give 'With a short reach' in the *Pandects* book twenty-three, the section entitled 'On the law of dowries,' the chapter beginning 'Although customarily': 'Whenever a third party releases a debtor in order to set up a dowry, if the marriage does not take place, release from the debt will be void unless by chance the creditor wanted to make a gift of the whole sum to the woman. For then one must believe that it had been given *Brevi manu* "With a short reach" [= "readily"] to the woman and then given by her to her husband.'[2]

* * * * *

2 Cicero *Brutus* 17.66
3 Erasmus reads *pudentem* 'modest'; the editions offer *pendentem*, literally 'hanging,' that is, 'in danger.'
4 Cicero *Pro Rabirio Postumo* 16.43

9 *Digest* (see nn1–2). Added in *1526*
1 *Digest* (*Pandects*) 46.3.79. On the legal texts used by Erasmus see *Adagia* IV ix 1n (419 below).
2 *Digest* (*Pandects*) 23.3.43.1

These expressions will be more attractive if applied to other circumstances. For example, a man who does nothing more than give promises
and only offers hope of their fulfilment, gives 'With a long reach.' He gives
you something for you to imagine receiving without your being able to take
it away on the spot. On the contrary, the man who immediately and personally provides what he promises gives 'With a short reach.' Children do
no more than show a penny to elephants and do not dare to stretch out and
give it to them.[3] I have discussed elsewhere 'Kings have long hands.'[4]

10 Iunge trahor
A wryneck draws me to it

Those who are attracted to something by a strong and uncontrollable desire are said to be 'drawn by a wryneck.' So Pindar in the *Nemeans* hymn
4: Ἴυγγι ἕλκομαι ἦτορ 'I am drawn in my heart by a wryneck.'[1] The scholiast adds the following story. Iunx is said to have been the daughter of
Echo or, according to some, of Peitho. When she had made Jupiter lust after
Io through love potions, Juno was angry and turned her into the bird that
women have been accustomed to use in love magic, as Theocritus tells us
in the *Pharmaceutria*: 'Through you, wryneck, may that man be drawn to
my home.'[2] Because the *iunx* continuously moves its tail, some translate the
word as *motacilla* 'wagtail.'[3]

* * * * *

3 Quintilian (6.3.59) reports that Augustus once said to a soldier who was reluctant to give him some document, 'Don't give it to me as if you are giving
a penny to an elephant.'
4 *Adagia* I ii 3

10 Pindar (see n1). A *iunx* is usually translated as 'magic wheel,' but originally it
is the name of a bird, the wryneck. This was attached to a rotating wheel and
was used as a love charm. The word was then applied to the wheel itself even
when there was no bird attached; see Gow on Theocritus *Idylls* 2.41. Added in
1526
1 Pindar *Nemeans* 4.35 (56) and scholiast ad loc
2 Theocritus *Idylls* 2.17
3 The scholiast on Theocritus *Idylls* 2.17 is somewhat confused; he says the bird
was called σεισιπυγίς 'rump-shaker' by the Romans because it kept twisting and
turning its neck(!) or its rump. Erasmus here echoes the etymology of *motacilla*,
given by Varro *De lingua Latina* 5.76.2, from *movere* 'to move' and, presumably,

11 **Dii omnia possunt**
The gods are all powerful

A hemistich from Homer: Θεοὶ δέ τε πάντα δύνανται 'But the gods are all powerful.'[1] It will suit monarchs who are quick to do whatever they fancy, whether it is right or wrong. Pindar in the *Pythians* hymn three: 'The god brings everything to fruition just as he wishes.'[2]

12 **Timidi mater non flet**
A cautious man's mother sheds no tears

In his *Life of Thrasybulus* Probus Aemilius attests that 'A fearful man's mother does not weep,' a rather puzzling expression, was a common saying. The meaning is that those who in war think lightly of their enemy and believe nothing is to be feared do not take enough precautions and are usually killed, causing their mothers great grief at the loss of their sons. Quite the opposite is the man who has some fear and takes nothing lightly; he employs safer counsels and rarely comes into danger. Thrasybulus declared war on the thirty tyrants who had taken control of Athens. When he had occupied Phile, a fortress of Attica, he had only thirty fellow soldiers. Probus says:

> This was the first step towards saving Attica, this was the force that led to the freeing of that most famous state. The tyrants thought lightly of him at first [*neque vero hic non contemptus*] and had no fears about him [*neque eius solicitudo*]. Their contempt of Thrasybulus, however, led to their destruction and his victory. For they were sluggish in hunting him down, while he and his men became stronger by being given time to prepare for the fray. There is all the more cause to keep in mind the precept that nothing should be taken

* * * * *

for the second part of the word, an unknown term that meant 'rump.' Giambattista Pio (*Annotationes*, Bologna 1505, B iii[r]) did not agree with the scholiast on Theocritus in identifying the *iunx* with the wagtail, and criticized Marsilio Ficino for giving *motacilla* as a translation of *iunx* at Synesius *De somniis* 2.132.

11 Homer (see n1). Added in *1526*
1 Homer *Odyssey* 10.306
2 Pindar *Pythians* 2.49 (not ode 3)

12 Nepos (see n1). Otto 1065. Added in *1526*

lightly in war, and that for good reason it is said that a fearful man's mother is not wont to weep.[1]

However, it is quite clear that this passage is corrupt, and I conjecture that it was originally written as follows: 'But the tyrants took lightly not only him [*neque vero hic modo contemptus*] but also the small number [*solitudo*] of his followers.' The word *modo* was corrupted into *non* and *solitudo* into *solicitudo*,[2] and then corruption precipitated more corruption, just as one opportunity leads to another.[3] Probus believes that Thrasybulus himself was despised by the tyrants because he was a man of modest rank and wealth, and then the fact that he had so few supporters added even more to their contempt. We have spoken elsewhere of the strength that 'breaks its string.'[4]

13 Teuthidum more
Like squids

Themistocles, as Plutarch relates, in his *Life of Themistocles*, once taunted an Eretrian for cowardice, saying, 'To be sure, you too can only speak about war since, "Like squids," you have a sword, but no heart.'[1] Some think that

* * * * *

1 Nepos *Thrasybulus* 2.1–4. The author's name is given as Probus Aemilius in the manuscript tradition.
2 It is far from clear that the passage is corrupt. Erasmus may have misunderstood the Latin and taken the second sentence in the quotation to mean 'the tyrants did *not* think lightly of him ...' Then there would be a contradiction between this and what follows. The reading *solitudo* (for *solicitudo*, which is a variant in the tradition) is the normal reading of modern editions. Erasmus' emendation of *modo* for *non* did not find favour.
3 Literally Erasmus says 'as one handle leads to another.' For 'handle' (*ansa*) in the metaphorical sense of 'opportunity' see *Adagia* I iv 4 To look for a handle.
4 Cf *Adagia* II vi 36 For fear it break the string. Erasmus' explanation there is that this proverb is 'suitable for those who are inconsiderate, rash, and headstrong, a quality that is often unsuccessful and sometimes leads to disasters.'

13 Plutarch (see n1). Added in *1526*
1 Plutarch *Themistocles* 11.6. The point of Themistocles' remark is that an inner bone of the squid or cuttlefish is called a sword, and that these lack internal organs such as the heart, here in the sense 'courage.' See Aristotle *Historia animalium* 4.1 (524b).

squids are what we call cuttlefish.[2] And indeed the cuttlefish belongs to the mollusc family, a family that I think has no heart.[3]

14 Samii literati
Lettered Samians

In his *Life of Pericles* Plutarch cites this verse from Aristophanes, the writer of comedy: Σαμίων ὁ δῆμος ἐστιν ὡς πολυγράμματος 'The Samians are a highly lettered people.'[1]

I think that this originated when the Samians branded Athenian prisoners with the mark of an owl and the Athenians retaliated by using the brand-mark of a *samaena* on Samian prisoners. In the *Collections* I think the word is Σάμη.[2] (A *samaena* was a kind of ship, broad-beamed and with the prow having the appearance of a boar's snout. This gave rise to the following verse: 'It was a swift ship, Samian, and with the appearance of a boar.'[3] It was called a *samaena*, because it was invented by the Samians.)

The saying will suit, therefore, those who are heavily scarred and covered with brand-marks. Hesychius and Suidas also say that in Aristo-

* * * * *

2 Hesychius T 684; *Suda* T 424
3 See Aristotle (n1 above).

14 Aristophanes by way of Plutarch (see n1). This adage, added in *1526*, is mentioned in *Adagia* IV i 89 You fear the punishments of the Samians. There were additions in *1533*: 'and criminals. In the *Casina* ... about the francolin we have spoken elsewhere,' and the final sentence of the essay.

As reflected in the translation, Erasmus probably thought that slaves, criminals, and enemy captives were branded. However, it may be that in the Greek and Roman world it was a question of tattooing rather than branding; see C.P. Jones '*Stigma*: Tattooing and Branding in Graeco-Roman Antiquity' *Journal of Roman Studies* 77 (1987) 139–55.

1 Plutarch *Pericles* 26.4, citing CPG 3.2 Aristophanes fragment 71
2 Zenobius (Aldus) column 156. This unhelpful remark about a different name was added in *1528*.
3 PCG 4 Cratinus fragment 14, cited by Hesychius Σ 147, from where Erasmus draws the information about the boat. This whole parenthesis is a digression that interrupts the sequence of thought. The next paragraph picks up the custom of branding prisoners.

phanes the expression was directed at the Babylonians as they came out of a mill, marked with brands.[4] Aristotle, however, points out a different origin for the saying.[5] After the Samians had been crushed by tyrants, there was a shortage of men who could govern the state. They were compelled, therefore, to allow some slaves to share in holding magistracies. So Aristotle.

To be branded is a distinguishing feature of slaves and criminals. In the *Casina* of Plautus ('If this lettered fellow would allow me') 'lettered' is applied to someone distinguished by brand-marks.[6] Pliny in book eighteen, chapter three, calls such persons *inscripti*: 'But now these same things are done by feet in chains, criminal hands, lettered faces.'[7] About the francolin we have spoken elsewhere.[8] Some give a quite different origin for the proverb – that the alphabet of twenty-four letters was invented in Samos by Callistratus.[9] So Andron in his *Tripod*. Callistratus also gave the Ionian alphabet to the Athenians.[10] It is probable therefore that the joke originated with the discovery and spread of writing and that it was then applied to branding. For the Samians not only took from elsewhere the use of brand-marks to indicate shameful behaviour but they also passed them on to others. There was a popular joke directed at Nicanor of Alexandria, a philologist; he was called Punctilious because he wrote in great detail on punctuation marks, which the Greeks call στιγμαί.[11]

* * * * *

4 Hesychius Σ 150, the source of the information 'as they came out of a mill'; *Suda* Σ 77, where a variant version of the story is given, namely, that the Athenians branded the Samian prisoners with the mark of an owl, and the Samians in return branded the Athenians with the mark of the *samaena*

5 Aristotle fragment 575 Rose. A similar explanation is also found in Apostolius 15.32.

6 Plautus *Casina* 401

7 Pliny *Naturalis historia* 18.21

8 *Adagia* IV iii 73 A francolin's new moon (44 above)

9 *Suda* Σ 77, followed by Erasmus in this and the following sentence

10 Andron of Ephesus fragment 7 in FHG 2.348. He wrote a work on the Seven Sages.

11 See *Suda* N 375. Nicanor wrote six books on punctuation in general, as well as individual books on the punctuation in certain authors (including Callimachus and Homer). The nickname he was given (Στιγματίας) was commonly used as a word for a slave since slaves were often branded (or tattooed).

15 Samii mores
Samian ways

Σαμιακὸς τρόπος, Samian ways. Some relate it to the vice of laying false accusations because, as has been said, the Samians not only branded some people but also suffered the same at the hands of others.[1] Others prefer to relate it to a new kind of ship that the tyrant Polycrates first made in Samos.[2] Accordingly it will suit those who have certain customs that differ from those of everyone else.

16 Λακκόπλουτοι
Pit-rich

A barbarian secretly pointed out to Callias a great store of gold that had been thrown into a pit.[1] Callias killed the informant (so that he would not divulge what he knew) and also took away the gold. This gained notoriety and it became a common joke in comedies for those who suddenly became rich by crooked means to be called Λακκόπλουτοι 'Pit-rich.' Plutarch recounts this in the *Life of Aristides*.[2] Hesychius also touched on it.[3]

* * * * *

15 Hesychius Σ 147. Added in 1526
1 Erasmus' reference to a Samian vice of bringing false accusations is based on a misunderstanding of ἐπὶ διαβολῇ τῶν Σαμίων in Hesychius' explanation of the phrase. Hesychius says that 'Samian ways' was a slanderous criticism made *against* the Samians (for their being effeminate), but Erasmus has taken the words to mean that 'Samian ways' related to slanderous criticism made *by* the Samians. He then fancifully links this alleged propensity for engaging in slander or false accusations with the use of brand-marks to indicate disgrace or shameful actions.
2 *Suda* Σ 77

16 Plutarch (see n2). Added in 1526
1 The Callias named here was an official in the celebration of the Eleusinian Mysteries.
2 Plutarch *Aristides* 5.6. Plutarch simply says that the term was applied to those descendants of Callias who were rich.
3 Hesychius Λ 210

17 Abydus, Abydenus
Abydus, an Abydenian

The customs and behaviour of the people of Abydus became proverbial,
since those who brought false charges or those who were soft and effeminate
men were called Abydenians.[1] Pausanias and Suidas mention the adage.[2]
The latter points out that Abydus was a term applied to worthless things
and pure rubbish (as we have recounted elsewhere when explaining 'Stuff
and nonsense').[3] The reason, I think, is that at that time Abydus was very
unattractive because it was old and run-down. Because of this Athenaeus
points out in book thirteen that the courtesan Sinope was commonly called
Abydus because she was old and could attract no clients.[4] Hesychius tells
us that someone is called Ἀβυδοκόμας by some poet because he prided himself on bringing false charges.[5] Suidas, if I am not mistaken, somewhere
cites this from Aristophanes.[6] Zenodotus gives the proverb in this form:
Ἄβυδος πόλις 'The city of Abydus.'[7] Stephanus points out that the proverb

* * * * *

17 Pausanias the Atticist and the *Suda* (see n2). Added in 1526. 'The reason, I
   think,' to the end was added in 1528.
1 Abydus is a city on the Hellespont
2 The Pausanias mentioned here is Pausanias the Atticist, a lexicographer, probably of the first half of the 2nd century AD, and often mentioned in the *Suda*.
   There is, however, no mention of Pausanias in the relevant entry in the *Suda*
   (A 101, also referred to here by Erasmus). Erasmus could have obtained this
   information from Eustathius 357.1–6. For an edition of the fragments of Pausanias see H. Erbse, *Untersuchungen zu den attizistischen Lexica* (Berlin 1950)
   152–221. The relevant fragment is α3. At *Suda* A 101 only sycophants are
   referred to. Eustathius mentions the alleged effeminacy of the Abydenians
   (μαλακία).
3 *Adagia* I ii 43 *Tricae; apinae*, which Erasmus explains as having arisen from
   towns named Trica and Apina.
4 Athenaeus 13.586A
5 Hesychius A 225. The poet is Aristophanes; see PCG 3.2 Aristophanes fragment
   755. There is no mention, however, in Hesychius that the word is used by a
   poet (see next note).
6 Aristophanes is named in Zenobius (see n7), not in the *Suda*.
7 Zenobius (Aldus) column 1; Zenobius 1.1. For 'Zenodotus' see *Adagia* IV iii 72
   n2 (44 above).

originally applied to the Milesian Abydenians.[8] For Abydus on the Hellespont was founded by Miletus. These matters, however, are more relevant
to the proverb we have already spoken of, 'Not rashly to Abydus.'[9]

18 Ἀθερίζειν
Not worth harvesting

In Greek something that is rejected and worth nothing is said Ἀθερίζεσθαι
'To be unharvested,'[1] a metaphor taken from the top of barley spikes, which
have sharp points, are worthless, and are lost in the harvesting. In Greek
they are called *atheres*. This was noted by that marvellous scholar Ermolao
Barbaro, drawing on Galen.[2] Some think that ears that are useless and discarded are called *atherices* because harvesters and threshers ignored them.[3]

19 Manuari
To put one's hand to

Thieves are skilled in many ways, and what they do has many different
names, for example, 'to swoop on' and 'to purse-snatch.' For the same idea

* * * * *

8 Stephanus of Byzantium sub Ἄβυδοι. Stephanus says that there were three
   places of this name, and that the proverb originated with the one on the
   Hellespont, founded by Miletus.
9 *Adagia* I vii 93

18 Erasmus' main source is *Etymologicum magnum* 24.29–32, but he also seems to
   have drawn on Hesychius (see n3). Added in *1526*
 1 The verb ἀθερίζω, which appears only in the middle voice, has the sense 'to
   think lightly of.' Erasmus links it to θερίζω 'to harvest' with a negative prefix,
   and takes it in a passive sense.
 2 H. Barbarus *Corollarii libri quinque*, Item no 309 *Triticum* (fol 33ʳ in the Cologne
   edition of 1530). On Barbaro, the renowned Venetian humanist, see CEBR 1:91–
   2.
 3 The word ἀθέριξ, the plural of which Erasmus uses here in transliteration,
   occurs only in Hesychius (A 60). The usual form of the word is ἀνθέριξ and
   the entry in Hesychius may be corrupt.

19 Laberius by way of Nonius Marcellus (see n1). This adage first appeared in
   1533.

Laberius, according to Nonius Marcellus, used *manuari*, and there is no doubt that this word was a popular humorous expression.[1] Even today, since the verb 'steal' is very offensive, people use a milder expression, 'he has fingered it,' if they want to point out that something has been stolen.[2] At the same time they want to avoid an action for slander: 'See here. Are you calling me a thief?' 'Not at all, you're a hand-merchant.'

Such obsolete expressions are not without charm, if they are used at the appropriate time and if prefaced with an apologetic remark[3] such as 'as the ancients used to say' or 'to use an ancient expression.'

20 Ad coronidem usque
Right to the final flourish

Μέχρι τῆς κορωνίδος, Right to the final flourish. When we mean the very end of something. Philologists think that this was taken from ships to which something with the appearance of a beak used to be added.[1] For in Greek *corone* means a crow, while *coronis* is the diminutive form.[2] In Homer κορώνη is used in the sense of a ring or anything else that is attached to a door, being added as an ornament when everything else has been completed.[3] This is why Eustathius points out that a happy ending to anything is often

* * * * *

1 CRF Laberius 39, quoted by Nonius Marcellus 205.1–2 Lindsay. Cf also Aulus Gellius *Noctes Atticae* 16.7.3.

2 Erasmus coins the Latin verb *digitare* 'to finger' to translate the Dutch verb *vingheren*, used in the sense of 'to steal.' See ASD II-8 29:212n and Suringar 259.

3 The word he uses (προεπίπληξις) is formed from a very rare verb (προεπιπλήτ-τειν) that means something like 'to rebuke beforehand.' Here the noun probably has the notion of self-rebuke, hence 'apologetic remark.' See Quintilian 8.3.37 and *Introduction* xiv of the *Adagia* (CWE 31 28). Erasmus says something very similar to this about archaisms in *De copia* (ASD I-6 40:295–6n), where he uses the verb προεπιπλήττειν.

20 Plutarch (see n4). Added in *1526*. 'And yet *coronis* ... or something similar' was added in *1528*. 'Finally, commentators ... in the shape of a beak' was added in *1533*.

1 Eustathius 73.21–6 on *Iliad* 1.170

2 *Etymologicum magnum* 530.34–5

3 For the reference to Homer see Eustathius (see n1). Cf *Odyssey* 1.441.

described as a golden flourish. Plutarch in his essay 'On the Fortune of Alexander' tells of how Philoxenus was thrown into the Quarries (that was what the most terrible prison was called) by Dionysius, who had given him a tragedy of his to correct.[4] Philoxenus 'marked it for correction from the very beginning right to the final flourish,' obviously indicating by the line he drew round it all that the whole play needed revision. Plutarch also in 'Against the Stoics': 'From the entrance and beginning right to the final flourish.'[5]

It will be more attractive when applied to intellectual matters, for example, if one were to say 'the flourish of someone's studies' and if one were to advise someone to add a golden flourish to an outstanding enterprise or if one were to ask that a life lived in the most praiseworthy way be given a golden flourish, in other words, a pious death.

And yet *coronis* is sometimes that which is added to a work that is complete, as in Martial, 'long with many an addition.'[6]

What the Greeks call ἐπιδορπίσματα or μεταδόρπια at banquets because they are added to dinners are called *bellaria* in Latin if I am not mistaken.[7] This word will also be attractive if applied to intellectual topics, such as an addition made to a problem that is being aired or to something similar.

Finally, commentators call it a *coronis* when in a play a character ends a speech with the same metre with which he began and they note it with a mark in the shape of a beak.[8] We touched on this proverb in 'From head to heel,' but only 'In three words.'[9]

* * * * *

4 Plutarch *Moralia* 334C *De Alexandri magni fortuna aut virtute*. The parenthesis in this sentence was added in *1533*.

5 Plutarch *Moralia* 1066A *De communibus notitiis adversus Stoicos*

6 Martial 10.1.1. The phrase applies to the length of a book. The text is quoted inaccurately by Erasmus (probably from memory). Modern editions read *seraque* (for *multaque*), 'long with a flourish that is late in appearing,' as did the Aldine edition of Martial.

7 See Athenaeus 14.664E–F and Plato *Critias* 115B. See also Aulus Gellius *Noctes Atticae* 13.11.7.

8 See the scholia on Aristophanes *Clouds* 1131, *Acharnians* 971. For other uses of the *coronis* to mark scenic action see J.W. White *The Verse of Greek Comedy* (London 1912) 393.

9 *Adagia* I ii 37, where the quotation from Plutarch's 'Against the Stoics' (see n5) is given at the end without comment, and *Adagia* IV iv 84 (117 above)

21 Sine ut incolumis redeat
Let the man live

An expression in Theocritus in the *Wayfarers* looks like a proverb: 'Come, say what you want to and allow our friend to return alive / To where he came from.'[1]

Even today we say to those who rant and rave at someone with threats and abuse, 'Ah! Come, let the man live.'[2] These are the words of Lacon to Comatas when the latter had spoken in arrogant terms about himself and had hurled a term of abuse at someone else.[3] However, the scholiast interprets the passage in different ways.[4]

22 E vestigio
On the spot

It is quite common to say in Latin of something done without delay and immediately (for which the ancients used the expression *extemplo*) that it was done *E vestigio* 'On the spot.' The same figure is found also in Greek: ἐκ ποδός for 'immediately,' for example in the *Spring Journey* of Theocritus: 'He immediately (ἐκ ποδός) created the fountain.'[1] About ἐκ ποδός, which means

* * * * *

21 Theocritus (see n1). Added in 1526. 'These are the words' to the end was added in 1533.
1 Theocritus *Idylls* 5.78–9: Εἶα λέγ' εἴ τι λέγεις, καὶ τὸν ξένον εἰς πόλιν αὖθις / Ζῶντ' ἄφες. The sense is 'and don't be the death of our friend.'
2 Suringar 211
3 Lacon and Comatas are the two herdsmen in Theocritus' poem; they quarrel and then engage in a contest. Comatas insults Morson, a woodcutter who has agreed to judge the contest.
4 In addition to the explanation given here the scholiast also suggests that the word ζῶντα might come from ζέω 'to boil' and that the sense is 'allow our friend to return quickly.'

22 Theocritus (see n1). Added in 1526
1 Theocritus *Idylls* 7.6. Gow in his commentary on this passage takes the expression literally to mean 'beneath his feet.' In myths springs are often created from the stamp of a hoof or foot. The usual title of this idyll is *Thalysia* (*First-fruits*), but *Spring Journey* is also given as an alternative title in the 1516 Aldine.

'from the very bottom,' as in 'from the feet up to the head,' I have spoken elsewhere.[2]

23 Quisquis tarde venit ad coenam
Whoever comes late to a dinner ...

The scholiast of Theocritus points out that the following iambic lines were spoken proverbially:

> Whoever comes late to a dinner to which he has been invited
> Is either lame or does not contribute to it.[1]

Theocritus reads as follows: 'Are you rushing to a dinner to which you have been invited?'[2] The scholiast adds that those who have been invited to a meal proceed more quickly, while those who have not been invited go more slowly.

To be sure, someone who has been invited to dinner and has promised to come thinks it impolite to cause delay for his host. A person who has not been invited arrives late either because of a sense of shame or because his hopes of a meal elsewhere have been dashed. A guest who has contributed to the meal hurries to avoid suffering a loss if he arrives late. The man who has not contributed is untroubled by the thought of a loss and strolls along as it suits him.

24 Gargara bonorum
Heaps of possessions

In antiquity a huge crowd of people or a huge amount of objects was called

* * * * *

2 Cited in *Adagia* I ii 37 From head to heel

23 Scholiast on Theocritus (see n1). Added in 1526
  1 Scholiast on Theocritus *Idylls* 7.24: "Οστις ἐπὶ δεῖπνον ὀψὲ κληθεὶς ἔρχεται / Ἡ χωλός ἐστιν ἢ οὐ δίδωσι συμβολάς. The two-verse fragment is *Adespota* fragment 153 (Kock 3.439).
  2 The text as printed in modern editions means '... to which you have *not* been invited.'

24 *Suda* Ψ 22 and the scholiast on Aristophanes *Acharnians* 3, where the prime meaning of the word is given as 'many, a large number.' Added in 1526. 'Macrobius ... of scribes' and 'Alexis is cited' to the end were added in 1528.

gargara, the word being fashioned, I imagine, from the sound made by a huge assembly of people or by many objects being flung about. Aristomenes in the *Helpers*, cited by Suidas and the scholiast of Aristophanes: 'There are γάργαρα "heaps" inside.'[1] Also cited is a writer of tragedy (Sophron, I think) who wrote, 'Heaps of money for us.'[2] Whence comes the verb γαργαίρω which means 'to make a great noise' because it connotes a large number of people. Cratinus: 'The whole city resounds with the sound of fine men.'[3] The following verse is cited from a play entitled the *Marshes*: 'The whole house resounds with the noise of men who have been brought there.'[4]

    In Homer, however, with a change of one letter κάρκαιρε is written for γάργαιρε: Κάρκαιρε δὲ γαῖα πόδεσσι 'The earth resounded with the noise of feet.'[5] Finally, crabs are thought to be called γαργαροί because of the number of their legs.[6] Macrobius in book five of the *Saturnalia* informs us that Gargara was a mountain and that a town of that name lay below the mountain, in Mysia, I think, an area that produces great harvests.[7] Because of this anyone who wanted to indicate a huge abundance of things called it 'Gargara.' He cites examples from Alcaeus and Aristomenes, but these have been omitted through the carelessness of scribes.[8] As a joke Aristophanes in *Acharnians* joined two words meaning a great amount: 'What pains have

*   *   *   *   *

1 PCG 2 Aristomenes fragment 1, quoted in the *Suda* and the scholiast of Aristophanes (see introductory note). The Greek title of Aristomenes' play is Βοηθοί.

2 The immediately preceding quotation in the *Suda*, not used by Erasmus, was ascribed to Sophron, but 'heaps of money' is cited anonymously as being only 'in tragedy'; see *TrGF* 2 *Adespota* 442.

3 PCG 4 Cratinus fragment 321

4 PCG 3.2 Aristophanes fragment 375. The title given in the sources, *Limnai*, means 'Marshes' and was the name of an area in Athens. The correct title, however, is *Lemnian Women*.

5 Homer *Iliad* 20.157

6 Again drawn from the *Suda* and the scholiast on *Acharnians* 3

7 Macrobius *Saturnalia* 5.20.9-12 citing PCG 2 Alcaeus fragment 19 and Aristomenes fragment 1

8 Erasmus probably means that the Greek quotations were missing from the edition of Macrobius that he was using. In early printed editions Greek was added by hand, but sometimes not all the Greek was inserted. This is the case, for example, in a copy of an edition of Macrobius, published in Brescia in 1485, that has been consulted. Quite a lot of Greek has been added by hand in this copy, but the spaces left for the quotations of Alcaeus and Aristophanes at this point have been left blank (fol y ii^r). The quotation from

I endured – sandy-thousands in number.'⁹ For in Greek ψαμμοσικόσια is an expression to denote a quantity that equals the number of the grains of sand, being based on the form of numerals such as τριακόσια 'three thousand' and ἑξακόσια 'six thousand.' Alexis is cited in Athenaeus book six: 'He bellowed at his one, solitary slave to come out, using sandy-thousand names.'¹⁰ The subject is a poor man who was pretending to be rich and was showing off his apparent wealth. Although he had only one slave, he called at the door for this same person under different names, so that his guests might believe that he had a large number of slaves in his home. Macrobius mentions this composite word in the passage we have just pointed out.¹¹

25 Onobatis
Ass-rider

In Cumae a woman caught in adultery was led into the market place. There she stood on a stone so that everyone could see her. Then she was placed on an ass and led round the whole town before being led back to the stone to be once again a spectacle for all. After this she was regarded as disreputable for her whole life, and to mark her disgrace she was called Ὀνοβάτις 'Ass-rider,' because she had ridden an ass. The stone on which the woman had stood was thought of as ill-omened and cursed. The term will suit anyone known to be a prostitute.

'An ass at Cumae' was a humorous proverb that we have spoken about elsewhere.¹ I should give a note here on the severity of punishment prescribed by law in the past. In Jewish law an adulteress was stoned.²

* * * * *

Aristomenes was available in the *Suda* and in the scholia on Aristophanes *Acharnians* 3.

9 Aristophanes *Acharnians* 3: Ἃ δ᾽ ὠδυνήθην, ψαμμοσικόσιγαργαρα.

10 Athenaeus 6.230c. What is quoted, however, is not from Alexis, the comic poet, but a comment (in prose) of the speaker in Athenaeus. The misunderstanding arose because these words immediately follow a citation from Alexis.

11 Macrobius *Saturnalia* 5.20.13

25 The first paragraph, except for the final sentence, is drawn from Plutarch *Moralia* 291D–F *Quaestiones Graecae*. The adage first appeared in 1526.

1 *Adagia* I vii 12

2 Deut 22:22–4; John 8:4–5

At Rome the *lex Iulia* was a deterrent for some time.[3] For the people of Cumae the extreme disgrace stood as punishment. Nowadays for Christians adultery is a game, even though marriage is a sacrament to them. All that is missing is a reward for those who have seduced many husbands' wives! At one time unchaste priestesses were buried alive; now it is an act of piety to violate a girl dedicated to Christ.[4] As far as the proverb is concerned, however, it is reported by Plutarch in his 'Problems.'[5]

26 Monophagi
Single-diners

Μονοφάγοι, Single-diners, can be applied to mean and inhospitable persons who never invite anyone to dine with them.

Of the Aeginetans who had gone to the Trojan war many perished in battle, and more had been lost in the storm at sea on their way home. When the relatives of the few who returned home in safety received them, they saw that the rest of the citizens were grief-stricken and in mourning for the loss of their family members. They did not think it was right either to display openly their own joy or to sacrifice to the gods in thanks for the safe return of their relatives. Instead, they received the family members who had returned safely into their own homes and there they privately feasted and gave thanks. They attended to their own fathers, kinsmen, brothers, and relatives on their own, and admitted no one who was not part of their family. It is in imitation of this that the Aeginetans feast privately in their own houses for sixteen days when they sacrifice to Neptune, holding what are called 'club-dinners'; no slave is allowed to be present. Then they sacrifice to Venus and end the festival. For this reason those who sacrificed in this way were called 'Single-diners.'[1]

* * * * *

3 *Digest* 48.5
4 The first half of this sentence is a reference is to the Vestal virgins. See for example Pliny *Letters* 4.11.6.
5 Plutarch *Moralia* 291F *Quaestiones Graecae*

26 Plutarch (see n1). Added in 1526
1 Plutarch *Moralia* 301D–F *Quaestiones Graecae*. As often, Erasmus incongruously gives the Roman names of gods even though the setting is Greek.

27 **Eamus Athenas**
Let us go to Athens

ΐωμεν εἰς ᾿Αθήνας, Let us go to Athens. Plutarch in his *Life of Theseus* tells
of how the Athenians were once sore-pressed simultaneously by the savage
aggressiveness of Minos and a shortage of food.¹ They made a treaty with
Minos, agreeing to send seven girls and boys to Crete every year. Some
think that these were usually killed by the Minotaur. Aristotle disagrees.²
Since the Cretans were bound by an ancient vow, they sent them to Delphi
as human first-offerings. As they were setting out, many young Cretan boys
joined them. However, they could hardly provide themselves with sufficient
food there because of the infertile soil, and travelled to that part of Italy that
was once called Iapygia. Then they set out for Thrace and were called Bottiaeans. This is why the girls of the Bottiaeans used to sing when they had performed a particular sacred rite, 'Let us go to Athens.' By these words they
showed how much they missed the land that they had left. Plutarch gives
Aristotle in his *Constitution of the Bottiaeans* as the source of this expression.

The expression can be used whenever we regret the loss of better
fortune.

28 **Abderitica mens**
An Abderan mentality

The people of Abdera became a byword for stupidity and madness. This is
clear from an epigram of Martial in book ten: 'If you think him brave, tough,
and impervious to pain, / You have the wits of the Abderans for a brain.'¹
The poem is about a condemned criminal who took the part of Mucius

* * * * *

27 Aristotle by way of Plutarch (see n2). Added in *1526*
1 Plutarch *Theseus* 15 (who says that the children were sent every nine years)
2 Aristotle fragment 485 Rose, referred to by Plutarch at *Theseus* 16.2–3. Plutarch
actually says that the Cretans gave their own children as first-offerings to the
gods and that descendants of the Athenian youths, who had lived in slavery,
joined them.

28 Based on Martial (see n1). Otto 1. Added in *1526*
1 Martial 10.25.3–4

Scaevola on stage and placed his hand in a fire.[2] He had been ordered to
do so, however, and was under the threat of even worse punishment if he
disobeyed.

I have spoken about the Boeotians and the Batavians elsewhere.[3] In
his books *On the Nature of the Gods* Marcus Tullius points out that the Abderans were particularly dim-witted by nature.[4] And Pliny informs us in
book twenty-five, chapter eight, that the pasturage near this city caused
madness in the horses that had grazed on it, as happens with asses in Potnia.[5] The city is in Thrace, was founded by Abdera, the sister of Diomedes,
and was named after her. It is the native land of Democritus, the natural
philosopher, according to Pomponius Mela.[6] Stephanus says that the town
was named after Abderitus, the son of Erimus, with whom Hercules was
in love and who was torn apart by the horses of Diomedes.[7]

29 Maritimi mores
As temperamental as the sea

'The way of the sea,' an expression used by Plautus in the *Casket Comedy*,
looks very much like a proverb, meaning a volatile and inconstant temper-

* * * * *

2 Mucius Scaevola was one of the legendary figures of early Roman history.
  When Lars Porsenna was besieging Rome in an attempt to reinstate the last
  king of the Romans, Scaevola tried to murder him. Unfortunately, he stabbed
  Porsenna's pay-clerk by mistake. When apprehended, he thrust his right hand
  into a brazier of fire to demonstrate Roman courage. We are told that Porsenna
  was so impressed that he abandoned the siege.
3 See *Adagia* I x 6 Boeotian pig; II iii 7 Boeotian brains; III ii 48 A Boeotian ear;
  IV vi 35 A Dutch ear (235 below).
4 Cicero *De natura deorum* 1.43.120
5 Pliny *Naturalis historia* 25.94, where the name of the town is Potniae, not Potnia.
  For Erasmus' reference to chapter 8 see *Adagia* IV iii 3 n3 (5–6 above).
6 Pomponius Mela 2.29, who also gives the information about Abdera, the sister
  of Diomedes
7 Stephanus of Byzantium sub Ἄβδηρα. Erasmus follows the Aldine edition in
  erroneously giving the name as Abderitus instead of Abderus. His father's
  name is given as Erimus in the MSS, correctly emended by Meinecke to Hermes.

29 Plautus (see n1). Added in *1526*

ament. This is generally true of lovers, who are carried along by intemperate passion but whose feelings are not consistent. In Plautus a young man complains about Love which causes different moods in him:

> These are all the moods I experience. What pleases me, displeases me a minute later. Love mocks me in my errors, drives me off, hounds me, goes after me, seizes me, holds me back, tosses me away, gives lavishly, does not give what he gives. Love makes sport of me. What he has just advised he warns against. What he has warned against he makes tempting. He makes trial of me by taking on the character of the sea.[1]

Just as the sea is never at rest and its appearance continuously changes, so sailors are said to take on something of the sea's nature. I have spoken about Euripus elsewhere.[2]

30 **Pecuniae pedibus compensantur**
Feet make up for funds

Among the sayings of Cato, which are frequently regarded as proverbs, there is 'Feet compensate for money,' although I have not yet found it in that author's works.[1] But it is possible that Marcus Tullius ascribed it to him as a joke. And it is quite probable that many of Cato's sayings that he did not write down but only uttered were well known. I shall append Cicero's words from his speech *In Defence of Lucius Flaccus*:

> If you fancied fertile land, you would have acquired it somewhere in this area at Crustumium or at Capena. But so be it! There is a saying of Cato, 'Feet make up for funds.' The rivers Tiber and the Caicus are very distant from each other.[2]

* * * * *

1 Plautus *Cistellaria* 213–21. Erasmus' text varies in several minor respects from that in modern editions. The quotation is printed as prose in the editions of the *Adagia*.
2 *Adagia* I ix 62 Man's a Euripus

30 Cato the Elder by way of Cicero. Otto 1402. Added in *1526*
1 Cato fragment 73 Jordan (page 110), quoted by Cicero *Pro L. Flacco* 29.72. The expression does not occur in the *Disticha Catonis*, which Erasmus edited in 1514.
2 Cicero *Pro L. Flacco* 29.71–2

I think the meaning is as follows. If an estate is rather remote, the owner incurs more costs and makes less profit from it; but this loss is made good by the owner's feet if he does not begrudge frequent visits to his estate.

31 Ne incalceatus in montes
Don't climb a mountain unshod

Theocritus in the *Herdsmen*: 'Battus, beware of climbing a mountain in feet that are bare, / For a mountain is all thick with bramble and tare.'[1] A person who chooses a particular kind of life should equip himself for the problems he will meet lest he repent of what he has undertaken.

32 Non incedis per ignem
You are not walking on fire

Οὐ γὰρ ἐπὶ πυρὸς βέβηκας, You are not walking on fire. Theocritus in the *Wayfarers*: 'Don't hurry, for you are not on fire.'[1] The scholiast points out that underlying these words there is a proverb that was used to signify that someone was in too much of a hurry. For the shepherd in the poem wants to begin the song contest just where he is. The other man does not approve of such haste and invites him to go to a more pleasant spot.

Those who go through fire do so hurriedly and the speed renders the fire harmless. No one is hurt if he quickly draws his hand through the middle of a flame or quickly snatches up a burning coal and throws it away. A person who is in a dangerous situation is also said to be walking through fire. I have spoken about this earlier.[2]

* * * * *

31 Theocritus (see n1). Added in *1526*
1 Theocritus *Idylls* 4.56–7: Εἰς ὄρος ὄκχ᾿ ἕρπεις, μὴ ἀνάλιπος ἔρχεο, Βάττε· / Ἐν γὰρ ὄρει ῥάμνοι τε καὶ ἀσπάλαθοι κομόωντι.

32 Theocritus (see n1). This adage is virtually a doublet of *Adagia* III x 94 You are stepping into fire. Added in *1526*. The first sentence (comprising the Greek adage and its translation) was added in *1533*. The same is true for 'For the shepherd ... pleasant spot' and the final sentence.
1 Theocritus *Idylls* 5.31: Μὴ σπεῦδ᾿· οὐ γάρ τοι πυρὶ θάλπεο. Erasmus draws on the scholiast ad loc for the actual proverb.
2 *Adagia* III x 94 You are stepping into fire

33 Calamoboas
Pen-shouter

When Carneades was attacking the Stoics with great forcefulness, Antipater would not and could not confront him face to face.[1] He therefore turned to writing and published many works that were abusive in tone and foolish in content. In these he contradicted Carneades on every page. Because of this he was given in common parlance the nickname Καλαμοβόας 'Pen-shouter,' because he shouted not with his tongue, but with his pen. Plutarch mentions this in his essay 'On Garrulity.'[2]

34 Non soli Atreidae amant uxores
Not only Atreus' sons love their wives

Whenever we want to mean that a man is hurt when he experiences wrong-doing, insults, or financial loss, and that no one ought to tolerate this without punishing the offenders, Homer's line from *Iliad* 9 will be suitable: Ἦ μοῦνοι φιλέουσ' ἀλόχους μερόπων ἀνθρώπων / Ἀτρεῖδαι; 'Surely not just the Atreidae love their wives?'[1]

Sextus Coelius, cited by Ulpian, adduces this as a common saying in the *Pandects* book forty-eight, the chapter entitled 'On the *Lex Iulia* concerning adultery,' the law that begins 'If a wife.'[2] Virgil imitated this in *Aeneid* book nine: 'Such anguish touches not only the Atreidae.'[3]

* * * * *

33 Plutarch (see n2). Added in *1526*
  1 Carneades was a philosopher of the 2nd century BC who became head of the Academy and opposed many aspects of Stoicism.
  2 Plutarch *Moralia* 514D *De garrulitate*

34 Homer (see n1). The sons of Atreus (the Atreidae) are Agamemnon and Menelaus, who were married to Clytemnestra and Helen respectively. It was, of course, to recover Helen when she had been abducted by Paris that the expedition to Troy was undertaken. Added in *1526*
  1 Homer *Iliad* 9.340–1
  2 Sextus Caecilius (not Coelius) at *Digest* (*Pandects*) 48.5.14.1
  3 Virgil *Aeneid* 9.138–9

35 Auris Batava
A Dutch ear

Just as the Greeks say Βοιώτιον οὖς 'A Boeotian ear,' referring to someone who is dull and stupid,[1] so in book six of his *Epigrams* Martial said *Batava auris* 'A Batavian ear,' of someone who was dour, unrefined, and graceless: 'Are you, says he, the poet Martial, / Whose risqué jests are plainly caught / By all but those with a Batavian ear?'[2] *Batavam* 'Batavian' is the reading of Domizio Calderini, although some had read *severam* 'austere.'[3]

The Batavians were a German tribe, part of the Catti, who were expelled as a result of civil war. They then occupied the northernmost part of the coastal region of Gaul, at that time uninhabited, and also an island situated between two stretches of water, being washed by the ocean at the front, and bounded by the Rhine at the sides and back.[4]

* * * * *

35 Martial (see n2). Tilley D 654 As dull as a Dutchman. This first appeared in *1508*, where it was placed in final position, serving a purpose similar to that of a *sphragis* 'a seal' placed at the end of a collection of poems in which the author identifies himself. It retained this position in subsequent editions up to and including *1526*. After this, however, new adages that were added in *1528* were placed after this one and it lost its privileged status. Erasmus' commentary on this adage is unusual since he more frequently criticizes his fellow Hollanders; see A. Wesseling 'Are the Dutch Uncivilized? Erasmus on the Batavians and his Natural Identity' ERSY 13 (1993) 68–102.

1 *Adagia* III ii 48
2 Martial 6.82.4–6
3 The printed work of the fifteenth-century humanist, Domizio Calderini, included commentaries on Juvenal, the *Silvae* of Statius as well as on Martial. See John Dunstan 'Studies in Domizio Calderini' *Italia medioevale e umanistica* 11 (1968) 71–150. The reading of the 1501 Aldine edition of Martial is *severam*.
4 Tacitus *Histories* 4.12. The next two sentences paraphrase part of this same section. Erasmus gives the reference as book twenty since Tacitus' *Annals* and *Histories* were numbered consecutively in the printed editions of the fifteenth and early sixteenth centuries. Hence the first book of the *Histories* was book seventeen, following what we now know as book sixteen of the *Annals*. ASD (II-8 37:436–44n) suggests that Erasmus' primary source was not Tacitus, but

This tribe was not only formidable in war, as a result of much experience in the Germanic wars, but it was also very wealthy, since its resources
were not drained by demands made upon them by the Roman army. The
tribe had an agreement with Rome to supply it with only men and arms.
This is what Tacitus tells us at considerable length in book twenty. Many
scholars agree (and there are no opinions to the contrary) that the island
mentioned by Tacitus is what is now called Holland, a land that I will
always honour and revere since I owe my life's beginning to it. I only hope
that the honour I can bring to it will match the pride it gives me. Although
Martial accuses this people of a lack of any sophistication and Lucan calls
them 'ferocious,' I think that both charges can be turned into praise, if they
actually apply to us. Which nation has not been rather primitive at some
time? And when was the Roman race more deserving of praise than when
the only arts it knew were warfare and agriculture? But if anyone will argue that what was once said against the Batavians applies to what we are
now, what higher praise can be given my dear Holland than for people
to say that it abhors Martial's humour, which even the author himself describes as indecent. I even wish that all Christians had 'Dutch ears' so that
they would not grant audience to that poet's corrupting witticisms or certainly not find them appealing. If anyone wishes to regard this as 'a lack
of sophistication,' we shall gladly admit the charge, one we share with the
high-principled Spartans, the ancient Sabines, the noble Catos. I think, however, that Lucan calls the Batavians 'ferocious' in the sense that Virgil calls
the Romans 'spirited.'[5] If one looks at how the Dutch conduct themselves
in everyday life, no other nation is more humane or generous and less wild
or fierce. By nature they are straightforward, free of treachery and deceit,
prone to no serious vices, although they are somewhat too fond of pleasure, particularly of feasting. The reason for this, I think, is the marvellous
abundance of everything that customarily stimulates the pursuit of pleasure. This abundance comes partly from the ease with which they can import goods (since the country is located at the mouths of two rivers, the
Rhine and the Meuse, and part of it is washed by the ocean), and partly
from the natural fertility of the region itself, since it is everywhere inter-
sected by navigable rivers that are well-stocked with fish, and it abounds in
rich pastures. Moreover, the marshes and glades provide an inexhaustible
supply of birds. It is said that no other region can be found that contains so

* * * * *

Raimondus Marlianus, a professor at Louvain, who compiled a repertory of
names in Caesar's *Civil War*.
5 Lucan 1.431; Virgil *Georgics* 3.346

many towns in such a small area. Admittedly, they are of modest size but they are unbelievably clean and attractive in appearance.[6] Merchants who have travelled over most of the world regard Holland as unequalled for the splendour of its domestic furniture. Nowhere is there a country with a larger number of moderately well-educated citizens, though not as many as one would expect are outstandingly erudite, particularly in ancient studies. The reason is either the luxury in which they live or their greater reverence for moral excellence than for distinction in scholarship. For it is indisputable, as many examples show, that they are not lacking in intellectual power. I, however, have this only to a modest, even tiny, degree, as is true of everything else of me.

36 Κρουνοχυτρολήραιον
Nonsense-spouter

Κρουνοχυτρολήραιον, Nonsense-spouter, was the name given by the Greeks to someone who chattered on in a foolish manner. It is a comic compound formed from κρουνός, which properly means 'a rushing spring,' and χύτρα 'a pot' and ληρεῖν 'to talk rubbish.' And in fact 'pots' is a term we apply to stupid persons. The word is given by Suidas.[1] It is to be found in Aristophanes in the *Knights*. He seems to have criticized excessive chatterers with this word.[2] For some people believe that fountains are also called λῆροι, from λίαν ῥεῖν 'to flow excessively.'[3] Ulpian points this out in his commentary on the *Third Olynthiac* of Demosthenes.[4]

* * * * *

6 Here 'clean and attractive in appearance' is a translation of *politia*, which has usually been taken to mean 'constitution, way of life' (= *politeia*, a transliteration of the Greek word). I follow the suggestion of Wesseling (see ASD II-8 42:470n) that *politia* here is linked with the adjective *politus* 'polished' and means something like 'elegance' and refers to the physical appearance of the towns in Holland.

36 *Suda* (see n1). This adage marks the beginning of a group of adages that first appeared in *1528* concluding with *Adagia* IV vii 58 (316 below).
1 *Suda* K 2485
2 Aristophanes *Knights* 89
3 Taken from the *Suda* (n1)
4 Scholia on Demosthenes *Olynthiacs* 3.29 (Dilts 1.99). But this is only one of two interpretations given by the scholiast at this point. Ulpian's scholia on Demosthenes were published in 1503 in Venice.

Elsewhere we gave the proverb 'Nightingales perching on trifles' (Ἀηδόνες λέσχαις ἐγκαθήμεναι).⁵ Later, however, I discovered that in Greek λέσχαι sometimes means some public benches on which Athenians used to sit with several others when they were at leisure, chatting about anything at all. These were rather like public meeting places.⁶ As testimony this verse from Homer is adduced: 'Do you not want to enter the brazen house and sleep / Or perchance you want to go to the lounging-place?'⁷

Cleanthes wrote that these benches were consecrated to Apollo.⁸ Some call that god 'Guardian of the Meetings in the Assembly Place.'

37 Fabarum arrosor
Gnawer of beans

Κυαμοτρώξ, Gnawer of beans, was the name given to those who sold their votes at the elections of magistrates and so loitered in the election area in order to make money. I only wish that this did not happen today when the leading princes of the church and the monarch of the world are being elected. In those days the general populace hurled abuse at those who accepted money to support the candidates for office. Nowadays huge rewards are openly given to the voters at the elections of the Pope or the Emperor.

* * * * *

5 *Adagia* II ii 3. There Erasmus mistranslated λέσχαι and the true meaning is 'Nightingales making their nests in public places.' Here he does not admit to his error, but covers it up by alleging that the normal meaning of the word is only one possibility. What follows is drawn from Harpocration (sub λέσχαι); see below n8.

6 'Public meeting places' is a translation of the Greek *hemikyklia*, literally, 'shaped in a half circle.' Erasmus may be referring to the actual benches of this shape rather than its sense (by metonymy) of 'meeting place.'

7 Homer *Odyssey* 18.328–9: Οὐκ ἐθέλεις εὕδειν χαλκήιον ἐς δόμον ἐλθὼν / Ἦ που ἐς λέσχην;

8 Cleanthes fragment 543 (SVF 1.123), quoted by Harpocration, who is also the source for the title of Apollo mentioned in the next sentence. Harpocration's *Lexicon* was published in the same volume as Ulpian's scholia to Demosthenes (see above n4). It was from Harpocration too that Erasmus learned the meaning of λέσχη.

37 *Suda* (see n1). Added in 1528. From 'It is found also in Aristophanes' to the end was added in 1533.

In fact, some princes themselves openly sell offices. Can we be surprised then at the moral deterioration in civic life?

Before the use of pebbles (ψῆφοι in Greek) for voting was invented, votes were cast with white and black beans. This is why those who made their living from selling their votes were said 'to live on beans.' Suidas quotes an iambic verse, but without naming the author, as is often the case: 'No Attic gnawer of beans will judge these men.'[1]

Hesychius too mentions the proverb, pointing out that it was the custom in Aetolia for the man who drew a white bean to take up the magistracy.[2] This is why the word κυαμεύειν in used in the sense 'to vote' or 'to draw lots.' A juryman was also called 'a caster of beans.' For even in some trials votes were cast, not verbally, but with pebbles. The custom has survived right up to the present day; at Epiphany a bean decides the choice of king of the feast.[3] It is found also in Aristophanes in the *Knights*: 'We have a master with the temper of a countryman, a bean-gnawer.'[4]

It can be applied to someone who is very poor and thrifty. For it was from this notion that the metaphor was taken and then applied to those who seek election or to those who try to make a living from their votes.

38 Manci Pera
Crippleman's Pouch

There is said to have been a place near Hymettus called Κυλλοῦ Πήρα 'Crippleman's Pouch.' In it there was a temple and a fountain, after drinking from which sterile women became fertile. Suidas points out that it was also called Κυλλοπήρα, a compound word.[1] He tells us that this was a proverb

* * * * *

1 *Suda* K 2578: Κρινεῖ δὲ τούτους οὐ κυαμοτρὼξ Ἀττικός. The author of the quoted verse is unknown.
2 Hesychius K 4339, 4342, 4343
3 In Holland the 'king' of the festival of Epiphany was sometimes chosen by the drawing of beans; see ASD II-8 45:510–11n.
4 Aristophanes *Knights* 41

38 *Suda* and Hesychius (see nn1–2). Zenobius (Aldus) column 108 gives two interpretations of this phrase. The first (reading κυλλοῦ 'crooked') means simply 'A beggar's pouch,' the second (reading κύλλου, with a different accent) was a place name. Also Zenobius (Athous) 2.37; see Bühler 4.283–90. Added in *1528*
1 *Suda* K 2672

directed at those who attempted to change the natural state of affairs by some stratagem or contrivance. Hesychius informs us that in his *Centaur* Aristophanes calls a brothel 'Crippleman's Pouch,' because the place of that name is steep and precipitous.[2]

The proverb will suit those who use onions and other medications as an aphrodisiac.[3] Some people use hellebore and certain memory-aiding drugs to improve their mental faculties.[4]

39 Undarum in ulnis
In the arms of the waves

Suidas quotes this iambic line from Aristophanes: Καὶ ταῦτ᾽ ἔχοντες κυμάτων ἐν ἀγκάλαις 'And that too when they were in the arms of the waves.'[1]

Those who were in the severest difficulties were said to be 'In the arms of the waves.' For the waves of the sea do not toss in any gentle way those who are held in their embrace. The expression refers to how nurses carry round children in their arms and rock them vigorously with the result that they become quite excited;[2] for infants, however, rocking is actually pleasant by its very nature and induces sleep. The tossing of the waves is quite different.

* * * * *

2 Hesychius K 4521, citing PCG 3.2 Aristophanes fragment 283. The reason for giving a brothel this name was presumably that a brothel was dangerous to its clients.

3 See *Adagia* III iv 44 He's looking for onions; IV ii 42 An onion would be no good at all.

4 See *Adagia* I viii 51 Drink hellebore; IV v 64 To drink mandrake (185 above).

39 Aristophanes by way of the *Suda* (see n1). Added in *1528*

1 *Suda* K 2675, quoting Aristophanes *Frogs* 704, which Erasmus describes here, as often, as a senarius instead of a trimeter. The scholiast of Aristophanes ad loc identifies Archilochus as the source of the expression (Archilochus fragment 213 West).

2 The sense of the Latin is not immediately clear. The translation is based on an assumed contrast between the vigorous rocking (*agitatione movere*) of young children (*pueri*) and the rocking of babies (*infantes*), which, one assumes, would be gentle, though Erasmus does not say so. The noun *infantes*, however, is at times interchangeable with *pueri* in Erasmus' writings (see for example *De pueris instituendis* ASD I-2 36:1–8n).

40 Fluctus mutus
A soundless wave

Κῦμα κωφόν, A soundless wave, was the description of a wave that had not yet given out a resounding crash but was already beginning to swell. For at first the sea swells and the waves make no noise, but then when the storm worsens the roar of the sea can be heard at a great distance. The expression can be said of a man's anger that has not yet exploded into open abuse but is silently beginning to burn. For example, if you were to say, 'Yield to the soundless wave,' meaning 'Cease arguing lest the dispute ends up in brawling,' or 'Withstand the soundless wave,' meaning 'Keep your boiling anger in check.'

41 Caricum vinum
Carian wine

Καρικὸς οἶνος, Carian wine. Suidas points out that this was a proverbial expression – referring, I think, to wine that was weak and did not produce any feeling of well-being. Similar to 'Carian Music,' of which I have spoken elsewhere. Anything or anyone that was cheap or doleful, or troublesome or querulous was called 'Carian.' I rather think that in Suidas οἶνος 'wine' may have been written for οἶμος 'path,'[1] but Hesychius refers briefly to Carian vines as being uncultivated and growing wild.[2] For this warlike race has no time for agriculture.

* * * * *

40 The source of the expression is Hesychius K 4531. Only the first sentence draws on Hesychius. The remainder is Erasmus' own contribution. Added in 1528

41 Added in 1528. The source of this adage is the 1499 edition of 'Suidas,' whose text Erasmus follows. But the correct reading (at *Suda* K 388) is Καρικὸς αἶνος, which means 'A Carian fable' or possibly 'Carian praise.' This latter meaning may derive from the practice of Carian women hiring themselves out as professional mourners. See Hesychius K 824; *Adagia* I viii 79 Carian music.

1 Erasmus does not explain what 'a Carian path' would mean. οἶμος has a metaphorical sense of 'course' or 'strain' of a song, but Erasmus may have been confused here and taken the word to mean 'lamentation.'

2 Hesychius K 817. Erasmus misconstrues the Greek of Hesychius, whose note on 'Carian' should be translated as 'faithless and also a kind of vine.'

42 Οἰόλυκος
Sheep-wolf

Reported by Herodotus in his *Melpomene*, that is, book four. When a certain Theres was preparing for a very long voyage and his son, a youth, said that he was not going to accompany him, he said, 'I shall leave him, therefore, as a sheep among wolves.' From these words the young man was given the name Οἰόλυκος 'Sheep-wolf,' a compound formed from Greek words for 'sheep' and 'wolf.' It may be said of a man who is completely on his own and has no one to help him.

Whoever says that this is not a proverb should accept it as an appendix to the proverb we have given elsewhere, 'You have entrusted a sheep to a wolf.'[1] For in all probability that proverb had its origin in this story.

43 Ναικισσορεύειν
To squawk like a jay

Ναικισσορεύειν, To squawk like a jay. This was said of those who were eager to disparage anything. Others think that 'you squawk like a jay' was said to a person who did not actually confess to something, although he seemed to do so; for he concealed his lies with obscure and ambiguous expressions, as heretics usually do when under cross-examination. The word seems to be a compound from ναί, which has asseverative force, and κίσση 'a jay' and ῥέω 'to flow.'[1] By their convoluted loquacity they deny what they appear to affirm, and affirm what they deny. It is Hesychius who mentions this expression.

* * * * *

42 Herodotus 4.149. Added in *1528*
  1 *Adagia* I iv 10, where this story is not mentioned

43 Hesychius N 22, whom Erasmus follows down to 'seemed to do so.' The proverb 'More talkative than a jay' (*Pica loquacior*) was mentioned by Erasmus in *Collectanea* 680 *Turture loquacior* (cf *Adagia* I v 30 As garrulous as a turtle-dove) as being current in his time. See Suringar 229. Added in *1528*
  1 This etymology seems to be Erasmus' invention.

44 Cui nullum negocium erat, Harmenen muro cinxit
He who had nothing to do, built a wall round Harmene

In his *Geography* book twelve Strabo reports the following proverb: "Οστις ἔργον οὐδὲν εἶχεν Ἀρμένην ἐτείχισεν 'The man who built a wall around
Harmene had nothing else to do.'[1] It is a trochaic tetrameter. He tells us that
Harmene was a village where the harbour of Sinope was located. Stephanus
too mentions it, pointing out that it was situated in Paphlagonia and was
called by some Ἀρμήνη,[2] a form that the metre does not permit here of
course.[3] Neither writer indicates the origin or meaning of the adage. One
may conjecture that someone surrounded a village with a wall to keep out
the cold. The result, however, was that in place of a cold village he created a little town that was equally cold! I say 'surrounded with a wall,' for
the text does not read ἔκτισεν 'he built,' which the translator seems to have
dreamed up when he translated the verb as *construxit*,[4] but ἐτείχισεν, which
means 'he surrounded it with a wall.'

45 Nec animans nec inanime
Neither animate or inanimate

Πάντων τῶν τε ἐμψύχων καὶ τῶν ἀψύχων, Everything, both animate and
inanimate. This proverb, meaning that nothing is excluded, is found in
Plato *On the Laws* book eight.[1] By a similar figure we say 'young and

* * * * *

44 Strabo (see n1). Added in *1528*
1 Strabo *Geographica* 12.3.10
2 Stephanus of Byzantium sub Ἀρμένη. Stephanus refers to Xenophon in his
  Anabasis for the alternative form of the name; see Xenophon *Anabasis* 6.1.15,
  17.
3 A word having its second syllable open with a short vowel is required in this
  position in a trochaic line.
4 Erasmus is referring here to Guarino da Verona (1374–1460), a prominent
  figure in Renaissance education, who translated Strabo as well as other Greek
  authors. See Strabo *De situ orbis* (Venice 1494) fol c ii[r].

45 Plato (see n1). Added in *1528*
1 Plato *Laws* 8.830c

old'[2] and 'the vilest of two-footed and four-footed beings,'[3] 'it pleases neither gods nor humans'[4] and 'he spares neither the living nor the dead.' We
have quoted the complete passage from Plato in 'Shadow-boxing.'[5]

46 In idem conspirare
To breathe in harmony for the same thing

Εἰς ταὐτὸν ξυμφῦσαι, To grow together (*coalescere*) and become one. Plato in
On the Laws book four: 'But for each of us *conspirare* "to breathe in harmony"
and, like a team of horses, *coalescere* "to grow together" and become one,
as the saying goes, needs much time and is very difficult to accomplish.'[1]
The translator renders ξυμφῦσαι by *unum et idem efflare* 'to breathe together
as one and the same,' although the word seems rather to come from φύω
'to be born' (*nascor*).[2] It is more appealing to me, therefore, to translate it as
coalescere 'to grow together.' However, I leave it to scholars to judge. If you
yoke together two horses that do not know each other, neither tolerates the
other. Only after a long time, when they have become accustomed to each
other and become used to the other's panting, do they act in unison. Therefore, to pant together under the same yoke produces concord. And Virgil
says, 'And they train them *inolescere* "to grow together" in the dank bark.'[3]

* * * * *

2 Cf Horace *Epistles* 1.1.55.
3 Cf *Adagia* I vii 42 Vilest of two-legged creatures.
4 Cf *Adagia* IV viii 76 Neither god nor man (403 below).
5 *Adagia* IV vi 48 (246 below)

46 Plato (see n1). Added in *1528*. The title of the adage is at odds with Erasmus'
   preferred translation 'to grow together' in his discussion, reflected at the beginning of the commentary. Apparently he did not seem confident enough to
   go the full way and to reject Ficino's Latin translation of the Platonic passage.
1 Plato *Laws* 4.708D
2 The translator to whom Erasmus refers is Marsilio Ficino (1450–99), the famous neo-Platonist; see *Adagia* IV viii 97 n2 (417 below). His translation is an
   accurate rendering of συμφυσῆσαι 'to blow together,' the correct reading in
   Plato (not ξυμφῦσαι), and is followed by Erasmus in his translation of it as
   conspirare. Erasmus is wrong in his interpretation of φύω. The Greek form that
   is equivalent to *nascor* would be the middle or passive form – φύομαι. The
   verb συμφύω means 'to make to grow together.'
3 Virgil *Georgics* 2.77 (of the grafting of trees)

47 Hic telam texuit, ille diduxit
One finished the web, the other took it apart

In Julius Pollux book seven, chapter ten, a senarius is quoted, without the author's name being given (unless perhaps he is Nicophanes in his *Pandora*): Ὁ δ' ἐξυφαίνεθ' ἱστούς, ὁ δὲ διάζεται 'One finished the web, the other takes it apart.'[1]

I think, however, that we should read ὁ μὲν ἐξυφαίνεθ' ἱστόν, ὁ δὲ διάζεται (or more probably διάζετο) since ἱστούς is also inadmissible for metrical reasons.[2] Now if some Greek weaver were to explain to us the meaning of διάζεσθαι, which, as Pollux points out, has the meaning of προφορεῖσθαι 'to pass the weft across the warp' in Attic Greek, it would not be difficult to explain the sense of the proverb. I say this, for all that Suidas gives us is 'διάζομαι the warp.'[3] Hesychius casts some light on the question, when he says the meaning of διέζετο is διεσχίζετο 'he split apart'[4] (though διέζετο should be part of the verb διάζομαι. If διάζεσθαι means 'to add what

* * * * *

47 Pollux (see n1). As in his treatment of the preceding adage, Erasmus here gives more than one explanation of the Greek without committing himself to any one. Added in *1528*

1 Pollux *Onomasticon* 7.33. The reference to chapter 10 agrees with the enumeration of chapters in the Aldine edition of 1502. Pollux quotes PCG 7 Nicophon fragment 13. Erasmus does not give a Latin translation of the Greek verse. One assumes it would have been similar to the Latin of the title. Erasmus gets the name of the Greek author wrong and does not make it clear that the suggestion about the author of the verse goes back to Pollux, who says 'Nicophon, I think, in his *Pandora*.'

2 The verse (an iambic trimeter) as cited by Erasmus has a 'heavy' syllable (the second syllable of ἱστούς) where a 'light' one is required. The point of 'also' is that, in addition to the metrical problem, the singular appears to make more sense than the plural. In fact in Pollux the reading is ἱστός (nominative singular), which is therefore the subject of the verbs, the sense being 'one web is being finished, another is being started.' The other change is simply a change of tense, from the present to the imperfect.

3 *Suda* Δ 549. The significance of Erasmus' remarks is that the entry in the *Suda* does not explain in any way the particular meaning of the verb.

4 Hesychius Δ 1011. This meaning ('he split apart') is the one that is reflected in the title of the adage (*diduxit*). In his edition of Hesychius (Copenhagen 1953) Kurt Latte suggests that in Hesychius at this point διέζετο is a corruption of

remains to the weft,' the sense will be 'One person began it, another completed it.'

48 Σκιαμαχεῖν
Shadow-boxing

Σκιαμαχεῖν, To fight with one's shadow. In antiquity this was said of those who laboured to no purpose. Plato in book eight of the *Laws*: 'Moreover, if ever we have no opponent, either living or lifeless and inanimate, because there is no one to train with, surely we will not refrain from shadow-boxing with ourselves?'[1] The same author in his *Apology of Socrates*: 'I simply have to shadow-box, both defending and accusing myself at the same time since no one has responded to what I say.' Also in the *Republic* book seven: 'We shall not be like several states that nowadays, as in a dream, are inhabited by those who fight with shadows and stir up disputes about who should hold office.' Perhaps what Florus writes in the epitome of book forty-nine of Livy is pertinent to this proverb.[2] For when Scipio was fighting bravely and successfully in Africa, Cato said in the senate 'that all the others who were serving in Africa were merely shadow-boxing; only Scipio was fighting with vigour.' Julius Pollux points out in book six that those who lived a soft and luxurious life were often called Σκιατρόφιαι, meaning 'People reared in the shade,' and because of this way of life they were unable to tolerate dust and sunlight.[3] He also says that those who are completely enervated by pleasures were said σκιατροφεῖσθαι 'to live in the shade.' For luxury and lust shun light and embrace darkness and secrecy.

An amusing performance of shadow-boxing survives even up to the present time. The person who performs it takes two parts, both his own and

* * * * *

δαΐζετο, 'he divided.' If he is correct, Hesychius Δ 1011 has nothing to do with this adage.

48 Plato (see n1). Added in *1528*
1 Plato *Laws* 8.830B–C; *Apology* 18D; *Republic* 7.520C
2 Livy *Periochae* 49.16. The author of these summaries of the books of Livy's history is unknown, but they were often attributed to Florus, who wrote an epitome of Roman history.
3 Pollux *Onomasticon* 6.185

his shadow's.[4] I thought I should mention this so that the passage we have cited from the *Apology* would be more readily understood. Lucian mentions the proverb in the *Sects*.[5] See the proverb 'To wrestle with ghosts.'[6]

49 Per fluvium traducere
To take across the river

Διαβιβάζειν τὸν ποταμόν, To take across the river. This was said of those who solved a difficult problem that was too much for weaker or less clever persons. A metaphor taken from rushing streams or from rivers that are too deep to be crossed by just anyone. And so those who are stronger and more experienced put the women, children, and others who are in any way enfeebled on their shoulders and take them across.

Plato in *On the Laws* book ten: 'As I have just done, I shall pick you up and take you across the river.'[1] The speaker is the Athenian traveller, who speaks these words when he hands over his role in the debate to Clinias and Megillus and promises that he will be at hand if they get stuck in any way.

50 Gangamon
A gangamon

Julius Pollux informs us in book ten, chapter forty, that this was a kind of net that was very long and winding with many pockets at different points,[1] called in Greek a γαγγάμων, from γῶ 'capture' as the Etymologist points out.[2] He thinks it is also called a γαγγάμη. Because of this those who fish with this

* * * * *

4 A reference to farces performed before or after dinner, both in Holland and elsewhere. See ASD II-8 51:627–9n.

5 Lucian *Hermotimus* 33. This sentence was added in *1536*, as was the final one.

6 *Adagia* I ii 53

49 Plato (see n1). Added in *1528*

1 Plato *Laws* 10.900C

50 Pollux (see n1). Added in *1528*

1 Pollux *Onomasticon* 10.132 who cites Aeschylus *Agamemnon* 361. The reference to chapter 40 agrees with the enumeration of the chapters in the Aldine edition of 1502.

2 *Etymologicum magnum* 219.17

kind of net are called γαγγαμουλκοί 'draggers of γαγγάμαι' and γαγγαμεῖς. This may be the same as a seine net or something very similar. Pollux cites Aeschylus, who called a situation that was complicated and difficult to resolve a γαγγάμων, in the way that we use the term *nassa* 'a fish snare.'[3] This is why the part of the stomach around the navel is called the γαγγάμων, because a network of muscles, so to speak, seems to surround the navel.[4] Perhaps the innards of the belly are also called this because the intestines are convoluted to prevent waste material flowing out immediately.[5]

51 Sacer manipulus
A sacred band

Ἱερὸς λόχος, A sacred band. In antiquity this was used in a similar way to 'The sheet-anchor needs to be dropped' or 'It is up to the third line now.'[1] Athenaeus says in book thirteen that at Thebes a part of the army was called the sacred band and was made up of men who were lovers.[2] The Thebans' greatest strength in war rested on these men because love gives men the greatest courage, emboldening them even to the point of thinking nothing of death.

An example of its use will be if anyone were to say that today Christendom depends on a sacred band, meaning monks.

52 Postico discedere
To leave by the back door

Galen in *On Natural Faculties* book twenty-two: 'If it consists of more, Τῇ κηπαίᾳ ... ἀποχωρήσαμεν "We have retreated to (or escaped) by the back

* * * * *

3 Cf *Adagia* IV iv 88 To seek food from a fishtrap (120 above).
4 Pollux *Onomasticon* 2.169
5 Hesychius Γ 1411

51 Athenaeus (see n2). Added in *1528*
1 *Adagia* I i 24 and I i 23
2 Athenaeus 13.561F–562A

52 Galen (see n1). Added in *1528*

door," as the saying goes, to Asclepiades' position.'[1] 'To leave by the back door' is said of someone who leaves secretly, stealing away without others' knowing it. So Horace: 'Escape from your client by the back door,' something that powerful men do even today.[2] The same author also said, using a different expression, 'I shall slip back secretly into the precepts of Aristippus.'[3] Thomas Linacre, a man of incomparable learning, translates κηπαία in Galen by *per horti posticum* 'by the garden door.'[4] A house with a garden has two doors, a front and a back. The front looks out on the public street, the back door leads to the garden. Those who wanted to leave secretly slipped away through the latter.

Some people are ashamed to recant their beliefs; instead, they secretly adopt someone else's views. Others take an opportunity to sneak away from troublesome affairs. The proverb will fit such persons.

53 Utres, thylaci
Wine skins, flour sacks

Ἀσκὸς καὶ θύλακος, Wine skin and floursack. Said of someone who indulged excessively in food and wine. For ἀσκός is a skin for holding wine, θύλακος is a container for flour. In book eleven Athenaeus cites these verses from the *Hesione* of Alexis, spoken by the character Heracles:

> He asked for a wine cup and when he got it he drank
> From it again and again, draining and emptying it;
> As the proverb says, it is ever good for a man to be a wineskin
> And a flour sack.[1]

* * * * *

1 Galen *De naturalibus facultatibus* 2.6.98 Helmreich
2 Horace *Epistles* 1.5.31 and then *Epistles* 1.1.18
3 Aristippus was a philosopher who was an associate of Socrates but espoused hedonism.
4 Thomas Linacre, the famous English humanist and physician (circa 1460–1524), and Erasmus held each other in high regard. Linacre's translations of six of the works of Galen were frequently reprinted. See CEBR 2:331–2.

53 Alexis by way of Athenaeus (see n1). Added in *1528*
1 Athenaeus 11.470E, citing PCG 2 Alexis fragment 88

Similarly Horace: 'If your belly is full and your body and feet are fine, / Will the wealth of a king give any greater boon?'[2]

I have spoken quite often about drunkards and gourmandisers elsewhere.[3]

54 Ignarium dare
To give a firestone

Seneca in *On Kindnesses* book four reports this as a popular saying.[1] He says, 'To give you pain, to make you consider more carefully what you say after this, I shall give you a firestone, as we are accustomed to say.' He is thinking of flint, if I am not mistaken, which some call 'living stone,' or 'firestone'[2] because it contains within it a great deal of fire, so that it burns one's fingers if one rubs it, and it is also very heavy. And so a person was said to give a firestone if he suggested something that would cause pain and thereby deter a man from going astray. Similarly, if you tie a stone to your finger, its weight or its rubbing does not allow you to forget why you had tied it. Marcus Tullius used a similar expression in his second *Philippic* against Antony: 'Surely you are not waiting for me to stick a goad in you? If you have one whit of feeling, this speech tears you to pieces, and covers you in blood.'[3] Terence: 'Don't poke me in the ribs.'[4] Persius: 'And someone nudging the person standing beside him with his elbow.'[5] For we use such gestures when we warn someone, in the same way that we pluck someone's ear, about which I have talked earlier.[6]

* * * * *

2 Horace *Epistles* 1.12.5–6
3 See, for example, *Adagia* II ii 65 A Sybaritic table; II iii 18 Wine hath no rudder; II viii 78 Idle bellies; IV v 99 Bellytalkers (207 above).

54 Seneca (see n1). Added in *1528*
1 Seneca *De beneficiis* 4.36.1, but instead of *ignarium* 'fire stone' the correct reading is *linguarium*, which means 'money paid as a forfeit for rash talk.'
2 Pliny *Naturalis historia* 36.138 and Jerome *Tractatus in psalmum 96* 107 (CCSL 78 160)
3 Cicero *Philippics* 2.34.86
4 Terence *Hecyra* 467
5 Not Persius, but Horace (*Satires* 2.5.41). The same phrase *cubito tangere* occurs, however, at Persius 4.34.
6 *Adagia* I vii 40 To pluck by the ear

55 In morbo consumat
Let him use it in sickness

Seneca in *On Kindnesses* book four says, 'It is only five hundred denarii. As the saying goes, "Let him use it in sickness."'[1] Zeno had promised to lend someone five hundred denarii.[2] Though warned by his friends that the fellow was completely untrustworthy, he lent the money all the same, since he had promised to do so and the amount was trifling. Therefore, when creditors realize that they have lent money to someone who will not pay it back and yet do not think it worthwhile to go to court for such a small amount, they are accustomed to say, 'Let him keep it. Let him use it in sickness.' The sense of these words is ambiguous. For it can be said by someone who does not want his friend to be short of money to spend if sickness befalls him. It can also be said by a scoundrel's enemy who prays for sickness to fall on him.

56 Vel Megaram usque
To go even to Megara

This kind of expression survives even to this day. For when we want to describe something that is very valuable and that we want very badly, we say, 'For this I would go even to India,' or 'This is so valuable that it is worthwhile to sail even as far as Ireland to get it.' Socrates in Plato's *Phaedrus*: 'To be sure what you say would be attractive and useful to the people. I for my part so want to hear it that I won't leave you even if you walk all the way to Megara and then, κατὰ Ἡρόδικον "in the manner of Herodicus," turn back again the moment you arrive at the walls.'[1]
    The meaning of the words κατὰ Ἡρόδικον is unclear.[2] For it is uncertain whether this was a saying of a certain Herodicus or whether there was a

* * * * *

55 Seneca (see n1). Otto 1138. Added in *1528*
1 Seneca *De beneficiis* 4.39.2
2 Incongruously, Erasmus talks in terms of Roman coinage although the setting is Greek. The denarius is usually thought to be the rough equivalent of a drachma.

56 Plato (see n1). Added in *1528*
1 Plato *Phaedrus* 227D
2 The phrase could mean 'according to Herodicus' or 'like Herodicus.'

Herodicus who turned back to Athens from the very walls of Megara, after completing such a long journey, either because he had forgotten something or had simply changed his mind. As a result of this he became the butt of a popular joke. (In the same way Terence's Phaedria turns back to the city at the very moment he reaches the actual cut-off for his country house.)[3] The phrase itself κατὰ Ἡρόδικον 'like Herodicus' has the appearance of a proverb, directed at someone who cannot make up his mind what to do or who is too late in changing his mind (too late, since there is need for careful deliberation before one undertakes anything).

The proverb is similar to 'Worth breaking bail for.'[4]

57 Omnem vocem mittere
To use every kind of tone

Πᾶσαν φωνὴν ἴεσθαι, To adopt every kind of tone. This was said of those who used everything at their disposal to persuade others. For certainly a person whose sole aim is to persuade others sometimes argues, sometimes upbraids; at times he flatters, at other times he promises; sometimes he threatens and assumes every kind of role in order to affect his listener. Plato in his *Laws* book ten:

> Far from it, stranger. If there is even a slight means of persuading you on such matters, in no way should one give up through exhaustion. This is especially true for the maker of laws if he is worth anything. No, rather, using every kind of tone, as the saying goes, he ought to defend the old belief, showing by his arguments that there are gods.[1]

The same author in *Phaedrus*: 'This makes it necessary for us to examine carefully all our arguments this way and that and see whether . . .'[2]

* * * * *

3 Terence *Eunuchus* 629–35
4 *Adagia* I viii 18

57 Plato (n1). This is very similar to *Adagia* IV v 76 In full voice (*Omni voce*), but there (191–2 above) the phrase is taken to mean speaking as forcefully and loudly as possible, the meaning that Erasmus discusses here at the end of the commentary. Added in *1528*
1 Plato *Laws* 10.890D
2 Plato *Phaedrus* 272D. The phrase which is relevant to the adage is πάντας τοὺς

The phrase seems to have originated in the way in which incantations were uttered; using this kind of delivery makes pleas that are not having much success more effective. Plato points this out somewhere, though the passage does not come to mind at the moment.[3] When it does, I shall point it out.

Perhaps *omnis vox* means 'to speak as vigorously as possible.' For lawyers usually raise their voice when pleading a case with all their passion. Something like this seems to have been meant by the apostle Paul in his letter to the Galatians, chapter 4, when he says, 'I wish I were among you and could modify my tone.'[4] For the man who employs at different times rebukes, flattery, preaching, humility, threats, and consolation – whatever may serve the interests of those for whose survival he is concerned – changes his tone all the time, like a skilled precentor, in order to persuade in some way or other.

58 Magadari
To play the Lydian flute

Μαγαδίζειν or μαγαδεύειν, To play the *magadis*, was said of those who were 'bilingual': from the same mouth came praise and abuse, flattery and condemnation, seemly expressions and indecent language. Athenaeus says a great deal about the *magadis* in book fourteen, and is inclined to think that it is a type of lyre or pipe.[1] Some think that it is the same as the sambuca, others the *pectis*.[2] But this has nothing to do with the proverb since it is generally agreed that the magadis is a two-pitched instrument, emitting two notes at the same time, one deep in pitch and one high, a combination that is called διὰ πασῶν.[3] This iambic line from Alexandrides is cited: Μάγαδιν λαλήσω μικρὸν ἄμα σοι καὶ μέγαν 'I shall play the *magadis*, the small and the

* * * * *

λόγους ἄνω καὶ κάτω μεταστρέφειν. Erasmus' translation of this phrase is *omnes rationes sursum deorsum versare.*

3 ASD II-8 55:741n suggests Plato *Republic* 2.364B–C as a possibility.

4 Gal 4:20. Paul means that he would be softening his tone. Erasmus cites the verse only in Greek. The Vulgate reads *mutare vocem.*

58 Athenaeus (see n1). Added in *1528*

1 Athenaeus 14.635A, on which Erasmus draws for most of the commentary here

2 The sambuca and *pektis* are two types of stringed instruments.

3 See Athenaeus 14.636C and Aristotle *Problemata* 19.39 (921a).

great at the same time.'⁴ Athenaeus says that this is an ancient type of instrument, invented by the Lydians. It got its name from a Thracian whose
name was Magdus. Others think that it was an invention of Sappho. Pindar calls the *magadis* a 'song for two voices,' as when men and young boys
sing together.⁵ We touched on this to some extent in the proverb 'Out of
one mouth to blow hot and cold.'⁶

59 Chalcenterus
With guts of bronze

In antiquity Χαλκέντερος was used to describe someone who had outstanding endurance and was indefatigable; such a person seemed to have guts
made of bronze, like the legendary Talus, who guarded the island of Crete.¹
This nickname was given to the grammarian Didymus because of the incredible number of books that he is said to have written.² For the same
reason Origen was called *adamantinus* 'man of steel.'³

60 Origanum tueri
The look of oregano

Ὀρίγανον βλέπειν, To have the look of oregano. This was said of a person
who showed great strength and a masculine spirit. Suidas cites this verse

* * * * *

4 Not Alexandrides, but Anaxandrides (PCG 2 fragment 36), quoted by Athenaeus. The name Alexandrides comes from the Aldine edition of Athenaeus.
5 Pindar fragment 125 Snell, quoted by Athenaeus at 14.635B
6 *Adagia* I viii 30

59 *Suda* Δ 872, X 29. Added in *1528*
1 In Greek myth Talus was a giant of bronze made by Hephaestus to guard
Europa when she was abducted by Zeus and then to guard the island of Crete
itself.
2 Didymus was a scholar of the Alexandrian school, living in the 1st century BC.
He was a prolific author, writing among other things commentaries on many
authors and lexicographical works. According to the *Suda* he wrote 3500 books.
3 Origen is described as *adamantius* (sic) by Jerome at *Letters* 33.4 PL 22 447, CSEL
54 255.

60 Aristophanes by way of the *Suda* (see n1). Added in *1528*

from Aristophanes, although the metre is faulty: 'I shall display a manly spirit and have the look of oregano.'[1] Taken from the bitterness of the herb, so that it is similar to 'The look of mustard' and to 'Cress,' mentioned elsewhere.[2] Some call the herb *cunila*, of the type that Dioscorides calls 'Heraclean.'[3] For there is another type called ὀνῖτις 'marjoram' and a third called 'Heraclean wound-wort.' So Dioscorides book three. Pliny tells us in book twenty, chapter fourteen, that oregano is not dissimilar to wild flea-bane.[4]

61 Thurium lema
A rushing resolve

Θούριον λῆμα, A rushing resolve, was an expression used to describe a disposition that was fearless and ready for war. For λῆμα, neuter in gender, means in Greek 'desire,' 'spirit' or 'purpose' or 'rank' or 'authority,' the word coming from λῶ 'to wish' (λῆμμα, written with a double mu, comes from λάβω or λαμβάνω 'to take, assume,' and is an argument that is assumed for a proof). Whatever is strong and warlike is called *thurios*. Whence Homer describes ἀλκή 'strength' as θοῦρις 'rushing.'[1] Moreover, even Mars himself is called θοῦρος, from θορεῖν 'to leap upon.'[2] Suidas quotes from Aristophanes.[3] We also find θούριος λόγος, meaning words that are powerful and divinely inspired, and used when anyone speaks fearlessly and with authority.[4]

* * * * *

1 *Suda* Λ 441, citing Aristophanes *Frogs* 601–3. Erasmus writes these three short lines as one verse. The Greek text that Erasmus offers here, from the *Suda*, differs in some respects from the text in modern editions.

2 Erasmus misquotes the proverbs 'To live on mustard' (*Adagia* IV v 74, 190 above) and 'Why can't you eat cress' (*Adagia* I viii 54).

3 Dioscorides *De materia medica* 3.27–9

4 Pliny *Naturalis historia* 20.156. For the reference to chapter 14 see *Adagia* IV iii 3 n3 (5–6 above).

61 Aristophanes by way of the *Suda* (see n3). Added in *1528*

1 Homer *Odyssey* 4.527; *Iliad* 7.164, 8.262

2 From the *Suda* Θ 420 and (for the etymology) the *Etymologicum magnum* 453.40–1

3 Aristophanes *Knights* 757 quoted at the *Suda* Λ 441

4 Julian *Letters* 152 Bidez-Cumont, but Erasmus' text of Julian is faulty and Θούριος λόγος is corrupt. The translation of the correct text of this phrase is 'the Thurian writer,' a reference to Herodotus.

62 Nec elephantus ebiberet
Not even an elephant could empty it

Οὐδ᾽ ἂν ἐλέφας ἐκπίοι, Not even an elephant could empty it. Said of a huge cup since an elephant can easily drink up an immense amount of water with its trunk. Athenaeus in book eleven quotes from Epinicus:

> An elephant carries round an elephant rhyton
> Holding two *choes*, so that not even an elephant
> Could drink it dry.[1]

A rhyton is a type of cup, shaped like a horn, that seems to have been made of ivory with the representation of an elephant at one end.[2] He adds,

> Neither are you different from an elephant

(this being therefore the fourth mention of an elephant in this passage). We have spoken previously of this proverb, without however citing this passage.[3] A *choa* is a type of measure.[4]

The phrase will be applied to a dull and long book that not even the hardiest of men could bear to read it in its entirety.

* * * * *

62 Athenaeus (see n1). Added in *1528*

1 Athenaeus 11.497A, citing PCG 5 Epinicus fragment 2. Erasmus does not translate into Latin the first line of the Greek quotation that he gives in the text. The verse is extremely corrupt and it is not clear how Erasmus would have understood it.

2 Where Erasmus got the information about a rhyton (he calls it a rhytos, masculine in gender) with the representation of an elephant (literally he says the rhyton was 'placed upon' the representation of an elephant, *impositum imagini elephanti*) is not known. One end of these drinking horns often took the shape of an animal or part of an animal, but none with the form of an elephant is known. Erasmus has probably misunderstood what was a joke in the text of Athenaeus, based on the fact that there was a drinking cup called an elephant (see Athenaeus 11.468F).

3 *Adagia* II ix 90 There's no difference between you and an elephant

4 The correct nominative singular form is *chous*, *choa* being the accusative singular.

63 Κναθίζειν
To be a wine-ladler

Those who indulged excessively in wine were said Κναθίζειν 'To ladle wine,' the same words as *cyathissare*,[1] like κωθωνίζειν,[2] of which I have spoken earlier.[3] Athenaeus pointed this out too.[4] I think it better suits those who drink a little at a time and do not quaff pint-pots, but become inebriated because they go back continually to sip from the ladle. Some individuals often make the following proposal: 'We shall each drink a half-pint, no more.' Often, however, their desire for drink gradually heats up and they consume more than they planned.

64 Sacer piscis
A sacred fish

Ἱερὸς ἰχθύς, A sacred fish, was the description applied to a fish that no one harmed and was subject to no constraints. Suidas points out that the phrase appears in Homer.[1] The ancients applied the term *hieros* 'sacred' to whatever they thought should be regarded as great and distinguished; for example, 'the sacred might of Alcinous' in Homer.[2]

* * * * *

63 Athenaeus (see n1). Added in *1528*. 'Some individuals' to the end was added in *1533*.
  1 The verb *cyathissare* is used by Plautus at *Menaechmi* 303, 305. The Greek verb κναθίζειν appears in a comic fragment quoted by Athenaeus at 11.503C (PCG 2 Antiphanes fragment 113), but there the meaning is 'to ladle water,' in other words 'to dilute the wine.' If Erasmus is basing his interpretation of the verb on this passage, he has misunderstood the meaning.
  2 The verb appears in Roman font in the *Adagia*-text as *cothonizin*. In the sense of 'to drink excessively' the verb is usually in the passive form (κωθωνίζεσθαι).
  3 *Adagia* III iv 65 The old woman is in her cups. See also IV vi 69 To be in one's cups (261 below).
  4 Erasmus here is referring to the use of κωθωνίζειν (or rather κωθωνίζεσθαι) to mean hard drinking, discussed by Athenaeus at 11.483F–484A.

64 Homer by way of the *Suda* (see n1). Added in *1528*
  1 *Suda* I 186 citing Homer *Iliad* 16.407
  2 Quoted by Athenaeus 7.284C, who is referred to in the final sentence. For the use of *hieros* see *Odyssey* 7.167; 8.4, 385; 13.20, 24.

It may be said of a very grand and highly regarded man, even if he is stupid and inarticulate. Athenaeus also mentions this proverb.

65 Φελλίνας
Cork-man

Φελλίνας means 'light' or *suberinus* 'made of cork.' For φελλός is tree-bark that always floats, the Latin equivalent being *suber*.[1] This is why φελλεύς is also used to describe ground that is rough and rocky, and more suited for pasturing goats than planting crops, because the terrain is like very shallow water whose surface floats, so to speak, just above rocks that lie below it.[2] This is also why what floats and does not have roots is said φελλεύειν 'to float like a cork.' Indeed, even today the English word for a man who is obliging and is in no way difficult is φελλεύς 'fellow.'[3] The Greeks call such easy-going behaviour εὐήθεια, a word that can have a pejorative connotation. Plato *Republic* book three:

> Good speech, then, proper behaviour, and elegant and graceful movement accompany a truly good disposition, not that disposition that we call by a flattering name (as if it were a mark of good character, when it is really foolishness), but a disposition that is truly equipped with fine and noble traits.[4]

We said a little about this in the proverb 'Lighter than cork.'[5] 'A deep furrow of the mind' has been discussed elsewhere.[6]

* * * * *

65 Hesychius Φ 280, 281, 283, 284, 289. Also in the *Suda* (Φ 189, 190). Added in *1528*
1 This sentence was added in *1533*.
2 In other words, there is hardly any top soil that can be cultivated. This etymological connection of φελλεύειν with φελλός seems to be Erasmus' own expansion of what is said at *Suda* Φ 190, that a region in Attica is called Phelleus because the terrain there is rocky and there is little topsoil. Erasmus also connects the Greek words with the Latin verb *fluitare* 'to float.'
3 Erasmus' etymology for English 'fellow' is fanciful to say the least.
4 Plato *Republic* 3.400D–E, exemplifying the good and bad senses of εὐήθεια
5 *Adagia* II iv 7
6 *Adagia* IV ii 23

66 Methysocottabi
Cottabus-drunk

Μεθυσοκόττάβοι, Drunk with the cottabus, was a common insult for drunk-ards. For the cottabus is a kind of wine-cup.[1] In book fifteen Athenaeus cites the following from some author (Aristophanes, if I am not mistaken): 'The young men drove off the whore Simaetha to Megara / And, cottabus-drunk, stole her away.'[2]

67 Ἴσον ἴσῳ
Half and half

Ἴσον ἴσῳ, Equal with equal. This expression was used to mean that some-thing had been modified so that it contained equal amounts of its ingre-dients. It is taken from drinkers, who often quarrel, sometime with fists and swords, about the proportions to be applied when mixing drinks. In antiquity equality meant that to the wine an equal amount of water was added. Athenaeus book eleven quotes from a play of Aristophanes entitled *Philonides*:

> Therefore my master recently gave me a round-shaped bowl
> Of highest quality among those made by Thericles,
> Filled to the brim with foam, splendid, mixed equal with equal.[1]

* * * * *

66 Aristophanes by way of Athenaeus (see n1). Added in *1528*
  1 Cottabus is more usually the name of a game played at Greek symposia, in which the participants threw the remains of their wine into a basin. Sometimes the word is used of the basin itself and this must be how Erasmus understood the word here.
  2 Athenaeus 13.570A (not book 15), citing Aristophanes *Acharnians* 524–5. Eras-mus mistranslates the first part of the quotation. The meaning is 'The young men went to Megara and, quite cottabus-drunk, stole the whore Simaetha away.'

67 Aristophon by way of Athenaeus (see n1). Added in *1528*
  1 Athenaeus 11.472C, but the name 'Aristophanes' is an error taken over from the Aldine edition of Athenaeus. The author is Aristophon (PCG 4 fragment 13). Thericles was a famous Corinthian potter.

From Straton, the writer of comedies, he cites these verses: 'The lot which some draw from a little wine-jug, / Others from a cask mixed half and half.'[2] The first trochaic line is flawed and I think προχοίδιον should be read here for προχίδιον.[3] Both are wine containers. Ἑρμῆς is used here of the lot that is drawn first, as we have shown elsewhere.[4] Athenaeus in the same book also quotes from Hermippus: 'I have drunk in the wine, without stopping to take breath, / Wine mixed in the sweetest way, half and half.[5]

We have given elsewhere the proverb *Par pari* 'Like to like.'[6] That one is concerned with how different things are considered to be of equal value, this one is concerned with equal mixture. These words ἴσον ἴσῳ are used absolutely, without regard to the syntactic construction, just as we say διὰ πασῶν 'diapason.'[7]

68 Recto pectore
With an upright heart

Ammianus Marcellinus book seventeen: 'When this letter had been considered for a long time, a response was given after great thought and, as the saying goes, "With an upright heart."'[1] 'With an upright heart' means

* * * * *

2 Ἑρμῆς, ὃν ἕλκουσ᾽ οἱ μὲν ἐκ προχιδίου, / Οἱ δ᾽ ἐκ καδίσκου ἴσον ἴσῳ κεκραμμένου. 'Straton' is also an error in the Aldine Athenaeus (11.473C). The correct name is Strattis (PCG 7 fragment 23), an emendation credited to Casaubon.

3 Both lines are iambic. For the first line to scan as an iambic trimeter the iota of the second syllable of προχιδίου must be long. By normal prosody, however, this vowel would be short. This is why Erasmus suggests *prochoidiou*, the second syllable of which satisfies the metrical requirements.

4 *Adagia* IV vii 2 May Mercury be with me (280 below). According to LSJ the phrase Ἑρμῆν ἕλκειν is proverbial with the sense 'to have a last drink before leaving a party.' The sense would be 'The last drink' rather than 'The lot.'

5 Athenaeus 11.502B, who quoted not Hermippus (as in the Aldine Athenaeus), but Alexis (PCG 2 fragment 246)

6 *Adagia* I i 35 To render like for like

7 This prepositional phrase functions as a noun in its own right, meaning the interval between first and last notes of the scale, an octave. See *Adagia* I ii 63 Double diapason.

68 Ammianus Marcellinus (see n1). Otto 1367. Added in *1528*

1 Ammianus Marcellinus 17.5.9

'sincerely, without dissimulation,' since 'True speech is simple.'[2] Those who approve of what ought to be approved and condemn what ought to be condemned speak 'With an upright heart.' Those who approve or condemn everything do not act 'With an upright heart.'

69 Cothonissare
To be in one's cups

Κωθωνίζειν or κωθωνίζεσθαι, To drink from a *cothon*, was said of those who drank heavily, and κωθωνισμός was the name given to a rather heavy drinking session. Mnesitheus, a doctor mentioned in Athenaeus book eleven, thinks that such a session is conducive to good health,[1] Plato believes that it is good for improving character,[2] Seneca says it lifts the spirits.[3] Nevertheless, they forbid complete drunkenness and they allow this to happen only rarely. Those who drank undiluted wine were called ἀκροκώθωνες or ἀκρατοκώθονες, as the word is written by whoever put together the *Etymology*.[4] Hesychius thinks that they are called ἀκροθώρακες.[5] For he explains this word as meaning μέθυσοι 'drunken.' But from Plutarch in 'Table-talk' and Aristotle in his *Problems* it appears that ἀκροθώρακες describes those who are not yet completely drunk; their whole body is inebriated, but their rational faculties are only partly affected.[6] The word ἀκροκώθωνες is mentioned by both Julius Pollux in book six, quoting from Hyperides,[7] and Athenaeus, citing the same author in his speech against Demosthenes.[8] Pollux cites

* * * * *

2 *Adagia* I iii 88 The plain speech of truth (but here I would prefer the translation 'True speech is simple')

69 Athenaeus (see n1). Added in 1528. 'Those who drank undiluted wine ... are only partly affected' was added in 1533.
1 Athenaeus 11.483F–484A. According to Mnesitheus wine purges the body through urination and it also relaxes the mind.
2 Plato *Laws* 1.637B–642A; 2.671A–672D
3 Seneca *De tranquillitate animi* 17.8–9
4 *Etymologicum magnum* 53.29
5 Hesychius A 2608
6 Plutarch *Moralia* 656C *Quaestiones convivales*, who quotes Aristotle *Problemata* 3.2 (871a) and 3.27 (875a)
7 Pollux *Onomasticon* 6.25, citing Hyperides (see Jensen page 24)
8 Athenaeus 11.483E

ἐπικωθωνίζεσθαι in the sense 'to drink intemperately' from Critias.⁹ A *cothon* is a type of cup, which we have touched on elsewhere.¹⁰

70 Τρυγόβιοι
Drinkers of dregs

In antiquity those who were mean and very thrifty were often jokingly called Τρυγόβιοι 'Those who live on dregs.' Those who live in a more splendid way open a new bottle when they get to the dregs of the one they are drinking. Yet I know some rich men who put nine-year-old lees on the table not only for their sons but also for distinguished friends.¹ Some people are by nature such cheapskates that they serve only wine that has turned sour or gone flat.

Pollux gives the adage in book six, chapter four.² Eustathius tells us that those who were very niggardly were called τρύσιβιοι, because they groaned and worried their way through life.³ In Aulus Gellius book eleven, chapter seven, a man provokes laughter when he says of a very frugal person, 'This Roman knight eats *apluda* and drinks *flocces*.'⁴ Farmers of old called the chaff of grain *apluda*, and the lees of wine crushed from grapeskins (like the dregs of oil from olives) they called *flocces*.

* * * * *

9 Pollux *Onomasticon* 6.31. For Critias see FHG 2.69.
10 *Adagia* II viii 24 To lift the elbow; III iv 65 The old woman is in her cups

70 Pollux (see n2). Added in *1528*
  1 This is almost certainly a reference to Andrea Torresani, the father-in-law of Aldo Manuzio. When Erasmus was in Venice in 1508 and preparing the new and enlarged edition of the *Adagia*, he lodged at Torresani's house. See the colloquy 'Penny-pinching' (*Opulentia sordida*) CWE 40 983–4, and CEBR 3:331–3.
  2 Pollux *Onomasticon* 6.27. The reference to chapter 4 agrees with the subdivision of books in the Aldine edition of 1502.
  3 Eustathius 1828.13–15 on *Odyssey* 17.455 (cf Aristophanes *Clouds* 421). Eustathius links the word with τρύω, which means 'to wear out, distress,' often used in the passive voice.
  4 Aulus Gellius *Noctes Atticae* 11.7.3–6. Gellius is criticizing those who use archaic or obsolete words and it is this practice that prompts laughter. The final sentence is a close paraphrase of Gellius.

71 Loquax talpa
A mole who never stops talking

It was a common insult to call a man who had no judgment but who talked interminably a mole who never stopped talking. It was first said of Julianus Capella when he had incurred the hatred of all his citizens.[1] The point of the insult is that the moles we are familiar with are not only blind but are also quite dumb. The same kind of person was also called Πίθηκος ἐν πορφύρᾳ 'An ape in purple,' which we have mentioned elsewhere.[2] Ammianus gives us the proverb in book seventeen.

72 Non contis aut ramulis
Not by poles or branches

Ammianus, in the same book, says of a certain Antonius who had been elevated to the honour of sharing the Persian royal table and had been given the right to vote, 'It was not by poles or *ramulis* "by branches," as the saying goes (in other words, not by ambiguous and obscure subterfuges), but at full sail that he attacked his country, and thereby urged on the king.'[1] However, I think *remulo* 'by little oar' should be read for *ramulo* 'by branch'; for when winds are adverse, sailors impel their ship with poles and oars.[2] This is really part of the adage that we listed elsewhere, 'With oars and sails,' rather than a new one.[3]

* * * * *

71 Ammianus Marcellinus (see n1). Added in *1528*. Erasmus added the Greek phrase Πίθηκος ἐν πορφύρᾳ in *1533*.
1 Ammianus Marcellinus 17.11.1. The point of the expression, as recounted by Ammianus, is that Julianus Caesar was very hairy. Ammianus says 'it was not a man, but a *capella* "a goat" that incurred hatred with his victories.' He goes on to say that Julianus, being hairy, was called a talkative mole and an ape in purple. Erasmus took *capella* to be one of Julianus' names.
2 *Adagia* I vii 10.

72 Ammianus Marcellinus (see n1). Otto 428. Added in *1528*
1 Ammianus Marcellinus 18.5.6 (not book 17)
2 Erasmus is right in rejecting *ramulis* 'by branches,' but the correct reading is *remulco* 'by tow-rope.'
3 *Adagia* I iv 18

73 **Extra calcem**
Off course

The same author in book twenty-one: 'So that our words will not bore the
future reader, by running *Extra calcem* "Beyond the mark," as the saying
goes, let us return to describing the events that had been foreseen.'[1] I think,
however, that there is a corruption here and that *extra callem* 'off the track'
should be read in the sense of *extra viam*, which we have spoken of elsewhere,[2] when anyone wanders from his intended purpose.

74 **Ex perpendiculo**
With a plumb-line

The same author in the same book used the expression 'With a plumb-line,'
meaning 'with precise judgment.' He says, 'He assigned the offices of the
palace with a plumb-line, as it were, and under him no one who was to
hold a lofty position was brought into the court suddenly or untested.'[1]
Related to this expression are those which, as well as occurring frequently
elsewhere, are to be found in Gellius book two, chapter one: *ad amussim
exigere* 'to demand a precise equivalent,' *librili perpendere* 'to weigh in the
balance,' *ad aequilibrium aestimare* 'to estimate an exact equivalent.'[2] Also in
Pliny book thirty-six, chapter twenty-five: *ad regulam ac libellam exigere* 'to
finish to rule and level.'[3] In addition there is *Digitis metiri* 'To count up on

* * * * *

73 Ammianus Marcellinus (see n1). Otto 309. Added in *1528*
  1 Ammianus 21.1.14. The *calx* was the finishing line of a race, marked by chalk.
    Here it is used by synecdoche for the course itself. There is no need to emend.
  2 *Adagia* I i 48 You are entirely on the wrong road; III i 84 He runs in vain

74 Ammianus Marcellinus (see n1). *Collectanea* no 773. Otto 102 (note). Cf Bras-
    sicanus no 97 (*Ad perpendiculum*); see *Adagia* IV iii 86 n2 (52 above). Added in
    1528. Most of the discussion was added in *1533*: 'Related to this expression . . .
    if applied to intellectual matters' and 'Marcus Tullius in the third speech' to
    the end.
  1 Ammianus Marcellinus 21.16.3
  2 Aulus Gellius *Noctes Atticae* 20.1.34 (not book 2)
  3 Pliny *Naturalis historia* 36.188. For the reference to chapter 25 see *Adagia* IV iii
    3 n3 (5–6 above).

one's fingers,' *Trutina pensare* 'To weigh in the scale,' *Ad unguem facere* 'To do something to the finger-nail' and others, some of which we have pointed out at the appropriate place.[4] All these expressions have more charm if applied to intellectual matters. The metaphor is taken from workmen's plumb-lines, with which they check whether a floor is level or a wall is perpendicular. An *amussis* is a string with a piece of lead attached to it at the bottom, and is fixed to the middle of a measuring rule consisting of two squares. With this they test whether the ground is level. Marcus Tullius in the third speech against Verres:

> 'You, Verres, have nothing to do here unless perhaps you wish to make sure that the columns are exactly plumb.' They tell him that there is scarcely any column that can be exactly plumb. 'Damn it then,' he says, 'let's do it. Let us demand that the columns be exactly plumb.'[5]

75 Acolo, non fico
Morsels, not figs

Ἀκόλῳ τὰ χείλη, οὐ σύκῳ βῦσαι, Put your lips on a morsel, not a fig. Suidas points out that this was said when good health was promised or when someone meant that one should face circumstances bravely.[1] For in Greek ἄκολοι refers to tiny pieces of food, sometimes even morsels of bread. It is derived from μὴ κολλᾶσθαι 'not to be joined' because the pieces do not stick together. Hesychius says that eating ἄκολοι gets rid of anger and makes one calm, while figs enflame the blood.[2] When Italians want to get rid of bile, we have seen them eat nothing for several days except a few morsels of bread dipped in a sauce made from water and a little fresh butter. Sometimes a few herbs or roots are added. The proverb encourages us to eat modestly.

* * * * *

4 *Adagia* IV v 86 To count up on one's fingers (200 above); I v 15 To be weighed on the same scales; I v 91 To the finger-nail
5 Cicero *Verrines* 2.1.51.133

75 *Suda* (see n1). Added in *1528*
1 *Suda* A 920
2 Hesychius A 2470. Cf Athenaeus 3.75B, 80B.

76 Πενταπλόα
A cup of five

Athenaeus book eleven mentions a kind of cup that in ancient times was called 'A cup of five,' used at public festivals.[1] Some youths used to take part in a race to Athens, carrying a vine branch laden with fruit as they ran. This was called an ὄσχος.[2] The race began at the temple of Bacchus and ended at the temple of Athena Scirras. The winner in this contest received a cup called 'a cup of five' and then leapt around in a group of dancers. The cup got this name because five kinds of things were mixed in it: wine, honey, cheese, ground barley, and a little olive oil.

The expression can be applied to a speech in which different arguments have been stitched together. There was a similar earthenware vessel (called a κέρνος 'tray' in Greek) that was used in the worship of Bacchus. In this were placed a greater number of things but these were kept separate in little cups that were joined together. Athenaeus lists about sixteen by name. Therefore, we can use the terms πενταπλόα or κέρνος as the equivalent of *farrago* 'a hodge-podge,' which we use to denote something that is multifaceted and composed of different kinds of things. About 'Horn of plenty' I have spoken elsewhere.[3] Quite similar to these expressions is what the ancients called *satyra*, of which I shall speak in its proper place.[4]

77 **More Carico**
In Carian fashion

Σχήματι Καρικῷ, In Carian form or fashion. This was said of anything that was done in a disgusting and crude way, particularly with respect to obscene matters. However, it can be applied to other things, such as unseemly

* * * * *

76 Athenaeus (see n1). Added in *1528*

 1 Athenaeus 11.495F

 2 Erasmus follows the spelling in the Aldine Athenaeus in reading ὄσχος (for the modern spelling ὤσχος) and also Σκιρράς (for Σκιράς).

 3 *Adagia* i vi 2

 4 *Adagia* iv vii 76 A hodge-podge (334 below). The final sentence was added in *1533*.

77 Hesychius K 822. Added in *1528*

and impolite manners or to a speech that is badly organized. We also find πλοίῳ Καρικῷ 'in a Carian ship.'[1]

78 Μυσικαρφί
Choking on straw

Μυσικαρφί was said of those who had a hard and austere life. The word seems to be fashioned from the Greek words μῦς 'mouse' and κάρφος 'straw' because a mouse expends a great amount of effort on insignificant things, unless we prefer a derivation from μύσσω 'to dry,' and μύσις 'suffocation,' in the sense that someone is suffocated by straw.[1] Hesychius points out that this word should be taken to be similar to ἀκονιτί 'without effort.' Used by Cratinus in the play entitled *Horae*.[2] Others think that there was some man called Μυσίκαρφος who was incapable of producing any witty sayings of his own, but nevertheless enjoyed laughing at what other persons said. There is mention of this name in Apollophanes, the writer of comedies.[3]

It will be applied therefore to a mean and miserly man or to one who tries unsuccessfully to be amusing.

79 Μύτης
A mutterer-fish

Someone who hardly ever said anything or who was rather loose in his sexual behaviour was called μύτης 'a mutterer' from mu, the only sound that mutes can make. I have spoken of this elsewhere.[1] A female fish of this

* * * * *

1 Hesychius K 821

78 Drawn from Hesychius M 1946, from where most of the discussion is derived. Erasmus does not give a Latin equivalent to the Greek word. Added in *1528*
1 The Greek word μύσις more often refers to the closing of the eyes than to the closing of the throat, as Erasmus takes it here.
2 PCG 4 Cratinus fragment 293
3 PCG 2 Apollophanes fragment 8, cited in Hesychius

79 Hesychius (see n2). Added in *1528*
1 *Adagia* I viii 2 He does not even say mu

name does not feed unless accompanied by its mate. Hence the proverb applies to lustful persons or to those who are too dependent on their wives, although more correctly it applies to women who are too dependent on their husbands. The source is Hesychius.[2]

80 Qui inspuerit in cavernam formicarum ...
Whoever spits on an ants' nest ...

The same author points out that there was a common saying ʽΩς ὁ πτύσας εἰς μυρμηκιὰν οἰδεῖ τὰ χείλη 'The lips of the man who spits on an ants' nest swell up.'[1] Whether it really happens that air is forced from an ants' nest, bringing some infection that affects the spitter's mouth or whether this is a foolish belief, it can be applied to those who stir up the hostility of a crowd of weaklings. Although these are weak individually, they are very numerous and can act together. Hesychius cites Dinolochus as the source. He was a writer of comedies, the son of Epicharmus.[2]

81 Nemo sibi nascitur
No one is born just for himself

This saying of Plato is used so frequently by all learned men that it can, with every justification, be listed among proverbs. Plato was the first to use it, in a letter that he wrote to Archytas:

> That too you must consider, that ἕκαστος ἡμῶν οὐχ αὑτῷ μόνον γέγονεν 'each of us is not born just for himself.' Our native land claims for itself part of us. A part of us is claimed by our parents, a part by all our other friends. Much is given too to the circumstances that befall us in our lives.[1]

* * * * *

2 Hesychius M 1990, from whom most of the information is drawn

80 Hesychius (see n1). Added in *1528*
1 Hesychius M 1903
2 This last sentence was taken from *Suda* Δ 338. Dinolochus was a writer of Doric comedy in the fifth century. See 1.149–51 Kaibel.

81 Plato (see n1). Tilley B 141 No man is born for himself. Added in *1528*
1 Plato *Letters* 9.358A

Marcus Tullius adduces this passage in *On Duty* book one.[2] He says, 'But since, as Plato wrote so brilliantly, we are not born just for ourselves, and our country, our parents and our friends all claim part of us.' Since Cicero translated this saying so clearly and appropriately, I am surprised that Seneca preferred to say *nemo sibi contigit* 'no one has yet found himself.' For he seems to have wished to render ἐγένετο in this way.[3] For this is what he writes in *To Lucilius* book five, letter thirty-two: 'Do you want to know what it is that makes mortals so greedy for the future? No one has yet found himself.'[4] For he seems to blame parents for the fact that we do not immediately search after what is finest. For he adds: 'And so your parents prayed for other things for you, but I pray that you may despise all these things that your parents wanted for you in abundance. Their prayers plunder many others to enrich you.' Quintilian seems to have had the same desire – to express differently everything that Cicero had said. Therefore he often writes more inelegantly and even more obscurely.

82 Pireus non fert vasa inania
The Piraeus does not have empty vessels

Julius Pollux in book six, chapter six, cites this from Aristotle: Τὸν Πειρέα μὴ κεναγγίαν ἄγειν 'The Piraeus does not have empty vessels.'[1] The Piraeus was the harbour of Attica, and ships laden with merchandise put in there. Young men who were going to have a party met in this same place. Antipho points this out in Terence's *Eunuch*: 'We young sparks met at the Piraeus to club together for a party today.'[2] The harbour of Corinth, where it is

* * * * *

2 Cicero *De officiis* 1.7.22

3 Erasmus means γέγονεν.

4 Seneca *Letters* 32.4. But Seneca's expression is probably not based on the Greek adage given here, and it has a different meaning: 'no one is or can be complete.'

82 Aristophanes by way of Pollux (see n1). The phrase κεναγγίαν ἄγειν means 'to fast.' Erasmus does not take the phrase in this sense. Added in *1528*

1 Pollux *Onomasticon* 6.31, quoting, not from Aristotle, but from Aristophanes: PCG 3.2 fragment 683. The reference to chapter 6 agrees with the enumeration in the Aldine edition of 1502.

2 Terence *Eunuchus* 539–40

generally agreed there was greater luxury,[3] has the same name.[4] This led to the proverb being used humorously of those who always take pleasure in being stuffed full of food and wine.

Consider whether Πειραιέα should be read in Pollux [for Πειρέα], referring to an individual, since Stephanus points out that a place and a man previously called 'Piraeus' later became Πειραιεύς.

83 Cradophagus
A figleaf-eater

As a joke the ancients used to describe a miserly man who lived in the country as a κραδοφάγος, in the sense of κραδαιοφάγος 'A figleaf-eater.' For κράδαια is the name given to the leaves of a fig-tree. The same persons were called βαλανοφάγοι, meaning those who ate acorns, as was done in early times.[1]

84 Sapiens divinat
A wise man prophesies

In his commentary on the *Mother-in-law* Donatus points out that 'A wise man prophesies' is a proverb.[1] By carefully examining all the evidence a wise man can deduce the truth not only about past events but also about future ones. In fact, in the play Laches goes completely astray in his conclusions. Yet Phidippus approves of them and says, 'This man has clearly second sight. For the situation is just as he says.' See the proverb 'He who guesses right.'[2]

* * * * *

3 Cf *Adagia* I iv 1 It is not given to everyone to land at Corinth; IV iii 68 To play the Corinthian (41 above).
4 Stephanus of Byzantium sub Πειραιός

83 Pollux *Onomasticon* 6.40. Added in *1528*
1 The phrase appears in the essay on *Adagia* III iii 27 A scion of Arcadia. See also IV iii 1 Milled fare (3 above).

84 Donatus (see n1). Otto 1582. Added in *1528*
1 Donatus on Terence *Hecyra* 696. In the play Laches and Phidippus are the fathers of the young married couple.
2 *Adagia* II iii 78

85 Iambizein
To iambicize

'Ιαμβίζειν, To iambicize. This was used by the ancients in the sense of 'to re-
vile' and 'to curse,' the word being derived from Iambe, a woman renowned
for her abusive language. More probably the word is derived from the
iambic measure that is found in invective, since this measure has the forcefulness of someone striking and attacking, the foot beginning with a short
element and ending in a long one. In the same way a wrongdoing may start
out as something minor but then result in great tragedy, as even Homer
also pointed out: ἤ τ' ὀλίγη μὲν τὰ πρῶτα 'small to start with.'[1] This is why a
fellow prone to invective is called ἰάμβηλος. This is very much what Suidas
and Hesychius say.[2]

86 Testaceum flagellum
An earthenware whip

Κεραμεικὴ μάστιξ, An earthenware whip. Another name for ostracism, about
which I have spoken at great length in the proverb 'The turning of a pot-
sherd.'[1] It was called 'a whip' because it was with this that men were driven
into exile, 'earthenware' because votes were customarily cast on potsherds.

87 Arietis ministerium
Doing a good turn to a ram

Κριοῦ διακονία, Doing a good turn to a ram. Suidas and Zenodotus say that
this was often said of doing a good turn for ingrates; for a ram butts the

* * * * *

85 Hesychius I 44. Added in *1528*
 1 Homer *Iliad* 4.442, misquoted both in the *Suda* (see next note) and by Erasmus.
   It should read "Η τ' ὀλίγη μὲν πρῶτα. Quoted in full at *Adagia* III viii 23 Greatest
   things from smallest beginnings
 2 *Suda* I 25 and Hesychius I 44, 45

86 Hesychius K 2266. Added in *1528*
 1 *Adagia* II i 51

87 The *Suda*, Zenobius, and Hesychius (see nn1–2). Added in *1528*. The second
   paragraph was added in *1533*.

person who feeds it.[1] Hesychius describes the expression as suiting those who serve unworthy masters in the hope of some trifling reward.[2] When we invite children to do a service for us, we promise them something: knuckle-bones or nuts, for example. Similarly (in some fable, I think) a ram said, 'Put oil on my food and I will give you knuckle-bones.'[3] The addition of an asterisk in the Aldine edition indicates that κατέλειψεν is a corruption.[4] I think that κατάλειψον 'dress with oil' from ἀλείφω 'to anoint' should be read. We mentioned this proverb in passing in 'The ram paid for its upbringing.'[5]

There is another proverb directed at ingrates that we have given earlier: 'In return for his kindness the Greeks bound Agamemnon,' which I came across without its source being identified.[6] Meanwhile I have discovered in *Notes on Greek Words*[7] that in the portico of the Stoa called 'Painted' and 'Royal'[8] there were several statues of Mercury, some erected by ordinary people, others by leading men. One of these had this verse inscribed in ancient letters. Then the expression became proverbial. This note, such as it is, should have been added at the appropriate place, but that page had already left my hands.[9]

88 In tuum ipsius caput
On your own head may it fall

Whenever misfortune redounds on the person who caused it, the Greeks say Εἰς τὴν αὐτοῦ κεφαλήν 'On your own head may it fall.' Demosthenes in

* * * * *

1 *Suda* K 2438 and Zenobius 4.63; Zenobius (Aldus) col 107
2 Hesychius K 4143
3 The words of the ram are given by Hesychius. It is Erasmus who guesses that the source is a fable.
4 The 1514 Aldine edition of Hesychius, which reads *κατέλειψε τοὺς ἀστραγάλους σοι δώσω*. The passage as now printed in modern editions means 'I shall leave (κατάλειψω) knuckle-bones for you,' δώσω being omitted as an interpolation.
5 *Adagia* II v 92
6 *Adagia* II vi 7 with 'punished' in place of 'bound'
7 This unusual title (*Scholia Graecanica*) is a reference to Harpocration's *Lexicon* (for the information given see sub Ἑρμαῖ). Harpocration's work was printed with Ulpian's scholia on Demosthenes in the 1503 Aldine edition.
8 These were in fact two distinct porticoes.
9 At *Adagia* II vi 7 (see n6 above)

88 Demosthenes and Plato (see nn1–2). Otto 347. Added in *1528*

his speech *On the Faithless Embassy*: 'This, then, was what that man prayed for and this was how he cursed his country. Now you should turn it on his own head.'[1] Ctesippus in the *Euthydemus* of Plato: 'If it were not rather boorish of me to do so, I would say "On your head."'[2] The sophist believed that those who wanted a young man to turn out wise were preparing his destruction, even though he was not yet wise; for what ceases to be what it was and begins to be what it was not is destroyed. So Maro: 'May the gods first turn that omen on you yourself.'[3] In Aristophanes in the *Plutus* Poverty reasons that if all men were to become rich Chremylus himself would be compelled to plough, to dig and to endure all the other labours.[4] He would live a harder life when rich than he had when poor. Chremylus, remembering the toils he had endured in poverty, expresses the hope that what was said will not come to pass and prays in turn for it to fall on the head of Poverty, saying 'On your head,' (with 'may it fall' to be understood).[5] Caelius to Marcus Cicero in book eight: 'But when Domitius put his fingers to his lips, on May 24 the loafers in the forum had spread it abroad that you had perished – may that fall on their heads.'[6]

89 **Iracundior Adria**
As angry as the Adriatic

A person who has a very unpleasant nature and an irritable disposition is proverbially compared to the Adriatic. So the girlfriend of Flaccus, from whom he had separated: 'You are more fickle than cork / And angrier than the terrible Adriatic.'[1] Horace himself admits that he is prone to anger: 'Quick to anger, but such that I can be appeased.' Also in the satire that begins 'I've been listening for some time now.'[2] Aeschines accuses Demos-

* * * * *

1 Demosthenes 19.130

2 Plato *Euthydemus* 283E

3 Virgil *Aeneid* 2.190-01

4 This sentence and all that follows it were added in *1533*.

5 Aristophanes *Plutus* 525–6

6 Cicero *Ad familiares* 8.1.4. The punctuation followed by Erasmus differs from that in modern editions, where a new sentence begins at 'on May 24.'

89 Horace (see n1). Added in *1528*

1 Horace *Odes* 3.9.22–3; followed by a quotation from *Epistles* 1.20.25

2 Horace *Satires* 2.7

thenes of being so truculent and unpredictable that it is easier to deal with the Adriatic than with him.[3] Not that this sea is stormier than any other – in fact, there is scarcely one that is more calm – but this was what the Italians thought. If they had sailed the English Channel or the Danish sea, they would admit that the Adriatic does not deserve to be called a sea.

90 Bos marinus
A sea-ox

Βοῦς ἐνάλιος, A sea-ox. Said of things that are huge, stupid, and of no use at all, like seals. All they do is eat, and they are useless for doing work or as food, quite the opposite of land oxen. The expression is reported by Suidas.[1] I suspect, however, that we should read βοῦς ἐναύλιος, so that it is the same as the one that follows immediately: Βοῦς ἐν αὐλίῳ κάθη 'you sit like an ox in the stable.'[2] For this is how it is given in the *Collections of Tarrhaeus and Didymus*.[3] It is the hemistich of an iambic trimeter.

91 Bos in stabulo
An ox in the stable

Βοῦς ἐν αὐλίῳ, An ox in the stable, described someone who was useless and spent his life in leisure. Hesychius points out that it was said by Cratinus in the play entitled the *Women of Delos*.[1] However, we have mentioned this proverb elsewhere.[2]

* * * * *

3 See Athenaeus 13.612D, where it is reported that Lysias says this of Aeschines.

90 *Suda* (see n1). Added in *1528*
  1 *Suda* B 458
  2 *Suda* B 459, the same as in Zenobius (Aldus) column 57. Cf *Adagia* II i 39 An ox at the manger.
  3 The title of the 1505 Aldine volume in which Zenobius' proverbs are given

91 Hesychius (see n1). Added in *1528*
  1 Hesychius B 969, citing PCG 4 Cratinus fragment 34
  2 *Adagia* II i 39 An ox at the manger

92 Canis ad cibum
A dog to food

Κύων ἐπὶ σῖτον, A dog to food. Said of those who hurry to their own destruction. A dog is enticed by food by those who wish to kill it. Hesychius
points out that this is like βοῦς ἐπὶ σφαγὴν 'an ox to slaughter' and ὗς ἐπὶ
δεσμά 'a pig to chains.'[1]

93 Bos in quadra argentea
An ox on a silver plate

Βοῦς ἐπὶ πίνακος ἀργυροῦ, An ox on a silver plate. Of those who give the
appearance that they do an outstanding service but are good only for enjoying themselves and looking down on others. It is very like the one we
have given elsewhere, 'The seventh ox.'[1] In antiquity sweets were served
in the shape of the horns of the new moon (for, when new and when wan-
ing, the moon looks like a horn). With respect to this proverb Suidas cites
a quite elegant epigram:[2]

> How is it that you, an ox, do not plough the field,
> But recline there, like a drunken peasant?
> Goat, why do you too not rush to pasture,
> But instead stand here, a silver image?
> I stand here, rebuking your idleness.

In book six, chapter eleven, Julius Pollux mentions this ox, pointing out
that this kind of food was customarily offered to Apollo, Diana, Hecate, and

* * * * *

92 Hesychius (see n1). Added in *1528*
 1 Hesychius B 971. See also Hesychius K 64 ('A dog to chains'). Cf *Adagia* II vii
   67 The dog asks for his chain.

93 *Suda* (see n2). Added in *1528*
 1 *Adagia* I x 63
 2 *Suda* B 457, on which the preceding sentence is based. The epigram has not
   been identified.

Moon.[3] Even today sweets are fashioned in the form of different animals. What the French call *roi de cartes* 'a paper king' (who is a king in name only rather than in wealth and power) is quite similar to this expression.[4]

94 Accepta candela
With candle in hand

Diphilus, cited in Athenaeus book fifteen, in the play entitled *Ignorance*: Ἄψαντες λύχνου λυχνεῖον ἐζητοῦμεν 'we snatched up the candle and then looked for the candlestick.'[1] You should have the candlestick at hand before you even touch the candle.

95 Vacuam inhabitare
To live in an empty house

Κενῷ ἐγκατοικεῖν δόμῳ, To live in an empty house. Said of those who put on a magnificent show of wealth, although they have not a single possession to their name. Plato quotes a trimeter, obviously one that was commonly spoken, since he does not give the author's name: 'Work at those things that will bring you wisdom, dropping those that are just for show, called nonsense or trifles as you will, "Things that will bring you to live in empty halls."'[1] Do not put great value on men who confute trifling arguments but rather value those who have substance and an honourable reputation and many other fine attributes.

* * * * *

3 Pollux *Onomasticon* 6.76. The reference to chapter 11 agrees with the enumeration of the sections of the book in the Aldine edition.

4 This French proverb is mentioned also at *Adagia* II v 79 A tragedy king.

94 Diphilus by way of Athenaeus (see n1). Erasmus mistranslates the Greek, which means 'having lit,' not 'having seized.' Rather oddly he gives the proverb as *accepta candela* ('having taken a candle') and not *arrepta candle* ('having snatched a candle') as in his translation. Possibly *accepta* is a misprint that was never caught. Added in *1528*

1 Athenaeus 15.700D, quoting PCG 5 Diphilus fragment 2

95 Plato (see n1). Added in *1528*

1 Plato *Gorgias* 486c–D. The verse quoted is Euripides fragment 188 Nauck.

We have spoken elsewhere about 'the empty box' of the *Graces*.[2]

96 Στηνιῶσαι
To Steniacize

Στηνιῶσαι, To Steniacize. This means to hurl fierce abuse at someone. In Athens there was a festival at which people were permitted to make fun of each other with witticisms and insults.[1] As a result of this, anyone who raved too freely at some individual was said 'To Steniacize.' The name of the festival was Στήνια. The word στηνόν properly describes something that is harsh and annoying to the ears.[2] So Hesychius[3] and the Etymologist.[4] Similar to 'Wagon-language.'[5]

97 A sexaginta viris venio
I'm coming from the Sixtymen

The Athenians took wondrous delight in those who could rouse laughter by their words or actions, so much so that sixty men used to gather in Diomeia[1] or in the temple of Heracles for this very purpose and were called 'the Sixtymen' (just as we say 'duumvirs,' 'triumvirs,' and 'decemvirs,' meaning magistracies). As a result of this, whenever anything funny had been said, an expression commonly used was, 'The Sixtymen said this' or Ἀπὸ τῶν

* * * * *

2 The *Graces* is the title by which Theocritus *Idyll* 16 is known. Erasmus refers to the phrase (Theocritus *Idylls* 16.10) at *Adagia* II ii 64 It's too late to spare when the bottom is bare.

96 Hesychius (see n3). Added in *1528*
1 This was a festival connected with Demeter.
2 There is no such word as στηνός. From where Erasmus drew this information is unknown.
3 Hesychius Σ 1825 and 1827, the source of most of what Erasmus says here
4 Nothing relevant to this adage has been found in the *Etymologicum magnum*.
5 *Adagia* I vii 73

97 Athenaeus (see n2). Added in *1528*
1 The name of an Attic deme. Erasmus follows the text of Athenaeus in the Aldine at this point (see next note). The text as emended in modern editions would be translated as 'in the temple of Heracles in the deme Diomeia.'

ἐξήκοντα ἔρχομαι 'I have just come from the Sixtymen.' Athenaeus tells of this in book fourteen.[2] In Athens there was a tribe called Διομῶν, named after a certain Diomus, son of Colyttus, whence Διομεῖον, as can be gathered from Hesychius.[3]

One can say ironically of a crude or graceless turn of phrase 'a phrase worthy of the Sixtymen' or of someone who tries to be witty in a foolish way one can say, 'This fellow has come to us from the Sixtymen.'

98 Capite gestare
To carry on our head

We are said 'To carry on our head' those whom we love dearly. Plato the *Republic* book ten: 'Because of their wisdom they are loved so deeply that their friends almost carry them around on their heads.'[1] It is clearly a metaphor taken from mothers and nurses who put their babies in cradles and carry them on their heads. Using a similar figure, Cicero said *oculis ferre* 'to carry in the eyes' meaning 'to love deeply.'[2] And 'we carry in our bosom' those on whom we lavish outstanding affection.[3]

99 Demissis auriculis
With ears lowered

Those who are dejected are said 'to have their ears on their shoulders.' So Plato in his *Republic* book ten: Τὰ ὦτα ἐπὶ τῶν ὤμων ἔχοντες 'Having their ears on their shoulders,' in other words, being dejected and unhappy.[1] Taken from work-animals who show how they feel by the movement of their ears, just as humans do with their brow and eyes.[2]

* * * * *

2 Athenaeus 14.614D
3 Hesychius Δ 1880

98 Platos (see n1). Added in *1528*
1 Plato *Republic* 10.600D: ἐπὶ ταῖς κεφαλαῖς περιφέρουσι.
2 Cicero *Philippics* 6.4.11; *Ad Quintum fratrem* 3.10; *Ad familiares* 16.27.2
3 See *Adagia* V ii 50 Carry in ones eyes, etc. (629 below).

99 Plato (see n1). Added in *1528*
1 Plato *Republic* 10.613C
2 Cf *Adagia* II iv 4 To see on the face of it; IV x 69 With honest brow (524 below).

For, as Pliny, says in book eleven, only to humans did nature give ears that do not move.[3] The ears of work-animals and almost all quadrupeds prick up when they are listening, are languid when they are tired, twitch when they are frightened, and almost completely prick up when they are angry; they droop when the animals are sick. This is why Flaccus writes, 'I droop my ears like an ill-tempered ass / When it takes up too heavy a load on its back.'[4] In fact, even today those whose hopes are disappointed are said 'to lower their ears' and 'to have droopy ears.'[5]

100 Ἀγαθοδαιμονίζειν
To be in the service of good luck

In antiquity those who drank sparingly were called 'Agathodaimonistae.' That is all Hesychius tells us, an author whose name matches his content, unless perhaps the work that we have is an epitome of what he actually wrote.[1] The story has come down to us that Socrates never drank from the first mixing bowl, but kept his thirst for the second.[2] The third bowl, however, was called Ἀγαθοῦ δαίμονος 'Here's to good luck,' as has been shown elsewhere.[3] And so those who kept their thirst for the third bowl were said 'To be in the service of good luck.'

The Italians rarely drink at a feast and only if their stomachs are ballasted with food, to use Plautus' expression.[4] We, however, begin the feast with drink, and end it with drink, while the doctors protest in vain.[5]

* * * * *

3 Pliny *Naturalis historia* 11.136
4 Horace *Satires* 1.9.20–1
5 Suringar 55

100 The Greek verb of the title is not attested. Erasmus has coined it from the noun Ἀγαθοδαιμονισταί in Hesychius A 252. Added in *1528*
1 Hesychius A 250. Hesychius' name means 'quiet,' matching the brevity of many of his explanations.
2 Plutarch *Moralia* 512F *De garrulitate*
3 *Adagia* I vi 53 Here's to good luck, or A blessing on it
4 Plautus *Cistellaria* 121. The Latin word is *saburratus*, the title of *Adagia* III vii 57 Full of ballast.
5 A criticism of his fellow Dutchmen

1 In frigidum furnum panes immittere
To put loaves in a cold oven

Ἐπὶ ψυχρὸν ἱπνὸν τοὺς ἄρτους ἐπιβάλλειν, To put loaves in a cold oven. Even today this is said of a person who tries to teach those incapable of learning or gives advice to those disinclined to take it or undertakes some other hopeless task.[1] It is to be found in Herodotus book five, the book entitled *Terpsichore*.[2] When the shades of the underworld were consulted, Melissa appeared and said that she would not reveal where a sum of money had been hidden, since she herself was cold and naked. For the clothes with which she had been buried had been of no use to her since they had not been burned. She gave credence to what she said by the following revelation: 'Periander put his loaves in an oven when it was cold.' When this puzzling statement was reported, only Periander understood it, since he knew that he had had intercourse with Melissa when she was dead.

I think this is enough to explain the sense of the proverb. We can use it in a less indecent and more seemly way.

2 Mercurio dextro
May Mercury be with me

Hesychius points out that in antiquity those who were about to throw dice were accustomed to address Mercury for good luck, just as 'Here's to good luck,' or 'To Zeus the Deliverer' was said at banquets.[1] I have spoken of these at the appropriate place.[2] The same author points out that when lots were

* * * * *

1 Herodotus (see n2). Added in *1528*

1 Suringar 92. Cf *Adagia* I iv 40 You teach a donkey to race with a bit.

2 Herodotus 5.92.7, which Erasmus closely follows in the following sentences. Melissa was the wife of Periander, the tyrant of Corinth, who had killed her, perhaps accidentally. Periander was trying to learn the whereabouts of money that a friend had given and that he had mislaid.

2 Hesychius (see n1). Added in *1528*

1 Hesychius E 5952. Erasmus translates a corrupt version of the text, as in the Aldine text of 1514, when he refers to the throwing of dice (πτῶσις). The correct text (πόσις) refers to a toast made to Mercury when someone was about to have a drink of wine.

2 *Adagia* I vi 53 (for the first of these). For the second cf *Adagia* II viii 1 A third to the Deliverer.

being drawn the first lot was customarily called 'Mercury.'[3] We can use it jokingly whenever we undertake anything new. Those who risk everything are said 'To cast all the dice,'[4] while those who are just beginning some enterprise can be said 'to be drawing Mercury.' In book six, chapter nine, Julius Pollux points out that when the meat of a sacrificial victim was being distributed the first portion was usually called Ἑρμοῦ κλῆρος 'Mercury's lot.'[5]

3 Ne Mercurio quidem credere
Not even Mercury would be believed

Ἦν οὐδὲν τῷ Ἑρμῇ πιστεῦσαι τις λέγοντι, Not even Mercury would be believed by anyone if he said this. Strabo in book two says this about a story that is scarcely believable.[1] However, the text of this passage is faulty, as is true of many others in this first edition.[2] Without any doubt οὐδέ must be read.[3] It will be appropriate to say this of those who have travelled on long and distant journeys and often tell of miraculous happenings. Mercury was regarded as the god of travellers.

4 Mercuriale
A gift of Mercury

In Greek, profit that befalls one unexpectedly was called a Ἑρμαῖον 'A gift of Hermes' from the first offerings for the god that used to be placed on

* * * * *

3 Hesychius E 5961
4 *Adagia* I iv 32
5 Pollux *Onomasticon* 6.55

3 Strabo (see n1). Added in *1528*
1 Strabo *Geographica* 2.4.2
2 The Venice edition of 1516 was the first to provide readers with the Greek text of Strabo. Up till then Erasmus depended on manuscripts or printed Latin translations.
3 Erasmus' translation of the Greek presupposes the reading he suggests: οὐδέ τῷ Ἑρμῇ 'not even Mercury.' The word he wants to replace, οὐδέν, would mean here 'in no way.' Erasmus is right in suggesting corruption in the text, but the correct reading is οὐδ᾽ ἄν.

4 *Suda* (see nn7–8 below). Added in *1528*. The last sentence (referring to Philostratus) was added in *1533*.

roads and were eaten by travellers. Others prefer to derive it from the piles of stones that were placed as a sacred offering to the god at points where it was not clear which road to take.[1] These cairns are referred to even in the Proverbs of the Hebrews: 'He who throws a stone on Mercury's heap is like the man who gives honour to a fool.'[2] This verse, however, has been translated in different ways in Greek. Some have rendered it in this way: 'He who ties a stone to his sling is like the man who gives honour to a fool.'[3] Instead of ἑρμαῖον 'Mercury's heap'[4] others give the translation πολυανδρεῖον,[5] which is a place set aside for many burials, and take 'stone' in the sense of 'jewel,' not referring to just any rock. There is little difference in translating the original term by 'cemetery' or by 'heap of stones,' for the graves of ordinary people were covered by a pile of stones. Whence Maro's words: 'Ballista is buried, covered under this mountain of stones.'[6] It is foolish to hurl a precious stone into a place of death and dirt. For a jewel does not enhance such a place, but is defiled by it. There is no point in throwing a stone on to a heap of stones, for in a cairn an individual stone serves no particular purpose. If, however, you throw a jewel on to a heap, you are much more foolish.

The most perceptive view, however, belonged to those who translated the word in question as 'sling.' For the meaning is that so far from doing what you are supposed to do, your action actually redounds to your misfortune; if you tie a stone to a fool's sling, you have provided the means for him to strike you.

* * * * *

1 One of Andrea Alciati's *Emblemata*, entitled *Qua dii vocant eundum*, refers to the cairn that marked the right road to take. On Alciati see *Adagia* IV ix 36 n2 (443 below).

2 Prov 26:8, here given by Erasmus in the Latin of the Vulgate: *sicut qui mittit lapidem in acervum Mercurii, ita qui tribuit insipienti honorem.*

3 Erasmus here quotes the Greek version from the Septuagint: Ὃς ἀποδεσμεύει λίθον ἐν σφενδόνῃ ὅμοιός ἐστι τῷ διδόντι ἄφρονι δόξαν. His Latin version follows the Complutensian Polyglot bible, that had been begun in 1514 but was not in circulation until several years later.

4 From the Latin version of Proverbs 26:8 one would expect the Greek original to have read ἑρμαῖον, translated in the Vulgate by *acervus Mercurii* 'Mercury's heap.'

5 The source of such a translation has not been identified.

6 According to Servius (in his preface to *Aeneid* 1) this was part of the first distich composed by Virgil.

The expression is not confined to this custom of heaping up stones. Suidas cites the following without giving the author's name: 'Unlike others, he is not obsessed with ἑρμαῖον "the love of profit" and does not think he is guiltless if he has bought at a profit something from someone who willingly sold it.'[7] He also reports this saying, again without naming the author: 'Whoever is gentle and kind is a ἑρμαῖον "a source of profit" to villains.'[8] For the gentleness of upright persons emboldens criminals. He also gives the following, apparently from the Damascan.[9] 'Whoever bumped into me thought that he had come upon a ἑρμαῖον "a windfall."' For a traveller who is lost takes fresh heart when he finds a cairn of Mercury. Such a cairn is also called λόφος Ἑρμαῖος 'a mound or hill of Mercury.'[10] Philostratus in the *Sophists* calls a treasure that had been discovered in a building a *hermaion*,[11] and elsewhere uses the term in the sense of a great profit that befalls one fortuitously.[12]

5 Filum nevistis et acu opus est
You have spun the thread; now you want a needle

A verse, clearly in anapests, that Julius Pollux gives in book ten from the *Fates* of Hermippus has the appearance of a proverb: Ῥάμμα ἐπέκλωσας· προσδεῖ καὶ ῥαφίδος 'The thread's been spun; now you want a needle.'[1]

The meaning is that it is not enough to have begun a task unless you complete it with equal effort. 'You have learned the art, what remains is to practise it.' 'You have learned grammar, dialectic remains.' 'You know the Bible, what remains is to lead a good life.'

* * * * *

7 *Suda* E 3030, citing Damascius fragment 122 Zintzen

8 *Suda* E 3032

9 Damascius fragment 341 Zintzen, cited in *Suda* E 3031. Erasmus gives the name as *Damascenus*.

10 Hesychius E 5939

11 Philostratus *Vita sophistarum* 2.548

12 Philostratus *Vita sophistarum* 1.525 and 2.617

5 Pollux (see n1). Added in *1528*

1 Pollux *Onomasticon* 10.136, citing PCG 5 Hermippus fragment 49. But only the first part of the line is from Hermippus. The second half ('now you want a needle') is Pollux's explanation of the preceding phrase.

6 Calvus quum sis
Although you are bald

Gregory the theologian, in a letter to the sophist Eustochius whom he had attacked: 'And I have not even followed the common proverb Φαλακρὸς ὢν "Although bald," which told me that I ought not to clash head to head with a ram or to stir up a wasps' nest against me; in other words, I ought not to provoke a tongue more ready to curse than to flatter.'[1]

I have spoken elsewhere about not stirring up hornets.[2]

7 Argenteus puteus
A silver well

Φρέαρ ἀργυροῦν, A silver well. Athenaeus in book eleven points out that in antiquity a huge wine bowl was customarily called 'a silver well,' since wine-ladles were quite small.[1] Even nowadays some take pleasure in draining wine from deep cups and 'in soaking their lips,' as the poet writes;[2] at the same time they say the proverb 'You need a lot of water to soak a beard.'[3] The joke comes from barbers who soak the beard with lots of warm water before shaving it.

8 Malo asino vehitur
Riding on a wretched ass

Ἐπ' ὄνου πονηρᾶς ὀχούμενοι, Riding on a wretched ass. Said of those for whom things are not going at all well. Suidas gives this expression, as a

* * * * *

6 Gregory of Nazianzus (see n1). Added in *1528*
1 Gregory of Nazianzus *Letters* 191.1
2 *Adagia* I i 60 To stir up hornets

7 Athenaeus (see n1). Added in *1528*
1 Athenaeus 11.461C; cf 5.192A. The point of the final part of the sentence is that drawing wine with small ladles from a large bowl was like drawing water from a well.
2 Persius *Prologus* 1
3 Cf Suringar 245. The Latin given here by Erasmus is *multa aqua ori admota probe macerari barbam* 'a beard is thoroughly soaked only when a lot of water is applied to the face.'

8 *Suda* (see n1). Added in *1528*

proverb, under the entry πονηρός.[1] The point of the expression is that those who are successful enjoy riding on fine horses so that they may reach their destination more quickly. It will be quite witty to use it of a man who is unhappily married.

9 Allium in retibus
Garlic in nets

Σκόροδον ἐν δικτύοις, Garlic in nets. This expression was used to describe cheap provisions. Its origin lies in a common practice of the people of Attica. Whenever they were preparing for a voyage or an expedition, they would buy up garlic, put it in nets, and take it with them. Garlic was also valuable when cities were being besieged, whence the following, quoted without source in Suidas: 'I lose garlic in the siege.'[1] The Thracians in particular like garlic since it is sharp-tasting and they live in a cold country. In fact even today garlic is a favourite of sailors, and country-people like it too, however much it was cursed by Horace.[2] A suitable occasion for the adage will be when someone is about to undertake the study of philosophy and you tell him he must prepare himself for a frugal way of living and for long nights of study and hard toil. Your advice will be 'Garlic in nets!'

10 Sybaritici sermones
Sybaritic style

Συβαριτικοὶ λόγοι, Sybaritic style. Hesychius tells of a Greek called Akopus (a man of Sybaris, I think), who worked extremely hard to acquire a

* * * * *

1 *Suda* Π 2041, but it is not explicitly described as a proverb.

9 *Suda* (see n1). Added in *1528*
1 *Suda* Σ 668, from which much of the first part of the essay is drawn. The quotation is from Aristophanes *Acharnians* 163–4: Ἀπόλλυμαι τὰ σκόροδα πορθούμενος, but Erasmus mistranslates. The sense is 'I am done for, now that I have lost my garlic.'
2 Horace *Epodes* 3

10 Hesychius (see n1). This adage is virtually a doublet of *Adagia* i vi 56 The language of Sybaris (*Sybaritica oratio*), and much of the commentary is repeated here. The Greek phrase probably means 'Sybaritic tales,' a type of fable (see n1). Added in *1528*

luxuriant and rich style of speaking to match his life-style.[1] This gave rise
to a humorous proverb that called an exquisite and highly polished style
'Sybaritic.' Such a style is usually not persuasive since 'the language of truth
is simple and short.'[2] 'As the man is, so is his talk.'[3] Examples of this are
Maecenas and Apuleius; the former lived luxuriously and was effeminate,
the latter was an African and a sorcerer.[4]

I have spoken of the magnificent splendour of the Sybarites in the
proverb 'A Sybaritic table.'[5]

11 Maturior moro
As soft as a ripe fig

Πεπαίτερος μόρου, Riper than a fig. Athenaeus in book two quotes a fragment
of Aeschylus in the *Phrygians* that refers to Hector: 'That fellow was softer

* * * * *

1 Hesychius Σ 2131. The name Akopus is taken from the 1514 Aldine edition of
   Hesychius. Modern editions correctly offer Aesopus (Aesop, the famous writer
   of fables, who came from Samos). Hesychius does not say that Akopus was a
   citizen of Sybaris. This is an inference of Erasmus. All Hesychius says is that
   Akopus was in Italy when he tried to acquire this style of speaking. Sybaris
   is a town in southern Italy, in the region called Magna Graecia, since many of
   the towns there had been Greek colonies. The Sybarites were renowned for a
   luxurious way of life. See final note.
2 Cf *Adagia* I iii 88 The plain speech of truth. Here Erasmus slightly expands
   the Latin of that proverb (to *veritatis simplex et brevis est oratio*).
3 *Adagia* I vi 50, also cited in *Adagia* I vi 56 The language of Sybaris
4 Seneca *Letters* 114.4–8 also took Maecenas, the advisor of Augustus, as a good
   example of how a person's style of speaking reflected his character and mode
   of life. Maecenas was renowned for his effeminacy and his foppish dress and
   behaviour. His poetry is said to reflect his 'preciosity and neuroticism' (E.C.
   Courtney *The Fragmentary Latin Poets* [Oxford 1993] 276–81). In contrast the
   style of the prose author Apuleius, which is described as 'the braying of an
   ass' by Lorenzo Valla and others (see *Ciceronianus* CWE 28 569 n445; ASD I-2
   649:15n), is rugged and unrefined. Erasmus also refers to Maecenas in *Adagia*
   I vi 50 As the man is, so is his talk.
5 *Adagia* II ii 65

11 Athenaeus (see n1). Added in *1528*. 'When the word . . . with an omicron' was
   added in *1533*.

than a ripe fig.'¹ It can be said of a man with a very mild disposition or of one who is effeminate or of someone who craves something, like a girl who is itching to marry. Athenaeus adds, from Nicander, that the fruit of this tree appears earlier than any other.² Small cuts are also made in the fruit to aid the ripening.³ When the word is written μόρον, with an omicron, it refers to a kind of fig, in my opinion.⁴

12 Flos cinis
A flower is but ash

St Augustine in his work *In Answer to the Letter of Petilianus*, at book two, chapter sixty-six, mocks his adversary because he boasted that the sky was filled with the souls of his followers and that the earth blossomed with the memory of their bodies.¹ In his reply he said, 'We certainly see the flowers of the earth issuing from the bodies of that vast number, but, as the saying goes, "A flower is but ash."' The Donatists regarded as martyrs those followers of theirs who had killed themselves or who had called upon others (who did not wish to die) to put them to death.² They constantly visited the martyrs' tombs, and this is why Augustine calls the flowers there 'ash.'

It seems to have been customarily said of the ephemeral nature of human existence. Today young men are in the bloom of life; tomorrow they will be in their tomb. And according to the prophet 'all flesh is grass.'³

* * * * *

1 Athenaeus 2.51C, quoting *TrGF* 3 Aeschylus fragment 264
2 Athenaeus 2.51D, citing Nicander fragment 75 *Georgica* in Nicander *Poems and Poetical Fragments* ed A.S.F. Gow and A.E. Scholfield (Cambridge 1953)
3 Athenaeus 2.51B–C. Erasmus says here that the tree is nicked. Athenaeus, whom the translation follows, more accurately says that it is the fruit to which a knife is applied.
4 The Greek word actually means 'black mulberry.' Erasmus is contrasting the Greek form with the Latin *morus* (with a long *o*) which means mulberry. There is, however, no Greek equivalent spelled with an omega instead of an omicron.

12 Augustine (see n1). Added in *1528*
1 Augustine *Contra litteras Petiliani* 2.71.160 CSEL 52 102, PL 43 309
2 The Donatists were a schismatic group in North Africa in the fourth and fifth centuries. Petilianus was a Donatist bishop of Cirta.
3 Is 40:6

13 Homo semper contradicens
It is human never to stop arguing

Galen, in the book in which he refutes someone called Julian who attacked
the *Aphorisms of Hippocrates*, quotes the following expression as a very common one: Οὐδέν ἐστιν ἀπεραντολογώτερον ἀνθρώπου 'There is nothing more
stubborn in arguing than a human being.'[1] Ἀπεραντολογία 'ceaseless talking' is a vice that does not permit one to know when to stop chattering.
     It suits those who never admit that they have been defeated in an
argument. The stupid and inexperienced suffer very greatly from this vice.

14 Insanire cum insanientibus
To take on the madness of the mad

Τοῖς μαινομένοις συμμαίνεσθαι, To share in the madness of the mad. This was
said of anyone who modified his own behaviour to match that of others, no
matter who they were. Galen used it in book one of *On the Natural Faculties*:
'Now that we have sufficiently indulged in trifles – not voluntarily, but
under compulsion "To take on the madness of the mad," as the proverb
says – let us return again to the investigation into urine.'[1]

15 Callipugos
Beautifully-buttocked

Those who had an elegant body were said to be Καλλίπυγοι 'Well-
buttocked.' Athenaeus in book twelve relates the origin of the proverb to

* * * * *

13 Galen (see n1). Added in *1528*
 1 Galen *Contra Iulianum* 2.3 Wenkebach

14 Galen (see n1). Added in *1528*
 1 Galen *De naturalibus facultatibus* 1.15.56–7 Helmreich. Erasmus has translated
    the Greek word διάκρισις, which here means 'secretion' of urine, by *discretio*,
    probably meaning 'separation' or 'differentiation,' here translated as 'inves-
    tigation.' Thomas Linacre, the English humanist and translator of Galen (see
    Adagia IV vi 52 n4, 249 above), construes the Greek word by *secretio*.

15 Athenaeus (see n1). Added in *1528*

the following story.[1] Two sisters, the daughters of a countryman, were vying with each other on a public road as to which of them was more beautiful. A young man came up. He was struck by their beauty and pointed
this out to his father.[2] He preferred the older sister and fell madly in
love with her. When he returned to the city he fell sick and explained
the cause of his illness to his younger brother, who went to the countryside and after seeing the girls fell in love with the younger one. The
father of the girls betrothed them to the other man's sons. The citizens
called the girls 'well-buttocked' because of their outstanding beauty. The
girls acquired wealth and this was used to build a temple to Venus who
was herself also called 'well-buttocked' after the girls. Athenaeus cites a
scazon of Cercidas about them: 'Once there was a well-buttocked pair in
Syracuse.'[3] An expression with similar meaning is πύγαργοι 'pale-bottomed
men,' as we have related elsewhere, in the proverb Λευκόπυγοι 'White-
bottomed.'[4]

16 Quod volumus sanctum est
Our wish is for what is holy

Saint Augustine in book four of *Against Cresconius the Grammarian*: 'No
longer is it a case of "Our wish is only for what is holy," as the old proverb
says. Instead, something is holy whenever we wish it and as long as we

* * * * *

1 Athenaeus 12.554C–D
2 Erasmus has mistranslated the text in his Aldine edition of Athenaeus at this
  point, which is the same as in modern editions. What Athenaeus says is that the
  two girls exposed themselves to a young man as he passed by. There is nothing
  at this point about the young man telling his father, although Athenaeus says
  that he had a father who was very rich.
3 Cercidas fragment 14 in J.U. Powell *Collectanea Alexandrina* (Oxford 1925). The
  scazon (literally 'limping') is the name of a verse similar to an iambic trimeter
  except that the second last element is long and not short.
4 Erasmus gives the wrong title. The proverb to which he refers is *Adagia* II i 43
  Mind you don't fall in with Blackbottom. In the accompanying essay there he
  says the terms 'white-bottomed' or 'pale-bottomed' were applied to effeminate
  and unwarlike men.

16 Augustine (see n1). Otto 1854. Added in *1528*

wish it.'[1] Elsewhere, if I am not mistaken, he cites it as being from Ticonius the Donatist.[2] The expression constitutes half of a dactylic hexameter.

Nowadays a class of men who do not measure piety by the rule of Christ but by their own desires hold sway in this world. They want whatever they passionately desire to be regarded as sacred too, marvellously deluding themselves as they indulge in what is by nature most foul. They say that just wearing the belt they do[3] is holy. Why? Because they wish to be regarded as holy with little effort on their part. But they do not wish to live in sobriety and purity, and they are unwilling to endure insults. Why so? Because that is hard and difficult.

17 Ne crepitu quidem digiti dignum
Worth not even the snap of a finger

Athenaeus in book twelve, speaking of the tomb of Sardanapalus: 'And in death, in the statue on his tomb Sardanapalus shows by his fingers how insignificant human affairs are, Οὐκ ἄξια ὄντα ψόφου δακτύλων "Worth not even the snap of a finger." '[1] Aristobulus, cited later in the same author, informs us that on the statue that had been placed on the tomb of Sardanapalus the fingers of the right hand had been brought together in the way that we do when we snap them.[2]

Both the gesture and the proverb survive up to the present day among our countrymen, when they say, 'I don't give this for it.'[3]

* * * * *

1 Augustine Contra Cresconium 4.37.44 CSEL 52 543, PL 43 572
2 Letters 93.43 (PL 33 342); Contra epistolam Parmeniani 2.13.31 CSEL 51 83. The floruit of Ticonius (or rather Tichonius) was 380–420. Cf Adagia I ii 15 What is one's own is beautiful, where the proverb is cited at the end.
3 The belt of a monk

17 Athenaeus (see n1). Added in 1528
1 Athenaeus 12.529D–E. This information from Athenaeus is given at Adagia I viii 7 I make it not worth a snap of the fingers. For Sardanapalus see Adagia IV vii 28 Don't eat an olive (296 below). See also III vii 27 A Sardanapalus.
2 Aristobulus was a historian of Alexander the Great and served him in a minor role. The fragment is FGrHist 39 F 9, quoted at Athenaeus 12.530B.
3 Suringar 131

18 Coriaceum auxilium
A leather prop

Σκυτίνη ἐπικουρία, A prop of leather, Prop of skin. The Greek expression described assistance that was weak and feeble. It is given by Hesychius.[1] Athenaeus book twelve points out that this was said of an extremely lean man called Sannyrion because he was nothing but skin and bone.[2] Also cited in Athenaeus, in book thirteen, is Antiphanes, who criticizes skinny philosophers: 'In the company of sophists who are, in heaven's name, lean, unfed, and nothing but skin and bones.'[3] That is how philosophers were in antiquity; today there are those who 'advertize their virtue by their sullen, downcast countenances.'[4]

19 Tanagraeus cetus
A Tanagran monster

Someone who was very fat and had a huge body mass was called a Ταναγραῖον κῆτος 'A Tanagran monster,' named after Tanagra, a city in Boeotia that Homer calls Γραῖα and Lycophron calls Poemandria, located on the

* * * * *

18 Hesychius (see n1). Added in 1528
1 Hesychius Σ 1199, whose interpretation of the proverb is ἐπὶ τῶν ἀσθενούντων βοηθημάτων 'applied to weak assistance'
2 Athenaeus 12.551C, quoting PCG 7 Strattis fragment 57. The expression – a pun on συκίνη ἐπικουρία 'fig-wood help,' also given by Hesychius (see n1) – probably refers to leather padding worn by Sannyrion in a vain attempt to conceal his thinness. Erasmus interprets the phrase differently.
3 Athenaeus 13.565F, quoting PCG 2 Antiphanes fragment 120.3–4
4 Erasmus is referring to the mendicant friars. Wesseling ('Dutch Proverbs' 364) identified the source of the last part of this sentence; it is an unacknowledged loose quotation of a line from a prologue that Angelo Poliziano wrote for Plautus' Menaechmi (Epistolae 7.15); see A. Politianus Opera omnia ed Ida Maier (Basel 1953) volume I page 95.

19 Athenaeus (see n2). Stephanus of Byzantium sub Τάναγρα is Erasmus' unacknowledged source for much of the information given here (but not for the adage itself). Added in 1528

coast.[1] The beaching of a huge sea-creature there gave rise to the proverb. The phrase is given by Athenaeus in book twelve.[2]

20 Legatus non caeditur neque violatur
An envoy is not beaten or violated

The scholiast on book four of the *Iliad* gives this proverb: Πρέσβυς οὐ τύπτεται οὐδὲ ὑβρίζεται 'An envoy is not struck or violated.'[1] The reason for the proverb is that in antiquity heralds were regarded as inviolate. This has come down into international law, so that envoys come and go under a general guarantee of safety, even if they deliver frightening messages, as the *fetiales* and the *patres patrati* once did.[2] Nowadays even in the middle of wars no harm is done to those who carry the insignia of an envoy.

The proverb can be turned so as to apply to anyone who gives good advice or counsel or harangues an assembly in an unrestrained manner: 'He is an envoy; he is reporting his prince's instructions' or 'He is engaged on state business; it is not right for him to be assaulted.'

21 Herculani lecti
Herculean couches

Ἡράκλειοι στρωμναί, Herculean couches. This was what soft and luxurious couches were called. Athenaeus in book twelve is the source of this.[1] The expression is extremely surprising since the Cynics claim Hercules as their

* * * * *

1 Homer *Iliad* 2.498 and Lycophron *Alexandra* 326, both quoted by Stephanus (see introductory note). Tanagra is a few miles inland. Stephanus gives another location that has this name, a part of the city of Oropos that is on the sea.
2 Athenaeus 12.551A

20 Scholiast on Homer (see n1). Added in *1528*. Tilley M 905 A herald should be neither beheaded nor hanged
1 Scholiast on Homer *Iliad* 4.394
2 The priests and representatives of the Roman people who conducted a ritual with other peoples that virtually marked the beginning of war. See Livy 1.24.

21 Athenaeus (see n1). Added in *1528*
1 Athenaeus 12.512F

champion, just as today the Carmelites claim the prophet Elijah for themselves.[2] In Athenaeus, however, the aim of the person who says this is to
persuade others that Hercules lived a soft and luxurious life, and that the
stories about his labours in the poets are pure figments of their imagination.[3] This is how we justify indulging our vices.[4]

22 Ἀποσκυθίσαι
A Scythian shave

Athenaeus in book twelve recounts that when the Scythians were being overwhelmed by many disasters they had the hair of all the peoples
they ruled over shaved close.[1] This they did as an amusing frolic. As
a result, all other peoples called a shave whose purpose was to arouse
shame and mockery 'A Scythian shave.' We read of something similar in
Second Kings chapter 10: 'Anon shaved off half the beards of David's
servants and cut off the lower part of their garments up to the but-
tocks,' clearly to cause them shame.[2] This action was the cause of a savage war.

The proverb will suit certain persons who have such a cruel disposition
that scarcely anyone can have dealings with them without coming away
humiliated.

* * * * *

2 For the Cynics, who lived in an extremely austere way, see Diogenes Laertius
   6.20–88 (on Diogenes of Sinope, traditionally the founder of the Cynics). The
   first Carmelites lived on Mt Carmel, as did Elijah.
3 The person cited by Athenaeus here is Megacleides, a fourth-century commentator on Homer.
4 By adducing famous persons or mythological characters to support our actions

22 Athenaeus (see n1). Added in *1528*
1 Athenaeus 12.524E–F. Erasmus misunderstands Athenaeus here. Athenaeus
   says that the Scythians cut off their *own* hair, something they also did when
   in mourning. Erasmus may have been confused by the Scythian practice of
   scalping their victims in war (see Herodotus 4.64).
2 2 Sam 10:4. Erasmus follows the designation in the Greek bible and in the
   Vulgate where the books of Samuel were named the first two books of Kings,
   forming a group of four with the ones we now know as First and Second
   Kings.

23 Macilentior Leotrephide
As skinny as Leotrephides

Λεπτότερον Λεωτρεφίδου καὶ Θαυμάντιδος, Thinner than Leotrephides and Thaumantis. Leotrephides was so extraordinarily lean that he provided the comic writers with an opportunity to use their wit. In Athenaeus book twelve the verses of Hermippus that are directed at him are given: 'They are now sacrificing heifers that are skinnier than Leotrephides and Thaumantis.'[1] The poet Cinesias was also criticized by many writers. He was tall, but so thin that he put on a girdle made of tree-bark to prevent his body bending over. For this reason Aristophanes called him 'linden.'[2] The poet Philetas also gained notoriety; he was so thin that he added lumps of lead to his feet so that the wind would not carry him away.[3]

The proverb will suit persons who are puny and very thin. It will be more pleasing if it is applied metaphorically to lack of talent or to a style of speaking that is dry, feeble and insubstantial.

24 Cape nihil et serva bene
Take nothing and watch it well

Λάβε μηδὲν καὶ κράτει καλῶς, Take nothing and watch it well. It appears to be said of those who give worthless information, yet tell their listeners to remember it. Galen *On the Principles of Plato and Hippocrates* in book three: 'For only in this way will I believe that the proverb "Take nothing and watch it well" applies here.'[1]

The proverb will suit false and useless teaching.

* * * * *

23 Athenaeus (see n1). Added in *1528*
1 Athenaeus 12.551A, quoting PCG 5 Hermippus fragment 36. Modern editions give the names as Leotrophides and Thoumantis. Erasmus follows the Aldine edition in giving the former as Leotrephides. The name Thaumantis is probably an error, either of Erasmus or the printer, since the Aldine has the correct spelling.
2 Aristophanes *Birds* 1377, also quoted by Athenaeus at 12.551D. The adjective 'linden' probably refers to the lightness of the wood.
3 Athenaeus 12.552B. The correct form of the name is Philitas.

24 Galen (see n1). Added in *1528*
1 Galen *De placitis Hippocratis et Platonis* 3.4.5 De Lacy

25 Μυιοσόβαι
Fly-flappers

Even today those who perform trivial services for someone are commonly called Μυιοσόβαι 'Fly-flappers.'[1] Athenaeus in book eleven points out that this had its origin in the luxurious customs of the Persians, who employed fly-repellers at banquets, as is now very common in Italy.[2] The verb μυιοσοβεῖν means 'to drive away flies.'

The expression will suit even those who love someone so tenderly that they are upset if their beloved suffers even the slightest inconvenience and agrees with what we cited elsewhere from Homer: 'Just as a mother brushes off a fly from her child when he lies quietly in soothing sleep.'[3]

26 Miserior monomachis
As doleful as a duellist

What Athenaeus quotes in book four from the comic writer Posidippus has the appearance of a proverb: Τῶν μονομαχούντων ἀθλιώτερος 'More wretched than those who fight in single combat.'[1] For these fight with each other under the cruellest of conditions: one of them must die. The verses are as follows: 'He who has never sailed has never seen any trouble; / We sailors are more wretched than duellists.'

In Latin such men were called *gladiatores* 'gladiators.' They provided the most barbaric of spectacles, but it was a favourite one of the Romans.

The expression will have more charm if it is applied metaphorically to a dispute that you are engaged in with the vilest of men, meaning that it is as if you are fighting with a gladiator.

* * * * *

25 Athenaeus (see n2). Cf *Adagia* III vii 60 Keeping off flies. Added in *1528*
  1 Wesseling (ASD II-8 85:241–2n) refers to a similar term in German that was used of courtiers, *Fliegenwedel*. Suringar 126
  2 Athenaeus 11.484D, where Menander fragment 437 Körte-Thierfelder is quoted to illustrate the word *labronia*. Athenaeus does not make any mention of 'fly-flappers' being a proverbial expression.
  3 Homer *Iliad* 4.130–1, cited also at *Adagia* III viii 20 Of one who loves tenderly

26 Athenaeus (see n1). Added in *1528*
  1 Athenaeus 4.154F, quoting PCG 7 Posidippus fragment 23

27 Zenonium est et lentem coquere
You are a Zeno even if you are cooking lentils

Timon of Phlius in Athenaeus book four: Καὶ Ζηνώνειόν γε φακῆν ἕψειν 'You are a Zeno even when cooking lentils.'[1] Zeno was the founder of the Stoics. He teaches that every action of the wise man is virtuous and that it does not matter what he does. The wise man is still the wise man whether he is engaged in the most trivial or most important activity. It follows from this that we need the wisdom of Zeno to cook lentils properly. Its origin is in an apophthegm reported by Diogenes Laertius.[2] For when Zeno was arguing that everything the wise man did was virtuous, someone laughed at him and rejoined, 'He'll be virtuous then even when he is cooking lentils!' Zeno agreed and approved of the comparison.

The proverb can be used in a serious vein when we want to say that a good man is true to himself even in the most insignificant of things or that an outstanding craftsman shows his skill whatever kind of material he is working in.

28 Olivam ne comedas
Don't eat an olive

In Athenaeus book ten the following expression from Chrysippus in his work *On the Good* is cited: Μὴ ποτε ἐλαίαν ἔσθι', ἀκαλήφην ἔχων χειμῶνος ὥρᾳ 'Never eat an olive when you have a nettle in winter-time.'[1] I be-

* * * * *

27 Timon of Phlius by way of Athenaeus (see n1). Erasmus misunderstands the Greek, in which Ζηνώνειον is an adjective agreeing with φακῆν. The sense is 'to make Zenonian lentil soup,' that is, following Zeno's recipe (of adding coriander). Added in 1528. 'Its origin is in an apophthegm . . . approved of the comparison' was added in 1533.

1 Athenaeus 4.158A–B, quoting PPF Timon of Phlius fragment 13 = fragment 22 Wachsmuth

2 This may be a reference to Diogenes Laertius 7.125: 'The wise man does all things well.' The source of the incident he now describes has not been identified.

28 Athenaeus (see n1). Added in 1528

1 Athenaeus 4.158B (not book 10), quoting Chrysippus fragment 709A (SVF 3.178). In modern editions 'in winter time' begins a new sentence, and ought to be detached from the adage.

lieve that he is thinking of the plant and not the fish.[2] I see no use for the adage unless we ever want to describe such extreme thrift in someone's diet that no condiment is added even to nettles.[3] He then adds that βολ-βοφακῆ is a favourite dish made, as the Greek word indicates, from onions and lentils: Βολβοφακῆν, βαβαί, βαβαί 'Onion and lentil soup. Wonderful! Wonderful!'[4] Nettles have a sharp taste, but are cheaper than oil.[5] He is implying that in the summer months there is no need of either olive oil or nettles.[6] Such a diet would suit those who think that they are like Paul or Antony[7] even though they are more like Sardanapalus in their luxurious fare.[8]

29 Olla lenticulam attigit
The pot has grasped the lentils

Epicharmus, as quoted in Athenaeus in the passage we have just cited: Χύτρα δὲ φακέας ἥψετο 'But the pot has grasped the lentils.'[1] It will suit those who have an insatiable desire for something. It is as if they are born to pursue what they desire, even if they have no opportunity of acquiring it. An earthenware pot is thought to love lentils and to come to them as

* * * * *

2 The Greek word translated as 'nettle' can also refer to a sea anemone.

3 Better sense would be given if the Latin meant 'that not even nettles were added as a condiment.' There may be a printing error in the Latin at this point: *condimenti* (genitive) instead of *condimento* (dative).

4 *Adespota* 367–8 Kock (3.477). Erasmus does not translate the Greek.

5 The point of the adversative 'but' seems to be that both olive oil and nettles add taste to food.

6 This odd inference of Erasmus arises from the punctuation that he follows (see n1).

7 Two hermits who lived in the Egyptian desert, and whom Erasmus often refers to as models of monastic asceticism. See Wesseling 'Dutch proverbs' 373 n56 and *Adagia* II ix 37 For they are no longer alive, and who are alive are no good. This is a jibe at the hypocrisy of the monks of Erasmus' time.

8 Sardanapalus was an eastern king renowned for his extravagant way of life; see *Adagia* III vii 27 A Sardanapalus.

29 Athenaeus (see n1). Erasmus mistranslates the Greek verb, which here means 'to boil' and not 'to grasp' or 'touch.' The expression means 'A pot was cooking lentils.' Added in *1528*

1 Athenaeus 4.158c, quoting Epicharmus fragment 33 Kaibel

if of its own accord. This proverb is like those we have given elsewhere – 'The pot picks its own greens,' 'The horse to the plain.'[2]

30 Qui non zelat
No jealousy, no love

'He who is not jealous does not love.' Saint Augustine in *Against Adimantus* at chapter 13 refers to this as a common expression.[1] Even today we say this when we mean that love cannot exist without jealousy.[2] It is true that jealousy springs from strong feelings of love, but it can also be prompted by sheer foolishness. In scripture God is called 'jealous,' because he wishes us to love him alone and does not permit anything to be loved other than himself, unless it is loved because of him.[3]

31 Lens deus
God Lentil

In Athenaeus book four this trimeter, apparently proverbial, is quoted: Φακός σε δαίμων καὶ φακὴ τύχη λάβοι 'May God Lentil and Fortune Lentil seize you.'[1]

Φακός means uncooked lentils, φακή cooked ones, as the Etymologist points out.[2] It will be suitable to use the expression when the same things are being repeated over and over *ad nauseam*.[3] In Greek *daimon* means fortune, so that those who are unlucky are called *cacodaemones*; τύχη means the same, the sole difference being that *daemon* is masculine and τύχη feminine.

* * * * *

2 *Adagia* I vii 60; I viii 82

30 Augustine (see n1). Otto 78. The full form of the adage is *Qui non zelat, non amat* 'No jealousy, no love.' Added in *1528*
1 Augustine *Contra Adimantum* 13.2 CSEL 25 146, PL 42 147
2 Suringar 189
3 As at Ex 20:5, 34:14

31 Athenaeus (see n1). Added in *1528*
1 Athenaeus 4.156F, quoting *TrGF* 2 *Adespota* 92
2 *Etymologicum magnum* sub φακή 786.40–1
3 The Latin reads *ad fastidium*.

32 Trabs in omnibus
A plank in everything

Δοκὸς δ᾽ ἐπὶ πᾶσι τέτυκται, A plank has been fashioned in all things. It seems to be a half-line from some poet.[1] It means that nothing is so certain that some doubts do not occur, compelling us to consider the situation more carefully. The gospel mentions a plank in the eyes.[2] The Greek work has a double meaning, 'plank' when it is pronounced δοκός, or 'opinion' when it is pronounced δόκος. The warning of Socrates, φρόντισον 'consider carefully,' is well known.[3]

Galen cites the expression in *On the Differences of Pulses* book three.[4] It appears to be drawn from ploughing, which is made difficult because the plough-beam continually meets resistance while the earth is being turned over.

33 Ex libro gubernatores
Steersmen from a book

Galen in the work that he wrote about his own books: 'Those, however, who have not learned under teachers but are, as the proverb says, Οἱ ἐκ βιβλίου

* * * * *

32 Galen (see n4). Erasmus has misconstrued the expression. What he translates as 'plank, beam' should be translated as 'opinion.' The proper sense of the phrase is 'everyone can have an opinion.' Added in *1528*

1 Xenophanes fragment 34.4 Diels-Kranz

2 Matt 7:3 'Why do you see the speck that is in your brother's eye, but do not notice the log that is in your own eye?' (Revised Standard Version); Luke 6:41. See also *Adagia* I vi 91 To cast a mote out of another man's eye.

3 The source of this is not known. In the *Suda* (Φ 731) there is a reference to Socrates and his followers being called φροντισταί because they never ceased from thinking. At *Adagia* II vii 95 A ruler should not sleep the whole night through, Erasmus relates the story from Plutarch *Moralia* 780c *Ad principem ineruditum* in which the king of Persia was commanded each morning to consider (φρόντιζε), but this story has nothing to do with Socrates.

4 Galen *De pulsuum differentia* 3.1 (8.637 Kühn)

33 Galen (see nn1–2). Added in *1528*

κυβερνῆται "Steersmen from a book" seek these things.'[1] The same author in book three of *On the Composition of Medicines*: 'Like those who are said in the proverb to be "Steersmen from a book."'[2] I have spoken elsewhere about 'Silent teachers.'[3]

34 Fractis auribus
Cauliflower ears

Galen against Thrasybulus: 'Those books of theirs that are carried around by Οἱ τὰ ὦτα κατεαγότες "Those with mangled ears" are wonderful.'[1] If I am not mistaken, he is thinking of boxers who later become doctors and write books, or, more likely, of the books of inexperienced doctors that are read by boxers. These boxers usually have mutilated ears like pigs, black eyes, and their whole face is marked with swellings – all this from the profession they practise. For Galen frequently vents his spleen on athletes.[2] Plato used this adage in the *Gorgias*, though in what sense it is not quite clear.[3] Socrates said that he heard that since Pericles had been the first to institute payment for public service it was he who had caused the moral decline of the Athenians; they became cowardly and timid, loquacious and greedy. Callicles replies, 'You hear this from those who have mangled ears.' I believe he is thinking of athletes and barbarians, who think that any one who is averse to the savagery of war is a coward. This is an interpretation of mine that I would like to be accepted only until something else is suggested after more

* * * * *

1 Galen *De libris propriis* 5.33 Mueller
2 Galen *De compositione medicamentorum* 3.2 (13.605 Kühn)
3 *Adagia* I ii 18

34 Galen (see n1). Added in *1528*. 'For Galen frequently vents his spleen ... after more detailed consideration' was added in *1536*.
1 Galen *Thrasybulus* 37 Helmreich
2 He engages in detailed criticism of athletes in his *Propempticus* (*Exhortatio ad medicinam* 9.1–14.3), a work that Erasmus translated into Latin in 1526. See A. Barigazzi ed *Galeni 'De optimo docendi genere'; 'Exhortatio ad medicinam' ('Protrepticus')*, *Corpus medicorum Graecorum* V 1.1 (Berlin 1991) page 51.
3 Plato *Gorgias* 515E. It is a reference to the oligarchs in Athens, who aped Spartan ways; see E.R. Dodds in his commentary (*Gorgias* [Oxford 1966]). Erasmus' interpretation is not plausible.

detailed consideration. On 'pierced ears' I have spoken elsewhere.[4]

It will suit a belligerent man, one who criticizes many people and is criticized in turn by many.

35 Corvus albus
A white crow

About things that are rarely found Juvenal said, 'Even rarer than a white crow.'[1] Ammianus in an epigram: Θᾶττον ἔην λευκοὺς κόρακας πτηνάς τε χελώνας / Εὑρεῖν 'Sooner will you find a white crow or a winged tortoise.'[2]

Galen in book one of *On the Natural Faculties*, reproaching a certain Lycus since he neither represented accurately the views of Erasistratus nor spoke the truth himself, says, 'Therefore since Lycus clearly neither tells the truth nor follows Erasistratus, he seems to be like a white crow. For this bird cannot mingle even with other crows because of its colour or with pigeons because of its size.'[3]

The term will suit a person who always has his own independent way of thinking and is opposed to what is generally believed by all. Some persons are ashamed to agree with anyone on any occasion, thinking that only the opposite of what is said can be true.

36 Asino fabulam
Telling a story to an ass

Galen *On the Natural Faculties* in book three: 'As for the others, what I have

* * * * *

4 Erasmus may be thinking of *Adagia* II iv 94 With well-washed ears (*Purgatis auribus*). There is no adage entitled 'Pierced ears' (*Perforatis auribus*).

35 Juvenal (see n1). Otto 232. Tilley C 859 A white crow (raven). Added in *1528*. 'Ammianus ... winged tortoise' was added in *1533*. Cf *Adagia* II ii 50 A white bird; II i 21 A rare bird.
1 Juvenal 7.202
2 Lucian (not Ammianus) *Anthologia Palatina* 11.436–7
3 Galen *De naturalibus facultatibus* 1.17.71 Helmreich

36 Galen (see n1). Otto 183. The full version of the adage, cited in the body of the text, had already been given in *Adagia* I iv 35 An ass to the lyre. Added in *1528*

written will be as useless as "Telling a story to an ass."'[1] In the *Collection of Greek Proverbs* one finds Ὄνῳ τις ἔλεγε μῦθον, ὁ δὲ τὰ ὦτα ἐκίνει 'Someone was telling a story to an ass, and it twitched its ears.'[2] Galen in *On the Difference of Pulses* book two: 'At this the old man shook his ears like an ass,' meaning, I believe, that he did not agree.[3] I think we have said something about this elsewhere.[4]

37 Sub aliena arbore fructum
Picking fruit under someone else's tree

'To pick fruit from someone else's tree.' This is said of those who enjoy the fruit of other persons' labours. So Fabius in Livy *From the Foundation of the City* in book ten.[1] Livy writes, 'Fabius thought it improper that someone else should pick the fruit from under the tree that he had planted.'[2] It is closely related to 'You are reaping another's harvest.'[3]

38 Milium terebrare
To drill a hole in a grain of millet

Κέγχρον τρυπᾶν, To drill a hole in a grain of millet. Said of those who toil over something that is very difficult to accomplish but is totally useless.

* * * * *

1 Galen *De naturalibus facultatibus* 3.10.180 Helmreich
2 Zenobius (Aldus) column 129 (= Zenobius 5.42); Diogenianus 7.30
3 Galen *De pulsuum differentia* 2.3 (8.573 Kühn). Estienne (LB II 1105) suggests a rather different interpretation of this passage from Galen. He thinks that the meaning of the proverb is that when the man shook his ears like an ass he was pretending to agree when in fact he understood nothing at all of what had been said to him.
4 *Adagia* I iv 35 An ass to the lyre

37 Livy (see n1). Otto 152. Tilley F 779 Stolen fruit is sweet. Added in *1528*
1 Livy 10.24.5, but with *dicere* 'said' for *ducere* 'thought,' already quoted in *Adagia* I v 32 Some sow, others will reap
2 The context is a dispute in 295 BC between the consuls Quintus Fabius and Decius Mus on whether Fabius should have the command in Etruria without the drawing of lots because of what he had previously done there.
3 *Adagia* I iv 41

38 Galen (see n1). Added in *1528*

Galen, in his work *On Foreknowledge*, says the following when he is criticizing sophists who think that the study of philosophy is quite worthless: 'Rather, they think that this is the most useless of all disciplines, ὁμοίως τῷ κέγχρον τρυπᾶν "like drilling a hole in a grain of millet."'[1] (This is how I think the text should read, although the published editions have τὸ κέγχρον.)[2] Millet is a small kind of legume that it would be difficult to drill through, as might be done with pearls. Even if pierced, however, it would be useless.[3] The activity of a man who from a far distance tried to throw millet grains through the eye of a needle was similar.[4]

39 Lanam in officinam fullonis
Wool to a fuller's workshop

To bring wool to a fuller's workshop. This is said of those who do something at an inappropriate time, for example, those who entrust a child to a theologian when he still needs to be educated in the basics of grammar. For the fuller's art is not applied to wool in its raw state, but to material that has already been woven. Galen *On the Difference of Pulses* book two:

> Whoever wants to deal with these in a precise manner, ought to be first well trained in categories. For it is a shrewd saying of Arcesilaus, Οὐδεὶς πόκον εἰς γναφεῖον φέρει 'No one brings wool to a fuller's workshop.' There is a sequence to be followed in intellectual disciplines, just as there is in the working of wool.[1]

Diogenes Laertius tells of Arcesilaus when he is talking about the philosophers of the Academy.[2] He was a person who did not usually tolerate those who took up the liberal disciplines at an inappropriate time – for example, if someone ignorant of grammar wished to learn about poetry or rhetoric.

* * * * *

1 Galen *De praecognitione* 1.15 Nutton
2 Erasmus' emendation of τῷ for the τὸ of the manuscripts is correct.
3 See *Adagia* II x 16 To turn millet on a lathe
4 Drawn from Quintilian 2.20.3, who uses it as an example of *vanus labor*. The source is identified by Wesseling (2001) 455.

39 Galen (see n1). Added in *1528*
1 Galen *De pulsuum differentia* 2.9 (8.624 Kühn)
2 Diogenes Laertius 4.36

40 De fumo ad flammam
From the smoke into the fire

Ammianus Marcellinus in book fourteen:

> And as the senses of human beings are wont to be blunted and crushed when fate lays hands on them, he was spurred on by these allurements to greater hopes. He left Antioch, on the orders of Melevus,[1] and hurried straight 'From the smoke into the fire,' as the old proverb has it.[2]

Said of a man who rushed from what was already a dangerous situation into one that brought immediate destruction. From Plautus we have given elsewhere 'Fire follows smoke.'[3]

41 Calicum remiges
Rowers of wine-cups

Κυλίκων ἐρέται, Rowers of wine-cups. An expression applied to those who drink continuously, drawing in wine as if pulling on an oar. So Dionysius, nicknamed 'The Brazen,' in his *Elegies*, as cited in Athenaeus book ten:

> Whoever in your crew, Bacchus, draw in the wine,
> Mariners of drinking, rowers of wine-cups.[1]

A huge goblet is like a bay, and to empty it such persons use their tongues, as oars are used in rowing; often they are shipwrecked, losing their money as well as their wits.

*****

40 Ammianus Marcellinus (see n2). Otto 667. Tilley s 570 Shunning the smoke he fell into the fire. Cf *Adagia* I v 5 Fleeing from the smoke I fell into the fire, of which this adage is a doublet. Added in *1528*
  1 In his text Erasmus read *Melevo dictante* 'on the orders of Melevus' for *numine laevo ductante* ('led by an ill-omened power') in modern editions.
  2 Ammianus Marcellinus 14.11.12
  3 *Adagia* I v 20

41 Athenaeus (see n1). Added in *1528*
  1 Athenaeus 10.443D, quoting Dionysius Chalcus fragment 5 West (2.58)

42 Ab unguibus incipere
To begin with the nails

Those who undertake some task by doing what is very insignificant and has very little relevance to the matter at hand are said Ἐκ τῶν ὀνύχων ἄρχεσθαι 'To begin with the nails.' So Basil in a letter: 'It is ridiculous to begin with the nails and not rather deal with the actual "heads" of the matter.'[1] The most important part of anything is called its 'head.'[2]

We can use this expression when we advise someone to put aside what is trifling and irrelevant and deal with the actual case; or when we advise anyone who wishes to improve the state of his country to begin with the leading men rather than with the low-born. For the latter play little part in ruining a city or in saving it.

43 Muscae
Flies

In antiquity those who took pleasure in someone else's food were called Mυῖαι 'Flies.' Plautus compares such men to mice that always eat food belonging to someone else.[1] In Athenaeus book six a parasite compares himself to a fly: 'I am a fly, since I love to dine uninvited.'[2] For this insect flies to someone else's food and can scarcely be driven away. Also in Athenaeus, Hegesander records how when Alexander said that he was being bitten by flies (his term for parasites) and was trying to drive them off, Cinesias, one such man who happened to be at hand, said, 'Surely other thirsty flies will

* * * * *

42 Basil (see n1). Added in *1528*
 1 Basil *Letters* 250 (Courtonne 3.88)
 2 See *Adagia* II i 61 The head.

43 Athenaeus (see n2). Otto 1182. Added in *1528*. The reference to Plautus *Mercator* 361–2 was added in *1533*, and was probably drawn from Brassicanus no 92 (*Musca est*); see *Adagia* IV iii 86 n2 (52 above).
 1 Plautus *Captivi* 77, cited in *Adagia* III v 68 Mouse fashion
 2 Athenaeus 6.238E, quoting from the *Ancestors* of Antiphanes (CPG 2 fragment 193 line 7). Erasmus' translation is loose. Antiphanes was a prolific poet of Middle Comedy. His first production was around 385 BC. The parasite became established as a stock character in Middle and New Comedy. His prime concern is to obtain food at no cost to himself.

assail you all the more once they have tasted your blood.'³ A fable survives
about a hedgehog who wanted to be a fly-repeller for a fox.⁴ Plautus in
the *Merchant* used the expression to describe a man who was curious and
rushed to be present at everything that was going on:

> My father's a fly. Nothing can be done without his knowing of it,
> Nothing sacred or profane without his being immediately present there.⁵

44 Baeon malus piscis
A tiddler is a worthless fish

Athenaeus in book seven attests that there was an Attic proverb Μὴ μοι
βαιών· κακὸς ἰχθύς 'No tiddler for me, it's a worthless fish.'¹ He does not
illustrate how the proverb is used, only pointing out that in Epicharmus
βαιών is the name of a fish. It seems to get its name from its small size.²
For huge fish are praised.

The expression can be used of a guest who is unwelcome and a nuisance.

45 De sportula coenare
A basket dinner

Τὸ ἀπὸ σπυρίδος δεῖπνον, The basket dinner. This was a Greek expression

* * * * *

3 Athenaeus 6.249D–E, quoting Hegesander fragment 6 (FHG 4.414), but the correct name of the individual in the story is Nicesias, not Cinesias. Erasmus
misinterprets the Greek. What the parasite says to Alexander in Athenaeus is
that such flies are better off than others in having tasted his blood.
4 Aesop 36 Halm. See also Aristotle *Rhetoric* 2.20 (1393b22–33) and Plutarch
Moralia 790C *An seni respublica gerenda sit.*
5 Plautus *Mercator* 361–2

44 Athenaeus (see n1). Added in *1528.* 'It seems . . . are praised' was added in *1533.*
1 Athenaeus 7.288A, citing Epicharmus fragment 64 Kaibel
2 The adjective βαιός is explained as meaning 'small' in Hesychius B 87 and
Etymologicum magnum 192.48–9.

45 Athenaeus (see n1). Added in *1528*

properly used whenever someone prepared his own dinner, put it in a basket and went off to eat it at someone else's house. So Athenaeus in book eight.[1] This custom lasts even today among frugal people, who do not wish to burden themselves or others with any expense.

The expression will have more charm if it is applied metaphorically to a man who comes to study under someone, but who can in turn make some appropriate contribution. In this way there will be an exchange of learning.

46 Tibicen vapulat
The flautist gets the beating

In Athenaeus in book nine Eubulus is cited as saying that it was the custom for the flautist to be beaten if the cook made a mistake.[1] Philyllius, also in Athenaeus: 'Whenever a cook makes a mistake, Τὸν αὐλητὴν λαβεῖν πληγάς "It's the flautist who gets the beating."'[2] In the same vein, also in Athenaeus, a cook says that he is not reporting some ancient belief, but one that he himself has made up. He then says, 'Not that I want the flautist to get a beating.'[3] The point of this, I think, is that it is not safe to beat cooks, in accordance with a saying that is cited somewhat later in Athenaeus: 'No one has escaped unscathed after wronging a cook.'[4]

However, the Greek verse is not free of error.[5]

* * * * *

1 Athenaeus 8.365A

46 Eubulus and Philyllius by way of Athenaeus (see nn1–2). The adage was added in 1528.
1 Athenaeus 9.380F–381A, quoting PCG 5 Eubulus fragment 60
2 Athenaeus 9.380F–381A, quoting PCG 7 Philyllius fragment 9
3 Athenaeus 9.380F where this cook begins by quoting Aristophanes *Clouds* 961
4 Athenaeus 9.383F, citing Menander *Dyskolos* 644–5: Οὐδεὶς μάγειρον ἀδικήσας ἀθῶος διέφυγεν (known as fragment 118 Körte-Thierfelder before the discovery of the *Dyskolos*)
5 The quotation is cited, correctly, in the Aldine edition of Athenaeus with a line break after οὐδὲ εἷς 'no one.' There is then no metrical problem with the second verse. The reading in the *Adagia*-text of ἀθρῶος, a non-existent form, instead of ἀθῶος, may be a printer's error.

47 Execrationes serere
To sow curses

Ἀρὰς ἐπισπεῖραι, To sow curses. This was said of those who laid curses on anyone. It arose from a custom of the Cyprians, who added salt whenever they were sowing barley and cursed those to whom they wished harm. So Hesychius.[1] Pliny tells us that some crops did not have good harvests unless one shouted abuse when they were being sown; when one kind of crop was dug into the ground, the earth was stamped down with the foot and a curse was added, 'May you never come out.'[2]

We have spoken elsewhere of 'A Lindian sacrifice.'[3]

48 Aqua et terra reddamini
May you become water and earth

Ὕδωρ καὶ γαῖα γένοισθε, May you be turned into earth and water, meaning 'May you be reduced to nothing and perish.' This hemistich is cited by Hesychius as if it were proverbial.[1] It was taken from the *Iliad* book seven. It is in these words that Menelaus taunts the Greeks for their cowardice because none dared to take up Hector's challenge of fighting in single combat with him: 'But may you all become water and earth.'

Plutarch explains it in his *Life of Homer*,[2] and Alexander of Aphrodisias, in book one, problem seventy-seven, gives the physical reasons for Homer's words.[3] Everything is created from earth and water and everything returns

* * * * *

47 Hesychius (see n1). Added in *1528*. The sentence beginning 'Pliny tells us' was added in *1533*.
  1 Hesychius A 6976
  2 Pliny *Naturalis historia* 19.120. The crops concerned were basil and cummin; see *Adagia* II i 5 n4 CWE 33 343. This reference to Pliny was added in *1533*.
  3 *Adagia* II v 19

48 Hesychius (see n1). This adage underwent considerable expansion in *1533*. Only the first two sentences and one other ('Everything is created ... to these elements') appeared in *1528*, where the adage was added to the collection.
  1 Hesychius Υ 97, quoting Homer *Iliad* 7. 99, but there is no mention of the expression being proverbial. That is Erasmus' inference.
  2 Pseudo-Plutarch *De vita et poesi Homeri* 93
  3 Alexander of Aphrodisias 1.79 (not 77)

to these elements. Very similar is what Plutarch quotes from Epicharmus in his 'Consolation to Apollonius': 'Everything was brought together or separated; everything returned whence it came, earth to earth and the soul upward into the air above. What is so terrible about this? Nothing.'[4] He is speaking about death, which is the separation of the body and the soul. In book three of his *Tusculan Questions* Cicero cites from Euripides:

> Earth must be given back to earth, then the life of all must be
> Harvested, like the grain. So Necessity commands.[5]

Antiochus writes that Chrysippus agreed with this view, but that Carneades disagreed. The Preacher of the Old Testament uttered the same thought in an enigmatic way.[6] Finally, Aristotle in his *Rhetoric* book two implies that those who accepted slavery were accustomed to hand over earth and water to their master, as if they were giving up all their rights and transferring them to him. He says, 'Because to give earth and water is to be a slave.'[7]

49 Mars communis
· Mars is on everyone's side

Ἄρης κοινός, Mars is common to all. This expression marked how uncertain and varied the outcome of a war could be. It was taken from Homer, *Iliad* book eighteen: 'Mars is impartial, and in turn destroys the destroyer.'[1]

This saying is mentioned by Aristotle in his *Rhetoric* book two as being a proverbial expression.[2] Homer, also in the same book: 'Victory falls

* * * * *

4 Plutarch *Moralia* 110A–B *Consolatio ad Apollonium*, citing Epicharmus fragment 245 Kaibel
5 Cicero *Tusculan Disputations* 3.25.59, giving a translation of Euripides fragment 757 Nauck, and also the information in the sentence that immediately follows
6 Eccles 3:20: 'All go to one place; all are from the dust and all turn to dust again.'
7 Aristotle *Rhetoric* 2.23.18 (1399b11–12)

49 Homer (see n1). Added in *1528*. A first (and quite different) version of this adage appeared in Erasmus' own copy of the 1526 edition (codex Chigianus R.VIII.62); see the critical apparatus in ASD II-8 95.
1 Homer *Iliad* 18.309: Ξυνὸς Ἐνυάλιος, καίτοι κτανέοντα κατέκτα.
2 Aristotle *Rhetoric* 2.21.11 (1395a15)

to one side, then the other.'[3] Titus Livius in book ten of the *Punic War*: 'Think not only of your resources but also of the power of fortune and of how Mars fights in war on both sides. Each side had[4] weapons and human bodies. In war more than in anything else the outcome does not match resources.'[5]

Again in book eight of *From the Founding of the City*: 'What would he have done if the battle had gone against him, the luck of war being what it is, and with Mars fighting on both sides?'[6] Again in the same book: 'Romans, no envoys' words, no arbitrator will resolve our differences. They will be settled by the Campanian plain, where we must join battle, by our weapons and by Mars who fights on all sides in war.'[7] And elsewhere in the same book: 'There in the councils Numitius, their general, by declaring that Mars who truly fights on all sides in war laid low both armies in equal slaughter, ...'[8] Again in book seven of *From the Founding of the City* he says, 'The Samnite war was fought with Mars favouring both sides.'[9] In the same author there is the common phrase 'They left the battle field, with Mars equal'[10] whenever neither side gained victory. Marcus Tullius, in *Philippics* eleven: 'But though I grant that the outcome of war is uncertain and that Mars fights on both sides, nevertheless we must fight for our freedom even at the risk of our lives.'[11] We touched on this proverb in the adage 'All things do change.'[12]

A further point. Mars is called Ἐννάλιος in Homer.[13] The name comes from Ἐνύω, which is thought to mean 'the fortune of war.'[14]

* * * * *

3 Homer *Iliad* 6.339 (not book 18): Νίκη δ᾽ ἀπαμείβεται ἄνδρας.

4 The manuscripts of Livy have the future tense.

5 Livy 30.30.20. The third decade of *Ab urbe condita* dealt with the Hannibalic War and was known as the *Punic War*, hence the book number and the title in Erasmus' citation.

6 Livy 8.31.5. Here Erasmus gives the title of the whole work.

7 Livy 8. 23.8

8 Livy 8.11.6 (where the correct name is Numisius)

9 Livy 7.29.2. The Latin phrase for 'with Mars favouring both sides' is *ancipiti Marte*: 'without a decisive result.'

10 Livy 2.40.14, 9.44.8, 25.19.5, etc. The phrase is *aequo Marte*.

11 Cicero *Philippics* 10.10.20 (not *Philippics* 11)

12 *Adagia* I vii 63

13 As at *Iliad* 2.651, 7.166 and 18.309

14 *Etymologicum magnum* 345.56–7

50 Lex in manibus
The law in one's hands

Ἐν χειρῶν νόμῳ, By the law of hands. This is said when something is done by force and not according to what law prescribes. Aeschines *Against Timarchus*: 'Those who support oligarchy, who do not favour equality in how the state is governed, must beware of those who destroy the constitution of our country by taking the law into their own hands.'[1] By 'the law of hands' he means violence or martial law.[2] Polybius used it in this sense in his *History* book one: 'Of all the enemies whom he had conquered, some he killed Ἐν χειρῶν νόμῳ "With violent hand." Those captives who were brought to him alive he threw to the beasts.'[3] Again in book two: 'Meanwhile it happened that the consul Gaius died "by the law of hands" while fighting bravely.'[4] I have spoken elsewhere about Αὕτη κυρία 'This is sovereign.'[5] In Plautus a slave threatens to bring a suit 'by hand.'[6]

51 Nihil inanius quam multa scire
Nothing is more useless than much knowledge

In Athenaeus book thirteen Hippon, who was given the name ἄθεος 'god-less,' is cited as the author of this verse: 'Nothing is more useless than much learning.'[1]

* * * * *

50 Aeschines and Polybius (see nn1, 3, 4). Tilley L 111 To have the law in one's own hand. Added in *1528*

1 Aeschines 1.5

2 'Martial law' a translation of *ius belli*, which normally means the conventions of behaviour in war, particularly with respect to the treatment of the conquered. This sentence and the following two quotations from Plutarch were added in *1536*.

3 Polybius 1.82.2

4 Polybius 2.28.10

5 *Adagia* I vi 28

6 This is perhaps a reference to Plautus *Truculentus* 618–64. Added in *1533*

51 Athenaeus (see n1). Added in *1528*

1 Athenaeus 13.610B: Πουλομαθημοσύνης, τῆς οὐ κενεώτερον οὐδέν, where the speaker Cynulcus wrongly ascribes the quotation to Hippon. It was actually an utterance of Timon of Phlius, PPF fragment 20.2 = fragment 65 Wachsmuth.

The same line is also quoted from Timon.[2] It will suit those who prefer to learn a lot of things rather than what is useful. The Preacher of the Hebrews expresses the same sentiments: 'He who increases knowledge increases sorrow as well, and in much knowledge there is great vexation.'[3] Hippias, however, was praised for his vast learning.[4]

52 Κύκλῳ περιέλκειν
To drag round in circles

Κύκλῳ περιέλκεσθαι, To be dragged round in circles. Said of those who have been led around so skilfully that although they think they have accomplished something they have actually accomplished nothing or they fall back into the same position from which they wanted to escape. So Plato in the *Charmides*: 'You scoundrel, you have been dragging me round in circles without my being aware of it.'[1] Through sophistry an opponent in an argument is led round by a wandering route to admit what he previously denied, or deny what he previously admitted. The metaphor is taken from horses that are led round and brought back to the place from which they earlier recoiled in fear. A similar deceit is practised in speeches called 'labyrinths.'[2] Related to 'You are caught in the same grip.'[3]

*　*　*　*　*

2 Quoted with slight variation from the preceding verse at Athenaeus loc cit
3 Eccles 1:18; a loose quotation. Also quoted in *Adagia* II x 81 In knowing nothing is the sweetest life
4 Apuleius *Florida* 9.24–5 (page 11.25–6 Helm). See also Plato *Hippias minor* 368B–D, where Hippias is praised as the wisest of men in most arts by Socrates, in the role of the *eiron*, however.

52 Plato (see n1). Added in *1528*
1 Plato *Charmides* 174B. The quotation as given by Erasmus distorts the sense of the Greek. 'Without my being aware of it' is a translation of ἀποκρυπτόμενος, but this goes syntactically with what immediately follows what is actually quoted: 'while concealing the fact that it is not the life according to knowledge that makes us happy ...'
2 See *Adagia* II x 51 A labyrinth ('a name ... for any speech or course of action which was excessively complicated and hard to unravel').
3 *Adagia* II i 36

53 Iovis lac
Jove's milk

The ancients called what was particularly sumptuous in the way of food
'Jove's milk.' Euripides, quoted in Athenaeus book fourteen:

> There is succulent cheese and Διὸς γάλα 'Jove's milk.'[1]

In Athenaeus there is frequent mention of Διὸς ἐγκέφαλος 'Jove's brain'
as an example of sumptuous food.[2] We have talked about this elsewhere.[3]
The Persians called extraordinarily luxurious food 'Jove's brain and the
king's' because the Persian king customarily gave a special prize if anyone
invented a new kind of dish.[4] Clearchus says much the same, as quoted
in Athenaeus book twelve, though in quite different words.[5] The ancients
seem to have wanted to attribute all that was very special to Jove. So from
a satire: 'And you keep these for the ears of Jupiter.'[6]

54 Maesonica dicteria
Maesonian quips

The ancients called σκώμματα 'witticisms' that were rather impudent Μαι-
σωνικά 'Maesonian quips' from a certain Maeson, a comic actor from
Megara, who invented a character that the Greeks called 'Maeson' after

* * * * *

53 Euripides by way of Athenaeus (see n1). Added in *1528*
1 Athenaeus 14.658C, quoting Euripides *Cyclops* 136. In the Euripidean manuscripts the line ends βοὸς γάλα 'cow's milk.' The reading of Athenaeus (Διὸς)
   is also found in Eustathius on *Odyssey* 4.88.
2 As at Athenaeus 14.642F
3 *Adagia* I vi 60 Jove's brain and the king's
4 Drawn from Athenaeus 12.529D, where he gives Clearchus as his source (see
   next note)
5 Athenaeus 12.514E, quoting Clearchus fragment 5 (FHG 2.304). Clearchus
   thought that the phrase was proverbial.
6 Horace *Epistles* (not *Satires*) 1.19.43–4

54 Athenaeus 14.659A–B is the source of this proverb and the commentary. Added
   in *1528*

him. For he first introduced the characters of a slave and cook to the
stage. In fact the ancient Greeks called a cook who was a fellow-citizen
a μαίσων, and one who was a foreigner a 'cicada.' Cooks in comedies
are always talkative, especially in Plautus. Philemon attests to this somewhere:

> It's not a cook I've taken into my house,
> But a male Sphynx. For I swear
> I cannot understand anything at all of what he says.[1]

It is similar to 'A testimonial in Hipponax' vein.'[2]

55 Necessitas magistra
Necessity is a teacher

Suidas cites this proverb from the *Carthaginian*: Χρεία διδάσκει, κἂν ἄμουσος
ᾖ, σοφόν 'Need as teacher turns even an ignorant man into a clever one.'[1]
Opportunity, experience, and necessity itself stimulate the mind to learn
skills. The same sense is given by the Greek aphorism Σοφία πενίαν ἔλαχεν
'Wisdom has drawn poverty as her lot';[2] in Aristophanes Poverty boasts
that she is the inventor of the arts.[3] In Persius the belly is called 'master
of art and bestower of wit.'[4] And, as Quintus Curtius says, 'Necessity is a
goad to cowardice.'[5]

* * * * *

1 PCG 7 Philemon fragment 114, quoted by Athenaeus 14.659B
2 *Adagia* II ii 56

55 *Suda* (see n1). Tilley N 60 Necessity is the best schoolmistress. Added in *1528*.
   The last sentence was added in *1533*.
1 *Suda* X 465, quoting Menander fragment 229 Körte-Thierfelder
2 Erasmus does not give a Latin translation for the Greek, which he misquotes,
   reversing the subject and object. See *Adagia* I v 22 Poverty has drawn wisdom
   as her lot.
3 Aristophanes *Plutus* 469, 532
4 Persius *Prologus* 10–11
5 Curtius 5.4.31

56 Victus spinosus
A thorny life

Βίος ἀκανθώδης, A thorny life. This describes a life that is rough, hard, and primitive, like the one led by those who had acorns in place of cakes. Suidas links this with Attic proverbs that we use to indicate a soft and luxurious life, the opposite of what this one means.[1] He also points out that βίος ἀβίωτος 'a life that is no life' (*vita non vitalis*), one that is miserable and unpleasant, has the same sense.[2] For in Latin *vivere* 'to live' is sometimes used not just of those who merely breathe but of those who have lives that are full of enjoyment.[3] Conversely, in Greek those who lack the necessities of life are said ἀβιώτως ἔχειν 'to be dead.'[4] Aeschines in *Against Timarchus*: 'Branding such a woman with shame and giving her a life that is no life.'[5] For to live in disgrace is the same as not living. It can be understood to refer to straitened resources as well. The same author in his speech *On the Treacherous Embassy*: 'I think the rest of my life is not worth living,' in other words, it is miserable and wretched.[6]

57 Bestia bestiam novit
Beast knows beast

Ἔγνωκε δὴ θὴρ θῆρα, A wild beast assuredly knows another. Aristotle in book one of his *Rhetoric* gives this proverb as one of those indicating simi-

* * * * *

56 *Suda* (see n1). This is mentioned in *Adagia* I viii 63 Living on a bed of thorns. Added in *1528*

1 *Suda* B 295

2 *Suda* A 49, where the following example is given: 'He had no life if he did not rule the city.'

3 See *Adagia* III v 66 While he lived he lived well.

4 The phrase occurs at Plutarch *Dion* 6.9, but there the sense is literal ('to be dead').

5 Aeschines 1.183

6 Aeschines 2.5

57 Aristotle (see n1). Added in *1528*

larity and affinity.¹ It seems to be part of an iambic trimeter, however corrupt it is as quoted by Aristotle. In Greek θήρ means 'beast,' but properly it refers to a wild or harmful one, such as boars, wolves and snakes. Therefore a man who is savage and uncivilized is described as θηριώδης 'beastlike.'²

It will be suitable to use when two persons equally wicked come together. Similar to 'Thief knoweth thief and wolf to wolf is known.'³

58 Caeci praescriptio
The orders of a blind man

Τυφλοῦ παρακέλευσις, The order (or exhortation) of a blind man. This means something that is absurd, as when the very man who gives an order does not understand what he is saying. Socrates in Plato, in *Theaetetus*, criticizes the absurd instructions given by Theaetetus when he tells those who already hold the correct notion of something to agree to this correct notion; he compares Theaetetus' words to an undecipherable message¹ or to a pestle that goes round and round for ever.² He thinks they should more correctly be called 'The orders of a blind man': 'But they would more correctly be called the orders of a blind man since to tell us to get hold of what we already have in order to learn what we already know clearly befits a fellow who is utterly blind.'³

* * * * *

1 Aristotle *Rhetoric* 1.11 (1371b16). There is no good reason to believe that the quotation is in verse. Modern editions read ἔγνω δὲ for ἔγνωκε δή.
2 As at Aristotle *Politics* 8.3 (1338b12)
3 *Adagia* II iii 63

58 Plato (see n3). Added in *1528* where it was the final adage
1 'Undecipherable message' is a translation of *lorum* (literally 'a leather thong'). A message was written on a strip of leather when it was wrapped round a staff. When the leather was removed, the message was undecipherable unless it was wrapped round a staff of the same size and shape.
2 This refers to a proverb, Ὑπέρου περιτροπή 'The turning of a pestle,' that was applied to persons or things that kept doing the same thing without bringing anything to completion; see *Suda* Υ 341.
3 Plato *Theaetetus* 209D–E

We have given elsewhere Horace's 'Though he is blind who shows you where to go'[4] and 'A blind man's watch.'[5]

Letter of dedication

TO CHARLES BLOUNT, A YOUNG MAN OF DISTINCTION AND HIGH RANK, ERASMUS OF ROTTERDAM SENDS GREETINGS.[1]
Most illustrious young man, your father was not only not annoyed that you had shared with him the dedication of the whole work in the last edition, but was actually very pleased.[2] He thought this was like a spur to your abilities, even though you run eagerly by your own inclination on the fields of the Muses.[3] A wise and pious man, he thought having you as his associate and equal in such an honour (which is enhanced rather than diminished by being shared) brought him considerable gain. Far from thinking that his blessings have been impaired in any way, he believes that his happiness has been marvellously doubled if he sees the qualities that shine in no ordinary way in him reproduced in his son. I thought it appropriate, therefore, to dedicate to you this addition to our work (an addition so large that it may be considered a volume in its own right) so that you may run all the more energetically and so that his joy may be all the greater. For in keeping with his singular love for you and his singular modesty he takes more pleasure in your virtues than in his own. Indeed the fine qualities he sees blooming in his son he thinks as his own, even more than those he knows have reached maturity in himself (for virtues

* * * * *

4 Horace *Epistles* 1.17.3–4, quoted in *Adagia* I viii 40 The blind leading the blind
5 *Adagia* I viii 41

Letter of dedication
Allen Ep 2726, first appearing in 1533. This is placed here, as a preface to the almost five hundred adages that make their first appearance in 1533.
1 The eldest son of Erasmus' patron, William Blount, Lord Mountjoy, and only seventeen years of age in 1533. The *Collectanea* and the successive editions of *Chiliades* were dedicated to the father until his death in 1534. The edition of 1536 was dedicated to Charles. See CEBR 1:154.
2 The reference is to the 1528 edition; see Allen Ep 2023.
3 The image of *Adagia* I ii 47 To spur on the running horse, is applied to Charles.

do not decline with old age). You are an outstanding young man; keep on developing your mind, press on with what you have begun, continue each day to increase your parent's pleasure and to fulfil your own happiness completely. You will achieve this if you engage in your studies following the model you have in your own home, combining true piety and liberal learning and not being distracted from your engagement with Philology by your family's fame or your good fortune or by your presence at court or by the love of a wife and the care of children.

If someone objects at this point that neither the human mind nor the constraints of time can allow one to undertake so many responsibilities, please consider how much of their lives other men waste in playing cards and in dice and how this time could be spent in reading fine authors at less expense, with greater pleasure and greater profit. And so, my dear Charles, try to be your father in every way, except in one thing. He is accustomed to keep whispering over his books from dinner right up to bed-time so that I am often surprised that he has not injured his health.

I am writing this in sorrow and with many a sigh, and in despondency, because I heard the news that William Warham, Archbishop of Canterbury, that incomparable giant of a man, has exchanged life for death;[4] no, rather, to express it better, he has left this life that is but a shadow[5] for the life that is true and eternal. It is my lot I bewail, not his. He was truly my 'sacred anchor.'[6] We had vowed συναποθνῄσκειν 'to die together,'[7] he had promised a common tomb, and I did not doubt that he would survive me, although he was the elder by fourteen years. To be sure it was not old age or disease that took him from us; rather his death was an unlucky disaster,[8]

* * * * *

4 William Warham was another of Erasmus' patrons. From him Erasmus received a benefice. See *Adagia* IV v 1 n11 Not even an ox would be lost (132 above).

5 Cf Ps 143:4, Chron 1 29:15, Job 8:9.

6 Cf *Adagia* I i 24 To let go the sheet-anchor. Erasmus refers elsewhere to Warham as his 'sacred anchor'; see Allen Epp 2735:41 and 2745:24.

7 Erasmus uses a verb that is the title of a play by Diphilus, a playwright of Greek New Comedy (Συναποθνῄσκοντες). Terence refers to it in his prologue of *Adelphoe*. It may refer to lovers who swear to die together.

8 Warham died in August 1532, apparently of natural causes, while visiting his nephew. Taken literally, Erasmus' words suggest that Warham died as a result of an accident (*casus infelix*) and not through old age or illness, but he may

unlucky more to learning, to religion, to his country, to the church than to him. He was so devout, so prudent in counsel, so generous in helping all. Now that heavenly soul reaps with Christ the harvest of what he sowed so well in this life.[9] I meanwhile am stuck here, half-alive, in default of the vow I gave. But, if I am not mistaken in what I sense will happen, I shall fulfil it soon. This agreement may seem to have been no more than a pact of friendship, but the truth proclaims that it was a serious covenant, since I am in such depths of despondency at his death and I cannot be lifted up by any intellectual diversions. Even with the passage of time itself, which often soothes the most bitter anguish,[10] this wound becomes more and more painful. To say no more, I feel that I am being called. I shall be pleased to share in the death here of that incomparable and irrecoverable patron if only through the mercy of Christ I can live with him there. He was a bright star of the church; now a brighter star has been added to heaven. I wish I could join him, my sun, as a tiny star!

This remembrance of him is not just a concession to my grief. I thought that it was useful for you too to revive the sorrowful memory of a prelate who was easily the most praiseworthy of all, so that you may more zealously organize your studies and your life on the model of two men, your father and your father's friend. Farewell.

Freiburg im Bresgau, October 1, 1532

59 Ibyci equus
Ibycus' horse

'Ιβύκειος ἵππος, The horse of Ibycus. This seems to have become a humorous proverb, said of those who were forced unwillingly into a dangerous enterprise that was beyond their age and strength to endure. Plato in *Par-*

* * * * *

be meaning here that Warham's death cannot be accepted simply as a normal death resulting from old age or disease, even if in fact that was the case. See CEBR 3:427–31; *Dictionary of National Biography* vol 20 (London 1909) 840.

9 Cf *Adagia* I viii 78 As you have sown, so also shall you reap.

10 A commonplace in a letter of consolation; see *De conscribendis epistolis* CWE 25 164 and Cicero *Ad familiares* 4.5.6. Cf *Adagia* II v 5 Time tempers grief.

59 Plato (see n1). Here begins the sequence of new adages that first appeared in 1533; see Preface (x above).

menides gives the origin of the expression.[1] The poet Ibycus had a horse, an old racing one, worn out by many contests. When it was being hitched to a chariot for a race, it showed great terror, obviously having experienced the danger of such games. When the populace laughed at this, Ibycus stood up and said, 'The horse is like his master. For I am old and yet still suffer the compulsion of falling in love.' He was comparing himself to his horse, since love affairs were no less unsuited to him because of his age than races were to his horse. For Suidas tells us this too, that Ibycus had a bad reputation for his love of boys.[2] Parmenides uses this comparison when he is complaining that he is an old man but is being forced to explain extremely difficult things. Horace seems to have alluded to this in his *Epistles*: 'My years are not the same, neither is my mind,' and

> If you are wise let loose the horse that is getting old,
> Lest he fail at the end amid jeers, straining his flanks for breath.[3]

Perhaps someone will think that I am not unlike the horse of Ibycus while I am being turned on this treadmill of adages.[4] I have spoken elsewhere about 'Ibycus' cranes.'[5]

60 In crastinum seria
Serious things are for the morrow

Εἰς αὔριον τὰ σπουδαῖα, Serious things are for tomorrow. Plutarch in his *Life of Pelopidas* says that this expression became proverbial among the

* * * * *

1 Plato *Parmenides* 137A. Erasmus misunderstands the passage in Plato, which refers to a poem of Ibycus (PMG Ibycus fragment 6, cited by the scholiast to the *Parmenides* passage) and not to a real horse that belonged to the poet, as Erasmus says. The details of the story (the laughter of the populace, and Ibycus rising to respond to it) are inventions of Erasmus.
2 *Suda* I 80
3 Horace *Epistles* 1.1.4, 8–9
4 Erasmus also applies this image to his work on the *Adagia* in III i 1 The labours of Hercules: 'Like a slave bound to the mill' (CWE 34 173).
5 *Adagia* I ix 22

60 Plutarch (see n1). Otto 534. Cf Appendix 2.58 'Serious things are for the dawn.' Added in *1533*

Greeks.[1] It originated with Archias, a rich and powerful man, but not a very sober one. At a banquet a letter was brought to him. The bearer advised him to read it immediately since it was concerned with serious matters. Then Archias, quite drunk, laughed and said, 'Serious things are tomorrow's concern.' At the same time he took the letter, placed it under the cushion on which he was sitting and continued with the conversation that he had begun with Phillidas.

Even today it is impolite to deal with serious matters at parties. When I was a young man in Holland I heard a story that is not irrelevant to this adage. A certain person at a party was reclining too near the fire, the result being that the bottom of his clothing was being burned. One of the guests noticed this and said, 'I have something to tell you.' Then the other said, 'If it is something sad, I don't want to hear it at a party where everything should be happy and gay.' 'It's not at all something happy.' Then the other said, 'Serious things are for after dinner.' When they had dined in festive spirit, he said, 'Now tell me whatever you want.' The other pointed out to him that the back of his clothing was extensively burned. Thereupon the fellow became angry because he had not been told of this at the time. 'I wished to do so,' the other said, 'but you told me not to: Μετὰ δεῖπνον σπουδαῖα "Serious things are for after dinner."'[2]

61 Cuniculis oppugnare
To assail with tunnels

Ὑπονόμοις πολεμίζειν, To wage war with tunnels. Said of someone who does not act with open force, but with stealth and deceit. On the contrary he who acts openly is said to act with siege-engines. When the power held by Julius Caesar was moving towards open monarchy, Catulus Lutatius,[1] a man of

* * * * *

1 Plutarch *Pelopidas* 10.4
2 By giving a Greek version without a Latin translation Erasmus seems to want to give this phrase the status of a proverb.

61 Otto 482. Most of the first paragraph is drawn from Plutarch *Caesar* 6.4. Added in 1533
1 After his consulship in 78 BC Catulus Lutatius ('Luctatius' is the form of the name in the printed editions of the *Adagia*) became the leader of the conservative group of senators (the *optimates*) and was hostile to both Pompey and Caesar. The context of this incident is the aedileship of Caesar (65 BC).

the highest standing among the Romans, rose in the senate and said, 'Caesar is no longer destroying[2] the republic with tunnels, but with war-machines.' Tunnels are built secretly; war-machines – that is, rams, catapults, missile-launchers – are employed openly.

The proverb will have more charm if applied metaphorically to matters of the mind; for example, if someone were to say that evil spirits sometimes attack us with war-machines when they openly frighten us or try to win us over, or that they sometimes assail us by tunnels whenever they use a false display of piety to trick us, creeping up on us unawares.

62 Exitii nulla ratio
Death deprives us of our wits

Ὀλέθρου οὐδεὶς λόγος, There's no rationality in death. Plutarch gives this in his *Life of Eumenes*. Eumenes was very busy with his responsibilities and had gone to Upper Phrygia, spending the winter at Celaenae. When he discovered that Alcetas, Polemon, and Docimus were determined to fight it out with him for the leadership, he said, 'Death has no rationality.'[1] He was thinking, I believe, that when death hangs over a man a god takes away his planning and reasoning. Ὀλέθρου δὲ οὐδεὶς λόγος seems to comprise half of an iambic verse. Similar to this is what we find in Quintilian, when talking about *coniectura*.[2] He says:

* * * * *

2 In Plutarch the correct verb used (αἱρεῖ) means 'is capturing, is taking over.' Erasmus, who translates the verb by *tollit*, seems to have confused two similar Greek verbs αἱρέω ('capture') and αἴρω ('raise, destroy'). Both ASD II-8 106:715 and LB II 1112 offer αἱρεῖ (a non-existent form) instead of αἱρεῖ or αἴρει.

62 Plutarch (see n1). The sense of the adage is somewhat ambiguous, depending on whether the genitive ('death') is subjective or objective. The sense of the former ('Death lacks any rationality') seems to be how Erasmus understood the expression. By the other interpretation the expression would mean that we have no understanding of death, of when or how it will occur, or that we ignore the possibility of dying prematurely. Added in 1533

1 Plutarch *Eumenes* 8.4

2 Quintilian 7.2.43 (not book 5) He is talking about a mode of argumentation, based on supposition.

Moreover, why would Milo have attacked him in that place, in that manner? (This is a point that is discussed with great detail in his defence.) If reason did not lead him, was he actually carried away by the impulse of the moment, having lost his wits? For there is a common saying: *Scelera non habere consilia* 'Crimes have no rational plan.'[3]

63 Qui lucerna egent infundunt oleum
Those who need a lamp pour oil in it

Plutarch in his *Life of Pericles* recounts that Anaxagoras was of great help to Pericles in governing the state. When the philosopher was worn out by old age and was being neglected by Pericles, who was engrossed in public affairs, he decided to starve himself to death. Pericles learned of this and hurried to the philosopher's house. He tried by pleas and tears to make him give up his plan – more for his own sake than for Anaxagoras'.[1] But Anaxagoras, already on the point of death, said, Ὦ Περίκλεις, καὶ οἱ τοῦ λύχνου χρείαν ἔχοντες ἔλαιον ἐπιχέουσιν 'Pericles, those too who need a lamp pour oil in it.'[2] He was rebuking Pericles for having neglected a friend from whom he had derived great benefit. Those who need a lamp for any purpose at all look after it; they clean it and fill it with oil. Those who need grain spread dung on their land.

64 In ventrem insilire
To kick in the belly

Ἐς τὴν γαστέρα ἐνάλλεσθαι, To leap on the belly. Said of someone who devotes all his energy to the question of food and drink. So Plutarch in his

* * * * *

3 The 'saying' from Quintilian is owed to Bonifacius Amerbach, who had sent Erasmus a list of proverbs that he had culled from various sources. See ASD II-8 105:729n.

63 Plutarch (see n2). Added in *1533*
1 Because he did not wish to lose Anaxagoras as his assistant (as Plutarch explains)
2 Plutarch *Pericles* 16.7

64 Plutarch (see n1). Added in *1533*

Life of Lucullus about that very man: 'Lucullus was not waging war openly or for mere display but, as the saying goes, "He was kicking the enemy in its stomach," doing everything to deprive it of its provisions.'[1] I shall not repeat here how Leonardo Giustiniano translated the passage.[2]

There are some whom you overcome only by attacking their stomach. Count Hermann of Neuenahr, distinguished by his learning as much as by his lineage, provided an example of this strategy.[3] He was attacked by a certain Dominican in a preface for supporting Capnion and thereby not living up to the character and piety of his ancestors.[4] He took issue with the defamer, threatening all kinds of things. The Dominican ranted and raved all the more. Finally the count's friends adopted the following plan. They informed the Dominican's college that they would hold the defamer's colleagues to be innocent if it expelled him. If the college did not do so, they intended to hold all responsible, on the grounds that it was with the agreement of them all that the slanderer had dared to act. When this threat was ignored, someone was sent to forbid any member of the order from collecting eggs or cheeses in the region governed by the count or his relatives.

* * * * *

1 Plutarch *Lucullus* 11.2

2 Leonardo Giustiniano was a Venetian poet who translated Plutarch's *Lucullus* and *Cimon*. He died in 1446. After the invention of the printing press many of the humanist translations of the individual *Lives* of Plutarch that had circulated in manuscript form in the first half of the fifteenth century were gathered together, published, and often re-published for several decades. The first edition of Plutarch's *Lives* in Greek appeared in 1517 in Florence. Here Erasmus appears to be faulting Giustiniano for the erroneous use of the reflexive pronoun *sibi* to refer to the enemy in the sentence when the grammatical subject is Lucullus.

3 Hermann von Neuenahr was a friend of Erasmus from about 1515 until his death in 1530. Along with Erasmus he supported Reuchlin in his defence of the study of ancient literature against the attack of the Dominican theologian Jacob van Hoogstraten, who taught in Cologne. The incident he describes here occurred in 1518, and Erasmus recalls it elsewhere: Ep 877:18–35 (CWE 6 148); Allen Ep 1892:56–62. For von Neuenahr see CEBR 3:14–15; for van Hoogstraten see CEBR 2:200–02.

4 The reference is to Van Hoogstraten's preface to von Neuenahr's *Apologia* against Reuchlin, here referred to by his humanistic name, Capnion, meaning 'smoky' from καπνός, a punning joke on his name and the German *rauchen* 'to smoke.'

The ban was ignored and the monks continued to go about begging for eggs and gathering cheeses. But after the count's servants attacked them and they barely escaped, dissension arose among the college members and the defamer was compelled to agree to the conditions of peace. He signed a declaration that he regarded the count as a learned, noble, and devout man, that he had always thought of him in this way and would always do so in the future. He admitted that he had written what they were alleging (for he could not deny what had appeared in print), but said that what he had written against the count applied only to a man who was degenerate and a supporter of heresy. The result of this was that his signed declaration simply added brazen impudence to his slanderous words. Nevertheless the count, noble-minded and a true Christian, was content with this apology, and I strongly approved.

I think that Terence had this idea in mind when he said, 'Punch him in the belly.'[5] For no part of a parasite can be hurt more than his stomach.

65 O domus Anti, quam dispari domino dominaris
O house of Antius, what a different master rules you

The verse of Ennius, cited by M. Tullius in *On Duties* in book one, ought, I think, to be regarded as a proverb: *O domus antiqua, quam dispari domino dominaris.* 'O ancient house, what a different master rules you.'[1]

This will suit an institution that has deteriorated because of the short-comings of its current members; for example, a house, a city, an academy, a monastery, or a college that declines from its earlier standards. And yet I suspect that the verse of Ennius has been corrupted in the manu-scripts and that one should read *O domus Anti, quam dispari domino domi-naris* 'O house of Antius, what a different master rules you,' so that the line criticizes the successor of Antius. The first syllable of *dispari* is long by nature, but if you suppress *s*, as Ennius frequently does, the syllable

* * * * *

5 Terence *Phormio* 988. In the context of the comedy the words are meant to be taken literally.

65 A fragment of drama by way of Cicero (see n1). The appearance of this adage (first in 1533) may have been prompted by Brassicanus no 61 (*O domus antiqua*); see *Adagia* IV iii 86 n2 (52 above).
1 Cicero *De officiis* 1.39.139, where it is not ascribed to Ennius. The quotation was thought to be a fragment from drama, and is now TRF *Incerta* 184–5.

becomes short and the metre is good.[2] (You may prefer to read *Anci* or *Anni*, whom Lucilius attacks on different occasions, instead of *Anti*.)[3] An ignorant scribe then thought that *Anti quam* was one word and changed it to *antiqua*; another one, not wishing to omit what was in most manuscripts, added *quam*.

Marcus Tullius had this in mind in the second *Philippic*: 'O wretched house, "With what a different owner." And yet how was such a man the owner? With what a different tenant, then.'[4]

66 Sortem et usuram persolvere
To pay off both principal and interest

Καὶ τὸν τόκον καὶ τὸ κεφάλαιον ἐκτίνειν, To pay off both principal and interest. Said of those whose punishment, though delayed, is more severe; or of those who postpone exacting punishment so that they may inflict more serious harm when the opportunity arises. For the interest increases if a loan is extended. Dio in his essay *On Distrust*:

Wild beasts are often quiet, either when sleeping or when they are filled with food, but they have not cast off their nature. Similarly these men too have not done harm on just any occasion, but whenever an opportunity presented itself, and, as the saying goes, they pay in full both the interest and the principal of their wickedness.[1]

* * * * *

2 What Erasmus means by 'long by nature' is that the first syllable of the word is closed ('heavy') and counts as a 'heavy' syllable for the purposes of metre. It is true that in Ennius a *final* 's' is sometimes suppressed, but only under particular circumstances. Erasmus' suggestion, which makes the line a dactylic hexameter, is implausible and unnecessary. The quotation probably constitutes the end of one line and the beginning of another, the metre being the iambic senarius.

3 Erasmus may be thinking of the dramatic poet Accius, whom Lucilius is said to have criticized more than once; see Lucilius 148 Marx (150 Krenkel) and Porphyrion on Horace *Satires* 1.10.53.

4 Cicero *Philippics* 2.41.104

66 Dio Chrysostom (see n1). Added in *1533*
1 Dio Chrysostom 74.11

67 Ad incitas
To a standstill

Those hard pressed by extreme necessity were said 'to have come to a standstill.' Plautus in the *Three-shilling Day*: 'Oh! How reduced to a standstill he is, the man who owns it' (understand 'farm'), meaning that he is reduced to extreme want.[1] The same author in the *Carthaginian*:

> Just be quiet,
> He'll reduce the pimp to a standstill, if he takes them away.
> I warrant he'll be done for and not move *unam calcem* 'one piece.'[2]

But probably one should read *unum calcum* 'one counter.'[3] Nonius Marcellus tells us that *incita* means 'want' and he is correct, but this meaning is only metaphorical.[4] For although the word does indeed denote extreme want in these two passages that he adduced from Plautus, *incitae* does not mean 'want' wherever it occurs. Lucilius seems to have used the form *incita* in the neuter: 'When that came *ad incita* "to a standstill" and utter destruction.' Also: 'He chewed him up and ruined him, reducing him to a standstill.'[5] But Isidore in book eighteen used the word in the masculine gender, saying, 'Sometimes counters are moved in order, sometimes at random. Those which cannot be moved at all are called *inciti*.'[6] The verb *cio* means 'to move' and so *inciti* means 'unmoveable,' ἀκίνητος in Greek.

It is quite clear that the proverb derives from a game of counters in which there were certain lines at which a counter, if forced back to that point, could no longer be moved. The proverb will suit those who are refuted by clear proofs and have nothing to reply – what the dialecticians call 'the utmost point of silence.'[7]

* * * * *

67 Plautus (see nn1–2). Otto 858. Added in *1533*
1 Plautus *Trinummus* 537, quoted by Nonius Marcellus (see n4)
2 Plautus *Poenulus* 906–8. Only 907 is quoted by Nonius (see n4).
3 The suggested emendation is unnecessary.
4 Nonius Marcellus 178.18–25 Lindsay
5 Lucilius 101 Marx (121 Krenkel); then Lucilius 513 Marx (516–17 Krenkel). Both of these are quoted by Nonius (see immediately preceding note).
6 Isidore *Origines* 18.67
7 The Latin here is *meta silentii*, but this phrase does not seem to be one known in medieval logic; see ASD II-8 109:824n.

68 Centro et spatio circumscripta
Limited by centre and radius

Plutarch in his 'Civil Precepts': 'If your resources are modest and limited for use Καὶ κέντρῳ καὶ διαστήματι "By centre and radius."'[1] He is thinking of resources that are so scant that unless they are disbursed in fixed portions they will not suffice for the necessities of life. For example, some calculate how much their annual income is and reckon how much they can spend each month, each week, and each day. But if a guest arrives or something similar occurs that causes rather more expense, they compensate for this by being thrifty on the following days so that their budget will hold good. The same author informs us in 'On Garrulity' that a reply ought to be circumscribed 'By centre and radius' so that no response should go beyond what the question requires.[2] For some persons reply about several things when asked about one. The metaphor is taken from a circle which is made with a pair of compasses. In the middle the centre is fixed and the distance from here to all points on the circumference is the same. Because of this things that are confined within fixed boundaries are also termed 'circumscribed.'[3]

69 Roscius
A Roscius

Roscius was such a successful actor that anyone who was distinguished in any activity was called a Roscius. Marcus Tullius points this out in the *Making of an Orator* book one: 'And so he had long reached such excellence that whoever excelled in his own profession was called a Roscius in his own field.' The same author in the *Making of an Orator* book two: ' I often wonder at the shamelessness of those who act when Roscius is in the audience. For who can make even a move on the stage without Roscius seeing his deficiencies?'[1] Again in *Brutus*: 'A spectator will think that the orator he

* * * * *

68 Plutarch (see n1). Added in 1533
1 Plutarch *Moralia* 822C–D *Praecepta gerendae reipublicae*
2 Plutarch *Moralia* 513C *De garrulitate*
3 See *Adagia* III vi 46 To enclose with a smaller pomerium.

69 Cicero (see n1). Otto 1553. Perhaps here Erasmus drew on Brassicanus no 42 (*Roscius*); see *Adagia* IV iii 86 n2 (52 above). Added in 1533
1 Cicero *De Oratore* 1.28.130, then 2.57.233

is listening to is like Roscius on the stage.'² This is the famous Roscius with whom Cicero used to have competitions and whom he complimented in the following way, saying that because he had been such an honourable man he alone should never go on stage and that because he was such a distinguished actor he alone deserved to be on stage.³

Therefore, just as we call someone who is very clever and inventive a Daedalus, one who can endure many toils a Hercules, one who is invincible in debate an Achilles, one who is unsurpassable in critical judgment an Aristarchus,⁴ so we use the same trope to call an orator who is outstandingly skilled in pleading cases a Roscius.

70 **Philotesius crater**
The cup of friendship

Κρατὴρ φιλοτήσιος, A cup of friendship. This is the name given to the cup at banquets by which friendships are made. This custom continues even now among the Germans who think it most shameful to mention old offences, however grave, once the cup of friendship has been taken. Neither would judges allow a suit for slander in these circumstances. In Plutarch's essay 'On the Fortune of Alexander' the king, who tried to bring a more humane and more just way of life to barbarians by force and to Greeks by public institutions, said, 'Mingling lives, customs, marriages, and ways of living as

* * * * *

2 Cicero *Brutus* 84.290
3 Cicero and Roscius had competitions to see whether Roscius could express by his acting some notion in more ways than Cicero could by his words; see Macrobius *Saturnalia* 3.14.12. The compliment is a paraphrase of Cicero *Pro P. Quinctio* 25.78, the point being that in general it was thought shameful for a Roman citizen to appear on the stage.
4 See *Adagia* II iii 62 The works of Daedalus; I vii 41 A second Hercules and III i 1 The labours of Hercules; I v 57 To mark with stars. To brand with an obelus (for Aristarchus). For Achilles as someone having skill in debating, not an attribute normally accorded him, see also the final sentence of I vii 41: '... they give the name Achillean to any argument or demonstration that cannot be surmounted or impugned' (CWE 31 92). The term 'an Achilles' is more suitably applied to someone who is intractable and cannot be won over by argument.

70 Plutarch (see n1). Added in 1533

if in a cup of friendship.'[1] In Plautus a drunk slave thinks that 'it is closest
to the gods ... to drink, with pure hand, to the most pleasant of friendships
from the cup of pleasure.'[2] Hesychius points out that this cup of friendship is
customarily brought out after dinner, when as a sign of friendship everyone
drinks the same wine from the same cup.[3] This custom survives even now
among us, but it is rarer because of the fear of syphilis, a disease from which
many suffer. Asconius Pedianus, commenting on the third speech against
Verres, thinks that Marcus Tullius charges Verres with this, that he drank
with his friend in Greek fashion.[4] For the common folk think that those who
drink copiously and in somewhat excessive measures drink like the Greeks.
Asconius himself, however, is inclined to favour a different view, that we
should understand 'to drink in Greek fashion' to mean 'to drink undiluted
wine.' It was the custom of the Greeks when they poured libations at a
banquet to toast the gods first, pouring out a little wine from the cup, then
to toast their friends. Whenever they called upon a god or those dear to them
by name they drank undiluted wine. This is what Pedianus says for the
most part. Some think that this cup is also called the cup to good fortune.[5]

71 Cithara incitat ad bellum
The lyre incites to war

Plutarch in book two of 'On the Fortune of Alexander' declares that the
following verse was customarily sung by the Spartans: Ἕρποι γὰρ ἄντα τῷ
σιδήρῳ τὸ καλῶς κιθαρίσδειν 'Sweet singing on the lyre stirs one to deadly
steel.'[1]

    By this they meant that certain tunes on the lyre calm the passions,
while others give strength for battle. When Alexander heard Antigenidas

* * * * *

1 Plutarch *Moralia* 329C *De Alexandri magni fortuna aut virtute*
2 Plautus *Pseudolus* 1258, 1262–3. The text as Erasmus quotes it is corrupt in
  some respects.
3 Hesychius Φ 529. He says nothing, however, about drinking from the same
  cup.
4 Pseudo-Asconius on Cicero 2.1.26.66 (Stangl 240)
5 See *Adagia* I vi 53 Here's to good luck.

71 Plutarch (see n1). Added in *1533*
1 Plutarch *Moralia* 335A *De Alexandri magni fortuna et virtute*, quoting PMG Alcman
  fragment 41, which varies somewhat from Erasmus' version of the line

playing tunes on the pipe that were called 'chariot tunes,' he was so stirred up that he stood up with his weapons and seized the men sitting closest to him.[2]

72 Bathyclis poculum
Bathycles' cup

Βαθυκλέους κύλιξ, Bathycles' cup. This seems to have been said of those who keep the enjoyment of their wealth to themselves and never give anyone anything. In Plutarch in 'The Banquet of the Seven Sages' a certain Ardalus says this to Aesop: 'Will you never hand over the cup here to us, when you see those men passing it to each other, like Bathycles' cup, but never giving it to anyone else?'[1] Aesop replies to him, 'But this cup is not public property. For it has been standing beside Solon alone for a long time.' In Greek 'Bathycles' means 'of deep glory,' apparently the name of a rich man who lived for himself and drank for himself.

73 Lunae radiis non maturescit botrus
Moon beams do not ripen grapes

Plutarch cites this iambic verse of Ion as if it were proverbial, arguing that since the moon has weaker rays than the sun it can induce grapes to swell with moisture but cannot ripen them: Μέλας γὰρ αὐταῖς οὐ πεπαίνεται βότρυς 'For the dark-clustered grapes are not ripened by them.'[1]

* * * * *

2 Erasmus mistranslates the Greek here (also from Plutarch *Moralia* 335A *De Alexandri magni fortuna aut virtute*), which means 'he jumped up and seized the weapons that lay close beside him.'

72 Plutarch (see n1). Erasmus' explanation of the expression is incorrect. The cup was one left by a certain Bathycles to be given to the most helpful of the seven sages. None of these claimed it for himself but passed it on to the next person. See Diogenes Laertius 1.28. Added in *1533*
1 Plutarch *Moralia* 155E–F *Septem sapientium convivium*. Aesop's reply is more witty in the original Greek, since he says that the cup is not 'democratic.'

73 Plutarch (see n1). Added in *1533*
1 Plutarch *Moralia* 658B–C *Quaestiones convivales*, citing *TrGF* 1 Ion fragment 57. Plutarch says nothing of the expression being a proverb.

This adage suits those who undertake what they cannot complete because they have insufficient strength. He also quotes this in his essay 'The Face on the Moon.'[2]

It will be more attractive if we say, 'For these do not ripen the dark-clustered grapes' when we wish to mean that human accomplishments do not bring happiness. With 'these' we must understand 'rays.'

74 Calliae defluunt pennae
Callias is shedding his feathers

There was a Greek called Callias who had gobbled up his patrimony in luxury and lust. A popular joke arose about him: Καλλίας πτεροῤῥυεῖ 'Callias is shedding his feathers.'[1] Sometimes this happens to birds either because of disease or because of the time of year, in the way that changes occur also in the coats and fur of quadrupeds. This is why those who have been stripped of their possessions are said to have been 'plucked' and 'sheared.'[2] The verb πτεροῤῥυεῖν is frequently used by Aristophanes in the *Birds* in a humorous sense.[3]

75 Ἐν πλάτει
In a broad way

In Greek a statement must be taken Ἐν πλάτει 'In a broad sense' when some concession should be made to what has been prescribed, especially when there is cause to show consideration; for example, if someone who

* * * * *

2 Plutarch *Moralia* 929A *De facie quae in orbe lunae apparet*

74 Scholiast of Aristophanes and the *Suda* (see n1). Added in *1533*
1 This is from a scholiast on Aristophanes *Birds* 284; also in the *Suda* K 215.
2 The Latin verbs used are *deplumare*, not found in Classical Latin, and *detondere*. The verb *tondere* 'to cut, shear' can mean 'to plunder,' but this sense is rare, as is true also of the Greek verb κείρειν. Wesseling (ASD II-8 113:909n) suggests that Erasmus may be thinking here of Dutch usage.
3 Aristophanes *Birds* 106, 284

75 Added in *1533*. The expression occurs in book 4 of Andrea Alciati's *De verborum significatione* (page 86 of the Lyon edition of 1537, the edition used in this volume) where a large number of proverbial expressions are given. The work was originally published in 1530 and Erasmus refers to it (inaccurately

has promised payment on August 10 gives the money on the following day. Julian in book forty-six of the *Pandects*, in the chapter entitled 'On performances and releases,' the part beginning 'The principal': 'The principal must ratify it as soon as he has been informed. But this ought to be taken in a broad sense and with some concession as to time.'[1] Ulpian also cites this passage of Julian in the same book, in the chapter entitled 'To hold the matter confirmed,' the part beginning 'For to what purpose.'[2] Again in book thirteen, in the chapter entitled 'On the obligations relating to fixed quantities,' the part beginning 'Under this action,' he says:

> Under this action, it is better what Servius says, that the time of condemnation ought to be considered. If death has ensued, the time of death should be considered, but understood 'In a broad sense,' according to Celsus. For the valuation should not focus on the very last minute of life.[3]

Again, in book twenty-two, in the chapter 'On proofs,' the penultimate part:

> And the question is not whether someone remembers on what day or under what consul the deed was done, but whether the date can be proved in some way. And the Greeks are accustomed to say 'In a broad sense.'[4]

So much for the *Pandects*.

* * * * *

as *De rerum significationibus*) and Alciati at *Adagia* IV ix 36 (443 below). Bonifacius Amerbach had drawn Erasmus' attention to the publication in a letter of October 1532 (no 1683 in *Die Amerbachkorrespondenz*, Basel 1953). Erasmus may have drawn, usually without acknowledgment, a dozen or so examples from it for his 1533 edition of the *Adagia*; as candidates Wesseling (ASD II-8 14 n48) lists this adage and the next two, as well as IV viii 21, IV viii 25, IV ix 36–38, IV ix 53, IV ix 60, IV x 32 and IV x 57. In all cases Alciati gives little or no explanation and the accompanying discussion of the proverbs is Erasmus' own. Alciati's *Emblemata* in turn draws material from Erasmus' *Adagia*. See *Adagia* IV ix 36 n2 (443 below).

1 *Digest* (*Pandects*) 46.3.13. On the legal texts used by Erasmus see *Adagia* IV ix 1n (419 below).
2 *Digest* 46.8.12
3 *Digest* 13.3.3
4 *Digest* 22.3.28

However, 'In a broad sense' is not recognized by the citizens of Calais.[5] Ordered to close the city gates at the eleventh hour, they shut them on the first chime of the bell, pushing back those who are outside or those who want to leave, although both groups are very close to the gate.

When a punishment is threatened against those who have not paid on the prescribed day, they are saved from catastrophe if they fulfil their pledge within fourteen days. This relates to the need for there to be equity in law.

76 Per satyram
A hodge-podge

A mixture of different ingredients that were heaped together at random and in no fixed order was called by the ancients a *satyra*.[1] The word is clearly derived initially from the wantonness of satyrs who leapt about wildly, now this way, now that. Then it was applied to a kind of food that was put together from different kinds of plants, then to a plate that was laden with different kinds of things and was offered in this form to the gods.[2] It is not unlike that goblet called πενταπλόον in Greek, from the five-fold ingredients, or κέρνος, from the fact that ingredients are mixed together. We have talked about this above.[3] Festus says that *satura* or *satyra* was the name given to food that was seasoned with different kinds of ingredients or to a law that was packed full of many different regulations.[4] The law was customarily passed with the terms 'Do not deduct or annul any part of the whole' (meaning that the whole law had to be kept). He cites Annius Luscus from a speech that he delivered against Tiberius Gracchus: 'The

* * * * *

5 This has the ring of a personal reminiscence. Erasmus was no stranger to Calais because of his visits to England. He was also in Calais in 1520 when Henry VIII and Charles V met.

76 Added in 1533. The phrase, like the preceding adage, appears in book 4 of Alciati's *De verborum significatione* (page 85 of the Lyon edition of 1537), but the essay is Erasmus' own work.
1 Based on Pompeius Festus 416.13–15 Lindsay
2 This sentence and the previous one are based on Diomedes (*Grammatici Latini* ed H. Keil 1.485.34–40).
3 *Adagia* IV vi 76 A cup of five (266 above)
4 Pompeius Festus 416.14–25 Lindsay, whom Erasmus follows down to 'like a *lex satura*'

authority that the plebs had given *per saturam* has been abrogated.'[5] He also cited Caius Laelius from the speech he delivered on his own behalf: 'On the next day his surrender is accepted, but on carefully worded terms, like a *lex satura*.'[6] A *lex satura* is explained as one that included many topics, just as Jugurtha's surrender was accepted with many terms laid out: he was to give thirty elephants, cattle, and many horses, as well as a considerable weight of silver.[7] Justinian used this adage in the preface of the *Pandects*:

> And this work was not issued to those reading in their first year following the order in the *edictum perpetuum*, but material has been gathered from everywhere and put together 'as a hodge-podge,' the useful being mixed with the useless, much the greater amount being devoted to the useless.[8]

In the same way Sallust in the *War against Jugurtha*: 'His surrender is accepted under terms as complex as a *lex satura*.'[9] Sallust says this of Jugurtha, and they do not appear in anyone's speech, not was there any Laelius present. Hence the passage in Festus must be lacunose. The words of Laelius have been lost along with Sallust's name.

77 Ne praeceps fueris ad iurandum
Do not rush to swear an oath

Some very learned scholars[1] think that what is cited by Ulpian in the

* * * * *

5 T. Annius Luscus fragment 5 (Malcovati 106). Luscus was consul in 153 BC.
6 The citation from Laelius (printed as Lelius), who was consul in 140 BC, is actually a quotation from Sallust *Bellum Jugurthinum* 29.5, as is suggested by Erasmus at the end of the essay. The error in Festus resulted from the loss of some text. See Malcovati 119 on Laelius fragment 19.
7 Here Erasmus is drawing from Sallust *Bellum Jugurthinum* 29.5–6, though with an interesting deviation (he gives 'a considerable weight' instead of 'a small weight' in the transmitted text of Sallust).
8 Justinian *Digest, praefatio* l–li Mommsen
9 Sallust *Bellum Jugurthinum* 29.5

77 Ulpian by way of the *Digest* (see n2). Added in *1533*
1 This is probably a reference to Andrea Alciati. The Greek expression appears in book 4 of his *De verborum significatione* (pages 85–6 of the Lyon edition of 1537). See *Adagia* IV vii 75n (332 above).

Pandects book twelve, in section 13 of the chapter entitled 'On oaths,' near the end, should be regarded as a proverb. He says:

> If, regarding a financial matter, anyone swears by the spirit of the emperor that he ought not to pay, or at least should do so only within a fixed time, and swears falsely that he ought to pay, or swears that he will pay within a fixed time and does not pay, it is held by rescript of the emperor and his father that he should be sent away to be flogged and that above him there should be displayed a sign with the words Προπετῶς μὴ ὄμνυε 'Do not rush to swear an oath.'[2]

This will have the ring of a proverb if one warns someone who has suffered harm, 'Do not rush to swear an oath.'

78 Ex syngrapha agere
To act by the letter of the law

In addition these formulas drawn from the law became proverbial: *Ex syngrapha agere* 'To act by the letter of the law,' and *Obsignatis tabulis agere* 'To act in accordance with sealed writings,' meaning to act 'rigidly and cruelly, but in accordance with what one is bound by.' Cicero in *In Defence of Murena*: 'Do you continue to deal with the people as if by the letter of the law?'[1] The Latin equivalent of *syngrapha* is *conscriptio* 'a writing together,' because the agreement is drawn up by and customarily given to two parties. *Syngraphae* differ in this respect from *tabulae* in that the latter are customarily retained by only one party. They differ from a *chirographum*, *tabulae*, and *codicilli* in that these contain only a record of what has been done, while in the *syngrapha* there is also a clause about the breaking of the agreement. And they are customarily written with the temporary acquiescence of the parties, without the payment having been calculated or without the

* * * * *

2 *Digest* (*Pandects*) 12.2.13. The text of Erasmus deviates somewhat from that in modern editions. Alciati names Ulpian as his source, but does not quote the passage. See *Adagia* IV ix 1n (419 below).

78 Cicero (see n1). Otto 1728. A *syngrapha* is a promissory note signed by both parties. Added in *1533*
1 Cicero *Pro L. Murena* 17.35

price having been completely paid. This is very much what Asconius Pedianus says in his commentary on the *Third Verrine*.[2]

79 Iniuria solvit amorem
Scorn breaks up love

In the Greek epigrams there is cited as a proverb "Ὗβρις ἔρωτας ἔλυσε 'Scorn (or abuse) breaks up love-affairs,' the point being that love, when slighted, generally turns into anger, and anger turns into hatred.[1] So Phaedria in a comedy: 'She has shut me out; she calls me back. Shall I return? Not even if she begs me.'[2] Similarly Horace:

> For if there is anything of a man in Horace
> He will not brook you giving night after night to a favoured rival,
> And in anger he will seek another mate.
> Nor, once certain pain has entered, will his resolve yield to your beauty,
> Proven odious on more than one occasion.[3]

In the epigram a lover complains that this common saying is untrue. He himself has been shut out by his girlfriend who has also heaped scorn on him. Although he had sworn that he would not return to her for a whole year, he came back to her the next day at dawn as a suppliant. The verses are as following:

> What they say is false, that scorn breaks up love affairs.
> For scorn stirs up my love-sickness even more.[4]

Nevertheless, in general, it is true that affection between persons is nourished by mutual assistance, and destroyed by scorn.

* * * * *

2 Pseudo-Asconius on Cicero *Verrines* 2.1.36.91 (Stangl 244–5)

79 *Anthologia Palatina* (see n1). Added in 1533
1 This is now *Anthologia Palatina* 5.256.3 but see *Adagia* IV v 57 n1 (181 above).
2 Terence *Eunuchus* 49
3 Horace *Epodes* 15.12–16. Erasmus reads *offensae . . . formae*, where *offensae* means 'giving offence,' that is 'odious.'
4 See n1.

80 **Diserte saltare**
To dance eloquently

'Orators speak without restraint, actors dance with eloquence.' According
to Cornelius Tacitus in his *Dialogue on Orators* this was a common insult directed at orators of his time.[1] In the wantonness of their words, the shallow-
ness of their thoughts and the undisciplined way in which their speeches
were organized they spoke like actors; and indeed they boasted that it was
praiseworthy and a sign of their glory and genius that their works were
chanted and danced to. The wit of the expression lies in this: orators were
speaking like actors, which was unseemly for them, while actors took over
the orators' style of delivery. The result was that orators spoke worse than
they had in the past and actors danced better. Dancing is part of an actor's
job, to speak is the orator's and those who do it skilfully are called eloquent.
The joke combines two opposites.

81 **Quod pulchrum idem amicum**
What is beautiful is also loved

Τὸ καλὸν φίλον, What is beautiful is loved. Among the proverbs relating to
those who become friends this one is given in Plato in *Lysis*:

> And I am inclined to think that, in accordance with an old proverb, 'What is
> beautiful is loved.'[1]

He who loves for his own advantage does not truly love. What is beautiful
is loved for its own sake. That is why, when someone asked Aristotle how it
was that we took more pleasure in conversing with handsome persons than
with ugly ones, he replied that only the blind could ask such a question.[2]
Nothing is more beautiful than virtue and therefore nothing can be more
loved.

* * * * *

80 Tacitus (see n1). Added in *1533*
  1 Tacitus *Dialogus de oratoribus* 26.2–3. Erasmus read *temere* 'without restraint'
    for *tenere* 'tenderly, effeminately,' an emendation of Lipsius, now generally
    accepted.

81 Plato (see n1). Added in *1533*
  1 Plato *Lysis* 216c
  2 The anecdote is given by Diogenes Laertius 5.20.

82 Mortuo leoni et lepores insultant
Even hares attack a lion when it's dead

There is a Greek epigram the topic of which goes back to Homer's *Iliad* book twenty-two, where the Greeks stood around the body of Hector defiling it after he had been killed by Achilles. Every one of them inflicted a wound on the corpse. For this is what we have in Homer:

> But the rest of the Greeks ran up and surrounded the corpse
> Of Hector, in awe of his outstanding body and appearance,
> Yet no one stood by the corpse without stabbing it.[1]

And a little later: 'So someone said, and as he stood by he inflicted a wound.' The epigram reads:

> Assail my body with your spears now that I am dead. Even a hare
> Dares to attack a dead lion.[2]

I have spoken elsewhere about those who inflict hurt on corpses, wrestle with ghosts, and fight with shadows.[3]

83 Lingua non redarguta
The tongue is not refuted

Plato in *Theaetetus*: 'But apparently, if you reply that it is possible, a verse of Euripides[1] will be relevant: Ἡ μὲν γλῶττα ἀνέλεγκτος ἡμῖν ἔσται 'Our tongue

* * * * *

82 *Anthologia Palatina* (see n2). Tilley H 165 'So hares may pull dead lions by the beard. Cf the proverb 'To pull the beard of a dead lion,' quoted in *Adagia* II iv 69 To pull by the beard. Added in *1533*
  1 Homer *Iliad* 22.369–71, and then 375
  2 *Anthologia Palatina* 16.4: Βάλλετε νῦν μετὰ πότμον ἐμὸν δέμας, ὅττι καὶ αὐτοὶ / Νεκροῦ σῶμα λέοντος ἐφυβρίζουσι λαγωοί.
  3 *Adagia* I ii 54 To cut a dead man's throat; III vi 41 The dead don't bite; IV vi 48 Shadow-boxing (246 above)

83 From here to no 99 in this century (excluding no 88) Erasmus draws on Plato for his examples. Added in *1533*
  1 The reference is to Euripides *Hippolytus* 612 'My tongue did swear it, but my heart is free.'

will not be refuted, but our mind will be.'² The adage will suit those who are refuted by arguments but do not yield. Instead they engage in evasion, fiercely resisting what they know in their hearts.

84 Pugno tenere
To hold in one's fist

Ἀπρὶξ ταῖν χεροῖν λαβέσθαι, To hold tightly in one's fist. So Plato in *Theaetetus*: 'Those who think that nothing is real except what that they can hold tightly in their two hands.'¹ He is talking about those who do not think that there is anything in the universe except what is physical and can be perceived by the senses. Actions or processes or other such things that are perceived by the intellect and not with the senses are just empty words in their opinion. Plato thought Diogenes was such a person. Diogenes said that he saw goblets and tables, but did not see the 'goblet-ness' or 'table-ness' that Plato talked about. This was the answer he received: 'To be sure you have eyes with which goblets and tables are seen; you do not have a mind to perceive "goblet-ness" and "table-ness."'² Plato says that such unperceptive persons ought to be kept away from the mysteries of philosophy because they are, so to speak, uninitiated. For what is not seen exists more truly than what is seen and we know with more certainty what we infer by reasoning than what we touch with our hands. For the judgment of the senses is deceptive.

85 Haud solide
No firm notion

Οὐ παγίως, Not firmly. I am surprised that Plato in *Theaetetus* gave this as a proverb, but perhaps it was because of the rather harsh metaphor that he

* * * * *

2 Plato *Theaetetus* 154D, quoted also in *Adagia* II v 41 My tongue did swear it

84 Plato (see n1). Added in *1533*
1 Plato *Theaetetus* 155E
2 Diogenes the Cynic. The incident is taken from Diogenes Laertius 6.53.

85 Plato (see n2). Added in *1533*

added, 'as they say.'[1] For Socrates is discussing there those things that are not constant in their own nature, but vary by contact with other elements and by reciprocal motions in such a way that they exist or do not exist. Examples are black and white, or acting on and being acted upon. This is how the passage reads:

> And we must think about the other things in the same way, namely, that each single thing has no being just in itself, as we said before, but that all things are created in all their variety through union with each other, that is, as a result of their motion. For we cannot have any firm notion, as they say, of what is active or passive in any single case.[2]

Aristotle in his *Rhetoric* in book two says that old men always have some diffidence because of their experience and are never dogmatic about anything, but always add 'perhaps' and 'perchance' or 'nothing is firm.'[3] What is solid is said to be πάγιον in Greek, from πήγω, meaning 'to fix' or 'to join together.'[4] From this we get παγίως, meaning 'solidly' and 'in a fixed fashion.' Accidental properties have some fluidity, while the essential nature of something is immoveable, and the function of those things that are called accidentals depends on other things. For this reason the property of being a father is lost if a man's son should die, since the nature of a father rests on nothing else.

In fact in Latin *res soli* 'things of the soil' are said to be immoveable possessions,[5] and it is from *solum* 'earth' that what is complete and firm is called 'solid.' (In Oscan *solum* is used in the sense 'whole.')[6] Juvenal: 'Noble birth is the sole and single virtue.'[7] St Jerome often uses this word

* * * * *

1 Erasmus frequently identifies expressions as proverbial simply on the basis of phrases like 'as they say' that accompany them.

2 Plato *Theaetetus* 157A

3 Aristotle *Rhetoric* 2.13.1–2 (1309b18); see *Adagia* IV viii 4n (354 below).

4 The Greek verb is πήγνυμι, not πήγω.

5 As for example at *Digest* 7.17

6 This is drawn from Pompeius Festus (372.26–8 Lindsay), but modern editions read *sollum* not *solum*. Erasmus connects the words *solus* 'alone,' *solum* 'soil, earth,' *solidus* 'firm, solid' and the Greek word ὅλος 'whole.'

7 Juvenal 8.20

in this way.[8] Because it can have this sense Sextus Pompeius Festus thinks that spears that are *wholly* made of iron are called *soliferrea*, that a man is called *solers* if he is skilled in *all* arts, and that what is done *every* year is described as *solemne*.[9] For the same reason we call the earth *solum* because it is fixed and firm, not moving around like air and water. The opposite of this is what we find in Marcus Tullius in *On Definitions of Good and Evil* book two: 'This can be said of the other virtues, the basis of which you place in pleasure alone, which is like water.'[10] The word comes from the Greek ὅλον 'whole,' the rough breathing changing into *s*, thus giving *solum*.

86 Aut abi aut exuere
Either go off or strip off

Plato points out in his *Theaetetus* that the Spartans had this custom of not compelling anyone to wrestle in the public games but promulgated a law Ἢ ἀπιέναι ἢ ἀποδύνεσθαι 'Either leave or strip off.'[1] In Greek those who prepare themselves for competition are said to strip off, because they wrestled naked except for a loin cloth. This is the reason that the very words 'strip off' have the force of a proverb whenever they are transferred to mental activities, such as debating or resisting the desires of the flesh. St Chrysostom and St Basil often use the word in this way.[2] It is similar to what we have discussed elsewhere, 'He must either drink or quit.'[3]

* * * * *

8 The point is that Jerome uses *solus* in the sense of 'whole.'

9 Pompeius Festus 372.28–31 Lindsay. The text of Festus reads *solliferrea, sollers,* and *sollemne*. The etymologies are based on compounds combining *solus* with *ferrum* 'iron,' *ars* 'art' and *annus* 'year.' That *so(l)lemne* has anything to do with *annus* is fanciful.

10 Cicero *De finibus* 2.22.72

86 Plato (see n1). Added in *1533*

1 Plato *Theaetetus* 169A–B. But Erasmus misunderstands the Greek which says in fact that the Spartans did force men to wrestle. Whoever refused was sent away. In addition, there is no mention of a law.

2 For example, Chrysostom *De sacerdotio* 3.10 (*Sources chrétiennes* 272 180); Basil *De gratiarum actione* 3 PG 31 892

3 *Adagia* I x 47

87 Crisonem Himeraeum praecurrere
To run faster than Crison of Himera

The amazing speed of Crison seems to have given rise to a proverb. For this is what Socrates says in Plato's *Protagoras*, when asked to complete the debate with Protagoras that had been undertaken: 'I would be willing to oblige you if I could do what you ask. But it's as if you are asking me to keep up with Crison of Himera, the famous runner, or run stride for stride with some miler or long-distance runner.'[1] Himera is a city in Sicily, although there is another one with the same name in Africa.[2] Crison was therefore called 'Himeraean.' He was famous for his fast running, comparable, as Pliny tells in book seven, to Philippides, Canistius of Sparta, and Philonides, Alexander the Great's runner.[3] Runners called *dolichodromi* ran twelve stades at full speed, *hemerodromi* ran the whole day from morning until nightfall without a rest.[4] (Pliny writes that there was a nine-year-old boy who ran continuously from noon until nightfall.)[5] This is why the Greek poets call the sun ἡμεροδρόμος: it completes its course each day,[6] resting, as it were, at night in the abode of Thetis.[7]

88 Charadrion imitans
Imitating a curlew

Χαραδριὸν μιμούμενος, Imitating a curlew. Customarily said of someone

* * * * *

87 Plato (see n1). Added in 1533
1 Plato *Protagoras* 335E. Erasmus mistranslates the Greek which says 'in his prime' for what he renders as 'the famous runner.'
2 Stephanus of Byzantium sub Ἱμέρα
3 Pliny *Naturalis historia* 7.84. Philippides and Canistius are the erroneous names found in early editions. In modern texts the names are Phidippides and Anystis.
4 For the *dolichodromos* see *Suda* Δ 1339; for the *hemerodromos* see Livy 31.24.4.
5 Pliny *Naturalis historia* 7.84. He says that the boy ran 75 miles from noon to nightfall.
6 Hesychius H 468. The word literally means 'he who runs for a day.'
7 The sea, Thetis being a Nereid. See Hesychius Θ 419.

88 Aristophanes (see n2). The impetus for including this proverb in the expanded edition of 1533 may have come from Brassicanus no 91 (*Vita charadrii*), where

hiding and concealing something useful. Suidas cites this scazon from Hipponax: 'And surely, pray tell, the vendor is not concealing a curlew?'[1] Also Aristophanes in the *Birds*:

> The hoopoe apparently entered the glade
> And hid itself, imitating the curlew.[2]

The scholiast on this passage is in general agreement with Suidas and says that this bird had a healing power; whenever those suffering from jaundice or *regius morbus* 'the royal disease,' as it is called in Latin, saw it, they were immediately cured. For this reason vendors hid the bird so that a buyer would not be cured before he actually purchased it. He adds that the bird changes colour to match its surroundings. Some, however, think that the cure comes not from seeing the bird, but from eating it. The word can be accented differently; for if you pronounce it with an acute on the final syllable (χαραδριός) it means the bird, if you put the acute on the penultimate[3] (χαράδριον, diminutive of χάραδρα), it means whirlpool or a chasm in the earth. The reason [for χάραδρα 'whirlpool, chasm' being similar to χαραδριός 'curlew'] is that when water flows into a chasm there is a melodious sound. We have been able to report only so much from what has been carelessly heaped together by Suidas. The comic writer also mentions this bird in the same play: 'The curlews brought water into the air from below.'[4] The

* * * * *

the passages from the *Gorgias*, the *Suda*, and the scholion on Aristophanes are quoted. Brassicanus also refers to Theodore of Gaza's translation of the word in Aristotle, not mentioned by Erasmus. See *Adagia* IV iii 86 n2 (52 above). As usual, in expanding the material offered by Brassicanus, Erasmus himself must have consulted the sources.

1 *Suda* X 90, citing Hipponax fragment 52 West. The text and punctuation of the fragment is uncertain, and Erasmus' translation is inaccurate in some details. The meaning is rather something like, 'You are not concealing it surely. Aren't you selling a curlew?' In the *Suda* the part of the verb 'to sell' is in the second person, while Erasmus seems to have taken it as a participle and to have interpreted καλύπτει as third person active, when it is in fact second person middle. Erasmus follows the *Suda* down to 'there is a melodious sound.'

2 Aristophanes *Birds* 266, with scholion. The translation 'hid itself' is erroneous. The Greek verb means 'made a whooping sound.'

3 This is presumably a slip for 'antepenultimate.' The form χαράδριον occurs in Strabo *Geographica* 16.4.13.

4 Aristophanes *Birds* 1140–01 and scholiast ad loc

scholiast adds that the bird was given its name because it liked to frequent whirlpools. In Plato in *Gorgias* Socrates enticed Callinices into admitting that a blessed life did not rest on abundance of possessions but on perpetual influx – for the man who is full or is not thirsty has the life of a stone rather than of a man, since he feels neither discomfort not pleasure. He adds the following: 'You mean the life of a *charadrion*, not of a corpse or of a stone.'[5] Marsilio translates the word as 'bird' although Socrates seems to be thinking of a chasm which is never filled, even if water runs into it unceasingly.[6] Unless perhaps the curlew is one of the greedy birds like the sea-mew and gets its name from *charadra* 'chasm.'

89 Quantum pedibus potes
As fast as your feet can carry you

Socrates in Plato's *Gorgias* says the following: 'We should pursue and practise temperance, while fleeing from intemperance ʽΩs ἔχει ποδῶν ἕκαστος ἡμῶν "As fast as our feet can carry us."'[1]

    If these words are not used literally with reference to corporeal things, they gain the status of a proverb, one that relates to speed. What the feet are to the body, the emotions, with which we long for or shun something, are to the mind.

90 Vasis instar
Like a pitcher

Ἀγγείου δίκην, Like a pitcher. Said of the way someone speaks when he can contribute nothing of his own to a discussion because of his inexperience

* * * * *

5 Plato *Gorgias* 494B, but the interlocutor's name is Callicles, not Callinices.
6 Marsilio Ficino, the famous Neoplatonist and translator of Plato; see *Adagia* IV viii 97 n2 (417 below). Here he was correct in translating the Greek word as *avis* in his Latin translation of the *Gorgias*.

89 Added in *1533*. Also taken from Brassicanus no 90 (*Quantum pedes nostri possunt*), though Erasmus has expanded what is quoted there from Plato's *Gorgias*; see *Adagia* IV iii 86 n2 (52 above).
1 Plato *Gorgias* 507D

90 Plato (see n1). Added in *1533*

but spouts what he has heard from others.A spring produces its own water,
a pitcher is dry unless you have poured something into it. Persons who lack
learning get filled through their ears. Socrates in Plato's *Phaedrus*: 'I thought
up nothing of these things by myself, I admit, since I am aware of my own
ignorance. All that is left to say, therefore, is that, like a pitcher, I have been
filled through my ears with someone else's streams.'[1]

91 Ut lupus ovem
As the wolf loves the sheep

'Ὡς λύκος ἄρνα φιλεῖ, As a wolf loves sheep. Of a person who pretends to
love for his own advantage (for this is commonly called 'love' although in
fact it is hatred). When a young man pursues a young girl to rob her of
her chastity, an incomparable treasure, to expose her to disgraceful gossip
instead of her enjoying a good name, to make her hated by her parents,
friends and all good persons, and finally to deprive her of a sound state of
mind, the most valuable possession of all – tell me, is there a worse thing
that enemies could do to each other? Socrates cites a verse in the *Phaedrus*
as if it were in popular use:

> As wolves love sheep, so a lover madly loves his boy.[1]

Maro:

> The savage lioness pursues the wolf, the wolf itself the goat,
> The sportive goat searches for the flowering clover.[2]

And Horace:

> I do not pursue you to mangle you
> Like a fierce tigress or an African lion.[3]

* * * * *

1 Plato *Phaedrus* 235D

91 Plato (see n1). Added in *1533*
1 Plato *Phaedrus* 241D
2 Virgil *Eclogues* 2.63–4
3 Horace *Odes* 1.23.9–10

92 In navibus educatus
Reared on ships

Ἐν νηυσὶν τεθραμμένος, Reared on ships. Said of a person who lacked any experience of anything and had no knowledge of social behaviour or of common moral standards. For generally sailors often become like the element they are familiar with because they live remote from contact with civilized men. So Plato in his *Phaedrus*: 'Or don't you think that he will think that he is listening to men brought up somewhere on ships.'[1] Plautus in the *Casket Comedy* calls uncivilized behaviour 'sea-like,' or rather this is what he calls unpredictable behaviour, because the sea ebbs and flows in alternating tides:

> So does Love mock me in my demented state, puts me to flight, hounds me, comes after me, snatches me, holds me, throws me, bestows largesse, does not give what he gives, tricks me. What he has just advised he advises against, he advocates what he advises against. He makes trial of me like the sea, to such an extent does he break my lover's heart.[2]

93 Quod utile honestum
What is useful is virtuous

Τὸ μὲν ὠφέλιμον καλόν, τὸ δὲ βλαβερὸν αἰσχρόν, What is useful is good, while what is harmful is disgraceful. Plato in book five of the *Republic* cites this as if it were a common saying: 'For this is and will be a most noble saying, what is useful is virtuous, what is harmful is disgraceful.'[1] He is discussing there the question of women being called to perform all the tasks that men do, provided they are found to be as useful as men to the state. He wants

* * * * *

92 Added in 1533. The proverb is probably derived from Brassicanus no 115 (*In navibus nutritus*), but Erasmus goes far beyond what is found there. On Brassicanus see *Adagia* IV iii 86 n2 (52 above).
1 Plato *Phaedrus* 243C
2 Plautus *Cistellaria* 215–22, printed as prose in 1533 and 1536. The passage is also quoted in *Adagia* IV vi 29 As temperamental as the sea (231 above).

93 Plato (see n1). Added in 1533
1 Plato *Republic* 5.457B

them, therefore, to be stripped naked as guardians of the state[2] and, if
they seem suitable, to exercise publicly alongside males. He is extremely
contemptuous of those who laugh at women whose sole purpose in being
naked is the public good. Marcus Tullius also considers it arguable whether
it is shameful for an upstanding citizen to dance naked in the forum if the
state can be saved by such dancing.[3] But the general populace inverts this
view, saying that whatever is useful is good, although philosophers think
that only what is good is useful.

94 Magis quam sol Heracliti
More quickly than Heraclitus' sun

Socrates in Plato in the *Republic* book six said that those who are failing without hope of recovery Μᾶλλον τοῦ Ἡρακλειτείου ἡλίου ἀποσβέννυσθαι 'Are ex-
tinguished more quickly than Heraclitus' sun.'[1] Heraclitus thought that the
sun was shaped like a skiff and that it suffered an eclipse whenever its in-
terior faced upwards, but it became bright again after turning over.[2] Xenophanes gave a rather similar silly explanation of the sun.[3] He thought that it
perished when it set and that when it rose again the sun was a newly created
one. But old men can never be rejuvenated to the level of having the strength
they had in their youth. Horace seems to have alluded to this in his *Odes*:
'The moon quickly replenishes its heavenly losses; / We when we set . . .'[4]

* * * * *

2 This is the sense of the passage in Plato that Erasmus is drawing on, where
Plato is talking about women being guardians of the state as well as men. However, instead of 'as guardians of the state' the Latin means 'for the guardians
of the state' or 'by the guardians of the state.'
3 Cicero *De officiis* 3.24.93

94 This first appeared in *1533* in the slightly different form *extinguitur magis quam
Heracliti sol*. It was changed in *1536*, as was the accompanying essay.
1 Plato *Republic* 6.498A, where the scholiast on the passage describes Heraclitus'
view of the sun's light, as given here. Socrates is talking there about old men,
who are not suited to master the difficulties of philosophy, since they have
been worn out by these in their youth.
2 Erasmus misrepresents the views of Heraclitus here when he says that Heraclitus thought the sun was like a skiff (*scapha*). In fact Heraclitus thought that
it was a bowl (σκαφίς); see Diogenes Laertius 9.9–10.
3 See Xenophanes fragment A 41 Diels-Kranz.
4 Horace *Odes* 4.7.13–14

95 Coenum barbaricum
Barbaric filth

Βόρβορος βαρβαρικός, Barbaric filth. This is used in the sense of great mental torpidity in Plato in the *Republic* book two.[1] There he is praising dialectic, which alone stimulates a mind that is immersed in ignorance and raises it from holding trivial beliefs to attaining a solid knowledge of the truth. He says, 'And it is quite true that dialectic gradually draws out the soul's eye that is immersed in barbaric filth and lifts it up.' The word *barbarus* seems to come from *borboros* 'filth' as a mark of contempt.[2]

96 Non e quercu aut saxo
Not from oak or rock

Οὐκ ἐκ δρυὸς ἢ ἐκ πέτρας, Not from oak or rock. Used when we want to indicate that something consists of spiritual qualities and not of physical material. For example, ordinary people mean by 'city' the walls and houses constructed from stones and timber, by 'church' the structure put together from similar material, when in fact a city consists of the character of its inhabitants and a church is the consensus of souls in true religion. Plato in the *Republic* book eight: 'Or do you think that states are made somehow from oak or from rock and not rather from the character of those who live in them?'[1]

97 Psallium iniicere
To put on a curb-chain

Ψάλλιον ἐμβάλλειν, To put on a curb-chain. Said of those who curb a wild disposition with some means of control. A metaphor taken from high-spirited horses. Plato in *On the Laws* book three: 'Your third saviour saw that the rulers were still being extravagant, noisy and unruly, and so he imposed

* * * * *

95 Plato (see n1). Added in *1533*
  1 Plato *Republic* 7.533D (not book 2), cited in *Adagia* II i 20 A barbarian from the roadside
  2 The etymology may have been Erasmus' own suggestion.

96 Plato (see n1). Added in *1533*
  1 Plato *Republic* 8.544D

97 Plato (see n1). Added in *1533*

on them, like a curb-chain, the power of the ephors.'¹ He is speaking of the
state of Sparta in which five ephors were appointed to modify the power
of the kings. The curb-chain is a small circular chain attached to the bridle,
and because of this the word is sometimes used also in the sense of 'bridle.'² But perhaps the expression was an allusion to bulls being led around
by an iron ring attached to their nostrils. Whence the proverb, 'To lead one
by the nose,' which we have talked about elsewhere.³

98 Principium, medium, finis
Beginning, middle, and end

Plato in *On the Laws* book four reports the following as if it were a very
common utterance: 'God embraces the whole universe, that is, the beginning,
middle, and end.'¹ For from God comes the beginning, the growth, and the
complete creation of all that exists. 'Let us say to them, "Sirs, God to be
sure, as the old proverb says, holds the beginning, end, and middle of all
that exists, and moves straight through the cycle of nature."'

99 Orphica vita
An Orphic life

Ὀρφικὸς βίος, An Orphic life. In *On the Laws* book six Plato says that this is a
life free of sin, one that is untouched by luxury and undefiled by food with
blood in it.¹ For Orpheus seems to have established such a way of living.
Not only did humans not defile the altars of the gods with the blood of
beasts, they also forbore from eating the flesh of any animal. Instead, they
sacrificed with cakes and grain sprinkled with honey, and they themselves
did not eat anything else. These are Plato's words: 'But your ancestors at
that time had "An Orphic life," as the saying goes.' Orpheus seems to

* * * * *

1 Plato *Laws* 3.692A
2 By metonymy. Cf Hesychius Ψ 43.
3 *Adagia* II i 19

98 Plato (see n1). Added in *1533*
1 Plato *Laws* 4.715E–716A. The Greek form of the proverb is ἀρχή τε καὶ τελευτὴ
καὶ μέσα τῶν ὄντων ἁπάντων.

99 Plato (see n1). Added in *1533*
1 Plato *Laws* 6.782C

have attempted in Thrace what Pythagoras tried in Ionia and Numa in Rome.[2]

100 Candidus sermo
White speech

Λευκὸς λόγος, White speech. This was a Greek expression for speech that is clear and easily understood, from the colour that has the greatest light of all. Therefore those who express their thoughts quite clearly are said λευκότερον εἰπεῖν 'to speak more brightly,' that is σαφέστερον 'more clearly,'[1] and a voice that easily reaches the ears of an audience is called a λευκὴ φωνή 'a bright voice.'[2] There are metaphors such as the one in this expression that draw from a closely related field, as when those who understand something are said 'to feel' or 'to see,' those who remember something are said 'to retain,' those who are suspicious are said 'to get a whiff,' those who err are said 'to be blind.'[3] The metaphors are drawn from a very closely related field when a function of the eyes is transferred to the ears, as in this one.

1 Ambrones
Ambrones

Ambrones was a term once commonly applied to people who lived by thieving and wickedness. Festus Pompeius gives the origin of the name,

* * * * *

2 The philosopher Pythagoras forbade the eating of animal flesh. According to Ovid *Metamorphoses* 15.477–51 Numa Pompilius, the second king of Rome, was influenced by the teachings of Pythagoras.

100 Added in *1533*. The Greek phrase is not found in ancient literature.
1 The use of the adverb λευκότερον in the sense 'more clearly' occurs in both Athanasius and Eusebius. For example, Athanasius *De decretis Nicaenae synodi* 19 PG 25 449A, 452B; Eusebius *Commentaria in Psalmos* PG 23 192C, 384B, 584A
2 See *Suda* Λ 332.
3 Cf *Adagia* I vi 81 Scenting out, where many more examples of such metaphors are given. The topic is discussed, under the heading of *deflexio*, in *De copia* CWE 24 333 (ASD I-6 62:758–67).

1 Brassicanus no 32; see *Adagia* IV iii 86 n2 (52 above). Erasmus supplements with material taken from the epitome of Livy book 68, wrongly ascribed to Florus, and from Plutarch's *Life of Marius* chapters 16 and 19–21. Added in *1533*

informing us that the Ambrones were a Gallic tribe driven out of their own territory by the flooding in of the sea, who then overran other people's lands and took to maintaining themselves and their dependents by looting and plundering.[1] Their army inspired terror, not only by reason of their numbers – thirty thousand is the figure given[2] – but by their savagery and method of fighting. They bore down on the enemy in close formation keeping in time together and shouting out in a kind of chant, 'Ambrones, Ambrones,' whether this was to keep their own troops together or to inspire terror in the enemy. They had defeated the Roman generals Manlius and Caepio,[3] but were themselves vanquished first of all by the Ligurians, afterwards suffering a crushing defeat at the hands of Gaius Marius, and were finally annihilated by him at Aquae Sextiae, together with the Cimbri and Teutones.[4] This is more or less what Julius Florus says in his epitome of book sixty-eight, also Plutarch in his life of Gaius Marius.

Similarly the name 'Cilician' developed into a term of abuse, implying pillaging and plundering.[5]

2 Vinaria angina
Wine-quinsy

We dealt earlier with ἀργυράγχη 'the silver-quinsy,' which causes many people besides Demosthenes to lose their voice.[1] Festus Pompeius tells us that it was jokingly said of those who choked over their wine that they were suffering from 'wine-quinsy,' which you could call οἰνάγχη in Greek.[2]

* * * * *

1 Pompeius Festus 15.29–16.2 Lindsay where 'Ambrones' is said to have become proverbial
2 As in Plutarch and ASD, but LB gives the figure as three hundred thousand.
3 The defeat of these generals in 105 BC was disastrous for the Romans, as large numbers of Roman troops were killed.
4 These were tribes from northern Europe who had been threatening Roman territory in Gaul and on the northern border of Italy for several years.
5 The Cilicians were pirates operating in the Mediterranean from various bases, especially Cilicia on the southern coast of Asia Minor. They were renowned for ferocity and cruelty; see *Adagia* III ii 25 A Cilician ending.

2 Pompeius Festus (see n2 below). Added in *1533*
1 See Plutarch *Demosthenes* 25 and *Adagia* I vii 19 He has the silver-quinsy, which recounts the Demosthenes story.
2 Pompeius Festus 25.25 Lindsay

I knew a man of considerable scholarship in Rome who actually died of this 'quinsy.' He was a Portuguese called Hermicus.[3] He was very fat and short of breath and he caught a fever. As he lay on his sick-bed, he was visited by Christopher Fisher, an Englishman, who said to him, 'Hermicus, you don't want to pay any attention to the stupid prescriptions the doctors give you. You'll wash this disease out of your system better with a pot of good wine.' So saying, he at once sent out for a bottle of four-year-old Corsican wine. He drank the invalid's health and told him to take heart. Thus persuaded, Hermicus took a deep draught, but immediately choked and began to breathe his last.

Drunkenness sometimes turns silent individuals into chatterers, sometimes makes people 'dumb as a fish,'[4] without however any permanent damage to their health. I wish this 'wine-quinsy' were not so prevalent among the Germans.[5]

3 Titivillitium
A tinker's cuss

Titivillitium was a word meaning nothing very definite, but when used as a sort of interjection it indicated utter contempt, like the Greek πεπαλό. Plautus uses *titivillitium* in a line cited by Festus Pompeius: 'I wouldn't give a tinker's cuss for talk like that.' (The line comes from the *Casina*.)[1] Festus gives another similar word, *buttubata*, used by Naevius for trifles and things of no value.[2] Nonius however thinks the word *pipalo* meant 'insult,' 'abuse,' as in the lines from Plautus' *Pot of Gold*: "So help me Laverna,[3] if you don't

* * * * *

3 The Portuguese humanist, Enrique Caiado. He had a reputation as a wit and a drinker. See Erasmus Ep 216 (CWE 2 153); CEBR 1:239; Erasmus *Poems* CWE 85 122 and CWE 86 521.
4 See *Adagia* I v 29 As dumb as the fishes.
5 The Germans were commonly depicted as uncivilized drinkers. See Erasmus *Colloquia* 'Inns' CWE 39 374.

3 Pompeius Festus and Nonius citing Plutarch and Naevius. This duplicates much of *Adagia* I viii 8 I would not buy it for a rotten walnut. Added in 1533
1 Pompeius Festus 504.1–3 Lindsay, citing Plautus *Casina* 347
2 Pompeius Festus 32.2 Lindsay, citing the third century BC Roman poet and dramatist Naevius (CRF Naevius 132)
3 The patron goddess of thieving, mentioned in *Adagia* IV viii 91 Make an offering to Coalemus (414 below). See also Nonius Marcellus 196.35 Lindsay.

have my pots brought back, I'll stand outside in the street and by yelling names *pipalo differam* 'I'll rip up your reputation.'"[4]

4 Nihil potest nec addi nec adimi
Nothing can be either added or taken away

Aristotle tells us in book two of the *Nicomachean Ethics* that people used to say this of a totally satisfactory creation: 'Accordingly people often say in connection with works of art that turn out well that Οὐκ ἀφελεῖν ἔστιν οὔτε προσθεῖναι "You can neither take away nor add anything."'[1] For excellence, the mean is required; excess or deficiency destroys it. Any one who adds, creates excess; anyone who takes away, generates deficiency. Horace wrote of Lucilius: 'There are things one would remove from his turbid stream.'[2] Of Demosthenes and Cicero it was said that 'nothing could be taken from the former, nothing added to the latter.'[3]

* * * * *

4 Nonius Marcellus 222.1–3 Lindsay, citing Plautus *Aulularia* 445–6. Nonius says *pipulo pro convicio,* implying that *pipulo* actually meant *convicio* 'with an insult,' and this fits the line of Plautus well. Cf Varro *De lingua latina* 7.103. Erasmus' text in both LB and ASD reads *Nonius autem putat pipolo convicii fuisse vocem,* 'But Nonius thinks *pipolo* was a term of abuse.' Possibly Erasmus misunderstood Nonius. It is difficult to see what interpretation he would put on the line of Plautus on this basis, but compare *Adagia* IV x 20 (497 below), where he leaves a difficult text to speak for itself. It seems to be his own idea that the word is Greek.

4 Johann Bebel published a new edition of Aristotle (ed S. Grynaeus) in 1531, for which Erasmus wrote the preface. This task required much reading in Aristotle (as can be seen from Ep 2432, preface), and the fruit of this is seen in the numerous citations from the *Rhetoric* and the *Nicomachean Ethics* in the 1533 enlargement of the *Adagia*: twenty-five examples in IV viii, six in IV ix, and two in v i; also three were added in 1533 to IV v and two to IV vii (all in this volume). Added in 1533

1 Aristotle *Nicomachean Ethics* 2.6 (1106b9); after the quotation Erasmus paraphrases the next section.

2 Horace *Satires* 1.4.11. Lucilius (second century BC) was Horace's predecessor in writing verse satire. Horace is here criticizing what he saw as Lucilius' unpolished and undisciplined style, which was however forceful.

3 Quintilian 10.1.106

5 Virtus simplex
Virtue is simple

It is not clear whether Aristotle, in the second book of the *Nicomachean Ethics*, was quoting a verse so well known that he did not need to name the author, or whether he wrote a pentameter verse by accident. It occurs in the passage where he is quoting Pythagoras' view that evil is infinite, virtue finite (for example, there is only one right track through a wood but one can go off it in a thousand ways).[1] Consequently, vice is easy, virtue is hard, just as missing the target is easy, hitting it difficult. Aristotle then goes on to say, Ἐσθλοὶ μὲν γὰρ ἁπλῶς, παντοδαπῶς δὲ κακοί 'Virtue itself is simple, vice comes in many forms.'[2]

6 Extra fumum et undam
Away from the smoke and the swell

In the same book, Aristotle cites an often-quoted line of Homer: 'Do you keep the boat Τοῦ . . . καπνοῦ καὶ κύματος ἐκτός "Away from the smoke and the swell."' He attributes the words to Calypso, who had advised Ulysses neither to sail too close to the shore-line, following the smoke, nor to entrust himself to the deep, but to cleave a way between the two. For on the one hand, there was danger from rocks and shallows, on the other, from great seas.[1] (Argyropylus in his translation attributes the words to Circe, I know not on what authority.)[2]

* * * * *

5 Aristotle (see n2 and *Adagia* IV viii 4n, 354 above). Cf Otto 161. Added in *1533*
1 Erasmus may be recalling the incident he records in *Adagia* IV viii 27 Like a whipping top (372 below).
2 Aristotle *Nicomachean Ethics* 2.6 (1106b29–35). The line in Aristotle actually says, 'Men are good in one way only, evil in all kinds of ways.' Erasmus himself doubts whether it is proverbial.

6 Aristotle (see n1 and *Adagia* IV viii 4n, 354 above). Added in *1533*
1 Aristotle *Nicomachean Ethics* 2.9 (1109a32), citing Homer *Odyssey* 12.219–20. Aristotle is still discussing the 'mean' (the material quoted in the previous adage is part of this argument), and advises choosing the lesser of two evils (ie Scylla rather than Charybdis).
2 Giovanni Argiropolo (1415–87); see CEBR 1:70–71. Erasmus mentions his translations of Aristotle into Latin in *Adagia* IV iv 34 (83 above) and Epp 456, 862, 2432. The translation of the *Nicomachean Ethics* (Cologne 1508) substitutes

7 Communis tamquam Sisapo
Jointly owned like Sisapo

This is without question a proverbial expression. In the second *Philippic*, Cicero says, 'Home, do I say? There wasn't a spot on earth where you could set foot on something[1] that you could call your own – apart from the one place at Misenum, and that you held in joint ownership with your partners like Sisapo.'[2] He meant that Antony did not own the estate at Misenum outright but held it on the same terms as an ore deposit bought up by concessionaires. Pliny tells us in book thirty-three, chapter seven, that red lead (which the Greeks call μίλτος, others 'cinnabar') was not only highly valued by the ancients but treated as a holy substance.[3] On festal days, the statues of the gods were daubed with red lead, as were generals celebrating a triumph (though Galba, who was old, would not let it be done to him, as Corneliius Tacitus tell us).[4] Sisapo is a place in Baetica, at one time a source of revenue to the Romans, where there were red-lead mines. Hardly anywhere else supplied Rome with the substance. Pliny tell us that 'the Romans supervised its production more carefully than anything else. It was not permitted to complete the process and refine it where it was produced. Up to ten thousand pounds in weight were sent to Rome per year under seal and purified there. The price at which it could be sold was controlled by law to prevent it rising out of all proportion.' But, as Pliny says, 'it was adulterated in many ways, providing rich pickings for the partnership.' Later on he says, concerning the

* * * * *

'Circe' for 'Calypso' here, correctly, for, in the relevant line of Homer, Ulysses himself is instructing his steersman on the course to take, based on the advice given him earlier by Circe. He decides to sail nearer to the cliffs of Scylla and so avoid the maelstrom of Charybdis. Aristotle seems to have misquoted from memory, and Erasmus too seems not to have checked with the original. Erasmus seems to think in Allen Ep 2432:255 that Argiropolo had available Aldus' *editio princeps* of Aristotle of 1495–8, but he was dead by 1487.

7 Erasmus draws on several of Cicero's *Philippics* in *Adagia* IV viii 7–14. These were fourteen speeches of invective directed at Mark Antony. Otto 1658, who doubts that it is proverbial; see also Otto 1394. Added in *1533*
1 Cf *Adagia* IV x 50 Tread on (513 below).
2 Cicero *Philippics* 2.19.48
3 Pliny *Naturalis historia* 33.111 and 118–20. The rest of the adage is almost entirely drawn from these sections.
4 Quotation not so far identified; Erasmus has probably misremembered.

adulterated substance, 'It is adulterated at the diggings of the partners.' This makes it clear that the whole area was divided up among many partners, just as today various contractors have a specified stretch of a gold or silver mine.

8 Quanta vix caelo capi potest
More than the heavens can contain

Cicero employed this hyperbole to express illustrious renown when speaking in the second *Philippic* of those who murdered Julius Caesar because he was aiming to set himself up as tyrant: 'Especially since these people have won for themselves such a glory that the heavens can scarce contain it.'[1] Virgil writes, 'His rule he extends to earth's extremes, / His glory to the stars.'[2] But he makes Daphnis 'famed even beyond the stars.'[3] Horace writes, 'I shall strike the stars with my exalted head.'[4] We often find in Cicero the expression 'to laud someone to the skies.'[5]

9 Modo palliatus, modo togatus
Now in pallium, now in toga

This phrase would provide a neat dig at an unreliable man of shifting loyalties and changing allegiance, someone, for example, who keeps altering his way of life and sometimes appears in ecclesiastical tiara, sometimes in general's uniform.[1] Cicero in the fifth *Philippic*: 'Will the presiding

* * * * *

8 Cicero (see n1). Added in *1533*
1 Cicero *Philippics* 2.44.114
2 Virgil *Aeneid* 1.287 (misquoted from memory)
3 Daphnis is the famed shepherd-poet; see Virgil *Eclogues* 5.43.
4 Horace *Odes* 1.1.36
5 Eg Cicero *De oratore* 2.128; 3.146; *Ad familiares* 10.26.2; *Ad Atticum* 6.2.9

9 Cicero *Philippics* 5.5.14. Cf *Adagia* IV v 45 From the toga to the pallium (171 above). The *pallium* was a simple Greek garment, consisting of a rectangular piece of cloth draped so as to leave the right arm free and reaching to the ankles. It was informal wear. The toga on the other hand was the traditional, heavy, semi-circular, elaborately-draped, Roman garment, which had to be worn on formal occasions and for all public activities.
1 Possibly yet another jibe at the militaristic pope Julius II, who personally led armies to reclaim the allegiance of Perugia and Bologna in 1506. Erasmus was in Bologna at the time.

magistrate accept the excuse of a Greek juryman, who appears sometimes in a *pallium*, sometimes in a *toga*?' The *pallium* is a Greek garment, just as the *toga* is Roman. Both however are civilian garb, just as the *sagum* is military.[2]

10 Ad saga
On with the soldier's cape

The *sagum* was a short cape worn by soldiers. Cicero several times uses an apparently proverbial expression, 'to don the soldier's cape,' meaning to prepare for war, to rush to arms. In the sixth *Philippic* he writes: 'Let them go quickly then, which I see they intend to do in any case. Do you however get out your soldiers' capes, since the House has passed a decree to the effect that "if he does not submit to authority, then capes will be donned."'[1] Again in the same speech: 'I proposed that a state of emergency should be declared, capes put on.'[2] Earlier, in the fifth *Philippic*: 'It is my view that a state of emergency should be declared and capes put on.'[3] Later, in the seventh: 'They called for arms, capes, war.'[4] In the eighth: 'Men have been called up all over Italy, no exemptions granted; tomorrow capes will be worn.'[5] Again in the same speech: 'For my part, honourable members of this House, though persons of my eminence usually wear civilian dress even when the whole country is under arms, I have nonetheless decided that at such a dreadful time, when the nation is in such turmoil, I must dress the same way as you and the rest of the Roman people.'[6] Again in the thirteenth: 'Levies are being raised throughout Italy,

* * * * *

2 The *sagum* was a coarse woollen cape worn, eg, by soldiers. See the next adage.

10 *Saga sumere* 'To put on capes' occurs as Brassicanus no 71, a short paragraph where Brassicanus names Cicero's sixth *Philippic* but gives no quotations. Erasmus illustrates with several extracts from this and other *Philippic Orations*. The phrase is so frequently used by Cicero that Erasmus takes it to be proverbial. On Brassicanus see *Adagia* IV iii 86 n2 (52 above). Added in 1533
1 Cicero *Philippics* 6.3.9
2 Cicero *Philippics* 6.1.2
3 Cicero *Philippics* 5.12.31
4 Cicero *Philippics* 7.8.21
5 Cicero *Philippics* 8.2.6
6 Cicero *Philippics* 8.11.32. Erasmus' text seems to have read *in armis*, 'under arms,' instead of *in sagis*, 'in military dress.'

consuls sent forth, Caesar honoured, capes being worn. Does all this not make you realize that you are seen as a public enemy?'[7] Similar phrases often occur in the fourteenth: 'We took to our capes'; 'we should don capes again tomorrow'; 'go away to put on capes'; 'to have put on capes and then returned to civilian dress.'[8] We find a similar string of phrases in the third *Verrine*: 'After you forced these wretched unfortunate men, despairing of Roman law and Roman justice, to resort to violence, to fighting, to weapons.'[9]

11 Igni ferroque minari
Threaten with fire and sword

Those who profess unmitigated hostility are said to 'Threaten with fire and sword,' an expression still in common use today.[1] Those who wage war in a civilized fashion confine themselves to looting and abstain from slaughter and putting to the torch. Cicero writes in the thirteenth *Philippic*, 'He will of course treat ambassadors with more respect than he does the two consuls, to whom he offers armed resistance, than the town of Mutina, which he is actually besieging, than his country, which he threatens with fire and sword.'[2] Again in the twelfth *Philippic*: 'who threatens this city with fire and sword.'[3] It will be even neater to use the phrase metaphorically referring to intellectual pursuits, like saying that philosophers 'threaten someone with fire and sword' when they propose to attack him mercilessly in writing. Likewise, we 'debar from fire and water'[4] those with whom we do not wish to have any dealings at all.

* * * * *

7 Cicero *Philippics* 13.10.23
8 Cicero *Philippics* 14.1.1–3
9 Cicero *Verrines* 2.1.32.82. The word *saga* does not occur here. The point seems to be the string of phrases in asyndeton, as in the examples from *Philippics* 7 and 13 (nn4 and 7 above).

11 Cicero (see nn2 and 3). Cf *Adagia* IV x 13 Sword and flame (491 below). Added in *1533*
1 Suringar 254
2 Cicero *Philippics* 13.21.47
3 Cicero *Philippics* 11.14.37 (not the twelfth)
4 This was the Roman formula for declaring someone an outlaw and so cutting him off from normal life in society. Cf *Adagia* IV ix 18 Fit for the sack (430 below).

12 Neque terrae motus timet, neque fluctus
He fears neither earthquake nor raging sea

In book three of the *Nicomachean Ethics*, Aristotle puts forward the view that people who fear nothing because they are naturally brutal, not because they are endowed with courage, should be called not brave but mad, stolid, insensate. He writes: 'A person would be mad and insensate εἰ μηθὲν φοβοῖτο, μήτε σείσμους μήτε κύματα "if he feared nothing, neither earthquake nor raging sea," as they say of the Celts . . .'[1] Nothing is more terrifying than the sea in turmoil; an earthquake seems to presage Hell bursting out into the world above. Yet some tribes of Gaul and Germany were so brutal that they had no fear even of what is naturally horrendous. Aristotle here equates 'mad' with 'insensate,' and I presume that Diogenes had the same idea in mind when someone asked him his opinion of Socrates and he replied, 'Mad'[2] – Socrates, who was in any case able to withstand all kinds of injury, had inured himself to any and every bodily discomfort.[3] Unless possibly Diogenes also attributed to insensitivity rather than virtue the fact that Socrates could not be provoked even by physical violence to lose his temper in the slightest.[4]

13 Calceos mutare
Change one's shoes

Cicero was apparently using a proverbial expression when he said of a certain person that he had 'Changed his shoes,' when, quite without justification, he took to himself the rank of senator, which entitled the holder to wear black boots with a crescent-shaped decoration at the ankle. What

* * * * *

12 Aristotle (see n1 and *Adagia* iv viii 4n, 354 above). Added in *1533*
  1 Aristotle *Nicomachean Ethics* 3.7 (1115b26)
  2 The reference is to Diogenes the Cynic philosopher; for the incident see Diogenes Laertius 6.54 ('Diogenes'), but there Plato is said to have described Diogenes the Cynic as Socrates gone mad. Either Erasmus has misremembered, or his text was faulty.
  3 See Xenophon *Memorabilia* 1.2.1–2; 1.6.; Plato *Symposium* 219E–220B. Cf *Adagia* v i 56 Socrates' cockerel or hide (572 below).
  4 See Diogenes Laertius 2.21 ('Socrates').

13 Cicero (see n1). Added in *1533*

Cicero said was: 'There is also some Asinius or other, a volunteer senator, self-appointed. After Caesar's death he saw the House wide open, he
changed his shoes, and all of a sudden became a senator.'[1]

A gold stripe on the toga was a sign of senatorial rank;[2] so also was
the black leather added at the ankle.[3]

14 Campana superbia
Campanian arrogance

Insolence usually accompanies prosperity. Many ancient writers tell us that
Campania was once easily the richest region in Italy. Pliny for example in
book three writes, 'Next comes the famous and fertile land of Campania.
From the gulf rise hills covered with vineyards, producing a noble tipple
with a fruitiness renowned throughout the world. As the ancients said,
Father Bacchus vies with Ceres for first place ...'[1] and so on, speaking

* * * * *

1 This is taken from Cicero *Philippics* 13.13.28; the example was added also to
   Adagia III i 4 in *1533*.
2 The distinctive dress of the senatorial class in the Republic and early Empire
   was a tunic with a broad purple stripe, *clavus*, (the knights wore a narrow
   stripe), and (if a magistracy had been held) a toga with a purple border, distinct from the normal plain one. Erasmus' gold stripe or braid is puzzling. He
   may be thinking of the more elaborate dress of the later Empire, or possibly *au-
   reus* should be emended to *purpureus*. Erasmus may, however, mean 'gold pin'
   or 'brooch.' *Clavus* means 'nail' or 'stud' as well as 'stripe,' and there was debate as to the meaning of *clavus* in the context of dress. See Lazare de Baïf *De re
   vestiaria* (Basel 1526). Erasmus knew this work; see *Ciceronianus* CWE 28 421. An-
   tiquarians were still discussing the problem in the eighteenth century; see, eg,
   Basil Kennett 'The Habit of the Romans' *Romae Antiquae Notitia* (London 1776)
   314: 'The whole Body of the Criticks are strangely divided about the Clavi.'
3 Senators also wore high leather boots adorned with a crescent-shaped ornament of ivory at the ankle. Erasmus has expressed this carelessly, in words
   recalling Juvenal 7.192: 'He sews on the crescent attached to the black leather.'

14 Cicero (see n4). Brassicanus no 54, quoting Cicero and Aulus Gellius (see nn4,
   5, 7, 8, 10) here expanded, and with additional material from Pliny and Livy.
   For Brassicanus see *Adagia* IV iii 86 n2 (52 above). Otto 313. Added in *1533*
1 Pliny *Naturalis historia* 3.60. Bacchus ... Ceres, ie wine and cereals, is a common
   metonomy, already cited in *De copia* CWE 24 339. See *Adagia* II iii 97.

not only of the fertility of Campania but of its delightfulness too. And indeed Capua[2] once challenged Rome for supremacy, with the result that 'Campanian pride, Campanian arrogance' became a by-word. Cicero in his speech against Rullus:

> That famous Campanian arrogance, that intolerable insolence, our ancestors deliberately and as a matter of policy reduced to utter indolence and apathy. They escaped the infamy of cruelty by refraining from destroying the finest city in Italy, yet at the same time took thought for the future by cutting all the sinews of the city[3] and leaving it limp and impotent.[4]

A little later in the same speech he calls Campania 'the home of arrogance, the seat of licentiousness' – his words are 'colonists selected and settled in Capua, in the home of arrogance, the seat of licentiousness.'[5] Again, in the speech he made to the senate after his restoration, Cicero says, 'Did you imagine you were consul – for you held that office at that time – in *Capua*, once the very home of arrogance?'[6] Again in the fragmentary speech attacking the same person: 'The place which by reason of its fertility and abundant supplies of everything needful is reputed to have spawned arrogance and hardness of heart.'[7] And shortly after: 'If the luxurious life-style corrupted Hannibal himself at Capua, if arrogance was born there, as they say, out of the haughty attitudes of the Campanians ...'[8] Livy writes in

* * * * *

2 The old capital of Campania, one of the most powerful cities of Italy until reduced by the Romans

3 The Romans abolished the Capuan magistrates, their assembly and their civic insignia, as a punishment for the city's defection to Hannibal in the Second Punic War.

4 Cicero *De lege agraria* 2.33.91. Erasmus accidentally wrote 'speech for Rullus' instead of 'against'; see n7 below.

5 Cicero *De lege agraria* 2.25.97

6 Cicero *Cum senatui gratias egit* 7.17

7 Cicero *De lege agraria* 1.6.18. Cicero made two speeches attacking the tribune Rullus and his land re-distribution bill, the first (now fragmentary) before the senate, the second before the assembly of the people.

8 Cicero *De lege agraria* 1.7.20. The discipline of Hannibal's victorious army was made slack by overwintering in Capua and enjoying its luxury and civilization. See Seneca *Letters* 51.5; also Livy 23.18.10–16.

the ninth book of his first decade that 'arrogance was endemic among the Campanians.'[9] Furthermore, Aulus Gellius in book eleven, chapter twenty-four, says that the boastful epitaph that Naevius composed for himself was 'full of Campanian arrogance.'[10] (But Naevius was, I think, *not* a Campanian.)[11] Just as any remarkable example of treacherous dealing was at one time commonly called 'Punic,'[12] so any piece of insolence was called 'Campanian.'

I will make no comment on the character of those who inhabit the region today, but when I travelled through Campania myself,[13] I found not a trace of that 'fruitiness renowned throughout the world,' never a drop of Falernian, Massic, Caecuban, of those famous wines from Cales, Sezza, Sorrento.[14] We all but choked with the 'wine-quinsy'[15] in the place today called Capua. We filled the whole cup with sugar, but the wine, sharper than vinegar, won the day. As a general rule, they boil the wine down because otherwise it won't keep until the next vintage. Where are those celebrated wines? The passage of time has destroyed their name and their place of origin. We drank in dust enough. Truly, nature allows nothing of man's works to endure.

15 Αὐτοβοᾶν
Self-crying

We dealt earlier with the saying Αὐτὸς αὑτὸν αὐλεῖ 'He is his own flute-player.'[1] The single Greek word Αὐτοβοᾶν 'Self-crying,' expresses a similar

* * * * *

9 Livy 9.6.5
10 Aulus Gellius *Noctes Atticae* 1.24.2 (not book 11)
11 Reading *non fuisse* with ASD; LB reads *fuisse*.
12 See *Adagia* I viii 28 Punic faith; *De copia* CWE 24 583.
13 During his stay in Rome in 1509, Erasmus took his pupil Alexander Stuart on a trip to Naples in the spring to visit the famous cavern of the Sibyl at Cumae; see Ep 756, *Adagia* v ii 20 Gathering sea–shells (613 below).
14 These are all fine ancient wines mentioned by Pliny in *Naturalis historia* 3.60 (see n1).
15 See *Adagia* IV viii 2 (352 above).

15 From the *Suda* (see n3 and *Adagia* IV iii 1 n1, 3 above). Added in 1533
1 In *Adagia* II v 86 He sings his own praises

idea, when someone recommends himself, or acts as his own auctioneer. Auctioneers cry up the skills and endowments of slaves for sale in order to make people eager to buy. But it is thought ridiculous for a man to cry up himself. The same idea is found in another saying we dealt with earlier, 'A home-grown witness,'[2] which is recorded in Suidas.[3] The Athenians in similar vein say, 'Down with you and all your prating.' Aristophanes in the *Knights*: 'Damn Paphlagon and all his plots'; and a bit later: 'together with all his lies.'[4]

16 Sterilem fundum ne colas
Don't cultivate barren land

Στεῖρον ἀγρὸν μὴ σπείρειν, Don't cultivate barren land. This is found in Plato's *Laws*. If I recall aright, in its context in Plato, the precept is a cryptic way of discouraging active male homosexual love. In the eighth book of the *Laws*, he says that they cast their seed on stones.[1] The saying can however be put to other uses: Don't teach the unteachable; Don't look for happiness in riches, for they do not bring real joy. Plautus in the *Amphitryo*:

> To lend your wife to another man is just the same
> As to rent out a barren field for sowing.[2]

* * * * *

2 *Adagia* II iii 6 Home-grown evidence
3 *Suda* A 4484
4 Aristophanes *Knights* 2–3 and 7, where the ancient commentator says that this type of phrase is an idiom characteristic of the Greek spoken in Athens

16 Cf *Adagia* I iv 52 You are sowing seed in the sand; Tilley s 89 To plough the sand. Added in *1533*
1 Plato *Laws* 8.838E, but the Greek form of the adage as Erasmus gives it is not found here.
2 Plautus *Amphitryo* 24–5 of the (spurious) supplement to the play. The long section missing from the original was supplied by a fifteenth-century humanist hand and was accepted into the editions as early as Venice 1495, though scholars continued to argue over the genuineness of this and other Plautine supplements; see Ludwig Braun *Scenae Suppositiciae oder, Der falsche Plautus* (*Hypomnemata* 64; Göttingen 1980) 16–37, 124. Erasmus several times quotes from the supplied lines, but without comment as to their genuineness.

17 Scarabaeus citius faciet mel
Sooner will a dung-beetle make honey

Two phrases found in an epigram of Palladas are examples of the type of expression classified as ἀδύνατα 'impossibilities':[1] 'Sooner will a dung-beetle honey make / Or else a gnat give milk.'[2]

18 Terram video
I see land

To signify that the end of some long hard task is at hand, people say Γῆν ὁρῶ 'I see land.' It is an expression taken from sea-faring. Quintus Curtius in book four: 'Just like those far out on the deep sea, they looked around for sight of land.'[1] Plautus, in the *Merchant*: 'And I thought I'd reached dry land.'[2] Cicero, in his speech on behalf of Lucius Murena: 'Those just sailing into harbour after a long sea voyage eagerly give advice to those who are leaving port about the likelihood of storms and the pirate situation and what all the different places are like, because it is natural to feel kindly towards those who are to face the perils we have just escaped. So what should be my feelings, who am just coming into sight of land after a terrible tossing, towards this man whom I see having to go out and face dreadful political storms?'[3] Cicero again in the *Elder Cato*: 'I seem to see land,' where Cato intimates that he feels the end of life

* * * * *

17 *Anthologia Palatina* (see n2). Added in *1533*
 1 Ie a figure by which the impossibility of something ever happening is asserted by associating it with something else of its nature quite impossible. See CWE 31 22 *Introduction* xiii 'On proverbial metaphors.' At *Adagia* I ii 42 Erasmus begins a long series of such sayings. See also IV iii 94 Mixing fire and water, IV iv 11 The stag drags off the hounds, IV v 69 Sooner will a dumb man speak (57, 67, 188 above).
 2 Not Palladas but Ammonius *Anthologia Palatina* 11.227

18 Brassicanus no 88; Erasmus' essay has mostly different examples. For Brassicanus see *Adagia* IV iii 86 n2 (52 above). Otto 1766; Tilley L 56 To see land
 1 Quintus Curtius 4.7.11
 2 Plautus *Mercator* 196
 3 Cicero *Pro Murena* 2.4

approaching.[4] When Diogenes was reading out from a very long scroll and reached the point where he could actually see the end of it, he said, 'All's well, friends. I can see land.'[5]

19 Incantatione quavis efficacius
More effective than any spell

Πάσης ἐπῳδῆς ἐνεργότερον, More effective than any spell. The ancients believed that immense power was inherent in the words of incantations. So the Psalmist speaks allegorically of 'the voice of charmers or of the cunning enchanter' and compares the people that would not obey the commands of the Divinity to 'the deaf adder that stops its ear.'[1] Plato, in the *Letter* to Hermias, Erastus, and Conscius: 'I believe that these words of mine will, through shame and a realization of what is right, reconcile you and restore you to your former amity more effectively than any magic spell.'[2]

20 Invidus vicini oculus
Envious is the neighbour's eye

Aliclytus to Eucymon: Δυσμενὴς γὰρ καὶ βάσκανος ὁ τῶν γειτόνων ὀφθαλμός, φησιν ἡ παροιμία 'Hostile and envious is the eye of neighbours, as the proverb says.'[1] This refers, I think, to what Hesiod says about potters,

* * * * *

4 Cicero *De senectute* 19.71
5 Diogenes the Cynic philosopher. The incident is recorded in Diogenes Laertius 6.38 ('Diogenes').

19 *Collectanea* no 629 *Quavis incantatione melius*. The Greek version may be Erasmus' own translation. Added in *1533*
1 Ps 57.5–6 (Vulgate)
2 Plato *Letters* 6.323B. Used again in *Adagia* v ii 17 Make stones weep (610 below)

20 Alciphron (see n1). Cf *Adagia* III i 22 Unfriendly and spiteful is the neighbour's eye. Added in *1533*
1 From Alciphron *Epistles* 1.18 (*Letters of Fishermen*). Alciphron was a second–third century AD sophist who composed fictitious letters (the *editio princeps* appeared in *Epistolarum Graecarum collectio, pars* II [Aldus: Venice 1499]). The names should read Halyctipus and Encymon.

singers, and neighbours, which I referred to earlier.[2] Ovid similarly says, 'Another's crops are heavier still than thine / And heavier udders grace thy neighbour's kine.'[3]

21 Eodem collyrio mederi omnibus
One salve for all sores

One should not apply the same rules, advice or reproaches to all situations, but adjust one's words to match different nationalities, times, natures. St Jerome, in his commentary on *Ephesians*, commends this versatility in the Apostle Paul,[1] who became 'all things to all people, that he might save all.'[2] Jerome's words are cited in *Distinctio* twenty-nine: 'He does not, like an inexperienced doctor, try to treat everybody's eyes with one salve.'[3] We have already quoted the saying from Galen, 'to fit the same shoe on every foot.'[4]

22 Funditus, radicitus etc
From the foundations, root and all, and similar phrases

Anything utterly destroyed beyond all hope of restoration is said to be removed 'From the foundations' and taken away 'Root and all.' The first phrase derives from buildings razed to the ground, the second from trees

* * * * *

2 *Adagia* I ii 25 Potter envies potter and smith envies smith
3 Ovid *Ars amatoria* 1.349–50, already used in *Adagia* I vi 72 The crop is heavier in another man's field

21 The title is derived from Alciati *De verborum significatione* IV 87 (see *Adagia* IV ix 36 n3, 443 below). Tilley s 82 He has but one salve for all sores; Otto 409. Added in *1533*
1 Jerome *Commentarius in Epistolam ad Ephesios, Prologus* PL 26 440A–B
2 See 1 Cor 9:20–22.
3 Ie in the first part of Gratian's *Decretum* (*Corpus iuris canonici*), which is divided into 101 *Distinctiones*; this is *Distinctio* 29.3. See *Adagia* IV viii 25 n2 (371 below).
4 *Adagia* IV iv 56 Putting the same shoe on every foot (100 above), quoting Galen *Therapeutike* 9.16

22 Alciphron (see *Adagia* IV viii 20 n1, 366 above) with Cicero. Added in *1533*

that not only have their branches lopped but have their trunks chopped right down or are even dug out, root and all.

When Acinetus wrote to his girlfriend Phoebiana complaining that she had stripped him of everything and then rejected him, he said, 'You have laid me in ruins, as the saying goes, and then reduced me to slavery.'[1] Plautus in the *Three-shilling Day* has:

> How that giddy fellow almost entirely overthrew
> My friend's wise plan, my careful stewardship,
> The entire secret business.[2]

In the *Haunted House* he uses a similar phrase, 'foundations and all':

> I don't see how I can
> Repair my house, prevent the whole thing falling down,
> Going to ruin, foundations and all,
> Nor can anyone help me.[3]

The Greek equivalent of Latin *radicitus* 'root and all' or *a stirpe* 'right from the base' is the verb ἐκπρεμνίζειν that is, *exstirpare* 'root out.' There is an example of *exstirpare* in Cicero's essay *On Fate*: 'but to have them *exstirpari* 'rooted out' and *funditus* 'totally' eliminated, so that the person ...'[4]

Here are other examples of *funditus* 'totally, absolutely' taken from Cicero. In his defence of Sextus Roscius: 'Titus Roscius did not merely abstract some trifling amount from the estate for his own benefit, but stripped my client absolutely of every possession';[5] in the fourth *Verrine*: 'I should run out of time, voice and lung-power if I were to expatiate at this point on the shame and iniquity of a festival in Verres' honour having to be celebrated by the very people who considered Verres entirely responsible for their being brought totally to ruination';[6] and in the fifth: 'the previous year had already dealt a serious blow to the farmers; the next one had utterly

* * * * *

1 Alciphron *Epistles* 2.6 (*Letters of Farmers*). This has already been quoted in *Adagia* III i 23 Total overthrow. The name should be Anicetus.
2 Plautus *Trinummus* 163–5
3 Plautus *Mostellaria* 146–8
4 Cicero *De fato* 5.11
5 Cicero *Pro Roscio Amerino* 39.115
6 Cicero *Verrines* 2.2.21.52

destroyed them';[7] in the speech he made before the priests, *Concerning his house*: 'so that you might utterly destroy the state from its very foundations';[8] and a little later: 'so that any reminder of the man who had plotted the destruction of the state should be utterly erased from the sight and from the thoughts of all';[9] in the first of his letters to his brother Quintus: 'If we kow-tow to them, we shall allow the people ... to perish utterly';[10] and, in another letter: 'We have absolutely lost our grip on the country.'[11] And an example of *radicitus* from the above speech: 'So you see I am not trying to tear out everything you did by the roots.'[12]

The phrase can be even more satisfactorily applied to the mind, if one says, for example, that ambition, avarice, and lust must be totally deleted, thoroughly extirpated from the mind.

23 In ore atque oculis
Before the face, in the sight of

Anything done publicly is said to be done 'Before the face' and 'In the sight of all.' Cicero in the fifth *Verrine*: 'Once you have admitted to these things that were done openly, in the Forum, at Syracuse, before the face and in full sight of the whole province ...'[1] Again, in his *Divination*: 'Has it never occurred to you to consider what an undertaking it is to embark on a public prosecution, to lay open another's whole life for inspection, to set it out not only before the minds of the jury but before the eyes and in the sight of all?'[2]

In the first example, Cicero perhaps used *os* 'face' to mean 'sight.' But generally the phrase *in ore omnium* means 'on the lips of all,' that is, to be the subject of common talk. We can also 'carry in our eyes'[3] those we protect and care for.

* * * * *

7 Cicero *Verrines* 2.3.18.47

8 Cicero *De domo sua* 13.35

9 Cicero *De domo sua* 43.114

10 Cicero *Epistulae ad Quintum fratrem* 1.1.11.32

11 Cicero *Epistulae ad Quintum fratrem* 1.2.5.15

12 Cicero *De domo sua* 13.34

23 Cicero (see nn1–2). Otto 1310. Added in *1533*

1 Cicero *Verrines* 2.2.33.81

2 Cicero *Divinatio in Quintum Caecilium* 8.27

3 See *Adagia* v ii 50 (629 below).

24 Myconiorum more
Like the Myconians

Μυκονίων δίκην, Like the Myconians. People who gate-crashed a party were said to turn up 'Like the Myconians.' Myconos is one of the Cyclades and the people were so poor they were obliged to push themselves in among the guests, hence the mocking proverb. Athenaeus cites Archilochus' lambasting of Pericles for thrusting himself uninvited into convivial gatherings 'like the Myconians.'[1] We have already treated this phrase elsewhere.[2]

Even today you still find traces of 'Myconian' behaviour among the Irish. On which subject, William Lord Mountjoy told me a rather amusing story, not, however, a fiction but something he saw with his own eyes.[3] A completely unknown Irishman entered the King's palace at the hour of dinner and sat down quite uninvited with the King's entourage. When they saw the exotic bird, they asked him where he came from. He named his country. They then asked whether he had any position at court. 'No,' he replied, 'but I would like to have one.' They were amazed at the fellow's impudence and told him to get up and go. 'Certainly,' said he, 'when I've had my dinner.' To cut a long story short, the Irishman did not retreat but carried the day by his sheer effrontery. Their anger turned to amusement and they asked him how he, a nobody and a foreigner, had the face to push himself in amongst the King's household. 'Well,' said he, 'I knew the King could afford to give me my dinner.'

25 Solem adiuvare facibus
Add light to the sun with torches

We have already dealt elsewhere with Τὸ φῶς ἡλίῳ δανίζεις 'You lend light

* * * * *

24 Athenaeus (see n1). *Suda* M 1400. Added in *1533*

  1 Athenaeus 1.7F citing Archilochus (fragment 124a West)

  2 In *Adagia* II i 7 Myconian baldpate, and III vi 39 A Myconian neighbour

  3 William Blount, fourth Baron Mountjoy (CEBR 1:154–6). For the dedication of the 1533 additions to the *Adagia* to his son Charles, see the Letter of Dedication printed after IV vii 58 (317 above).

25 This was taken from Alciati *De verborum significatione* IV 88, where it is briefly explained. See introductory note to *Adagia* IV vii 75 (332 above) and IV ix 36 n2 (443 below). Tilley s 988 To set forth the sun with a candle. Otto 1665. Added in *1533*

to the sun.'[1] Very similar is this other phrase quoted by Gratian from Pope Anacletus in cause six, question one, where he attacks those who in this world think they have the right to dispense the judgment of God which no man shall escape.[2] The judgments of men are indeed unsure and, compared to the judgments of God, are like torches compared to the sun. 'If everything in this world,' he writes, 'received its just deserts, there would be no place for divine judgment. It is wasted effort to seek to add light to the sun with torches ...' Though in common copies of the work, scribes have corrupted *facibus* 'with torches' to *fascibus* 'with faggots.'

26 Censoria virgula
The obelus of censure

Scholars very commonly use the term 'Obelus of censure' for authoritative judgment, especially when expressing disapproval.[1] This is derived from the Roman magistrate [the censor]. We can class with this Jerome's words in the dialogue against the Luciferians: 'No one can lay claim to the palm of Christ, no one pass judgment on men before the day of judgment.'[2] Jerome seems to be alluding to Deuteronomy twenty-five, where the palm of justice is a palm given by the judges to one who had proved his innocence and won his case.[3] This palm Christ truly has, and he does not give it to any undeserving person, since he alone never errs in judgment, whereas in human judgments there is plenty of error and darkness.

* * * * *

1 *Adagia* I vii 58
2 Gratian *Decretum* 2. Cause 6, Question 1, canon 7. Gratian's *Concordantiae discordantium canonum* or *Decretum* (*Corpus iuris canonici*), most important for the collection of legal texts of different periods and origins which it incorporated, became available probably in 1148, and became the standard text in universities for the study of Canon Law. The second part consists of 36 *causae*, subdivided into *quaestiones* (ie cases proposed for solution and the several questions raised by each), which are in turn divided into canons.
   For Erasmus' use of extracts from the Roman jurists in the 1533 expansion of the *Adagia* see the introductory note to *Adagia* IV ix 1 (419 below).

26 *Collectanea* no 765. Otto 370. Added in 1533
1 See Quintilian 1.4.3. Cf *Adagia* I v 57 To mark with stars. To brand with an obelus, and *Adagia* I v 58 To be marked with the finger-nail, etc.
2 Jerome *Altercatio Luciferi et orthodoxi* 22 PL 23 186B
3 Deut 25.1: *quem iustum esse perspexerint, illi iustitiae palmam dabunt*

27 Trochi in morem
Like a whipping-top

Βέμβικος δίκην, Like a whipping top, said of inconstant and changeable people. A *bembix* is a top which boys whip to make it spin. Suidas cites a line from Aristophanes: 'must be just like a whipping-top.'[1] (The line is from *Birds*.) Hesychius thinks it refers to someone running away who does not keep to the right path but goes round in circles.[2] This happened to me once when I was going from Sélestat to Basel. I fell in with another horseman and led by him rode about in a certain wood for ages. Eventually I asked him if he was sure of the way, and he assured me that he was. When there seemed no end of it, I said, 'We must have gone wrong somewhere. We've been in this wood for three hours now, and it usually takes only an hour to get through it.' To cut a long story short, it turned out that we were almost back where we started. A whipping-top moves with great energy, but in a circle, so that it flees but does not escape. Sirach, the wise Hebrew, chapter thirty-three, uses a similar figure to describe the inconstancy of the fool: 'The heart of the foolish is like a cart-wheel; and his thoughts are like a rolling axle-tree.'[3] Plautus sometimes says someone 'turns quicker than a top' or 'than a potter's wheel.'[4]

28 Praestat canem irritare quam anum
Better provoke a dog than an old woman

There is a line in Menander which says, 'Worse by far it is an old woman to rouse than a dog.'[1] According to the sayings of the Hebrews, there is no anger more violent than a woman's.[2] The whole sex is easily provoked and

* * * * *

27 Brassicanus no 18 *Turbine versatilior* 'Turning quicker than a top' (see *Adagia* IV iii 86 n2, 52 above). Erasmus shares with Brassicanus the references in n1. Cf Otto 1556. Added in *1533*
  1 *Suda* B 236, citing Aristophanes *Birds* 1461
  2 Hesychius B 503
  3 Ie Ecclus (the Book of Sirach) 33:5
  4 Plautus *Epidicus* 371

28 Menander by way of Stobaeus (see n1). Added in *1533*
  1 Stobaeus 73.44 Gaisford citing Menander fragment 587 (Körte-Thierfelder)
  2 Ecclus 25:23

vindictive, partly through irrationality, partly through pettiness. The truly great spirit will ignore certain injuries and think it beneath him to be angry with all and sundry. Woman, however, is a formidable creature when to the normal faults of the sex are added advancing years. A dog when roused merely barks, sometimes even bites; but old hags not only have poisonous tongues but skill in evil arts as well, in poisonings and spells. Many have discovered to their cost the truth of Menander's words.

29 Pecuniosus damnari non potest
A rich man cannot be found guilty

In the second part of his attack on Verres, Cicero says that it was universally acknowledged 'not merely among Romans but among foreign nations as well, that, with the courts constituted as they now are, no man with well-lined pockets, however guilty he might be, can be convicted.'[1] And in the third part: 'The guilt of the accused is indubitable. If he is convicted, men will no longer say that in these courts money is the thing that matters. If he is acquitted, I for my part shall no longer oppose the transference of the courts to others.'[2] Similar to this is the idea occurring several times in Sallust's *Jugurthine War*: 'In Rome everything has its price.'[3] Rome has now lost its empire. I wish that the saying did not still stick.

30 Inter manum et mentum
Between the hand and the chin

Festus records this as a proverb in use among the Romans but ultimately de-

* * * * *

29 Cicero (see n1). Added in *1533*
  1 Cicero *Verrines* 1.1.1. Erasmus no doubt classifies this as a proverb because Cicero says that 'it was universally acknowledged.'
  2 Cicero *Verrines* 2.1.2.6
  3 See Sallust *Bellum Jugurthinum* 35.10, where Jugurtha says, as he escapes from Rome: 'A city for sale, which will soon be destroyed, once it finds a purchaser.' Jugurtha was a Numidian prince with both supporters and enemies in Rome, and involved in the political rivalries of the time. Bribery is one of the themes in this monograph of Sallust's.

30 This is given as a proverb in Festus (see n1), where, as Erasmus remarks, the text is incomplete. One full version of the story is given in Zenobius (Aldus)

rived from a Greek one, Πολλὰ μεταξὺ πέλει κύλικος καὶ χείλεος ἄκρου 'Many a thing befalls between the cup and the brush of the lips.' He records its origin as follows: 'Chalcas was planting vines when a seer who lived in the neighbourhood happened to pass by and remarked that Chalcas was under a misapprehension – it would not be granted to him [to taste] the new wine.'[1] That's all we can gather from the fragmentary text, which is all that somebody or other's stupidity has left us of this author who is so thoroughly knowledgeable on every subject. The proverb reminds us that there is nothing certain in human life. Very often the very thing that we think we have in our grasp some unexpected chance snatches away. It is like someone holding a cup so close that there is only a small space between the hand and the chin and even so, as sometimes happens, dying before he can drink. The proverb is explained in various ways, and different writers give different accounts of its origin, all of which I treated in some detail above when discussing the proverb 'There's many a slip 'twixt the cup and the lip.'[2] I have introduced it here because Festus gives it in different words, which in the Latin have a nice alliterative ring, *manum* 'hand' and *mentum* 'chin.'

31 Colophonium calciamentum
Colophonian footwear

Κολοφώνειον ὑπόδημα, Colophonian footwear, was a name for clogs. The ancients usually wore a simple sandal that only protected the sole of the foot. I have seen among my own countrymen a form of footwear made of

* * * * *

column 143 and Diogenianus 7.46, and Erasmus himself has already given several versions of it (see n2). Otto 1035; Tilley T 191 Many things fall between the cup and the lip. Added in *1533*

1 Pompeius Festus 132.18–22 Lindsay. The *editio princeps* lacks a required verb. Erasmus supplies *degustare* 'to taste.' In the next sentence, however, Erasmus may be referring to the loss in Festus of the rest of the story (see introductory note).

2 *Adagia* I v 1; see also I v 2 Between mouth and morsel.

31 The probable source is Hesychius K 3391 and Σ 625. Κολοφώνειον (sc ὑπόδημα) is also found in Rhinthon, a comic poet of the third century BC (fragment 4 Kaibel, page 185). The second part of this essay is based on Brassicanus no 73 *Calcei Sicyonii* 'Sicyonian slippers,' with which it shares the passage from Cicero (see n4). For Brassicanus see *Adagia* IV iii 86 n2 (52 above).

hollowed-out wood, called in the vulgar tongue a 'hollow block.'[1] This is why the term can be applied to a thick, clumsy, rustic fellow. This kind of footwear is appropriate if you have to make your way through mire. So you could wittily say of someone who was about to work on texts containing filthy material that he needed 'Colophonian clogs.'

The opposite of this is 'Sicyonian shoes,' named after Sicyon, a town in the Peloponnese, as we are told by Stephanus[2] and Sextus Pompeius Festus mentions them too,[3] though neither explains the saying. Cicero gives us to understand that 'Sicyonian shoes' were very pretty, more suitable for women and fops than for men. This is what Cicero says: 'Again, when Lysias, the eloquent speaker, brought Socrates a ready-written speech, which he could learn off if he wanted and use it to defend himself at his trial, he read it willingly enough and said it fitted the circumstances very nicely, "but," said he, "if you had brought me Sicyonian shoes, I would not wear them, however comfortable and well-fitting they were"; that is, he thought the speech eloquent and one that did credit to Lysias as an orator, but he did not consider it manly or courageous.'[4]

32 Manduces
Jaws

Manduces, Jaws, was a name for people who were always hungry, or for those who inspired terror with empty threats. Festus tells us that at one time in processions, as well as other extravagant and frightening figures, there

* * * * *

1 Erasmus gives the name in Latin, *cavus truncus*, a translation of the Dutch *holsblok* 'clog.'
2 Stephanus of Byzantium sub Σικυών. Stephanus' work, *De urbibus*, was a list in 60 books, giving the names of places and the adjectives derived from them, occasionally with some additional information, which was extracted from the works of Stephanus by an epitomator. A considerable number of manuscripts was made during the Renaissance period, and Aldus published the *editio princeps* of the Greek text in 1502.
3 Pompeius Festus 455.7–8 Lindsay
4 Cicero *De oratore* 1.54.231. This material is briefly referred to again at *Adagia* v ii 18 (612 below).

32 Pompeius Festus (see n1). The form should be *manduci*, as in Festus. Added in *1533*

would be an effigy with huge jaws gaping wide open and making a great clacking with its teeth, called *Mandux* 'Jaws.'[1] In Plautus' play the *Rope*, the professional toady, Charmides, says, 'Suppose I hire myself out somewhere as a Mandux at the games? For why? My teeth are gnashing nicely.'[2] He had just swum ashore from a shipwreck and was shivering all over with cold. A little later, he says his voice has 'got the rattles.'[3] Martial was thinking of this figure or something like it when he wrote: 'Worked in red clay, a Dutchman's phiz am I. / I move your laughter, but make the children cry.'[4] The Greeks call this sort of bogey μορμολύκιον 'fright-wolf,' because they used to frighten children with the spectacle of a wolf to make them stop crying.[5]

33 Ubi tu Caius, ibi ego Caia
Where you are Gaius, there I am Gaia

In his 'Roman Questions,' Plutarch discusses the origin of the custom according to which those who conducted the bride to her husband bade her speak the words, 'Where you are Gaius, there I am Gaia.'[1] His first suggestion is that the ancients desired the bride, in speaking these words, to enter into an agreement with her husband that they would share everything and have equal authority in the household, saying in effect, 'Where you are lord and master of the house, there I am lady and mistress.' The form of the saying is derived from the Jurisconsults, who use 'Gaius Sestius' and 'Lucius Titius' as any two representative people, as the philosophers use 'Dion' and 'Theon.' (Hence the adage which I cited earlier from Varro, 'Accius and Titius take alike,'[2] meaning that they had equal rights.) Plutarch's

* * * * *

1 Pompeius Festus 115.20–4 Lindsay, quoting Plautus (see n2)
2 Plautus *Rudens* 535–6
3 Erasmus has misremembered; it is earlier, line 526.
4 Martial *Epigrams* 14.176. For the translation, see *The Epigrams of Martial* (Bohn's classical library, London 1911).
5 The etymology is based on Μόρμω, a she-monster (hence μορμολύττεσθαι 'to terrify') and λύκειος 'of a wolf.' See Lucian *Pseudologus* 2 on Mormo as a bogey to frighten children.

33 Plutarch supplemented by Pompeius Festus (see nn1 and 3). Added in *1533*
1 Most of this section down to 'laid up in his temple' is derived from Plutarch *Quaestiones Romanae* 30 (*Moralia* 271E).
2 *Adagia* I x 77

second suggestion is that the woman is called Gaia as a good omen, because there was a certain Gaia Caecilia, previously called Tanaquil, who was both beautiful and virtuous. She was married to one of the sons of Tarquin, Tarquinius Priscus in fact.[3] The Romans placed a bronze statue of this lady in the temple of Sanctus (that at any rate is the form of the name given in Plutarch's text).[4] He was a god at one time worshipped under this name by the Romans, one of the twelve special divinities. In ancient times the lady's sandals and distaff were laid up in his temple. The sandals were a sign that she stayed at home and looked after the household, the distaff indicated her industry, in diligently performing the work of women and applying herself to her spinning. The use of the name Gaia reminded the bride to be to her husband what Gaia Caecilia was to hers. Among other observances connected with ancient marriage ceremonies was the belief that it was ill-omened to call bridegroom or bride by their proper names. Even today it is customary for the bride to give up her own family name and take her husband's name, just as Andromache is addressed as 'Andromache of Hector.'[5] The saying, which originated with the married state, should remain special to husband and wife, though it could be adapted to brother and sister.

34 **Rumor publicus non omnino frustra est**
General report not always groundless

In the seventh book of his *Nicomachean Ethics*, Aristotle quotes some well-known lines from Hesiod: 'Rumour dies hard that many folk have uttered.'[1]

* * * * *

3 Erasmus has probably taken this supplementary information from Festus Pompeius 85.3–7 Lindsay, whence comes also Caecilia's devotion to spinning.

4 Erasmus questions the form *Sanctus*, and Plutarch's text should possibly be emended to *Sancus*. There was an ancient Sabine deity called Semo Sancus (supposed to be a Sabine name for Hercules), associated with the Roman Dius Fidius, a god of oaths. There is some support for an alternative form Semo Sanctus. The earliest temple dedicated to this divinity in Rome was believed to date from the time of the first kings (eighth century BC).

5 Virgil *Aeneid* 3.319

34 Hesiod quoted by Aristotle (see n1). Adages 34–40 use material derived from Aristotle *Nicomachean Ethics* (see *Adagia* IV viii 4n, 354 above).

1 Aristotle *Nicomachean Ethics* 7.13 (1153b28), quoting Hesiod *Works and Days* 763–4, given by Erasmus in Greek: Φήμη δ' οὔτοι πάμπαν ἀπόλλυται ἥντινα

The philosopher adduces this brief poetic extract as a probable argument in support of the view that pleasure is the supreme good because men as well as beasts pursue it.

35 Quadratus homo
A four-square man

In the first book of his *Nicomachean Ethics*, Aristotle takes issue with those who equate human happiness with external blessings, which come and go at the whim of fortune. He says that, according to this line of thought, our happy man appears as a kind of chameleon, being sometimes happy, sometimes unhappy, according as his circumstances change, just as the chameleon changes colour if placed on a different coloured background. True happiness on the other hand lies in the blessings of the mind, from which he deduces that there is no reason why the truly happy man should not remain happy all his life. He goes on:

> For the person who will always or as far as possible act and think in a way consonant with virtue and suffer the mishaps of fortune as well as can possibly be done, in an absolutely consonant manner, will be the person who is truly good, a four-square man, free from all that can be faulted.[1]

(In the third book of his *Rhetoric*, he uses this same phrase, 'a four-square man,' to illustrate a type of metaphor.)[2] Now a square remains a square, whichever side it falls on. In the same way, the wise man remains unchanged in his essential self, however events fall out. It will be even neater to apply the term 'four-square' to the actual mind of the wise man, which remains unshaken in face of fortune's blows.

* * * * *

λαοί / Πολλοὶ φημίζωσιν. This has already been used in *Adagia* I vi 25 What is in every man's mouth is not spoken wholly without cause, and will reappear in v i 76 Rumour makes all things known (585 below).

35 Aristotle (see n1 and *Adagia* IV viii 34n above). The chameleon has already been treated in I i 93 Adopt the outlook of the polyp, and in III iv 1 As changeable as a chameleon; 'four-square' appears again in v ii 39 To square up (623 below). See also IV iii 6 A barrel rolls easily (7 above).

1 Aristotle *Nicomachean Ethics* 1.10 (1100b6)

2 Aristotle *Rhetoric* 3.11.2 (1411b27). The metaphor is a non-vivid one, because the image is static.

36 Merces amico constituatur
Let the price be agreed for a friend

In his *Life of Theseus*, Plutarch tells us of a certain Pittheus, the maternal grandfather of Theseus and instructor of the famously chaste Hippolytus. Pittheus was famous for his wise saws, which at the time were held to enshrine the highest sapience. This is supposed to be one of them: Μισθὸς δ᾽ ἀνδρὶ φίλῳ, εἰρημένος ἄρκιος ἔστω 'Agree the price and make it fair when dealing with a friend.'[1] Aristotle tells us in the ninth book of his *Nicomachean Ethics* that Protagoras never settled with his students in advance what fees they should pay, but once they had acquired the knowledge they desired, he told them to reckon how much they thought it was worth and then he would accept whatever they gave him.[2] Aristotle thinks that people of this persuasion would find the precept of Pittheus perfectly adequate in transactions of this sort, since he recommends fixing a fair and just reward for a friend. It would be a good thing if doctors too did not fix a fee in advance but accepted what they were offered, once the patient had recovered. In the same passage, Aristotle tells us that certain sophists[3] would not admit anyone to their courses unless the fee were paid cash down, and then, having pocketed the money, failed to deliver what they had promised.[4] We sometimes see shady doctors and surgeons doing exactly the same thing. The ones who demand an enormous fee and will not lift a finger unless the whole sum or at least the greater part of it is actually paid on the spot are usually discovered to be quacks.

37 A bonis bona disce
Learn goodness from the good

In the ninth book of his *Nicomachean Ethics*, Aristotle is demonstrating that

* * * * *

36 A saying from Hesiod, half-quoted by Aristotle without attribution as obviously too well known to need the full text (see nn1 and 2 and *Adagia* IV viii 34n, 377 above.)
1 Plutarch *Life of Theseus* 3.1–2. The saying is well known from Hesiod *Works and Days* 370, and it is presumably from there that Aristotle quotes it (see n2).
2 Aristotle *Nicomachean Ethics* 9.1 (1164a23–6)
3 See *Adagia* IV x 64 n2 Ass looks lovely to ass and pig to pig (521 below).
4 Aristotle *Nicomachean Ethics* 9.1 (1164a30–32)

37 A well-known line from Theognis, half-quoted by Aristotle (see n1 and *Adagia* IV viii 34n, 377 above). Apostolius 11.50. Otto 277. Added in *1533*

virtue is learnt best from the company of good men, since friends correct each other if any error is committed and find themselves spurred on to virtuous action by the presence of others. To support this argument, he quotes as if well-known some words of poetry: 'goodness from the good.'[1] The quotation is actually from Theognis, and it also occurs in Xenophon's account of the sayings and doings of Socrates.[2] Socrates was saying that the best of all perfumes was the oil used by athletes. Oil of marjoram and spikenard[3] were best left to women. When asked what old men should smell of, he replied, 'Integrity.' When asked in turn where this perfume could be purchased, he quoted in reply these words from a line of Theognis: 'From the good do thou goodness learn.' Our own writer of maxims says in similar vein: 'Learn, but only from those who have been well taught.'[4]

38 Asinus stramentum mavult quam aurum
The ass prefers straw to gold

In the tenth book of the *Nicomachean Ethics*, Aristotle is saying that plea-

* * * * *

1 Aristotle *Nicomachean Ethics* 9.12 (1172a13), citing in part Theognis 35. For similar material, see *Adagia* III iii 78 Neither a blind guide nor a witless counsellor, and v i 84 Let one who has learned teach others (591 below).

2 This suggests Xenophon's *Memorabilia* or 'Socratic memoirs,' and the quotation from Theognis does occur there at 1.2.20 in a comparable context, but the succeeding passage is from Xenophon *Symposium* 2.3, which gives the two-line Theognis quotation in full.

3 Ie *amaricinum* and *foliatrum*. For the suggested identifications see Pliny *Naturalis historia* 13.15; 21.37; 21.163.

4 Ie *Disticha Catonis* 4.23. This compilation of moralizing verses attributed to the elder Cato served as an introductory Latin reader for centuries. Erasmus had produced editions of the work in 1514 and 1515, and there were many reprints during his life-time. See Erasmus Ep 298. Estienne points out (in a note printed at LB II 1131F) that Erasmus has twice mistranslated Greek διδάξεαι (a future indicative) in the Theognis quotation by an imperative, thus obscuring the meaning 'for you will learn goodness from the good' (ie naturally, by association). The verb does not occur in the half line quoted by Aristotle but in the full text in Xenophon (see nn1 and 2). (The notes by Estienne incorporated into LB are taken from his 1558 edition of *Adagia* with *Animadversiones*.)

38 *Collectanea* no 29. Heraclitus quoted by Aristotle (see n1 and *Adagia* IV viii 34n, 377 above). Added in *1533*

sure is not the same for all creatures, since the dog, the horse, the man, take pleasure in different things. He then quotes from Heraclitus: 'Asses would choose straw in preference to gold, because food gives them more pleasure than gold.'[1] Here indeed asses are wiser than men. Asses judge things according to their usefulness, we set great price on useless or even harmful things because of some preconceived notion. Everyone knows the fable about the barnyard cock who spurned the gem he uncovered in the dung-hill.[2] A cock prefers a perishable barleycorn to a pearl or a diamond. Likewise those who are slaves to their bellies think more of drunken revelry than all liberal disciplines.

39 Iocandum ut seria agas
Play in order to be serious

In the same book, Aristotle cites the criticism of Anacharsis,[1] directed at those who treat trivial pursuits as serious business, as for example putting a life-time of effort into becoming a good dancer or a skilled wind-player. Play is really something that should be indulged in only from time to time in order to make possible concentration on serious subjects.[2] Aristotle actually says, 'It looks foolish and very childish to treat what is only a pastime as something that matters and to devote a great deal of energy to it. But to play in order to achieve something worthwhile is, according to Anacharsis, quite acceptable.'[3]

* * * * *

1 Aristotle *Nicomachean Ethics* 10.5 (1176a5–8), citing the philosopher Heraclitus (fragment 9 Diels-Kranz)
2 Phaedrus 3.12 (Mueller)

39 Anacharsis quoted by Aristotle (see nn1 and 3, and *Adagia* IV viii 34n, 377 above). Added in *1533*
1 A fabled Scythian prince exemplifying 'the wise barbarian,' who was sometimes numbered among the Seven Sages of Greece. Various wise sayings were attributed to him. See eg Diogenes Laertius 1.8 ('Anacharsis').
2 Erasmus believed that relaxation was not only permissible but necessary, especially in education. See eg Allen Ep 2431:227–33; *Adagia* v ii 20 Gathering sea-shells (613 below).
3 Aristotle *Nicomachean Ethics* 10.6 (1176b32–36); the passage continues: 'Amusement is a sort of relaxation, and relaxation is necessary because they cannot work continuously.'

40 Cyclopum more
Like the Cyclopes

In the same book again, Aristotle calls 'Cyclopean' a life subject to no public regulation, where everyone does what he chooses: 'In the majority of cities there is no action taken on these matters (that is, the education of children), but everyone lives as he sees fit, like a Cyclops determining for himself how wives and children are to be treated.'[1] The Cyclopes, it is said, lived scattered over the mountains with no semblance of civilized life, but each doing what he pleased in his own cave. Nor did they have any kind of religion. I have already dealt with the saying, 'To live like the Cyclopes.'[2]

41 In leporinis
Live on hare-pie

Ἐν λαγῴοις. Those who lived in ease and luxury were said to 'Live on hare-pie.' Martial is evidence for the fact that hare's meat was once considered a delicacy: 'Of birds the thrush, if I my thoughts declare, / Of quadrupeds, the glory is the hare.'[1] There is also the proverb: 'A hare thyself, and goest in

* * * * *

40 Aristotle (see n1 and *Adagia* IV viii 34n, 377 above)
1 Aristotle *Nicomachean Ethics* 10.9 (1180a26)
2 *Adagia* I x 69

41 From here to the end of century VIII, Erasmus has twenty-nine entries extracted from the comedies of Aristophanes. His primary source appears to be the ancient commentaries ('scholia') on the plays. These were printed together with the plays (excluding *Thesmophoriazusae* and *Lysistrata*) in the Aldine edition (ed M. Musurus) of 1498. Erasmus' common practice is to translate or paraphrase most of the entry, often supplementing it with a quotation of the relevant lines of text, and adding miscellaneous information from elsewhere. The material in the scholia is often to be found repeated in the *Suda* and the proverb collections of Apostolius, Zenobius, and others in CPG.
In this adage Erasmus is using the ancient commentator on *Wasps* 707–10 (see n3), who explains *puon* and *pyarites* and quotes the supplementary line of verse (see n4). See also *Suda* Π 3179 and Brassicanus no 6 *Inter meros lepores* 'Nothing but hare's meat.' See *Adagia* IV iii 86 n2 (52 above). Added in *1533*
1 Martial 13.92 (see *Adagia* IV viii 32 n4, 376 above)

quest of game?'² Aristophanes says in the *Wasps*: 'A thousand cities pay us tribute. If each one of them were ordered to provide for twenty men, then:'

> Twenty thousand of the common folk
> Would live on meat of hares,
> With all sorts of garlands.
> First milk and curdled beastings.³

(The Greek word for 'first milk,' which is taken from the animal when it has just borne its young, is *puon*, and a clotted form of this is called *pyarites*.) The ancient commentator on this passage of Aristophanes cites a line (from Homer, I think): 'Feasting on first milk, gorging on beastings.'⁴ In Aristophanes again, when Cleon and his rival are vying with each other in promising a really magnificent meal to the people, among all the other fancy foods, they promise hare's flesh as something very special and a great delicacy.⁵

42 Matrem sequimini porci
Piglets, after your mother

Ἔπεσθε μητρί, χοῖροι, Piglets, after your mother. This is found several times, for example, in Aristophanes' *Plutus*.¹ The ancient commentator tells us

* * * * *

2 Treated in *Adagia* I vi 7. The line (from Terence *Eunuchus* 426–8, where it is identified as a proverb) is addressed to a youth making advances to an older woman when he is young enough to be desirable himself.

3 Aristophanes *Wasps* 707–10. Erasmus translates the first two lines and quotes the other two in Greek.

4 The line is not from Homer but from Cratinus, a Greek comic poet of the fifth century BC (PCG 4 Cratinus fragment 149). Porson attributed it to the play *Odysses* (*Odysseus and his Companions*) and it appears to be similar in content to Homer *Odyssey* 9.162, with which it shares the word δαινύμενοι 'feasting,' and this has caused Erasmus to attribute it (from memory) to Homer.

5 Aristophanes *Knights* 1192

42 Aristophanes *Plutus* together with the ancient commentary (see n1 and *Adagia* IV viii 41n, 382 above). Added in 1533

1 Aristophanes *Plutus* 315. This follows on from the line quoted below in the next adage, 43, and like that refers to Aristyllus' perversions. In both places, Erasmus extracts only the dull and innocuous part of the ancient commentary.

it's a proverbial joke directed against the stupid and ignorant. According to another proverb, the sow is the opposite of Minerva.[2] One could say, 'Piglets, after your mother,' to the ignorant students of an ignorant teacher. The saying also fits those who are slaves to gullet and belly.[3]

43 Aristylli more
Like Aristyllus

Aristophanes again, in the same passage from the *Plutus:* 'You'll be an Aristyllus and say with jaw half-agape ...'[1] The ancient commentator on the passage tells us that Aristyllus was a poet with a facial deformity that made his mouth always hang open. Aristophanes makes fun of him elsewhere, for example in the *Women in Parliament.*[2] Now actors employing tragic diction do open the mouth unnaturally wide, but to my way of thinking, Aristyllus was really taken to task for speaking without opening his mouth properly, so that he spoke through his nose with a shrill squeal like a pig's.[3] We know people who speak and sing in that way.

44 Citeria
Citeria

Citeria was a term of abuse at one time directed at people who talked too much. Cato, in his speech against Marcus Caelius: 'What more need I say? He'll be paraded about at the Games, I suppose, as a Citeria, and will bandy

* * * * *

2 See *Adagia* I i 40 The sow teaches Minerva. Minerva is the patron goddess of learning and all the arts.
3 This is probably suggested by the explanation of the phrase by Macarius 4.6: 'referring to people who suck up to someone for the sake of their keep.'

43 Aristophanes *Plutus* together with the ancient commentary (see n1 and *Adagia* IV viii 41n, 382 above). Added in *1533*
1 Aristophanes *Plutus* 314, the line previous to that quoted above in adage IV viii 42
2 Aristophanes *Ecclesiazusae* 647; for Aristyllus' coprophilic tendencies see *Aristophanes. Ecclesiazusae* ed and comm R.G. Ussher (Oxford 1973) 165–6.
3 An explanation suggested by the line quoted in the previous adage, which also refers to Aristyllus.

44 The elder Cato quoted by Pompeius Festus (see n1). Added in *1533*

words with the on-lookers.' Festus tells us that this Citeria was an amusing and loquacious figure, carried along in procession to raise a laugh, making a great noise and racket all the time.[1] These clown figures are no longer carried about in processions, but many people have them at home, making a great deal more noise than the artificial ones.

45 Ostrei in morem haeret
Sticks like a limpet

῞Ωσπερ λεπὰς προσίσχεται, Sticks like a mollusc or shellfish.[1] Aristophanes says of an old woman who can hardly be dragged away from a young man: 'Jupiter, how tightly the old hag / Sticks to the lad like a limpet.'[2] There is a type of mollusc which bind themselves together with filaments so as to have more protection against the motion of the waves.

46 Hodie nihil succedit
Nothing's going right today

In the play named after him, Plautus' Amphitryo uses these words, which he takes to be proverbial: 'Not a thing, as they say, can go well today.'[1] He is referring to the popular belief that some days were lucky for doing things, some unlucky.[2] If one or two things go wrong, they judge the whole

* * * * *

1 Pompeius Festus 52.17–21 Lindsay, quoting this fragment from a speech of the elder Cato (Malcovati fragment 116). Erasmus had previously added this material in *1515* to *Adagia* II vii 44 Archytas' rattle.

45 Aristophanes *Plutus* with the ancient commentary (see n2 and *Adagia* IV viii 41n, 382 above). Added in *1533*
1 In Erasmus' text *ostrei sive conchylii*; the word *ostreum* is taken from the explanation of the scholiast on the line quoted below (see n2). It can mean 'mollusc' generally, as well as 'oyster' specifically. The addition of the synonym *conchylium* 'shell-fish' suggests that Erasmus was unsure of the precise meaning of *ostreum* here. The two words do often occur together in Latin.
2 Aristophanes *Plutus* 1095–6

46 Plautus (see n1). Added in *1533*
1 Plautus' *Amphitryo* 120 of the spurious supplement; see *Adagia* IV viii 16 n2 (364 above).
2 Cf *Adagia* IV x 88 No day is bad from start to finish (535 below).

day by that and say, 'Nothing will go right today,' and refrain from doing anything important.

47 Nec currimus nec remigamus
Neither running nor rowing

In the *Women in Parliament*, Aristophanes has the women plotting to take over the state, because hitherto they have been prevented from performing any function and have done nothing: 'Now we neither run nor drive with oars.'[1] The metaphor is taken from sea-farers, and applied to the running of the state. Sailors are said 'to run' before a following wind, 'to drive' when the wind fails and they have to use oars to propel the ship. This is called ὁ δεύτερος πλοῦς, 'the second sailing.'[2] The women feel that they are not asked to do anything in either peace or war. The saying can be neatly applied to those who make no progress in spite of all their efforts, because fortune is against them.

48 Ut luti baiuli
Like carriers of mortar

Ὥσπερ πηλοφοροῦντες, Like carriers of mortar. The women in Aristophanes' *Women in Parliament* complain that the citizens of Athens will no longer come to the assembly unless they get a coin in the hand, although previously they would pay their own expenses when debating matters of public concern.[1] 'Carrying mortar' is the lowest of all ways of earning a living.

* * * * *

47 Aristophanes (see n1 and *Adagia* IV viii 41n, 382 above). Added in *1533*
　1 Aristophanes *Ecclesiazusae* 109. This material was added in *1533* also to *Adagia* III iv 71 The next best way to sail.
　2 Ie the next best way or a second attempt, the first having failed; see *Adagia* III iv 71, the Greek form of which is ὁ δεύτερος πλοῦς.

48 Aristophanes (see n1 and *Adagia* IV viii 41n, 382 above). Added in *1533*
　1 Aristophanes *Ecclesiazusae* 310. Erasmus forgets that his readers have not the original Greek passage before them, so his comment is not entirely clear. The Greek lines say, 'When they do some service for the common weal, / Like mortar-carriers they want pay to buy a meal.' By this time, the payment for attending the assemblies of the people had risen from one obol to

The words of the saying can be applied to any who use a respected position as an opportunity for sordid gain, for example, those who preach, perform the Mass, bury, or minister the sacraments, but refuse to function unless something is slipped into their hand, 'like carriers of mortar.' There is the well-known passage in the Bible about the children of Israel being slaves to the Egyptians, 'with hard service in mortar and brick.'[2]

49 Tam multa quam sapiens
As much as a man of sense

In book three of the *Rhetoric*, Aristotle advises the speaker not to employ a continuous succession of enthymemes, but to mix them with other matter. He then quotes the apparently well-known line of verse (from Homer, unless I am mistaken):

> Since, my friend, you have said as much
> As a man of discretion would say ...[1]

This could be addressed to someone who speaks at length but not to the matter in hand. 'As much,' says Aristotle, but not 'in such a way.' What matters is not how much we say, but how relevant it is. In similar vein a philosopher once remarked that we should consider learned not those who have learned a great deal but those who have learned something of use.[2]

* * * * *

three obols per day. See *Adagia* IV x 5 Worth a penny (487 below). 'Mortar-carriers,' ie labourers on a building site, were, it seems, the butt of jokes then as now.

2 Exod 1:14

49 From here to number 64, Erasmus draws much from Aristotle's *Rhetoric*, books two and three. See *Adagia* IV viii 4n (354 above). Not all the chosen examples are obviously proverbial. Added in *1533*

1 Aristotle *Rhetoric* 3.17 (1418a8), citing Homer *Odyssey* 4.204

2 Ie Aristippus; see Diogenes Laertius 2.71 ('Aristippus'); Erasmus *Apophtheg-mata* III Aristippus 18. This is Aristippus the Elder, an associate of Socrates, possibly founder of the Cyrenaic school of philosophy. See *Adagia* IV viii 60 n2 (396 below).

50 **Hoc iam et vates sciunt**
Even the seers know it now

A little further on, Aristotle is saying that it is much more difficult to put
one's case to the people than to make a speech in the courts.[1] The man who
is trying to win support for his proposals has to talk about things that have
not yet happened, whereas a prosecutor or defending counsel talks about
past realities, and, what's more, has the law as a starting point. With this as a
basis, it is easy to develop your line of argument. In passing, Aristotle quotes
the saying of Epimenides of Crete: 'That (what has already happened) is
a matter of knowledge even to the diviners.' He adds that Epimenides did
not make pronouncements about future events, which cannot be known,
but about ones in the past that were however not known about. This too is
a form of divination. (St Paul calls Epimenides a prophet.)[2] This sarcastic
comment can be used about something hitherto unknown which has at long
last come to light.

51 **Novi nummi**
New coinage

It is clear from a passage in Plautus that it's nothing new to find every fresh
issue of coinage more debased than last year's. This is what he says in the
Prologue to the *Casina*:

> Those who drink old wine I consider wise.
> And those who go to see the plays of older days.
> Since you appreciate the words and deeds of ancient times,

* * * * *

50 Aristotle (see n1 and *Adagia* IV viii 49n, 397 above). Added in *1533*
  1 Aristotle *Rhetoric* 3.17 (1418a21–6), citing Epimenides, a half-mythical poet of
    the sixth century BC (fragment 4 Diels-Kranz)
  2 Titus 1:12: 'It was one of them, their very own prophet, who said, "Cretans are
    always liars, vicious brutes, lazy gluttons."' Cf *Adagia* I ii 29 To play Cretan
    with a Cretan, where Erasmus attributes this line to Epimenides' work *On
    oracles*, on the authority of St Jerome's commentary on the epistle PL 26 606
    (706B). (See *FGrHist* 457 F1, F2 for both these fragments of Epimenides.)

51 Plautus (see n1). Added in *1533*

It's likely you'll prefer as well the older plays.
For those new comedies that come upon the stage
Are more debased by far than is our latest coinage.[1]

52 Θράττειν
To play Thracian

I have already written about Κρητίζειν 'To play Cretan,'[1] which has become
a by-word indicating treachery. To say Θράττειν 'To play Thracian' is a
somewhat cryptic way of saying the same thing. The ordinary meaning of
this in Greek is 'to create a disturbance, be a nuisance,' but a glance back
at the entry Θρᾷτται 'Thracian slave-girls' suggests the meaning 'deceiving
and acting with Thracian guile.' Theodorus said of Nicon, the harp-player,
θράττει σε. And indeed, Nicon was Thracian. If you don't know this, you
don't see the joke. This is in Aristotle's *Rhetoric* book three.[2] I think Aristo-

* * * * *

1 Plautus *Casina* 5–10

52 Aristotle (see n2 and *Adagia* iv viii 49n, 387 above). Cf *Adagia* iv ix 58 To romance (458 below), for more information on the bad character of the Thracians.
See also Macarius 4.70; Zenobius (Aldus) column 97 (two entries) 32, 37.
The earlier part of this adage uses two consecutive entries in the *Suda*, Θ 464–5
and, later, 476. The verb θράττειν is there glossed as meaning 'disturb, trouble,
upset.' The previous entry, Θρᾷττα, simply 'a Thracian slave girl,' says nothing directly about (female) Thracian guile, but it refers the reader to Aristophanes *Acharnians* 272, where a Thracian slave girl (Thracian women were often slaves in Athenian families) is thieving and saucy. Erasmus seems to have
consulted the Aristophanes passage. His whole paragraph is too compressed
for clarity. The Greek verb θράσσω, θράττω, which did indeed mean 'trouble'
or 'destroy,' is probably connected with the words θράσυς, θαρσέω 'bold, be
bold,' if anything, not with Thracians. This last connection seems to be Erasmus' own idea. Added in *1533*
1 *Adagia* i ii 29
2 Aristotle *Rhetoric* 3.11 (1412a34). Aristotle is dealing in this passage with jokes
dependent on various sorts of word play, and as so often happens in such
cases, the Greek text has become corrupted. Various emendations and interpretations have been suggested by modern editors, eg that the Greek could
mean 'you're thrashed' and could also mean 'you're a Thracian (slave) girl.'

phanes was after the same idea in the *Knights*, where Nicias is urged to say
what he has to say with boldness. He replies, Ἀλλ᾽ οὐκ ἔνι μοι τὸ θρέττε 'I
haven't any thrash.'[3] The ancient commentator tells us that the word used
here, θρέττε, is a foreign word meaning 'confidence,' used to give people
courage, like saying to someone 'Assume Thracian boldness.'

53 Neque dicta neque facta
Never said and never done

Μήτε δεδραμένα μήτε εἰρημένα. We are obviously using a proverbial turn
of phrase when we say of something totally false 'Never said and never
done.' Similarly, 'Never written and never drawn.' Where truth is mingled
with falsehood, we say 'Some things done, some not done.'[1] Aristophanes
in the *Women in Parliament*: 'Now just discourse on things never done or
said before.'[2] The character in the play is jokingly telling the other person to make sure everything she says is new, because people don't want
to hear about what is old. Something never said or done before must be
really new, because, as the wise man of the Hebrews said, 'There is nothing new under the sun.'[3] In his speeches, Cicero often uses the phrase
novo more 'without precedent' for something which has never occurred
before.[4]

* * * * *

The joke is relevant here insofar as it turns on the verb θράττειν and the noun
Θρᾷξ 'Thracian,' with its implications of barbarity, guile, and untrustworthi-
ness. Erasmus' version of the section in Aristotle suggests that he could not
see the point of the pun in the form presented by his corrupt Greek text. Accordingly, he offers no comment on, or translation of, the Greek phrase, and
readers are left to make of it what they will.

3 Aristophanes *Knights* 17, with the scholiast. The *Suda* (Θ 476) and Hesychius
(Θ 725) gloss θρέττε as 'that which is daring, manly, bold.'

53 Aristophanes (see n2). For this adage, cf the earlier one, *Adagia* III vi 85 Said
and done. Added in 1533
1 Virgil *Aeneid* 4.190
2 Aristophanes *Ecclesiazusae* 578–9
3 Eccles 1.9
4 Eg Cicero *Verrines* 2.2.27.67; *De lege agraria* 2.10.26 (Erasmus' text presumably
read *novo more* here)

54 Salvete equorum filiae
Hail, daughters of stallions

This is a popular joke, directed at those who flatter in return for money. Aristotle records the story in book three of the *Rhetoric*.[1] When the victor in a mule-race offered Simonides only a small fee for writing a victory ode, he refused the commission, saying that he resented the idea that his poetry should celebrate half-asses. When however the victor offered him a fee he considered adequate, he wrote the following line: 'Hail, ye daughters of stallions, galloping fast as the storm.' He passed over the fact that they were the offspring of asses too, and concentrated on the more creditable feature, calling them 'daughters of stallions.'

55 Mithragyrtes, non dadouchos
An itinerant priest of Mithras, no Torchbearer

Anyone who is allotted a humble and despised rôle at any function can be called 'An itinerant priest of Mithras, no Torchbearer.'[1] That is what

* * * * *

54 Aristotle (see n1 and *Adagia* IV viii 49n, 387 above)
  1 Aristotle *Rhetoric* 3.2 (1405b24–8). There is nothing here to suggest the saying is proverbial.

55 Aristotle (see n1 and *Adagia* IV viii 49n, 387 above). Added in *1533*
  1 The 'saying' is extracted from Aristotle *Rhetoric* 3.2 (1405a20). Aristotle is there dealing with the substitution of words in the same semantic field with either enhancing or belittling force (cf Erasmus *De copia* I, chapters 27 and 29 [CWE 24 342–3]), eg to substitute 'beg' for 'pray' (or vice versa) or 'mistake' for 'crime,' or, the example used here, 'Metragyrtes' for 'dadouchos,' both of which are terms connected with the worship of a goddess, the second complimentary, the first contemptuous. Erasmus seems to have consulted the text hastily and missed the point. Also it is Callias who retorts that Iphicrates must be uninitiated, or he would have called him *dadouchos* and not *Metragyrtes*. The first name here should be Metragyrtes 'a mendicant priest of the Great Mother'; Erasmus' text read *Mitragyrtes*, as Estienne comments in a long, critical footnote (LB II 1135D). Consequently Erasmus explains the word with reference to the god Mithras, and not to Cybele, the Great Mother of the Gods. Her mendicant priests were generally treated with contempt, whereas a Torchbearer

Iphicrates called Callias, meaning that he had not been initiated into the sacred rites, though he wanted to give the impression that he had. Among the Persians, the sun is called Mithras and they consider him the supreme god. So 'itinerant priests of Mithras' would seem to refer to those who travel about with fake religious objects, deceiving the ignorant. The existence of such types even in ancient times is confirmed by Apuleius when he was in ass-form.[2] They are very like those characters today who carry round relics of St Antony, St Cornelius or John the Baptist, not as aids to piety but as a source of gain.

56 Sibi parat malum qui alteri parat
He that plots ill for another lays up ill for himself

In book three of the *Rhetoric*, Aristotle quotes the following verse from Democritus of Chios: 'Each man that fashions another's ill, fashions ill for himself.'[1] No one can injure another without first injuring himself. A man

* * * * *

was an important and revered functionary in the secret rites of Demeter and Persephone at Eleusis, to which only initiates were admitted. Callias was head of the family which traditionally filled that office.

2 In Apuleius' novel *Metamorphoses* (popularly known as the *Golden Ass*), the hero is accidentally transformed into a thinking ass, in which guise he has many adventures and meets all kinds of people. In one episode he is sold to some odious mendicant priests of the Dea Syria, who employ the ass to carry about the image of their goddess, by which they hope to extract small sums from the ignorant and superstitious (8.24–5). Apuleius himself was charged with (and acquitted of) sorcery and murder, and this, together with some apparently autobiographical elements in the novel, gave his fellow-countryman St Augustine a pretext for claiming that Apuleius was himself turned into an ass, or at least pretended to have been (*Civitas Dei* 18.18). Erasmus, who disapproved both of Apuleius and his Latin style, here repeats the jibe; see *Ciceronianus* CWE 28 569 n445.

56 Aristotle citing Democritus (see n1 and *Adagia* IV viii 49n, 387 above). Cf *Adagia* I ii 14 Bad advice; Tilley H 830 He that hurts another hurts himself. Added in *1533*

1 Aristotle *Rhetoric* 3.9 (1409b28). Democritus did not compose the line in question, but cites Hesiod *Works and Days* 265–6 for a satiric purpose, adding two of his own.

who cheats another of money, robs himself of peace of mind and harms
himself more than the other. So it is very true that 'he that seeks to hurt
another hurts himself.'

57 Trabem baiulans
Carrying the plank

In book three of the *Rhetoric*, Aristotle is discussing examples of words
that need emphasis and gesture to get their effect. Otherwise, he says,
it's a case of 'the man that carries the plank.'[1] This applies to separate
words, especially proper names and pronouns, and to repeated words,
which carry more than their surface meaning. For example: '*Thersites* despises *Achilles*?';[2] 'Do *you* call *me* an ass?' Also in the figure of asyndeton,
for example, 'I came, I saw, I conquered,'[3] and other similar expressions, all
of which lose their effect if not enhanced by dramatic delivery. For example, in Terence: 'Shut out! Called back! Return?';[4] and a little further on: 'I
her – ? who *me* – ? who won't – ?'[5] Terence again, this time from the *Brothers*: 'Storax! Aeschines didn't come home from the party last night.'[6] The
character starts off by shouting for Storax, so that has to be delivered in a
much louder voice, the rest he says to himself. I believe that the words ὁ τὴν
δοκὸν φέρων 'the man carrying the plank' come from some play or other, because they form the end of an iambic trimeter.[7] A person carrying a plank
can't be expected to do any acting, he just has to concentrate on carrying
it. Some such figure, I imagine, was introduced into a comedy to raise a

* * * * *

57 Aristotle (see n1 and *Adagia* IV viii 49n, 387 above). Cf *Adagia* IV v 14 Like a
   bodyguard (148 above). Added in *1533*
 1 This occurs in Aristotle *Rhetoric* 3.12 (1413b18–31), a passage discussing dramatic versus wooden delivery. Ὁ τὴν δοκὸν φέρων 'The man that carries the
   plank' seems to refer to a stiff, dull speaker. Erasmus has summarized the
   passage rather hastily and supplied illustrative examples of his own.
 2 Thersites, the ugliest man at Troy, who jeered at Achilles, the noblest warrior
   on the Greek side, in the (now lost) epic poem *Aethiopis*
 3 *Veni, vidi, vici*, Caesar's terse comment on his lightning five-day campaign and
   victory over the kingdom of Pontus; see Suetonius *Divus Julius* 37.
 4 Terence *Eunuchus* 49
 5 Terence *Eunuchus* 65
 6 Terence *Adelphi* 26
 7 A metre used for ordinary dialogue in Greek drama

laugh.[8] Sometimes σκευοφόροι 'baggage carriers' appear in a play, like the ones in the *Woman of Andros*, who are told, 'Get that stuff inside!'[9] Or Sosia, in the *Mother-in-Law*.[10] These are the sort of characters who either aren't given anything to say, or only words that don't require dramatic delivery. Possibly Aristotle was thinking of the figures of Atlas which are placed under the supporting beams of a building,[11] because they appear to be making a great effort, but are not actually moving. Delivery is the life of a speech, and the sign of life is movement. The equivalent of 'baggage-carriers' in tragedy is δορυφόρημα 'spear-carriers' or 'bodyguard.' They simply stand about the stage doing nothing.[12] Perhaps Aristotle originally wrote ὁ δορυφορῶν 'carrying the spear' not ὁ δοκὸν φέρων 'carrying the plank.' This is just a suggestion – Aristotelian scholars can look into the problem.[13]

58 Quae quis ipse facit
What anyone does himself

In book two of the *Rhetoric*, where Aristotle is discussing emotions, he quotes the following apparently popular saying: 'They say that whatever anyone does himself, he doesn't resent his neighbours doing.'[1] The corollary of this is the line in Terence: 'There really is nothing more unfair than an ignorant man – he doesn't approve of anything that he doesn't do himself.'[2] Some people disparage anything that they can't achieve themselves.

* * * * *

8 George of Trebizond (see Monfasani 472; see *Adagia* v i 82 n4, 590 below) suggested that this refers to the comic situation of trying to get a plank through a door sideways.

9 Terence *Andria* 28

10 Sosia is a slave who comes from the harbour, presumably carrying his master's luggage, and has a few unimportant lines to say in Terence *Hecyra* 415–25.

11 Erasmus no doubt suggests this because the Greek word for 'beam' in this passage, δοκός, means 'a supporting beam.'

12 Cf *Adagia* iv v 14 Like a bodyguard (148 above).

13 The Greek words for 'spear,' δόρυ, and 'beam,' δοκός, perhaps have sufficient similarity to make such a textual emendation possible, but there seems no reason to question the transmitted text.

58 Aristotle (see n1 and *Adagia* iv viii 49n, 387 above). Added in *1533*

1 Aristotle *Rhetoric* 2.6 (1384b3–4)

2 Terence *Adelphi* 98–9

59 Cognatio movet invidiam
Kinship generates resentment

In the same book, Aristotle tells us that resentment is felt towards what is
near and related to us. No one feels resentment towards those who have
long been dead, or are quite different, or vastly superior or inferior. To
support his argument he quotes the following line: 'Kith and kin know
what resentment is.'[1] Those who have reached such heights that their very
distinction makes any ill-will ineffective are said to be 'beyond all hazard
and out of envy's range.'[2]

60 Sapiens non eget
The wise man is never in need

In the same book, where he is discussing maxims, Aristotle quotes the following line:

The man with sound mind endowed never is in need.[1]

This is true, either because the possession of a sound mind is in itself wealth,
or because it is easy for the wise man to become rich if he so desires. See

* * * * *

59 Aristotle citing Aeschylus (see n1 and *Adagia* iv viii 49n, 387 above). Cf *Adagia* iv viii 73 From home to home (402 below) and iv viii 20 Envious is the
neighbour's eye (366 above).
 1 Aristotle *Rhetoric* 2.10 (1388a7), citing a fragment of Aeschylus (*TrGF* 3 Aeschylus fragment 305)
 2 See Pliny *Naturalis historia* preface 7; *Adagia* i iii 93 Out of range.

60 Aristotle citing Euripides (see n1 and *Adagia* iv viii 49n, 387 above). Added in
1533
 1 Aristotle *Rhetoric* 2.21 (1394a29), where the quotation is defined as a maxim.
Erasmus however cites only the first of the pair of lines quoted there by
Aristotle (Euripides *Medea* 294–5). In its context the first line means something
quite different from the interpretation Erasmus puts on it here, ie 'The man
of sense has never any need / To have his sons taught to be over-wise.' He
added both lines (the author again unrecognized) in *1526* to *Adagia* iv 1 100
I hate striplings who are precociously wise, but there he translates the lines
correctly.

for example Aristippus, who found people to give him hospitality after he was shipwrecked. On another occasion, when he asked Dionysius for a considerable sum of money, Dionysius said, 'Did you not teach that the wise man was never in need?' Aristippus replied, 'Give me the money and then I will give you your answer.' The ruler gave him the money and demanded the answer to his question. Aristippus then said, 'Wasn't I right to say that the wise man is never in need?'[2]

61 Multa incredibilia
Much that seems beyond belief

In the same work, Aristotle quotes the following line of verse as proverbial: 'Much that is unbelievable comes true for mortal men.'[1] He suggests that this saying should be employed by a speaker who enjoys making false statements and wants his words to be accepted as the truth. A little later, he quotes some lines of Agathon expressing a similar sort of idea:

> Well might one say that this is probable –
> Much that is improbable will truly come to pass.[2]

* * * * *

2 Ie Aristippus the Elder; see *Adagia* IV viii 49 n2 (387 above). He became a member of the court of Dionysius I, autocrat of Syracuse in Sicily. Many stories were current illustrating his love of money and luxury; see Diogenes Laertius 2.66, 69, 76–7 ('Aristippus'), and Xenophon *Memorabilia* 2.1. For the shipwreck story, see the longer version at Erasmus *Apophthegmata* III Aristippus 58 (from Diogenes Laertius 2.82). The point is that, as a philosopher, he soon finds likeminded persons to welcome and help him.

61 Aristotle citing Euripides and Agathon (see nn1 and 2 and *Adagia* IV viii 49n, 387 above). Added in 1533
1 Aristotle *Rhetoric* 2.23 (1397a19), quoting Euripides *Thyestes* (fragment 396 Nauck). Erasmus quotes the line in Greek without translating it, but his remarks in this paragraph suggest that he understood it as translated in the English text. Aristotle does not say what Erasmus ascribes to him here – he is actually discussing arguments from contraries. This is the kind of application of a saying that Erasmus himself often proposes.
2 Aristotle *Rhetoric* 2.24 (1402a10–11), quoting the tragic poet Agathon (fragment 9 Nauck)

62 Lecythum habet in malis
She has the bottle by her chops

Ἔχειν λήκυθον πρὸς ταῖς γνάθοις, To have the bottle by one's chops. This is
a veiled and cryptic jibe at old women who disguise their wrinkles with
thick make-up, like the courtesan Phryne, who did not retire from the business even when she was old. See Aristophanes in the *Women in Parliament*:
'Phryne holding the bottle to her chops.' By her 'bottle,' Aristophanes means
a small container for cosmetics. Phryne used to say that many still drank
the dregs because the wine had been superlative.[1] So great was her fame
that many a client came to her when she was *passée*,[2] simply to be able to
boast that he had had an assignation with Phryne.

63 Piscis eget sale
Fish needs salt

Ἰχθὺς δεῖται ἁλός, Fish needs salt. For something ridiculous and unbelievable.
It is not very likely that fish that spend their lives in the sea should need
salt. When Androcles of the deme Pitthus was pointing out the deficiencies
in a particular law and said, 'Laws need a law to put them right,' the people
shouted back, 'Yes, and fish need salt.' The purpose of laws is to provide a
standard by which men's actions can be corrected, but if the laws themselves
require correction, they cease to be laws. That is as ridiculous as salt-water
fish requiring salt. This is all to be found in Aristotle's *Rhetoric*.[1]

* * * * *

62 The paragraph is based on Aristophanes *Ecclesiazusae* 1101, supplemented from
   Plutarch *Moralia* 125B *De tuenda sanitate praecepta*. Added in 1533
  1 Erasmus' text of Plutarch (see introductory note) seemingly read τρύγα
   πλειόνους 'many bought the dregs,' whereas modern texts offer τρύγα πλείονος
   πωλεῖν 'she sold the dregs for more.'
  2 Phryne was famous in her day and many well-known persons (Philip, Alexander, Apelles, Praxiteles) were numbered among her admirers.

63 Aristotle (see n1 and *Adagia* IV viii 49n, 387 above). Added in 1533
  1 Aristotle *Rhetoric* 2.23 (1400a9–13). Again Erasmus seems to have read his
   Aristotle rather hastily. 'Fish need salt' was said not by the people but by
   Androcles in support of his argument: even fish that live in salt water need
   salt (ie when they are eaten); likewise, even cakes of pressed olives need olive
   oil (to make them soft and usable). See next adage. (Estienne has a long note
   to this effect [LB II 1137D–F]).

64 Bacae egent oleo
Olives need oil

This is the same sort of saying as the previous one and follows on from it in Aristotle.[1] Again, it is not very credible that the source of oil should itself need oil – oil is produced by pressing olive-berries. It is very like a saying I discussed earlier: 'The springs themselves are thirsty.'[2]

65 Avis ex avibus
Bird of a long line of birds

Ὄρνις ἐκ τῶν ὀρνέων, Bird descended from birds. A 'proverbial' saying used by Aristophanes to make mock of a man of noble birth, supposedly 'a good man of a long line of good men': 'This hoopoe, a bird descended from a long line of birds.'[1] Those who pride themselves on their nobility trace their descent back through generations of ancestors. Nobility acquired by purchase or only recently achieved is no such great thing.

66 Da lapidi volam
Give the rock a kick

The ancient commentator on Aristophanes tells us that when boys see birds they say, 'Give the rock a kick and they'll all fall down.'[1] This is a useful saying when someone is aiming at something he cannot achieve or threatening people he cannot harm. In the comedy, one of the characters says he'll make a noise and rouse the birds. The other jokingly replies, 'Kick

* * * * *

64 Aristotle (see n1). Added in *1533*
  1 Aristotle *Rhetoric* 2.23 (1400a13–14); see previous adage, IV viii 63 n1. Estienne (footnote at LB II 1138E) comments that the Greek word used here στέμφυλα means not 'olives' but the residue of pressed olives.
  2 *Adagia* I vii 59

65 Aristophanes (see n1). Added in *1533*
  1 Aristophanes *Birds* 16. Erasmus quotes from this play here and in *Adagia* IV viii 66 (next adage) without naming it. He returns to it below in *Adagia* IV viii 79–87.

66 Aristophanes and the ancient commentator (see n1). Added in *1533*
  1 Material derived from Aristophanes *Birds* 54–5 and the ancient commentator on the passage

the rock then.' This of course is not going to incommode the birds in the slightest, only hurt his foot or hand when it strikes the rock. So the first man tells the other to bang his head against the rock and make twice the noise.

67 Ne quaeras deus esse
Seek not to become God

Μὴ ζήτει θεὸς γενέσθαι, Seek not to become God. A saying directed at a man who has every blessing in this life. Pindar in the fifth *Olympian* ode:

> If a man has established sound prosperity
> And enjoys his good in quiet content
> And to those blessings adds fair fame,
> Let him not pray heaven to make him God.[1]

My own countrymen often say, 'You're well enough off. What are you after? Do you expect to be God?'

68 Operi incipienti favendum
Applaud the first beginnings

It's a well-known saying that 'Honours nourish arts,'[1] also that 'Virtue grows with praise.' Pindar in the sixth *Olympian* ode: 'To a fresh start must a

* * * * *

67 Erasmus here embarks on a run of material, *Adagia* IV viii 67–78, extracted from Pindar's victory odes, elaborate choral works commissioned by various victors at the four main Greek athletic festivals (Olympian, Pythian, Nemean and Isthmian), to be performed in their home cities in celebration of their success. Zacharias Calliergis had published an edition of Pindar with the ancient commentaries in 1515 (Rome) and Erasmus had acquired a copy of Pindar (possibly this edition) in 1518; see Epp 642:5; 832:34. He ordered a copy of Aldus' *editio princeps* of 1513, possibly in 1525; see Allen 7 547 (Appendix xx). He had however become acquainted with Pindar in manuscript while in Venice in 1507–8 and quotes him throughout the *Adagia* (see Phillips 87 and 400).
1 Pindar *Olympians* 5.53–5

68 The adage is a prosaic rendering of a passage in Pindar (see n2). Otto 169. Added in *1533*
1 *Adagia* I viii 92

brilliant face be given,'² that is, one must applaud those starting out on some splendid project, both in order to encourage them and to stir others to emulate them. As it is, most people carp and criticize if anyone tries to achieve something out of the ordinary. One can also take the saying to mean, 'Anyone who desires to win fame must start off with something really remarkable.'³ It matters a great deal how you first make your name.

69 Nec apud homines nec in mari
Neither among men, nor yet upon the sea

In the same hymn, Pindar writes some other lines with a proverbial ring: 'Distinction won without venture receives no honour, / Neither among men nor yet in hollow ships.'¹ The sentiment agrees with the oft-quoted line of Hesiod: 'Toil is the price of excellence – Heaven wills it so.'² No one ever achieved great fame without risk. That is why Pindar calls war κυδιάνειρος 'the bringer of glory to men.'³ We have a proverbial turn of phrase in the words 'Neither by land or sea' and also in fighting 'By land and sea.'⁴

70 In hoc calciamento pedem habet
He has his foot in this shoe

In the same ode, Pindar brings in yet another proverbial sentiment: 'He may be sure his blessed foot is in this *pedilon* "shoe," '¹ that is, he knows that this

* * * * *

2 Pindar *Olympians* 6.4–5: ἀρχομένου δ᾽ ἔργου πρόσωπον χρὴ θέμεν τηλαυγές.

3 Cf Plutarch *Moralia* 804D *Praecepta gerendae reipublicae*, where similar sentiments are expressed.

69 Pindar (see n1 and *Adagia* IV viii 67n, 399 above). Added in *1533*
  1 Pindar *Olympians* 6.9–11: ἀκίνδυνοι δ᾽ ἀρεταὶ / Οὔτε παρ᾽ ἀνδράσιν οὔτ᾽ ἐν ναυσὶ κοίλαις / Τίμιαι.
  2 Hesiod *Works and Days* 289
  3 Not Pindar but Homer, eg in *Iliad* 4.225
  4 This sentence refers back to 'men and ships' above. *Adagia* I iv 25 and IV x 26 (500 below); Otto 1762

70 Pindar (see n1 and *Adagia* IV viii 67n, 399 above). Added in *1533*
  1 Pindar *Olympians* 6.8: ἴστω γὰρ ἐν τούτῳ πεδίλῳ δαιμόνιον πόδ᾽ ἔχων.

praise belongs to him. In ancient times shoes and sandals could be items of great luxury. The Greek *pedilon* was a brightly coloured embroidered sandal, so called because it is 'fastened round the foot,' *ped-* in Greek.[2] The same shoe does not fit every foot.[3] Even so the same praise is not appropriate to any and every person.

71 Virtus gloriam parit
Virtue begets glory

Pindar again, in the same victory ode: 'Those that value virtue walk the path of fame; / Each man's activity proclaims him.'[1] The poet gives us to understand that the true glory proceeds from deeds of virtue, not from wealth, and that there is more than one way to achieve distinction. Each person becomes famous for his own particular prowess. Homer is remembered for his poetry, Demosthenes for his eloquence, Aristides for his incorruptibility, Themistocles for his military successes; and many others have made a name for themselves, each in their own separate way.

72 Bonum est duabus niti ancoris
Safe riding at two anchors

Pindar again, in the same ode: 'Good it is in wintry night / From the swift ship / Two anchors to let down,'[1] that is, it is good to have two lines of defence, so that if one fails us, we may fall back on the other. The recipient of this victory ode had two homelands,[2] so that if disaster befell the one,

* * * * *

2 The etymology is based on *Etymologicum magnum* 658.51–2 πέδιλα.

3 Cf *Adagia* IV iv 56 Putting the same shoe on every foot (100 above).

71 Pindar (n1 and *Adagia* IV viii 67n, 399 above). Tilley v 70 He that sows virtue reaps fame; P 541 Praise is the reflection of virtue. Added in *1533*

1 Pindar *Olympians* 6.72–4, but the heading is a paraphrase.

72 Pindar (n1 and *Adagia* IV viii 67n, 399 above). Tilley R 119 Good riding at two anchors men have told / For if one fail the other may hold. Added in *1533*

1 Pindar *Olympians* 6.100–1: ἀγαθαὶ / Δὲ πέλοντ᾽ ἐν χειμερίᾳ / Νυκτὶ θοᾶς ἐκ ναὸς ἀπεσκίμφθαι δύ᾽ ἄγκυραι.

2 See *Adagia* IV viii 73 n1 (next adage).

he could betake himself to the other. I have already treated this under the heading, 'Secured by two anchors.'[3]

73 E domo in domum
From home to home

Several times in Pindar and Aristophanes, we find the phrase Οἴκοθεν οἴκαδε 'From home to home,' meaning that someone has of his own innate abilities and powers won some special glory for his family or country. For example, in the same victory ode we have: 'From home to home, from the walls of Stymphalos.'[1] A particular ability is more easily accepted, is less cause for resentment, when it is handed down through the generations from distant ancestors.

74 Quod dici solet
The usual

In the same play, Plautus uses a roundabout expression to suggest something too lewd to be named directly. One of the characters swears by all the gods that another character has absolutely nothing to do with the girl in question. He isn't having dinner with her, walking with her, kissing her, or doing 'the usual.'[1]

* * * * *

3 *Adagia* i i 13

73 Pindar (see n1 and *Adagia* IV viii 67n, 399 above). Added in *1533*
  1 Pindar *Olympians* 6.99, see also 7.4. The recipient of this victory ode actually had two homes. He originated from Stymphalos in Arcadia but had moved to a new home in Syracuse in Sicily, where he became a supporter of the ruler Hieron and an important person in the city. So, though the phrase is proverbial and means something like 'with security and ease' (LSJ s.v. οἴκοθεν), there is this additional literal meaning here.

74 Plautus (see n1). Added in *1533*
  1 Plautus *Bacchides* 896–7, but this play has not been quoted in *Adagia* IV viii. In fact Plautus has not been quoted at all since *Adagia* IV viii 51 (388 above, *Casina*). The adage strangely interrupts the extracts from Pindar *Olympians*. It has perhaps been misplaced and should occur as IV ix 74, where it would follow another extract from *Bacchides* (467 below).

75 Domi pugnans more galli
As aggressive as a cock in his own backyard

'Ενδομάχας ἄτ' ἀλέκτωρ, Aggressive at home like a barnyard cock.[1] A saying directed at a man who skulks at home and never ventures out to join
in any war or conflict – the cock is an aggressive creature, but only on his
own territory. Such a man contributes nothing to his country and his battles are inglorious. (So the commentators explain it, but all the same I wonder whether the true reading is ἐνδομύχας 'lurking within.' 'Ενδομάχης is a
new word, made up of ἐντός 'within' and μάχομαι 'fight.')[2] The saying will
fit people who are always quarrelling at home but are peaceable enough
outside. This is like the saying I discussed earlier, 'Lions at home.'[3]

76 Nec deus nec homo
Neither god nor man

We often find these two words linked in a proverbial-type figure in the
poets: 'in defiance of gods and men'; 'by the faith of gods and men.'[1] There
the words mean 'divine and human.' In Horace we have: 'That the gods
allow not, neither men, / Nor yet the booksellers' stalls.'[2] In Pindar's third

* * * * *

75 Pindar (see n1 and *Adagia* IV viii 67n, 399 above). Cf *Adagia* IV iv 25 A cock
    has most power on his own dunghill (76 above). Added in 1533
  1 Taken from Pindar *Olympians* 12.14
  2 Erasmus no doubt feels his suggested emendation is more complimentary and
    more appropriate to the recipient of this victory ode, Ergoteles, who was a
    political exile from his homeland in Crete. He might have stayed ingloriously
    there, but he moved to Himera in Sicily and eventually became an Olympian
    victor. This suggested reading is not acknowledged in modern editions. The
    proposed word may have been suggested to Erasmus by its appearance in
    Cicero *Ad Atticum* 5.14.3; 5.21.14.
  3 Cf *Adagia* IV v 80 Peace-time lions (193 above).

76 Pindar (see n3 and *Adagia* IV viii 67n, 399 above). Otto 511, who doubts its
    proverbial nature; *Adagia* I i 74 With the applause of gods and men; IV vi 45
    Neither animate nor inanimate (243 above). Added in 1533
  1 Examples of Erasmus' phrases can be found at, eg, Terence *Heautontimorou-
    menos* 61; Plautus *Epidicus* 580; also in prose.
  2 Horace *Ars poetica* 373. Horace is ironically saying that nobody allows poets
    to be mediocre.

Pythian: 'No god, no man, can him deceive, by counsel or by deed.'³ He is praising Apollo, who, though he knows all things, yet will have nothing to do with deceit.

77 Apud matrem manere
Tied to his mother's apron-strings

Παρὰ ματρὶ μένειν, To stay at their mother's side, was said of those who always stay at home and never venture on any bold enterprise out of cowardice. Pindar, in the fourth *Pythian*: 'Lest any be left at home safe / From danger at his mother's side.'¹ He is speaking, I think, of the Argonauts who sought glory in bold exploration, inspired by Juno. In the time of Augustine, weak and effeminate persons were called 'Mammy's boys.'² This could mean 'brought up by Grandmother' (in Greek, *mamme*), as grandmothers always bestow a more indulgent affection on the grandchildren than the children's mothers do; or *mamme* could be a diminutive meaning 'Mummy.' Even today a youth brought up too soft is commonly known as a 'mother's boy,' and such persons used to be said 'to take after their mothers.'³

78 Sine canibus et retibus
Without dogs and nets

Ἄνευ κυνῶν τε καὶ λίνων, Without dogs and hunting-nets. In *Nemean Odes* three, Pindar used this form of words to indicate supreme swiftness of foot. For what ordinary person could keep up with deer on foot unless

* * * * *

3 Pindar *Pythians* 3.29–30. This material was added in 1526 to *Adagia* II x 23 You need great knowledge, if you would deceive God with it.

77 Pindar (see n1 and *Adagia* IV viii 67n, 399 above). Suringar 15. Added in 1533
1 Pindar *Pythians* 4.185–6
2 See Augustine *Commentarius in Psalmos* 30:12 CSEL 38 210. Augustine says they were children who refused to be weaned.
3 Erasmus seems to have invented the word *matrisso* by analogy with *patrisso* 'to take after one's father,' which occurs in Terence *Andria* 564. Nonius Marcellus (199.5–6 Lindsay) offers *matresco* 'to become like one's mother' from Pacuvius. For Erasmus' views on the freedom of modern writers to form new words see *De copia* CWE 24 338.

78 Pindar (see n1 and *Adagia* IV viii 67n, 399 above). Added in 1533

they were slowed down by dogs or caught in the nets? The saying will however fit people who capture their prey by stealthy moves. What Pindar says is: 'Slaying the deer without dogs or snaring nets.'[1] It will also apply to people who do something without outside help, in their own strength.[2]

79 Et Scellii filium abominor
I can't bear Scellius' son either

If anybody absolutely loathes somebody or something, it's a natural reaction for him to avoid using not only the actual name but any word that sounds like it. Aristophanes has a nice example in the *Birds*. One character there says, 'It's clear you like aristocracy.' The other replies, 'No, I don't. I can't bear Scellius' son either.'[1] Scellius' son was called Aristocrates. Anyone who detested aristocracy would obviously find the name Aristocrates obnoxious, because it reminded him of the thing he found odious.

80 Larinum verbum
A fat and lardy word

Λαρινὸν ἔπος, A fat and lardy word,[1] meaning something large and out of the ordinary. The usage originates from the fact that in Larissa the cattle are very large and well-fleshed.[2] Another explanation is that very large

* * * * *

1 Pindar *Nemeans* 3.51, describing the young Achilles, who performed various physical feats while yet a boy, such as running down deer by sheer fleetness of foot.
2 See *Adagia* iv x 31 Under my own auspices (503 below).

79 Next we have a run of material derived from Aristophanes *Birds*, together with the ancient commentators on the play (*Adagia* iv viii 79–87). Added in 1533
1 Aristophanes *Birds* 125–6

80 For this adage see the scholia at Aristophanes *Birds* 465; also Apostolius 10.45 and the *Suda* Λ 121.
1 Aristophanes *Birds* 465 (quoted below). The Greek word λαρινός means 'fatted' and is possibly cognate with English 'lard.'
2 Larissa was the name of many old Greek cities. The form of the word possibly suggested a connection with λαρινός; in the *Suda* Larissa (Λ 123) follows closely on λαρινοὶ βῶες 'well-fleshed cattle.'

fat people were called 'lardy' after a shepherd called Larinus, who was enormous. There is a breed of very large cattle in Epirus, descended from the cattle of Geryon.[3] Aristophanes in the *Birds*: 'I've long been itching to say a mighty word, a lardy one.'[4] It's worth adding that the Greeks add 'ox' to words to express the idea of hugeness, as in 'ox-eating,' meaning 'with an enormous appetite.' Similarly, the early speakers of Latin used the word *luca* to mean 'large.'[5]

81 Herniosi in campum
Up, ye castrated, and to the fields

Κόκκυ, ψωλοί, πεδίονδε, Cuckoo! Up, ye castrated, and to the fields. Aristophanes quotes this as a proverbial saying in the *Birds*: 'So that's what the saying really means, "Cuckoo! Up, ye castrated, and to the fields!"' with 'come' understood. The cuckoo begins to call shortly before harvest time, as if summoning the farmers to the labour of harvesting. See Hesiod's line: 'When the cuckoo first calls "Cuckoo."'[1] When Aristophanes uses the word 'castrated' (Greek ψωλοί) for farmers, he is in passing

* * * * *

3 Briefly mentioned by the scholiast on Aristophanes, but see Apostolius and the *Suda*. A shepherd called Larinus who lived in Epirus stole some of the well-favoured cattle which Hercules was bringing back to Greece after taking them away from Geryon (the three-bodied monster who lived in the far west) in one of his 'Labours.' For the excellence of Epirote cattle see Varro *Res rusticae* 2.10: 'Epirote cattle are not only the best in Greece but even better than Italian ones,' and again the *Suda*.

4 See n1 above.

5 See Varro *De lingua latina* 7.39, for an explanation of the term *luca bos* 'elephant,' which Erasmus is probably thinking of here. According to one interpretation, this phrase meant 'Lucanian cow,' as the Romans first confronted elephants in Lucania during the war with Pyrrhus, who had a squadron of war-elephants: 'They called the creature *bos* "cow" because that was the name for the largest quadruped they knew.' Erasmus accordingly chooses to interpret *luca* as 'large.' (The true etymology of *luca* is not known.)

81 Aristophanes *Birds* (see n1). Added in 1533

1 Aristophanes *Birds* 507, quoting Hesiod *Works and Days* 486 (though there, exceptionally, the cuckoo's call precedes spring ploughing)

making a jibe at the Egyptians, most of whom had been 'cut,' and who were all compelled to get into the fields when the cuckoo called.[2] In the play, he makes out that Cuckoo once ruled in Egypt before he was turned into a bird. Even today undersexed men who find themselves sharing their wives with other men are commonly called 'cuckolds.' I have discussed elsewhere Horace's passage about passers-by calling out 'Cuckoo!' to those who only started tending their vines when they heard the cuckoo.[3] The cuckoo calls only when spring is well on, emerging late from its nest. It builds this in winter in hollow trees, pulling out its feathers and wrapping itself in them, feeding off a store of apples and pears.[4] The ancient commentator on this line of Aristophanes tells us that 'Cuckoo! Up, ye castrated, and to the fields' is a proverb. It is one to be used when the very lateness of the hour compels the idle to bestir themselves.

82 Μελλονικιᾶν
Hang about like Nicias

People complained that Nicias was a 'delayer' when it came to military action, just as Fabius is said to have been among the Romans. So the Old Comedy invented a joke word μελλονικιᾶν, made up of μέλλειν 'to be always on the point of, to delay,' and Νικίας, the Athenian commander's name. Aristophanes in the *Birds:*

* * * * *

2 Erasmus has extracted this rather dull explanation about farmers in Egypt from the earlier part of the ancient commentator on the above line in Aristophanes. The commentator also identifies the saying as proverbial. For another (and more amusing and also more likely, because obscene) meaning, only hinted at in the scholia, see *Aristophanes. Birds* ed and comm N. Dunbar (Oxford 1995) 346–7. Erasmus, ignoring the obscene possibilities, seems to interpret ψωλοί as 'castrated.' See ASD II-8 169:893n and *Adagia* III i 54 Why castrate Galli?, where he uses the same verb, *exseco* 'cut,' as here.

3 *Adagia* IV v 84 Cuckoo! (197 above), quoting Horace *Satires* 1.7.31. See also Pliny *Naturalis historia* 18.249. Pruning vines is a task that should be completed before the cuckoo begins to call.

4 The source of this information has not been identified.

82 Aristophanes *Birds* (see n1). Added in 1533

This is no time for us to doze
Or hang about like Nicias.
We must do something fast.[1]

83 Fumus
Smoke

Καπνός, Smoke, is a word for magnificent, empty promises, hence the say-ings, 'To sell smoke,' 'to blow out smoke.'[1] *Kapnos* was the name given to one Theagenes. He was poor, but tried to give the impression that he was a rich and important businessman, so he was known as *Kapnos* 'Smoke' or 'Hot Air.' The ancient commentator on Aristophanes gives as his authority for this Eupolis, in his comedy *Demoi*.[2]

84 Pariter remum ducere
All pull together

Oarsmen have to row to a definite rhythm in order to keep the oars moving together, otherwise they will get nowhere. Aristophanes in the *Birds* used the verb ὁμορροθῶ 'I'm pulling with you,' meaning, 'I agree, I have the

* * * * *

1 Aristophanes *Birds* 639–41. The play was produced in 414 BC, when Nicias was one of the Athenian generals sent to Sicily the year before to besiege the city of Syracuse. He had been reluctant to support the sending of the expedition, and his caution and inactivity there (partly caused by illness) were to result in a serious defeat. Erasmus calls him *cunctator* 'delayer,' in order to compare him with the famous Roman commander Fabius, nicknamed 'Cunctator' for his successful delaying tactics against the triumphant Carthaginian commander Hannibal in the Second Punic War. The name Nicias is connected with the word νίκη 'victory,' so the joke verb in the lemma both means 'hang about like Nicias' and suggests 'always be going to win in the future.'

83 Aristophanes *Birds* (see n2). See *Adagia* III iii 54 Theagenes and his shrine of Hecate; Tilley s 575 To feed oneself with smoke. Added in *1533*
1 See *Adagia* I iii 41 To sell smoke.
2 Ie the scholiast on Aristophanes *Birds* 822–3, which also mentions rowing in time together. See the next adage, IV viii 84.

84 Aristophanes *Birds* (see n1). Added in *1533*

same aim as you.' This word is made up of ὁμοῦ 'at the same time' and
ῥοθέω 'I rush.' The full line says: 'I pull with you, my will concords, I have
consented.'[1] The ancient commentator tells us that the word was taken from
Sophocles' *Peleus*.[2]

85 Ipsis et Chiis
And for the people of Chios too

Αὐτοῖς καὶ Χίοις. It is clear that these words were traditionally employed
by ordinary people whenever anyone was praying for blessings for himself
and his friends. One of the birds in Aristophanes prays as follows:

> On the Cuckoolanders please bestow
> Safety and health, and on the Chians too.[1]

The ancient commentator tells us that this style of words was derived
from a regular feature of Athenian public life – whenever they besought
the gods for blessings on the state in their solemn supplications and sac-
rifices, they used to add the words, 'and for the Chians too.'[2] He gives as
his authority for this statement Theopompos in the *History of Philip* book
twelve.[3] It was, I presume, because the Athenians benefited considerably
from Chios. Anyone who prays for himself alone, not mentioning friends
and benefactors, may facetiously intone, 'and for the Chians too.'

* * * * *

1 Aristophanes *Birds* 851
2 The point of his remark is that Sophocles' *Peleus* was a tragedy, and the word
ὁμορροθῶ is normally only found in tragedy. Aristophanes is indulging in
paratragedy. See *TrGF* 4 Sophocles fragment 489.

85 Aristophanes *Birds* (see n1). Added in *1533*
1 Aristophanes *Birds* 878–9
2 The inhabitants of Chios were so honoured because they had a special status
among the Athenian allies, being autonomous and allowed to contribute actual
ships and men for the Athenian navy rather than paying tribute.
3 Theopompos was an historian of the fourth century BC. He was important in
ancient times and a prolific author, but his work survives only in fragments
and indirect references, such as this one in the ancient commentator on Aristophanes (*FGrHist* 115 F 104).

86 Alas addere
To lend wings

People were commonly said Ἀναπτερεῖν 'To lend wings' when they embold-
ened others and made them enthusiastic. Aristophanes in the *Birds*:

> You must have heard
> Fathers in the barber's shop say to the lads,
> 'Diotrephes has by his words supplied my boy with wings
> And made him wondrous keen on horses.'[1]

We are told that Diotrephes was a very rich man who was a fanatical breeder
of horses, because of which he was later appointed Commander of Cavalry.
His example and encouragement fired many young men with a passion
for horses, but the fathers hated this enthusiasm on the part of their sons
because it was a very expensive hobby.

87 Χηναλώπηξ
Fox-goose

Theagenes was as clamorous and stupid as a goose and as slippery as a fox,
so he was popularly known by the nickname *Chenalopex*, made up of two
Greek words meaning 'goose' and 'fox.' Didymus[1] prefers the explanation
that he was called 'Goose' because he was excessively fond of eating birds,

* * * * *

86 Aristophanes *Birds* (see n1). Added in *1533*
1 Aristophanes *Birds* 1439–43, with the scholiast

87 This adage is based on Aristophanes *Birds* 1295, with the ancient commentary.
All Aristophanes says is that Theagenes was nicknamed 'Chenalopex' ('goose-
fox'). See also *Adagia* IV viii 83 (408 above). For the identity of the bird, Egyptian Goose or Ruddy Shelduck, see D'Arcy W. Thomson *A Glossary of Greek
Birds* (Oxford 1895) 195–6, and Dunbar (IV viii 81 n2, 407 above) 641.
1 Didymus was a prolific scholar of the first century BC to the first century
AD, who compiled a commentary on Aristophanes preserving much work of
earlier scholars as well as incorporating his own notes. His work is lost, but
excerpts from it are preserved in other ancient commentaries, eg, as here, on
Aristophanes, whence Erasmus has extracted this information. According to
modern texts, Didymus said that Theagenes looked like the bird, not that he
ate it. Either Erasmus' text was faulty or he has misinterpreted it.

especially a goose – just like a fox. (Goose-liver was a great delicacy in the ancient world.) Aristophanes mentions the nickname briefly in the *Birds*.

88 Concinere
To sing in concert, to agree

Tὴν ξυναυλίαν κλαίειν means 'to moan in concert.' Aristophanes in the *Knights*: 'So we can moan in concert to one of Olympus' tunes.'[1] By ξυ-ναυλία 'concert,' the Greeks meant either several *auloi*[2] playing in unison or one *aulos* accompanying a lyre. Olympus[3] was a pupil of Marsyas,[4] and wrote about sorrowful music. The words 'Olympus' tunes,' referring to songs of lament, have a proverbial ring, like 'sing like Ialemus,' 'Carian music.'[5]

89 Respublica nihil ad musicam
Politics is not for the man of culture

Educated, able men are not suited to be political leaders. Many in the ancient world believed this and the same view is commonly held today. Plato

* * * * *

88 Erasmus now has a run of extracts from Aristophanes' *Knights*, *Adagia* IV viii 83–93, 95, where he again makes use of the ancient commentators (see IV viii 79n, 405 above). *Adagia* IV x 9 Make the same complaint (489 below), duplicates the material in this adage.
1 Aristophanes *Knights* 8–9, with the comments of the scholiast
2 The ancient Greek *aulos* (Latin *tibia*), was a straight-bore instrument like a recorder, but reeded like a shawm or an oboe. Its tone had an edge to it. It is difficult to find a modern equivalent; 'pipe' might suffice.
3 A musician credited with the creation of the Phrygian and Lydian modes in music, both supposedly employed in music of a sad nature
4 A mythical figure, supposed to have invented the double-aulos. His expertise as a performer led him to challenge the god Apollo to a musical contest, which Marsyas of course lost. He was flayed alive for his presumption and his pupil Olympus lamented him. See Ovid *Metamorphoses* 6.382–400 for the story and Plato *Symposium* 215c for the lasting power of Olympus' melodies.
5 See *Adagia* II x 86 Tedious as a dirge; I viii 79 Carian music.

89 The material at the end of this adage quoted from Aristophanes' *Knights* makes this part of the series based on Aristophanes (see *Adagia* IV viii 79n, 405 above, and the introductory note to the preceding adage). Added in *1533*

abstained from political involvement, Socrates had an unsuccessful attempt at it,[1] the political careers of Demosthenes and Cicero brought them disaster.[2] The mother of Nero urged her son not to study philosophy, as it was deemed to be of no use to one who was destined to occupy the chief position in the state.[3] On the other hand, in his *Letters* St Augustine demolishes the arguments of certain people who put forward the view that the philosophy of the Gospel was incompatible with effective government.[4] Aristophanes puts the first idea nicely in the *Knights*. A character there refuses the position of ruler because he knows nothing of music. He gets the reply, 'Leading the people is no job for a man / Who's musical or whose character is sound.'[5] Under 'music' the ancients included every discipline that forms part of a liberal education.

90 Verbis coquinariis
With cookery words

In the same play, Aristophanes amusingly uses the phrase Ῥήματα μαγειρικά 'Cookery words' to mean soft, sweet, enticing words. Cooks use flavourings to sweeten something that is naturally rather bitter. In the play, one of the characters is being encouraged to butter up the Athenian people by saying things that will please them. The line reads: 'Cajoling them with little bits

* * * * *

1 Socrates had one brief period of participation in public life in 406–4 BC when he held an executive position and put his life in danger by refusing to vote for a popular but illegal proposal and by ignoring an order from the Thirty Tyrants to arrest an innocent citizen. See eg Plato *Apology* 32.
2 See Juvenal 10.118–121. Demosthenes, at the end of a brilliant if controversial career as orator and politician, went into exile. After his return to Athens, he was condemned to death for corruption and committed suicide. Cicero, the greatest of Roman orators, was, as a result of his handling of the Catilinarian conspiracy, likewise sent into exile for a time. In the turmoil following the assassination of Julius Caesar, he was murdered in 43 BC by a follower of Mark Antony, in revenge for the *Philippic Orations* (the name recalling Demosthenes' attacks on Philip of Macedon); see *Adagia* IV viii 7n (356 above).
3 See Suetonius *Nero* 52.
4 Augustine *Letters* 138.9–15 PL 33.528–32, CSEL 44 133–42
5 Aristophanes *Knights* 191–2

90 Aristophanes *Knights* (see n1). Added in 1533

of cookery words.'[1] Aristophanes used the adjective 'cookery' instead of 'sugary.' A good use for this phrase will be to say that the philosophy of Epicurus seduces the minds of ignorant people 'with cookery words,' because he asserts that pleasure is the highest good.[2]

91 Liba Coalemo
Make an offering to Coalemus

Σπένδε τῷ Κοαλέμῳ, Make an offering to Coalemus. This is a saying for someone who has done well out of behaving outrageously. The comic poet pretends that this is the name of a wicked spirit, inspiring effrontery.[1] It's like someone saying 'Sacrifice to Folly,' if a person plays the fool and is advanced to wealth and position. The Greek word κοάλεμος basically means 'stupid, foolish.'[2] The verb κοέω has the same meaning as νοέω 'perceive, think.' (Callimachus wrote ἐκόησεν, equivalent to ἐνόησεν 'he was so minded.')[3] So, by analogy, κοῦς, equivalent to νοῦς 'mind,' which is put together with ἀλέω 'flee,' because he is 'out of his wits.' Similarly, people are

* * * * *

1 Aristophanes *Knights* 216
2 Epicureanism did indeed posit pleasure as the supreme good and goal in life, a doctrine which was easily misunderstood, especially by uninformed people, as a licence for self-indulgence, and Erasmus often speaks of it in these conventional terms. Various Renaissance thinkers had attempted to reinstate the philosophy of Epicurus by showing what he really meant by pleasure, as Erasmus was well aware, and in his Colloquy 'Epicureus' (cwe 40 1075) he makes the startling equation of true Epicureanism with the following of Christ. He did not however find Epicureanism congenial, no doubt because of its teaching of the indifference of the gods to human affairs and the disintegration of the soul at death, and he hardly ever quotes the Epicurean poet Lucretius: eg, three times in the first chiliad of the *Adagia*, some doubtful echoes in other works. Erasmus seems to find the Epicurean atomic theory ludicrous: see *Adagia* III vi 3 Whatever falls on the ground.

91 Aristophanes *Knights* (see n1), together with the *Suda*. Added in 1533
1 Aristophanes *Knights* 221
2 This and the etymology given below, 'out of his wits,' are taken from the *Suda* K 1893–4 and E 523, supported by the scholiast on the above line of Aristophanes. Cf Hesychius K 3168.
3 Information from the *Suda* (E 523)

said to have 'made an offering to the Graces,' when they have been blessed in winning friends.[4] Drunkards have their god Comus, and thieves their goddess Laverna. So one could say jokingly to someone who had grown rich by dishonesty, 'Make an offering to Laverna.'[5]

92 Spirat Caecias
Blowing north-easterlies

I have already written about the Caecias, the north-east wind that attracts clouds.[1] Aristophanes was referring to the nature of this wind when he wrote in the *Knights*, 'He's blowing squally north-easterlies and betrayed-winds now!'[2] The ancient commentator remarks on the proverbial use, but Aldus' Greek text[3] wrongly reads κακίας 'wickednesses,' not Καικίας 'north-easterlies,' though the metre will not admit of this. By 'north-easterlies' the poet meant commotions and law-suits. Cleon is here being pilloried as a layer of information and a bringer of charges.

93 Latum et angustum
Broad and narrow

It is quite obvious, I think, that Aristophanes is using a proverbial phrase when he puts these words into Cleon's mouth in the *Knights*. Cleon had just been accused of behaving like a nurse and not feeding the people properly, but chewing over the food first and popping a morsel into their mouths but swallowing most himself. He replies, 'True, by Jove! So skilled

* * * * *

4 See *Adagia* II vii 50 Naked are the Graces, where Erasmus links the Graces with friendship.
5 See *Adagia* IV viii 3 n3 A tinker's cuss (353 above).

92 Aristophanes *Knights* (see n2) with the ancient commentator. Added in *1533*
1 *Adagia* I v 62 Attracting trouble as the north-easter draws clouds. The name of this north-easterly wind, Caecias, was explained as 'bringing down evils' (κακά): see Diogenianus 4.66.
2 Aristophanes *Knights* 437
3 See *Adagia* IV viii 41n (382 above). The reading is probably a misprint.

93 Aristophanes *Knights* (see n1). Added in *1533*

am I / That I can make the people Ἐυρὺν καὶ στενόν "Broad or narrow."' [1]
Indeed, ill-fed children grow thin but they fatten up again if properly
fed. The saying might well be turned to fit those who teach the young
well or badly, or to an orator who harangues the people skilfully or otherwise, for these things contribute greatly to establishing good or bad public
morals.

94 Scarabaeo citius persuaseris
You would sooner persuade a dung-beetle

Θᾶσσον ὁ κάνθαρος ἂν μεταπεισθείη, You would sooner get a dung-beetle to
change its mind. A saying applicable to those who have got used to what
is bad and cannot be induced to give it up because, out of familiarity with
it, they have come to believe it the best. Lucian in the *Pretended Critic*: 'No
censure of mine would ever make you improve, any more than a dung-
beetle could ever be persuaded to give up rolling those things, now it has
grown accustomed to them.' [1] The dung-beetle rears its young in dung,
especially goat-dung, feeds on dung, lives in dung. These beetles shape
the excrement into little balls and roll these along to the nest, with their
heads down to the ground and their back legs raised up. [2] No one is easily
detached from vices when he is born and brought up amidst them. Long
familiarity makes things which are actually disgusting seem attractive and
agreeable.

95 Alienis soleis uti
Wear someone else's slippers

Ἀλλοτρίοις βλαυτίοις χρῆσθαι, Wear another person's slippers, was said of
those who copy others' ways for their own ends. Aristophanes in the *Knights*:

* * * * *

1 Aristophanes *Knights* 719–20, with the ancient commentator

94 Lucian and the elder Pliny. Added in *1533*
1 Lucian *Pseudologista* 3
2 For this information see Pliny *Naturalis historia* 11.98.

95 Aristophanes *Knights* (see n1). Added in *1533*

Not at all! But like a chap who's drinking at a party
And needs a visit to the loo, I grab my neighbour's slippers –
And take your ways for my own.[1]

The character says he is not tricking the Athenian people, but doing what
people at a party do when they have to go out suddenly to answer nature's
call, and pick up somebody else's shoes, either because they are in a hurry or
because they are drunk. The character he is addressing was playing on the
nature of the Athenian people, who were willing to be bribed with hand-
outs and were more ready to listen to what was pleasing than to what was
good for them. The Greeks it seems took off their foot-gear when reclining at
table, and 'asked for their sandals' when ready to go home.[2] This gave great
scope to the stealers of clothes. Some people even reclined at dinner naked.

96 Longum prooemium audiendi cupido
The preamble is long when one is eager to hear

In Plato, *Republic* book four, we have Μακρὸν τὸ προοίμιον τῷ ἐπιθυμοῦντι
ἀκοῦσαι 'The preamble is long when one is eager to hear.'[1] This sounds like
a proverb. Anyone who is eager to get to the nub of the matter finds any
preamble long. See also the line in Terence: 'Oh dear, he's starting off with a
preamble (*prooemium occeptat*)!'[2] At Athens, the official who told the speakers
that they could now deliver their addresses used to instruct them, before
they started, to do so 'without preamble or emotional appeal,' because such
things are extraneous to the matter in hand.[3]

* * * * *

1 Aristophanes *Knights* 888–9, with the ancient commentator
2 See eg Aristophanes *Wasps* 103; Plautus *Truculentus* 363, 367.

96 The century concludes with extracts from Plato's dialogues (*Adagia* IV viii 96–
8, 100). Added in *1533*
1 Plato *Republic* 4.432E
2 The words *prooemium occeptat* do not occur in Terence. The phrase may be a
confused memory of Terence *Andria* 709 *Narrationis incipit initium* 'he's starting
a rigmarole,' quoted in *Adagia* III iii 96 (see n3); Terence *Heautontimoroumenos*
318–19 *quas ... ambages ... narrare occipit?* 'What's this roundabout tale he's
starting?'; Plautus *Menaechmi* 916 *occeptat insanire* 'he's starting to go mad.'
3 See Lucian *Anacharsis* 19, referred to in *Adagia* III iii 96 Why such great prefaces on little themes?

97 Omnia praeclara dicis
Well said, all of it

In Plato's *Euthydemus*, where Socrates is being ironical in his usual way. The person with whom he is arguing had drawn some absurd conclusions, namely that Socrates knew what he did not know and did not know what he knew. Socrates says to him: Εἶεν, ὦ Εὐθύδημε, τὸ γὰρ λεγόμενον, καλὰ δὴ πάντα λέγεις '*Esto* "let it be so" then, Euthydemus, for, as the saying goes, "Well said, all of it."'[1] In his translation of the work, Marsilius[2] does not here use *esto*, the Latin for 'let it be so,' but *en* 'See that!' Presumably his Greek text read, not εἶεν 'let it be so,' but εἰν or εἰνί, the Greek equivalent of Latin *en*, 'See that!' This makes the remark express ironic admiration. I think this is what Plato really wrote. For 'let it be so' does not fit the context – Socrates concedes nothing but mockingly expresses admiration as at something unheard of, to say nothing of the fact that εἶεν does not express concession, 'let it be so,' but a wish, 'may it be so.'[3] Plato uses 'Well said' in several places as a common saying, a phrase which I think he has taken from some poet or other. In Theocritus, for example, Praxinoe says, 'Indeed! Truly said!'[4]

* * * * *

97 Plato (see n1). Added in 1533

1 Plato *Euthydemus* 293D

2 Ie Marsilio Ficino, 1433–99, an influential philosopher, also a physician and theologian, with a particular interest in Plato and Neo-Platonism. He was a leading member of Cosimo de' Medici's Platonic Academy in Florence. His many writings included commentaries on some of the major dialogues of Plato (Florence 1496) and translations into Latin of Plato's complete works (1463–1482). See *The Letters of Marsilio Ficino* (London 1981–) vol 3 38 and 91 and CEBR 2:27–30.

3 Erasmus proposes emending εἶεν to εἰν or εἰνί, first on the basis of Ficino's translation of the word by Latin *en*, equivalent to Greek ἤν. Estienne in a note (printed at LB II 1144F) points out that εἰν and εἰνί are, as far as he knows, never used as the equivalent of Greek ἤν 'see!' but are poetic forms of the preposition ἐν 'in.' Secondly, Erasmus rejects εἶεν on the grounds that anything expressing concession does not fit this context. Εἶεν, however, is a particle meaning 'very well then; to proceed,' and *esto* seems to express that idea well enough.

4 Theocritus *Idylls* 15.38 (with a different reading in modern texts)

98 Quod recte datum est
What's once given

You should not ask something back that you have once given away. Plato
tells us in *Philebus* that this was a saying used by children: 'We say to you
what children say to each other – "No taking back once you've given it!"'[1]
He said this because it was Socrates' habit to go back to where the argument
had started and call into question again points that had already been con-
ceded. Even today children have much the same kind of retort. So we see
sayings like this coming right down to us over the ages via so many nations.

99 Funiculum ad lapidem
Lay the line against the stone

People who are endeavouring to make sure that the state is being governed
as it should be are said Τὴν σπάρτην πρὸς τὸν λίθον ἄγειν 'To apply the line
to the stone.' St Chrysostom, in section thirty-five of his sermon on the First
Epistle to the Corinthians: 'See how he again applies the line to the stone,
seeking in all things the edification of the Church.'[1] The idea is taken from
master-builders, who don't rely on the eye but test the regularity of the
stonework with a plumb-line. This is what careful exactitude requires.

100 Hoc tu mihi dices
You'll tell me

In Plato's *Republic*, book nine, when Socrates asks how a tyrannous man
lives, Adeimantus replies, 'As people say when they want to tease someone,
Σὺ καὶ ἐμοὶ ἐρεῖς "You'll tell *me*."'[1] This can be used when a reply that would
not be welcome is turned back on the questioner, or when the questioner is
someone who ought to know the answer better than the one he questions.

* * * * *

98 Plato (see n1). Suringar 192. Added in *1533*
1 Plato *Philebus* 19E. The speaker is Protarchus.

99 Chrysostom (see n1). Added in *1533*
1 St Chrysostom *Homiliae in Epistolam I ad Corinthios* 35.3.17 PG 61 300

100 Plato (see n1). Added in *1533*
1 Plato's *Republic* 9.573D

1 Nummo addicere
To knock down for a penny

In the Jurisconsults, we find the proverbial phrase 'To knock down for a penny,' meaning 'to sell for a trivial sum.' This is actually a subterfuge, designed to circumvent laws prohibiting gifts. Ulpian in the *Pandects*, book nineteen, title 'On lease and hire': 'If anyone shall lease for one penny, the lease is void, because this has the semblance of a gift.'[1] Again, in book one, title 'On matters brought to judgment': 'Where anyone hires something and asks that he may possess it by tenancy at will, if he hired it for one penny, there is no doubt that he holds it only by tenancy at will ...'[2] I rather think however that in these examples one should read not *conduxit, conductio* 'hires, hiring' but *condixit, condictio* 'contracts, contract.' Suetonius, in his life of Julius Caesar, writes, 'During the Civil War, in addition to other presents, he knocked down some splendid estates to her for a penny.'[3] Valerius Maximus, in book two, section *On gratitude*, says that the undertakers contracted 'to provide all the necessaries for the funeral for a penny piece.'[4] Likewise Plautus, in the *Pseudolus*, writes, 'You will never be a penny piece the richer.'[5] By 'a penny piece' he meant the smallest possible amount.

* * * * *

1 Erasmus quotes a number of extracts from Roman legal texts in *Adagia* IV viii, in IV ix especially, and in v ii. His sources are Gratian's *Decretum* (see *Adagia* IV viii 21 n3 and IV viii 25 n2, 367 and 371 above) and also the *Codex Justinianus*, the *Digest* or *Pandectae*, and the *Institutes*, which were sections of the vast compilation and codification of the whole of Roman law attempted on the orders of the emperor Justinian (AD 527–565). The compilers of the *Digest* made excerpts from texts originating with various earlier jurists such as Gaius and Ulpian and, in the *Codex*, promulgations by previous emperors, and such extracts are cited under their authors' names. Erasmus cites them in the same way (see eg nn1 and 2 below). For Justinian see *Adagia* IV v 1 n22 (136 above). Erasmus received suggestions regarding possible legal texts for use in the *Adagia* from the legal experts Andrea Alciati and Boniface Amerbach (see Epp 2709, 2710, 2730). Tilley s 636 To sell for a song. Added in *1533*
1 *Digest* (*Pandects*) 19.2.46
2 *Digest* (*Pandects*) 41.2.10.2 (not book 1), title 'On the acquisition and loss of possession'
3 Suetonius *Divus Julius* 50.2
4 Valerius Maximus 5.2.10 (not book 2)
5 Plautus *Pseudolus* 1323

2 Vero verius
Truer than truth

Though nothing can be truer than truth, all the same we use the proverbial
expression 'Truer than truth' for something which we want to be taken
as absolutely indubitable. Martial attacks a certain Gallicus, who forever
had on his lips the words: 'Tell me, Marcus, tell me the truth, I pray.' He
replies, 'To what is truer than the truth then lend an ear – You do not like,
Gallicus, the truth to hear.'[1] Similarly we say, 'surer than sure.'[2] Though
it is perfectly possible for one thing to be surer than another. Ulpian, in
book twenty-three of the *Pandects*, title 'On testamentary guardianship': 'It
is surer than sure that testamentary guardians may not be compelled to
give security for the preservation of the property.'[3]

3 Vento vivere
Live on the wind

Even today people commonly say that those who live without visible means
of support 'Live on the wind,' and, they add, 'like a catfish,' as it is widely
believed that the catfish feeds on air,[1] as the chameleon is supposed to do.[2]
The emperor Alexander, in book five of the *Codex*, title 'On the maintenance
to be provided for those under puberty': 'Nor is any young person to be
upheld, who, in spite of being visibly present, educated and maintained, if
he cannot demonstrate that he has received these benefits through another,
denies that any expenditure has been incurred, as if he has lived on the
wind or has not been given the education proper to a gentleman.'[3]

* * * * *

2 Martial (see n1) and *Digest* (see n3). Otto 1878 and 376. Added in *1533*
1 Martial 8.76.1 and 7–8
2 Plautus *Captivi* 643
3 *Digest* (*Pandects*) 26.2.17 (not book 23)

3 *Codex Justinianus* (see n3). Otto 1865; Tilley w 435 To live by the Wind; Suringar
235. Added in *1533*
1 Whether catfish or sheat-fish (Latin *silurus*) is not easy to identify. Possibly the
catfish, which has a pronounced air-bladder, some species travelling overland.
Or it could be the sturgeon, at one time believed to feed on air.
2 See Pliny *Naturalis historia* 8.121; *Adagia* III iv 1 As changeable as a chameleon;
see also IV viii 35 A four-square man (378 above).
3 *Codex Justinianus* 5.50.2.2. See *Adagia* IV v 1 n22 (136 above).

4 Tuas res tibi habeto
Take your things and go

In book forty-four of the *Pandects*, title 'On divorce and repudiation,' the jurisconsult Gaius shows that it was customary for a man divorcing his wife to employ the words: 'Take your things and go; manage your own affairs.'[1] The first form of words returned the dowry, the second renounced the function of guardian in respect of the wife's property. This mode of expression was prescribed to prevent the divorce being invalid if no formal phraseology were employed, or to prevent the proceedings turning unpleasant and inauspicious if intemperate language were used. Likewise, in repudiating a betrothal, the prescribed words were: 'I do not accept your proposal.'[2] We can use these formulae like well-worn sayings politely to reject someone's offer of friendship, but it will be rather amusing to transfer them to the things of the mind. For example, if we say, 'He has taken up the monastic life; he has told the world to take its things and go, to look after its own affairs.' If someone that we do not think has anything to offer us is seeking our acquaintance, we can say to him, appropriately enough, 'I do not accept your proposal,' instead of, 'I do not accept your friendship.' Plautus has a nice application of the words in *Three-shilling Day*, where young Lysiteles is complaining about the miseries endured by lovers and is considering expelling love from his mind: 'On your way, Love, if you please. Take your things and go. / Never, Love, shall you consort with me.'[3] In *Amphitryo* Plautus used the formula in its literal sense: 'Good-bye! Take your things and give back mine.'[4]

5 Gamma Betam persequitur
Gamma chases after Beta

In book three of the *Vandal War*, Procopius tells us that the children of Carthage used to chant an old saying, 'Gamma comes chasing after Beta, and

* * * * *

4 The material in the first sentence was added in *1528* to *Adagia* II iii 4 He bade a long farewell. It was inserted here to introduce a new adage in the *1533* expansion of the *Adagia*.

1 *Digest* (*Pandects*) 24.2.2.1 (not book 44). See *Adagia* IV ix 1n (419 above).

2 *Digest* (*Pandects*) 24.2.2.3

3 Plautus *Trinummus* 267–8

4 Plautus *Amphitryo* 928

5 Procopius (see n1). Added in *1533*

then comes Beta chasing Gamma.'[1] I think these words used by children in fun really referred to the fact that neighbours often quarrel, but the childish saying was made to apply to actual historical events, namely that Gaiseric drove out Boniface and then later on Belisarius drove out Gelimer.[2] The saying did not arise from the events, but the riddling words chanted by the Carthaginian children were a kind of prophecy of what happened thereafter.

6 Pulchrum sepulcri elogio
A fine thing to have upon one's tomb

I would not class this as a proverb if it were not specifically referred to as such by Procopius, in book one of the *Persian War*, where the Empress is represented as addressing her husband Justinian to the following effect: 'So, noble Emperor, if you wish to preserve your life, you can undoubtedly do so, and easily enough. We have an enormous supply of money, the sea is close at hand, we have plenty of ships. Consider however that you may save yourself and then find that you have exchanged the happiness of life

* * * * *

1 This is taken from Procopius *De bellis* 3.21.14–16. Procopius was a sixth-century historian who wrote in Greek a history of the wars waged on behalf of the emperor Justinian. The Greek text was not published until 1607 (D. Hoeschel, Augsburg), though there had been various translations into Latin. Christoforo Persona's version of *De bello Gothico*, printed, together with a version of Agathias, (see *Adagia* IV ix 7, 423 below) in 1516 and 1519 (Rome, Jacobus Mazochius) and Raffaele Maffei of Volterra's version of both *De bello Gothico* and *De bello Vandalico* (Rome 1509) were edited in 1531 by Beatus Rhenanus (Basel, Herwagen). Erasmus quotes Procopius in the *Adagia* only among the 1533 additions, in this adage and the next one and at *Adagia* IV ix 77 (469 below). The surrounding extracts from Justinian's legal codification probably brought Procopius to mind here, as well as Agathias, quoted at *Adagia* IV ix 7 (423 below).
2 Boniface (Beta), the Roman general in the province of North Africa from 423 AD onwards, was generally believed to have invited the Vandals, under their king Gaiseric (Gamma), to come to Africa from Spain to support him in his quarrel with the Roman imperial government at Ravenna. He could not control his new allies, who by 439 had captured Carthage, the capital of the Roman province, and established a Vandal kingdom in North Africa. Belisarius (Beta) reconquered Africa in 533–4, capturing the last Vandal king, Gelimer (Gamma).

6 Procopius (see n1). Added in 1533

for the bitterness of death at the last. To me at any rate the old proverb rings true: A fine thing it is to have upon one's tomb – the title "Emperor!"'[1]

I have known people who at the very end of their lives have at great expense bought themselves the cardinal's hat, so that the title 'Cardinal' could be inscribed upon their tombs.

7 Primum apes abigendae
First you must drive off the bees

Agathias in book three of the *Gothic War* writes, 'What was said pleased Ulilagus, headman of the Heruli. Consequently this proverb came into popular use, a barbarian saying of no great moment, but a useful one nonetheless and marked by a certain vigour. He was for ever proclaiming "First you must drive off the bees, then you may take the honey." Buzes was well aware that they must first clear the advancing enemy host out of the way, if they were to gain control of Asia.'[1] The saying is derived from bee-keeping. Bee-keepers drive off the bees with smoke or by some other means, in order to extract the honey from the hives.

8 Porrigere manus
Extend a helping hand

'Extend a helping hand' for 'to lend assistance' is a common enough expression, but a stylish one too. Ulpian in book forty-two of the *Pandects*,

* * * * *

1 Procopius *De bellis* 1.24.36–7 (see previous adage IV ix 5 n1). This extract refers to a time of riots and sedition during which a rival emperor had been declared and Justinian feared for his life.

7 Agathias (see n1). Added in *1533*
1 Agathias *Histories* 3.6.5. See *Adagia* IV ix 5 n1 (422 above). Agathias (circa AD 532–580) wrote the *Histories* as a continuation of Procopius' history and it was likewise written in Greek. The Greek text was not printed until 1594 (Lyon) (when it appeared with a Latin version by Bonaventura Vulcanus; see R. Keydell ed *Agathiae Myrinaei historiarum libri quinque* [Berlin 1967] xv). This is the only place where Agathias, here named as 'Agathius' by Erasmus, is quoted in the *Adagia*. The translation used by Erasmus seems to be based on a text differing from modern ones.

8 *Digest* (see n1) supplemented by Cicero (see n2). Added in *1533*

title 'On matters brought to judgment': 'If the buyer to whom the pledges
were assigned by the judge's decision does not pay the purchase price,
we must see whether the same judges who made the decision should extend a helping hand to call the purchaser to account.'[1] Cicero, in the speech
delivered after his return from exile: 'When I lay in the depths of misery and affliction, he was the first to extend a helping hand to me, to offer me the support of a man of consular rank.'[2] It will be wittier to use the
phrase metaphorically, saying, for example, that 'Philosophy extends a helping hand to the depressed spirit,' or that 'To someone floundering amidst
the difficulties raised by theology, dialectic – or linguistic expertise – often
extends a helping hand.'[3]

9 **Optima quidem aqua**
Water is indeed the best of things

Ἄριστον μὲν ὕδωρ, Water is indeed the best of things. This seems to have
become a proverbial saying for use when we advance something as being
better than something else that is highly thought of. Pindar starts off his
Olympian Odes by saying that water is indeed a very good thing, but he then
gives the preference to gold because it gleams by night like fire.[1] Water and
fire are two chief elements, which is why those we consider unfit to live
are debarred from fire and water.[2] Aristotle, in book three of the *Rhetoric*,
cites the saying as being in common use: 'This,' he says, 'is why they say,
"Water is the best of things."'[3] Some things are rated highly for their rar-
ity value. In general however water is more necessary than gold. Plutarch
has these words in mind in his essay, 'Whether Fire or Water is More

* * * * *

1 *Digest* (*Pandects*) 42.1.15.7 (see *Adagia* IV ix 1n, 419 above)

2 Cicero *Post reditum in senatum* 9.24

3 This hints at the current controversy between those who applied the scholas-
tic method in biblical exegesis and the humanistic language-based approach
practised by Erasmus and others.

9 Pindar (see n1) and Aristotle (see n3). Added in *1533*

1 Pindar *Olympians* 1.1–2. See *Adagia* IV viii 67n (399 above).

2 The standard formula by which persons were outlawed at Rome; see *Adagia*
IV viii 11 (359 above) and *Adagia* IV ix 18 (430 below).

3 Aristotle *Rhetoric* 1.7 (1364a28, not book 3). The next two sentences paraphrase
Aristotle's previous words.

Useful.'[4] If someone is praising philosophy inordinately, a person who agrees that philosophy is indeed an excellent thing but still inferior to theology, can wittily sing along, intoning this fragment from Pindar, 'Water is indeed the best of things.'

10 Non oportet hospitem semper hospitem esse
The stranger must not ever stranger be

Aristotle, in book three of the *Rhetoric*, cites the following words, without however naming any author, as something commonly said: 'The stranger must not ever stranger be.'[1] People are called strangers when they are not familiar with the place where they live. However, it is shameful to live a long time in the same city and remain always a foreigner. (The words seem to form a faulty iambic trimeter.) It is shameful to spend a long time studying the same subject and know nothing.

11 Moriendum priusquam etc.
One must die before ...

In the same place, Aristotle cites, as something well known and popular, a line from Alexandrides:

> Good it is to die before you do
> What makes death come deservedly to you.[1]

As Aristotle himself tells us, this means: 'The right thing is to die when you do not deserve to die,' or 'Death is honourable when you have done nothing deserving of death.'

* * * * *

4 Plutarch *Moralia* 955D *Utrum aqua an ignis sit utilior*

10 Aristotle (see n1 and *Adagia* IV viii 4n, 354 above). Added in *1533*
  1 Aristotle *Rhetoric* 3.11.8 (1412b15) quoting PCG 8 *Adespota* fragment 97: Οὐ δεῖ τὸν ξένον ξένον αἰεὶ εἶναι.

11 Aristotle (see n1 and *Adagia* IV viii 4n, 354 above). Added in *1533*
  1 Aristotle *Rhetoric* 3.11.8 (1412b16), quoting Anaxandrides (not Alexandrides), a fourth century BC comic poet: Καλόν γ᾽ ἀποθανεῖν πρὶν θανάτου δρᾶν ἄξιον (PCG 2 Anaxandrides fragment 65).

12 Sustollere manus
Raise hands on high

Those who are absolutely delighted because things have turned out as they want, apparently by divine agency, are said to 'Raise their hands on high.' Cicero, in book seven of his *Letters*: 'Balbus and I raised our hands on high. The thing was so opportune that it seemed not accidental but a gift from the gods.'[1] Again, in *Academic Questions*: 'Hortensius was absolutely amazed, as he had been all the time Lucullus was speaking, so much so that he often raised his hands on high.'[2] Horace in his fifth satire: 'Day in, day out, he wants your praise – then keep at him / Till he raises hands on high and "Hold, enough!" exclaims.'[3]

13 More Romano
In blunt Roman fashion

Cicero was, it seems, using a proverbial expression, when, in the same letter, he employed the phrase *More Romano* 'In Roman fashion,'[1] meaning 'straightforwardly, without misrepresentation, not cleverly.' Such were those famous Romans of old, quite different from the Greeks.[2] Cicero writes, 'I guarantee, not using that previous phrase of mine, which you quite properly made fun of, when I wrote to you about Milo, but in blunt Roman fashion as used by men who are not at all socially gauche, that there isn't a sounder, better, more sensible fellow.' The Romans saw 'truth' as unsophisticated. A 'truth' of this sort is brought into book two of Cicero's book on *Definitions of Good and Evil*: 'Our teachers argue strongly that the future philosopher has no need of an advanced education. Just as our ancestors summoned the great Cincinnatus from the plough to become dictator, so you collect from all kinds of primitive societies men who may well be good, but are certainly not

* * * * *

12 Cicero is much used in *Adagia* IV ix 12–23 and 29–32. Added in *1533*
1 Cicero *Ad familiares* 7.5
2 Cicero *Academica priora* ('Lucullus') 2.63
3 Horace *Satires* 2.5.96–7

13 Cicero (see nn1, 4, and 5). Otto 1550. Added in *1533*
1 Cicero *Ad familiares* 7.5.3
2 Erasmus several times records without dissent disparaging Roman remarks about contemporary Greeks, who were allegedly quite different from the heroes of old. See *Adagia* I vii 95, I viii 27; Juvenal 3.78.

always men of education.'[3] Cicero again, writing to Trebatius in book seven: 'Balbus assured me you were going to be rich. I will find out later whether he said this in plain Roman fashion, meaning you were going to make a lot of money, or whether he was talking like the Stoics, who say that anyone is rich who can enjoy the sky and the earth.'[4] By 'plain Roman fashion' he meant 'unsophisticated and simple.' The Stoic definition of 'rich' and 'poor' was a subtle one. A little later, writing to the same Trebatius, Cicero says, 'When Balbus comes to visit, I will recommend you to him in frank Roman fashion.'[5]

14 Lacryma nihil citius arescit
Nothing dries faster than a tear

In the first book of his *On Invention* Cicero tells the orator that once he has stirred pity in the hearts of the jury, he should not linger over this 'pathetic appeal,' quoting in support of this recommendation the precept of Apollonius:[1] Οὐδὲν θᾶσσον ξηραίνεσθαι δακρύου 'Nothing dries faster than a tear.'[2] People have soon had enough of strong emotion.

* * * * *

3 Cicero *De finibus* 2.4.12. The text should read not *nostri* 'our teachers' but *vestri* 'your teachers.'
4 Cicero *Ad familiares* 7.16.3
5 Cicero *Ad familiares* 7.18.3

14 Cicero (see n2). Tilley N 288 Nothing dries sooner than tears. Otto 903. Added in *1533*
1 Probably Apollonius of Alabanda (second century BC), who won a great reputation as a teacher of rhetoric in the island of Rhodes. The place became famed for rhetorical studies and many distinguished Romans went there to study. Cicero was a student there under Apollonius' successor, Apollonius Molon, who may be the one meant here.
2 Cicero *De inventione* 1.56.109. See also *Rhetorica ad Herennium* 2.31.50; Quintilian 6.1.27. Erasmus quotes the maxim in Greek, but the Greek form does not appear in any of these sources, nor does it seem to be known from Aristotle or the late Greek writers on rhetoric. The Greek form is quoted and attributed to Apollonius sub ξηραίνω in Estienne's *Thesaurus Graecae linguae* of 1572 (enlarged edition Didot, Paris 1865) and is given also in Gisbertus Longolius' edition of *Rhetorica ad Herennium* (Cologne 1539). See G.D. Kellogg 'Study of a proverb attributed to the rhetor Apollonius' *American Journal of Philology* 28 (1907) 301–10. It looks as if Erasmus himself reconstructed the Greek form, which was then reproduced by Longolius and Estienne as genuine.

15 **Ex potestate exisse**
Gone out of control

People who have lost their senses and are swept along, deaf to the voice of reason, blindly following where their cravings lead, are said to have 'Gone out of control.' Cicero, in the third book of the *Tusculan Disputations*, writes, 'We must consider sane those people ... So the best thing is to say of these that they are "out of control," using the expression commonly applied to people who lose their grip on themselves and are carried away by lust or anger.' And a little further on: 'People who are said to be "out of control" are so described because they are not under the control of the mind, which nature has appointed as governor of the non-physical part of man.'[1] So Cicero writes. We accordingly speak of people being *compos mentis* or *non compos mentis* 'in control' or 'not in control of their senses,' and people are said to be 'uncontrollably deranged' when their mental processes are not under their control but are at the mercy of their emotions. The basic form of words comes from the jurists: children born of lawful marriage are 'subject to the control of parents,' unless they are emancipated[2] or the father dies. Those who are emancipated 'have gone from the control of parents.'

16 **Gallonius**
Gallonius

Some people like Aesopus[1] and Apicius[2] have actually become famous for

* * * * *

15 Cicero (see n1). Added in *1533*
  1 Cicero *Tusculan Disputations* 3.5.11. Erasmus' eye seems to have slipped in copying the passage as a necessary section is omitted: 'whose mind is not disturbed by agitations which are a kind of sickness. Those on the other hand who are so affected we must call insane.' Cicero remarks that 'gone out of control' was a common Latin idiom.
  2 A technical term signifying the release from paternal power (by a juridical act)

16 Cicero (see nn4, 6, and 8). Added in *1533*
  1 Not the writer of fables but the wastrel son of the famous tragic actor Aesopus, a contemporary and friend of Cicero
  2 There were several Roman gourmets of this name, the most famous being Marcus Gavius Apicius (first century AD), who was renowned for the prodi-

their extravagant life-style. The Gallonius who appears in Lucilius' poem[3] was honoured with mention by Cicero, and in more than one place at that. In the speech in defence of Caecina, for example, Cicero writes, 'So what follows? This does not mean that we go on to accept the idea that the lives and fortunes of respectable citizens should be at the mercy of persons who have abandoned the self-control exercised by decent men and chosen to emulate the getting and spending of a Gallonius.'[4] He mentions him in the speech in defence of Quinctius as well,[5] and also in book two of *Definitions of Good and Evil*, where he quotes the following lines from Lucilius:

> Publius Gallonius, says he, you swill food down like a drain,
> Yet in all your life, poor fellow, you never a good meal attain,
> For all that you squander on sea-food dishes
> And sturgeon of monster size.[6]

Lucilius puts these words into the mouth of Laelius,[7] who dined off sorrel, addressing Gallonius, a glutton measuring everything by the pleasure it afforded to gullet and belly. Cicero mentions Gallonius again in book two of *Definitions of Good and Evil*, where he says, 'I have no time for someone

* * * * *

gality and inventiveness of his culinary creations. He was well remembered in anecdote. After squandering a fortune on procuring unusual and exotic foods, he found he had left only 10 million sesterces (in his eyes an inadequate sum to live on), so, fearing starvation, committed suicide. (See Seneca *Consolatio ad Helvetiam* 10.9; Martial 3.22.) A cook-book went under his name, but it was a later fourth-century compilation. It was popular with Renaissance humanists and physicians (*editio princeps* Le Signerre, Milan, 1498); see the edition by B. Flower and E. Rosenbaum *Apicius: The Roman Cookery Book* (London 1958).

3 See n6 below.
4 Cicero, not from *Pro A. Caecina*, but *Pro P. Quinctio* 30.9
5 See previous note; Erasmus seems to have misremembered.
6 Cicero *De finibus* 2.8.24, quoting Lucilius 1238–40 Marx (1135–7 Krenkel), the second century BC satirist, whose works survive only in fragments quoted by others. See *Adagia* IV ix 54 Every tenth one (456 below).
7 Gaius Laelius (circa 190–129 BC), a member of the so-called 'Scipionic circle,' a group of prominent Romans gathered round P. Cornelius Scipio Aemilianus, who favoured the dissemination of Greek culture and philosophy at Rome. Laelius was nicknamed *Sapiens* 'the Wise.'

who lives with pleasure as his yardstick, like Gallonius, and at the same
time talks like Piso the Uncorrupt.'[8]

17 Vultu saepe laeditur pietas
Even a look can strike a blow against filial respect

In his speech in defence of Roscius, Cicero makes passing reference to a
saying often on the lips of wise men. 'If,' he says, 'as the wise have so strik-
ingly expressed it, "Even a look can strike a blow against filial respect," can
one find a punishment sufficiently severe for a man who has actually murdered the parent for whom every sanction, human and divine, demanded
that he should sacrifice his own life, should that be necessary?'[1] The saying
reminds us that we must devote such scrupulous care to maintaining our
love and respect for our parents that we do not offend them with an angry or rebellious look, let alone with insolent words or deeds. The eyes, the
brow, the face, all speak their own language. The Gospel goes even deeper,
to the depths of the heart, where anger has its origin.[2] Anger bursts out in
an exclamation of resentment which as yet does not say anything definite.
The next stage is open abuse, the third murder.

18 Culleo dignus, aut, Non uno culleo dignus
Fit for the sack, or, One sack is not enough

We use the phrase 'Fit for the sack,' of somebody we consider utterly wicked.
'The sack' was the punishment reserved for a parricide, that is, someone who
had killed a parent. In early times 'parricide' meant killing any other human
being. The word was derived from *par* 'equal,' that is, a man killing a fellow
man.[1] This was in the period when it was considered a savage deed to kill

* * * * *

8 Cicero *De finibus* 2.28.90. The reference is to Lucius Calpurnius Piso Frugi (second century BC), who earned his nickname *Frugi* 'Uncorrupt' for his probity.

17 Cicero (n1). Added in 1533
1 Cicero *Pro S. Roscio Amerino* 13.37
2 See Mark 7:21–2.

18 Cicero (see n3). Added in 1533
1 For the proposed original meaning of the word, see Pompeius Festus (247.19–
24 Lindsay). The etymology of the word is unknown. The derivation from
par 'equal' is suggested, among other possibilities, in Priscian *Institutiones*

an ox, a goose, a barnyard cock.[2] Then, when killing people became commonplace, the word 'parricide' was limited in meaning to refer only to the supreme act of impiety. 'The sack' was a sack of leather, into which the person who had murdered a parent was sewn, together with a snake, a monkey, and a barnyard cock. Then the whole thing was thrown into running water. Cicero says in his speech in defence of Roscius of Ameria, 'How much wiser did our own ancestors show themselves! They realized that nothing was so sacred that man's audacity would not one day profane it, so they thought up a special punishment for parricide, intending that those whom natural feeling could not hold to their duty should be deterred from the supreme deed of wickedness by the enormity of the penalty. They wanted such persons to be sewn into a sack alive and then thrown into a river. What remarkable wisdom those judges displayed! By cutting off the perpetrator in one move from sky, sun, water, earth, they expelled and excised him from the natural world, so that the killer of the one who had given him life should be himself deprived of all those elements which are themselves the source of all life.'[3] Juvenal magnifies the enormity of this act of impiety on the part of a certain person by saying that one serpent, one sack is not enough for him.[4] Suetonius tells us that some persons put a leather bag over Nero's statue, and wrote on it, 'You deserved this. But what can I do?'[5]

19 Ratio quidem apparet
The accounts are clear enough

Plautus, in the *Three-shilling Day*: 'But these accounts don't seem clear.' To which Stasinus replies, 'Good Lord, the accounts are clear enough; it's the

* * * * *

Grammaticae 1 33 (ed Martin Hertz, in Heinrich Keil ed *Grammatici Latini* vols 2 and 3 [Leipzig 1855, repr Hildesheim and New York 1981]).

2 See eg Ovid *Metamorphoses* 15.75–110.

3 Cicero *Pro S. Roscio Amerino* 25.70–26.71. Roscius was charged with the murder of his father.

4 Juvenal 8.213–4, referring to Nero's arranging to have his own mother murdered

5 Suetonius *Nero* 45.2 (misquoted, presumably from memory). This was a secret protest at Nero's murder of his mother. See n4 above. Erasmus offers a possible explanation of the words at *Apophthegmata* VI Nero 14.

19 Cicero quoting Plautus (see nn1 and 3). Very similar to Brassicanus no 72 *Ratio apparet, argentum* οἴχεται; see *Adagia* IV iii 86 n2, 52 above. Added in *1533*

money that's cleared off.'[1] This is the true reading here, though various people have thought up different ways of corrupting it.[2] Cicero used this same line in his speech attacking Piso: 'If you inspect these accounts, you will realize that I more than anyone have profited from receiving an education. They are written out so expertly, with such style, that the treasury clerk who recorded them, after copying them out, scratched his head with his left hand and muttered to himself, "Good Lord, the accounts are clear enough; it's the money that's cleared off."'[3] Terence's Geta says something similar in *Phormio*: 'It wasn't calculation that was missing, just the cash.'[4] Cicero, writing to his brother Quintus in the last letter in book two: 'Although it's easier said than done.'[5] We can include with this, 'Fine words!'[6]

20 Omnia praeter animam
Everything bar the soul

When we want to express the idea that nothing has been held back, saving only life itself, we say, 'Everything bar the soul.' Cicero, in his speech defending Roscius of Ameria says, 'If you have no justification for wishing to inflict such misery on this unfortunate man, if he has surrendered everything to you bar his soul, if he has kept back nothing that was his father's, not even a memento ...'[1] A similar phrase, 'to owe one's very soul,'

* * * * *

1 Plautus *Trinummus* 418–9. The correct form of the name is Stasimus.
2 See n3. Erasmus is using the Plautine commentary of Giambattista Pio; see *Adagia* IV iii 40 n2 (27 above).
3 Cicero *In L. Pisonem* 25.61, quoting the above line from Plautus (n1 above). 'Cleared off' translates a Greek word (οἴχεται) in the Latin text, which, as so often, occasioned corruptions in the MSS. The correct reading is *argentum* οἴχεται, but various readings are found in the *In Pisonem* passage, such as *et doctum, argutum, te thece, oechetae, oechete*. Of these, the humanists had emended *et doctum* to *decoctum*, which appears in some editions of Plautus also. (See Cicero *In Pisonem* ed R.G. Nisbet [Oxford 1961] 125.)
4 Terence *Phormio* 299
5 Cicero *Ad Quintum fratrem* 1.4.5 (not book 2)
6 The relevance of the last two examples is not clear. See *Adagia* I x 55 Fine words! and IV viii 97 Well said, all of it (417 above).

20 Cicero (see n1). Added in *1533*
1 Cicero *Pro S. Roscio Amerino* 50.146

is used of those who owe more than they are worth: Terence: 'What if he owes his very soul?'[2] Or, the other way round, 'He owes everything bar his own soul.'

21 De reduvia queritur
He complains of a whitlow

Περὶ τῆς παρωνυχίας μέμφεται ὁ τῷ μείζονι ἔνοχος κακῷ, A man suffering from a serious illness complains of a whitlow. Used when somebody from a false sense of shame seeks a remedy for some trivial complaint and conceals a serious one. Many people act like this. They even try to deceive the doctor, especially sufferers from gout. Plutarch tells of a man who consulted a doctor about a whitlow, when it was obvious from his complexion that he was suffering from a diseased liver. The doctor saw through his foolish embarrassment and said to him, 'The whitlow is the least of your problems. You are seriously ill.'[1] Cicero refers to this in his speech in defence of Roscius of Ameria: 'I am well aware that I am being premature in discussing this matter at this point and am probably making a mistake in attending to a whitlow when I should be finding a remedy to save Sextus Roscius' life.'[2]

22 Ad libellam debere
To owe according to the balance

A person who owes cash of a specified amount is said to owe 'precisely,' that is, 'according to the balance.' For cash payments were in times past made using scales, not by counting out individual coins. This is the origin of common expressions such as Latin *expendere* 'incur expense,' *expensum ferre* 'enter expenses as paid,' *dependere* 'expend,' *rependere* 'pay in recompense,'

* * * * *

2 Terence *Phormio* 661. This has already been used; see *Adagia* I x 24 He owes his own soul.

21 Plutarch and Cicero (see nn1 and 2). Otto 1512. Added in *1533*
1 Plutarch *Moralia* 73B *Quomodo adulator ab amico internoscatur.* Another version of the story is given in *Moralia* 43A *De recte ratione audiendi.*
2 Cicero *Pro S. Roscio Amerino* 44.128

22 Cicero (see n2). See *Adagia* IV vi 74 With a plumb-line (264 above).

impendere 'spend on.'[1] Cicero in the speech defending Roscius of Ameria writes, 'Unless he can prove that fifty-three thousand sesterces precisely is the sum he is owed, he loses his case.'[2]

23 Hoc municeps aut vicinus nunciavit
Some fellow-townsman or a neighbour brought the news

In the same speech, Cicero says, 'When you hear something like this, gentlemen of the jury, your immediate response is always to say that someone from the same town or a neighbour brought the news.'[1] The misdeeds of neighbours or citizens are always most likely to be betrayed by neighbours or inhabitants of the same place. Even today, people commonly say that it's fellow-countrymen and neighbours that are responsible for someone being disgraced. If some misfortune occurs, or some slip-up, they will tell of it, because they know.

24 Dea excogitavit
The goddess thought of it

Aristophanes in the *Knights*: Τὸ μὲν νόημα τῆς θεοῦ, τὸ δὲ κλέμμ᾿ ἐμόν 'The goddess it was that thought of it; the theft was mine entirely.'[1] This apparently proverbial saying was directed at orators who boasted to the people that Minerva[2] had suggested to them the policy which they were trying to put across and then claimed the credit when it turned out well. The general idea comes from Homer where any deed for which there is no rational ex-

* * * * *

1 All these Latin words are derived from the root *pend-* 'to weigh,' a word which is only implied by Erasmus' previous remark.
2 A mistake: the quotation is from Cicero's speech defending his friend, the actor Quintus Roscius Gallus, *Pro Q. Roscio comoedo* 4.11.

23 Cicero (see n1). Suringar 253. Added in *1533*
1 Cicero *Pro S. Roscio Amerino* 37.105

24 Aristophanes (see n1). Added in *1533*
1 Aristophanes *Knights* 1203, together with the ancient commentator on the passage. See *Adagia* IV viii 41n (382 above).
2 The Roman goddess equated with the Greek goddess Pallas Athene. Erasmus prefers to use the Latin equivalents rather than the Greek names.

planation is said to have been inspired by Pallas. Pallas was the protecting
deity of Athens. The comic poet in the line quoted above substitutes 'theft'
for 'deed,' so as to make a joke about Cleon's rapacity.

25 Usus est altera natura
Habit is a second nature

No saying is better known than the following: Ἔθος ἄλλη φύσις 'Habit
is a second nature.' Nothing is more effective or more powerful than
nature. As the Satirist puts it, 'Nature more potent than any guardian or
care.'[1] In book one of the *Rhetoric*, Aristotle is discussing pleasure and
says that pleasure arises either from what accords with the natural condition, or from the nearest thing to this, that is, from what is habitual. He
thinks the only difference between nature and habit is the difference between 'always' and 'mostly.'[2] Anything implanted by nature is permanent,
what is instilled by habit is usual. So it was admirable counsel given by
the man who said that we should from our earliest days always choose
what is best.[3] In later years this will through habit become pleasurable
as well.

26 Necessitas molesta
Necessity is disagreeable

Immediately after the passage cited above, Aristotle quotes a well-known
line to the effect that anything that does not come naturally is disagreeable.
Compulsion is at odds with nature and so everybody finds irksome something they are forced to do. 'This is a very true saying,' he goes on. Πᾶν

* * * * *

25 Aristotle (see n2 and *Adagia* IV viii 4n, 354 above). Otto 426; Tilley C 932
   Custom (Use) is another (a second) nature; Once a use and ever a custom.
   Added in *1533*
1 Juvenal 10.303
2 Aristotle *Rhetoric* 1.11 (1370a3–9), paraphrased by Erasmus. Aristotle does not
   actually say Ἔθος ἄλλη φύσις 'Habit is a second nature,' but ὅμοιον γάρ τι τὸ
   ἔθος τῇ φύσει 'Habit is something rather like nature.'
3 See Quintilian 1.8.4, and cf *Adagia* II iv 20 Long will a crock. See also the next
   adage.

26 Aristotle (see n1 and *Adagia* IV viii 4n, 354 above). Added in *1533*

γὰρ ἀναγκαῖον πρᾶγμα ἀνιαρὸν ἔφυ 'That which must be done is of its nature hateful.'[1] However, we do not accustom ourselves to what is best unless some compulsion is applied at the beginning. The thing that was forced upon us at the start and was then hateful, as we get used to it, ceases to be burdensome and finally becomes actually pleasurable.

27 Jucunda malorum praeteritorum memoria
The remembrance of past sorrows is pleasurable

In the same section, Aristotle goes on to cite the following proverbial sentiment from some poet or other: 'Pleasure it is, when delivered, past sufferings to recall.'[1] He also cites this: 'Great pleasure it gives a man past sorrows to remember / When he has much endured and many a deed performed.'[2] I have already treated this subject earlier.[3]

28 Suffragium optimum
To the best of one's judgment

In the first book of the *Rhetoric*, Aristotle touches on a phrase that was much used in judicial contexts, 'To the best of one's judgment.' While there are many methods of winning assent dependent on material drawn from outside the case, called by the Greeks ἄτεχνοι 'not of the art,' that is, given proofs, such as laws, witnesses, contracts, evidence obtained under torture, and oaths,[1] the best proof is that using 'probabilities,' for which the Greek

* * * * *

1 Aristotle *Rhetoric* 1.11 (1370a9–11), citing a fragment of Evenus (a fifth-century BC elegiac poet), *Elegi* fragment 8 West

27 Aristotle (see n1 and *Adagia* IV viii 4n, 354 above). Tilley R 73 The remembrance of past sorrow (dangers) is joyful. Added in *1533*
1 Aristotle *Rhetoric* 1.11 (1370b4–6), citing a line from Euripides' lost tragedy *Andromeda* (fragment 133 Nauck). See *Adagia* II iii 43 Past labour is pleasant, where the line is attributed to Euripides on the authority of Cicero.
2 Homer *Odyssey* 15.400–1. Erasmus quotes the lines as they appear in Aristotle.
3 See n1.

28 Aristotle (see nn1 and 2, and *Adagia* IV viii 4n, 354 above). Added in *1533*
1 Aristotle *Rhetoric* 1.15 (1375a22–4)

word is εἰκότα. What Aristotle says is, 'If witnesses are lacking, the speaker will argue that the judges have to base their decision on probabilities, acting, as they say, Γνώμη τῇ ἀρίστη "To the best of one's judgment."'[2]

29 Tamquam ad aram
As if to an altar

I have written elsewhere of 'the sheet-anchor.'[1] Very like this is the saying, 'To an altar,' meaning, 'the last resort.' Those who were in desperate straits used to take refuge at the altars of the gods, and to drag anyone away from there was an offence against heaven – hence our phrase. Cicero, in his speech in defence of Roscius the actor, says, 'The same thing happened recently in the case of Eros, the comedy actor. When he was not merely hissed off the stage but subjected to a barrage of insults, he took refuge, as at an altar, in the house of this man, subject to his instruction, protected by his name.'[2] Again, in book three of *On the Nature of the Gods*, he writes, 'When you cannot do so, you resort to the supernatural, as if to an altar.'[3] Again, in the fourth part of his attack on Verres: 'They endured injustices from many a magistrate of ours, yet never before this did they as a community betake themselves to the altar of the laws and claim your protection.'[4] Ovid, in book four of the *Epistles*: 'Thou, the sole altar for my

* * * * *

2 Aristotle *Rhetoric* 1.15 (1376a18–19). Erasmus' compressed paragraph has obscured Aristotle's argument (as Estienne points out in two footnotes at LB II 1150D). Aristotle is discussing techniques of argument in forensic cases and does not actually say that arguments based on probabilities are best, but simply that they can be effectively used in the absence of witnesses (who constitute one of the ready-supplied or non-technical ἄτεχνοι means of corroborating the speaker's contention).

29 *Adagia* IV ix 29–32 consist almost entirely of material derived from Cicero. This one is based on Brassicanus no 38 *Ara* 'The altar' and uses almost all of Brassicanus' illustrative examples, with no additional material. For Brassicanus see *Adagia* IV iii 86 n2 (52 above). Added in *1533*
1 *Adagia* I i 24 To let go the sheet-anchor
2 Cicero *Pro Q. Roscio comoedo* 11.30
3 Cicero *De natura deorum* 3.10.25
4 Cicero *Verrines* 2.2.3.8

fortunes found.'[5] Plautus, in the *Haunted House*: 'You've taken refuge at the altar.'[6]

30 Ad asylum confugere
Flee to sanctuary

Very similar to the last is *Ad asylum confugere* 'Flee to sanctuary.' Cicero, in the third part of his attack on Verres, writes, 'He used to say that, when quaestor, he had been prevented from removing from the shrine of Diana his own slave, who had taken refuge in that sanctuary.'[1] If you use these phrases metaphorically to refer to things of the mind, they will be more engaging and παροιμιωδέστερα[2] 'more proverbial.'

31 Arx
Citadel

Related to the last is the metaphorical use of the word 'citadel,' meaning the strongest and most secure defence. Cicero, writing in the sixth part of his attack on Verres: 'This same man turns to you now, gentlemen of the jury, as a private individual, appealing to the law under which this court is constituted, the law which acts as a universal citadel for all communities associated with us.'[1] Later on in this same speech: 'This is the one place of refuge whither our allies may flee, this is their harbour, this their citadel, this their altar.'[2] Similarly, in the speech in defence of the actor Roscius: 'This is a law for the benefit of allies, this is a sanction devised to help

* * * * *

5 Ovid *Tristia* (not *Epistulae ex Ponto*) 4.5.2
6 Plautus *Mostellaria* 1135; here the phrase is used literally.

30 Cicero (see n1). Cf *Adagia* IV x 79 Not even if to Jove's temple (530 below).
1 Cicero *Verrines* 2.1.33.85. The quaestorship was the lowest of the regular Roman magistracies. The duties of quaestors were in large part financial and they were often attached to Roman governors abroad. The reference is to the world-famous shrine of Diana of the Ephesians.
2 A word apparently culled by Erasmus from his reading in later Greek authors

31 This adage consists mostly of extracts from Cicero. Added in *1533*
1 Cicero *Verrines* 2.4.8.17
2 Cicero *Verrines* 2.5.48.126 (not 'the same speech')

foreign nations, this is their citadel, not as secure to be sure as it used to be, but all the same ...'[3] Again, in the speech in defence of Sulla: 'By the execution of five mad and desperate men, I saved the lives of everyone, the security of the world, this city in fact which is the home territory of all of us, the citadel of foreign nations and kings, a light to their peoples and the home of empire.'[4] Cicero again, in a letter addressed to P. Lentulus, calls the real point at issue the 'citadel of the matter.'[5] Aristotle, in the preface to his *Rhetoric* addressed to Alexander, writes, 'Since they knew full well that the consideration of what is expedient, based on reason, is the ἀκρόπολις "citadel" of salvation.'[6]

32 Ne vestigium quidem
Not even a vestige or trace

Whenever we want to say that someone or something has been completely destroyed, we say that 'Not a vestige' remains. Cicero, in the third part of his attack on Verres: 'If we felt the same indignation over others' wrongs as we do over our own, there would not be a vestige of him left in the forum.'[1] Again, in the fifth: 'You have to take great care that not a trace of lust is to be found in your own life.'[2] Again, in his speech attacking Rullus: 'Hardly a vestige of Corinth was left.'[3] And another example from the same speech: 'that even the site should preserve the signs of the calamity that overtook the people who measured themselves against this city for dominion of the world.'[4] Cicero again, in the speech defending Cluentius: 'And meantime you can find no vestige of any cash that can be traced back to Cluentius.'[5]

* * * * *

3 A mistake; actually Cicero *Divinatio in Quintum Caecilium* 5.18
4 Cicero *Pro P. Sulla* 11.33
5 Cicero *Ad familiares* 1.9.8
6 Aristotle *Rhetorica ad Alexandrum*, Preface 9 (1421a1; *1533, 1536*, and LB mistakenly read *oratione* for *ratione*). This quotation appears in briefer form in *Adagia* II i 61 The head.

32 This adage consists entirely of extracts from Cicero. Added in *1533*
1 Cicero *Verrines* 2.1.44.113
2 Cicero *Verrines* 2.3.2.4
3 Cicero *De lege agraria* 2.32.87
4 Cicero *De lege agraria* 2.19.51
5 Cicero *Pro A. Cluentio* 30.82

Again, in the speech in support of the measure proposed by Manilius: 'His legions went into Asia in such a way that not only did no hand in all that army injure anyone who did not resist, but not even traces of its passage did them any harm.'[6] Again, speaking on behalf of Flaccus: 'Our representatives thrown into prison, the very memory of the name of Rome together with every vestige of our rule deleted not merely from Greek settlements but from Greek records.'[7] Again, speaking on behalf of Sulla: 'The man who a short time before had been consul designate suddenly found himself without a trace of his former status.'[8] Cicero again in book five of his letters, writing to Plancus: 'Not a vestige of my former standing is left to me.'[9] Again in book nine, writing to Papirius Paetus: 'Think what you will, I am much taken with witticisms, especially those in our native Roman style, especially when I observe such wit to have been contaminated, first of all by the territory round Rome as outsiders poured into our city, and nowadays by wearers of trews and dwellers beyond the Alps, so that no trace of the old elegant wit remains.'[10] In the fifth *Philippic*, he uses 'shadow' instead of 'vestige': 'Unless these measures are repealed by authority of the Senate, now that we have begun to hope for a restoration of the republican constitution, not a shadow of a free state will be left.'[11] Cicero again, in a letter to his brother Quintus: 'You would not have seen your brother, not the man you knew, not the man you sent back as he escorted you on your way, both of us in tears, not a semblance, just the ghost of the living dead.'[12] He expressed the same idea again in different words in the fourth book of his letters to Atticus, in the one beginning, 'You can tell how preoccupied I am': 'We have lost, my dear Pomponius, not merely the substance, the life-blood of our former country, but even its semblance and appearance.'[13] Again, in the first letter in the tenth book of *Letters to Friends*: 'Not a semblance, not a vestige, of the free state.'[14]

* * * * *

6 Cicero *Pro lege Manilia* 13.39
7 Cicero *Pro L. Flacco* 25.60
8 Cicero *Pro P. Sulla* 32.91
9 Cicero *Ad familiares* 4.14.1 (not book 5)
10 Cicero *Ad familiares* 9.15.2
11 Cicero *Philippics* 5.4.11
12 Cicero *Ad Quintum fratrem* 1.3.1
13 Cicero *Ad Atticum* 4.18.2
14 Cicero *Ad familiares* 10.1.1

33 Diobolares
Twopenny fellows

Diobolaris, Worth two obols, was the ancient word for someone of no account, the obol being a small bronze coin. The word referred at first to common prostitutes who could be had for a very small sum, but was later used for anybody or anything that was vile and contemptible. Festus Pompeius records the usage.[1] Plautus calls a low prostitute *diobolarium* 'a twopenny slut.'[2]

34 Equitandi peritus ne cantet
The horseman should not take to singing

Ἱπποσύνην δεδαὼς μὴ ᾄδῃ, The horseman should not take to singing. A sentiment originating with some poet or other and directed at a person who, after practising a serious occupation, turns to frivolities. Horsemanship is a soldier's skill and relates to war. Musicians are useless in war and their sole concern is pleasure. Gregory the Theologian writes in a letter to Eudoxus, the teacher of rhetoric, 'The poem will not have a horseman making music, for you may finish up a failure both as a horseman and as a musician.'[1] I have not yet identified the source of the quotation, but the saying seems to have been directed at the Thebans, who studied two skills in particular, horsemanship and playing the pipe, though one does not really go with the other.[2]

* * * * *

33 Pompeius Festus (see n1). Cf *Adagia* I viii 10 A three ha'penny fellow; II ix 2 I wouldn't give four obols for it. Added in *1533*
1 Pompeius Festus 65.8–9 Lindsay
2 Plautus *Poenulus* 270

34 Gregory of Nazianzus (see n1). Added in *1533*
1 Ie Gregory of Nazianzus (circa 329–389), one of the four great Doctors of the Church, in *Epistolae* 178.4 PG 37 289. The poem referred to is *Anthologia graeca* 9.537.
2 The Thebans of the fourth century BC were a formidable fighting force under their leader Epaminondas. They were also highly appreciative of skill on the aulos; Pronomos, one of the most distinguished aulos-players of fifth-century Greece was Theban. The precise source of Erasmus' comment has not been identified.

35 Spartae servi maxime servi
Nowhere more a slave than at Sparta

In his *Life of Lycurgus*, Plutarch records an apparently well-known saying, 'Among the Spartans a free man is freer than anywhere else, but a slave is a slave absolutely.'[1] At Sparta free-born persons were prohibited from learning or practising any trade or engaging in business or agriculture. All these activities were performed by Helots, a type of slave, who were forbidden to learn or practise any liberal art. These Helots the Spartans treated harshly. They were compelled to be present at dinner-parties and there to drink until intoxicated, sing ridiculous songs, and perform lewd dances, so that the free-born might learn from their example how disgusting and shaming drunkenness was. Moreover, when the Ephors[2] entered on their office, they used to declare war on the Helots, thus making it no wrong to kill them. All this reduced the Helots so such a state of servitude that they dared do nothing without the consent of their masters. Indeed, when the Thebans made an incursion into Spartan territory and captured some Helots, they bade them sing the songs of Terpander, Alcman, and Spendon, the Spartan poets,[3] but the Helots replied that their masters' daughters did not permit it. I have dealt elsewhere with the saying, 'As spirited as a Spartan.'[4]

36 Vespertilio
A bat

People who are so deeply in debt that they·stay at home during the day to

* * * * *

35 Plutarch (see n1). Added in *1533*
  1 See Plutarch *Lycurgus* 28 for all of this paragraph. Much of the material is also found in Erasmus *Apophthegmata* I and II (translated from Plutarch): 'Sayings of Spartans' 70, 116, 189; 'Ancient Customs of the Spartans' 25; 'Sayings of Spartan Women' 40.
  2 Spartan officials wielding great authority, first appointed in the seventh century BC, at first three in number, later increased to five. They were elected from influential families to hold office for a year.
  3 Musicians and poets active at Sparta in the early period. Terpander's and Alcman's poems have survived only in fragmentary form. Nothing further is known of Spendon (not Spondon, as in LB).
  4 *Adagia* II viii 61

36 *Digest* (*Pandects*) and Andrea Alciati (see nn1 and 3). Added in *1533*

prevent their creditors presenting them with a demand for payment, coming out only at night, are called 'bats' or 'fly-by-nights.' Ulpian, in book twenty-one of the *Pandects*, title 'On evictions,' writes:

> If anyone gives a guarantee when so requested that the slave is of sound mind, no thief, no bat etc ... Some are of the opinion that to ask for such a guarantee is useless, because if the slave in question is in such a case, the master cannot make the declaration, and if he is not, there is no point in his doing so. In my opinion the declaration 'not to be a thief, to be of sound mind, not to be a bat' does have a use; the essential point is that it is of concern to the buyer that he should be or not be any of these things.[1]

In this extract, some people read not *vespertilio* 'bat' but *vespillo* 'corpse-robber,' or *versipellis* 'were-wolf.' Alciati,[2] who has the most extensive knowledge of any among the jurisconsults, says in his commentaries on nomenclature that *vespertilio* 'bat' signifies, as I said above, a person who skulks by day for fear of his creditors and comes out only by night.[3] The bat is called *vespertilio* in Latin because *vesperi volat* 'it flies in the evening,' an etymology found in Nonius Marcellus.[4] The usage seems to be derived from one of Aesop's fables, or more likely one written by some imitator, as it does not seem good enough for Aesop.[5] This fable tells how a bat, a gull, and a bramble went into partnership, pooling their assets and trading as a group. The bat contributed money he had raised on loan, the gull goods of some sort, the bramble clothing. After they had been shipwrecked and had escaped with nothing but their lives, the bat took to hiding by day for fear of his creditors and flying only by night, the gull haunted the

* * * * *

1 *Digest* (*Pandects*) 21.2.31; see *Adagia* IV ix 1n, 419 above.

2 Andrea Alciati, 1492–1550, the distinguished jurist, classical scholar, historian, antiquarian, and, most famously, creator of the Renaissance emblem. Erasmus and Alciati corresponded but did not meet. For Erasmus' high opinion of him, see *Adagia* I v 45 Nothing to do with verse and I iii 59:16n Inheritance without rites CWE 31 284.

3 Based on a selection of Alciati *De verborum significatione* book IV (see *Adagia* IV vii 75n, 332 above). This adage, *Vespertilio*, offers a considerable development of the short paragraph in Alciati (page 86 of the 1537 edition), which, after explaining the word, summarizes the fable and in passing rejects the readings *vespillo* and *versipellis*.

4 Nonius Marcellus 67.30–1 Lindsay

5 Aesop *Fables* 250 (Chambry)

shores, ducking his head in the water to see if he could find his merchandise either cast up on the shore or caught on the bottom, the bramble clung to the clothes of passers-by, in case he could discover any garment that was his own.

It might seem unlikely that a slave could be in debt, for who would lend to a slave? – though in Terence we do find that Davus has repaid Geta what he owed him.[6] It seems to me however that the word *vespertilio* 'bat' could also be applied to a runaway slave, as a runaway slave usually absconds from his master during the night and hides away somewhere while there is any danger of his being recognized. In the next section, Ulpian has, instead of 'bat,' the terms 'runaway' and 'fugitive.' He writes, 'when anyone guarantees that he is no thief, fugitive, or runaway.'[7] In early times the word 'bat' had a different meaning, that is, a man of dubious loyalty, belonging neither to this group or to that but playing along with both. The bat likewise is double-natured and does not belong with either birds or mice: it has wings but no feathers; it flies, but only at dusk; it has teeth, which no bird has.[8] Nonius cites a line of Varro's *Agatho*: 'To say no more, I have become a bat – I'm neither mouse nor bird.'[9] 'Bat' can also be used to disparage lovers who flit about by night. Plautus in the *Three-shilling Day* refers to them as 'lurkers in the shadows': 'Love likes nice things. He's a despoiler, and a perverter of men / Who hang about in shady places.'[10]

37 **In folle offerre**
    Proffer in a purse

In the *Pandects*, book thirty-five, title 'On conditions and particularizations,' chapter 'When a slave,' Callistratus writes:

* * * * *

6 Terence *Phormio* 35–8; Davus and Geta are two slave characters in the play.
7 See above n1.
8 See A. Alciati, *Emblemata* 62 *Aliud* (Padua 1621), which contains similar material.
9 See above n4.
10 Plautus *Trinummus* 240

37 Developed from Alciati *De verborum significatione* IV page 87; see *Adagia* IV vii 75n (332 above) and iv ix 36 n2 (443 above). Added in *1533*

It is our opinion that the condition is not simply one of giving something or doing something, but is a condition of mixed content. For if he offers the rest 'in a purse,' he will in no way be free. For the testator did not intend this, but meant him to present his accounts as a slave usually does, that is, to present them first of all so that they can be read, and secondly in a manner that allows the figures to be checked, so that it is possible to see whether the calculations have been correctly recorded or not and the credits properly entered.[1]

It looks as if the phrase 'in a purse' means 'not examined, not explained, unclear,' like someone supplying documents and money concealed in a bag.

38 Malus choraules, bonus symphoniacus
Bad accompanist, great chorister

In a letter to Aurelianus (and you will find the words cited in the *Decretum* Cause 16, Question 1, canon beginning, 'I have read your letter'),[1] Augustine quotes the popular saying, 'Bad accompanist, great chorister.' This refers to someone who is despised in his original calling, but later on proceeds to a higher one and comes to be highly thought of, for example, a bad poet becoming a distinguished doctor. Augustine actually says, 'A grievous wrong is done to the order of clergy if deserters from the monasteries are to be enrolled in the ranks of the secular clergy, since it is our practice to receive into the clergy only the best and most highly regarded of those who actually abide steadfastly in their monasteries; unless maybe the same ordinary folk who say, "Bad accompanist, great chorister," are also to laugh at us and say, "Bad monk, great cleric."'[2] The idea seems to come from Cicero, who says in his speech in defence of Murena, 'I get the impression that at the outset they saw this as much more desirable, but when they

* * * * *

1 *Digest* (*Pandects*) 35.1.82; see *Adagia* IV ix 1n, 419 above.

38 Quoted in Alciati *De verborum significatione* IV page 88; see *Adagia* IV vii 75n (332 above). Added in *1533*. Otto 383, 207. Cf *Adagia* II iii 44 Let him be a flute-player who could not play the lyre.

1 *Decretum* (ie *Corpus Iuris Canonici* pt 1) 2. Cause 16, Question 1, canon 36; see *Adagia* IV viii 25 n2, 371 above.

2 Augustine *Letters* 60.1 (PL 33 228, CSEL 34 221) to Pope Aurelius

could not achieve a high enough standard, they settled for the other thing instead. Among Greek musicians, we find that pipe-players are those who were unable to master the lyre. Likewise, we observe quite a number of failed orators who have taken to jurisprudence.'[3]

39 **Nutu atque renutu**
By a nod or shake of the head

To indicate that someone has supreme power, we say that everything happens according to a nod or shake of his head. It's a great thing to get what you want done by a mere word, but it's even more to achieve it 'By a nod or shake of the head.' Cicero, in the third part of his attack on Verres, writes, 'Unless it is ready there at your nod, unless it submits to your lust and greed . . .'[1] Again, speaking in defence of Caecina: 'Can any more incontrovertible charge be brought against anyone than a charge which he doesn't attempt to refute even by a shake of his head?'[2] Again, attacking Rullus: 'that all should still pay sums of money over to you on the nod.'[3] Again, in the eleventh book of his *Letters to Friends*: 'The king is dead, but we still observe the king's every nod.'[4] Again, in the first letter in book thirteen: 'He does not doubt that I could with a mere nod get you to agree to this.'[5] In the same book, writing to the propraetor Silius: 'with the result that you can get whatever you want done with a mere nod, with the full cooperation of the Greeks.'[6] Pliny makes it clear in the first book of his *Letters*, writing to Octavius Rufus, that the phrase originates with Homer, who represents Jove granting or rejecting the prayers of men 'with a mere nod.' To quote what Pliny says: 'See what a pinnacle you have set me on, when you attribute to me the same power and dominion that Homer attributes to Jupiter Great-

* * * * *

3 Cicero *Pro L. Murena* 13.29; this material was used earlier, in *Adagia* II iii 44 (see introductory note).

39 We now have another run of Ciceronian material (*Adagia* IV ix 39–53), much of it derived from Cicero's speeches, especially the *Verrine Orations*.
1 Cicero *Verrines* 2.1.31.78
2 Cicero *Pro A. Caecina* 10.29
3 Cicero *De lege agraria* 2.36.98
4 Cicero *Ad familiares* 12.1.1 (not book 11)
5 Cicero *Ad familiares* 13.1.5
6 Cicero *Ad familiares* 13.65.1

est and Best,[7] saying "Part of his prayer did the Father grant him, / At the other he shook his head." For I too can respond to your entreaty with a similar nod or shake of my head.'[8]

40 Ne bestiae quidem ferre possent
Not even wild beasts could stand it

Cicero uses an exaggerated expression of a proverbial nature in the fifth part of his attack on Verres: 'More than that, the stench emanating from Apronius' mouth and person, so revolting that not even wild beasts, as they say, could stand it, he alone found sweet and pleasant.'[1] This is like the line we discussed earlier, 'Balbinus loves the polyp that he sees on Agne's nose.'[2] Cicero again, in his third invective directed against Catiline: 'Those times inflicted such searing pain that now wild beasts, it seems to me, could not endure such things, let alone men.'[3] He has a variation on this idea in book one of his *Letters to Atticus*, the one that begins 'You ask me . . .': 'a thing which not only men but the very cattle know to be a fact.'[4]

41 Cossi
Grubs

In times past people with creases in their flesh were popularly called by the insulting term 'grubs,' from their similarity to a sort of worm living in stumps of wood. These creatures have natural creases to enable them to draw themselves up and stretch out again. Pliny mentions these grubs in several places, for example, book eleven, chapter thirty-three, and book thirty, chapter thirteen. In book seventeen, chapter twenty-four, he tells us that larger specimens were in early times used for food and even considered

* * * * *

7 The cult title by which the Romans referred to their supreme deity
8 Pliny *Letters* 1.7.1, citing Homer *Iliad* 16.250

40 Cicero (see nn1 and 3). Otto 251. Added in *1533*
1 Cicero *Verrines* 2.3.9.23
2 *Adagia* I ii 15 What is one's own is beautiful, quoting Horace *Satires* 1.3.39–40
3 Cicero *Catilinarians* 2.9.20 (not 3)
4 Cicero *Ad Atticum* 1.16.6

41 Pompeius Festus (see n4) and Pliny (n1). Added in *1533*

a delicacy.[1] Jerome also mentions this in book two of his *Against Jovinianus*.[2] The Greek word προφερεῖς 'premature' is used for young people who look far older than their years.[3] The information about the word *cossi* comes from Festus Pompeius.[4]

42 Menia columna
The Maenian Column

We speak of someone being 'out of the gutter' or 'off the block' to mean 'utterly contemptible.' We find a similar idea in Cicero, who writes, in the first part of his attack on Verres, 'Do you think me so bereft of friends that I have to have someone to sign the accusation allocated to me, not from among the gentlemen I have brought with me, but out of the general populace? And are you so short of people to prosecute that you have to try to take this case away from me, instead of finding guilty persons of your own sort to prosecute out of the crowd at the Maenian Column?'[1] Asconius Pedianus tells us that petty criminals, such as thieves or bad slaves, were tried before the *triumviri capitales* at Maenius' Column. The landmark got its name from one Maenius, who 'sold his house to the censors, Cato and Flaccus, so that the site could be used for a basilica, but reserved to himself the right of constructing a column with a roof and projecting wooden balconies, from which he and his posterity could watch the gladiatorial games, which even then were still laid on in the forum.'[2] This is why it was called Maenius'

* * * * *

1 Pliny *Naturalis historia* 11.113; 30.115; 17.220
2 Jerome *Adversus Iovinianum* 2.7 PL 23 334
3 See Stobaeus 101.4 Gaisford (quoting Aristoxenus), meaning 'precious.'
4 Pompeius Festus 36.11–12 Lindsay

42 Cicero (see n1). Otto 1006. Added in 1533. For 'out of the gutter,' 'off the block' see Cicero *Pro L. Murena* 6.13, *In Pisonem* 5.35; *Adagia* III i 67 Bought off the block.

1 Cicero *Divinatio in Quintum Caecilium* 16.50. This speech dealt with the preliminary question of who was to speak for the prosecution in the Verres case, whether Cicero himself or Quintus Metellus Caecilius Creticus, a noble who supported Verres for political reasons.

2 Quintus Asconius Pedianus (AD 3–88) wrote commentaries (which have survived only in part) on some of Cicero's speeches. That dealing with the Verrine speeches is now held to be a later compilation and not by Asconius. See

Column. Only the lowest of court hacks were brought in to act in the sort of cases that were tried there.

43 Circeo poculo
Circean cup

I have already written about Circe's magic wand.[1] Cicero used a similar phrase, 'Circean cup,' when talking about someone suddenly transformed. In the first part of his attack on Verres, he says, 'But all of a sudden, in a flash, as if by some Circean cup, he turned from being a man into a Verres; he became himself again, and reverted to his normal character.'[2] We have a play on words concealed here: 'Verres' has a double meaning, since *verres*, in addition to being a personal name, is also the word for an uncastrated hog.[3]

44 Ex sinu illius
His bosom friend

We say that someone is so-and-so's 'bosom friend' to mean that they are on the closest possible terms. Cicero writes, in the third part of his attack on Verres, 'The moment Verres set foot in the province, he sent a letter to Messana, summoned Dio to appear, and put in some of his bosom pals to act as accusers and make a false declaration that the inheritance in question had been forfeited to the Venus of Mount Eryx.'[1] Cicero again, in the fourth part: 'Do you think this sum was large enough, this sum demanded in the name of the goddess of love by this man who was so devoted to her service,

* * * * *

Adagia I v 56:12n CWE 31 434. Erasmus quotes the text of the commentary on Cicero's speech (see n1 above) verbatim.

43 Cicero (see n2). Otto 390. Added in *1533*
  1 *Adagia* I viii 30 Out of one mouth to blow hot and cold
  2 Cicero *Divinatio in Quintum Caecilium* 17.57
  3 The joke is that the sorceress Circe, by her potions and magic wand, turned men into pigs; here Verres, who has been acting like a human being for once, turns back into Verres (*verres* is Latin for 'hog').

44 Cicero (see nn1 and 3). Added in *1533*
  1 Cicero *Verrines* 2.1.10.27

who tore himself from Chelidon's bosom to go to his province?'[2] Again, in his second speech attacking Catiline, Cicero says, 'The last group are not merely by their numbers but in their type and their manner of life Catiline's specials, recruited by him, his closest associates, friends of his bosom.'[3] Plutarch uses a similar phrase in his *Life of Cato of Utica*: 'Gabinius Paulus, ἐκ τῶν Πομπηίου κόλπων "one of Pompey's bosom friends."'[4] I cited this passage before, when discussing the proverb 'To rejoice in one's bosom' but the sense of that is somewhat different.[5] I have already discussed 'One of that gang.'[6] Cicero several times uses the word *gregales* 'members of the same company' for 'cronies in the same group.'[7]

45 Circumpedes
Foot-servants

Those who attend a person closely and stand about him ready to do his will are said to be 'about his feet,' that is, 'Foot-servants.' Cicero, in the third part of his attack on Verres, writes, 'But the foot-servants who were good-looking and educated, he said were his own, that he had bought them.'[1] So Cicero used this phrase *circumpedes* for servants in a long-standing close relationship, just as we call our domestic servants 'handmaids' and 'footmen.'

46 Ne tempestas quidem nocere potest
Not even a storm can harm

Cicero used this apparently proverbial expression in the fifth part of his attack on Verres, with reference to people who owned nothing, who were quite without possessions: 'Don't expect to hear anything from the other

* * * * *

2 Cicero *Verrines* 2.2.9.24; Chelidon was Verres' mistress in Rome.
3 Cicero *Catilinarians* 2.10.22
4 Plutarch *Cato* 33.4
5 *Adagia* I iii 13 To rejoice in one's own bosom
6 *Adagia* III vi 86 He is from that flock
7 Eg Cicero *De domo sua* 28.75; *De haruspicum responso* 25.53; *Pro P. Sestio* 52.111

45 Cicero (see n1). Added in *1533*
1 Cicero *Verrines* 2.1.36.92

46 Cicero (see n1). Added in *1533*

inhabitants of Leontini, as not even storms could damage their farms, let alone Apronius. They suffered no misfortune – in fact, in all those rampagings and plunderings of the boorish Apronius, they were at an advantage and came off well.'[1] There is a joke here – the name Apronius suggests the Calydonian Boar.[2] People who have possessions or own land or go to sea can be harmed by a storm. Someone whom 'no storm can harm' neither owns land, like a farmer, nor has cargoes on shipboard, like a merchant.

47 Ballio
Ballio

Some people have been so remarkably wicked that their names have become proverbial. Sometimes they are real people, sometimes characters in comedies. Cicero several times refers to a certain Gaius Fannius Chaerea in his speeches as 'Ballio,' for example, in his speech defending the actor Roscius: 'He always has his hair and eyebrows shaved off, so that no one can say there is "even a hair"[1] of a good man on him. Roscius has often portrayed this character well on the stage, but doesn't get the thanks for this service that he deserves. When he acts Ballio, that scoundrelly, lying pimp, he is acting Chaerea. That hateful, foul, polluted character in the play becomes alive and real in Chaerea's nature, manners, activities.'[2] Later on in the same speech, Cicero says, 'Upon my word, Fannius, you would hardly dare to ask such a thing of Ballio and his like, nor would you be likely to get it.'[3] Ballio is a character in Plautus' *Pseudolus*, a vicious, grasping, unprincipled pimp. The name has been invented on the basis of Greek βάλλειν 'to hit,' because a pimp is always on the look-out for some prey or other; or

* * * * *

1 Cicero *Verrines* 2.3.46.109. The point Cicero is making is that the inhabitants of Leontini did not own any farms in the surrounding countryside and so could not be plundered.
2 This was a huge boar (*aper*), sent by the goddess Diana to devastate the countryside round Calydon. It was killed in the famous hunt, described, eg, in Ovid *Metamorphoses* 8.260–424.

47 Cicero (see nn2 and 3). Added in 1533
1 See *Adagia* i viii 4 I count it not worth a hair.
2 Cicero *Pro Q. Roscio comoedo* 7.20
3 Cicero *Pro Q. Roscio comoedo* 17.50

of Greek βαλλίζω 'to jump about, have a ball,'[4] because he is the impresario of licentiousness and wild activities.

48 Ostiatim
Seriatim, in detail

Cicero employs a neat and apparently well-established usage when he uses *Ostiatim* 'From door to door,' with the meaning 'one by one, in detail, specifically.' This is found in the sixth part of his attack on Verres: 'Don't expect me to go through this accusation *ostiatim* "in detail": a bowl filched from Aeschylus, an inhabitant of Tyndaris; a plate from Thrason, also of Tyndaris, etc.'[1] It will be even nicer if the word is used in an intellectual context, if for example someone looking for proof texts and corroborative statements in separate books or chapters of various authorities is said to do so *ostiatim* 'knocking on successive doors.' Cicero uses a comparable Greek expression κατὰ λεπτόν, when writing to Atticus in the letter which begins, 'I've received several letters from you.' He says, 'Don't ask κατὰ λεπτόν "in detail" about the situation. The whole thing has got to such a state that there is no hope.'[2]

49 Domi nobilis
A man of standing in his locality

Cicero on several occasions uses the phrase 'A man of standing in his locality' of a man who is not merely rich and influential but a member of a family of quality. In the third part of his attack on Verres, he writes, 'He had a fire made from damp green wood in an enclosed space and there subjected to the torture of suffocation from breathing in smoke and left more dead than alive a man of free birth and of considerable standing in the area, an associate and recognized friend of the Roman people.'[1] Again, in the fourth part: 'There was a certain Sopater from the town of Halicyae, a rich and

* * * * *

4 This etymology seems to be Erasmus' own idea. He probably derived it from Athenaeus 8.362A–C, where it is said to be a word for wild dancing.

48 Cicero (see n1). Added in *1533*
1 Cicero *Verrines* 2.4.22.48
2 Cicero *Ad Atticum* 2.18.12

49 Cicero (see nn1, 3, and 4). Added in *1533*
1 Cicero *Verrines* 2.1.17.45

highly respected person in his local area ...'[2] Again, in the fifth part: 'So
when Philenus of Herbita, a wise and eloquent man, a person of standing
in the area ...'[3] Again, in his speech defending Cluentius: 'These letters
Aulus Aurius, a courageous and enterprising man, much respected in the
neighbourhood ...'[4] Writing to his brother Quintus in a letter in book two,
he recommends one Marcus Orfius, a Roman knight, whom he describes as
a man 'of some consequence on his home territory and influential in wider
circles as well.'[5] The phrase will fit anyone who is great and distinguished
by reason of his native qualities.

50 **Obtorto collo**
With one's neck in a noose, by the throat

Anyone who is subject to violent compulsion is said to be dragged off 'With
his neck in a noose.' Cicero writes, in the sixth part of his attack on Verres,
'That was the origin of the "Festival of Verres." During the celebratory party,
he had Sextus Cominius dragged in, he tried to throw a goblet at him and
then ordered him to be haled off to the chains and darkness of prison with
his neck in a noose.'[1] Cicero again, speaking in defence of Cluentius: 'So
he at once set off after him and dragged him back to court in a headlock,
so that he could deliver the rest of his oratorical tour de force.'[2] Plautus
had a variant on this phrase in the *Amphitryo*, *obstricto collo*: 'For that reason
I'll thrash you and wring your neck.'[3] And again in the same play: 'Why
don't I grab Amphitryo by the throat and drag him off?'[4] Plautus again,
in the *Carthaginian*: 'Why don't I take myself off to the devil / Before I'm
haled off by the throat to face the magistrate?'[5] Plautus, in the *Rope*: 'Say

* * * * *

2 Cicero *Verrines* 2.3.34.80
3 Cicero *Verrines* 2.2.28.68
4 Cicero *Pro A. Cluentio* 8.23
5 Cicero *Ad Quintum fratrem* 2.12.3

50 Cicero (see nn1–2) and Plautus (see nn5–7). Otto 408. Cf *Adagia* II i 19 To lead
one by the nose. Added in *1533*
1 Cicero *Verrines* 2.4.10.24
2 Cicero *Pro A. Cluentio* 21.59.
3 Plautus *Amphitryo* 139 of the spurious supplement, for which see *Adagia* IV
viii 16 n2 (364 above).
4 Plautus *Amphitryo* 953
5 Plautus *Poenulus* 789–90

quick now, would you rather be hauled off / With your neck in a noose, or dragged off?'[6] And a little later: 'Help me, Charmides! I'm being dragged off with my neck in a noose.'[7]

51 Canes venatici
Hunting dogs

Keen huntsmen have dogs which are sent on ahead. These track down the prey by scent and reveal its whereabouts by baying. I have already discussed the Corycaeans.[1] In the sixth part of his attack on Verres, Cicero writes, 'He laid on one of his "dogs" to state that he intended to arraign Diodorus of Malta on a capital charge.'[2] A little further on: 'As soon as he arrived in a town anywhere, those Cibyrian hounds of his were unleashed, and they tracked down and investigated everything.'[3] He calls the two brothers 'Cibyrian hounds' because in his depredations Verres employed their eyes, but used his own hands. Breeds of dog are usually named after the area they come from, for example, Maltese. A little earlier Cicero writes, 'After they arrived there, they so wonderfully sniffed out and tracked down everything – you'd have said they were hunting dogs – that . . .'[4]

52 Mercennarium praeconium
Self-interested commendation

Praises which are not heartfelt but offered by way of flattery to gain some advantage are called by Cicero 'Self-interested commendation.' This is in

* * * * *

6 Plautus *Rudens* 852–3
7 Plautus *Rudens* 867–8

51 Cicero (see n4). Added in 1533
1 See *Adagia* I ii 44 A Corycaean was listening. The people living round Mt Corycus were notorious eavesdroppers, who listened to merchants' talk and betrayed them to pirates.
2 Cicero *Verrines* 2.4.19.40
3 Cicero *Verrines* 2.4.21.47
4 Cicero *Verrines* 2.4.13.31

52 Brassicanus no 27 *Chorus domesticus* 'A home-grown chorus,' mentioning the example from Cicero (see nn1–2)

the third attack on Verres: 'After you had tricked out that particular clause with so much verbiage, so much self-interested commendation, did any praetor who ever came after you reproduce that wording?'[1] I am well aware that widely used printed texts here read *prooemium* 'preamble' rather than *praeconium* 'commendation,' but whether rightly or no, scholars may judge.[2]

53 Manus pretium
Labour costs, fee

Cicero, in the third attack on Verres: 'A certain amount of marble had to be cut and prepared, using the proper tools. No stone, no timber, was transported to the site. There was nothing more involved in the job than the wages of a few masons, the fee, the tools.'[1] Cicero seems to use the phrase *manus pretium* for payments made not for materials but as a fee to the architect for his professional skills. Cicero again, in his attack on Piso: 'It was not by a senate that begged and coerced you but by a reluctant senate under duress, not with the enthusiastic support of the Roman people but by a vote in which not a single free-born man participated, that that province was handed over to you as a fee for overturning, nay utterly destroying, the state.'[2] Gaius, 'On the meaning of terms,' in the section beginning, 'Woman': 'Since there is often more in the paid-for workmanship than in the actual article.' This follows on from: 'As Sabinus says, a view in which Pedius concurs, property is considered lost when the substance remains but the form is changed; accordingly, if property is damaged or altered, it is treated as lost, since . . .'[3] This can be applied to those who by their instruction either mould their pupils to virtue or change them for the worse.

* * * * *

1 *Cicero Verrines* 2.1.43.111
2 The OCT edition of Cicero reads *prooemium* for *praeconium*. Brassicanus (see *Adagia* IV iii 86 n2, 52 above) uses the same passage in no 27 *Chorus domesticus,* also reading *praeconium*.

53 Inspired by the brief treatment in Alciati *De verborum significatione* IV page 86 (see *Adagia* IV vii 75n, and IV ix 36 n2, 332 and 443 above). Added in *1533*
1 Cicero *Verrines* 2.1.56.147
2 Cicero *In L. Pisonem* 24.57
3 Ulpian (not Gaius) at *Digest* 50.16.13.1 (see *Adagia* IV ix 1n, 419 above)

54 Decumanum
Every tenth one

In times past, people used phrases like 'the tenth egg,' 'the tenth wave,' to mean 'huge,' because farmers and sailors observed that every tenth egg laid was bigger than the previous nine and every tenth wave was more powerful than the ones preceding it. So Ovid writes:

> The onslaught of the tenth wave comes crashing
> Down upon the ship.[1]

Consequently, anything huge came to be called 'tenth,' for example Lucilius' phrase: 'tenth sturgeon,' that is, 'monstrous.'[2]

55 Palmarium facinus
A crowning deed

Palmarium facinus, A deed that takes the palm, a crowning achievement, a phrase equivalent to 'special, worth a triumph,' is used by Terence in the *Eunuch*: 'Then there's this second thing, which I see as my crowning deed.'[1] Cicero uses *palmae* 'palms of victory,' that is, 'prize achievement' to mean the same thing, for example, in his speech in defence of Sextus Roscius of Ameria: 'If he presents himself as a witness, which is what I hear they have arranged between them, he will learn of other prize achievements on his part.'[2] Again, in his eleventh *Philippic* oration: 'It is difficult, even for a gladiator, to carry off the palm for the sixth time in Rome; but that was the judges' fault, not mine.'[3] Plautus uses *palma* 'prize' with a pejorative meaning in the *Haunted House*: a young man who had previously behaved in a most exem-

* * * * *

54 Some of this material is to be found in Pompeius Festus 62.27–9 Lindsay (*Decumana ova*), but it is also discussed at greater length by Poliziano in chapter 85 of his *Miscellanea*. Added in *1533*
1 Ovid *Metamorphoses* 11.530
2 See *Adagia* IV ix 16 n6 (429 above). The line is quoted by Cicero *De finibus* 2.8.24.

55 Terence (see n1). Added in *1533*
1 Terence *Eunuchus* 929–30
2 Cicero *Pro S. Roscio Amerino* 30.84
3 Cicero *Philippics* 11.5.11, referring to his failure to get Gaius Julius Caesar Vopiscus acquitted a sixth time

plary manner had taken to behaving in a quite disgraceful way and a character in the play remarks, 'Now he takes the prize for quite the opposite thing.'[4]

56 Commovere sacra
To stir the holy objects

In *Pseudolus* Plautus uses the phrase *Commovere sacra* 'To stir the holy objects'
to mean 'to try the last line of defence.'[1] When the situation is desperate,
men flee to the protection of the gods, hence this phrase. Nowadays in
Paris, for example, when the Seine rises and overflows its banks, the bones
of Sainte Geneviève are carried from the church at Montaigu down to the
cathedral of Notre Dame.[2] It's possible that, instead of *sacra*, the phrase here
should read *commovere saga* 'to shake out the soldiers' capes,' meaning 'to
take to arms,' a usage I discussed earlier.[3] I suggest this because the next
line in Plautus says, 'You know how I can create quite a tidy commotion,'
and the character then goes on to make a mock declaration of war:

> Now let no one say he was not notified.
> To all able-bodied persons here present in this assembly,
> To all the people, to all friends, to all that know me,
> I make this proclamation – this day they must
> Beware of me and trust me not.[4]

And the speaker, a slave, continues to spout war-talk in the next section of
the play.

* * * * *

4 Plautus *Mostellaria* 32

56 Plautus (see n1). Added in 1533
1 Plautus *Pseudolus* 109–10
2 Erasmus witnessed such a ceremony in Paris on January 12th, 1497, when
the Seine overflowed its banks after three months of continuous rain. See Ep
50 (CWE 1 105). The shrine of Ste Geneviève was originally preserved in the
church of the Holy Apostles, built by King Clovis on the highest point of the
Left Bank, known as Montagne Ste Geneviève. (The eighteenth-century church
of Ste Geneviève is now known as the Pantheon.) The Collège de Montaigu,
which Erasmus entered when he first went to Paris in 1495, was opposite the
abbey of Ste Geneviève.
3 *Adagia* IV viii 10 On with the soldier's cape (358 above)
4 Plautus *Pseudolus* 125–8

57 Quasi dies dicta sit
As if waiting for one's case to come to trial

At one time people awaiting trial would go about long-faced and unkempt, like people in mourning, hoping to stir pity in the hearts of the judges.[1] Hence the line in Plautus' *Comedy of Asses*:

> You look as doleful as if you're waiting
> For your case to come to trial.[2]

58 Βεργαίζειν
To romance

Stephanus tells us that Ἱβέργη was a town in Thrace, or, according to Strabo, a village.'[1] The bad character of the inhabitants became proverbial, so that people who never said anything reasonable were said Βεργαίζειν 'To romance.' The Thracians as a whole were spoken ill of on many counts, but mainly for their belligerence and treachery.[2] Polymnestor was a Thracian – he was the man who 'joined the winning side, murdered Polydorus, and thus by violence secured the gold.'[3]

59 Summo pede
Dip the toes

Ἄκρῳ ποδί, Dip the toes, is the same kind of expression as 'Touch with the

* * * * *

57 Plautus (see n2). Added in *1533*
  1 Cf *Adagia* IV ix 78 (470 below).
  2 Plautus *Asinaria* 838

58 Brassicanus no 13, with the same reference to Stephanus of Byzantium (see n1). For Brassicanus see *Adagia* IV iii 86 n2 (52 above). Added in *1533*
  1 Stephanus of Byzantium sub Βέργη. Strabo *Geographica* 7 fragment 30 (Loeb)
  2 Cf *Adagia* IV viii 52 To play Thracian (389 above).
  3 A paraphrase of Virgil *Aeneid* 3.54–5, though the name of the treacherous Thracian king is supplied from Euripides *Hecuba*. Erasmus had published a translation of this play, together with Euripides *Iphigenia in Aulide*, in 1506.

59 Plato (see n2). Added in *1533*

finger-tips.'[1] A person is said to have not 'dipped his toes' into a subject,
when he has never entered into it, never even touched the threshold. The
Greek phrase is found in Plato's *Laches* and I have, I think, already quoted
it elsewhere.[2]

60 Usurae nauticae
Bottomry interest

In the Jurisconsults, a high rate of interest, such as twelve percent per an-
num, is called 'bottomry interest.' Businessmen often borrow a capital sum
to finance a venture. Because a merchant-venturer entrusts himself and all
he has to the winds and waves, the money-lenders demanded a higher rate
of interest. Sometimes the merchants took out the loan in one city and arranged to repay it in another, like borrowing money in Venice to be repaid
in Bruges. Any arrangement of this sort which involves a risk to both parties
is called in Greek ἀμφοτερόπλους. A general loan of this kind was generally
called δάνειον ναυτικόν 'a shipping or bottomry loan,' a phrase which occurs
in Demosthenes' speech against Dionysiodorus. It is also called ἔκδοσις 'an
out-loan' (a term which Demosthenes uses in his speech against Aphobus),
because it is lent on ships and goods going abroad.[1] There is a title on bottomry interest in book twenty-two of the *Pandects* – Modestinus calls the
sum involved 'a transmarine loan.' Paulus speaks of 'maritime interest,' and

* * * * *

1 See *Adagia* I ix 94; also IV ix 73 With the tips of two fingers (467 below).
2 Plato *Laches* 183B, quoted earlier in *Adagia* IV iii 66 To walk on tiptoe (39 above)

60 Suggested by Alciati *De verborum significatione* IV page 87 (see *Adagia* IV vii
75n and iv ix 36 n2, 332 and 443 above), and expanded with material from
Harpocration. Added in *1533*
1 The material from 'Sometimes the merchants' to 'going abroad' is based on
Harpocration (1.29.7 and 107.10 Dindorf), which quotes Demosthenes *Adversus Dionysiodorum* 56.6 and *Adversus Aphobum* 27.11 and 29.35. The term
ἀμφοτερόπλους really means 'covering both the outward and the inward journey.' Erasmus has been misled by the entry in Harpocration.
Aldus published the *editio princeps* of Harpocration's *Lexicon in decem oratores
Atticos* in 1503, together with scholia to Demosthenes. The editor incorporated
into the text glosses to Harpocration found in the *Suda* (Suidas), which were
thus easily available to Erasmus, though he seems to have had access to the
Suda in any case. These insertions were removed by Dindorf in his edition.

so do others.[2] The same title occurs in book four of the *Codex*.[3] As I am only explaining an adage, I need not go into further detail. Anyone who wants more information can consult the sources just mentioned.

61 Philosophari
Philosophizing

The Greek word Φιλοσοφεῖν 'Philosophize' or 'moralize' is used of people who utter weighty and sententious remarks. We find it so used several times in Plautus. The meaning was then extended to refer to any strongly-felt and serious concern. We find it with this meaning in Isocrates' speech *On the Peace*, and Menander writes in the *Thrasyleon*, 'This is all his philosophy, to bring about this match.'[1] Chrysostom often uses 'philosophize' to mean keeping the emotions under control and facing up to misfortune with a mind unmoved, and he calls such discipline of the spirit 'philosophy.' St Basil and Gregory of Nazianzus also like using the words in this way. Cicero writes in the second book of his letters to Atticus, 'But why do I bother with all this? – I want to have done with it and devote myself wholeheartedly and without distraction to philosophizing.'[2] And, writing to Atticus again: 'But one has to philosophize'[3] – meaning that one must endure things with equanimity. (Horace says in similar vein, 'So I wrap my virtue round me.')[4] Cicero uses the word in the same way in quite a number of places, for example, in the fourth book of letters: 'I can exercise my philosophizing on you,'[5] meaning, 'I can find such pleasure in your friendship that I can bravely make light of everything else.' The word is found several times in

* * * * *

See Dindorf 1 xi. Erasmus uses Harpocration quite extensively but without acknowledgment, except in *Adagia* v i 81 All-spiny (588 below), where he is called *qui adiecit scholia in Demosthenem* 'the ancient annotator on Demosthenes.'
2 *Digest* (*Pandects*) 22.2.1 and 6. For this and the *Codex Justinianus* see *Adagia* iv ix 1n (419 above). Added in *1533*
3 *Codex Justinianus* 4.33

61 Harpocration (see n1 of immediately preceding adage). Added in *1533*
1 Taken from Harpocration (1.301.9 Dindorf), which quotes Isocrates *De pace* 16 and Menander *Thrasyleon* fragment 204 Körte-Thierfelder
2 Cicero *Ad Atticum* 2.5.2
3 Cicero *Ad Atticum* 1.16.3
4 Horace *Odes* 3.29.54–5, cited from memory
5 Cicero *Ad Atticum* 4.18.2

Plautus too, when something weighty and sententious is said, for example, in the *Prisoners*: 'All's well! He's not just telling lies now, he's moralizing!'[6]

62 Doribus Dorice loqui
Dorians may speak the Doric

Gorgo, in Theocritus' *Syracusan Women*, seems to be using a proverbial expression, when she says to a stranger who tells her and her friend to stop cooing like turtle-doves, 'Dorians, I suppose, may speak the Doric!'[1] This saying will fit people who are natural chatterboxes, or whose manner of speaking corresponds to their character and nature, if, for example, a Carthaginian speaks deceitfully,[2] or a pimp says what you expect pimps to say.[3]

63 Somnium hibernum
A winter dream

Χειμερινὸς ὄνειρος, A winter dream. This refers to a long, tedious narrative, because in winter the nights are long and so dreams go on longer as well. Lucian, in the *Dream*: 'As I was speaking, someone remarked, "Heavens! What a long dream, a real lawcourt one!" And someone else interposed, "Yes, a winter dream indeed!"'[1] By calling it a 'lawcourt' dream, the speaker meant either that two figures are involved in the argument, or that the water-clock has to run through many times before a law-suit reaches its conclusion.[2]

* * * * *

6 Plautus *Captivi* 284. For another example see Plautus *Pseudolus* 974.

62 Theocritus (see n1). Added in *1533*
1 Theocritus *Idylls* 15.93
2 For Carthaginian duplicity, see *Adagia* I viii 28 Punic faith.
3 See eg *Adagia* IV ix 90 (478 below).

63 Lucian (see n1). Added in *1533*
1 Lucian *Somnium* 17 (*The Dream* or *Lucian's Career*). Lucian relates a dream in which Sculpture and Education offer themselves as alternative careers, each making a speech in support of her claims.
2 The water-clock was a device for marking the passage of time by the flow of water from a vessel. In the lawcourt a specified number of units was allocated to speeches for prosecution and defence. See *Adagia* IV ix 70 (465 below).

64 Alios tragoedos provocat
He challenges the other tragedians

Τοὺς ἑτέρους τραγῳδοὺς ἀγωνιεῖται, He readies himself[1] to compete against the other tragedians. This comes from the speech of the sophist Lycurgus against Demades. Didymus tells us that the phrase was applied to people who collect their thoughts and prepare themselves to face the opposition.[2] It seems to originate in the contests in honour of Bacchus, in which the rivalry of the tragedians reached fever-pitch.[3]

65 Deserere vadimonium
Break bail

At one time it was reprehensible and damaging 'To break bail,' and the guarantor was exonerated only for very weighty reasons. Cicero writes in his second speech attacking Catiline, 'As for that "army," compared with our Gallic legions and the men recently enlisted by Quintus Metellus in Picene and Gallic territory, compared with the forces which we are assembling daily, I see it as utterly contemptible, an assemblage of desperate superannuated men, peasants on the rampage, penniless rustics, bankrupts, men who chose to break bail rather than miss out on joining that army.'[1] And that non-stop talker in Horace who was due to appear in court can't make up his mind whether to break bail or let Horace slip.[2] I have already

* * * * *

64 Cf *Adagia* III vi 90 He's imitating his tragic friends, where Erasmus was translating a faulty reading. Except for the last sentence, this adage is a translation of the entry in Harpocration (1.291.8 Dindorf), citing Lycurgus (fragment 17 Conomis).
1 The Greek verb is actually future tense.
2 On Didymus, see *Adagia* IV viii 87 n1 (410 above). (Didymus' explanation of the saying has been mistakenly transferred to the previous entry, *Torone*, a place name, in Apostolius 17.18.)
3 Ie the Great Dionysia at Athens, dramatic festivals for which nearly all surviving Greek drama was written

65 Cicero (see n1). Added in *1533*
1 Cicero *Catilinarians* 2.3.5
2 Horace *Satires* 1.9.36–41. Erasmus uses this same incident in *Adagia* I viii 18 Worth breaking bail for, and v ii 15 To lose one's action (605 below).

discussed 'Worth breaking bail for,' a phrase used to refer to something of the greatest importance.[3]

66 Πομπεύειν
Ribaldry

For the ancients, πομπεύειν 'processing,' came to mean 'jeering, abusing,' and πομπεῖαι 'processions' meant 'raillery.' This was because in the processions in honour of Bacchus some people sat on wagons and hurled abuse at others and were themselves assailed in turn. The following lines are cited from Menander's *Woman of Perinthos*: 'When the wagons are rolling, some mighty/ Powerful abuse is heard.'[1] I have already discussed 'Wagon-language.'[2]

67 Securim inicere
Lay the axe

People are said to 'Lay the axe' when they do serious harm and damage. Cicero, defending Lucius Murena: 'Do you realize, Servius, how you laid the axe to your candidature when you made the electorate afraid ...?' A little earlier, instead of using the word 'axe,' he spells it out more clearly with 'blow': 'And you struck the greatest blow of all to your own candidature, one which I warned you about ...'[1] Again, when defending Plancius: 'How could they more effectively lay the axe to the country ...?'[2] Cicero again, in the second book of letters to his brother Quintus: 'The independence of the people of Tenedos was chopped off short with an axe from

* * * * *

3 See n2 above.

66 A translation of the entry in Harpocration (1.253.2 Dindorf), which quotes Menander (see n1 below). Added in *1533*
1 Menander *Perinthia* (fragment 4 Körte-Thierfelder)
2 *Adagia* I vii 73

67 Brassicanus no 65, which already has the examples from Cicero (nn1 and 2) and Plautus *Mostellaria* (n5); for Brassicanus see *Adagia* IV iii 86 n2 (52 above). Otto 469. Added in *1533*
1 Cicero *Pro L. Murena* 24.48; 23.48
2 Cicero *Pro Cn. Plancio* 29.70

Tenedos.'³ Demosthenes used to call Phocion 'the pruning knife of his arguments.'⁴ Plautus often uses figurative phrases like 'hurl the spear, throw the javelin, shoot the arrow.'⁵ Cicero spoke of 'every weapon being trained on the country' in his speech on the consular provinces.⁶

68 Sale nihil utilius
Nothing more beneficial than salt

I find that scholars treat the following as a maxim: 'Nothing is more beneficial to the human body than salt and sun.'¹ Even today we put salt on all our food, and doctors in the past set great store by sunshine. The Jews were forbidden to offer any sacrifice without salt.²

69 Apud equum et virginem
At 'The Horse and Girl'

In his speech against Timarchus, Aeschines tells us that there lived a man at Athens so strict that when his daughter behaved shamelessly and lost her virginity before marriage, he took her away to a lonely place and there shut her up with a horse and left her to die of hunger. He tells us that in his time the foundation of the building was still there, and was called from the incident Παρ᾽ ἵππον καὶ κόρην 'At "The Horse and Girl."'¹ The phrase can be used to signal some instance of excessive severity.

* * * * *

3 Cicero *Ad Quintum fratrem* 2.9.2. See *Adagia* IV i 6 A man of Tenedos and I ix 29 An axe from Tenedos. This latter meant a short, sharp, summary decision.
4 See Plutarch *Demosthenes* 10.4, *Phocion* 5.4.
5 Eg Plautus *Pseudolus* 407; *Epidicus* 690; *Mostellaria* 570; *Poenulus* 919
6 Cicero *De provinciis consularibus* 9.23

68 Pliny (see n1). Otto 1570. Added in *1533*
  1 The idea that this is a maxim is based on Pliny *Naturalis historia* 31.102, where Pliny remarks 'herein is especially applicable the saying . . .'
  2 Lev 2.13: 'with all your offerings you shall offer salt.'

69 There are a number of extracts from Aeschines' speeches in *Adagia* IV ix (and a few in IV x and v i). It is clear that Erasmus quotes directly from the text of Aeschines and not only from secondary sources. Added in *1533*
  1 Aeschines 1.182

70 Ad vinum diserti
Orators over the bottle

In his speech defending Caelius, Cicero applies the phrase 'Orators over the bottle' to men who are poor speakers on serious issues but find plenty to say over their cups where such eloquence is unnecessary: 'who will never extricate themselves if they once get into that spot. They are really witty and great conversationalists at parties, over the bottle they quite often become real orators – but the dining-room is one thing, the courts are another.'[1] Horace has a well-known line: 'Was ever any man not made more eloquent / By the fructifying cup?'[2] Cicero's passage also hints at the ancient practice of using water to measure the time allocated to the conduct of the case. The water was divided into three portions and poured into water-clocks, one portion being allocated to the prosecution, one to the defence, one to the judge. Those who are 'Orators over the bottle' become practically dumb 'over the water.'

71 Sicco iunco
With a dry rush

We find what appears to be a proverbial expression in Aeschines' speech *On the False Legation*: Ὁλοσχοίνῳ ἀβρόχῳ 'With a dry rush or rope.' He says, 'Now he declared that he had well-springs of argument and would say such things concerning our rights over Amphipolis and the origin of the war, that he would sew up Philip's mouth with a dry rush.'[1] A thing can be called ἄβροχος either because it is dry and not full of moisture or because it is free

* * * * *

70 Cicero (see n1). Added in *1533*

1 Cicero *Pro M. Caelio* 28.67

2 Horace *Epistles* 1.5.19. Erasmus added this example in *1515* to *Adagia* II vi 2 Water drinkers are not powerful thinkers.

71 From Harpocration (1.221.4 Dindorf), supplemented by Hesychius (see n3); but see *Adagia* v i 81 All-spiny (Ὀλοέχινος, 588 below) where Erasmus returns to the subject. Added in *1533*

1 Aeschines 2.21; the reference is given by Harpocration, but Erasmus has added the Greek text. The phrase 'with a dry rush' has been taken to mean 'with no trouble,' not even needing to be soaked. See LSJ sub ὁλόσχοινος.

from knots.[2] For rushes both like moist conditions and are sometimes used to weave ropes. Hesychius tells us that ὁλόσχοινος is the same as ὀξύσχοινος 'the sea club-rush.' He adds ὁλότροχος 'turnable,' and then περιφερὴς λίθος 'a rounded stone that rolls easily.'[3] So the learned reader may well ask himself whether he might not interpret ὁλόσχοινος ἄβροχος as 'salty words,' salty, not with sea-water, but with sharp and telling arguments. There is even a proverbial saying lurking in the phrase 'well-springs of argument,' if it means 'an abundant supply.' This metaphorical use of πηγή 'well-spring' occurs often in Chrysostom.[4]

72 Supercilium salit
My eyebrow twitches

Whenever some happy expectation tickles our fancy, we can say that 'our eyebrow twitches.' In Plautus' play *Pseudolus* (so called after its chief character), the young man in love asks where the money is going to come from, and Pseudolus replies, 'From where it comes I've no idea. / I only know that come it will, my eyebrow twitches so.'[1] This saying arises from the superstitious belief held by many ordinary people, who interpret physical sensations as a sign of what is going to come, if, for example, one has an unexplained itch somewhere, if one's right eye twitches, if there is a ringing sound in one's right ear. I am well aware that the text of Plautus can be read differently, but the sense of the passage and the requirements of

* * * * *

2 To understand Erasmus' proposed etymologies, it is necessary to supply the Greek words which he fails to mention, ie βρόχη 'moisture' or βρόχος 'slip-knot,' either word combined with privative ἀ- 'without.'

3 Hesychius O 632. Erasmus includes what is actually the next entry in alphabetical order. He seems to think the two entries belong together.

4 Chrysostom *Homilia cum fuit presbyter ordinatus* PG 48.693; *Homilia in Sanctum Bassum* PG 50.719; *Homilia* XL *in Matthaeum* PG 58.791. Erasmus had been working on some sermons of Chrysostom for an edition and translation which appeared in 1533 (see Ep 2774), but he had had a long acquaintance with various texts of that author.

72 *Collectanea* no 231. Plautus (see n1). Otto 1713; Suringar 156. Added in *1533*

1 Plautus *Pseudolus* 103–7, already quoted in *Adagia* II iv 37 My right eye twitches, which anticipates much of this

the metre show that the way I wrote it above must be correct. The metre is iambic senarii, and the lines should be read as follows:

> Have no fear, I'll not desert you in your love affair.
> I trust, today, from somewhere, by my good offices, or this hand of mine
> To get you some assistance – of the money kind. –
> But that will come from where? – From where it comes I've no idea.
> I only know that come it will, my eyebrow twitches so.[2]

73 Duobus digitis primoribus
With the tips of two fingers

When we seize upon something avidly, we take it 'with the whole hand,' or, as the saying goes, 'with both hands.' Whereas those who take something in a niggardly manner, do it 'with two fingers.' Plautus in the *Bacchis Sisters*: 'What, you fool! When you had the chance which / I engineered for you, to take just what you fancied, / Did you pick with just two fingers?'[1] I imagine he means the thumb and index finger. Again in the *Carthaginian*: 'You've got it! – Upon my word, hardly with our finger-tips, the thing's so small!'[2] If transferred to a non-material thing, the phrase will be rather pleasing: 'You should not have picked at such an opportunity with two finger-tips, but rather embraced it with your whole body.'

* * * * *

2 *Verum ego te amantem, ne pave, non deseram. / Spero alicunde hodie me bona opera aut hac mea / Tibi inventurum esse auxilium argentarium. / At id futurum unde? Unde dicam nescio, / Nisi quia futurum sit, ita supercilium salit.* The fourth line of the quoted passage is not now usually divided between the two speakers but assigned wholly to Pseudolus: 'I have no idea wherever in the world it's coming from' (*undeunde* as one word, 'wherever'). Iambic senarii are lines consisting of six iambic units and provide the usual metre for dialogue in Roman comedy.

73 Plautus (see nn1 and 2). Zenobius 1.61. Zenobius (Aldus) column 19. For similar material, see earlier *Adagia* I ix 94 To touch with the fingertips; I ix 16 To take with both hands; IV ix 59 Dip the toes (458 above). Otto 546. Added in *1533*

1 Plautus *Bacchides* 673–5

2 Plautus *Poenulus* 565–6

74 Madusa
A booze-up

In Plautus' *Pseudolus*, the tipsy slave says, 'Oh, *habeo madusam* "I am having myself a really lovely booze-up."'[1] From Festus Pompeius we learn
that *madusa* was an old word meaning 'tipsy, drunk.'[2] He suggests it could
be Greek in origin (μέθυσος is Greek for 'drunk'), or else it could come
from the Latin word *madere* 'to be soaked,' as the word used for people
who are absolutely inebriated is *madidi* 'soaked.' But if *madusa* means
'drunk,' not 'drunkenness,' it does not make sense to say *habeo madusam*
'I'm having a drunk.' So I think the text should read in this line not *habeo
madusam* but *habeo madusa*: 'I'm having lots of drinky-winkies with lovely
things to eat ...' In his inebriated state, the slave thinks himself really
happy, free from all fear and care, with all his misfortunes forgotten. You
may well ask, 'What has this to do with proverbs?' Well, just as foreign
phrases become sayings because of their novelty value, so do obsolete ones
sometimes.

75 Talum reponere
Put the counter back

Τὸν πεττὸν ἀναθέσθαι Put the counter back, take back the move. People are
said to do this when they put right something that had not turned out
as they intended, with 'a second try,' as the saying goes. Antiphon, in his

* * * * *

74 Plautus with Pompeius Festus (see nn1–2). Added in *1533*
  1 Plautus *Pseudolus* 1252
  2 Pompeius Festus 113.9–10 Lindsay. The word is given there in the form
    madulsa, not *madulsam* as in Plautus. Festus seems to think it an adjective
    as he equates it with Latin *ebrius* 'drunk.' He suggests that it comes from the
    Greek verb μαδάω 'to be soaked,' or, alternatively, links it with Latin *madidus*
    'drenched.' (Erasmus has expanded Festus' brief entry.) It is not immediately
    obvious what Erasmus' emended text is supposed to mean; *madusa* is presum-
    ably a neuter plural, object of *habeo*. J.J. Scaliger and J. Lipsius proposed *abeo
    madulsa* 'I'm on my way, quite tipsy,' (see *Plauti Fabulae* [Plantin, Lyons 1598]
    587). Possibly Erasmus similarly emended both words.

75 Harpocration (see n1). See earlier *Adagia* I iii 38 Better luck next time; I v 55
  To take back a move. Added in *1533*

speech on concord, says, 'One cannot cancel a move in life as one can a move in a game.'[1] It is not granted us to replay life once it has passed. All the same, as Micio says in Terence's play, one can with better deeds rectify the mistakes of earlier life.[2] Once life is lost there is nothing you can put right.

76 Dorice concinere
To sing together in Dorian mode

Of people who disagree, it is said that they do not 'Sing together in Dorian mode.' The saying seems to be used to twit those whose words do not accord with their deeds; Plato in *Laches*: 'From what you say, Laches, you and I are not singing together in Dorian mode. For our deeds do not accord with our words.'[1] Among the various species of music, the Dorian was the most highly thought of, its character being intermediate between the Lydian and the Phrygian.[2]

77 Praesentibus rebus consulendum
Take thought for the here and now

Procopius, in book one of the *War against the Goths*: 'A really old saying comes to mind which bids us take thought for the here and now.'[1] I think this is essentially the same as the saying I quoted earlier from Plato: δεῖ τὸν παρὸν εὖ τιθέναι 'Make the best of what you have.'[2] What is once done cannot be recalled and made undone;[3] all kinds of contingencies interfere

* * * * *

1 This paragraph is based on Harpocration (1.31.1 Dindorf sub ἀναθέσθαι), which cites Antiphon *De pace* (fragment 8 Gernet).
2 Terence *Adelphi* 739–41

76 Plato (see n1). Added in *1533*
1 Plato *Laches* 193D
2 See earlier *Adagia* II v 93 From Dorian to Phrygian; *Suda* Δ 1461.

77 Procopius (see n1). Added in *1533*
1 Procopius *De bellis* 5.13.25. See *Adagia* IV ix 5 n1 (422 above).
2 See *Adagia* II ix 83, quoting Plato *Gorgias* 499C (where the words are identified as proverbial).
3 Cf *Adagia* IV ix 75 Put the counter back (468 above).

with our plans for the future; one's first thoughts must be for the demands of the immediate situation.

78 Mutare vestem
To change one's clothes

In addition to its everyday meaning, this phrase often occurs in Cicero with reference to people who were either mourning a death or were accused of some crime. These were all said 'To change their clothes,' because not only mourners but also people about to stand trial used to go about in dark or deliberately dirtied clothes. In the case of these last it was a stupid custom. What was the point of lamenting before they were condemned, and when they were, very often, innocent? Yet the Senate too sometimes expressed its unhappiness by 'changing clothes.' Cicero, in his speech in defence of Sestius: 'The bill was passed, the Forum being empty and deserted, abandoned to thugs and slaves, a bill moreover which the Senate had tried to block by appearing "in changed dress."'[1] Again: 'The Senate was plunged in grief, the whole country was in its mourning clothes, everyone had by general consent "changed dress."' Again: 'when the two consuls suddenly issue a decree that the Senate should return to its normal dress.' And shortly after: 'not show the sorrow they felt by "changing dress," whether the purpose of that change of garb was to express their own grief or to make an appeal ...?'[2] Cicero again, in book two of the letters to his brother Quintus: 'Cato carried a bill cancelling Lentulus' command. His son "changed clothes."'[3] And another phrase from the same speech: 'though they had not defended him when in normal dress.'[4] 'In normal dress' means 'not having changed clothes.' You can give the expression a proverbial turn by saying, 'An event not worth changing clothes for,' that is, not worth shedding tears over.

* * * * *

78 This adage consists of material from Cicero. Added in 1533
1 Cicero *Pro P. Sestio* 24.53
2 Cicero *Pro P. Sestio* 14.32 (3 examples)
3 Cicero *Ad Quintum fratrem* 2.3.1
4 Cicero *Pro P. Sestio* 19.44. Erasmus' text reads *ne vestitum quidem defendissent;* the modern reading is *ne vestitu quidem defendi rempublicam sissent* 'would not have allowed the state to be defended even by a change of dress.'

79 Fumosae imagines
Smoke-darkened portraits

Καπνώδεις εἰκόνες, Smoke-darkened family portraits, a phrase used to deride those who bragged about the centuries-old nobility of their family. Cicero, in his speech attacking Piso: 'You sneaked into office by misjudgment on the part of the voters, commended by those smoke-darkened family portraits, which you resemble in no way, apart from your colour.'[1] Juvenal calls these family portraits 'ancient waxen forms': 'Though ancient waxen forms adorn your halls on every wall / The one and true nobility is – virtue.'[2] Earlier in the same poem, he pokes fun at 'famous Curii, half gone, / And Corvinus with his nose chipped off.'[3]

80 Sal et mensa
Salt and table

I have already written about the ancient view of hospitality as a most sacred rite.[1] It was established by the sharing of 'Salt and table.' In the same way, amongst the Germans, to accept the cup when one's health is drunk abolishes any right to initiate legal proceedings for injury.[2] Aeschines, in the speech *On the False Legation*: 'For he says he values highly the city's salt and its public table.'[3] I had not forgotten that I had commented on this proverb before, but this last example urges on us a reverence for the rite of hospitality when provided publicly, not privately, so I thought it worth

* * * * *

79 Cicero (see n1). The Greek version may be Erasmus' own translation. Added in *1533*
1 Cicero *In L. Pisonem* 1.1
2 Juvenal 8.19–20
3 Juvenal 8.4–5 (Erasmus has misremembered the second quotation). Members of noble Roman families displayed in the *atrium* of their houses wax portrait masks of distinguished ancestors. Over the years these became smoke-blackened and fragile.

80 Aeschines (see n3 and *Adagia* IV ix 69, 464 above). Added in *1533*
1 See *Adagia* I vi 10 Transgress not salt and trencher.
2 See *Adagia* IV vii 70 The cup of friendship (329 above).
3 Aeschines 2.22

bringing in. Traces of this public rite of hospitality survive until the present day among the Germans.

81 Saliares dapes
Banquets fit for Salian priests

The Salii or Leaping Priests were a very ancient Roman priesthood, so called because they used to perform a ritual leaping dance as they carried round the *ancilia*, which were supposed to have fallen from heaven.[1] Any particularly rich and splendid banquet was called 'Salian' after them. See Horace in the *Odes*:

> Now is the time to drink, to beat
> With merry foot the earth; high time,
> My friends, before the sacred couch
> To spread a banquet Salian.[2]

'Salian' banquet here means 'priestly,' I think (*species* for *genus*).[3] All sacred rites involved much magnificent pomp and circumstance, and the supervision of all this was delegated to the *septemviri epulones* 'the Seven Banquetmen.' People found fault with Aristippus for enjoying a luxurious life-style when he professed to be a philosopher. 'If there were anything wrong in that,' he replied, 'the gods would not allow it in their worship.'[4] I have written elsewhere of 'A dinner for a pontiff.'[5]

* * * * *

81 Horace (see n2). See *Adagia* III ii 37 A dinner for a pontiff. Added in 1533
1 For the *ancilia*, twelve shields of archaic shape, and the ancient priesthood of the Salii who had their custody, see Livy 1.20.4; Plutarch *Numa* 13.
2 Horace *Odes* 1.37.1–4
3 The ancient Roman priesthoods, which were filled by members of noble families, involved much archaic ritual, usually and most importantly including banquets in honour of the deity or deities concerned, whose presence with their worshippers was symbolized in some rites by the physical presence of the cult statue laid on a richly decorated couch. These priestly banquets were proverbial for their splendour and extravagance. 'Salian' is a sub-species of 'priestly.'
4 For Aristippus see *Adagia* IV viii 60 n2 (396 above). For this anecdote, see Diogenes Laertius 2.68 ('Aristippus').
5 *Adagia* III ii 37

82 Falsum probrum
A sneer without foundation

Aeschines expresses a proverbial sentiment in the speech *On the False Lega-*
tion when he says that Τὸ ψευδὲς ὄνειδος 'A sneer without foundation' goes
no further than the ears.[1] If a man is the butt of taunts which he secretly
knows to be justified, he is cut to the heart, but anyone assailed by sneers
which have no foundation does not mind so much. Such sneers do not
thrust so deep into the heart of a man whose conscience is clear.

83 Ne insciens quidem verum dicit
He doesn't tell the truth even by accident

A little further on, Aeschines uses an exaggerated expression of a proverbial
nature: 'In these political activities I have got involved with a man beyond all
measure tricky and unprincipled, Ὃς οὐδ' ἂν ἄκων ἀληθὲς οὐδὲν εἴποι "Who
couldn't tell the truth even by accident." '[1] This figurative expression draws
attention to the man's total unreliability, as on the whole even people to
whom lying comes naturally sometimes either by a slip of the tongue or by a
moment's inattention do say something true. There's a saying used nowadays
by my own countrymen about someone who can't be relied on: 'He's lucky
if he tells the truth.' As if he would never tell the truth except by accident.
Anything that happens without our intending it is ascribed to fortune.

84 Capillis trahere
Seize by the hair

Τῶν τριχῶν ἕλκειν, To seize by the hair, a phrase used of those who compel by
force. Nowadays we also say 'To drag by the ears.' Aeschines, in the speech
I have just quoted: 'that I would not have put up with the insult, but would

* * * * *

82 The next four adages draw on the same speech of Aeschines (see n1). Tilley
   c 597 A clear conscience laughs at false accusation. Added in 1533
 1 Aeschines 2.149

83 Aeschines (see n1). Suringar 133. Added in 1533
 1 Aeschines 2.153

84 Aeschines (see n1). Suringar 37. Added in 1533

have blazed up, when we were actually being entertained by the member of Philip's entourage who was entrusted with organizing hospitality for guests, and would have seized a captive woman by the hair, taken a strap and thrashed her.'[1] In the *Two Menaechmuses*, Plautus writes, 'But who is this who by the hair tears me from my car?'[2] I think there is a reference here to Pallas Athene in Homer, who stops Achilles fighting by pulling at his hair.[3] Plautus again, in the *Merchant*: 'I'll drag that girl by her hair out into the street, / Unless he takes her hence.'[4] I have already discussed 'Lead by the nose,' 'With one's neck in a noose,' 'With one's throat in a stranglehold.'[5] It will be nice to apply the metaphor in a less physical context and say something like 'One must seize licentious living by the hair and tame it by fasting and toil.'

85 Scytha malus
An evil Scythian

The Scythians were so barbaric and brutal that their very name became proverbial, just as we today call a cruel man 'a Turk,' and a dreadful deed 'a Turkish act.' Aeschines, in the speech *On the False Legation*: 'I beg you, save me, do not hand me over to that speech-peddler, that evil Scythian.'[1]

86 Mali principii malus finis
Ill beginning, an ill ending

Ἀρχῆς κακῆς τέλος κακόν, An ill start, an ill ending. This is said to be an

* * * * *

1 Aeschines 2.157; Erasmus seems not to have looked at the context of the passage. *Xenodocus* is a proper name here, not someone in charge of guests, and the optative forms are not potential in force, as Erasmus' translation suggests, but occur in past reported speech.
2 Plautus *Menaechmi* 870
3 Homer *Iliad* 1.97
4 Plautus *Mercator* 798–9
5 See *Adagia* IV ix 50 (453 above) for the last two, II i 19 for the first.

85 Aeschines (see n1). Suringar 204. Added in *1533*
1 Aeschines 2.180: Σκύθῃ κακῷ παραδοῦναι (modern texts omit κακῷ)

86 Stobaeus (see n1). Added in *1533*

iambic dimeter from the poet Aeolus.[1] Things well set up at the beginning still reach a happy conclusion eventually, even if problems intervene on the way; but things that start off wrong ultimately come to a bad end, even if they go well at first.

87 Laureolam in mustaceis quaerere
To look for the sprig of bay in the must-cake

Cicero, writing to Atticus: 'Bibulus has started looking for the bay-sprig in the must-cake,'[1] that is, is trying to squeeze a little bit of minor notability out of insignificant activities. *Mustaceus* or *mustaceum* is a kind of cake made with the grated bark of the bay and cooked on a bed of bay-leaves, as it says in Cato's book *On Agriculture*.[2] (In consequence, Pliny, in book fifteen, chapter thirty, thinks that *mustaceus* is the name given to a third species of bay used for that purpose.)[3] Generally speaking, bay was associated with triumphs and was used to adorn the residences of leading citizens and priests. Those who could not win bays of that sort used 'To look for the bay-sprig in the must-cake.' Cicero, writing to Atticus in the letter in book five that begins, 'On the morning of the Saturnalia ...': 'Bibulus, I believe, wants to get this empty title in order to be equal with me. In that same territory of Amanus, he's started looking for the bay-sprig in the must-cake.'[4] Cicero had had some real achievements in the province, Bibulus was quite ineffective. Cicero again, in the second book of letters, writing to

* * * * *

1 Erasmus has been misled by his text of the entry in Stobaeus 4.11 Gaisford. It actually refers to Euripides' lost play *Aeolus* (fragment 32 Nauck).

87 Based on Brassicanus no 81, a short paragraph, but containing the references to Cicero and Pliny (nn1 and 3). For Brassicanus see *Adagia* IV iii 86 n2 (52 above). Otto 1186. Added in *1533*

1 Cicero *Ad Atticum* 5.20.4. Must-cake was a kind of cheese pastry made with unfermented grape-juice (*mustum*) and including the grated or shredded bark of the bay. Cicero's phrase is not found elsewhere, but seems to mean 'look for something requiring no effort to find.'

2 Cato *De agri cultura* 121

3 Pliny *Naturalis historia* 15.127. For Erasmus' reference to chapter 30 see *Adagia* IV iii 3 n3 (5–6 above).

4 See n1 above.

Marcus Caelius Rufus, calls a triumph[5] of any sort 'a sprig of bay': 'You say you would like me to have just enough trouble to earn a sprig of bay.'[6]

88 Si tu proreta
If you're the look-out

'If you're the *proreta* "look-out" on that ship, then I'll be the *gubernator* "steersman."' So Plautus writes in the *Rope*,[1] and the words look just as much like a proverb as one fig looks like another fig.[2] You can use this one when you have two people, neither of whom will give way to the other in the matter in hand. The prow is the part of the ship which strikes the shore when coming in to land; the poop is the stern section, and the one who controls the rudder sits there. Every member of the crew has his allotted function, and the most important are the look-outs and the steersmen. Hence the proverb 'Stem and stern.'[3] *Prora* 'prow' is a Greek word, and the man who is in command there is called by them πρωρεύς or πρωράτης, from which comes the verb πρωρατεύεσθαι 'to control the prow.' I suspect that, in this line, Plautus made the second noun Greek as well, to correspond with the other Greek word. If you read the Latin term *gubernator* here, the trochaic line will have a short syllable in the antepenultimate position, which the metre does not allow.[4] So read: *Si tu proreta isti navi es, ego* κυβερνήτης *ero*. But I leave

* * * * *

5 This was the splendid and costly triumphal processional entry into Rome voted to military commanders in celebration of victories won (in theory) only in a major campaign. To be granted one was the height of a Roman noble's ambition, and it was often sought on inadequate grounds.

6 Cicero *Ad familiares* 2.10.2. A bay wreath was held over the victor's head.

88 Plautus (see n1). Added in *1533*

1 Plautus *Rudens* 1014. At this point in the play, two characters are having a tug-of-war over a chest which one of them has just fished up from the sea. Neither will let go or give up his claim.

2 See *Adagia* II viii 7 As like as two figs; I v 10–11 As like as one egg to another.

3 *Adagia* I i 8

4 In Latin dramatic verse, various syllabic patterns were allowed in the earlier part of the verse, but the rhythmic pulse was clearly defined at the end. The trochaic septenarius (which we have here) was required to close with the syllabic pattern long-short-long. *Gubernator* in Classical Latin had the syllabic value short-long-long-short, but in the time of Plautus, the shortening

this point for scholars to discuss. The poop is the more significant part of the ship, which is why we find Aeneas in Virgil standing 'on the lofty poop';[5] and Cicero, writing to Cornificius in book twelve of the letters, says, 'So, my dear Quintus, embark with us, and what's more, join us on the poop.'[6]

89 Hedera lascivior
More wanton than ivy

These words have a very proverbial ring, because it is the nature of ivy to wind round things and bind them fast. So Horace in the *Odes*, describing the courtesan's clinging embrace, says, 'Tighter than the ivy binding, about the lofty holm-oak twining, / Your soft arms about me winding.'[1] In another place, he writes, 'Tighter than / Wanton ivies twine the tendrils of your embrace.'[2] Ivy kills trees with its embrace and girls of easy virtue do the same to their lovers. For this reason, the Flamen Dialis at Rome was forbidden to touch ivy, or for that matter, even to name it.[3] By this riddling prohibition, the ancients proclaimed how pure and chaste a priest must be, and indeed how free, for the passion of love is nothing but slavery. He was not allowed to wear a ring that was a complete circle or to have any kind of knot about his person, as Festus Pompeius tells us,[4] the reason being, I imagine, that a priest should be free from all vexation of spirit and have a totally clear conscience.

* * * * *

of the final syllable had not taken place. The values of (*guberna*)*tŏr ērō* would therefore be long-short-long, which provides the necessary pattern. Erasmus' emendation is unnecessary. (LB II 1162C reads *isti navis*, which is probably a misprint.)

5 Virgil *Aeneid* 10.261
6 Cicero *Ad familiares* 12.25.2

89 Based on Horace (see nn1–2). Added in *1533*
1 Horace *Epodes* 15.5–6
2 Horace *Odes* 1.36.20
3 The Flamen Dialis was the holder of an ancient Roman priesthood assigned specifically to the worship of the supreme god, Jupiter, and surrounded by many archaic tabus. For the tabu on ivy, see Plutarch *Moralia* 290E–291B *Quaestiones Romanae* 112; Aulus Gellius *Noctes Atticae* 10.15.
4 Pompeius Festus 72.23–6 Lindsay

90 **Nugae theatri**
Stage nonsense

Plautus uses the phrase 'Stage nonsense' in the *Pseudolus* to refer to the
standard insults which characters in comedy were always throwing at tarts,
pimps, and professional toadies. In the play, the pimp Ballio is asked what
somebody or other had said to him and he replies:

> Just stage nonsense, things that people always say
> To a pimp in comedy, things known to every boy –
> That I'm a scoundrel, steeped in wickedness,
> And never keep my word.[1]

So says the pimp. Such insults are not to be taken any more seriously, for
Heaven's sake, as Socrates used to say, than the rather uninhibited comments bandied about at a grand dinner.[2] In fact, the whole business of comedy could be called 'stage nonsense' – young men falling in love, old men
being grumpy, slaves getting the better of their masters, bawds being fond
of the bottle, and so on. Cicero has a somewhat different idea when he uses
the word 'theatre' to imply 'show, attention-seeking.' In the speech on behalf of Rabirius, he says, 'I am well aware of Caesar's many virtues, great
and incredible as they are, but the rest are displayed in greater theatres and
are popular in their appeal – strategic choice of camp-site, etc.'[3] Accordingly,
any line of conduct calculated to win popular favour can be called 'theatrical' or 'stagey.'

91 Ἐν ἐπιτομῇ
In brief

Cicero writing to Atticus in the letter in book five which begins, 'On the

* * * * *

90 Plautus (see n1). Added in *1533*
  1 Plautus *Pseudolus* 1081–3. For examples of pimps breaking their word, see
    Plautus *Rudens* 1353–5, 1373–4.
  2 See Erasmus *Apophthegmata* III Socrates 83; Plutarch *Moralia* 10C–D *De liberis
    educandis.*
  3 Cicero *Pro C. Rabirio Postumo* 15.42

91 Cicero (see n2). Added in *1533*

morning of the Saturnalia[1] ...': 'You can take it that with this army in this place such mighty deeds were not to be done. You will learn ἐν ἐπιτομῇ what deeds were done, for according to your last letter you allow me that.'[2] Cicero used Ἐν ἐπιτομῇ with the same meaning as another Greek phrase διὰ βραχέων 'In short,' 'in summary form,' 'cutting out the inessentials.' Hence the Greek verb ἐπιτέμνειν 'to shorten, cut back.' The opposite of Ἐν ἐπιτομῇ is Ἐν πλατεῖ 'in a broad way,' which I have already discussed.[3]

92 Iuxta cum ignarissimis
No more than the most ignorant of men

In Plautus' *Pseudolus*, old Simo uses a proverbial sort of expression when Ballio asks him, 'Don't you see what's going on?' and he replies, 'No, no more than the most ignorant of men.'[1] He knows he knows nothing, not a scrap more than those who know nothing at all. The ancient Romans often used another similar type of expression,[2] which could be used of people, as in 'You're as dear to me as the dearest can be'; or of time, as in 'Pamphilus was then as deep in love as ever he was';[3] or of a thing, as in 'That good turn was as gratifying as the most gratifying thing there is,'[4] or, 'I hate drunkenness as a thing most hateful.'

* * * * *

1 Ie a winter festival of merriment celebrated on December 17 and the following days
2 Cicero *Ad Atticum* 5.20.1
3 *Adagia* IV vii 75 (332 above)

92 Plautus (see n1). Added in *1533*
1 Plautus *Pseudolus* 1161
2 Erasmus here gives examples of a Latin idiomatic expression which is difficult to represent closely in English. The common feature is that in all cases a superlative adjective or adverb appears in a subordinate clause expressing a comparative idea, which is introduced by words such as *quam, quantus,* or *ut* (the general meaning being 'as ... as the most ...'). The examples are relevant here insofar as the construction, like the phrase in the heading, provides a means of intensifying a positive concept; see Erasmus *De copia* 1 46 'Varying the expression of the superlative' (CWE 24 384), where very similar examples are given.
3 See Terence *Hecyra* 115.
4 See Cicero *Ad familiares* 13.3.

93 Pleno modio
In full measure

I have already discussed the phrase 'In handfuls,' used of something done generously and unstintingly.[1] Cicero uses a similar phrase, 'In full measure,' in the first letter to Atticus in book six: 'If they already have these satisfactions in full measure – addressed in complimentary terms, frequently invited . . .'[2] He had just before written that he had expressed in extravagant terms his approval of the interest rate charged by the tax-collectors.

94 Agninis lactibus alligare canem
Tie up a dog with lamb's chitterlings

Ballio, in Plautus' play *Pseudolus*:

> If I lent to you, it would be just the same
> As tying up a dog that runs away
> With lamb's chitterlings for rope.[1]

Anyone who ties up a dog with lamb's entrails not only loses the dog, but gives the runaway something to run off with into the bargain. Likewise, anyone who makes a loan to someone whose credit is bad loses his money and any hold he has over the other fellow is worthless because he hasn't the means to pay. Chitterlings are the softer entrails of an animal.[2]

95 Superavit dolum Trojanum
Better than that Trojan trick

In Plautus' *Pseudolus*, the old man is praising his slave for thinking up a

*****

93 Cicero (see n2). Added in *1533*
  1 *Adagia* II i 16
  2 Cicero *Ad Atticum* 6.1.16

94 Plautus (see n1). Otto 324. Added in *1533*
  1 Plautus *Pseudolus* 319
  2 Nonius Marcellus 521.26–7 Lindsay

95 Plautus (see n1). Added in *1533*

new dodge and tricking the pimp Ballio by getting someone to come and play a part in an elaborate hoax he's set up. What he says is: 'It was better than that Trojan trick; the victory goes to Pseudolus.'[1] He's referring to that Trojan horse made out of planks of wood, which I've mentioned often enough.[2] The Greeks deceived the Trojans by coaching Sinon in his part. Pseudolus likewise deceived the pimp through Harpax.

96 Laryngizein
To roar

The Greeks use the verb λαρυγγίζειν of people who don't speak in a natural way but dilate their throats and let out a great roar. Some people even sing like that. Demosthenes finds fault with Aeschines for doing just that, accusing him of straining his voice unnaturally because he was not speaking from the heart.[1] It is not the job of an orator to stir his audience by shouting, but by argumentation and setting the thing vividly before them.

97 Oculis ac manibus
By eye and hand

Something that has been thoroughly and completely ascertained is grasped 'By eye and hand.' Cicero, in the speech in defence of Cluentius: 'When he had actually intercepted the poison which Oppianicus, his step-father, had prepared for him, and the affair was not now a matter of conjecture but was "grasped by eye and hand," and when there could not be any dubiety in the matter, then he brought the accusation.'[1] People believe their eyes rather than their ears, and some people are so δυσπειθεῖς 'hard of persuasion' that

* * * * *

1 Plautus *Pseudolus* 1244. Erasmus is following Pio's Milan 1500 text of Plautus; see *Adagia* IV iii 40 n2 (27 above). Modern texts read not *atque vicit Pseudolus* but *atque Ulixen Pseudolus* 'Pseudolus has surpassed Ulysses.'

2 Eg *Adagia* IV ii 1 A wooden horse; IV x 70 A Trojan pig (525 below)

96 From Harpocration (1.190.14 Dindorf), citing Demosthenes (see n1 below). Erasmus has supplied the content of the passage referred to.

1 Demosthenes 18.291

97 Cicero (see n1). Added in 1533

1 Cicero *Pro A. Cluentio* 7.20

they will not believe unless they can actually handle with their hands, as we are told of Thomas Didymus in the Gospel narrative.[2]

98 Ut herba solstitialis
Like the solstice plant

In Plautus' *Pseudolus*, the young man in love suddenly has his hopes dashed and says, 'Just like the solstice plant, I lasted but a moment: / I sprang up of a sudden and as quickly died.'[1] I have written elsewhere of the *ephemeron*, the little insect that lives only a day.[2] Some people interpret this 'solstice plant' as the heliotrope,[3] but although the heliotrope turns and keeps its face towards the sun, we do not read anywhere that it dies the same day as it appears. It's more likely that Plautus was thinking of the *ephemeron*, a plant which Dioscorides mentions in a number of places, such as book four, chapter 698, and *passim*.[4] In book six, chapter 111, he posits two types, one the

* * * * *

2 John 20:25

98 Plautus, supplemented by Pliny and Dioscorides (see nn1, 3, and 4). Otto 1670. Added in *1533*

1 Plautus' *Pseudolus* 38–9

2 *Adagia* IV ii 87 To live as long as Ephemerus

3 For the heliotrope see Pliny *Naturalis historia* 22.57; Dioscorides 4.193. The suggestion that the heliotrope is the plant in question comes from Giambattista Pio's Plautus commentary of 1500; see *Adagia* IV iii 40 n2 (27 above).

4 The simplest explanation of Plautus' line is that it refers to any plant that withers quickly in the heat of Mediterranean countries at the time of the summer solstice (June 21). Erasmus prefers a specific reference to the plant *ephemeron*, so called because its flowers naturally last only one day. The name *ephemeron* was applied both to *colchicum autumnale* 'autumn crocus,' and *iris sylvestris* 'meadow saffron.' Erasmus' information concerning these two is conflated from Dioscorides 4.84 and 85, and Pliny *Naturalis historia* 25.170. The saffron bulb had many medicinal applications (Pliny *Naturalis historia* 21.140), like various other edible bulbs including the lily (Dioscorides 3.116 and 200), and as these were taken internally it was important not to confuse them with the bulb of the autumn crocus, every part of which is poisonous. These mishaps obviously occurred frequently as both Dioscorides and Pliny (*Naturalis historia* 28.129) specifically recommend milk as an antidote to autumn crocus, as well as its general use as an antidote to various poisons (*Naturalis historia* 28.160). In northern European latitudes both the autumn crocus and the meadow saf-

colchicum, so called because it grows in abundance in Colchis. The inhabitants call it the 'wild' or 'meadow' bulb. Towards the end of autumn, it produces a whitish flower, not unlike the saffron. The other is called 'wild iris,' has leaves like a lily but finer, and a similar stem. Its flowers are blueish and pungent. Pliny describes it in book twenty-five, chapter thirteen. Because it is similar to edible bulbs, the colchicum attracts the unwary and causes death, as poisonous fungi do – but cow's milk is an effective antidote. There is no doubt that Plautus was really thinking of this plant, as Dioscorides says that it appears around the end of autumn,[5] that is, I presume, about the time of the winter solstice, for autumn comes later with the Romans and Greeks than with us. Theophrastus thinks this plant is called *ephemeron* because the flower doesn't live more than a day, attributing the same characteristic to the plant as Aristotle attributed to the creature of the same name.[6]

99 In herbis
In the blade

We use the phrase 'In the blade' of things that have not yet reached maturity, but merely hold out good hopes of what they will become. Cicero, in his speech in defence of Marcus Caelius: 'I am not speaking of wisdom, which one does not expect to find in a person of this age. I am speaking of ardour, the passionate desire for victory, the burning impulse to win glory, enthusiasms which are properly somewhat circumscribed in men of our age, but in youth presage, 'in the blade' as it were, the fine characteristics that maturity will bring, the harvest of vigorous activity yet to

* * * * *

fron flower in September; in Greece, the autumn crocus appears in December–January. Dioscorides says (4.84) that it appears at the end of autumn.

None of Erasmus' references to Dioscorides indicate that he had the text in Greek, though this had been printed several times by now: Aldus (Venice 1499); Andrea Torresani of Asola (Venice 1518); J. Cornarius (Basel 1529). Latin translations had been available since 1478 (J. Allemannus, Colle in Toscana). One by F. Ruellius appeared in 1516 (Paris). A combined Greek and Latin text was printed at Cologne in 1529.

5 For Erasmus' references to Dioscorides and Pliny, see nn3 and 4.

6 Theophrastus mentions the plant *ephemeron* at *Historia plantarum* 9.16.6, but does not discuss the name there; for the insect (the may-fly) see Aristotle *Historia animalium* 1.5 (490a34), 5.19 (552b23).

99 Cicero (see n1). Added in *1533*

come.'[1] I do remember that I have discussed this proverb before,[2] but I have decided to add it here. If this does the reader any harm, he has grounds for complaint, but if he is simply raising the frivolous objection that I am just trying to make up the numbers, he will hold his tongue once he considers the countless proverbs included in with others to which I have not given a separate number.

100 Nullius coloris
Of no colour

I wrote earlier about the saying, 'I know not whether you are dark or fair,' used of someone totally unknown.[1] Very similar is the remark made by Harpax in Plautus:

> What Pseudolus, what trick are you on about?
> He's a man of no colour as far as I'm concerned.[2]

This is putting it more strongly than saying, 'whether he's dark or fair.' A little further on in the play, instead of saying, 'I don't know the fellow,' he says, 'As for that Pseudolus, who on earth he is, I don't know, / Nor have I any idea.'[3] We have a similar sort of idea elsewhere in the play: 'Their own cash they call in, other people's they return to – not a mother's son.'[4] Again, in the *Rope*: 'The owner for this, make no mistake, apart from me is / – Not a mother's son.'[5] Again, in the *Haunted House*: 'I'll see it's done – just as if not a mother's son / Were living in the house.'[6] The same phrase in another line from the same play: 'Not a mother's son inside the house.'[7]

* * * * *

1 Cicero *Pro M. Caelio* 31
2 In *Adagia* II ii 89 To be in the blade, but different examples are used there.

100 Plautus (see n2). Added in *1533*
1 *Adagia* I vi 99 I know not whether you are dark or fair; see also III ix 24 Utterly unknown.
2 Plautus *Pseudolus* 1195–6
3 Plautus *Pseudolus* 1212
4 Plautus *Pseudolus* 297
5 Plautus *Rudens* 969–70
6 Plautus *Mostellaria* 401–2
7 Plautus *Mostellaria* 451

1 Et praedam et praemium
Plunder and prize

Whenever we want to say that something must be appropriated by any and every possible means, whether right or wrong, we will use the phrase 'seize prize and plunder.' A 'prize' is awarded on merit, 'plunder' is something taken by force or craft. In the play I quoted above, Ballio says, 'So it's taken off me, the prize I promised as a joke.' The old man replies, 'From villains it is only right to take both prize and plunder.'[1] He means that evil men should be robbed at every opportunity, because a bad thing done to a bad man is a good deed, just as an abusive remark directed at someone who deserves it is something well said.

2 E natali emortualem facere
Turn birthday into funeral day

In the same play, the pimp Ballio is forced to pay over the money and he says, 'I've decided to make today my funeral day instead of my birthday.'[1] 'Funeral day' here means dismal and disastrous, whereas 'birthday' is happy and successful.

3 Catone hoc contenti sumus
Satisfied with Cato as he is

Suetonius records a number of sayings that the emperor Augustus liked to use in everyday conversation. Among these is one he used to mean that one must be satisfied with things as they are: 'We are satisfied with Cato as he is.'[1] Cato of Utica endeavoured to preserve the Republic as it

* * * * *

1 Plautus (see n1). Added in *1533*
1 Plautus *Pseudolus* 1224–5. The play was quoted three times in *Adagia* IV ix 100 (484 above).

2 Plautus (see n1). Added in *1533*
1 Plautus *Pseudolus* 1237. It really is the pimp's birthday; see line 165.

3 Brassicanus no 35 (see *Adagia* IV iii 86 n2, 52 above), who quotes Suetonius (see n1). Otto 359. Added in *1533*
1 Suetonius *Divus Augustus* 87.1

was and resist the transfer of power to a single individual, but without success.[2] The party triumphed that apparently favoured rule by one man. Augustus so far agreed with Cato in not desiring any change in the constitutional arrangements of his own time, and so was a kind of contemporary Cato. I have already quoted in my *Apophthegmata* the incident recorded in Macrobius where the emperor Augustus came to the house where Cato once lived. Thinking to please Augustus, Strabo started to inveigh against Cato's obstinacy in preferring to take his own life rather than submit to the victorious Julius Caesar. Augustus replied, 'Anyone who does not wish for any change in the existing constitution is both a good citizen and a good man.' These words paid tribute to Cato's memory, but also served Augustus' own purposes, as indicating that no future change in the political order was to be countenanced.[3]

4 Edax triremis
Hungry trireme

Ἀδδηφάγοι τριήρεις, Hungry triremes, so called because their maintenance involves great expense.[1] The idea has been transferred to ships from thoroughbred horses, which are reared and fed for use in racing and very properly have enormous appetites. The phrase occurs in the orator Lysias. Alcaeus also uses the word in a tragicomedy, where he calls thirsty lamps ἀδδηφάγοι, because they 'consume a lot' of oil. The words will have a proverbial ring, like the 'greedy racing-car' that I discussed earlier,[2] if they are applied to a spendthrift fellow who squanders vast sums of money.

* * * * *

2 The Younger Cato (95–46 BC), an adherent of the Stoic philosophy, a man of intransigent principle and a staunch republican
3 Erasmus *Apophthegmata* IV Augustus 32, citing Macrobius 2.4.18

4 A reorganization of the entry in Harpocration (1.10.2 Dindorf), which quotes Lysias (fragment 39 Thalheim) and Alcaeus (PCG 2 Alcaeus comicus fragment 21). For Harpocration, see *Adagia* IV ix 60 n1 (459 above).
1 Triremes were the warships of the ancient Greeks, with a complement of oarsmen, marines, etc of about 200. A rich Athenian citizen would be called on to maintain a trireme for a year, a costly service. Cf Aristophanes *Knights* 910–18.
2 *Adagia* II iv 64 Greedy as a racing-car

5 Obolo dignus
Worth a penny

Ἄξιος ὀβελοῦ, Worth a penny, jokingly said of someone who wants to be thought of some account.[1] The phrase derives ultimately from the Athenian custom whereby those whom the council of elders admitted to the list of adult males and who were accordingly described as δόκιμοι 'approved,' received one obol 'penny,' a day from the public purse. So Aristotle tells us in the *Politics*.[2] Some authorities say it was two obols, and it is possible that the small emolument was later doubled. Lysias refers to this obol payment in the speech *On Behalf of the Disabled Person*,[3] and probably Aristophanes was alluding to it in the line in the *Knights*: '... has been such a man to most of those who get the penny dole.'[4] Persons who were incapacitated for three months were classified as ἀδύνατοι 'disabled.' Likewise, those who were on scrutiny not admitted to the ranks of men nor yet considered worthy of the penny were called ἀδοκίμαστοι 'not approved.'

* * * * *

5 Appendix 1.33; *Suda* A 2819. Harpocration quoting Aristotle. Added in 1533. Erasmus expands the heading with a muddled paragraph in which he seems to be confusing various types of payment made by the Athenian state. The addition is based on entries in Harpocration ἀδοκίμαστος 'not approved' and ἀδύνατοι 'disabled' (1.10.13 and 11.12 Dindorf), combined with Erasmus' general memories from elsewhere. The ἀδύνατοι entry refers to Aristotle *Athenaion Politeia*, not *Politics*: Erasmus does not seem to have consulted Aristotle directly. One function of the Athenian boule or council was to investigate claims for state maintenance on grounds of disability, the payment being two obols per day according to Aristotle (*Athenaion Politeia* 49.4) and Hesychius A 1217, one obol per day according to Lysias (see n3) and Harpocration quoting Aristotle. On this matter, Erasmus was misled by the Aldine text of Harpocration, which read μηνῶν 'for three months.' Harpocration (and Aristotle) wrote that the disabled claimant must own property worth 'less than three minae' (μνῶν). See *Adagia* IV viii 48 Like carriers of mortar, and n1 (386 above) for public payment for jury service; IV x 27 To out-leaf (also using Harpocration, 501 below), for the council's scrutiny of its own members.

1 Cf *Adagia* V ii 44 Begin to count for something (626 below).
2 Aristotle *Athenaion Politeia*, not *Politics*; see introductory note.
3 Lysias 24.4.13.26 (from Harpocration)
4 Aristophanes *Knights* 945

6 Areopagita taciturnior
Closer than an Areopagite

Ἀρεοπαγίτου στεγανώτερος, Closer than an Areopagite, said of one who
guards well a secret entrusted to him.[1] Alciphron writes in one of his *Letters*, 'Become now for me closer than an Areopagite.'[2] 'Close' in this sense
means not simply holding one's tongue but specifically keeping a secret, not
blabbing it abroad. The Greek word for this, στεγανός, was originally used
of pots that were solid, not leaking anywhere. In Athens, capital charges
were brought before the Areopagus and the case was heard at night, with
scrupulous attention. Maybe it was strictly forbidden for the members of
the council to talk openly about the proceedings there. Today there are sur-
vivals in Westphalia of this kind of judge, popularly known as 'The Sure,'
and those admitted to this group take a solemn oath of silence, for there is
some way of detecting crime known only to these who have so sworn.

7 Ἀδελφίζειν
To call brother

This means trying to ingratiate oneself with others by addressing them as
if they were members of one's family. This is very common today among
the Italians – they address those they want to please as 'little brother.' This
Greek verb ἀδελφίζειν 'to call brother,' is the same kind of formation as
εὐδαιμονίζειν καὶ μακαρίζειν 'to call happy and blessed.' Horace writes in
the *Satires*, 'And tack on "brother, father," / According to his age, merrily
make him your relation.' Again, in the same work: 'When we were together,
you heard me call you "father"; / And in your absence I called you "father"
still.'[1] There is an example of this usage in Aristophanes' *Knights*,[2] and there

* * * * *

6 Brassicanus no 4 *Areopagita subticentior*, quoting Alciphron (see n2); see *Adagia*
  IV iii 86 n2 (52 above). Suringar 19. Added in *1533*
1 Cf *Adagia* I ix 41 An Areopagite, for an account of the Areopagus, the highest
  court in Athens.
2 Alciphron *Epistles* 1.16.1. See *Adagia* IV viii 20 n1 (366 above).

7 This is basically Harpocration (1.9.9. Dindorf), but Erasmus has expanded the
  entry and supplied his own examples. Suringar 3. Added in *1533*
1 Horace *Epistles* (not *Satires*) 1.6.54–5; 1.7.37–8
2 Aristophanes *Knights* 725 (the use of 'father')

are several in Plautus, including one in *Pseudolus*. There the young master
in love effuses over his slave, saying, 'Tell me, Pseudolus, tell me do, shall
I call you "father" / Or call you "mother dear"?'[3]

8 Veterata vaticinari
Trot out the same stale prophecy

I have already discussed the phrase ἀρχαῖα λέγειν 'to talk rubbish.'[1] In Plautus' play *Pseudolus*, when the other two characters hurl the most shocking abuse at him, Ballio replies, 'Out you trot the same stale prophecy.'[2]
The phrase can be used of persons who offer nothing new, but only something that has long been common knowledge, for the true function of the
prophet is either to declare something new that has not yet occurred, or
to reveal something not known to anybody. Indeed, some persons with
the gift of foreknowledge divine wonderful things about times gone by.[3]
There is nothing new in a pimp hearing himself called 'villain, perjurer,
irreligious.'[4]

9 Eadem queri
Make the same complaint

Ξυναυλίαν κλαίειν, To moan in concert. This phrase is used of people who
join together to bemoan the same woes. The phrase derives from the practice
in ancient times of two *aulos*-players sometimes playing the same melody
together in concert. Aristophanes in the *Knights*: 'So we can moan together to
one of Olympus' tunes.'[1] This Olympus was some pupil or other of Marsyas.

* * * * *

3 Plautus *Pseudolus* 709. Erasmus seems to have quoted this from memory, some-
    what inaccurately.

8 Plautus (see n2). Added in 1533
1 *Adagia* I v 24 You are talking of things older than the diphthera
2 Plautus *Pseudolus* 363
3 Cf *Adagia* IV viii 50 Even the seers know it now (380 above).
4 See *Adagia* IV ix 90 Stage nonsense (478 above).

9 Aristophanes (see n1). This adage mostly repeats material in *Adagia* IV viii 88
    To sing in concert (see 411 above, with notes).
1 Aristophanes *Knights* 8–9

He wrote about doleful music for the *aulos*. Marsyas' music did him no good, so the pupil composed laments in honour of his master.

10 **Schoenicolae**
Wearers of rush-scent

Festus Pompeius tells us that this was at one time used of common low-class prostitutes, referring to the cheap perfume they drenched themselves in.[1] Plautus, in the *Carthaginian*: 'Wretched creatures, stinking of cheap scent, rank with rush-pong, unwashed . . .'[2]

11 **Luto lutulentior**
Fouler than filth

We call misers and people obsessed with making a profit 'shabby' and 'dirty.' Plautus expresses the same idea hyperbolically in the *Carthaginian*: 'Filth itself couldn't be filthier than that pimp Lycus, her boss.'[1] The word 'filth' often means 'wicked' or 'corrupt' rather than plain 'dirty.' Cicero, in the speech about his house made before the priests, calls someone 'Scum! Monstrosity! Villainy!'[2] And somewhere or other, as I recall, he refers to Piso as 'filth.'[3] His use of 'filth' here is just like his frequent use of 'blot,' 'smut,' for a villain. Likewise, he often calls someone who disturbs public order 'a firebrand,' 'a whirl-wind,' 'a tempest.'[4]

* * * * *

10 Pompeius Festus, quoting Plautus (see nn1 and 2). Added in *1533*
1 Pompeius Festus 442.7–9 Lindsay, paraphrased by Erasmus
2 Plautus *Poenulus* 267. A cheap perfume was derived from a species of rush. Erasmus follows the reading in the Milan 1500 edition of Plautus. The modern reading is not *schoenicolas* but *servilicolas* 'mean and cringing' (*Oxford Latin Dictionary*). Festus also quotes *schoenicolae* from Plautus *Cistellaria* 407.

11 Plautus (see n1). Otto 998. Cf *Adagia* IV x 38 Stain, blot (506 below). Added in *1533*
1 Plautus *Poenulus* 157–8 (reading *domino non*, not *domi non* as in LB and ASD, a haplography)
2 Cicero *De domo sua* 18.47
3 Cicero *In L. Pisonem* 26.62
4 Eg Cicero *Philippics* 11.5.10, *De domo sua* 38.102, 53.137

12 Διακωδωνίζειν
Shake the bell at

Demosthenes used this Greek term in the sense of 'try out,' 'examine.'[1] It is
thought to come from those who go round the watch at night with a bell to
make sure that no one is asleep, or so that the watchmen can indicate that
they are awake when the bell sounds. Or else from those who try out quails
with a bell to see whether they are good for fighting,[2] as Aristarchus has
it.[3] Some prefer to explain it as derived from the similar practice of testing
horses to see whether they can stand the noise of trumpets and battle. At
one time candidates for initiation into the mysteries were tested in a similar
way with verbal abuse, and the theological schools still preserve remnants
of this custom.

13 **Ferrum et flamma**
Sword and flame

A totally destructive war, we say, is waged with 'Sword and flame,' or
'Sword and fire.' Cicero, in his speech for Lucius Flaccus: 'Good God! What
could be worse than this? A situation in which we, who wrested sword and
flame from the hands of Publius Lentulus now trust to the judgment of the
ignorant multitude.'[1] Or later in the same speech: 'Oh that night, the one
that almost brought eternal darkness on this city, when the call went out to

* * * * *

12 This paragraph down to 'as Aristarchus has it' is translated from Harpocration
   sub διεκωδώνιζε (1.96.13 Dindorf), with additions from the scholiast on Aristophanes *Birds* 842. The 'testing of horses' is from the scholiast on Aristophanes
   Frogs 78. Added in *1533*
 1 Demosthenes 19.167, from Harpocration.
 2 The ancient Greeks kept quails as pets and for the sports of quail-fighting and
   quail-tapping (the latter described in Pollux, 9.102, 107). See also *Aristophanes.
   Birds* ed N. Dunbar (Oxford 1995) 707, 1298.
 3 Presumably the great Alexandrian scholar and literary critic. The reference is
   taken from Harpocration.

13 Cicero (see nn1–4). Otto 665; Suringar 254. Cf *Adagia* IV viii 11 Threaten with
   fire and sword (359 above). Added in *1533*
 1 Cicero *Pro L. Flacco* 38.97

the Gauls to make war, to Catiline to march on the city, to the conspirators to seize sword and flame.'[2] Again, in the speech on behalf of Sulla: 'whose sword I so recently blunted, whose flame I quenched.'[3] In the speech about his house he adds 'rocks': 'Then when he had brought devastation upon my house with rocks and fire and sword.'[4] Again, speaking on behalf of Plancus: 'Throughout that year you saw their sword in the forum, their flame in the buildings, their violence throughout the city.'[5]

14 Montes frumenti
Mountains of grain

I have already discussed 'mountains of gold.'[1] Now, we can use the word 'fly' in any context to indicate that we have absolutely nothing of whatever it is; for example, 'There isn't a fly in the house.'[2] Likewise, 'mountains' can be used for anything of which there is a huge abundance; for example, Plautus in the *Pseudolus*: 'They've all got heaps, great mountains of grain.'[3] 'Mountains' is really superfluous here, but it has been added because it is such a familiar usage and reinforces the idea of abundance. Similarly, *oppido* came to be used for 'very much,' when farmers wanted to say they had as much of something as would be enough *oppido* 'for a town.'[4] In the *Haunted House*, Plautus says *mons erroris* 'a mountain of a perplexity,' meaning a serious worry:

* * * * *

2 Cicero *Pro L. Flacco* 40.102
3 Cicero *Pro P. Sulla* 30.83
4 Not *De domo sua* but Cicero *De haruspicum responso* 8.15, a speech on a related topic
5 Cicero *Pro Cn. Plancio* 29.71

14 Plautus (see n3), from whom most of the material in this adage is derived. Otto 1133. Added in *1533*
1 *Adagia* I ix 15 To promise mountains of gold, where the example from Plautus *Miles Gloriosus* 1065 was already used
2 Plautus *Truculentus* 284. See *Adagia* II i 84 Not so much as a fly.
3 Plautus *Pseudolus* 189
4 Erasmus has taken this explanation from Pompeius Festus (201.9–12 Lindsay). The relation, if any, of the adverb *oppido* 'absolutely, exceedingly' to *oppidum* 'town' is not clear.

Salvation herself cannot save me now if she would.
For sure, another huge mountain of perplexity I've just seen
Down at the harbour. Master's back from abroad. Tranio's had it.[5]

If you insert *mox* and read *ita mox alium* 'for sure, this very minute, another
. . .' the proper rhythm of the trochaic verse will be restored. In the *Braggart
Soldier*, Plautus writes 'mountains of silver': 'He has mountains of silver,
not mere lumps of it.'[6]

15 Post homines natos
Since the human race began

To express the idea of 'the whole human race,' we say 'Since the human
race began.' Cicero, in the speech he made before the priests concerning his house: 'Well then, who gave this fellow, the most foul, wicked,
and degraded person ever seen since the human race began, who gave
him that rich, fertile province of Syria, allowed him to bring war on
people living totally at peace, who turned over to him, forcibly diverted
from Caesar's legislative measures, money earmarked for purchasing land,
who gave him power without limits?'[1] Later on in the same speech: 'The
thing I was accused of was not only no crime but the finest deed since
the human race began.'[2] Cicero again, speaking in defence of Cornelius
Balbus: 'Since very few have been found since human kind began, who
would expose their lives to the enemy's fire for their own country without the inducement of some reward . . .'[3] Again, speaking in defence of
Milo: 'The bravest man since the human race began.'[4] Again, attacking

* * * * *

5 Plautus *Mostellaria* 351–3. Erasmus was obviously not happy with the text
   of 352 (*ita alium erroris montem maxumum*), hence his suggested emendation.
   Modern texts read *ita mali, maeroris montem maxumum* 'such a great mountain
   of misfortune and misery.'
6 Plautus *Miles Gloriosus* 1065

15 All the material in this adage is derived from Cicero. Added in *1533*
   1 Cicero *De domo sua* 9.23
   2 Cicero *De domo sua* 35.95
   3 Cicero *Pro L. Cornelio Balbo* 10.26
   4 Cicero *Pro T. Annio Milone* 26.69

Antony: 'The two most disgusting and abominable individuals since the human race began, Dolabella and Antony.'[5] Again, in his book on the ideal orator: 'By far the best since the human race began,'[6] and also in *Brutus*: 'Servilius Glauca was by far the most unconscionable since the human race began.'[7]

16 Post hominum memoriam
In all human memory

Very similar to the last is the phrase 'In all human memory.' Cicero, in the speech made before the priests concerning his house: 'This is a grave and serious accusation, the gravest, in fact, in all human memory, since courts were first established to deal with cases of extortion.'[1] Again, in his speech dealing with the reply given by the College of Diviners: 'In response to the motion put by you, the finest, the most courageous consuls in all human memory.'[2] Again, speaking on behalf of Plancus: 'The Senate stood by me and, what's more, adopted mourning dress,[3] the only occasion on which this was done officially for a single individual in all human memory.'[4] For Plancus again: 'Nothing more magnificent in all human memory.'[5] And again: 'The foulest and wickedest consuls in all human memory.'[6] And writing to Plancus, in the tenth book of his letters to friends: 'Nothing more magnificent, more welcome in all human memory, nothing more opportune in its timing, have I ever seen turn up than your letter, my dear Plancus.'[7] Again,

* * * * *

5 Cicero *Philippics* 11.1.1
6 Cicero *De optimo genere oratorum* 17, quoting *post homines natos* from Lucilius 152 Marx (154 Krenkel). See *Adagia* II v 98 Esernius versus Pacidianus.
7 Cicero *Brutus* 62.224

16 All the material in this adage is derived from the Ciceronian corpus. Added in *1533*
1 Not *De domo sua*, but Cicero *Verrines* 2.3.56.130
2 Cicero *De haruspicum responso* 8.15
3 See *Adagia* IV ix 78 To change one's clothes (470 above).
4 Cicero *Pro Cn. Plancio* 35.87
5 Not in the speech, but from a letter to Plancius repeated below; see n7.
6 Cicero *Pro Cn. Plancio* 35.86
7 Cicero *Ad familiares* 10.16.1

in the eleventh book, writing to Brutus: 'You at any rate need no one to urge you on, seeing you felt no need of anyone to encourage you even in performing the greatest deed that ever was done in all human memory.'[8] Speaking on behalf of Sestius: 'Out of all human memory, what could anyone select that was more honorific than having all good men by private consent and the whole senate by official decision go into mourning dress on behalf of myself, one individual citizen?'[9] Again, when attacking Catiline: 'In this one war, the greatest and most vicious in all human memory';[10] and from another place in the same speech: 'An internal, civil war, the most vicious, the greatest, in all human memory.'[11] Again, speaking on behalf of Rabirius when charged with treason: 'No case of more significant import in all human memory.'[12] Speaking in support of Manilius' proposed legislation: 'Everything done without any precedent to be found in all human memory, anywhere among all mankind.'[13] Finally, in his enquiry into Vatinius' suitability to give evidence: 'Absolutely unheard of in the whole of human memory.'[14]

17 Ἐξορχεῖσθαι
Dance off

Those who run away and take themselves off to something other than the matter in hand are said in Greek Ἐξορχεῖσθαι 'To dance off.' The metaphor comes from dancing, especially dancing as part of a religious ceremony, as it was ill-omened to break off from that. This is shown by the proverb, 'All's well: the old man dances.'[1] There is a well-known story in Herodotus about Hippocleides, who lost the girl he expected to marry by dancing in

* * * * *

8 Cicero *Ad familiares* 11.5.1
9 Cicero *Pro P. Sestio* 12.27
10 Cicero *Catilinarians* 3.10.25
11 Cicero *Catilinarians* 2.13.28 (not the same speech)
12 Cicero *Pro C. Rabirio* 2.4
13 Cicero *Pro lege Manilia* 21.62
14 Cicero *In P. Vatinium* 14.33

17 The starting point of this seems to be Harpocration (1.117.9 Dindorf), referring to Demosthenes 22.68. Added in *1533*
1 *Adagia* III i 40

an indecent manner, and was rewarded with the remark, 'You have danced away your marriage.'[2]

18 Peristromata Campanica
Campanian curtains

Origen called a work of his that dealt with miscellaneous topics, *Stromateis* 'Tapestries,'[1] a metaphorical application of the word used for the embroidered hangings and coverlets which were at one time a source of great delight to the rich. The phrase can be applied to an inconstant person, as hangings show different patterns according as they are spread out or pleated, or arranged in various other ways. In Plautus' play *Pseudolus*, the pimp threatens his servants in these words: 'I'll use my strap and paint such a fancy pattern on your ribs / That curtains from Campania won't be near so colourful.'[2] Campania in its heyday indulged excessively in soft living and luxuries.[3] (Plautus mentions Alexandrian carpets as well as Campanian curtains.) I have spoken earlier of the francolin.[4]

19 Fors domina Campi
Lady Luck, ruler of the hustings

In the appointment of magistrates, it was not always the best candidate who was successful, but the one that fortune favoured, for everything depended

* * * * *

2 Herodotus 6.129. See *Adagia* II x 12 Hippocleides doesn't care.

18 Plautus (see n2). Added in *1533*
  1 Much of Origen's considerable output survived only in fragments of the Greek text or in Latin translations. Erasmus used what he was able to locate for his own biblical commentaries. *Stromateis*, the title of a lost work, is mentioned without any further information by Jerome (*Letters* 84.7 PL 22 749, CSEL 58 130). Erasmus' suggestion as to its contents possibly derives from Aulus Gellius *Noctes Atticae*, *Preface* 7, who lists *Stromateis* as a title for a work of miscellaneous content.
  2 Plautus *Pseudolus* 144–6
  3 Cf *Adagia* IV viii 14 Campanian arrogance (361 above).
  4 *Adagia* IV i 5 Woodcock; IV iii 73 A francolin's new moon (44 above). The francolin is included here because of its speckled plumage.

19 Cicero (see n2). Added in *1533*

on the popular vote. Cicero, attacking Piso, says, 'I am not dwelling on the
way either of us got elected – granted that Lady Luck rules the hustings[1]
after all – there is more scope for congratulation in discussing what we did
while we held the office of consul.'[2]

20 Fulmentum lectum
Choice fulmentum

Nonius Marcellus tells us that there was a proverbial saying often used by
Varro, *Fulmentum lectum scandunt* 'They climb the choice fulmentum.'[1] But
he doesn't explain what *fulmentum* is or give the sense of the proverb. He
merely says that the word occurs either as a neuter form *fulmentum*, or as a
feminine *fulmenta*.

21 Parthi quo plus biberint
The more a Parthian drinks

There's an old proverb about the Parthians, 'The more they drink, the
thirstier they get.'[1] It's typical of people who are drunk that, once the palate
has got beyond registering taste, they just want to swill down more and
more. The proverb can be used of misers, or indeed of students, because
as one acquires knowledge so the desire for learning grows.

* * * * *

1 'Hustings,' literally 'The Plain,' the Plain of Mars (*Campus Martius*), an open
 area used among other things for the assembly of citizens gathered to elect
 consuls and other senior magistrates of the Roman state
2 Cicero *In L. Pisonem* 2.3. This reference was added in *1533* to *Adagia* I vi 28
 This is sovereign.

20 Nonius Marcellus (see n1). Otto 729. Added in *1533*
1 Nonius Marcellus 304.26–7 Lindsay, citing Varro *Menippeae* 586 Buecheler.
 Erasmus includes this because Nonius expressly says it is proverbial, though
 he is clearly nonplussed by it because of the inferior reading offered by his
 text. Possibly he takes *lectum* as a participle. The modern reading is *Fulmenta
 lectum scandunt* 'The bed-legs get onto the bed,' that is, things are back to
 front, upside down.

21 Pliny (see n1). Otto 1351. Tilley M 1149 The more one drinks (eats) the more
 one may; D 625 Ever drunk ever dry. Added in *1533*
1 Taken from Pliny *Naturalis historia* 14.148

22 Scraptae
Gob-hawkers

A term of popular abuse applied to low-class women of no account, derived from the verb *screo* 'to hawk,' that is, noisily to clear the mouth of purulent matter. *Screa* 'phlegm' was likewise used for anything worthless and contemptible. One could possibly use the word of old women who are always hawking and coughing. That is Festus' explanation.[1] Nonius thinks it's a term of abuse for unattractive prostitutes, and cites a line from Plautus' play, the *Travelling-Bag*: 'gob-hawkers, with knobbly ankles, unsteady on their feet, unclean.'[2]

23 Ex Phelleo
To come from Phelleus

People who rose to eminence from obscurity and difficult circumstances were said Ἐκ Φελλέως ἐλθεῖν 'To come from Phelleus.' In Greek, φελλεύς was a word meaning 'hard, stony, and barren,' applied to an area suitable for pasturing goats, as goats are happy to feed in this kind of place. In the *Clouds*, Aristophanes writes, 'When you bring in the goats from Phelleus, / Clad like your father in a jerkin of leather.'[1] There is a hilly, stony place in Attica actually called Phelleus, mentioned by Stephanus also, though he calls the hill Phellas, which may be a mistake in writing.[2] I have touched on this material already in the adages 'Lighter than cork' and 'Phellinas.'[3]

* * * * *

22 Pompeius Festus and Nonius Marcellus (see nn1 and 2). Added in *1533*
1 Pompeius Festus 448.4–8 Lindsay
2 Nonius Marcellus 248.9–11 Lindsay. See further Varro *De lingua Latina* 7.65. The line is now attributed to Plautus' lost play *Nervolaria* (fragment VII Lindsay OCT). The *Travelling-Bag* (*Vidularia*) survives only in fragments.

23 Based on Aristophanes (see n1). Added in *1533*
1 Aristophanes *Clouds* 71–2, with the ancient commentator, from which most of this derives. See also the scholiast on Aristophanes *Acharnians* 272.
2 Stephanus of Byzantium sub Φελλεύς
3 *Adagia* II iv 7 Lighter than cork; the last paragraph there speaks of rising above adversity. The Greek word for 'cork' is φέλλος; see *Adagia* IV vi 65 Cork-man (258 above).

24 In foro veritas
No deception in the market-place

Ἐν ἀγορᾷ ἀψευδεῖν, Refrain from misrepresentation in the market-place. The Athenians had a law which required the avoidance of all dishonesty in the market-place. Theophrastus tells us in his books *On the Laws* that the market controllers were concerned with ensuring two things in particular: first, that all the business of the market was carried on in an orderly manner, free from all disturbance, and second, that both the sellers and the buyers refrained from deception. This is the context of Anacharsis' comment, recorded in Diogenes Laertius: he said he was surprised that the Athenians had a law against cheating in the market-place, when they cheated and lied more often and more impudently there than they did anywhere else.[1]

25 Oculum excludere
Knock my eye out

People use this colloquial turn of phrase to inform someone making a request that he hasn't a hope. They say, 'If I say yes, knock my eye out, knock my tooth out.' The old father in Plautus' *Pseudolus* says:

> 'Pon my word, knock my eye out if I give it you.[1]

He means that the last thing he'll do is give the slave the money to buy his son's light-o'-love. Similarly, Phormio in Terence's play of that name: 'Knock an eye out if you like – there's somewhere I can make you pay for this.'[2]

* * * * *

24 Translated from the entry in Harpocration (1.170.17 Dindorf), which cites Theophrastus *De legibus* (fragment 98 Wimmer). Added in *1533*
1 Diogenes Laertius 1.104 ('Anacharsis'), though Anacharsis is there censuring Greeks in general. See also Erasmus *Apophthegmata* VII Anacharsis 9.

25 Plautus and Terence (see nn1–2). Otto 1266. Added in *1533*
1 Plautus *Pseudolus* 510
2 Terence *Phormio* 989 (*vel oculum excludito*). Modern editions favour the variant *exsculpe* for *exclude / excludito* in early editions, but the meaning remains the same.

26 Aut terra aut mari
By land or sea

In *Pseudolus*, Plautus wrote 'By land or sea,' meaning 'in any way what-soever.'[1] The phrase comes from the historians, who record exploits per-formed by land and sea, nations defeated in battle by land and sea. Cicero, in his speech for Cluentius: 'who has so many achievements to his credit by land and sea.'[2] Again, speaking in support of Manilius' proposed legis-lation: 'What mighty exploits of his have we seen at home and abroad, by land and sea, how many missions brought to a successful conclusion!'[3] An-other example from the same speech: 'So that at last we were truly seen to rule all peoples and nations by land and sea.'[4] Again, in the second of his speeches attacking Verres: 'though many plots were laid against me by Ver-res by land and sea.'[5] In the seventh book of his letters to Atticus: 'How can I follow by land or sea a person whose whereabouts I don't know?'[6] Demosthenes, in the closing section of his speech on behalf of Ctesiphon: 'If they are so beyond redemption, consign these same people and these alone to complete and utter destruction by land and sea.'[7] Plautus uses the phrase like this:

> I'll dredge up the money for you somehow by land or sea
> Within the next three days.[8]

In the fifth book of his work on *Definitions of Good and Evil*, Cicero adds a third term: 'One part deals with speaking, one with living, and in the third the natural world is so thoroughly investigated by them that no part in air, land, or sea, to use a poetic phrase, has been passed over.'[9] He says 'poetic,' because the poets list only the three elements, as, for example,

* * * * *

26 A very common expression, illustrated from Plautus and Cicero. This is briefly treated in *Adagia* I iv 25 By land and sea. Otto 1762. Added in 1533
1 Plautus *Pseudolus* 317. See full quotation below.
2 Not *Pro A. Cluentio* but Cicero *Pro lege Manilia* 23.68
3 Cicero *Pro lege Manilia* 16.48
4 Cicero *Pro lege Manilia* 19.56
5 Cicero *Verrines* 1.2.3
6 Cicero *Ad Atticum* 7.22.2
7 Demosthenes 18.324
8 Plautus *Pseudolus* 316–17
9 Cicero *De finibus* 5.4.9

Ovid: 'Before there was sea or land or sky that overarches all';[10] Terence: 'O heaven! O earth! O Neptune's seas!';[11] Plautus, in the *Amphitryo*: 'All things now, sea and earth and sky, seem to me to be conspiring.'[12]

27 Ἐκφυλλοφορῆσαι
To out-leaf

Those who lost the right to vote and were removed from the list of jurymen were said to be 'Out-leaved,' just as soldiers who lost the right to be in the fighting force were said to be 'out-warranted.' Originally votes were cast not with pebbles[1] but with leaves, so it's like saying that they were 'excluded from casting leaves.'

28 Lacunam explere
Fill up the gap

Cicero's use of the phrase *Lacunam explere* 'To fill up the gap,' to mean 'make good the loss,' in his fourth speech attacking Verres, has a proverbial look about it: 'The censors did exactly what people in this country always do when they have secured their office through bribery: they proceeded to use their position of authority so as to fill up the gap in their financial resources.'[1] He calls the reduction in their assets 'a gap.' Again, writing

* * * * *

10 Ovid *Metamorphoses* 1.5
11 Terence *Adelphi* 790
12 Plautus *Amphitryo* 1055

27 This appears to be based on Harpocration (1.109.1 Dindorf). See also the *Suda* E 721–2 and the scholion on Aeschines 1.111 (Dilts 41). Erasmus has omitted much that makes the content clear. The paragraph refers to the obligation of the Athenian boule or council to investigate ineligible or unworthy members and expel them. The archaic practice of using olive-leaves as voting papers was employed for this procedure.
1 For the ancient use of pebbles in voting, see *Adagia* I v 53 To add a white stone; IV vi 37 Gnawer of beans (238 above). The Greek verb ψηφίζειν 'to vote' means 'to cast a pebble.'

28 Brassicanus no 64, a longer essay than Erasmus', but using the same examples in the earlier section (see nn1–3); see *Adagia* IV iii 86 n2 (52 above). Added in *1533*
1 Cicero *Verrines* 2.2.55.138

to Atticus: 'See that there's no gap in the gold,'[2] that is, that there is no shortfall. Aulus Gellius in book one, chapter three of his *Attic Nights*, calls a stain on one's reputation a 'gap': 'That slight stain, that kind of a gap that his reputation will incur, is made up for by the advantages won for his friend.'[3] In texts, a 'fault' occurs where the reading is corrupt, whereas a 'gap' or lacuna occurs where there is something missing. One is emended, the other supplied.

29 Nullam corporis partem
No part of his body

Aeschines, in the speech *On the False Legation*: 'Indeed, Οὐδὲν ἄπρακτον ἔχων μέρος τοῦ σώματος "Letting no part of his body lie idle," not even the part where his words come streaming out, acting like an Aristides, the man who fixed the tribute-quotas for the Greeks and earned the nickname "The Just,"[1] he gets all indignant and spits out the word "bribes." '[2] Consider, learned reader, whether one should here read not ἄπρακτος 'idle, inactive,' but ἄπρατος, that is, 'unsold,' meaning that every part of his body could be bought, even his mouth and voice. Though indeed ἄπρακτος can mean 'making no demands,' giving one to understand that he grabbed not only with his hands but with his whole body.

30 Purus putus
Clean and clear

In the *Pseudolus*, Plautus used the phrase 'Clean and clear' to mean 'absolutely, sure as anything': 'Clean and clear, it is he – I know him – the mas-

* * * * *

2 Cicero *Ad Atticum* 12.6.1
3 Aulus Gellius *Noctes Atticae* 1.3.23

29 Aeschines (see n2). Added in *1533*
1 See *Adagia* IV viii 71 (401 above); Plutarch *Moralia* 186A–B
2 Aeschines 2.23. Estienne (in a footnote at LB II 1169F) strongly supports Erasmus' tentative emendation, which is accepted in modern texts, though parts of the text as quoted by Erasmus are now omitted.

30 Much of this is based on Pompeius Festus (241.3–7 Lindsay), though *putamina* is from Nonius Marcellus (39.19–22 Lindsay). See also Varro *De lingua Latina* 6.63; Aulus Gellius *Noctes Atticae* 7.5. Otto 1492. Added in *1533*

ter Polymachaeroplacides.'[1] It's like saying 'his absolute and very self.' The overtones of the word still reflect the way it was used in early times, as the ancients used *putus* to mean 'cleansed,' hence *putare* 'to cleanse' or 'prune' vines, and the discarded shells from nuts and such-like are called *putamina* 'cleanings.' The phrase seems to have originated with goldsmiths, who coined 'Clean and clear' just as the jurisconsults did *Sarta tecta* 'Wind-proof and water-tight.'[2]

31 Meis auspiciis
Under my own auspices

'Under my own auspices,' that is, by my own choosing, depending on my own resources. So Virgil, in *Aeneid* book four: 'But if the fates allowed me of my own choosing to conduct my life / And soothe my heart-ache as I myself should will.'[1] The phrase originates with Roman commanders who joined battle only after consulting the auspices. Any subsequent fighting was then said to be done 'under the auspices' of the person in supreme command. Very similar to this is the phrase I discussed earlier, 'By our own prowess.'[2] Cicero, in the fifth of his Verrine speeches: 'Especially since you have plenty of all these things, thanks to your own prowess.'[3] A thing happens 'thanks to our own prowess' when no outside help is required to bring it about.

32 Vestigiis inhaerere
Tread in the tracks of

A man who follows the example of his forebears is said to 'Tread in his

* * * * *

1 Plautus *Pseudolus* 989. The name in modern editions is 'Polymachaeroplagides.' Erasmus follows the text of Giambattista Pio's 1500 edition; see *Adagia* IV iii 40 n2 (27 above). Added in *1533*
2 *Adagia* IV v 37 (166 above). The phrase may have been taken from Alciati *De verborum significatione* IV page 86 (see *Adagia* IV vii 75n, 332 above).

31 Virgil (see n1). Added in *1533*
1 Virgil *Aeneid* 4.340–1
2 *Adagia* I vi 19
3 Cicero *Verrines* 2.3.4.9

32 Inspired by Alciati *De verborum significatione* IV page 87, where the phrase is quoted (see *Adagia* IV vii 75n, 332 above). Added in *1533*

ancestors' tracks.' Cicero, in his speech for Publius Sestius: 'A man who should have been standing in the tracks made by his ancestors.'[1] The saying comes from travellers who mark carefully the tracks of those who have gone before, so that they do not go off the path. Similarly, those who fall away from the example of their forefathers or their teachers are said to 'abandon their tracks.' People who produce nothing original but stick to what others have discovered are said to 'tread in others' tracks.'

33 Dulce et amarum
Sweet and bitter

Plautus is using a proverbial expression in *Pseudolus* when he writes 'Sweet and bitter' for 'happy and sad.' The young man in love says about the note from his girlfriend, 'You bring me sweet and bitter mixed together.' Later on in the same play: 'Sweet and bitter, I've confided all to you. / You know my passion, you know my problem, you know my lack of cash.'[1] Plautus again in *Truculentus*: 'Now I know the sweet and bitter, the things that money brings.'[2]

34 Hyberno pulvere, verno luto
Dust in winter, mud in spring

Festus Pompeius cites a line from an old poem without naming an author, from which we can deduce that it was a piece of popular wisdom. In it we find a father giving his son instruction in farming, and he says, 'Dust in winter, mud in spring – fat barley-ears, my boy, you'll reap.'[1] I think this means that if barley is sown in a clear bright winter followed by a wet spring a good crop results.

* * * * *

1 Cicero *Pro P. Sestio* 3.7

33 Plautus (see nn1–2). Otto 1083. Added in *1533*
1 Plautus *Pseudolus* 63, 694–5
2 Plautus *Truculentus* 345–6

34 Pompeius Festus (see n1). Added in *1533*
1 Pompeius Festus 82.16–22 Lindsay

35 Αἰξωνεύεσθαι
Talk Aexonian

We have already listed many proverbial sayings derived from national characteristics.[1] Here we have another, Αἰξωνεύεσθαι 'Talk Aexonian,' applied to
people who can't stop making slanderous accusations. The people of Aexonia were lampooned for this trait in Old Comedy, as Stephanus tells us,
adding the information that Aexonia is a place in Magnesia.[2] He also mentions Αἰξωνή, with an accent on the final syllable, the name of a deme in
the Cecropian tribe.[3] The adjective Αἰξωνεύς 'Aexonian' could be derived
from either. This information about the Aexonians is supported by references to Menander's the *Basket-Bearer*, and to Plato's dialogue on courage:
'I will say nothing to that, though I could easily do so, or you might well
call me Aexonian.' Marsilius translates 'Aexonian' as 'foulmouthed' and
'slanderous.'[4]

36 Gallam bibere oportet
He needs to drink gall-nut

Those who over-indulged belly and gullet were humorously told 'To drink
gall-nut.' Gall-nuts are fruits which develop on trees, especially oaks, in
the autumn and look like round nuts. There is a good deal of information

* * * * *

35 Brassicanus no 12 (see *Adagia* IV iii 86 n2, 52 above). Stephanus of Byzantium
sub Ἀιξωνεία, with Harpocration (1.9.1. Dindorf), supplemented by Apostolius
1.67. These sources include the references to Menander (fragment 222 Körte-
Thierfelder) and Plato *On Courage* (ie *Laches* 197C). Added in 1533
1 Eg Thessalians: *Adagia* I iii 10 and 12; Scythians: IV ix 85 (474 above); Thracians:
IV viii 52 (389 above), IV ix 58 (458 above); Boeotians: V i 77 (585 below);
Carthaginians: I viii 28
2 Magnesia is a district in Thessaly.
3 In 1533 Erasmus read *Cercopidis* 'Cercopian,' thinking of the Cercopes, a tribe
notorious for violence and insolence. He changed it in 1536 to *Cecropidis* 'of
Cecropis.' Cecropis was an Athenian territorial division. See Wesseling (2001)
456.
4 Marsilio Ficino, in his translation of Plato. See *Adagia* IV viii 97 n2 (417 above).

36 Pompeius Festus citing Lucilius (see n2). Added in 1533

about them in Pliny, Dioscorides, Galen, and Theophrastus.[1] Their effect is astringent and drying, and for that reason they have many applications. Hence that line of Lucilius, where he bids spendthrifts and guzzlers 'drink gall-nuts and take a tuck in the belly,'[2] that is, reduce their appetites. Sextus Pompeius Festus quotes the line. Horace has a line of similar import, where he writes that 'spendthrifts' bellies should be branded with a red-hot iron.'[3]

37 Sontica causa
Compelling reason

The poet Naevius, in a trochaic tetrameter catalectic cited by Festus, uses the phrase *sontica causa*, meaning a really compelling reason: 'There must be some compelling reason why / You should destroy the woman.'[1] The word originates in the Twelve Tables,[2] where an illness is called 'compelling' if it is not an everyday complaint but one so serious that a defendant cannot be forced to appear in court.

38 Macula, labes
Stain, blot

Cicero often calls a notorious evil-doer 'stain, blot, filth, dirt.'[1] Festus cites a line from Plautus where the word *suasum* occurs with similar meaning: 'Be-

* * * * *

1 See Pliny *Naturalis historia* 16.26–7; 24.9; Galen *De simplicibus medicinis* 7.22; Dioscorides 1.146; Theophrastus *Historia plantarum* 3.7.45.
2 Pompeius Festus 85.8–10 Lindsay quoting Lucilius 501 Marx (506 Krenkel)
3 Horace *Epistles* 1.15.36–7

37 Naevius by way of Pompeius Festus (see n1). Added in *1533*
1 Pompeius Festus 372.2–7 Lindsay, citing CRF Naevius 128, and also giving *sonticus morbus* 'compelling disease' from the Twelve Tables. Erasmus in passing identifies the metre in Naevius as trochaic tetrameter catalectic, which is one used for more impassioned monologue and dialogue in Roman comedy.
2 The Twelve Tables were an early Roman codification of miscellaneous legal regulations, surviving only in fragments, often preserved for the archaic forms and words they contain. See *Adagia* v ii 15–17 (608–10 below).

38 Cicero (see n1). Added in *1533*
1 Cicero *Ad Atticum* 1.16.11, *In L. Pisonem* 26.62. See above *Adagia* IV x 11 Fouler than filth (490 above).

cause, you shameful wretch, you've stained your dress with *suasum* "lamp-black."'[2] Festus thinks *suasum* is a stain made by smoky drip onto a white garment. Plautus' tetrameter could be applied to those who have an honest name, either handed down from their forebears or won by good deeds, but who stain it with some wickedness.

39 Capere crines
Seize the locks

In the *Haunted House*, Plautus writes 'Seize the locks' for seizing the opportunity offered and making the most of it. The phrase comes either from the god the Greeks call Καιρός 'Opportunity,' who is represented with hair on the front of his head but bald at the back,[1] or from the custom of holding onto the hair of someone you don't want to get away. What Plautus writes is as follows:

> If you're sure he'll be yours for ever,
> That you'll hold your lover all your life,
> Then I suppose you'd better put yourself
> At his disposal only, seize the fellow's locks, as the saying goes,
> And make your money that way.[2]

40 Nihil est miserius quam animus conscius
Nothing is more miserable than a guilty conscience

'Even a gardener oft speaks to the point,' as the proverb goes.[1] In Plautus'

* * * * *

2 Pompeius Festus 392.25–8 Lindsay, citing Plautus *Truculentus* 271

39 Plautus (see n2). Added in *1533*
1 For Opportunity, which must be seized by the forelock, see *Adagia* I vii 70 Consider the due time.
2 Plautus *Mostellaria* 224–7. The words are spoken to a prostitute. Erasmus' text, and consequently his interpretation, drawn from Pio's commentary (see *Adagia* IV iii 40 n2, 27 above), differs from that of modern editions, where, with a change of speaker, the last two lines are taken to mean 'Get your plaits (your wedding hair-do). – As a person's reputation, so can he make his money.'

40 Plautus (see n2). Tilley C 601 Conscience is a thousand witnesses. Added in *1533*
1 *Adagia* I vi 1

play, the *Haunted House*, Tranio, who is a slave of shocking character, utters a sentiment worthy of any theologian: 'Nothing is more miserable than a guilty conscience.'[2] This agrees with the Hebrew saying 'A cheerful heart has a continual feast,'[3] and with this: 'Conscience is a thousand witnesses.'[4] Horace considers that happiness consists in 'a conscience that does not accuse, no guilty thought to pale one's cheek.'[5]

41 Celei supellex
Celeus' goods and chattels

A line from Virgil's *Georgics*, book one, shows that simple rustic equipment could be called 'Celeus' goods': 'You'll need as well what's made of withies, / Celeus' goods of little worth.'[1] See the story related in Ovid's *Fasti*:

> Places too have their allotted fate.
> That now called Eleusis, Ceres' place,
> Once was the farm of aged Celeus.
> He was returning home with load of acorns,
> Berries too from brambles plucked,
> Dry wood to burn upon his hearth.
> His little daughter from the hills
> Was bringing home the goats,
> And in his cradle lay his baby son, unwell.[2]

Celeus was king of Eleusis, and the father of Triptolemus, to whom Ceres revealed the principles of agriculture, because Celeus offered her hospitality. Plautus has a line: 'Like Celio's goods and chattels, peg next to peg.'[3]

* * * * *

2 Plautus *Mostellaria* 544
3 Prov 15:15
4 *Adagia* I x 91, quoting Quintilian 5.11.41
5 Horace *Epistles* 1.1.61

41 Virgil (see n1). Added in *1533*
1 Virgil *Georgics* 1.165
2 Ovid *Fasti* 4.507–12
3 Plautus *Menaechmi* 404, but modern texts read *suppellex pellionis* not *suppellex Celionis*, that is, 'a tanner's tools,' not 'Celio's goods.' Erasmus' interpretation

It's surprising that Plautus here gives Celio a long first syllable when the name has a short syllable elsewhere. There is nothing unusual in having *Celio* for *Celeus*: compare the two forms *scorpio, scorpius* 'scorpion.'[4]

42 Ampullacea
Flask-rich

Plautus seems to use the word *ampullacea* in *The Two Menaechmuses* to describe a woman who is splendidly dressed and well kitted out. The text actually says, 'Since he keeps you well found in jewellery and clothes, with flask hope (*ampula spem*). / They're quite right when they say, my girl, it's better to be sensible.'[1] It's quite obvious that the words *ampula spem* are corrupt. Some people keep the reading *ampullosam* 'with many a flask,'[2] but that does not fit the trochaic metre. *Ampullaceam* fits both metre and sense. The word occurs in Pliny book fifteen, where he is listing types of pears, though possibly the text is corrupt there too. What Pliny says is:

> The myrrh-pear, the bay-leaf pear, the nard-pear are so called from their smell; the barley-pear from the season when it is ripe, the *ampullacea* 'flask-pear' from its long neck, and the Coriolan ...[3]

* * * * *

is based on Pio's notes on the text, which had the corrupt reading. For Pio see *Adagia* IV iii 40 n2 (27 above).

4 *Scorpio, scorpius* is an example of enallage; see *De copia* (CWE 24 329).

42 Plautus (see n1). Added in *1533*
1 Plautus *Menaechmi* 801–2, but modern texts read *ancillas penum / recte praehibet* 'provides servants and provisions,' (not *ampula spem. / Recte perhibent*, the reading of the Milan 1500 edition; see previous adage, n3), an improved reading known in better earlier texts (see the annotator at LB II 1171F). Erasmus does not really explain his suggested reading *ampullacea*, but presumably he is thinking of *ampulla* 'flask,' a container for cosmetics and perfumes. The common suffix *–aceus* implies, in one of its senses, 'made of,' so possibly 'a woman absolutely made of scent-bottles.'
2 This is another dismissive reference to material in Giambattista Pio's Plautus commentary; see *Adagia* IV iii 40 n2 (27 above).
3 Pliny *Naturalis historia* 15.55

43 **Cyatho non emam**
I wouldn't give a dram

The soldier in Plautus' play, the *Carthaginian*, is using a proverbial expression when he says, 'Pshaw! Hot air! I wouldn't give a dram for seven nights with her!'[1] He is speaking of a girl who gives herself airs but is not particularly good-looking. By 'dram' the soldier means the smallest possible amount. Being a soldier, he's used to measures of drink. The dram-measure (*cyathus*)[2] is the smallest size of drink, the bowl (*crater*) is considerably larger.

44 **Rex sum**
I'm a king

At one time, to indicate great good fortune, people said, 'I'm a god,' or 'I'm in heaven.' Plautus similarly says in the *Carthaginian*, 'I'm a king, if I can get him to my place today.'[1] He puts the words into the mouth of the pimp Lycus, who hopes his fortune will be made if he can entice some man with plenty of ready money into his establishment.

45 **Cribro crebrius**
Through more slots than a sieve

An amusing phrase used by Plautus with a kind of proverbial ring:

* * * * *

43 Plautus (see n1). Added in *1533*
  1 Plautus *Poenulus* 274. Modern texts again present a different reading: *quoius ego nebulai cyatho septem noctes non emam*, possibly, 'I wouldn't pay a cup of fog for seven nights of her.' Erasmus interpreted *MIL.* (indicating the speaker) as *miles* 'soldier,' whereas it really stands for *Milphio*, the name of a slave character. Consequently his comment is ill-founded.
  2 The definition is to be found in Hesychius κ 4334–5.

44 Plautus (see n1). See *Adagia* I v 99–100 To be a god. To make a god of someone. To be in heaven. Otto 1533. Added in *1533*
  1 Plautus *Poenulus* 671, added in *1533* to *Adagia* III v 41 A king or an ass

45 Plautus (see n1). *Cribro crebrius* is mentioned in Brassicanus no 4 *Areopagita subticentior* (used at *Adagia* IV x 6 Closer than an Areopagite, 488 above). Otto 465; Suringar 46. Added in *1533*

'Through more slots than a sieve,' meaning 'in very many places, all over': 'I see I must re-roof the whole of my house – / As it is, it lets in daylight through more slots than a sieve.'[1] A stupid chatterbox is commonly said to be 'as watertight as a sieve.'

46 Et operam et retiam perdere
Waste both toil and net

Plautus in the *Rope*: 'As it is, he's making mock of toil and net as well.'[1] Here it is meant quite literally by the old master, as he had sent his slave Gripus fishing in spite of the great storm the night before. It will be more satisfying to use it metaphorically with reference to a person hoping to extract a legacy from someone, but whose hunting fails to net the bird. Plautus here used the old form *retia* for later *rete* 'net.' This saying is related to the ones I discussed earlier, 'I have wasted both oil and toil' and 'Care and cost lost.'[2]

47 Virtute duce, comite fortuna
Guided by virtue, fortune attending

Cicero, writing to Plancus, in the tenth book of his *Letters to Friends*: 'You have achieved all that is best – "Guided by virtue, fortune attending."'[1] This is such a worthy sentiment and so neatly expressed that some people have adopted it as their public motto.[2] Virtue chooses what is best, but if the undertaking does not succeed, in noble endeavours as in great ones, even to have shown the will is a fine thing.[3] If however success does follow, praise is due in the first instance to virtue, who leads the way in deeds of note, secondly to fortune, as one that follows in virtue's train.

* * * * *

1 Plautus *Rudens* 101–2

46 Plautus (see n1). Added in *1533*
1 Plautus *Rudens* 900
2 Both sayings in *Adagia* I iv 62 I have wasted both oil and toil

47 Cicero (see n1). Added in *1533*
1 Cicero *Ad familiares* 10.3.2
2 The motto was adopted by Sebastian Gryphius. He was the Lyon printer who published a number of unauthorized editions of Erasmus' works.
3 *Adagia* II viii 55 In great enterprises even to have shown the will is enough

48 Croesi pecuniae terunciam addere
Add a penny to Croesus' millions

Cicero in book four of *Definitions of Good and Evil*: 'With regard to objects
which are so small that they have to be searched out, it is often the case
that we have to say it doesn't matter to us whether they exist or not, just as
"Adding a torch to the light of the sun"'[1] (the example you adduced) is of no
significance, or adding a penny (*teruncius*) to Croesus' millions.'[2] The *teruncius* was so called because it was worth three times (*ter*) an ounce piece (*un-
cia*),[3] and became a proverbial example of something of little value.[4] Croesus, king of Lydia, was famous for being one of the world's inordinately
rich men.

49 Barbati
Wearers of the beard

It seems that the Romans had a proverbial joke phrase, 'Wearers of the
beard,' which they used to refer to men of old-fashioned simple ways
and rustic honesty. The Romans did in fact adopt the practice of shaving or trimming the beard only late on. According to Pliny, it was Publius
Ticinius Mena who first imported a barber from Sicily in the four-hundred-
and-fifty-fourth year of Rome's history.[1] Until that time they had let their
beards grow. Cicero, in the fourth book of his *Definitions of Good and Evil*,
writes:

> You should have said that you couldn't accept the belief of those ancient
> thinkers, those 'Wearers of the beard,' as we might call them, using that phrase

* * * * *

48 Cicero (see n2). Otto 1767. Added in *1533*
  1 *Adagia* IV viii 25 Add light to the sun with torches (370 above)
  2 Cicero *De finibus* 4.12.29 (the modern text gives the sense 'indistinctness re-
    sults' for 'they have to be searched out'). For Croesus' millions, see *Adagia* I
    vi 74 As rich as Croesus or Crassus.
  3 The etymology is from Varro *De lingua latina* 5.174.
  4 *Adagia* I viii 9 He did not spend a farthing

49 Cicero (see n2). Added in *1533*
  1 Pliny *Naturalis historia* 7.211. The year was 299 BC.

we have for some of our own contemporaries. This belief of theirs was that a good man, who lived a decent life and also enjoyed good health and a good reputation and had adequate means to live on, would have a preferable life of better quality and more to be desired than a man, equally good, but also, 'in many a way,' like Ennius' Alcmaeon, 'by sickness, exile and poverty ensnared.' Those ancient thinkers rather naively considered the more desirable life to be superior, happier. The Stoics, however . . .'[2]

This line of Juvenal illustrates the same idea: 'It's easy to deceive a bearded king.'[3]

50 Vestigium ponere
To tread on

Vestigium ponere, To tread upon, come across, was used by Cicero in book five of his *Definitions of Good and Evil*: 'Although there is an endless supply in this city – wherever we go, we tread on some bit of history.'[1] There's an amusing tale told of someone, Stratonicus, I think, who was walking about on tiptoe in some town or other, looking round as he did so, and when he was asked what he was doing, he said he was afraid of treading on a town-crier, hinting at the excessive numbers of town-criers in the place.[2] Cicero, again in book five of the above work: 'Why! Wisdom wouldn't have a place to set her foot if you take away all the duties of life.'[3] I know I have already discussed the proverb 'He has no place to set his foot,'[4] but at the time I didn't remember this example, and it's too good to be passed over, as it illustrates a nice metaphorical use of the phrase, applied to the things of the mind. Cicero means that there is no place for wisdom if there is no weighing of duties.

* * * * *

2 Cicero *De finibus* 4.23.62, citing Ennius (*Scenica* 22 Vahlen)
3 Juvenal 4.103

50 Cicero (see n1). Added in *1533*
1 Cicero *De finibus* 5.2.5
2 Stratonicus was a musician and a joker. The story is told, along with other examples of his witticisms, in Athenaeus 8.349B.
3 Cicero *De finibus* 4.25.69 (not 5)
4 *Adagia* I v 7

51 Priscis credendum
Believe the ancients

In his fragmentary work *On the Universe*, Cicero says, 'We must of course
believe the men of old, the ancients, as they say, who claimed they were the
offspring of the gods.'[1] It is not clear whether Cicero means that the whole
expression was commonly bandied about, or whether he was marking just
the word 'ancient,' which we use for persons belonging to a far distant
age, whose origin was unknown to their descendants and so was usually
ascribed to the gods.

52 Omnes intus
Everyone's inside

As Theocritus wrote in the *Syracusan Women*: Κάλλιστ'· ἔνδοι πᾶσαι ὁ τὰν
νυὸν εἶπ' ἀποκλάξας 'Splendid! Everyone's inside – as the young man said,
shutting the door on his bride.'[1] The ancient commentator tells us that we
have a proverb here. My guess is that its origin was as follows: the husband
got weary of his wife and shut her out of the house. When she knocked
at the door and asked to be taken back, the husband replied, 'Everyone's
inside!' Or maybe, when the bride was conducted according to custom to
her husband's house, he shut the door and spoke these words. This can
be given a more serious application if someone unworthy to be received
as a friend is angling to be accepted into one's circle. One can then reply,
'Everyone's inside.' Or – a more likely explanation – we will use it to mean
everything is safe and secure, since the Greek verb ἀποκλείω can mean not
only 'to shut out,' but also 'to shut in' something we want to be set aside and
kept safe. Hence the Greek noun ἀπόκλεισμα, meaning 'guard-house.' So it
is possible that the bridegroom shut his bride into the marriage-chamber

* * * * *

51 Cicero (see n1). Added in *1533*
1 Cicero *Timaeus* 11.38

52 Between here and the end of this century, Erasmus introduces sixteen adages
culled from the *Idylls* of Theocritus. He was using the edition of Zacharias
Calliergis (1516), which included the ancient scholia on the text. Added in
1533
1 Theocritus *Idylls* 15.77

and excluded all the other females, saying, 'Everyone's inside.' One woman is enough for the bridegroom, so he excluded the rest as supernumerary! Κλάξ is the Sicilian word for 'key,' hence ἀποκλάζω for ἀποκλείω.[2]

53 Esurienti ne occurras
Don't go near a hungry man

There is a line at the end of the same *Idyll* which looks like a proverb. Gorgo is anxious to get home because her husband is short-tempered, and she adds: Πεινῶντί γε μηδὲ ποτένθῃς 'Don't go near a hungry man.'[1] Hunger makes the temper worse. So in Plautus somebody asks a person talking crossly how long it is since he had a meal.[2] Also in Plautus we find: 'Being kept waiting for a meal when one is hungry drives the bile up one's nose.'[3]

54 Opus ad opus
Toil on toil

Here's another one from the same poem: Ἔργον ἐπ᾽ ἔργῳ 'Toil on toil,' meaning no end to the task.[1] Here the woman is complaining about her husband because he had bought dirty, coarse wool, involving her in a lot of work. Virgil too, speaking of the cultivation of vines: 'On this there is never spent of pains enough.'[2]

* * * * *

2 Κλάξ 'key' appears earlier in the poem (line 33); ἀποκλάξας (see quotation) is a form of ἀποκλάζω, which is the Doric form of Attic ἀποκλείω. (Theocritus was employing the Doric Greek of Syracuse.) Erasmus' cryptic comments are based on the ancient scholiast at lines 33 and 77.

53 Theocritus (see n1). Added in *1533*
1 Theocritus *Idylls* 15.148
2 Plautus *Stichus* 318
3 Plautus *Amphitryo*, line 81 of the spurious supplement (see *Adagia* IV viii 16 n2, 364 above). The line supplies the title of *Adagia* II viii 60.

54 Theocritus (see n1). Added in *1533*
1 Theocritus *Idylls* 15.17
2 Virgil *Georgics* 2.398 (already used in *Adagia* II vi 62 A spring in the field)

55 Tredecim cubitorum
Over eight feet tall

Very tall men are laughed at even today for being slow and useless. Like many other things, this has worked its way down to us from antiquity. In that same poem, Praxinoa calls her husband ἀνὴρ τρισκαιδεκάπηχυς 'a fellow over eight feet tall,' exaggerating his height, because he was so stupid he went to the market and brought home salt instead of soap.[1] I have already written about 'The boot of Maximinus.'[2] The ancients jokingly called very tall men 'long-shanks.' Varro in *Tripalus*, cited by Nonius: 'I say nothing; the fellow in front of me, some long-shanks, is taking care of it all.'[3]

56 Volam pedis ostendere
Show the sole of one's foot

Τὸ κοῖλον τοῦ ποδὸς δεῖξαι, To show the hollow or sole of one's foot. This is said of those who take to flight in battle. In the Roman historians, we very frequently find the Latin equivalent 'turn the back,' that is, turn tail. The Greek proverb is reported in Hesychius.[1] Even today we say of runaways that they 'show a clean pair of heels.'[2]

57 Factum transactum
Done and dealt with

The Jurists are constantly using the phrase *Factum transactum* 'Done and

* * * * *

55 Theocritus (see n1). *Adagia* III iv 58 Big and foolish. Suringar 226. Added in 1533
  1 Theocritus *Idylls* 15.20
  2 *Adagia* I i 21
  3 Nonius Marcellus 191.27–9 Lindsay, citing Varro *Menippeae* (562 Buecheler, *Triphallos*) where the modern reading differs in several respects from Erasmus' text

56 Brassicanus no 114 *Cavum pedis ostendere* (see *Adagia* IV iii 86 n2, 52 above), quoting Hesychius (see n1). Suringar 241. Added in 1533
  1 Hesychius K 3240
  2 Erasmus uses a non-classical word, *calcaneum* 'heel,' which is first attested in Tertullian and is common in later and Ecclesiastical Latin.

57 Cicero and Terence (see nn1–2). Added in 1533

dealt with,' to mean that nothing relevant to the business in hand has
been omitted. Cicero, in his third speech attacking Catiline: 'The thing that
needed to be done first of all has been done and dealt with.'[1] The phrase
occurs in Terence too,[2] and many other reputable authors.

58 Maeandri
Meanders

When some business is carried through not straightforwardly but with deceitful and devious machinations, we speak of 'Meanders,' a metaphor derived from the river Meander, which twists and bends in its course, and gets
its name from this, as it 'wanders about seeking human communities.'[1] Cicero, in his speech attacking Piso: 'What meanderings, as you threaded your
way through every uninhabited district, what diversions, what roundabout
routes did you choose?'[2] Prudentius uses the word in one of his hymns[3]
which I quoted above in the adage 'A labyrinth.'[4] The Meander is a river
which waters Lydia, bending and flowing back on itself. Pliny writes of it in
book five, chapter twenty-nine: 'The Meander has its source in a lake in the
mountainous region of Aulocrene. It flows close by many towns, and is often
enlarged by tributaries. Its curves are so tortuous that it is often believed to
flow backwards. Its course takes it first through the region of Apamena, then
that of Eumenia, then the Bargyliotic Plains, and finally Caria. It is a tranquil river, irrigating all those lands with extremely fertile deposits of mud.

* * * * *

1 Cicero *Catilinarians* 3.6.15. This example was added in 1533 to *Adagia* I iii 40
  To consider a thing done. Cf the passage at Alciati *De verborum significatione*
  IV page 87, where the same Cicero example is adduced (see *Adagia* IV vii 75n,
  332 above).
2 Terence *Andria* 248

58 Cicero (see n1). Otto 1005. Cf *Adagia* II x 51 A labyrinth, which had material
  about 'meander' added in 1515. Added in 1533
 1 This explanation of the name Meander as derived from the words for 'seek'
  and 'men,' in Greek μαίομαι, ἄνδρες, was perhaps suggested to Erasmus by the
  two successive entries in Hesychius, Μαίανδρος 'Meander' and μαίεσθαι 'seek'
  (M 65–6).
 2 Cicero *In L. Pisonem* 22.53
 3 Prudentius *Cathemerinon* 6.142. Erasmus wrote a commentary on this hymn in
  1523.
 4 *Adagia* II x 51

About ten stades from Miletus it gently debouches into the sea.'[5] 'Meander' is also the name of an embroidery pattern put round the borders of cloaks, consisting of an intertwining line wrapped round on itself like a labyrinth. See Virgil *Aeneid*, book five: 'To the victor, a gold-embroidered cloak with border wide / Of Meliboean purple, where two meanders intertwine.'[6]

59 Masculum
Masculine

The ancients used the word *masculus* 'masculine' not only to signify gender but also for anything vigorous, solid, and robust. Nonius Marcellus cites an example from one of Varro's *Satires*, called Ὄνος λύρας 'The ass hears music':[1] 'I am convinced there's nothing masculine for the business.'[2] The grammarians think Horace meant 'firm and solid,' when he wrote of 'a male yolk.' This is in the *Satires*, where he writes as follows of long-shaped eggs: 'For they are thicker shelled and contain a male yolk.'[3] Virgil too describes the white and better sort of frankincense as 'masculine.'[4] It will have a nice touch if you transfer the word to abstract things, for example, calling a noble and strong spirit 'masculine.'

60 Intra labia risit
He kept his laughter within his mouth

I have already written of the 'Sardonic grin.'[1] Theocritus writes of something similar in his *Thalysia*: 'And calmly he addressed me, his lips just part-

* * * * *

5 Pliny *Naturalis historia* 5.113. For Erasmus' reference to chapter 29 see *Adagia* IV iii 3 n3 (5–6 above).
6 Virgil *Aeneid* 5.250–1. This, together with the 'Greek key' pattern, is taken from Nonius Marcellus 203.2–204.7 Lindsay.

59 Nonius Marcellus (see n2). Added in *1533*
1 See *Adagia* I iv 35 An ass to the lyre.
2 Nonius Marcellus 205.7–9 Lindsay, citing Varro *Menippeae* 369 Buecheler
3 Horace *Satires* 2.4.14. 'The grammarians' means the ancient commentator Acron on this passage.
4 Virgil *Eclogues* 8.65. See also Pliny *Naturalis historia* 12.60, 61.

60 Theocritus (see n2). Added in *1533*
1 *Adagia* III v 1

ing and with twinkling eye, / And the laughter stayed within his mouth.'[2]
Homer calls a bitter laugh 'sardonic.'[3] Theocritus is describing a civilized,
friendly laugh, which becomes an unseemly hoot if it is allowed to break
out.[4]

61 Pingui mensura
With fat measure

Πίονι μέτρῳ, With fat measure, used by Theocritus in the same poem, meaning ample and generous: 'For indeed with measure fat / The goddess has
piled high their threshing-floor with barley.'[1] This is similar to the adages
I discussed earlier, 'In handfuls' and 'To take with both hands.'[2]

62 Fato Metelli
By fate the Metelli

In his commentary on Cicero's speech in defence of Milo, Asconius Pedianus[1] cites a senarius of the poet Naevius aimed at the Metelli and implying that they became consuls not on their merits but at the whim of Fortune, ruler of the hustings,[2] as they call her. The line runs: 'By Fate here in
Rome Metelli become consuls.'[3] This annoyed the Metellus who was consul
at the time and he replied in a hypercatalectic senarius, a verse form which
Asconius says was also called a Saturnian: 'Evil will the Metelli bring on

* * * * *

2 Theocritus *Idylls* 7.19–20: Γέλως δέ οἱ εἴχετο χείλευς.
3 Homer *Odyssey* 20.301–2
4 See *Adagia* II vi 39 Shaking with laughter.

61 Theocritus (see n1). Added in *1533*
1 Theocritus *Idylls* 7.33–4
2 *Adagia* II i 6 and I ix 16

62 Much of this paragraph is derived from the commentary of Pseudo-Asconius
(for whom see *Adagia* I v 56:12n CWE 31 434) on a line in Cicero's first speech
in his action against Verres (see n1). Added in *1533*
1 Pseudo-Asconius commentary on Cicero *Verrines* 1.10.29, quoted below (see
n5), not the commentary on *Pro Milone*.
2 See *Adagia* IV x 19 Lady Luck, ruler of the hustings (496 above).
3 The line of Naevius may be found in E.H. Warmington ed *Remains of Old Latin*
(Loeb edition, Cambridge, Mass 1936) II page 154.

poet Naevius.'[4] Cicero makes an oblique reference to this exchange when he says, 'Unlike the rest of your family, you were not "By Fate" . . .'[5] This amusing gibe at the Metelli can be turned against anyone advanced beyond his merits to wealth and honour.

63 Non habet cui indormiat
He hasn't a thing to sleep on

Theocritus in the *Wayfarers*: Οὐδὲ γὰρ Εὐμάρᾳ τῷ δεσπότῃ ἦς τοι ἐνεύδειν 'For not even your master Eumaras had a skin on which to sleep.'[1] The shepherd Lacon makes this tendentious remark to insinuate the utter poverty of some goatherd or other who didn't have even a goatskin on which to sleep. The ancients used to lie on animal skins both at table and in bed. In Homer the suitors are lying on ox-skins as they feast.[2] Even today we say, 'He hasn't a bed, or a mattress, to sleep on.'

64 Asinus asino et sus sui pulcher
Ass looks lovely to ass and pig to pig

Ὄνος ὄνῳ κάλλιστον An ass looks most lovely to another ass. Likes attract

* * * * *

4 The Saturnian was an early Latin verse form of which a number of examples survive, mainly fragments of Livius Andronicus' translation of the *Odyssey* into Latin and Gnaeus Naevius' epic poem on the First Punic War (both third century BC). The principles on which its versification was based are still a matter of debate. The Latin iambic senarius was a quantitative metre consisting of six units fundamentally of the syllable pattern short/long (or light/heavy); 'hypercatalectic' means having an extra syllable after the last complete unit.

5 Cicero *Verrines* 1.10.29. Cicero is here citing a jibe reportedly made by Verres himself, but Erasmus has been misled by Pseudo-Asconius.

63 Theocritus (see n1). Suringar 147. Added in *1533*

1 Theocritus *Idylls* 5.10. The goatherd accuses Lacon of stealing his skin jacket. Lacon replies that even the master Eumaras didn't have a skin, let alone his goatherd.

2 Possibly a memory of *Odyssey* 3.38, but the guests there, not suitors, lie on fleeces.

64 Diogenes Laertius (see n1). See *Adagia* I ii 21–4 Like rejoices in like, etc. Added in *1533*

each other. Diogenes Laertius quotes a number of extracts which Alcimus
assembled out of Plato and the comic writer Epicharmus, by which he hoped
to show that the philosopher had filched a great deal from the comic writers.
Among these we find the following lines in iambic metre:

> It is no wonder that we speak thus,
> That we admire ourselves, and think
> Ourselves fine creatures, for to a dog
> Another dog looks good, and to an ox an ox.
> One ass to another lovely seems, and pig to pig.[1]

This can be used when disreputable persons strike up a relationship
based on their similarity of character and way of life, for example, soldiers
together, or gamblers, or drinkers, or sophists.[2] It's surprising that Epicharmus didn't bring in the ape, since no other animal is more satisfied with its
own kind.

65 Pediculi Platonis
Plato's lice

Οἱ Πλάτωνος φθεῖρες, Plato's lice. These have become proverbial, as Myronianus gives us to understand. In his work on *Parallels*, as cited by Diogenes
Laertius in his life of Plato, Myronianus deduces that Plato died of the louse
disease, because people commonly speak of 'Plato's lice.'[1] The Greek name
for this disease is *phthiriasis*. It is a disgusting and painful condition. Lucius

* * * * *

1 Diogenes Laertius 3.9 and 16 ('Plato'). The lines cited are Epicharmus fragment
   173 Kaibel.
2 Erasmus is always disparaging about the sophists, an attitude that goes back
   to Plato. These were teachers of rhetoric in Greece from the fifth century
   BC onwards who professed, for a fee, to promote fluency, confidence, and
   success in life. See eg *Adagia* IV v 31 Catch with both hands, and IV v 33 An
   enemy within (162 and 163); v i 39 n1 (564 below); *Apophthegmata* I 'Sayings
   of Spartans' 1; II 'Sayings of Nameless Spartans' 17; VIII Preface.

65 Diogenes Laertius (see n1). This adage, with some of the material here, somewhat differently worded, appeared in 1526 and 1528; see ASD II-8 255, critical
   apparatus on 603–12.
1 Diogenes Laertius 3.40 ('Plato')

Sulla died of it as well,[2] though we do find in the ancient writers differing opinions as to the manner of his death.[3] Myronianus says nothing about the use of the proverb. One can however deduce that it was directed at those of dirty habits, because philosophers pay very little attention to polishing the outer man, being absorbed in the cultivation of the mind.

66 Vates secum auferat omen
Let the prophet keep his doom

We can apply to those who threaten us with dire consequences or prophesy a nasty fate these lines of Theocritus from his poem, *The Rustic Singing-Match*: 'But the seer Telemos, threatening me with doom, / May take home his doom and save it for his children.'[1] The Cyclops had sworn by his one eye, which, he said, saw everything and always would. The seer Telemos however had predicted that Ulysses would put out that eye. The Cyclops turns the prediction back on the seer and his children. Similarly in Virgil: 'That prediction may the gods turn back on him that made it!' And again: 'Such sufferings may the gods reserve for him and his children's children!'[2] Also Homer in *Iliad* book four: 'With their own heads, with their wives and their children they pay.'[3] This is like Plato's expression, 'on your own head.'[4]

67 In ultimas terras
To the ends of the earth

Ἐπ᾽ ἔσχατα γῆς, To the ends of the earth, that is, an extremely remote place. Theocritus in his *Idyll* about the Syracusan women: 'That's my fine man for you! He goes to the end of the world / And takes not a house but a den

* * * * *

2 Plutarch *Sulla* 36.2–3
3 See eg Cicero *Ad familiares* 15.17.2 (proposing assault or gastric problems).

66 Theocritus (see n1). Added in *1533*
1 Theocritus *Idylls* 6.23–4
2 Virgil *Aeneid* 2.190–1; 8.484
3 Homer *Iliad* 4.162
4 Plato *Euthydemus* 283E. See *Adagia* IV vi 88 On your own head may it fall (272 above).

67 Theocritus and Cicero (see nn1–6). Added in *1533*

for beasts.'[1] The wife is blaming her husband for taking a house in a very remote place, and, what's more, something fit for beasts rather than human habitation. Cicero often uses the phrase 'To the ends of the earth,' as in his sixth speech attacking Verres: 'How did you think other nations were going to react to this, what impression did you imagine the news of this deed of yours would make when it reached the realms of other kings and spread to the ends of the earth?'[2] Cicero again, speaking in defence of Sulla: 'What an incredible, what a ridiculous idea, to think that the person who wanted to stage a massacre in Rome, who planned to send the city up in flames, would pack his closest associate off and give him a job to do at the ends of the earth!'[3] And in the thirteenth *Philippic*: 'How can I pass over Saxa Decidius, a man haled from nations on the edge of the world?'[4] Again, writing to Publius Lentulus in the first book of his *Letters to Friends*: 'Just call to mind the people for whose benefit you sent from the ends of the earth, and don't be afraid ...'[5] Again in the fifteenth book, writing to Marcus Marcellus: 'Though we are far away and dispatched by you to the ends of the earth.'[6] St. Jerome often uses the phrase, for example, 'a monster to be relegated to the ends of the earth.'[7] Plautus, in the *Haunted House*: 'I've been to desert lands as well, sailed past the furthest shores.'[8]

68 Talia gignit bellum
Such things are born of war

In book two of his letters to his brother Quintus, Cicero quotes the following line from a Greek play, obviously assuming it to be well known: Τοιαῦθ' ὁ τλήμων πόλεμος ἐξεργάζεται 'Such deeds does dreadful war engender.' In the context, he means that many farcical situations arise from the dissensions of those in power. His actual words are: 'There is absolutely no movement on

* * * * *

1 Theocritus *Idylls* 15.8–9
2 Cicero *Verrines* 2.4.30.68
3 Cicero *Pro P. Sulla* 20.57
4 Cicero *Philippics* 13.13.27
5 Cicero *Ad familiares* 1.9.19
6 Cicero *Ad familiares* 15.9.1
7 See eg Jerome *Contra Vigilantium* 8 PL 23 347
8 Plautus *Mostellaria* 995–6

68 Cicero (see n1). Added in *1533*

the political front, but this is because the country is in decline rather than happy with the situation. The views I expressed in the Senate are more likely to convince other people than convince myself. "Such dreadful deeds does war engender."'[1] If transferred to private quarrels, the phrase will be even more satisfactory.

69 Vera fronte
With honest brow

Anything said or done sincerely and without dissimulation is said to be done 'With honest brow.' Cicero, when defending Gaius Rabirius: 'If they then spoke the truth with totally honest brow, they are now lying; if they then lied, let them tell us the truth.'[1] Conversely, anything done with dissimulation we say is done 'with deceitful brow.' Cicero, writing to his brother, if the letter is correctly ascribed to him,[2] says that 'brow, eyes, face, often lie, words oftenest of all.'[3] The brow and the eyes best reveal what the mind is thinking. Words can be falsified without difficulty, but, as Ovid says, 'How hard it is for guilt to wear a guiltless face!'[4] Dido in Virgil 'wears false hope upon her face, and crushes down her trouble deep within her heart.'[5] Terence, in the *Self-Tormenter*: 'Bah! The villain even invents faces.'[6] And in the *Phormio*, Geta helps Antiphon to put on the right expression to meet his father, but the lad cannot keep it up.[7]

* * * * *

1 Cicero *Ad Quintum fratrem* 2.13.5, quoting Euripides *Supplices* 119

69 Cicero (see n1). Cf *Adagia* IV vi 68 With an upright heart (260 above); II iv 4 To see on the face of it; IV vi 99 With ears lowered (278 above). Added in *1533*
1 Cicero *Pro C. Rabirio Postumo* 12.35
2 The authenticity of this letter is still questioned, but most people now accept its genuineness. See Cicero *Epistulae ad Q. fratrem et M. Brutum* ed D.R. Shackleton-Bailey (Cambridge 1980) 147; David Magie *Roman Rule in Asia Minor* (New York 1975) II 1244.
3 Cicero *Ad Quintum fratrem* 1.1.15
4 Ovid *Metamorphoses* 2.447, used in *Adagia* I x 91 Conscience is a thousand witnesses
5 Virgil *Aeneid* 1.209, but the line refers to Aeneas, not Dido. It is used again in *Adagia* v i 53 Put on an appearance (571 below).
6 This is possibly a misremembering of Terence *Heautontimoroumenos* 887.
7 Terence *Phormio* 200

70 Porcus Troianus
A Trojan pig

The ancient architects of gastronomic extravagance even thought up the idea of serving at dinner a whole ox or camel stuffed with all kinds of other creatures. They also invented the 'Trojan pig,' which has gone into popular speech, so called because it concealed within its womb various species of living creatures, just as the Wooden Horse concealed the armed warriors.[1] In book three of the *Saturnalia*, Macrobius tells us that when Cincius was making his speech advocating the passing of the Lex Fannia (the purpose of which was to curb extravagance), he slated his contemporaries for serving the Trojan Pig at their dinners.[2] If I had the choice, I would rather have the Trojan Pig than the Trojan Horse! The saying will fit either splendid banquets or a man stuffed with all kinds of delicacies.

71 Pilus in medio
A hair in between

We speak of things being 'A hair's breadth apart,' when we mean that the difference is minimal. This is a stronger expression than saying 'a straw's breadth.'[1] Theocritus, in his *Idyll*, *Thyonicus*: 'I'll maybe find I've gone mad. Θρὶξ ἀνὰ μέσσον "I'm only a hair's breadth off it."'[2] The speaker is a man in love who fears his passion may send him mad, and he's so close to it that there is hardly 'A hair in between.' Plautus has a similar use in the *Haunted House*: 'It doesn't matter a feather whether patron or client is the better

* * * * *

70 Developed by Erasmus from a quotation from Macrobius (see n2) at the end of Brassicanus no 67 *Equus Troianus* 'The Trojan horse,' and made into something quite different. Added in *1533*

1 Erasmus uses a phrase *Durius equus*, based on Greek δουρεῖος/δούριος ἵππος, found in Aristophanes *Birds* 1128 and Plato *Theaetetus* 184D. See *Adagia* IV ii 1 A wooden horse and IV ix 95 Better than that Trojan trick (480 above).

2 Macrobius *Saturnalia* 3.13.13. The Lex Fannia (161 BC) restricted the amount to be spent on dinners, the number of guests attending, and the types of food served.

71 Theocritus (see n2). Added in *1533*
1 See *Adagia* I v 6 A nail's breadth.
2 Theocritus *Idylls* 14.9

man. / A man without any boldness in his breast . . .'[3] 'It doesn't matter a feather' means 'it is quite irrelevant.' Asinius Pollio in a letter to Cicero: 'I won't stir a foot's breadth away from you.'[4]

72 Musopatagos
Muse-struck

Μουσοπάταγος is a word used of someone who is 'smitten' or 'struck' by the wild inspiration of the Muses. See Virgil in the *Georgics*: 'whose holy offerings I bear, smitten with love for them.'[1] It can also be used of those who love their own poetic creations as parents love their offspring. See Cicero in the second book of letters to his brother Quintus: 'Good heavens, no Muse-struck person ever reads his latest poem with more pleasure than I feel when listening to you.'[2] Compare Horace's line: 'He loves poetry; this is his sole concern.'[3]

73 Ut Phrygius amavit Pieriam
As Phrygius loved Pieria

We learn from Plutarch's book 'On Noble Deeds Performed by Women' that even in his day women were still praying to be loved by their husbands 'As Phrygius loved Pieria.' This is the story behind the words. Some of the Ionians who had migrated to Miletus rebelled against the sons of Neleus, took themselves off to Myous, and settled there. They suffered much at the hands of the inhabitants of Miletus, who maintained a state of war against them because of their defection, but the war was not prosecuted with total

*****

3 Plautus *Mostellaria* 407–9
4 Cicero *Ad familiares* 10.31.6

72 Cicero (see n2). The word should be *Musopataktos*, as Estienne points out, in a footnote at LB II 1176F. He also rejects Erasmus' explications of the word. Added in *1533*
1 Virgil *Georgics* 2.476 (quoted from memory)
2 Cicero *Ad Quintum fratrem* 2.8.1
3 Horace *Epistles* 2.1.120

73 Plutarch (see n1). Added in *1533*

ferocity, nor was all communication between the two communities at an
end, but quite often on festal days the women from Myous would go to
Miletus. One of those who seceded was a man called Pythes, who had a
wife called Hippygia and a daughter Pieria. On one feast-day in Miletus,
sacrifice was being offered to Diana, who is there called Neleis, and Pythes
sent his wife and daughter, who had begged to be allowed to attend the
festival. By far the most powerful of the sons of Neleus was Phrygius. He
fell in love with Pieria, and was wondering what he could do that would
best please her. She said that nothing could please her more than if he
would make it possible for her to come to Miletus frequently and bring
many girls with her. Phrygius understood from this that she was asking
for peace and friendship for her fellow-citizens, so he declared an end to
hostilities. Consequently, Pieria was highly honoured in Miletus as well as
Myous, so that all the girls who were getting married used to pray, as a
good omen, 'May I be loved by my husband as Phrygius loved Pieria.'[1]

74 Vita hominis peregrinatio
The life of man is a time of exile

Παρεπιδημία τίς ἐστιν ὁ βίος, Life is a sort of time in exile. In Plato's *Axiochus*,
Socrates adduces this sentiment as a popular saying known to everybody –
though this dialogue is considered spurious.[1] Its author was more likely a
Christian who wanted to imitate Plato, as this sentiment is often found in
Holy Scripture, namely, that this life is life as an exile, life as an alien, life
in a land that is not our true home.[2] Though even Socrates as depicted by
Plato does say that the souls of men have fallen from heaven and endeavour
to return there by the study of philosophy.[3]

* * * * *

1 Plutarch *Moralia* 253F–254B *De mulierum virtutibus* 16, which Erasmus here
   translates closely; but it is the festival of Diana, not Diana herself, which
   is there called Neleis. Neleus and his sons (the founders of Miletus) belong to
   early Greek tradition (about the time of the Trojan War). Plutarch was writing
   in the first to second centuries AD.

74 Pseudo-Plato (see n1). Tilley L 249 Life is a pilgrimage. Added in *1533*
 1 Pseudo-Plato *Axiochus* 365B
 2 See eg 1 Chron 29:15, Ps 119:19, 1 Pet 2:11, Heb 11:13.
 3 See possibly Plato *Phaedrus* 248–9.

75 Tota hulcus est
The whole thing is a festering sore

In the same dialogue, after someone has praised agriculture, Socrates replies: ''Ἀλλ᾽ οὐχ᾽ ὅλη ὥς φασιν ἕλκος "But isn't the whole thing a festering sore," as they say, always producing some reason for grief?'[1] Horace's Vulteius agreed with that sentiment.[2] Anything that is a trial and tribulation we call a sore, an abscess, a canker. We read that Caesar Augustus used to call the two Julias, his daughter and grand-daughter, and Agrippa, whom he first adopted and later repudiated, his three 'abscesses,' his three 'cankers.' He so hated their extravagant behaviour that whenever they were mentioned he used to cry out, adapting Homer's words: 'Would that I had never wed, that I had childless died.'[3]

This verse too could well be treated as proverbial and used by men who have made an unhappy marriage or found themselves with disappointing children. The head phrase will do also for a man of unpleasant character. In his *Lament for Adonis*, Theocritus calls a bitter grief 'a festering wound in the heart': 'Deep, deep is the wound dealt to Adonis' groin; / Deeper still the wound that festers in Cytherea's heart.'[4]

76 Ex cohorte praetoris
The governor's squad

Those who stand ready to obey every nod and are given authority to carry out this or that task are, as we are told, referred to as 'The governor's squad.' Cicero, in the first letter to his brother Quintus: 'As for the private associates and personal attendants you have chosen to accompany you, the

* * * * *

75 Pseudo-Plato (see n1). Added in 1533

1 Pseudo-Plato *Axiochus* 368c

2 See Horace *Epistles* 1.7.86–9. Vulteius is a man who has a short but disastrous venture into farming.

3 See Suetonius *Divus Augustus* 65.4, where Augustus adapts Homer *Iliad* 3.40. Agrippa Postumus was Augustus' grandson, son of his daughter Julia.

4 Bion 1.16–17, wrongly attributed to Theocritus. The correct author was first suggested by Kammermeister in 1530, followed by Estienne in 1566 (see M. Fantuzzi *Bionis Smyrnaei Adonidis Epitaphium* [Liverpool 1985] 139).

76 Cicero (see n1). Added in 1533

ones that people usually refer to as a sort of "governor's squad," we have to take responsibility not only for what they do but even for what they say.'[1] A governor's subordinates need no other excuse than to say they were carrying out orders, so that any complaint is directed at the governor, not at themselves as his agents. The same kind of control is exercised over persons who are so beholden to someone for their keep and various obligements that they dare not say no to any request.

77 Lucernam accendere possis
You could light a lantern

This is Theocritus' exaggerated way of describing furious anger in his *Thyonicus*: 'She went bright red. Εὐμαρέως κεν ἀπ᾽ αὐτᾶς καὶ λύχνον ἅψαις "You could easily have lit a lantern at her face."'[1] The words are spoken by a lover who is complaining about his girlfriend's provoking behaviour. When she refused to speak at the party, someone said to her, 'Lost your tongue? Seen a wolf?'[2] and at the word 'wolf' she went red as fire, because there was present a young man she fancied, called Wolf. Angry people are said to burn. We have a similar, if cruder, exaggerated expression today: 'He was so hot with rage you could have fried an egg on his face.'[3]

78 Semper aliquem virum magnum
Ever for some great man ...

Ἀλλ᾽ αἰεί τινα φῶτα μέγαν: Cicero quotes this half line as something very well known in the letter to his brother Quintus that begins, 'Statius came to see me':

* * * * *

1 Cicero *Ad Quintum fratrem* 1.1.4.(12)

77 Theocritus (see n1). Suringar 108. Added in *1533*
1 Theocritus *Idylls* 14.23. Erasmus sketchily paraphrases the whole section.
2 To be seen by a wolf before seeing it yourself was supposed to deprive one of the power of speech. See, eg, Virgil *Eclogues* 9.54; *Adagia* I vii 86 The wolves have seen him first, and also IV v 50 Wolf in the story (175 above).
3 Erasmus is thinking of the Dutch expression 'you could fry an egg on his arse,' but has toned it down in the interests of decency. See ASD II-8 261:n765–6.

78 Cicero (see n1). Added in *1533*

His arrival did away with all the expectation that would have attached to yourself and all the crowds that would have gathered if he had left together with you and had never been seen before. And that seemed to me no bad thing. People have said all they had to say, and much of it was to the effect that 'ever for some great man ...' I am glad that all this was over and done with while you were still away.[1]

It's not clear where this half line comes from. Possibly instead of αἰεί 'ever,' one should read αἴτει 'ask for,' or αἰτεῖ 'he asks for' or 'he seeks.'[2]

79 Ne si ad Iovis quidem aulam
Not even if to Jove's temple

Those who fear some harm take refuge at a sanctuary, at an altar, at a citadel,[1] at the emperor's statues, at the temples of the gods. But there is no place where one can take refuge from death, a thought which Sophocles expressed in the following lines:

Whensoe'er the hour of death shall hard upon you press,
Go even to Jove's temple if you will, but still escape you cannot.[2]

The words that look proverbial here are Οὐδ᾽ ἂν πρὸς αὐλὰς Ζηνός 'Not even to Jove's temple,' meaning the safest place of sanctuary. It was here that the eagle took refuge when persecuted by the beetle.[3]

* * * * *

1 Cicero *Ad Quintum fratrem* 1.2.1
2 Cicero is citing Homer *Odyssey* 9.513. As Estienne explains in his note at LB II 1178E–F, the Cyclops is speaking here after being blinded by Odysseus. He says that he had received a prophecy that someone would come and blind him but that he 'always looked for some great man,' not someone physically unimpressive, like Odysseus. It is odd that Erasmus did not recognize the line, considering his familiarity with the text of Homer.

79 Stobaeus, quoting Sophocles (see n2). Added in *1533*
1 See *Adagia* IV ix 29–31 (437–8 above).
2 Stobaeus 118.12 (Gaisford), quoting *TrGF* 4 Sophocles fragment 951.3–4
3 See *Adagia* III vii 1 A dung-beetle hunting an eagle.

80 Oracula loqui
Speak oracles

Χρησμοὺς λέγειν, To speak oracles, applied to those who say things that are unquestionably true. Theocritus in the *Syracusan Women*: 'The old lady spoke some oracles before she went.'[1] I have already discussed 'Straight from the tripod' and 'A leaf from the Sibyl's book.'[2] Cicero, in the letter to Brutus which begins, 'My letter was already signed and sealed,' says, 'You may take this as an oracle straight from Pythian Apollo.'[3] Cicero again, in the fifth book of his *Definitions of Good and Evil*: 'Because, I replied, when Zeno makes the magnificent statement, coming straight, as it were, from the oracle's mouth, "For the purpose of the happy life, virtue needs nothing outside itself . . ."'[4]

81 Non ab Hymetto
Not from Hymettus

In a letter from book two of the letters to his brother Quintus, Cicero speaks of 'philosophy from the Syrian district,' meaning 'simple and home-spun,' the sort we learn from mixing with ordinary, humble folk, not from the treatises of Zeno and Plato. The relevant section reads: 'We are scholars of such a sort that we can even live with the workmen. We got this philosophy not from Hymettus but from the Syrian district.'[1] Hymettus is a hill in Attica; it's where the honey of Hymettus comes from. He contrasts with Hymettus the 'Syrian district,' which thus suggests uncultured simplicity, especially as he had been speaking of sophisticated, cultivated conversation

* * * * *

80 Theocritus (see n1). Added in *1533*

1 Theocritus *Idylls* 15.63

2 *Adagia* I vii 90 and 91

3 Cicero *Ad M. Brutum* 1.2.1 and 3. The two sections appear as one letter in the manuscripts, but nowadays they are attributed to two fragmentary letters. This section appears as letter 843 in *The Correspondence of Cicero* ed R.Y. Tyrrell and L.C. Purser (Dublin 1899) 6.113, and letter 6 in *Cicero, Epistulae ad Q. fratrem et M. Brutum* ed D.R. Shackleton-Bailey (Cambridge 1980) 109.

4 Cicero *De finibus* 5.27.79

81 Cicero (see n1). Added in *1533*

1 Cicero *Ad Quintum fratrem* 2.8.3

just before. It seems that Cicero had had some building work done on his property at the time. Though I do wonder whether the text is corrupt here, as various readings are offered in the editions. The learned reader might consider whether instead of *area Syra* 'the Syrian district' one should read *ex hara Syra* 'from the Syrian sty.' Compare what Cicero says in his speech attacking Piso: 'product of the sty, not the school.'[2] The Syrians were as famous for their lack of civilization at that time as the Athenians were for their cultured wit.

82 Cymbalum mundi
The world's cymbal

In his *Preface* addressed to the Emperor Vespasian, Pliny the Elder tells us that Apion, the literary scholar, was called by the Emperor Tiberius 'The world's cymbal,' no doubt because of the fame he enjoyed, though, Pliny adds, he would be better thought of as 'the drum of the world's reputation.'[1] This Apion used to say that he bestowed immortality on anyone to whom he dedicated a work. It was in reference to this that Tiberius called him 'The world's cymbal,' meaning that he bestowed on people fair fame, which resounded pleasingly round the world. Because of his arrogance, Pliny thought he should be called 'the drum of the world's reputation,' because he bestowed fame, but not necessarily fair fame. A drum resounds, but the noise is not attractive. There is also the thought that drums are made of ass-skin.

83 In beato omnia beata
With the rich all things are rich

The rich do everything magnificently, the poor sparingly. In Theocritus'

* * * * *

2 Cicero *In L. Pisonem* 16.37 (already quoted in *Adagia* 1 i 40 The sow teaches Minerva). The passage in the letter does seem to be hopelessly corrupt and various scholars have suggested emendations. Erasmus' suggestion has not been adopted.

82 Pliny the Elder (see n1). Added in *1533*
1 Pliny *Naturalis historia* preface 25. Modern texts however read *propriae famae tympanum*, ie, he would be better thought of as 'the drum of his own reputation.'

83 Theocritus (see n1). Added in *1533*

Graces, Praxinoe is praising Ptolemy for celebrating the festival of Adonis magnificently, with no expense spared, and says, apparently using a proverbial expression, 'With the rich, all things are rich.'[1] You can adapt this idea by saying a scholar does all in a scholarly way, a pious man in a pious way, a king in a kingly way.[2]

84 Digitum qua proferat
Nowhere to put a finger out

Cicero was using a proverbial figure of speech when he said in his speech defending Aulus Caecina, 'It has "Nowhere to put a finger out,"'[1] an exaggerated expression, meaning that there is absolutely nothing that can be said or done. The whole passage reads as follows: 'In short, that excessive influence which holds sway elsewhere in the state, in this one type of case has no effect; it does not know how to proceed, how to get at the jury, where to put a finger out.'[1] The phrase is derived from the gestures used by orators, the various types of which are described by Quintilian.[2] The simplest gesture is pointing the finger, used by common, unmannered people.

85 Tristis littera
The sinister letter

Cicero, speaking in defence of Milo: 'He was well aware that a defendant who admits to a crime may nonetheless be acquitted. Otherwise, seeing that we admitted to the charge, he would never have ordered a trial, nor would you have had this life-giving letter to vote with, as well as the sinister

* * * * *

1 Theocritus *Idylls* 15.24: Ἐν ὀλβίῳ ὀλβία πάντα. The *Graces* is now the title of *Idyll* 16, but this was probably in origin the dedicatory epistle and the title included the whole collection of poems.
2 'A king' could be a colloquial term for a rich man. See *Adagia* IV x 44 I'm a king (510 above).

84 Cicero (see n1). Otto 548. Cf *Adagia* I iii 21 I would not turn a hand, I would not raise a finger, where some of the material used here was added in *1526* and *1536*; also I v 7 He has no place to set his foot. Added in *1533*
1 Cicero *Pro A. Caecina* 25.71
2 Quintilian 11.92–106

85 Cicero (see n1). Added in *1533*

one.'[1] 'The sinister letter' is the Greek θ, the 'life-giving' one, τ. The latter was used to acquit the defendant, the former to condemn. I have already said something about this in the adage 'To prefix a theta.'[2] It is Asconius Pedianus who says (that is, if the texts are free from error) that θ was used to condemn, τ to acquit, and *NL* (that is, *non liquet*) to give a verdict of 'not proven.'[3] Livy used the phrase 'a more sinister mark.'[4]

86 Iovis germen
Scion of Jove

'Εκ Διὸs ἔρνοs, Scion of Jove, a phrase used of a man endowed with remarkable ability. A shepherd so addresses another shepherd who is wonderfully skilled in music, and to whom he makes the gift of a club[1] to do him honour. The club is the typical accoutrement of Hercules, offspring of Jove, and the ancients observed that the poets always depict the sons of Jove as civilized and humane, the sons of Neptune on the other hand as fierce and wild. Music indeed teaches civilized behaviour. The poem says, 'Since you are in all truth a scion formed of very Jove.' However, the ancient commentator on the passage thinks that the line refers to the fact that those who speak truth are said to be the offspring of Jove, and to support this view, he quotes the words that Homer gives to Jove:

> Nothing of mine can be recalled, nor can it ever deceive
> When once I give it my nod.[2]

* * * * *

1 Cicero *Pro T. Annio Milone* 6.15
2 *Adagia* I v 56
3 Pseudo-Asconius *In Divinationem in Caecilium* 7.24; *Verrines* 2.1.9.26. Stangl (pages 193 and 231) reads 'C' and 'A' ('C' for *condemno* and 'A' for *absolvo*). See *Adagia* I v 56 To prefix a theta.
4 Apparently misremembered. Cf Livy 4.29.6, *nulla tristi nota* 'with no sinister mark,' added in 1533 to *Adagia* I v 54 To mark with chalk, with coal.

86 Theocritus *Idylls* 7.43–4, with the ancient commentator (see *Adagia* IV x 52n, 514 above; see n2 below). Added in 1533
1 The word can mean 'shepherd's crook' as well as 'club.'
2 Homer *Iliad* 1.527–8. Calliergis expanded the quotation in the ancient scholiast and Erasmus quotes and translates (and corrects) Calliergis' version. For Calliergis see *Adagia* IV x 52n (514 above).

The shepherd is at this point being praised for modestly rejecting any comparison between himself and famous musicians. Virgil shows him in a similar light:

> The shepherds say
> That I'm inspired, but I'm not one to believe them.[3]

87 Musarum aves
Birds of the Muses' flock

Μουσῶν ὄρνιθες, Birds of the Muses. In his *Idyll*, *Thalysia*, Theocritus applies this apparently proverbial expression to poets, the reason being that they are like nightingales, singing their songs unceasingly.[1] The commentator on the passage remarks that all song birds are 'Birds of the Muses' flock,' but Theocritus gives us to understand that he hates those poets who are arrogant enough to pit their cuckoo-calls against Homer.

88 Nullus dies omnino malus
No day is bad from start to finish

Astrologers mark certain days as lucky or unlucky for doing this or that. But no day should be spent in idleness, because no day is so inauspicious that it cannot be good for something, if one makes proper use of the time thus made available. A day that is not propitious for fighting or sailing can be well spent on sorting out one's private affairs. And there isn't any day that isn't favourable for improving one's mind. The sentiment comes from Hesiod's *Works and Days*: 'Never is the day entirely bad.'[1]

*****

3 Virgil *Eclogues* 9.33–4. In Virgil however the words are given to Lycidas; in Theocritus they are spoken by Simichidas to Lycidas.

87 Theocritus (see n1). Added in *1533*
1 Theocritus *Idylls* 7.47, in the line following on from the passage discussed above in *Adagia* IV x 86. Erasmus' comment is not clear, divorced from the text of Theocritus, but see IV vi 4 Birds of the Muses (211 above), which anticipates most of this.

88 Hesiod (see n1). Added in *1533*
1 Hesiod *Works and Days* 813: καὶ οὔ ποτε πάγκακον ἦμαρ.

89 Guttam adspergere
Add a drop of dressing

When a small amount is sliced off a lucrative deal for someone, we can
say he's had 'a drop of dressing added.' See Cicero, speaking on behalf
of Aulus Cluentius: 'And the one who cooked up the whole business also
added a drop of dressing to this Bulbus. Consequently, anyone who got
a little smack of hope from what he was saying didn't think him at all a
distasteful fellow.'[1] (A 'speck' of gold is a similar sort of phrase for a very
tiny amount.) Apart from the proverbial turn of phrase in Cicero's words,
there is also an amusing pun on the names. Stelemus had promised a large
sum of money to one of the jurors called Bulbus – the name means 'Onion.'
This Stelemus,[2] who was cooking up the whole business – he's called in
Latin *conditor* with the second syllable long, that is, 'seasoner,' not *conditor*
with a short syllable, 'originator' – adds to Bulbus another juror who was
called Gutta, which means 'Drop.' This livened Bulbus up, for cooks add
seasonings to edible bulbs, which are a sort of onion, to take the sharpness
off, and Cicero is suggesting this when he says that he seemed by no means
'a distasteful fellow.' Anything that happens gradually is said to do so 'drop
by drop.' See Plautus, in the *Merchant*: 'My heart will melt away drop by
drop, like salt put in water.'[3] Anyone who makes frequent but tiny gifts
gives 'a drop at a time.'

90 Rectam instas viam
You're on the right track

'You have touched the issue with a needlepoint'[1] is very like 'You're on the
right track,' which occurs in Plautus' play, the *Comedy of Asses*: 'Isn't it as I
say, Libanus? – You're on the right track. That's how it is.'[2] Those who are

* * * * *

89 Cicero (see n1). Added in *1533*
1 Cicero *Pro A. Cluentio* 26.71
2 Better texts read *Staienus*, as is pointed out in the footnote at LB II 1180F.
3 Plautus *Mercator* 205

90 Erasmus now has a run of material derived largely from Plautus, which continues until *Adagia* v i 25. Suringar 225; Otto 1886. Added in *1533*
1 See *Adagia* II iv 93.
2 Plautus *Asinaria* 54–5

mistaken are said to be right off track,[3] and those who have a good idea what's going on are said to be 'on the right track.' This is a very common colloquial expression even today. There's a very similar turn of phrase in *Casina*: 'At least I'm back on track,'[4] meaning, 'I really understand things now.'

91 Aeacidinae minae
Threats worthy of Achilles

In the same play, the trader says:

> He can come bursting with threatenings and wrath fit for Achilles,
> But if your angry chap lays a finger on me, your angry chap
> Will get a thrashing.[1]

This seems to be a proverbial phrase for dreadful overbearing threats. The verse form would indeed allow the reading *Aeacinae* 'fit for Aeacus' rather than *Aeacidinae* 'fit for Achilles,'[2] and some people have proposed this reading, but Plautus is most likely thinking of Aeacus' descendant Achilles, whom Homer constantly represents as short-tempered and aggressive, as, for example, at the beginning of the first book of the *Iliad*, where he is

* * * * *

3 See *Adagia* I i 48 You are entirely on the wrong road.
4 Plautus *Casina* 469

91 Plautus (see n1). Added in *1533*
1 Plautus *Asinaria* 405–6, the play mentioned first in *Adagia* IV x 90 above
2 Erasmus is commenting on the variant reading proposed by the commentator on his text of Plautus here, ie Giambattista Pio (for whom see *Adagia* IV iii 40 n2, 27 above). The adjectival form *Aeacidinus* in the text is only attested in this one place, hence the commentator's desire to emend it. It is presumably derived from *Aeacides* 'descendant of Aeacus,' a common substitute for the name of Achilles in the figure of *antonomasia* (see Erasmus *De copia* CWE 28 331) and so would mean 'worthy of (the famous) descendant of Aeacus.' Aeacus was appointed a judge of the dead by Zeus as a reward for his justice and piety in this life, and the adjective *Aeacinus* would presumably mean 'worthy of Aeacus, the wrathful judge.' This word is not attested elsewhere either, and the reading is not recognized in modern texts. Erasmus exhibits his usual dismissive attitude to Pio's suggestions, and produces arguments in support of the transmitted reading.

so incensed against Agamemnon that he lays his hand on the hilt of his sword and would have moved from angry words to actual blows if Pallas Athene had not caught him by the hair and held him back.[3] The whole work in fact starts with Achilles' wrath – the very first words are, Μῆνιν ἄειδε, θεά 'Wrath, o goddess, is the theme ...'[4] I can't see the relevance in this context of the remarks some commentators make about Aeacus, the judge of the dead. Besides, anything indomitable and invincible is called 'Achillean.'

92 Oleo nitidius
Shiny as oil

The shine of oil has become so proverbial that even Sacred Scripture bids us anoint our faces and conceal the gloom of fasting.[1] In *Truculentus*, Plautus speaks of a courtesan all dressed up in her best as follows: 'She glows! She's all flowers! She's as shiny as oil!'[2] Oil adds brightness and lustre to everything.

93 Herculis quaestus
Hercules' profits

In the *Haunted House*, Plautus speaks of 'Hercules' profits,' meaning 'huge spending':

> – He spends enough money to lay on a banquet!
> – He's ruined his father!

* * * * *

3 Homer *Iliad* 1.188–198
4 Homer *Iliad* 1.1

92 Plautus (see n2). Added in 1533
1 Matt 6:17
2 Plautus *Truculentus* 353–4. Erasmus follows the text of Pio's Milan 1500 edition of Plautus; see *Adagia* IV iii 40 n2, 27 above. The modern reading is *Ver vide, / Ut tota floret, ut nitide nitet.* 'Look at her! Here comes the Spring, all flowers and sweet smells. How radiantly she shines!'

93 Plautus (see n1). Added in 1533

– That one single slave, that Tranio, sharpest of fellows,
  Could easily squander the profits of Hercules.[1]

I have already recorded that most people in ancient times were accustomed to dedicate a tenth of their profits to Hercules, convincing themselves that their business would flourish through Hercules' favour.[2] All these tenths necessarily added up to a huge sum of money. Plautus humorously calls it 'Hercules' profits,' as if Hercules sold his favour.

94 **Posterius dictum**
   Told too late

'You are teaching the taught, reminding the mindful, talking to one who knows' and other similar phrases have been discussed earlier.[1] Plautus expresses the same idea in an amusing way in the *Comedy of Asses*. Demaenetus is complaining about his wife and says, 'I must admit that she's unreasonable and difficult.' Libanus replies, 'You told me that after (*posterius*) I believed you,'[2] that is, 'I knew that before you said it.' I do not see why Nonius here explains *posterius* 'after' as meaning *minus* 'less.'[3] The following line in Plautus has a proverbial sound too: 'You are the first to feel it, but we knew it before.'[4] As the Satirist says, 'He will be the last to know the shame brought on his house.'[5] And Terence: 'He's the only one who doesn't know it all.'[6] Even if we know of others' misfortunes before they do, it doesn't grieve us. It is the people it affects who have a real sense of the misfortune, others merely know of it.

* * * * *

1 Plautus *Mostellaria* 982–4
2 *Adagia* I i 73 With Hercules at my side or Hercules being my friend

94 Plautus (see n2). Added in 1533
1 *Adagia* I ii 12
2 Plautus *Asinaria* 62–3
3 Nonius Marcellus 597.11–13 Lindsay. Nonius gives, as equivalents of *posterius*, first of all *tardius* 'later' and *secundo* 'secondly,' and then adds *minus*, 'less,' rather as an afterthought. This perhaps does not relate to the example from Plautus, but Nonius' bald note is far from clear.
4 Actually the preceding line, Plautus *Asinaria* 61
5 Juvenal 10.342
6 Terence *Adelphi* 548

95 Tamquam de specula
As if from a watch-tower

Those who foresee future events long before they happen are said to see them in advance 'As if from a watch-tower.' Cicero, writing to Servius Sulpicius in book four of his *Letters to Friends*: 'I saw the storm that was coming long before it happened, as if from a watch-tower.'[1] Not only towns and fortified positions have their look-out posts, but ships too, and from them skilled captains can observe in advance that winds and storms are imminent.

96 Verbis conceptis peierare
Perjure oneself in set form of words

At one time a person who was taking an oath had to repeat a prescribed form of words dictated to him, so as to make the oath more binding. Plautus, in the *Comedy of Asses*: 'times when you merrily and consciously perjured yourself in set form of words.'[1] Again, in the *Bacchis Sisters*: 'I gave an undertaking in set form of words / That I would this day give to the woman ...'[2] Sometimes the person taking the oath grasped an altar to increase the solemn binding force of the oath. So, when they wanted to indicate an oath of the most solemn kind, they could say something like, 'Even if you swear with your hands on the altar, I won't believe you.' Cicero, for example, in the speech defending Lucius Flaccus: 'Is a man whom no one would believe if he swore with his hands grasping the altar, going to get us to accept what he wants without any oath, just by writing a letter?'[3]

* * * * *

95 Cicero (see n1). See *Adagia* IV iii 95 As if from a watch-tower (58 above). Added in *1533*
  1 Cicero *Ad familiares* 4.3.1

96 Plautus (see n1). Added in *1533*
  1 Plautus *Asinaria* 562
  2 Plautus *Bacchides* 1028–9
  3 Cicero *Pro L. Flacco* 36.90

97 Agones
Agones

I have already told how King Antigonus, grandson of Demetrius, was given the humorous nickname *Doson* by his soldiers, because he was always making promises, saying (in Greek) δώσω 'I'll give' and then not always fulfilling his promise.[1] The Romans had a similar sort of word, *Agones*, a name for the officiants who killed the sacrificial victim, because it was customary for them to ask the people before striking the blow, '*Agon*?' that is, 'Am I to proceed?' See Ovid in his versified calendar: 'Always he asks whether he should proceed, and never / Does he proceed unbidden.'[2] Lactantius writes about *Agones* in his commentary on Statius.[3] The word will be appropriate to ditherers, who are always considering and never actually embarking on any course of action.

98 Fungus putidus
A rotten mushroom

In the *Bacchis Sisters*, Plautus calls a useless, witless old fellow 'A rotten mushroom.' Mushrooms, though naturally rather tasteless, were at one time considered a delicacy, and still are in Italy, but only if fresh and tender. Nothing is more unpalatable than stale ones. Plautus writes:

> He walks around, cumbering the earth,
> Witless, senseless, as useless as a rotten mushroom.[1]

The words 'cumbering the earth' themselves have a proverbial ring, like, 'a useless weight upon the earth.'[2] Again in the same play, 'mushroom' is

* * * * *

97 Lactantius Placidus with Ovid (see nn2 and3). Added in *1533*
1 *Adagia* IV v 92 *Dosones* Shall-givers (204 above)
2 Ovid *Fasti* 1.322. See also Varro *De lingua Latina* 6.12.
3 Lactantius Placidus *In Statii Thebaida commentarius* 4.463, the only citation of the noun

98 Plautus (see n1). Otto 735–6. Added in *1533*
1 Plautus *Bacchides* 820–1. See *Adagia* IV i 38 A mushroom.
2 See Homer *Iliad* 18.104; also *Adagia* I vii 31B A burden on the earth.

one of the abusive words Plautus uses for stupidity: 'Silly, stupid, moronic mushrooms, doddering, drivelling dolts.'[3] In the *Haunted House*, he uses 'thicket' to call someone 'thick': 'You don't talk sense or truth, you thicket.'[4] Other trees can be seen as an image of dignity and intelligence, but thickets grow haphazard, know nothing of cultivation, and either bear no fruit or only what is wild and useless.

99 Vivum noveris
Know a man while he's alive

I have already discussed 'One should remember the living.'[1] The courtesan in Plautus' *Truculentus* gives a new twist to the idea, treating her lover as a dead man now he's stopped being a source of presents. She says:

> While a man's alive, you may know him.
> Once he's dead, you may let him be.
> You I knew when you were alive.[2]

According to Hesiod, it's cash that gives men life.[3] Once that's gone, a fellow's dead.

100 Lippo oculo similis
Like a runny eye

There are people of such a nature that you find it difficult to put up with them, but they are so active and so eager to do you service that whenever the occasion arises you can't prevent yourself from giving them something

* * * * *

3 Plautus *Bacchides* 1088
4 Plautus *Mostellaria* 13

99 Plautus (see n2). Added in *1533*
1 *Adagia* I ii 52
2 Plautus *Truculentus* 164–5, added in *1523* to *Adagia* I ii 52 One should remember the living
3 Hesiod *Works and Days* 686

100 Plautus (see nn1–2). Added in *1533*

to do for you. A sore eye gets worse if you rub it and yet it's natural to put your hand to the place that hurts. Plautus writes in the *Persian*:

> I'm not a willing slave and I'm not as my master would have me be.
> But I'm like a runny eye to him – he still can't keep his hands away,
> He has to give me orders and make use of me
> To bolster up his plans.[1]

Plautus again, in the *Bacchis Sisters*:

> That slave is like a runny eye. If you haven't got one
> You don't want it, don't feel the lack of it,
> But if you get one, you can't prevent yourself from touching it.[2]

1 Tu in legione, ego in culina
You in camp, I in the kitchen

In Plautus' *Truculentus* the soldier is making horrible threats and the cook replies:

> You may be a great fighter in camp if you please,
> But here in my kitchen I'm Ares himself.[1]

The cook takes the word 'fighter' up a notch, for Ares is the god of war. As for the use of Greek 'Ares' for Latin 'Mavors' it's nothing unusual for Plautus to mix Greek words in with Latin. Though some texts read here, instead of *Ares*, either *aves* 'birds' or *aries* 'ram,' which are obviously wrong.[2]

* * * * *

1 Plautus *Persa* 10–12
2 Plautus *Bacchides* 913–15

1 Plautus (see n1). Added in 1533
1 Plautus *Truculentus* 615. The text is corrupt here and various emendations have been proposed. Modern readings are markedly different from Erasmus'.
2 This is information based on Giambattista Pio's commentary on Plautus (Milan, 1500; see *Adagia* IV iii 40 n2, 27 above). He corrected *aves* to *Ares*, and commented that some read *aries*.

2 **Citius quam formicae papaver**
Quicker than ants move poppy-seed

This line from Plautus' *Three-shilling Day* seems to incorporate a proverb:
'It disappears quicker than poppy-seed put before ants.'[1] The words are
spoken by the slave Stasimus, who is describing how forty minae disap-
peared in a fortnight, spent on dinners, drinking-parties, visits to the baths,
fish-merchants, pastry-cooks, butchers, cooks, greengrocers, perfumers, and
poulterers, just like putting poppy-seed in the way of a column of ants. The
heap melts away as each ant takes its own little grain.

3 **Itidem ut Acheronti**
As in the grave

In the same play, when the lover demands his gifts back, the tart replies,
'Our accounts are kept like the grave's – what once is brought in / And
written in the ledger, never goes out again.'[1] She means that what once
enters the tart's establishment never returns to the lover, anymore than the
dead return from the grave. As Catullus says, 'Thence they say no one
returns.'[2]

4 **Mus non uni fidit antro**
A mouse keeps more than one hole

One of the most common popular sayings today is 'It's an unhappy mouse
that only has one hole.' Plautus has the same idea in *Truculentus*:

> Just consider how wise a creature is the little mouse,
> Who never to one hidey-hole alone entrusts his life.
> If siege is laid to one, he finds at another his defence.[1]

* * * * *

2 Plautus (see n1). Otto 692. Added in *1533*
1 Plautus *Trinummus* 409–10

3 Plautus (see n1). Added in *1533*
1 Plautus *Truculentus* (not the same play, *Trinummus*) 749–50.
2 Catullus 3.12

4 Plautus (see n1). Suringar 127; Tilley M 1236 The mouse that has but one hole
    is quickly taken. Added in *1533*
1 Plautus *Truculentus* 867–70

This adage will find a place if we advise someone to provide himself with abundance of friends or to give thought to philosophy as well as to material well-being, so that if Fortune removes what is hers, learning may provide some defence.

5 Post rem devoratam ratio
To start reckoning up when the money's been squandered

Help that comes too late is called 'Help when the war is over.' Likewise, economy applied too late is 'Counting up when the money's all gone.' Stasimus in Plautus' *Three-shilling Day*:

> Too late and stupid – what should have been thought of before –
> To start doing his accounts now, when he's used up all the capital![1]

The slave is talking to the young master, who is now counting up his assets when he has liquidated his entire resources through folly. This really is numbering the waves that have passed, when one should be counting those that are coming.[2]

6 Coena popularis
A dinner for the people

Phormio, in Terence's play of that name, speaks of 'A doubtful dinner,' that is, one offering so many dishes that you are 'doubtful which one to try first.'[1] Similarly, Plautus' character Philto applies the phrase 'A dinner for the people' to a splendid, sumptuous, and, what's more, free dinner, like those provided for the whole community. Plautus says:

> Suppose you went to a temple for a dinner
> And found yourself beside a wealthy man;

* * * * *

5 Plautus (see n1). See *Adagia* III vi 17 Help when the war is over; II ii 64 It's too late to spare when the bottom is bare. Added in *1533*
1 Plautus *Trinummus* 416–17. Erasmus is following the division of parts in the Milan 1500 edition of Plautus. Philto, not Stasimus, says these words.
2 See *Adagia* I iv 45 You are counting the waves.

6 Plautus (see n2). Added in *1533*
1 Terence *Phormio* 342; see also *Adagia* II iv 23 A doubtful dinner (also in *Adagia* III ii 37 A dinner for a pontiff).

The banquet's served, standard of a people's dinner,
Before him lots of tasty dishes by his clients piled.[2]

7 Apud mensam verecundari neminem decet
No one ought to hold back at table

Another saying occurs soon after the passage quoted above, one that has been 'Passed down from hand to hand'[1] right from those early days and still is in common use today: 'No one ought to hold back at table, / For things human and divine are there in question.' Except that the vulgar add 'or in bed!' These are no words of a philosopher, but the words of Stasimus, a slave in comedy,[2] for in reality bed and table are the two places where restraint needs to be exercised more than anywhere else. Though there are people who are embarrassing guests to have at a dinner because of their gauche fear of putting themselves forward, always waiting for others to offer them food and putting back what they are given. The words 'things human and divine are there in question'[3] are also proverbial, being a figurative expression for 'matters of supreme import are involved.' This saying befits a slave who placed felicity 'Stem and stern'[4] in filling his belly.

8 Salillum animae
A little salt-cellarful of soul

In the same scene Philto speaks of man as 'A little salt-cellarful of soul,' meaning that the life of man is very brief, comparable to the small amount

*****

2 Plautus *Trinummus* 468–71. Free dinners for the population of Rome were laid on, for example, by triumphing generals as part of the victory celebrations. Their splendour enhanced the giver's reputation and advanced his political career. Banquets were often associated with religious ceremonies involving sacrifice of animal victims to the gods. See *Adagia* IV ix 81 Banquets fit for Salian priests (472 above).

7 Plautus (see n2). Suringar 16. Added in *1533*
1 *Adagia* IV v 28 To pass down from hand to hand (160 above)
2 Plautus *Trinummus* 478–9
3 The phrase 'things human and divine' also occurs at Plautus *Amphitryo* 258.
4 *Adagia* I i 8

8 Plautus (see n1). Added in *1533*

of salt served to each guest at a dinner. Plautus here says:

> The gods are rich – wealth and social connections are for them.
> But we poor mannikins are just a salt-cellarful of soul,
> And the moment that has gone from us, the beggar and the millionaire
> Count the same in Hell, once dead.[1]

The last line is two syllables short – maybe read 'the millionaire Pelops' or 'the millionaire Croesus' or some such thing.[2]

9 Nummus plumbeus
A lead penny

Like the *as*, the *obol*, and the *teruncius*, 'A lead penny' became proverbial for something of little value.[1] Plautus in *Three-shilling Day*: 'If it were a matter of life and death, I wouldn't ever trust him with a lead penny.'[2] Again in *Casina*: 'A fellow that hasn't saved a single lead penny to this day.'[3] Coins of bronze are known even today in Flanders, and England has lead ones. Cicero, in the fifth book of his *Letters to Atticus*, calls Vatinius a despicable villain, 'a half-penny fellow': 'At the same time that half-penny fellow took up arms against me.'[4] And somewhere or other we have the

* * * * *

1 Plautus *Trinummus* 490–4
2 Erasmus' text varies in several places from modern ones, which accept the reading *censetur censu* 'count the same in cash,' with *censu* supplying the two necessary syllables. Erasmus offers two two-syllable names as possible supplements to the line; see *Adagia* I vi 23 The talents of Pelops and *Adagia* IV x 48 Add a penny to Croesus' millions (512 above).

9 Plautus (see nn2, 3, and 6). Added in *1533*
1 The *obol* (a Greek weight or coin), and the Roman bronze coins, the *as* and *teruncius* 'three-ounce piece,' were all of little value. See *Adagia* I viii 10 A three-ha'penny fellow, 11 A threepenny man; II ix 2 I wouldn't give four obols for it, IV ix 33 Twopenny fellows (441 above); III vii 52 Not a lead penny (where some of this material has already been used).
2 Plautus *Trinummus* 962
3 Plautus *Casina* 258
4 Cicero *Ad familiares* 5.10.1. Erasmus is mistaken here, both about Cicero's work (*Letters to Friends*, not Atticus) and about who the 'half-penny fellow' is. It is Vatinius who writes to Cicero about a pirate he has captured. Cicero and

phrase 'a threepenny donkey man,' meaning 'contemptible.'⁵ In the *Haunted House* Plautus writes, 'Shut up, you coiner of leaden pennies.'⁶

10 **Basilica facinora**
Right royal doings

As I have already recorded, the adjective βασιλικός 'royal' was applied to anything splendid, for example, enjoying health βασιλικῶς 'fit for a king.'¹ Also splendid buildings were called *basilicae*. In the *Three-shilling Day*, Plautus says of a slave, a worthless fellow who is nonetheless spouting some fine sentiments, 'Good heavens! Now he's got onto right royal doings!'² There is a well-known story about Porus and Alexander. After he had defeated Porus in battle, Alexander asked him, 'How am I to treat you?' and Porus replied, 'Like a king.' Alexander then asked him, 'And what besides?' Porus answered that the words 'like a king' were all-inclusive.³ Kings should indeed do nothing ignoble. Plautus has a rather less natural use of the last phrase in *Epidicus*: 'Ye gods! I'm done for *basilice* "right royally!"'⁴

11 **Nec caput nec pedes**
Neither head nor feet

The ancients said that any business so involved that you don't know how to straighten it out or get rid of it had 'Neither head nor feet.' So Cicero jokingly replies to his friend Curio, 'I gather from your letter that you didn't

* * * * *

Vatinius were now on friendly terms, though they had been opposed earlier and Cicero had attacked him in the lawcourts.
5 Persius 5.76
6 Plautus *Mostellaria* 892. The line here refers to 'stale' or 'leaden' jokes.

10 Plautus (see n2). Added in *1533*
1 *Adagia* II viii 86 To be as fit as a pancratiast
2 Plautus *Trinummus* 1030
3 See Plutarch *Moralia* 181E *Regum et imperatorum apophthegmata*, Erasmus *Apophthegmata* IV Alexander 31 (LB IV 199D).
4 Plautus *Epidicus* 56

11 Cicero (see n1). Otto 344; Apostolius 2.2. Added in *1533*

greatly need Sulpicius' assistance, as your affairs were in such a heap that, as you yourself say, they had "Neither head nor feet." For my part, I wish they did have feet, so that you would come back one of these days.'[1] I spoke earlier of Plato's phrase, 'A story without a head.'[2]

12 Somnum non vidit
He never saw sleep

Since sleep is not seen but in fact closes the eyes, it is quite obvious that we have one of those proverbial figures of speech in the words 'He never set eyes on sleep,' which express the idea of supreme vigilance. Cicero, writing to Curius in the eighth book of *Letters to Friends*, says, 'You can take it from me that during Caninius' consulship not a single person ever had lunch. Nor were any crimes committed while he was consul. He was in fact wonderfully vigilant, as he never saw sleep during his whole period of office.'[1] The point of the joke is that he was consul only for one day. Sayings depend on the use of figures.[2]

13 Manum ad os apponere
Put one's fingers to one's lips

This gesture is a sign that we know something that we don't want to noise abroad. Caelius, writing to Cicero in book 8 of the *Letters to Friends*: 'But when Domitius put his fingers to his lips, the loafers in the forum, on their own heads be it, had spread it abroad that you had perished on May 24th.'[1]

* * * * *

1 Cicero *Ad familiares* 7.31.2 (to Curius, not Curio)
2 Plato *Laws* 752A; *Phaedrus* 264C. See *Adagia* I i 14 A story without a head. It is interesting that Erasmus did not here include *nec pes nec caput* 'nor foot nor head' from his favourite Horace (*Ars poetica* 8).

12 Cicero (see n1). Added in *1533*
1 Cicero *Ad familiares* 7.30.1 (not book 8)
2 See CWE 31 21 *Introduction* xiii.

13 Cicero (see n1). Added in *1533*
1 Cicero *Ad familiares* 8.1.4–5 Already used in *Adagia* IV vi 88 On your own head may it fall (272 above). See n6 there.

14 Emendus cui imperes
If you want to give orders, you must buy a slave

Anyone may lord it over his own slaves, but not over anyone else's, nor over free men. So Stasimus in Plautus' play, the *Three-shilling Day*, says to his master who is imperiously telling him to come back (either because he doesn't know it is his master or is pretending not to know), 'You'd better buy someone to give orders to.'[1] Again, in the *Persian*: 'You need to buy someone if you want him to obey you.'[2] A line in Theocritus which I discussed earlier is relevant here: 'I'm not bothered. Don't you level off what is empty!'[3] The woman is taking exception to being reprimanded by a man to whom she is neither maidservant nor wife. She also says, 'You're telling Syracusan women what to do,'[4] that is, not women you have any rights over, but free women.

15 Omnium quos sol videt
Of all whom the sun beholds

Here are some other proverbial figures of speech: 'Of all the earth supports' or 'Of all the sun beholds, the worst or the best.' Plautus in *Stichus*:

> You'll soon find a woman worse than she was, father,
> And with not so nice a nature. A better one
> You'll never find; the sun doesn't look upon her like.[1]

* * * * *

14 Plautus (see nn1 and 2). Otto 598. Cf *Adagia* IV iv 24 Give orders to those you have fed (75 above). Added in *1533*
1 Plautus *Trinummus* 1061
2 Plautus *Persa* 273
3 Theocritus *Idylls* 15.95. According to the scholiast here, 'To level off what is empty' means to smooth off with a stick a measure of dry goods that is not full and so does not need levelling off, in other words, to waste one's efforts. See *Adagia* IV iii 28 Don't level off what is empty (20 above), where Erasmus had earlier tentatively offered a different explanation of the phrase. In *1533* he expanded that essay, incorporating this explanation and another.
4 Theocritus *Idylls* 15.90

15 Otto 1669, 1671. Added in *1533*
1 Plautus *Stichus* 109–10

Again, in the *Bacchis Sisters*:

I know this for sure,
Vulcan, Moon, Sun, Day, the Four Gods,
Never shone down on a greater villain.[2]

Virgil: 'O sun, that lightest with thy flames all the works of earth.'[3] Hence the sun is called 'the eye of the world.'[4] Another similar expression is 'whatever meets the foot,' for example in the last letter of book 9 of Cicero's *Letters to Friends*, 'I enjoy going out to dinner. There I can talk about "whatever meets the foot," as they say, tears and smiles.'[5] Cicero is saying that over dinner he can talk about anything at all, happy or sad. I have already cited this phrase, quoting it from the first book of *On the Nature of the Gods*.[6] I didn't at the time recall this second example,[7] but it does serve to establish the words as proverbial. Plautus in the *Carthaginian*: 'The nastiest villain of all that walk upon the earth.'[8]

16 Sale et aceto
With salt and vinegar

A thrifty, meagre lunch is being described by the fisherman Gripus in the *Rope*, when he says, 'My lord will have his lunch flavoured with vinegar and with salt, not a piece of something tasty.'[1] Poor people have salt and vinegar in place of something more substantial. Cicero, writing to Papirius Paetus in book 9 of his *Letters to Friends*, makes mention of something called

* * * * *

2 Plautus *Bacchides* 254–7
3 Virgil *Aeneid* 4.607
4 Ovid *Metamorphoses* 4.228
5 Cicero *Ad familiares* 9.26.2
6 Cicero *De natura deorum* 1.23.65, quoted in *Adagia* III vi 3 Whatever falls on the ground. It is debatable what the words *quicquid in solum* actually mean; *solum* could be 'ground' or 'sole of the foot.'
7 See n5.
8 Plautus *Poenulus* 90

16 Plautus (see n1). Otto 1571. Suringar 197. Added in *1533*
1 Plautus *Rudens* 937. Gripus has been out fishing and has caught no fish.

tyrotarichus, apparently a cheap and popular savoury dish. It was a broth made with cheese, a dish still found in Italy today under the name 'menestra.'[2] Cicero also mentions there the pilot-fish, a coarse species like the gudgeon. What he says is 'What's all this about a pilot-fish, about a shilling, about a dish of tyrotarichus?'[3] Pliny often mentions the pilot-fish.[4] I suspect that *denarius*, the word for 'shilling' in the Cicero passage, is corrupt. Certainly I don't as yet see what it means. 'Vinegar' is quite often used in the sense of 'sharpness' or 'shrewdness,' as for example in the phrase from Plautus, 'vinegar in his bosom,'[5] or in Persius, 'well-washed with biting vinegar.'[6] Nonius cites lines from Varro's *Better than Ulysses*: 'Carneades mapped out another road to virtue, drawing on "tubs of sharp vinegar."'[7] He means 'with great subtlety.'

17 Cassa glande
An empty acorn

Along with various other examples of phrases meaning 'of little worth' I have already quoted 'I wouldn't buy it for a rotten nut.'[1] Plautus used a similar figurative expression, 'An empty acorn,' in the *Rope*.[2] Here the character Gripus is offering information for money. Labrax offers thirty pounds. *Gripus*: 'Rubbish!' *Labrax*: 'Forty.' *Gripus*: 'Stuff and nonsense!' *Labrax*: 'Fifty.' *Gripus*: 'Empty acorns!' *Labrax*: 'Sixty.' *Gripus*: 'Squiggly

* * * * *

2 See *Adagia* IV vi 70 Drinkers of dregs (262 above); also Erasmus *Colloquia* 'Penny-pinching' CWE 40 987, thought to be a reference to the meagre fare provided by Andrea Torresani when Erasmus lodged with him in 1508.

3 Cicero *Ad familiares* 9.16.7

4 Pliny *Naturalis historia* 9.51; 32.153

5 Plautus *Pseudolus* 739, already used in *Adagia* II iii 52 He has vinegar in his bosom

6 Persius 5.86, already used in *Adagia* II iv 94 With well-washed ears

7 Nonius Marcellus 117.21–3 Lindsay, citing Varro *Menippeae* (fragment 484 Buecheler)

17 Plautus (see n2). Otto 1258. Added in *1533*

1 *Adagia* I viii 8 I would not buy it for a rotten walnut. See also *Adagia* IV x 43 I wouldn't give a dram (510 above); *Adagia* IV x 98 A rotten mushroom (541 above).

2 Plautus *Rudens* 1323–5. For 'rubbish,' *tricae*, see *Adagia* I ii 43 Stuff and nonsense.

wrigglies!' An empty acorn is rotten, just an empty shell with nothing inside.

18 Vervecea statua
A sheep-brained piece of statuary

Hegio, in Plautus' play the *Two Captives*, calls a stupid slave 'A sheep-
brained piece of statuary,' that is, a brutish tongue-tied fellow. He says, 'You
two go inside. Meantime I'll question this sheep-brained piece of statuary /
And find out what happened to my younger son.'[1] Some people[2] read here
not *vervecea* 'sheep-brained,' but *verberea*,[3] so that Plautus wrote 'whipping-
block' instead of 'marble-block,' that is, a rascal constantly getting flogged.
Certainly the form *vervecea* disturbs the trochaic rhythm, as there is an
extra syllable, unless one reads *-cea* with the two vowels contracted into
one syllable by synaeresis.

19 Hoc age
Attend to the business in hand

When we bid someone pay attention, we say, 'Be right here'[1] or 'Attend to
the business in hand.' The Emperor Caligula heard those who had come to
assassinate him say 'Attend to the business.'[2] Plautus in the same play uses
a plural version, 'Let's attend to business.'[3]

* * * * *

18 Plautus (see n1). Added in *1533*
1 Plautus *Captivi* 951–2. In some early editions the title is given as *Duo Captivi*.
2 A comment based on Giambattista Pio's commentary in his edition (see *Adagia*
  IV iii 40 n2, 27 above)
3 From *vervex* 'wether' or *verbera* 'blows'

19 Suetonius and Plautus (see nn2–3). Otto 43. Cf *Adagia* II vii 84 Though present
  he is far away. Added in *1533*
1 A phrase from Augustine *Soliloquia* 2.6.9 (CSEL 89 57)
2 See Suetonius *Caligula* 58. The words were originally addressed to the assembled people to get attention and quiet when a sacrifice to the gods was being
  performed (see Plutarch *Life of Numa* 14.2). So they are grimly humorous in
  the mouth of an assassin. The phrase was so familiar it was used in everyday
  speech. There are several examples in Plautus and elsewhere.
3 Plautus *Captivi* 930, 967, the play quoted in the immediately preceding adage

20 **Quam in tragoedia comici**
   Comic characters in a tragedy

'Comic characters brought on in a tragedy.' We can use this phrase when someone is operating in a field not his own. Tragedy and comedy are very different genres, and it is not allowed to bring on tragic characters in comedy, or vice versa.[1] In Plautus' play the *Carthaginian* we have a line 'Why, to be sure, I'm less well trained than comic characters in a tragedy.'[2] The word in the text here is *indoctior* 'more untrained,' but in my opinion we should read *inductior* 'brought on more.' Colabiscus' words picked up what Milphio had just said: 'Now you just make sure that you've got some words *conducta* "brought in" to suit this bit of trickery.' Colabiscus jokingly retorts, 'Actually I'm *inductior* "more brought on,"' in other words 'I'm better rehearsed.'

21 **Non magis quam canem**
   No more than a dog

The word 'dog' is used in common speech to indicate hatred and contempt. Horace says, 'He hates worse than a dog.'[1] Plautus in *Amphitryo*:

> AMPHITRYO: Have you kept well? Are you pleased to see me back?
> SOSIA: Never saw anyone more welcome!

* * * * *

20 Brassicanus no 96 (see *Adagia* IV iii 86 n2, 52 above), which contains the reference to Plautus *Poenulus* (see n2). Added in *1533*
1 See perhaps Horace *Ars poetica* 89–92, on appropriate diction and characterization.
2 Plautus *Poenulus* 580–1. Erasmus is struggling to make sense of a faulty text and his emendation is not very happy. He bases it on one of the meanings of the verb *inducere*, 'to bring (performers) onto the stage,' 'to put on (a play).' Modern editions read *condocta ... condoctior* 'well-learned,' (a reading known to the commentator at LB II 1185F, who also points out that the slave's name is Collybiscus), and there are other differences from Erasmus' text. The commentator in LB adds, 'I have often had occasion to remark that this greatest of men has been frequently misled by bad editions.'

21 Plautus (see n2). Otto 315–33. Added in *1533*
1 Erasmus quotes Horace *Epistles* 1.17.30–31 from memory, giving *odit* 'hates' instead of the correct reading *vitabit* 'will shun.'

No one's any more pleased to see him back than to see a dog![2]

I think we need this reading to fit the metre, which is trochaic tetrameter catalectic.

22 **Gralatorius aut testudineus gradus**
Stilt-walk or tortoise walk

Plautus in *Amphitryo*:

> BLEPHARO: We couldn't stride our steps out with a bigger stretch.
> AMPHITRYO: Whether it was 'Stilt-walk or tortoise walk,' I'm sure we've
> lost the villain.[1]

Plautus again, in the *Carthaginian*: 'You'd have outrun a stag, outstepped a stilt-walker.'[2] *Gralae* 'stilts' are poles on which it is possible to prop oneself up and walk. The Latin name for stilt-walkers was *gralatores*. The Greeks called them καλοβάται, just as tight-rope walkers are called σχοινοβάται. The higher the foot-rest on the stilt is from the ground, the bigger the step that can be taken. So much can be deduced from a Nonius passage which is very corrupt, especially in the Aldine edition.[3] Plautus again, writing in the *Two Menaechmuses*: 'Just look at him tripping along! Get that ant's pace of yours moving!'[4] Ants appear to be scuttling along without making much progress. Plautus, in the *Carthaginian* again: 'You beat a snail in a slow-race.'[5] In the same play, he calls people who come slowly 'sticky-footed, slower than cargo-boats in a dead calm.'[6] Then he

* * * * *

2 Plautus *Amphitryo* 679–80. In the last verse Erasmus read *quisquam* for *quicquam* in modern texts: 'she welcomes him not a bit more warmly ...'

22 Plautus (see nn1 and 2). Added in *1533*
1 Plautus *Amphitryo* line 94 of the spurious section (see IV viii 16 n2, 364 above)
2 Plautus *Poenulus* 530
3 Nonius Marcellus 165.18–23 Lindsay. Erasmus cites the Aldine edition of Nonius four times by name in *Adagia* v i 1–100 where there is a textual problem (adages 22, 56, 59 and 64).
4 Plautus *Menaechmi* 888
5 Plautus *Poenulus* 532
6 Plautus *Poenulus* 506–7

says their steps must have been passed through a flour-sieve[7] – because the flour trickles slowly through the tiny holes.

23 Daedaleum remigium
Oarage of Daedalus

To indicate speed, Plautus in *Amphitryo* uses the phrase 'By oarage of Daedalus,' meaning 'flying': 'I couldn't have done it quicker if I'd brought myself by oarage of Daedalus.'[1]

24 Argentum accepi, imperium vendidi
I took the money, sold my authority

There is nothing more frequently trotted out than this saying: 'Accept a favour and lose your liberty.' Demaenetus puts it neatly in the *Comedy of Asses*: 'I took the money and for a dowry sold my authority.'[1] He was poor and had married a wife with a large dowry, but found he had no authority over her. Nausistrata in Terence's play *Phormio* is just such another wife.[2]

25 Despuere malum
Spit away the evil

Even today it is a popular custom for people to spit to avert the evil omen if they hear of something dreadful that they don't want to happen to themselves. This is a survival of an ancient superstition whereby people believed that spitting was a protection against looming evils, especially against the

* * * * *

7 Plautus *Poenulus* 513

23 Plautus (see n1). See *Adagia* III i 65 The wings of Daedalus. Otto 498. Added in 1533
1 Plautus *Amphitryo* line 92 of the spurious section (see IV viii 16 n2, 364 above)

24 Plautus (see n1). Suringar 246. Added in 1533
1 Plautus *Asinaria* 87
2 See Terence *Phormio* 990–1053.

25 Pliny with Plautus (see nn1, 2, and 3). See *Adagia* I vi 94 Spit into your own bosom. Added in 1533

'assembly disease,' so called not only because attacks are more likely to occur in crowded places, but because it caused the assembly to be abandoned.
Also in the application of remedies, it was thought that spitting three times
increased their effectiveness, and it could also counteract spells, according
to Pliny,[1] and the same superstitious belief led people to spit three times
in their own bosom to avert the mischief attracted by overweening hopes.
We have a section in a play of Plautus that goes as follows:

– And he suffers attacks of that disease, the one that gets spat on.
– You wretch! So I've got that disease that means I need to be spat on?
– Never mind! Many a man's tormented by that disease, and spitting
  Has helped him back to health.[2]

Plautus again in *Amphitryo*: 'Please, for heaven's sake, spit away the
words you spoke!'[3]

26 Χρήσει καὶ κτήσει
By use and possession

Anyone who wanted to express the idea of belonging wholly to someone,
could say, 'I am yours Χρήσει καὶ κτήσει,' that is, 'By both usufruct and
ownership.' With regard to possessions, it is often the case that ownership
rests with one person, the usufruct with another. Curius, writing to Cicero
in book 8 of his *Letters to Friends*, says, 'I hope you are in good health, for I
am yours by usufruct, by ownership I belong to our friend Atticus. So the
enjoyment is yours, the ownership his.'[1] Curius means that he is bound to
Atticus without being any the less well-disposed to Cicero. Cicero's reply
expands on this: '. . . if I didn't have our dear Atticus as a companion in
my studies. When you write that you belong to him by bondage and debt-
slavery, to me by use and enjoyment, I am content with that, for what

* * * * *

1 Pliny *Naturalis historia* 28.35
2 Plautus *Captivi* 550–5. 'The disease that gets spat on' is epilepsy.
3 Plautus *Asinaria* (not *Amphitryo*) 39

26 Erasmus now embarks on a long series of adages (*Adagia* v i 26–53) derived
   almost exclusively from Cicero's *Letters*, mostly *Ad Atticum*, though he has
   been using the *Letters* less intensively since v i 9. Added in *1533*
1 Cicero *Ad familiares* 7.29.1 (not book 8)

someone uses and enjoys is his.'² Cicero's joke with the lawyer shows that ownership could be established in two ways, by bondage and by debt-slavery, but he does not want that kind of right so long as he has use and enjoyment, because as long as the right of use and enjoyment exists, it is as if the thing were one's own.

27 Ferire frontem
Beat one's brow

Anyone who is thoroughly exasperated and angry is said 'To beat his brow.' Cicero, in his first letter to Atticus, writes, 'I imagine all that will make you laugh or groan. To make you beat your brow, some people think Caesonius too will stand ...'¹ He considered what he had just written fit to raise a laugh or groan, but his news about Caesonius was so unacceptable that Atticus ought 'To beat his brow.' Anyone who thinks this isn't a proverb will have to reject 'To wipe off your blushes' and 'Thumbs down' and many other sayings referring to physical gestures.²

28 Virtutem omnem explica
Lay out all your powers

In a letter from the same book he quotes a very well-known line from Homer: Παντοίης ἀρετῆς μιμνήσκεο, and do all you can to ensure that I am generally popular and approved of.'¹ The Greek may be translated as 'Bring now to mind every power of which you are possessed,' in other words, 'In this matter exert all your strength, strain every mental nerve.'²

* * * * *

2 Cicero *Ad familiares* 7.30.2. The joke is perhaps that Manius Curius, who, like Atticus, was a banker (not a lawyer), owed Atticus a lot of money. Erasmus seems to be thinking of Cicero's legal friend Trebatius, with whom he often bandied legal jokes (for example, Cicero *Ad familiares* 7.18). See *Adagia* v ii 15 (608 below).

27 Cicero (see n1). Otto 720. Added in *1533*
  1 Cicero *Ad Atticum* 1.1.1
  2 These sayings are found at *Adagia* i viii 47 and 46.

28 Homer by way of Cicero (see n1). Added in *1533*
  1 Cicero *Ad Atticum* 1.15.1, quoting Homer *Iliad* 22.268
  2 See *Adagia* i iv 16 With every sinew; iii ix 68 With every nerve.

29 Clemens lanista
A soft-hearted manager of gladiators

I have already recorded the Greek proverb Εὔνους σφάκτης 'A well-wishing murderer.'[1] Very similar to this is the phrase 'A soft-hearted manager of gladiators,' used by Cicero when writing to Atticus in the letter in book 1 that begins 'You ask . . .':

> After the challenging of the jury had taken place amidst a great deal of up-roar, with the prosecuting counsel, like a good censor, rejecting those of bad character, and the defendant, like a soft-hearted manager of gladiators, set-ting aside the respectable, when the jury took their places, decent men began to feel very apprehensive.[2]

30 Praepostere
Back to front

When we think something is 'Back to front,' like the people telling the rulers what to do, or students instructing their teachers, it will be appropriate to use Cicero's words in this same letter: 'I will answer your questions Homeric fashion, ὕστερον πρότερον.'[1] This is a figure of style that the grammarians call πρωθύστερον 'hindmost foremost' or ὑστερόπρωτον 'latter first,' in which what naturally comes first is put second, for example 'Cornelia brought up the Gracchi and brought them into the world.' This figure occurs frequently in Homer.

31 Consessus in talario ludo
A music-hall assembly

The same letter contains another phrase that looks proverbial, 'A music-hall assembly,' referring to a gathering of persons of not very reputable

* * * * *

29 Cicero (see n2). Added in *1533*
 1 *Adagia* III ii 7 Well-wishing murderer
 2 Cicero *Ad Atticum* 1.16.3

30 Cicero (see n1). Added in *1533*
 1 Cicero *Ad Atticum* 1.16.1

31 Cicero (see n1). Added in *1533*

character. *Consessus* 'assembly,' συνέδριον in Greek, is properly used for a session of senators or jurymen, who are usually selected from men of good standing. In a music-hall assembly the most disreputable takes the leading role. Cicero says:

> There was never a more disgraceful 'Assembly in a music-hall' – senators under a cloud, knights who had lost their status, treasury tribunes who are not so much paying-out officers as paying-in officers, as people are calling them. There were however a few honest men . . .[1]

This last joke can also be called proverbial as Cicero says these men were popularly called not 'paying-out' officers, but 'paying-in' officers. In other words, they were in debt; or else they had paid themselves well out of the public purse.

32 Contrahere vela
Take in one's sails

In the same letter, Cicero uses the phrase 'Take in one's sails,' meaning 'check oneself, go carefully.' 'I took in my sails,' he says, 'when I realized the financial straits of the jurymen, and I didn't say anything in my testimony that was not already so well known and sworn to that I couldn't leave it out.'[1] Horace says something similar:

> But also
> Draw in, when favouring winds too strongly blow,
> Your billowing canvas.[2]

The metaphor is derived from sailors, who take in the sails when the wind blows too strongly, so as to avoid danger; and when it drops, they spread the sails to catch the breeze.

* * * * *

1 Cicero *Ad Atticum* 1.16.3. It is clear that Cicero is making a pun on *aerarii* and *aerati*, but there are problems with the text here. See *The Correspondence of Cicero* ed R.Y. Tyrrell and L.C. Purser (Dublin 1904) 1.210.

32 Cicero (see n1). *Collectanea* no 776. Otto 1857. Added in *1533*
1 Cicero *Ad Atticum* 1.16.2
2 Horace *Odes* 2.10.22–4

33 Ἔσπετε νῦν μοι
Tell out now

In the same letter, Cicero continues his narrative of events with an amusing quotation from Homer: 'Tell out now, ye Muses, as you told what went before.'[1] This will be nice to use when relating some laughable incident. In the Aldine edition, only the first half of the line is quoted: 'Tell out now, ye Muses.' This half-line occurs more than once in Homer, with variants in the second half, for example, 'Tell out now, ye Muses, that dwell on Olympus' heights,' from book 2.[2]

34 **In dierectum**
Get crucified

We tell someone to whom we wish ill to 'go and be hanged' or to 'be off to the crows' or 'to Cynosarges.' The early Romans said, 'Go and get crucified,' using a word *dierectus*, which means 'crucified.' Nonius cites a line from Varro: 'Get that madness out of our house *in dierectum* "and onto a cross." '[1] Nonius thinks the word *dierectus* means 'erected into the day,' (that is, *in diem erectus*). Perhaps Nonius really wrote *in dium erectos* 'erected under the open sky,' as those who are crucified are displayed in the open, especially as Varro adds, 'out of our house.' Anything carried out of the house is taken into the open. Varro's word for madness here, *insanitas*, not *insania*, is supported by Cicero's use of it,[2] so there is no need to suspect a corruption.

* * * * *

33 Homer quoted by Cicero (see n1). Added in 1533
　1 Cicero *Ad Atticum* 1.16.5, where Cicero quotes the first half of each of the two lines of Homer *Iliad* 16.112–13. The Aldine edition of Cicero's letters offers only the first half-line (112) and Erasmus seems to have completed the line with a confused memory of the opening of line 113.
　2 Homer *Iliad* 2.484, also the true reading of *Iliad* 16.112 (see n1)

34 Nonius Marcellus quoting Varro (see n1). See *Adagia* II i 96 Off with you to the crows; III i 70 Off with you to Cynosarges. Added in 1533
　1 Nonius Marcellus 70.24–6 Lindsay, citing Varro *Menippeae* (fragment 133 Buecheler). The etymology of the word *dierectus* is not known. Plautus uses it several times, eg *Poenulus* 347 *i dierecte in maxumam malam crucem*. A connection with διαρρήγνυμι 'to break,' as suggested by the humanist commentators on Plautus (see the note at LB II 1187F), is possible.
　2 Cicero *Tusculan Disputations* 3.5.10

35 Mittere sanguinem
Letting blood

At one time, soldiers who were guilty of a grave misdemeanour had a vein opened to humiliate them. This was called 'Letting blood.' Cicero, in the same letter as above: 'The vein of ill-will was opened without any pain.'[1] He means that his unpopularity was diminished to some extent, because the evidence he produced at the trial had carried no weight, and that this happened without any grief on his part, because everybody knew the jury had been bribed. Again, in the first letter in book 6: 'Appius had treated the province by means of reduction, let blood, removed whatever he could, handed it over to me at the point of death . . .'[2] The phrase 'treated by means of reduction' is a kind of saying, as it is here used of a greedy rapacious man. It is a metaphor derived from doctors, who in certain conditions empty the body, removing superfluous matter, either by a regime of fasting or by blood-letting.

36 Faba nummus
Bean-currency

I have said elsewhere that at one time votes were cast using beans,[1] and Pythagoras is thought to have had this in mind when he forbade the eating of beans. So in the following passage, Cicero is referring to electoral corruption in a witty metaphorical way: 'But mark you! If he's elected, our consulship, which Curio used to call a positive apotheosis, will become bean-currency.'[2] Where beans become money, there votes have been bought.

37 Nihil est, aut nihil curae est
He is nothing, or cares for nothing

In the same book of letters, in the one beginning 'After I got back from

* * * * *

35 Cicero (see nn1–2). Added in *1533*
1 Cicero *Ad Atticum* 1.16.11, the letter last quoted at *Adagia* v i 33 (561 above)
2 Cicero *Ad Atticum* 6.1.2

36 Cicero (see n2). Otto 1117. Added in *1533*
1 *Adagia* I i 2 CWE 31 37 (*A fabis abstineto*); IV vi 37 Gnawer of beans (238 above)
2 Cicero *Ad Atticum* 1.16.13. The reading here is problematic.

37 Rhinthon quoted by Cicero (see n1). Added in *1533*

my place near Pompeii,' Cicero quotes an obviously well-known line of
Rhinthon: 'I would have you know,' he writes, 'that since the death of Cat-
ulus I maintain this optimate road with no protection and no support. As
Rhinthon, I think, says, "These are nothing, the others care for nothing."'[1]
He means he is without the support of the big names, because they were
either powerless or indifferent.

38 E terra spectare naufragium
View the shipwreck from the shore

I wrote earlier about 'Judging the Achaeans from the tower,' that is, ob-
serving other people's danger from a safe place.[1] Cicero with a touch of
humour finds another metaphor to express this same idea. In the second
book of his *Letters to Atticus*, the one beginning 'About the *Geography*,' he
writes, 'Now that I am compelled to abandon ship, not taking my hand off
the tiller but having it torn from my grasp, it is my intention to observe
from the shore the shipwreck those people are going to make. I desire, as
your friend Sophocles says, "beneath my own roof-tree to harken, free from
care with mind at peace."'[2] In some texts this fragment of Greek verse appeared in a different version, but one equally corrupt. Other texts omitted

* * * * *

1 Cicero *Ad Atticum* 1.20.3, quoting Rhinthon, a third-century BC writer of plays,
  whose works survive only in fragments. But this line was probably wrongly
  ascribed to him; see Kaibel page 189.

38 Cicero (see 2). Added in *1533*
1 *Adagia* III ii 93 Why judge the Achaeans from the tower?
2 Cicero *Ad Atticum* 2.7.4. Estienne pointed out (see the long note at LB II
  1188E–F) that Erasmus was misled about the metre of the extract from Sophocles quoted by Cicero because he believed it to consist of one line only, not
  a line and a half. Estienne cites in Greek the complete three-line extract from
  Sophocles *Tympanistae* (*TrGF* 4 Sophocles fragment 636; see Stobaeus 59.12
  Gaisford): 'What greater pleasure could you e'er receive than this, / Having
  attained the shore, beneath your own roof tree / To harken to the pounding
  rain with mind at peace.' This version has (πυκνῆς) . . . ψακάδος '(to the pounding) rain,' instead of εὔκηλος 'free from care.' The corrupt (and meaningless)
  ψάκαλος on which Erasmus comments is obviously based on the former. As
  the line appears here, it has indeed (in εὔκηλος) one syllable too many for a
  trochaic tetrameter catalectic, but the correct text reveals the metre as one and
  a half lines of iambic trimeters.

it. The line seems to be trochaic catalectic. Instead of the word εὔκηλος 'free from care,' some texts had ψάκαλος but I do not know what this could be. Εὔκηλος doesn't fit the metre. However, the sense seems to be that Cicero desires to listen from home to the commotion affecting others, himself being uninvolved and unconcerned.

39 Qui prior laesit
The first to wound

In the same book of letters, in the one beginning 'When Caecilius suddenly informed me,' Cicero quotes a line from Homer, threatening vengeance on someone who was the first to pick a quarrel: 'As for myself, it is my intention, if your crony Publius will allow it, to play the sophist.[1] If he is even thinking of upsetting me at all, I will do what goes with the sophist's stance, and I proclaim that I will "ward off any man that is the first to injure." '[2]

40 Quod datur
What you're given

Nonius Marcellus cites this verse from Caecilius' *Plocium*: 'Put up with what they give, as they don't give what you want.'[1] The line in Latin contains the form *danunt*, an old form for *dant* 'they give.' This sentiment agrees with something I cited from Cicero earlier: 'Make the best of what you've got,'[2] and other similar phrases.

* * * * *

39 Homer quoted by Cicero (see n2). Added in *1533*
  1 In their public demonstrations of debating skills, the sophists did not initiate the discussion, but waited for someone to put forward a proposition to which they would respond *extempore*.
  2 Cicero *Ad Atticum* 2.9.3, quoting Homer *Iliad* 24.369. Erasmus treats the second part of the verse as an adage, that is (Ἄνδρ᾽ ἀπαμύνεσθαι) ὅς τις πρότερος χαλεπήνῃ, translating as *qui prior laesit*, no doubt recalling Terence *Eunuchus* 6, though the text there reads *quia laesit prior* 'because he injured first.'

40 Caecilius by way of Nonius Marcellus (see n1). Added in *1533*
  1 Nonius Marcellus 138.20–1 Lindsay, citing CRF Caecilius 76
  2 Cicero *Ad Atticum* 6.5.2, cited in *Adagia* IV ii 43 What is given. The phrase in Cicero is actually in Greek, τὰ μὲν διδόμενα.

41 Chimaera
A chimaera

Cicero humorously denotes an inconstant man of unpredictable behaviour or a work that does not hold together with a line from Homer: 'As to what you write about brother Quintus' letter, I too found it "forepart lion, behind a dragon, in between a chimaera." I don't know what to make of it. The first few lines he spends complaining so forcefully about having to stay out there that anyone would feel sorry for him. Then he slackens off and asks me to edit his *Annals* and get them published.'[1] Cicero calls this inconsistent letter 'A chimaera.'

42 Nihil dulcius quam omnia scire
Nothing nicer than being in the know

In book four of his *Letters to Atticus*, in the one beginning 'I was delighted to receive,' Cicero quotes an apparently well-known line of Greek verse: Οὐδὲν γλυκύτερον ἢ πᾶν εἰδέναι 'Nothing nicer than knowing all.'[1] As it stands, the verse is faulty, but this can be healed by the insertion of ἐστιν 'is': 'Nothing is nicer than πάντ᾽ εἰδέναι "knowing all things."' Or one can read at the end πᾶν εἰδέναι 'knowing all.' Cicero goes on: 'So treat me as a fellow consumed with curiosity and write and tell me about what happened on the first day, on the second, tell me about the censors, about Appius, about that pet of the people, the unsexed Appuleius.' One also finds in Cicero's letters another Greek phrase, πάντα περὶ πάντων 'everything about everything.'[2]

* * * * *

41 Cicero quoting Homer (see n1). See *Adagia* II vi 82 A Bellerophon letter. Added in *1533*
  1 Cicero *Ad Atticum* 2.16.4, quoting, in Greek, Homer *Iliad* 6.181; but modern texts of Cicero limit the quotation to the first half of the line: '"Forepart lion, behind ..." – I don't know what.' Erasmus is following the Basel 1528 edition of Cicero.

42 Cicero (see n1). Added in *1533*
  1 Cicero *Ad Atticum* 4.11.2. The Greek verse has been ascribed to Menander *Epitrepontes* (fragment 2 Körte). Erasmus' emendation seems right.
  2 Cicero *Ad familiares* 15.17.1; 12.20.1. The contexts suggest that the phrase implies 'make full amends.'

43 **De statu demigrare**
Abandon one's position

I have already discussed 'To be pushed off the step,'[1] meaning 'to be made
to abandon one's stance.' Similarly, in the fourth book of his letters to
Atticus, in the one beginning 'You will gather how busy I am,' Cicero wrote,
'Abandon my position,' meaning 'give up my principles of action.' He says,
'Those who were not happy that I had any powers at all may burst with
fury. I find comfort in many things, nor am I really abandoning my position
– I am returning to the life that is most natural to me.'[2] The metaphor seems
to be derived either from athletes, or from battles, where it is considered
praiseworthy not to have retreated from one's position.

44 **Strumam dibapho tegere**
Cover a swelling with a purple robe

In a letter to Atticus, Cicero used the phrase *Strumam dibapho tegere* 'Cover
a swelling with a purple robe' to mean 'disguise infamy with office.' He
says, 'Conceal Vatinius' tumour with the purple robe of priesthood.'[1] The
word for the purple robe, *dibaphon*, means 'double-dyed.' The word *struma*
means some swelling of the body, such as a hump. That deformity is sometimes camouflaged with the purple.[2] Again, writing to Marcus Caelius in
book 2 of the *Letters to Friends*: 'Our friend Curtius has thoughts of the
purple robe, but the dyer is keeping him waiting.'[3] By 'purple robe' here
he means a magistracy, as holders of such offices were entitled to wear

* * * * *

43 Cicero (see n2). Added in 1533
 1 *Adagia* II iii 98
 2 Cicero *Ad Atticum* 4.18.2. The extract is not nowadays assigned to the letter
   (*Ad Atticum* 4.14) whose opening Erasmus cites.

44 Cicero (see n1). Added in 1533
 1 Cicero *Ad Atticum* 2.9.2. Vatinius suffered from scrofula, a swelling of the
   glands.
 2 Erasmus was possibly thinking of the English king, Richard III (d 1485), who
   was generally believed to have a crooked back. See (the earliest reference to
   this) *The Complete Works of Thomas More* (New Haven 1963), *Historia Richardi
   Regis* 7.
 3 Cicero *Ad familiaes* 2.16.7

the double-dyed *dibaphon*, but he jokes that things were not turning out as Curtius hoped, because the dyer was behind schedule. Indeed, one way of obliterating ill repute is to inhibit accusation by the eminence of the position one holds. Modest rank is open to the attacks of enmity. This maybe has motivated some who have striven to attain the cardinal's mitre and hat.

45 Multa in medio
Much in between

I have already written about 'There's many a slip 'twixt the cup and the lip.'[1] Cicero has another metaphorical expression for this idea in book 6 of his *Letters to Atticus*, in the letter beginning 'Although I had nothing new.' There he writes, 'Not that you could help me. The matter is in train, and you are far away across the world. Πολλὰ δ᾽ ἐν μεταιχμίῳ / Νότος κυλίνδει κύματ᾽ εὐρείης ἁλός.'[2] Cicero feels that many upheavals would take place before Atticus, who was far away, could come to his aid. The Greek is in iambic verse and could be translated, 'And many the waves in the space between / Rolling before the wind, over the outspread sea.'

46 Preces armatae
Requests backed by force

Cicero again, in the letter in book 9 that begins 'I received your letter on the twenty-third,' uses a Greek word πειθανάγκη, meaning 'suggestion linked with compulsion and power.'[1] The requests of rulers have this character, and Ovid puts this neatly, when speaking of Jove: 'And being a king, he joins with his entreaties threats.'[2] Here is what Cicero writes: 'I am not so much

* * * * *

45 Cicero (see n2). Added in *1533*
 1 *Adagia* I v 1
 2 Cicero *Ad Atticum* 6.3.1, quoting an unidentified fragment of Greek verse. This was used earlier in *Adagia* IV iii 74 A long distance (45 above).

46 Cicero (see n1). Otto 1458. Apostolius 4.97. Added in *1533*
 1 Cicero *Ad Atticum* 9.13.4, quoting Plato *Letters* 7 (329D). The opening words of Cicero quoted by Erasmus are not at the beginning of the letter in modern editions but in paragraph 2.
 2 Ovid *Metamorphoses* 2.397

afraid of his manipulative ability as of his πειθανάγκη, the compulsion that accompanies his requests. As Plato says, "The requests of tyrants come, as you know, with power to compel."' See also the famous line from the mime writer: 'When the more powerful make requests, their request compels.'³

47 Libero lecto nihil iucundius
Nothing nicer than a bed to oneself

Cicero, writing to Atticus about Quintus in the fourteenth book of *Letters to Atticus*, in the one beginning, 'My dear Atticus': 'He is so opposed to taking a wife that he says nothing is nicer than a bed to oneself.'¹ Quintus had had experience of a wife, and now that she had died, he was greatly worried about paying back the dowry. So he was thinking that a bachelor life was best, and he calls this 'a bed to oneself,' since, as Juvenal says, 'Little sleeping is done in a bed that holds a wife.'²

48 Benefactis pensare delicta
Make up for failings with noble deeds

In the same book of letters, in the one beginning 'When Pilia told me,' Cicero quotes the following Greek senarius. He does not give the author, but clearly considers it well known: Ἄλλοις ἐν ἐσθλοῖς τὸν δ᾽ ἀπωθοῦνται ψόγον 'By other noble deeds they fend off this blame.'¹ He is presumably speaking of Brutus and Cassius, who had assassinated Caesar. The passage runs as follows: 'So the Ides of March do not comfort me as much as they

* * * * *

3 He means Publilius Syrus. This is one of the many sayings that are falsely attributed to him, being no 54 in Friedrich's list of such verses. See O. Friedrich *Publilii Syri sententiae* (Berlin 1880) 97.

47 Cicero (see n1). Added in *1533*
 1 Cicero *Ad Atticum* 14.13.5. The marriage of Quintus and Pomponia was never happy.
 2 Juvenal 6.269 (quoted wrongly from memory). See *Adagia* IV ii 35 If he has no disputes he's a bachelor, where it is quoted correctly.

48 A line of Greek verse quoted by Cicero (see n2). Added in *1533*
 1 *Fragmenta tragica adespota* 105 Nauck

did, for they contain a great mistake, even if those young men "by other noble deeds" . . .'[2] This saying agrees with 'You speak ill while doing well.'[3]

49 Tempestas rerum
A stormy situation

To indicate a troubled situation, we may make use of the lines from Homer which Cicero cites in book 3 of the *Letters to his Brother Quintus*:

> When on an autumn day, Zeus a lashing rainstorm sends,
> Impatient grown with mortal men and grievously displeased.

He goes on with the next lines, to indicate that evil is sent from the gods to punish men's injustice: 'For in the meeting-place they set law at naught / And crooked judgments give, but for themselves / They lay up vengeance, scorning Heaven's command.'[1]

50 Altius Oromedonte
Higher than Oromedon

Theocritus writes in his *Idyll* entitled *Thalysia*:

> Just so I hate a builder who strives a house so high to raise
> That it challenges Oromedon's high peak.[1]

* * * * *

2 Cicero *Ad Atticum* 14.22.2. This is assumed to refer to the mistake of the conspirators in not murdering Antony at the same time as Caesar.
3 Quoted from memory. It is *TrGF* 4 Sophocles fragment 855, cited in Plutarch *Moralia* 504C *De garrulitate* 4 and 810B *Praecepta gerendae reipublicae* 14.

49 Homer by way of Cicero (see n1). Added in *1533*
1 Cicero *Ad Quintum fratrem* 3.5.8, quoting Homer *Iliad* 16.385–8. Erasmus translates the Greek very freely.

50 Theocritus (see n1) with the scholia; see *Adagia* IV ix 51 (514 above). Added in *1533*
1 Theocritus *Idylls* 7.45–7. Cf *Adagia* IV x 87 Birds of the Muses' flock (535 above), which treats the line immediately following these.

We have here a proverbial expression containing a metaphor, its purpose being to deter from the arrogance of setting oneself above those with whom one has no point of comparison. The ancient commentator tells us that Oromedon was a mountain in the island of Cos. I think there is here an allusion to the 'Poet of Cos,' for in the next line he calls Homer the Coan poet.

51 Primas tenere
Hold first place

Writing to his brother Quintus in a letter in book 3, Cicero quotes a line of verse as something well known and proverbial. 'That ideal,' he writes, 'that always inspired me as a boy, αἰὲν ἀριστεύειν καὶ ὑπείροχον ἔμμεναι ἄλλων, has totally perished.'[1] He is complaining that, with constitutional government suppressed, there is no opportunity for exercising one's talents or even for maintaining one's status. I think the line comes from Homer, and may be translated, 'Always to hold first place and excel all others in praise.' He uses it again in book 13 of the *Letters to Friends*, writing to Caesar.[2]

52 Auriculam mordicus
Bite off an ear

Even today the ignorant crowd say, 'I could have gladly bitten off his ear,' giving vent to passionate hatred and a burning desire for vengeance. Cicero, writing to his brother Quintus in one of the letters in book 3, says, 'There would have been an open breach of relations; there might have been a fight like the one between Pacideianus and Eserninus the Samnite; possibly he would have bitten off my ear; certainly he would have been reconciled to Clodius.'[1] That is how Cicero uses it, but it will be more fittingly used of a man who, however angry he is, has more desire to hurt than ability to do

* * * * *

51 Homer by way of Cicero (see n1). See *Adagia* II iv 18 Alpha of those who wear the cloak. Added in *1533*
1 Cicero *Ad Quintum fratrem* 3.5.4, citing Homer *Iliad* 6.208 or 11.784
2 Cicero *Ad familiares* 13.15.2

52 Cicero (see n1). Suringar 21. Added in *1533*
1 Cicero *Ad Quintum fratrem* 3.4.2

so, for it is women and boys who bite off an ear.[2] I discussed 'Esernius (or Eserninus) versus Pacideianus' earlier, using Horace as my authority.[3]

53 Φαινοπροσωπεῖν
Put on an appearance

Cicero seems to have liked this word, as he uses it several times in his letters.[1] It means to wear an expression of cheerfulness and good will when one's real feelings are very different. Hence the line in Virgil: 'She wears false hope upon her face and crushes down her trouble / Deep within her heart.'[2]

54 Faciles partus
Children that come easily

In his *Encomium* of Ptolemy, Theocritus writes, 'To them 'Ρηίδιαι ... γοναί "Children come easily," but the offspring never / Bear the father's features.'[1] According to the Jurists, there is a legal presumption that the husband is the father of any child, but the offspring does not always look like the mother's husband. So, as Horace writes, 'The father's face in the babe honour to the mother brings.'[2] Though here too nature makes sport with variety, as in almost all things.[3] The child does not always look like its mother or its father, but sometimes like its paternal or maternal grandfather, or its grandmother, or its father's brother or indeed its great-grandfather's brother!

* * * * *

2 See Erasmus *Apophthegmata* II 41 (LB IV 138F).
3 *Adagia* II v 98. The source given there is not Horace but Lucilius, his predecessor in satire 149–52 Marx (151–4 Krenkel).

53 Cicero (see n1). Added in *1533*
1 In fact, twice: Cicero *Ad Atticum* 7.21.1, 14.22.2. The word, coined by Cicero, is thought to mean 'put in an appearance' rather than 'put on an appearance.' See *Adagia* II i 70 Shame is in the eyes.
2 Virgil *Aeneid* 1.209, already used in *Adagia* IV x 69 With honest brow (524 above, with n5)

54 Theocritus (see n1). Added in *1533*
1 Theocritus *Idylls* 17.44
2 Horace *Odes* 4.5.23
3 See Erasmus *De copia* CWE 28 302.

55 Praeficarum more
Like hired mourners

Praeficae was the word used for women hired to wail at a funeral, to sing the praises of the deceased and lead the rest in their lamentations. They were called *praeficae* because they were, so to speak, *praefectae* 'put in charge.' The word can be used jokingly of those who feign love or grief when they are really motivated by greed. Nonius cites Lucilius: 'Those women hired to mourn at a stranger's obsequies / Tear their hair and cry far more than all the rest.' Horace imitated this in the following: 'Those weeping at a funeral for hire, say and do / Almost more than those who grieve from the heart.'[1] Nonius also cites Plautus' *Frivolaria*: 'They surpass hired mourners with their never-ending noise.' The words will fit those who, out of jealousy, cannot bear to praise anyone except the dead. Naevius, quoted by Festus: 'Upon my word, I think she's been hired for the job, / She praises him so, now he's dead.' It's common practice for wives to praise a dead husband without end, in order to spite their second. The words will also fit those who themselves have nothing worthy of praise, but try to make themselves seem something by praising others. Plautus, in *Truculentus*: 'A citizen of ready tongue but without worth, to me / Is but a women hired to praise others, who cannot praise herself.'[2]

56 Socratis gallus aut callus
Socrates' cockerel or hide

Nonius Marcellus cites an example from Varro where 'Socrates' cockerel,' is used to indicate 'hairlessness': 'Though he went to sleep as smooth as

* * * * *

55 *Adagia* v i 55–66 use material from Nonius Marcellus supplemented by Pompeius Festus. For this adage see *Adagia* II vii 11, where some of this material has already been used. It is derived from Nonius Marcellus (92.27–93.7 Lindsay), who cites Lucilius 954–5 Marx (959–60 Krenkel) and Plautus (line 81 of the fragments in the OCT of W.M. Lindsay); also from Pompeius Festus (250.7–10 Lindsay), who cites CRF Naevius 129 and gives the supposed etymology of *praeficae*. Otto 1461. Added in *1533*
1 Horace *Ars poetica* 431–2
2 Plautus *Truculentus* 495–6

56 Varro by way of Nonius Marcellus (see n1). Suringar 32. Added in *1533*

Socrates' cockerel, he found himself turned into a hedgehog with bristles and snout.'[1] Whoever is speaking here means to say that when he went to bed, his skin was smooth and he had no hairs anywhere, but in his sleep he was turned into a hedgehog, which is bristly all over and has a snout such as pigs have. I know that the text is corrupt here, and I am well aware of the reading of the Aldine edition, which has not *gallus* 'cockerel,' but *calvus* 'bald.' A possible reading would be to replace *calvus* with *callus* or *callum* 'hide,'[2] that is, 'When he went to sleep as hairless as Socrates' hide, he found himself turned into a hedgehog.' Socrates had a tough body, hardened to every kind of toil; he walked bare-foot, slept on the ground.[3] Hence the joke about 'Socrates' hide.' I know the story about the plucked cockerel that Diogenes, if I remember aright, released into Plato's school,[4] but it is more satisfactory to read *callus* 'hide' than *gallus* 'cockerel.' The letters 'c' and 'g' are related and it is easy for one to change to the other. The parts of the body covered with thick skin, such as the sole of the foot and the palm of the hand, do not grow hair. The common people, to indicate that they have nothing to give, show the palm of the hand and say, 'Pluck a hair from there.' The saying will fit the poor and destitute.

57 **Ut ex bulga matris**
As from our mother's bag

Nonius Marcellus cites the following trochaic tetrameter catalectic from Lucilius: 'Just as each one of us was from our mother's bag thrust into the light.'[1] This can be introduced when speaking of a total lack of possessions, utter destitution, or of the basic equality of the process that gives us life.

* * * * *

1 Nonius Marcellus 151.15–18 Lindsay, quoting Varro (*Menippeae* 490 Buecheler)
2 Mueller's edition (and also Buecheler's) reads not *gallus* or *callus* but *calva* 'a bald head'; Lindsay reads *calvum* 'bald.'
3 See Plato *Symposium* 219E–220B; Diogenes Laertius 2.27–8 ('Socrates'); Xenophon *Memorabilia* 1.6.2.
4 A story about Diogenes the Cynic, related in Diogenes Laertius 6.40 ('Diogenes'); see Erasmus *Apophthegmata* III Diogenes 59 (LB IV 178C).

57 Lucilius by way of Nonius Marcellus (see n1). Suringar 153. Added in *1533*
1 Nonius Marcellus 109.12–13 Lindsay, quoting, among other examples, Lucilius 623 Marx (676 Krenkel)

The manner of birth does not distinguish a Croesus from an Irus,[2] a king from a commoner. A queen and a beggar-woman both cry out in labour. The babe as it enters the world wails equally, whether it is an emperor or an insignificant nonentity. The cavity from which a queen's child emerges is no cleaner than that which produces a servant's brat. Festus tells us that the word for 'bag,' *bulga,* comes from the Gauls, who used this word for leather sacks or purses or pouches, that is, those made of animal skin.[3] Lucilius, with a satirist's lack of inhibition, calls the female reproductive organ or womb 'a bag.' The Greek notion 'Naked as he came from his mother' has already been discussed.[4]

58 Esurienti leoni praedam exsculpere
To prise the prey from a hungry lion

Nonius Marcellus cites the following line from Lucilius: *Ut esurienti leoni ex ore exsculpere praedam* 'As from a hungry lion's mouth its prey to prise away.'[1] This line can be made to scan if you remove *ut* 'as' at the beginning, or, a more likely solution, replace it by *vi* 'by force,' and if the *-ti* in *esurienti* is shortened, or the word emended to *esuriente.* The line is harsh, as it has no caesura, but it is not uncharacteristic of Lucilius' style.[2] The adage is

* * * * *

2 Stock examples of the multi-millionaire and the beggar. See *Adagia* I vi 74 and 76.
3 Pompeius Festus 31.20 Lindsay. Erasmus adds the definition of 'leather' in order to explain the word *scorteus,* used here by Festus for 'leather.' He is drawing on a later entry in Festus (443.7 Lindsay): 'everything made of skins is called *scorteus.'*
4 *Adagia* II viii 44

58 Lucilius by way of Nonius Marcellus (see n1). Otto 935. Added in *1533*
1 Nonius Marcellus 146.24–5 Lindsay, citing Lucilius 286 Marx (277 Krenkel). Two of Erasmus' suggestions are adopted in modern texts: excluding *ut* and reading *Esuriente leoni.*
2 The metre is dactylic hexameter and poets later than Lucilius (2nd century BC) produced a smoother movement by usually incorporating a break between words (*caesura*) in the third measure or foot. Here there is no such break, but the third and fourth measures are occupied by *–ōn(i) ex ōr(e) ex–* where the words are run together in 'elision.'

similar to ones I discussed earlier: 'Wrest the club from Hercules' hand'
and 'Snatch the lamb from the wolf.'[3]

59 Halopanta
Romancer

This was a word the ancients used for someone who tells lies all the time.
Plautus in *Curculio*:

> Well! Phaedromus has got himself a fine spinner of yarns in this fellow.
> I don't know whether to say he's *halopanta* 'romancer' or *sycophanta* 'trickster.'[1]

At this point in the play, the soldier is complaining about Curculio, who had
used the soldier's signet ring to trick the pimp. Nonius Marcellus quotes the
extract, saying '*halopanta* or *sycophanta*, a despicable class of men, hired for
a small fee, because of their ability to string lies together.'[2] Festus explains
as follows: 'A *halopanta* means one who tells lies all the time.'[3] In Greek,
πάντα means 'all,' ἀλιτόμενος means 'deceiving.' Though how much credulity
should be accorded to fragments of this sort, which are as corrupt as they are
truncated, I do not know. The Aldine edition offered another etymology, but
one equally blemished. For if *halopanta* is derived from ἀλέω or ἀλιτεύομαι
'to err, transgress,' neither of these words has an initial aspirate and in both
the first vowel is short, whereas the word in Plautus has the first vowel long,
as required by the trochaic metre. If it is derived from ἅλς 'salt,' we have
an initial aspirate, but this word too has a short vowel in its first syllable.
There is also the further problem in *halopanta*, that it is unusual to form
a compound with a nominal stem in second place. It would be easier if
the form were πανθαλήτης 'all-wandering.'[4] The two words in the line in

* * * * *

3 *Adagia* IV i 95; II vii 80

59 Nonius Marcellus with Pompeius Festus (see nn2–5). Added in *1533*
  1 Plautus *Curculio* 462–3. Erasmus is following the Milan 1500 text of Giambat-
    tista Pio (see *Adagia* IV iii 40 n2, 27 above), which gives the words to the sol-
    dier, not to the Choragus as in modern texts.
  2 Nonius Marcellus 172.8–9 Lindsay
  3 Pompeius Festus 90.24 Lindsay
  4 This suggestion is based on the rest of Festus' explanation (above n3).

Plautus demonstrate the figure of προσονομασία, and there would be a better play on words if we had *sycophanta* and *halophanta*, rather than *halopanta*.[5] A 'halophant' would appear to be someone who informed against those trying to cheat the customs-officers of their dues, just as a sycophant was someone who reported those exporting figs from Athens. If we read ἀλλοφάντην [from ἄλλος 'other'], meaning someone who says something alien and tells all kinds of lies, the word fits the metre but we have to reject the initial aspirate. The line will scan, however, if you treat *halophanten aut sycophanten* as Greek words, as then there will be an anapaest instead of a spondee in first position. Plautus often does as the Greeks do in his plays.[6] But I leave all this for the consideration of scholars.

60 **Quadra propria**
Your own slice of pie

Even today we commonly say, 'Nothing tastes as good as your own home fare.' Nonius cites half a line from Catullus' *Priapea*: 'A longing to lick up something I myself provide.'[1] 'Lick up' here means 'to eat with enjoyment.' Though Homer's gods prefer to be invited out to the aroma arising from burnt offerings, rather than live at their own expense at home![2] Nonius also cites Plautus' play the *Persian*: 'To guzzle at his own expense, if he has the wherewithal at home.'[3]

* * * * *

5 Lindsay's text of Nonius Marcellus does read *halophantam* as suggested by Erasmus, and this appears in Lewis and Short, *A Latin Dictionary*, as 'a salt-informer' (by analogy with *sycophanta*, 'a fig-informer'); see *Adagia* II iii 81 A sycophant. Both words seem to have acquired the meaning 'trickster, imposter.' *Halophanta* has since antiquity given rise to many ingenious emendations and explanations; see Blanche Brotherton, *The Vocabulary of Intrigue in Roman Comedy* (New York and London 1978) 112–18.

6 An anapaest is a metrical unit of the pattern short, short, long, and this would obviate the problem of a short initial syllable in trochaic metre (essentially long, short).

60 Erasmus seems to have invented the phrase on the basis of Juvenal 5.2 *aliena quadra* 'someone else's pie.' Suringar 180. Added in *1533*

1 Nonius Marcellus 195.27–8 Lindsay citing Catullus fragment 2 (in the OCT)

2 See Lucian *De sacrificiis* 9.

3 Plautus *Persa* 122, cited in Nonius Marcellus 263.21 Lindsay

61 **Mansum ex ore dare**
Give pap from your own mouth

If we love someone dearly, we are said to 'Give them pap from our own mouths,' a phrase borrowed from mothers and nurses. Nonius cites Lucilius: 'Hoping, if he could show the same years, / He'd give pap from his own mouth.'[1] Cicero and Gellius, however, use *praemandere* in a rather different sense, 'predigest,' as I indicated earlier.[2]

62 **Medullitus, oculitus**
From one's very bones, as dear as one's eyes

The ancients had various ways of expressing deep affection: from the heart, from the soul, heart and soul (which I have already discussed),[1] deeply, from the depths of one's being, from one's very bones, as one's very soul, as one's very eyes. Nonius cites a line from Plautus' *Crows:* 'Hold my maid Sedulium as dear as their very eyes.'[2] Lovers call the object of their affection their 'eye.' In the *Haunted House*: 'Oh good, my dearest eye!' or 'I wish to please my dear Philolaches, the apple of my eye, my dear protector.'[3]

63 **Sapientia gubernatur navis**
The ship is steered by judgment

The wisest of men have said that even in war counsel carries more weight

* * * * *

61 Lucilius by way of Nonius Marcellus (see n1). Added in *1533*
1 Nonius Marcellus 204.12–14 Lindsay, citing Lucilius 1045–6 Marx (1001–2 Krenkel), with a significantly different reading from Erasmus'.
2 *Adagia* II x 33 Spoonfeeding (*Praemansum in os inserere*)

62 Plautus by way of Nonius Marcellus (see n2). Added in *1533*
1 *Adagia* I iv 26 With the whole heart
2 Nonius Marcellus 215.22–3 Lindsay, citing Plautus' lost play *Cornicula* (line 64 in the fragments in the OCT by Lindsay). The Nonius entry contains the last three of the phrases listed here by Erasmus: *medullitus, animitus, oculitus*.
3 Plautus *Mostellaria* 311, 167

63 Titinius by way of Nonius Marcellus (see n2). Added in *1533*

than force.[1] Titinius, as cited by Nonius, puts this neatly: 'The steersman turns the ship by judgment, not by strength.'[2]

64 Novum cribrum novo paxillo
A new sieve on a new peg

This quotation from Varro's *Eumenides*, cited in Nonius, quite unmistakably contains a popular saying. It says, 'Zeno was the first to hang a new school on a new peg.'[1] He is censuring Zeno, who introduced to Athens the Stoic sect with its novel theories and its paradoxes. Varro again, in *Bimargus*: 'A new sieve must hang from a new peg.'[2] I follow the reading of the Aldine edition.[3] The saying will fit those thinking up something new.

65 Sarcinator summum centonem
The patcher with his last patch

Nonius Marcellus also cites this verse from Lucilius: *Sarcinatoris esse summum suere centonem optime* 'It is for a stitcher of patches to sew his last bit of patchwork best.'[1] The metre appears to be trochaic tetrameter catalectic, and the line scans correctly with the elision of final *-s* in *sarcinatoris* 'the

* * * * *

1 See *Adagia* III x 75.
2 Erasmus quotes the line with *in sapientia* 'in wisdom'; Nonius cites it three times, without *in* (28.17–19, 274.26–7, 807.4–6 Lindsay) from the *Setina* (CRF Titinius 127). Titinius was a dramatist probably of the early second century BC, of whom only a few fragments survive.

64 Varro by way of Nonius Marcellus (see nn1–2). Otto 464. Added in 1533
1 Nonius Marcellus 224.4–6 Lindsay citing Varro *Menippeae* fragment 164 Buecheler
2 Nonius Marcellus 224.7–8, citing Varro *Menippeae* fragment 69 Buecheler
3 The Latin text as quoted by Erasmus reads *Novum ut*. The Aldine edition of 1513 reads *Ut novum cribrum ... pendeat*, as also the Venice 1478 edition, a reading followed by Marx, Buecheler and Lindsay.

65 Lucilius by way of Nonius Marcellus (see n1). Otto 371; *Adagia* I ii 35. Added in 1533
1 Nonius Marcellus 258.1 Lindsay, citing Lucilius 746 Marx (799 Krenkel), reading *sarcinatorem*

stitcher of patches.' The word *sarcinator* is derived from *sarcina* 'a bundle,' not from *sarcire* 'to repair.'[2] This saying comes in the same category as one I mentioned earlier: 'A good poet is at his best in the last act.'[3] But Lucilius' version has a more convincing and nicer proverbial ring.

66 Proelio victus non bello
Lose the battle but not the war

It is not the one who gets the upper hand in one or two phases of the action who is necessarily the victor, but the one who triumphs overall. A battle is a particular military engagement, a war is the whole period of conflict, even if there is no actual fighting for a time, or if a truce intervenes. Only peace brings a war to an end, a truce suspends hostilities. Nonius cites these lines in trochaic rhythm from Lucilius:

> As the Roman people, oft subdued by might
> And in many a battle worsted by the foe,
> Never yet a war did lose, wherein lies the whole.[1]

This belongs with 'He that fights and runs away may live to fight another day.'[2]

67 Curre denuo
Take another run

Τρέχ᾽ αὖθις, Take another run. Lucian introduces this phrase into his tragedy *Okypus* as a saying supposedly originating in a barber-shop.[1] And yet this

* * * * *

2 Erasmus' etymology comes from Nonius Marcellus 79.22–4 Lindsay sub *sarcinatricis*.

3 *Adagia* I ii 35 To add a last act to the play

66 Lucilius by way of Nonius Marcellus (see n1). Added in 1533
1 Nonius Marcellus 703.14–18 Lindsay, citing Lucilius 613–14 Marx (683–4 Krenkel). Nonius makes the distinction between 'battle' and 'war.'
2 *Adagia* I x 40

67 Lucian (see n1). Added in 1533
1 Lucian *Okypus* 56–9. Erasmus' emendation (below) is accepted today.

little work in verse is full of faults and hasn't a grain of Lucian's wit. We meet here a young man suffering from gout, who nevertheless wanted to be thought ὠκύπους 'fast-foot.' When an old man asked him why his foot hurt, he replied that he had sprained his ankle when running very fast, and was in agony as a result. The old man replied, '"Take another run," as one of the customers said, / Sitting and plucking his beard under the barbers' arms,' that is, submitting to the barber's ministrations. (If that is, one reads εἶπεν ὃς 'one said, who ...') People with gout seek relief from barbers, but they do not want the condition to be recognized as gout, preferring it to be thought the result of some kind of injury, caused for example by too much running. Meantime, one of those getting barbered, realizing that this is just a tale, says, 'Take another run.' For that's the way of treating sprains etc., because the pain subsides as the tendons heat up with vigorous movement. One can see this any day in horses, which after a gallop either do not limp or do not limp so noticeably. It's more likely however that instead of κουρέων 'of the barbers,' we should read κουριῶν the present participle of the verb κουριᾶν meaning 'to be hairy' and in need of a barber, the sense being 'as someone said, sitting in the barber's shop, and plucking the shaggy mass of hair luxuriating in his armpits.' The barber's shop is the place where idlers meet and chatter. As Horace says, 'Leisurely trimming his own nails with a knife.'[2] If anyone does not fancy this suggestion of mine, he can pursue something that appeals to him more, but it is of no great matter.

68 Nutricis pallium
A nurse's dress

As nurses handle babies, their clothes are often stained with food, dribble, urine and faeces. So Plautus writes in the *Bacchis Sisters*: 'If you'd got one syllable wrong, your skin would have / As many blotches as a nurse's dress.'[1] The Scriptures often mention 'the cloths of a menstruous woman.'[2]

* * * * *

2 Horace *Epistles* 1.7.51. The person in question is sitting in the barber's shop in the evening when the rush is over.

68 Plautus (see n1). Otto 1325. Added in *1533*
1 Plautus *Bacchides* 433–4
2 For example, Isa 30:22; 64:6

69 Cum ramento
Filings and all

This proverbial expression can be used of someone who has handed over all with no deductions of any kind. The phrase apparently originates with metal-workers, who take for themselves what they file off. Plautus, in the *Bacchis Sisters*: 'For I have handed it over totally to my father, filings and all.'[1] 'Filings and all' is added for the sake of emphasis. He then gives a kind of explanation, saying: 'Every bit. Absolutely.'[2] I have already discussed 'Dust and all,' 'Rust and all.'[3] Plautus, in the *Rope*: 'He'll sweep me up entirely, dust and all.'

70 Mortuo vilior
Of less account than a corpse

Nothing is more worthless than a dead body. In the same play, Plautus writes, 'Come on, cheer up! – How can I? A dead man is worth more than I am.'[1] In the *Persian*, one character insults another by calling him 'a slab of dead flesh': 'Heavens! I wouldn't feel afraid, even if I punched / Your face in, you slab of dead flesh!'[2]

71 Quam Clinia ex Demetrio
More than Clinia heard from Demetrius

In the same play, Plautus writes:

* * * * *

69 Plautus (see n1). Otto 1503. Added in *1533*
 1 Plautus *Bacchides* 680, 681
 2 The Latin for 'absolutely' is *oppido*, for which see *Adagia* IV x 14 Mountains of grain (492 above).
 3 *Adagia* II viii 85, which cites this same Plautus quotation, *Rudens* 845

70 Plautus (see n1). See *Adagia* I iii 44 I am nothing. Added in *1533*
 1 Plautus *Bacchides* 630, the play which provides the chief examples in *Adagia* V i 68–71
 2 Plautus *Persa* 283

71 Plautus (see n1). Added in *1533*

You'll hear more hard words from me this day
Than ever Clinia heard from Demetrius.[1]

Some scholars think that one should read *Lamia* instead of *Clinia*.[2] It's quite true that Lamia was passionately loved by Demetrius, king of Macedonia, and on account of this he was much criticized by the people, but we never read that the king abused her verbally. In any case, *Lamia* does not fit the metre. It's more likely that it's taken from the comedy by Turpilius, called *Demetrius*,[3] or from some other play where a father bitterly and at great length reproaches his son. In the *Self-Tormentor* we have just such a Clinia, whose father censures him so often and so bitterly that he eventually runs away to join the army.[4] Maybe Plautus is alluding to this story. It's possible that Terence changed the name of the father from Demetrius to Menedemus. The fact that Terence is later than Plautus does not raise a problem, because the Greek author of the original play was earlier than both of them.[5]

72 Pleno gradu
At a quick march

Those who have just sampled anything are said to have dipped their toes in,[1] whereas those who have tackled something with great enthusiasm are said to have approached it 'At a quick march.' Trebonius, writing to Cicero in book 12 of his *Letters to Friends*: 'He is mentally prepared and marching quick step, as I can see, but I will keep on encouraging him, and then he will continue to make daily progress in his studies and exercises.'[2]

* * * * *

1 Plautus *Bacchides* 911–12
2 Another reference to Giambattista Pio's Plautine commentary (see *Adagia* IV iii 40 n2, 27 above)
3 Turpilius was a writer of comedies in Latin of the 2nd century BC. Only a few fragments survive (see CRF). The title *Demetrius* is preserved in Pompeius Festus 158.34 Lindsay.
4 Terence *Heautontimoroumenos* 99–117
5 The Greek author is Menander. The plays of both Plautus and Terence were based on Greek originals.

72 Cicero (see n2). Added in *1533*
1 See *Adagia* IV ix 59 Dip the toes (458 above).
2 Cicero *Ad familiares* 12.16.2

73 Ad pila ubi ventum
When it comes to the pikes

Cicero, in his little treatise *On Military Terms* (if this work is correctly attributed to him), says, 'The first and second lines, when, as the saying goes, "It comes to the pikes," bear the full brunt of the fighting.'[1] The pike is a kind of short Roman spear, so when the fighting has got to close quarters, they say 'It has come to the pikes.'[2] I have a feeling I have already used this adage, but I can't at the moment recall where.[3]

74 Velatis manibus orare
Pray with veiled hands

Those who make suppliant entreaty are said to 'Pray with veiled hands,' a phrase derived from the ancient custom whereby spokesmen who came to treat for peace carried an olive branch before them. I think that *velati* 'veiled' is here equivalent to *vittati* 'swathed with *vittae*.'[1] Plautus writes in *Amphitryo*:

> Next day come the chief men from the town to our camp,
> Weeping, begging us with veiled hands to pardon their wrongdoing.[2]

* * * * *

73 Pseudo-Cicero (see n1). Added in *1533*
  1 The treatise *De vocabulis rei militaris* was actually a thirteenth-century abbreviation of Vegetius' fourth-to-fifth century AD treatise on Roman military practice, which circulated under the name of Modestus in the fifteenth century. Its authenticity as a Ciceronian work had been questioned by Siccus Polentonius, 1376–1447 (R. Sabbadini *Le scoperte dei codici latini e greci ne' secoli* XIV *e* XV [Florence 1914] 215). It was nonetheless printed among Cicero's works in the edition by Junta in 1516. Cratander, however, included it as a doubtful work in his edition of Cicero (Basel 1528), which Erasmus is using here as elsewhere; see ASD II-8 301:696n.
  2 See *Adagia* IV v 39 To put foot to foot (see 168 above).
  3 See *Adagia* I i 23 Back to the third line.

74 Plautus (see n2). Added in *1533*
  1 The *vittae* were strands of wool with which the olive-branch of the suppliant was intertwined. Erasmus forgets to add this necessary piece of information.
  2 Plautus *Amphitryo* 256–7

75 Cicadae sibi canent
The cicadas will sing to themselves

Οἱ τέττιγες ἑαυτοῖς χαμόθεν ᾄσονται, The cicadas will sing to themselves on
the ground. Aristotle in book 3 cites this from Stesichorus as an example of
a figure in which the real meaning is not the literal meaning of the words.[1]
Aristotle doesn't add anything that would help to elucidate the true meaning, though I suspect that the poet in these words threatens those who had
injured him, giving them to understand that, if he could not avenge himself in any other way, certainly he would use his poetry to destroy their
reputation. Aristotle quotes it again in book 2 among enigmatic sayings:
'As Stesichorus said when among the Locrians, "One shouldn't act with insolent effrontery, or the cicadas will sing on the ground."'[2] Cicadas represent poets; 'on the ground' refers to their poverty and humble status. Every
creature uses what means nature has given it to present a threatening as-
pect. Poets have nothing but their verse, but by this they can hand a man
down to posterity as a 'dark or fair man.'[3] This is why Plato is said to have
advised his friends never to make an enemy of a man of poetic bent.[4] For,
as Horace said, 'Bards are an irascible tribe,'[5] and some of them 'have hay
on their horn.'[6] A number of scholars prefer quite a different explanation of
Stesichorus' saying.[7] As Virgil tells us, cicadas usually sing in trees,[8] so it
appears that, by this riddling saying, Stesichorus was politely warning the

* * * * *

75 Steisichorus by way of Aristotle (see n1). Added in 1533
  1 Aristotle *Rhetoric* 3.11.6 (1412a), citing Stesichorus, an early Greek lyric poet
    of the sixth century BC (PMG fragment 104b)
  2 Aristotle *Rhetoric* 2.21 (1395a)
  3 *Adagia* I vi 99 I know not whether you are dark or fair
  4 This (unidentified) quotation, together with the Horace extract, *Epistles* 2.2.102,
    was previously used in *Adagia* I ix 28 You have taken a grasshopper by the
    wing.
  5 See n4.
  6 A sign to indicate that a bull was dangerous. Horace uses it of mordant poets,
    Satires 1.4.34. Cf *Adagia* I i 81 He has hay on his horn. It is used again in *Adagia*
    III vii 53 Luxury breeds brutality.
  7 Estienne has a long note here (LB II 1195F), pointing out that this alternative ex-
    planation is to be found in the treatise Περὶ ἑρμηνείας attributed to Demetrius
    of Phalerum (3.284 Spengel), and also in the scholiast's comment on this pas-
    sage of Aristotle (2.21).
  8 Virgil *Eclogues* 2.3: 'The stands of trees re-echo with cicadas' song.'

Locrians not to keep on harrying their neighbours out of arrogance and aggressiveness, or they would drive them to take up arms against them; their
neighbours would invade their territory and cut down everything growing out of sheer hostility, and then the cicadas would start singing on the
ground, as there would be no trees for them to perch in. Possibly Gregory
of Nazianzus reports something of the sort. I saw his commentaries on this
work when I was in Venice.[9]

76 Fama prodit omnia
Rumour makes all things known

In his speech against Timarchus, Aeschines quotes a line from Euripides:
'Rumour makes known the righteous man, even in the hollows of the earth.'[1]
He explains this as meaning that it is not only the living whose virtues are
celebrated by common report, but the dead and buried also. Earth may
cover the body, but the talk of men does not allow a man's good deeds
in life to be covered over. In the same passage, he cites lines from Hesiod,
which I have used before: 'Rumour dies hard that many folk have uttered; /
Rumour herself's a kind of deity.'[2] He quotes these lines again in the speech
On the False Legation.[3]

77 Boeotissare
Act Boeotian

Among all the other accusations which Aeschines hurls at Demosthenes,
he taxes him with shouting out in an uncontrolled and unseemly manner,
like Boeotians: 'As I was saying this, Demosthenes shouted out extremely

* * * * *

9 While he was staying in the house of Aldus in 1507–8, Erasmus had access
  to a considerable number of Greek manuscripts belonging to members of the
  Aldine circle, but his memory seems to be at fault here. There is no evidence
  that Gregory of Nazianzus wrote such a commentary on the *Rhetoric.*

76 Euripides by way of Aeschines (see n1). Added in *1533*
 1 Aeschines 1.129, quoting Euripides (fragment 865 Nauck)
 2 Aeschines 1.129, citing Hesiod *Works and Days* 763–4, used before at *Adagia* I
   vi 25 and IV viii 34 (377 above)
 3 Aeschines 2.144

77 Aeschines (see n1). Added in *1533*

loudly, as all those who were on the embassy with us know. For indeed, in addition to all his other crimes, Βοιωτιάζει "He acts Boeotian."[1] The 'shouting out' contains an allusion to the mooing of bovines.[2] Though 'Act Boeotian' could be taken as meaning 'to follow a pro-Boeotian policy.'

78 Surculus surculum ferens
Twig supporting twig

Individuals are weak, but joined together in concord they acquire great strength. See Ennius, as cited by Festus: *Unus surus surum ferret, tamen defendere possent* 'One twig would carry but another twig, and yet they could defend.'[1] As Festus tells us, *surus* was the form of the word used in ancient times; we now use the diminutive *surculus*. I am well aware that the text of this line of verse is corrupt, even in the Aldine edition.[2] Perhaps it should read *Si unus surum surus ferret* 'If one twig should carry but another twig,' *eum* (or *se*) *defendere posset* 'it could defend it (or, itself), or *possent* 'they could defend it,' or, 'they could defend each other.' A branch is strong; twigs have no strength except when bundled together.

79 Salacones
Salacons

Because of their poverty, Irus and Codrus became stock examples of indigence.[1] Likewise, a certain Salacon was so impoverished that all persons in extreme penury came to be called 'Salacons' and poverty itself was called

* * * * *

1 Aeschines 2.106
2 The name 'Boeotia' was believed to be connected with βόες 'cattle,' either because of its rich pastures, or in commemoration of the cow (βοῦς) which led Cadmus to the place where he was to settle (*Etymologicum Magnum* 203.14–24).

78 Ennius by way of Pompeius Festus (see n1). Added in 1533
1 Pompeius Festus 383.12–14 Lindsay, citing Ennius *Annales* 525 Vahlen, 540 Skutsch.
2 The meaning of the line remains problematic. Many emendations have been suggested but none has won acceptance.

79 Hesychius (see n2). Added in 1533
1 See *Adagia* I vi 76 and v i 57 (573 above).

salaconia. This information comes from Hesychius, but he also tells us that the same word was used for a conceited person who put on airs, and this gave rise to the verb σαλακωνίζειν or σαλακωνεύειν 'walk in a mincing or foppish manner.' There is also the evidence of Theophrastus, who said a 'Salacon' was a person who squandered his possessions.[2] From all this we may conclude that the censure carried in the adage is not directed at any and every poor person, but only at those reduced to indigence by self-conceit and extravagance. The word seems to come from the verb σαλάξαι, which means 'to totter,' 'to be on the point of collapse.'

80 Archilochi melos
Archilochus' song

Ἀρχιλόχου μέλος, Archilochus' song. This was the name for a song that could be adapted to many subjects, such as Archilochus is supposed to have invented. He was earlier than Pindar and other such lyric poets who composed celebratory odes specific to individual victors. Archilochus' song was the same for everybody and was played on the lyre. The lyre-player simply sang in the name of the victor at intervals throughout the music. If he were praising Hercules, for example, he would bring into his song 'Tenella Kallinike, hail Lord Hercules,' or some other name, if he was praising somebody else. Rather similar is Horace's story of the painter who painted a cypress tree and asked the sailor if he wanted anything added.[1] This phrase will fit anything crude and primitive.[2] 'Archilochus' song' is mentioned by the commentators on Pindar and on Aristophanes.[3] It comes from the seventh of Pindar's Olympian triumphal odes: 'The song of Archilochus, sung out at Olympia, "Kallinikos."' The commentaries on this passage report

* * * * *

2 Hesychius Σ 98, 99, 100, quoting Theophrastus, but the text is not known from elsewhere.

80 This is a paraphrase of various remarks of the ancient commentators on Pindar *Olympians* 9.1–3 (see West 1.104–6). Added in *1533*

1 Horace *Ars poetica* 19. See *Adagia* I v 19 To paint a cypress. Erasmus adds information from the ancient commentator (pseudo-Acron).

2 Pindar says in *Olympian* 9.4 that Archilochus' song was good enough in the old days. (Erasmus names *Olympian* 7 below by accident.)

3 See the scholia on Aristophanes *Birds* 1764, where Aristophanes incorporates 'Tenella Kallinike' into a concluding triumphal ode.

various suggestions that have been thought up, but it doesn't seem necessary to my present purpose to reproduce them here.

81 Ὀλοέχινος
All-spiny

I have already discussed the word ὁλόσχοινος (in the phrase ὁλόσχοινος
ἄβροχος) from a speech by Aeschines. The lexicographers however have
here not ὁλόσχοινος but ὁλοέχινος. The ancient annotator on Demosthenes
cites this speech of Aeschines, that is, the one *On the False Legation*, attacking Demosthenes, and also Theophrastus, book four.[1] I found the form
ὁλόσχοινος in the Aeschines passage. Likewise, Theophrastus, in book four
of *On Plants*, where he is discussing water-loving plants, distinguishes (as
the ancient commentator tells us) three species of σχοῖνος 'esparto' or 'rush.'
One is the *iuncus acutus*, the sharp rush, also called 'male,' here meaning
'infertile'; the second is fertile, and from its dark fruits is called μελαγκρανίς
'black' bog-rush; the third is the ὁλόσχοινος, the club-rush, which surpasses
the others in stoutness, height, and toughness. Theophrastus thinks this
last is better for weaving ropes because it is more pliable and fleshier.[2]

* * * * *

81 Erasmus here returns to a phrase from the orator Aeschines (cited in Harpocration 1.221.14 Dindorf ὁλόσχοινος) which he first discussed in *Adagia* IV
ix 71 (465 above). He had been puzzled because the Aldine text of Harpocration nonsensically read ὁλοέχινος rather than ὁλόσχοινος. He had corrected the
reading there by referring directly to the sources quoted by Harpocration,
that is, Aeschines and Theophrastus, as he tells us here. Although, as he says,
it is not very relevant to *Adagia*, he records his investigation of the problem,
together with miscellaneous information gathered on the way, for example,
some from Dioscorides. Aldus had published the *editio princeps* of Dioscorides'
De materia medica in 1528, but none of the references to Dioscorides in *Adagia*
after that date suggests that Erasmus was using the Greek text (see *Adagia* II
vii 62 n1 CWE 34 327).
1 By 'The ancient annotator' Erasmus means Harpocration, the text of which
was printed with Ulpian's scholia on Demosthenes in Aldus' edition of Demosthenes; see *Adagia* IV ix 60 n1, 459 above. This is the only direct reference
Erasmus makes to Harpocration, though he often uses his material.
2 Theophrastus *Historia plantarum* 4.12.1–2. Erasmus translates considerably
more than the brief extract given in Harpocration.

Dioscorides, in book four, classifies them somewhat differently, but he does tell us that the third species, the one called ὁλόσχοινος, is rougher and tougher than the others.[3] I think the reason why some persons preferred to write ἐχῖνος 'hedgehog' instead of σχοῖνος 'rush' was that Theophrastus spoke of its 'fleshiness,' as if it were anything unusual to speak of the 'flesh' of an apple or cherry. The land *echinos*, or 'hedgehog,' does share with the *holoschoinos* the characteristic of being bristly.[4] The skin of a hedgehog, if removed complete with spines, can be used to clean pots. So the word 'all-spiny' can be used of harsh domineering words, which we dash in someone's face, so to speak. Even if some of this is somewhat of an appendix, I wanted to pass it on to my readers.

82 Apologus Alcinoi
A story for Alcinous

Ἀπόλογος Ἀλκινόου, A story for Alcinous, is recorded in the Greek proverb collections, as I noted earlier.[1] On that occasion, I surmised that it was derived from Homer's *Odyssey*, where Ulysses is represented as telling a whole lot of tall stories about himself at the feast.[2] This is not a silly suggestion, if 'A story for Alcinous' can mean a fictitious tale told in the presence of Alcinous. However, Aristotle, in book three of the *Rhetoric*, happens to mention this tale and writes in such a way that he appears to be censuring some writer who wrote an imaginary speech to Penelope, bringing in all the things that could have happened in the course of many years, and treating fiction as truth. Perhaps the writer, called Alcinous, introduced the figure of Ulysses telling Penelope a lot of things which he was supposed to have experienced either in the war or on his journey home.

* * * * *

3 Dioscorides *De materia medica* 4.52
4 *Echinos* is the word for both the sea-urchin and the hedgehog, both having the appearance of spiny balls.

82 *Collectanea* no 146. A doublet of *Adagia* II iv 32 A story for Alcinous, drawn from Diogenianus 2.86. Added in *1533*
1 *Adagia* II iv 32
2 Aristotle *Poetics* 16 shows that Erasmus' earlier surmise was correct. In January 1533 he asked Bruno Amerbach if he had any information on the phrase (Ep 2752).

Aristotle writes, 'Besides, one must speak of events as past and done, ὅσα μὴ "except for" those that arouse either pity or indignation if represented as happening now. An example is the story of Alcinous, when it is presented to Penelope as if covering sixty years.'³ George of Trebizond's translation of the passage gives one to understand that he read, 'One must speak of μὴ πεπραγμένα "events that have not actually happened," such that, if represented as happening now ...'⁴ But even so, the text is not free from fault. So I shall suspend judgment until I can find something more definite either in the commentaries of Gregory of Nazianzus on the *Rhetoric*, or elsewhere.⁵

83 Virtus aeterna
Virtue lives forever

Pindar records a similar sentiment in *Olympian* eight: Ἀΐδα τοι λάθεται / ἄρμενα πράξας ἀνήρ 'A man that performs fitting deeds / Gives no thought to Hades.'¹ Life is short, but the memory of good deeds never dies, and for that reason those who have done splendid things that deserve to be remembered for ever depart this life more contentedly and are not so appalled by death, because they know they will live on in the minds of future generations through the glory of their name.

* * * * *

3 Aristotle *Rhetoric* 3.16 (1417a)
4 A reference to George's translation of Aristotle's *Rhetoric*, made in 1443–5, first published circa 1475 (Petrus Caesaris et Io. Stol, Paris,). Aldus produced an edition of this translation in 1523, in a volume containing various rhetorical works. George also made annotations on Aristotle's text. See John Monfasani ed *Collectanea Trapezuntia (Texts, Documents and Bibliographies of George of Trebizond)* Renaissance Society of America, Renaissance Texts Series vol 8 (Binghampton, NY 1984) 698–9. George seems to have read the negative at an earlier point in the text. Modern texts have the same reading here as Erasmus. Erasmus' erroneous interpretation of the second sentence seems due to the fact that he, like George of Trebizond, read here ἔτεσι 'years' rather than ἔπεσι 'lines.'
5 See *Adagia* v i 75 n9 (585 above).

83 Pindar (see n1). Added in *1533*
1 Pindar *Olympians* 8.72–3

84 Doceat qui didicit
Let one who has learned teach others

Pindar again, in the same victory ode: Τὸ διδάξασθαι δέ τοι / εἰδότι ῥᾴτερον
'Easier it is for one who knows to teach.'[1] This is like 'Learn, but only from
those who have been well taught.'[2] No one can more easily pass on a skill
to another than the person who is thoroughly versed in it. He knows how
to compress a great deal of information into a few words, he knows how
to cast light on obscurities. The reason why some teachers take their pupils
round in circles and keep them from making progress is either the desire
to make more money, or else spite, or, finally, lack of skill.

85 Celeritas in malis optima
When evils strike, speed is best

In *Antigone*, Sophocles writes, Βράχιστα γὰρ κράτιστα τὰν ποσὶν κακά 'When
evils are upon us, 'tis best when they are short.'[1] These words are addressed
by the chorus to Creon, who longs to be removed from this life when faced
by all the griefs that have befallen his house. There is much to be said for
dying quickly if one is weary of life. Nothing is worse than enduring the
mental torture of seeing some evil approaching which cannot be avoided.
The best thing is to make sure that it doesn't last long.

86 Nullus sum
I am nothing

Sophocles again, in the same play: 'Take me away, / Τὸν οὐκ ὄντα μᾶλλον ἢ
μηδένα "One who no more exists than one who is already nothing."'[1] This

* * * * *

84 Pindar (see n1). Added in 1533
 1 Pindar *Olympians* 8.59–60
 2 *Disticha Catonis* 4.23. See *Adagia* IV viii 37 n4 (380 above); III iii 78.

85 Erasmus now embarks on twenty-three examples taken from Sophocles
  Antigone, extending into *Adagia* v ii.
 1 Sophocles *Antigone* 1327

86 Sophocles (see n1). Added in 1533
 1 Sophocles *Antigone* 1324–5

idea signifies destruction without hope of recovery. I know I have already discussed 'We Trojans have ceased to be' and 'I am nothing,'[2] but I decided to add this example because it puts the idea in a new way.

87 Prima felicitatis pars sapere
Wisdom the chief part of happiness

In the closing section of the same play: Πολλῷ τὸ φρονεῖν εὐδαιμονίας / πρῶτον ὑπάρχει 'Wisdom is by far the foremost part of happiness.'[1] This was said in reference to Creon who chose to follow the dictates of passion rather than clear thinking, and brought destruction on himself and those nearest him. Without wisdom, great good fortune easily turns to great misfortune. A little earlier in the play, Sophocles expresses the same idea from the opposite point of view. Speaking of Haemon, who had taken his own life, the poet says, 'Proclaiming to the world how rashness divorced from thought / Becomes the greatest evil that can befall a man.'[2]

88 Sero vidit iustitiam
He has too late recognized the right

Sophocles again, in the same play: Οἴμ᾿ ὡς ἔοικας ὀψὲ τὴν δίκην ἰδεῖν 'Alas! Too late you seem to realize what is right.'[1] This is said with reference to Creon, who earlier on would not give way to Tiresias or any of his people, but, having learnt his lesson through dreadful happenings, now blames his folly. We find the same sentiment again in the closing lines of the play, expressed differently: 'Exacting dreadful vengeance for overweening words / The gods teach men in old age to be wise.'[2] This agrees with 'The Phrygians learn wisdom too late.'[3]

* * * * *

2 See *Adagia* I ix 50 and I iii 44.

87 Sophocles (see n1). Added in *1533*
1 Sophocles *Antigone* 1348–9
2 Sophocles *Antigone* 1242–3

88 Sophocles (see n1). Added in *1533*
1 Sophocles *Antigone* 1270. Erasmus omits ὡς in the quotation, presumably by accident, since the line does not scan without it.
2 Sophocles *Antigone* 1351–3
3 *Adagia* I i 28

89 Vindicta velox
Swift recompense

There is quite a number of proverbs about the slow vengeance of the gods, which I have recorded above.[1] Sophocles' lines about the swift vengeance of heaven suggest that we should come to our senses promptly if we have fallen into some wickedness. The chorus is addressing Creon:

> Do it with all speed, O King. For swift-footed mischief from the gods
> Seizes evil-minded men and cuts them off.[2]

That is what happened to Creon, for vengeance fell on him almost before Tiresias had finished his prophesying.

90 Fato non repugnandum
Fight not against fate

In the same play, Creon says, Ἀνάγκῃ δ᾽οὐχὶ δυσμαχητέον 'Fight not against the fates, for that fight is hard.'[1] We have cited this same sentiment elsewhere, culled from various authors.[2] No one can escape what God sends us, and what can't be avoided must be endured, not railed against. 'For the fates lead the willing man, the unwilling man they drag,' as the writer of the tragedies says.[3]

* * * * *

89 Sophocles (see n2). Added in 1533
1 *Adagia* IV iv 82 The gods' mill grinds slow (116 above)
2 Sophocles *Antigone* 1103–4: ποδώκεις . . . βλάβαι

90 Sophocles (see n1). Added in 1533
1 Sophocles *Antigone* 1106. The Greek says 'that fighting is doomed to failure.'
2 *Adagia* I iii 14
3 The Younger Seneca, better known as a Stoic philosopher, wrote a number of tragedies in verse. They are the only Latin tragedies to have survived complete. Erasmus expressed doubts as to Seneca's authorship of the plays in his 1529 edition of Seneca's works, hence his non-specific reference here. This quotation is however not from Seneca's tragedies but from his verse translation of part of the Stoic philosopher Cleanthes' well-known *Hymn to Zeus*, to be found at Seneca's *Letters* 107.11. See Tilley F 82 Fate leads the willing but drives the stubborn.

91 Vati non conviciandum
Do not revile a prophet

In the same play, when Tiresias becomes impassioned in the manner of prophets and attacks the king rather too boldly, Creon replies, Οὐ βούλομαι τὸν μάντιν ἀντειπεῖν κακῶς 'I will not return evil words for evil to a prophet.'[1] Horace's words, 'Bards are an irascible tribe,' do not apply to poets only but even more so to people with prophetic powers.[2] You have to wheedle to get anything out of them, and if you offend them, their prophecy is entirely bad. We can use this phrase when somebody assails us with uncontrolled abuse, being in the grip of a sort of madness, and when we are unwilling, out of respect for his position, to return insult for insult, though there is much that we might say by way of reply; or when we permit anger, as a kind of derangement, to say what it will. It is as much use to enter into a contest of insults with a man in the grip of anger as with a madman. This is very like a saying I recorded earlier, 'Hands off the holy man.'[3] Also, 'Were you not my father,' which occurs in this same play, addressed to Creon by Haemon.[4]

92 Vatum genus avarum
Prophets are a greedy tribe

In the same scene, Creon says to Tiresias, Τὸ μαντικὸν γὰρ πᾶν φιλάργυρον γένος 'Prophets as a tribe are money-lovers, each and every one.'[1] In the past, augurs and soothsayers had this bad reputation, and I wish that when the same accusation is levelled against those who handle the things of God today, the charge were not deserved.[2] No one who takes gifts and is thereby induced to say what people want to hear can be relied on to speak the truth at all times.

*****

91 Sophocles (see n1). Added in *1533*
1 Sophocles *Antigone* 1053
2 Horace *Epistles* 2.2.102, quoted at *Adagia* v i 75 (584 above). The Latin word *vates* used here means both 'prophet' and 'bard.'
3 *Adagia* II ix 61
4 Sophocles *Antigone* 755. The line continues, 'I would have said you are not in your right mind.' See *Adagia* II vii 16.

92 Sophocles (see n1). Added in *1533*
1 Sophocles *Antigone* 1055
2 Cf *Adagia* IV viii 48 Like carriers of mortar (386 above).

93 Non movenda loqui
To speak what should be left undisturbed

In the same passage of the play, Tiresias is provoked into threatening Creon with the following words: Ὄρσεις μὲ τἀκίνητα διὰ φρενῶν φράσαι 'You will make me utter what lies quiescent in my thoughts.'[1] We can use this phrase when the outrageous behaviour of an opponent drives us to say something about which we had decided to keep silent. Creon had angered Tiresias with the insult 'A skilful prophet you may be, but you love unjust accusation.'[2] This in its turn can be used of a man who is shrewd or learned, but unprincipled. Related is the saying 'You move what should not be moved.'[3]

94 Mortuos rursus occidere
To slay the dead again

Again in *Antigone*, the following words are given to Tiresias as he tries to persuade Creon to let Polynices' body be buried:

> Make concession to the dead. Do not stab
> A man who is no more. What prowess is it
> Τὸν θανόντ᾽ ἐπικτανεῖν 'To slay the dead again?'[1]

This is like a saying I discussed earlier, 'To cut a dead man's throat.'[2]

95 Deo nemo potest nocere
No one can injure God

It is a pious sentiment to say, Θεοὺς μιαίνειν οὔτις ἀνθρώπων σθένει 'No mortal man has power to violate (or pollute) the gods,' but when Creon

* * * * *

93 Sophocles (see n1). Added in *1533*
  1 Sophocles *Antigone* 1060
  2 Sophocles *Antigone* 1059
  3 *Adagia* I vi 61

94 Sophocles (see n1). Added in *1533*
  1 Sophocles *Antigone* 1029–30
  2 *Adagia* I ii 54

95 Sophocles (see n1). Added in *1533*

utters these words he is being impious.[1] The ancients believed that offence was given to the gods of the underworld if a dead person were denied burial, and to Jove, the protector of suppliants, if a suppliant's plea were rejected. Creon thought that nothing of this sort was of any concern to the gods, because no mortal could injure them. Some people think it improper for God to lie concealed in the Virgin's womb and to come into the world from a woman's belly, just like the rest of mankind. Others think the Body of the Lord is polluted because it goes down into the foul human stomach. To all these one can intone in reply, 'No mortal man can the gods pollute.' The sun is not polluted, though its beams fall on sewers and swamps.

96 Auscultandum bene loquenti
Listen to a man who says what is sound

Tiresias, in the same speech addressed to Creon, says:

> I mean you well, and speak to bring you good.
> Pleasant it is to learn, when he who speaks
> Wishes well and says what will bring advantage.[1]

Haemon had said the same thing earlier in the play: 'Right and proper it is to listen to good advice.'[2] This agrees with 'Listen to a man who speaks from the heart,'[3] and also with that line from Hesiod, which expresses approval of the man who follows good advice.[4]

97 Fortunae novacula
On the razor's edge of fate

The same Tiresias addresses Creon, warning him to take thought in the

* * * * *

1 Sophocles *Antigone* 1044

96 Sophocles (see n1). Added in 1533
  1 Sophocles *Antigone* 1031–2: Εὖ σοι φρονήσας εὖ λέγω· τὸ μανθάνειν / δ᾽ ἥδιστον εὖ λέγοντος, εἰ κέρδος λέγει.
  2 Sophocles *Antigone* 723
  3 *Adagia* I x 46
  4 Hesiod *Works and Days* 295, quoted in *Adagia* II v 52

97 Sophocles (see n1). Added in 1533

crucial situation in which he finds himself: 'Think, now that once again / You tread Ἐπὶ ξυροῦ τύχης "Upon the razor's edge of fate."'[1] On the heels of the calamity brought upon the community by the quarrel of Eteocles and Polynices has come this one, engendered by Cleon's offence against heaven. I have already quoted this line in the course of discussing the proverb 'On the razor's edge.'[2]

98 Exemplum utile
A useful example

Creon threatens his son Haemon, when he remonstrates with him too freely: 'Senseless yourself, you shall as you repent / Teach others to have sense.'[1] When wrongdoers pay the penalty for their folly, though they themselves are not bettered by it, they are nonetheless a warning to others not to fall into similar disaster through thoughtless action.

99 Pervicacia stultitiae dat poenas
Stubbornness pays the penalty that its folly deserves

In the same tragedy, Tiresias warns Creon not to hold to his own view of things with rigid obstinacy, and says, Αὐθαδία τοι σκαιότητ᾽ ὀφλισκάνει 'The stubborn mind pays the penalty of its mindlessness.'[1] That kind of intractable ferocity is usually the prelude to some great disaster, as it says in the Hebrew Book of Proverbs: 'Pride goes before destruction, and a haughty spirit before a fall.'[2] Haemon put forward the same view as Tiresias earlier in the play, tellingly expressing it through metaphors taken from trees and sailors:

> You see how trees that grow beside the streams
> Which winter rains have to torrents turned,

* * * * *

1 Sophocles *Antigone* 996
2 *Adagia* i i 18

98 Sophocles (see n1). A better form of the adage would, from the context, be 'Punishment is a useful example.' Added in *1533*
1 Sophocles *Antigone* 754

99 Sophocles (see n1). Added in *1533*
1 Sophocles *Antigone* 1028
2 Prov 16:18

If they yield, their branches keep intact.
Those that resist are torn out root and branch.
Likewise, the master of the ship, holding
The sheets too tight, his boat capsizes,
And on his journey goes, clinging to upturned benches.[3]

100 Navigationis socius
A fellow-sailor

I have already recorded 'To be in the same boat,' said of those who share a common danger.[1] Ismene has the same idea in mind when she says she is quite prepared to share the same danger as her sister Antigone: 'In this your misfortune, I am not ashamed / Ξύμπλουν ἐμαυτὴν τοῦ πάθους ποιουμένη "To board your boat and share your suffering."'[2]

1 Nuncio nihil imputandum
Don't blame the messenger

Human beings are so constituted that they round on someone who brings bad news as fiercely as if he were responsible for it. When Creon rails at the messenger for bringing unwelcome tidings, he replies, 'He who has done the deed wounds your soul; I trouble only your ears.'[1] He also says, 'No one ever loves the bearer of bad tidings.'[2] This saying can be used in a situation where it is necessary to reprimand someone for committing a fault, so that the guilty person then vents his anger on himself rather than on the one who applies the necessary rebuke. The rebuke is unwelcome at the time, but a guilty conscience pricks for ever.

* * * * *

3 Sophocles *Antigone* 712–17

100 Sophocles (see n2). Added in *1533*
  1 *Adagia* II i 10
  2 Sophocles *Antigone* 540–1

1 Sophocles (see n2). Added in *1533*
  1 Sophocles *Antigone* 319
  2 Sophocles *Antigone* 277: Στέργει γὰρ οὐδεὶς ἄγγελον κακῶν ἐπῶν.

2 **Quod fieri non potest nec incipiendum quidem est**
Do not even begin what cannot be achieved

I have already listed Ἀδύνατα θηρᾷς 'You pursue the impossible.'[1] Sophocles expressed the same idea in different words in *Antigone*:

> It is not right even to start upon a hopeless quest.[2]

Here Ismeme is trying to deter Antigone from burying Polynices in defiance of the king's order.

3 **Cor calidum in re frigida**
A hot heart in a cold task

The same Ismene, when trying to persuade Antigone to abandon her bold plan, says, 'Hot is the heart you bring to this cold task.'[1] I have already noted that 'a hot deed' is one that is bold and precipitate.[2] By 'cold' here she means 'unlikely to be carried through.'

4 **Frustra niti dementiae est**
Folly it is to strive to no good purpose

Again in the same play, Ismene says, 'There is no sense at all in doing what is needless.'[1] It is folly not only to do what is not right, but also to do what is not necessary. Sometimes there is something to be gained from the unjust deed, but never from the unnecessary.

* * * * *

2 Sophocles (see n2). Added in *1533*
1 *Adagia* i x 7
2 Sophocles *Antigone* 92: Ἀρχὴν δὲ θηρᾶν οὐ πρέπει τἀμήχανα.

3 Sophocles (see n1). Added in *1533*
1 Sophocles *Antigone* 88: Θερμὴν ἐπὶ ψυχροῖσι καρδίαν ἔχεις.
2 *Adagia* ii v 50, including this line

4 Sophocles (see n1). Added in *1533*
1 Sophocles *Antigone* 67–8: Τὸ δὲ / Περισσὰ πράσσειν οὐκ ἔχει νοῦν οὐδένα.

5 Principi obtemperandum in omnibus
The prince must be obeyed in all things

The following words of Creon in the same tragedy have a proverbial ring:
'Of that one man, whosoe'er he be, / Chosen by the city as its ruler, / Every
command must be obeyed, / Small things, just things, and their opposites.'[1]
But these are the words of a tyrant, not a prince, for he who commands
injustice is no prince.

6 Civitas non civitas
A city and no city

When Creon begins to speak and act like a tyrant, Haemon stings him with
the following words: 'What one man owns can never be a city.'[1] Creon
had just said that he and no other had the right to rule the land. Haemon
replies that there cannot be a city where the supreme power is in the hands
of a single individual. The Greek word for city, *polis*, comes either from a
Greek word meaning 'to go about in,' or from one meaning 'many.'[2] The
Latin term is *respublica* 'republic.'[3] It is not a republic where everything
proceeds and is done according to the decision of one individual. So when
Creon replies that the city belongs to him that rules it, Haemon retorts,
'Yes, if you rule alone an empty land.'[4] The proper function of a king is
to command free men and not attempt anything without the consent of the
citizens.

* * * * *

5 Sophocles (see n1). Added in *1533*
1 Sophocles *Antigone* 666–7: Ἀλλ᾽ ὃν πόλις στήσειε, τοῦδε χρὴ κλύειν / Καὶ σμικρὰ
καὶ δίκαια καὶ τἀναντία, already used in *Adagia* II vii 89, with a different Latin
version, apparently based on a different Greek text

6 Sophocles (see n1). For 'a city and no city' see CWE 31 23 *Introduction* xiii, On
proverbial metaphors. Added in *1533*
1 Sophocles *Antigone* 736–7. Line 737 (Πόλις γὰρ οὐκ ἔσθ᾽, ἥτις ἀνδρός ἐσθ᾽ ἑνός)
was used in *Adagia* I vii 94.
2 The suggested etymologies are taken from *Etymologicum Magnum* 680.5–8,
based on the Greek words πέλω and πολλοί, ie 'many people go about the
city,' or 'consisting of many people.'
3 The English word 'republic' has lost the meaning of the Latin word, 'that
which concerns everyone,' as opposed to 'private affairs.'
4 Sophocles *Antigone* 739

7 Mens caeli terraeque regina
Mind, queen of heaven and earth

In the *Philebus* Plato represents Socrates as saying 'All philosophers agree, and in so doing they enhance their own standing, that "The mind is the queen of heaven and earth."'[1] His view is that everything is directed by wisdom rather than pleasure. After Philebus had argued that happiness depends on a combination of wisdom and pleasure, the discussion then moved on to the question of which of the two was of more significance for the attainment of the happy life. Plato's remark that everyone agreed on this hints at its being a common saying. Sophocles' character Haemon expresses a comparable idea: 'Father, it is the gods that grant men wisdom, / The noblest thing of all that they possess.'[2]

8 Primas iactare hastas
Throw the first spears

In book two of his work the *Making of an Orator*, Cicero uses the phrase 'To throw the first spears' in the sense of 'to start the preliminary skirmishing.' He applies this to the orator, whose opening words should be low-key and unimpassioned, so that his speech is able to take fire as it goes along. In this passage he censures the orator Philippus for being in the habit of rising to speak without knowing what was the first word he was going to utter. Philippus used to say that he didn't start fighting until he had got his arm warmed up, but, as Cicero comments, Philippus did not notice that the very gladiators from whom he took his simile did indeed throw those self-same 'first spears,' even if they did so without exerting a lot of force at this point, their aim being to display graceful movement while saving their strength for later.[1] This becomes proverb-like if it is transferred to the opening section of a discussion or dispute. One can express the same idea with the simple word 'to skirmish.'

* * * * *

7 Plato and Sophocles (see nn1–2). Added in 1533
1 Plato *Philebus* 28c: Νοῦς ἐστι βασιλεὺς ἡμῖν οὐρανοῦ καὶ γῆς.
2 Sophocles *Antigone* 683–4

8 In *Adagia* v ii 8–24, Erasmus draws mainly on Cicero's rhetorical works, especially *De oratore*. He returns to them for v ii 37–46. Otto 795n. Added in 1533
1 Cicero *De oratore* 2.78.316

9 Omissis fontibus consectari rivulos
Ignore the fountain-head and follow along the stream

In the same book, Cicero uses another proverbial expression when he says, 'Follow along the stream,' meaning to ignore the essential point and say things not particularly relevant.[1] Jerome seems to have been very fond of using 'streams' in this metaphorical way.[2] Cicero says, 'It is the sign of thick-wittedness to follow along the stream and not see its source. But by this time persons of our maturity and experience will fetch what we want from the fountain-head and see whence flows this material.'

10 Res palaestrae et olei
A thing of oil and the wrestling-school

Activities which have no serious purpose but are intended only for relaxation and display are said to be 'Things of oil and the wrestling-school.' The contenders in the wrestling-school strove unarmed but oiled. The oil made it more difficult to grip an opponent and easier to escape from his hold; also it made the body shine, as they wrestled naked. In the *Making of an Orator*, book one, Cicero writes, 'They use glossy, luxuriant words which belong more to oil and the wrestling-school than to the hurly-burly of politics and the lawcourts.'[1] Some oratorical schools practise this kind of well-worn sophistic oratory, which teaches a man how to triumph in an artificial, show-piece debate, but makes him useless for genuine law-suits. So one of the characters in this same book is quite right to say that speaking needs to be brought out of the domestic, sheltered training-ground into the middle of the action, into the dust and shouting, the camp, the battle-line of the courts.[2] Likewise, in book two, where he is speaking of Isocrates' stu-

* * * * *

9 Cicero (see n1). Added in *1533*

1 Cicero *De oratore* 2.27.117, used again at *Adagia* v ii 37 (622 below). Cicero is actually talking about the invention of proofs by rote on the part of the student orator.

2 As at Jerome *Letters* 27.3 and 28.5 (CSEL 54 224 and 229); *Commentarius in Zachariam prophetam* 2.8 (CCSL 71A 820)

10 Cicero (see n1). Added in *1533*

1 Cicero *De oratore* 1.18.81

2 Cicero *De oratore* 1.34.157

dents: 'Some of them had ambitions to excel in display, others in battle.'[3] A passage in book one of *On the Laws* deals with the same subject: 'Antipater was contemporary with Fannius. He blew a bit harder and displayed some strength. This may have been rough and unpolished, without any sign of gloss or the exercise-ground, but he was able to show the others that they should take more care with their writing.'[4] Here Cicero uses 'gloss' instead of 'oil' as above. In the work on famous orators, he uses 'glossier' in the sense of 'more brilliant': 'By now a glossier and showier style of speaking had come in.'[5] Again, in the *Orator*, a work he addressed to Brutus: 'Rhythm was not yet out in the open and had no necessary relationship or connection with prose. So it was only later, once it had been observed and recognized, that it brought to prose style the finishing touch, something of the wrestling-school.'[6] By 'wrestling-school' here he means a certain attractiveness of movement, introduced purely to give pleasure. In this last passage there is another proverbial expression, *extrema lineamenta* 'the finishing touch,' a metaphor derived from painting.[7]

11 Operarii
Hired labourers

In the same book, Cicero is employing a proverbial turn of phrase when he applies the words 'Hired labourers' to people who plead cases without any knowledge of philosophy. An architect says how a building is to be constructed, using his expert knowledge; the day-labourers do not use their own judgment, but merely apply their labour where they are directed. Someone with philosophical expertise is equipped to speak properly on any topic out of his inner resources. Cicero says, with reference to Mnesarchus, 'The men whom we call orators he said were nothing but a kind of hired labourer, with quick and practised tongues. No one could be an orator unless he were a philosopher.'[1] Again in *Brutus*: 'I am not so concerned about

* * * * *

3 Cicero *De oratore* 2.22.94
4 Cicero *De legibus* 1.2.6
5 Cicero *Brutus* 20.78
6 Cicero *Orator* 56.186
7 For 'the finishing touch' see *Adagia* I ii 32–5.

11 Cicero (see nn1–2). Added in 1533
1 Cicero *De oratore* 1.18.83

your collecting together all these "hired labourers." I imagine some people would gladly be dead in order to qualify for inclusion in your list of orators.'[2] In the book *On Famous Orators* he says this kind of orator mostly 'has the power of human speech': 'We don't want to leave out anyone with the power of human speech, so let's include Gaius Cosconius Calidianus.'[3] This word 'labourer' could be used of preachers who are not sufficiently expert in the Scriptures and so learn up something out of books of extracts, which they can then thunder at the people with much waving of arms; or those who boom out in choir what they don't understand. Not preachers, but hired labourers; not choristers, but hired labourers.

12 E schola cantorum
A sing-song from the schools

As I recorded earlier, Plautus calls 'stage-nonsense' the things always being trotted out in comedy.[1] Cicero calls 'A sing-song from the schools' a piece of declamation suited to students, more a demonstration of technique than an expression of sensible content. The phrase comes in a passage from the book quoted above: 'You must oblige our young friends, Crassus. They don't want a piece of stock fluency from some Greek or other, no sing-song from the schools. They want something from the wisest and most eloquent of men, and what's more, one shown to be supreme in counsel and eloquence, not in minor literary productions, but in causes of the greatest import, right here in this very seat of empire and glory.'[2] The phrase can be applied to those who have never made the acquaintance of good authors, never drawn solid learning from the fountain-head, but simply keep to the old themes chanted over and again in the schools. Examples are: 'I would not believe the Gospel, if the authority of the Church did not compel me'; 'No offering is acceptable to the Holy Spirit if what is needful is omitted'; 'The Lord Jesus did many other things which have not been written down'; 'No forgiveness of the sin without restitution of the thing.'

* * * * *

2 Cicero *Brutus* 86.297
3 That is, Cicero *Brutus* 69.242

12 Brassicanus no 41 (*Cantilena ex scholis*), quoting Cicero (see n2); see *Adagia* IV iii 86 n2 (52 above). Cf Otto 338. Added in *1533*
1 *Adagia* IV ix 90 (478 above)
2 Cicero *De oratore* 1.23.105

13 A deo ficti
Fashioned by heaven

Of those who seem especially fitted by nature for something in particular, we say, using a proverbial expression, that they are born, made, fashioned, for whatever it is. In the same book Cicero used a neat expression for such remarkable natural ability: 'There are others who are so well fitted in all these points, so well supplied with natural gifts, that they seem to be not just born but fashioned by some divinity.'[1] There is an allusion here to Pandora, who was fashioned by Vulcan, with all the other gods each conferring on her his or her own gift.[2]

14 E circulo
Out of a group in the street

'A fellow out of the gutter' – so we speak of a low-class contemptible person. Cicero has a phrase, 'Out of a group in the street.' This 'group in the street' is a gathering of men chatting together in the town centre or in the squares. Crassus, in the book I have just cited, says, 'I have poured out before you all my thoughts on the subject. If you had picked any ordinary family man out of a group in the street, possibly he would have given the same answer to your question.'[1]

15 Causa cadere, formula cadere. Ex iure manu consertum.
To lose one's action, to lose one's case on a fault in the formula. To lay on hands according to law.

In the old Jurisconsults, a person against whom a suit was brought was

* * * * *

13 Cicero (see n1). Added in *1533*
 1 Cicero *De oratore* 1.25.115
 2 The myth about Pandora is told at *Adagia* I i 31.

14 Cicero (see n1). Added in *1533*
 1 Cicero *De oratore* 1.34.159

15 Cicero (see nn3–5) and Justinian (nn7–8). In the phrase *ex iure manu consertum* here, and in all the illustrative texts as cited by Erasmus in the adage, the reading is *manu*. Modern texts read *manum*, but *manum* and *manu* alternate in the manuscripts. The meaning is the same. Added in *1533*

said to be summoned *Ex iure manum consertum* 'To lay on hands according to the law.' Also, a person who lost the right of raising an action by
raising it wrongly was said *Causa cadere* 'To fall from the case,' that is,
to lose the action. Either of these phrases can be treated as proverbial if
used metaphorically; for example, 'The theologians never stop summoning
Lorenzo Valla "to lay on hands according to law," because, although a literary man, he has seized on theological territory.'[1] Both phrases are put into
the mouth of Scaevola in Cicero's book, the *Making of an Orator*: 'As for
the assumption you made at the end of your discourse, apparently assuming yourself to be within your rights so to do, namely, that the orator can
deal more than adequately with any topic whatsoever under discussion, if
we were not in your own kingdom,[2] I would not have let it pass. I would
be putting myself at the head of a whole company of people prepared to
dispute with you by interdict, or summon you "To lay on hands according
to the law."'[3] And then a little further on: 'When Hypsaeus was going on
at great length and at the top of his voice, trying to get the praetor, Marcus Crassus, to rule that the person he was defending should be allowed
causa cadere "to withdraw from the action," and Gnaeus Octavius, a man
of consular rank, was, in a speech equally long, objecting to the opposing
party *causa cadere* "so withdrawing ..."'[4] Cicero again, in the speech in defence of Lucius Murena: 'If you think it reflects badly on you, if a person
to whom you have given legal advice and whom you later oppose in court
should then *causa cadere* "lose his action" ...'[5] Quintilian is thinking of this
in book seven, chapter four. The ancients stuck religiously to the procedure
by which anyone who made even a verbal error in raising an action auto-
matically 'lost his action.'[6] There are considerable traces of this blind sticking to the rules in England, where sometimes a whole legal document is

* * * * *

1 The famous humanist Lorenzo Valla (1407–57) was much admired by Erasmus
  for his notable work on Classical Latinity and on the text of the Vulgate New
  Testament. He also wrote controversially on law, philosophy, and theology,
  thus 'invading others' territory.' See CEBR 3:372–3.
2 *Adagia* I vii 48
3 Ie Cicero *De oratore* 1.10.41. Scaevola was a distinguished orator and jurist.
4 Cicero *De oratore* 1.36.166. The praetor is urban praetor, a senior Roman magistrate who exercised jurisdiction over all civil claims.
5 Cicero *Pro L. Murena* 4.9
6 Quintilian 7.3.17 (not chapter 4). Erasmus does not quote, but paraphrases
  Quintilian's words.

rejected because a name is written with a mistake in a single letter. Justinian in book four of the *Institutes*, title 'On actions,' section beginning 'If anyone':

> If a plaintiff included in his statement of claim more than appertained to him, *causa cadebat* 'he lost his action,' meaning that he lost the cause of action and was only with difficulty restored to his original status, unless he was under twenty-five years of age ...

In the next paragraph, he demonstrates four aspects of this 'overclaim': thing, time, place, cause; 'thing,' if twenty gold pieces are claimed instead of ten; 'time,' if the demand is made before the date specified or before stated conditions are fulfilled; 'place,' if payment is demanded in Rome when it was promised in Ephesus; 'cause,' if a person promised to hand over either Stichus or twenty gold pieces, and there is a straight demand for Stichus when the promissor or debtor-party has the right of election.[7]

The phrases *rem amittere* 'lose the cause of action,' *litem perdere* 'lose the case,' *formula cadere* 'lose the case on a fault in the formula' seem to mean much the same thing as *causa cadere*. See Justinian in book four, title 'On defences' in the paragraph beginning 'Defences are styled': 'When they rashly brought the issue into litigation and thereby destroyed it, whereby *rem amittebant* "they lost the cause of action ..."'[8]

Horace in *Satires*:

> As it so happened, it was already time for him
> To answer a summons to the court:
> If he did not himself present, *perdere litem* 'his case was lost.'[9]

Quintilian, in chapter eight of book three: 'I am well aware that there are many changes to the basis of action in all those cases where someone is said "to lose on a fault in the formula." The questions asked are whether this person is entitled to bring the case, to bring it against this person, to do so under the provisions of this law, in this court, at this time.'[10] In

* * * * *

7 Justinian *Institutes* 4.6.33. For this and the next reference, see *Adagia* IV ix 1n (419 above).
8 Justinian *Institutes* 4.13.10
9 Horace *Satires* 1.9.36–7, used in *Adagia* I viii 18 and IV ix 65 (462 above)
10 Quintilian 3.6.69 (not chapter 8)

the forty-ninth letter of the sixth book, Seneca is speaking of philosophers who make a parade of their erudition by employing verbal trickery. 'What is your object,' he says, 'when you deliberately lead the person you are interrogating to make contradictory statements, if not to make it appear that he has *formula cecidisse* "lost his case on a fault in the formula"? But just as the praetor "restores" the man in a law-suit "to his original status," so does philosophy restore these.'[11]

This very phrase *in integrum restituere* 'to restore to the original status,' meaning 'to start afresh,' can be considered as a saying if it is transferred from its legal use and applied metaphorically to other things. Likewise, *causa cadere* 'to lose his case' can be used metaphorically of a man who has lost the right to censure his son because he has more or less provoked him into a dissolute way of life either by his own example or by giving him too much money.

The formula 'lay on hands according to the law' actually comes from the Twelve Tables, according to Aulus Gellius in book twenty of the *Attic Nights*, chapter nine. In ancient times, those who were in dispute about a field or some such thing used to go out to the actual site and, in the presence of the praetor, by way of claiming ownership, would 'apply hands,' that is, each would seize the other's hand.[12] But when the boundaries of Italy were extended, the praetors were unwilling to go long distances to oversee this procedure, and 'so the practice grew up of the parties to the dispute not "laying on of hands according to the law" in the presence of the praetor, but summoning to a "laying on of hands according to the law," that is, each would summon the other "to lay hands on" the thing in dispute according to the law, and then they would go together to the property in question and bring back some soil, or even a single sod, to the praetor's court in the city, and there lay claim to that sod as if to the whole field.'[13] In book seven of the *Letters to Friends*, Cicero is writing to Trebatius, who was a Jurisconsult. He says, 'I am just afraid that your skills will not be of much use to you. From what I hear, the people there:

* * * * *

11 Seneca *Letters* 48.10 (not 49)

12 A definition influenced by the explanation given by Varro. See n17.

13 Aulus Gellius *Noctes Atticae* 20.10.7–9. Erasmus quotes only the later section *verbatim*, paraphrasing the earlier part. In so doing, he leaves out, after 'the practice grew up,' the necessary words 'by silent consent and contrary to the Twelve Tables.' For the Twelve Tables, see *Adagia* IV x 37 (506 above) and v ii 16 (609 below).

Claim not the thing by law, by laying on of hands,
But by the sword; dominion they desire,
By solid violence they proceed.'[14]

Cicero paints a humorous picture of this kind of procedure for claiming ownership in his speech in defence of Lucius Murena:

They were furious because they were afraid that once it was generally known and understood on what days the courts could sit people would be able to go to law without their assistance. So they thought up some formulae, so that their presence would be necessary on every occasion, though the following procedure would have done very nicely. 'The Sabine farm is mine.' 'No it isn't, it's mine.' Then the judgment. What they preferred was: 'The farm which lies in the territory that is called Sabine' – plenty of words there! So, what next? 'I declare it to be mine according to the law.' And then? 'On that account I summon you there to the laying on of hands according to the law.' The man against whom the claim was being raised was at a loss to know what to say to such a loquacious litigant. So the legal expert crosses over to the other character, like the Latin flute-players[15] on the stage. He then says, 'On that matter on account of which you have summoned me to lay on hands according to the law, on that same account I summon you there in return.'[16]

The phrase is itself metaphorical, derived from warfare, where those who fight at close quarters are said 'to join hand-to-hand,' as Varro tells us in book two of the *Latin Language*.[17]

16 **Herciscere**
To apportion

Certain words have acquired proverbial status by being obsolete or pecu-

* * * * *

14 Cicero *Ad familiares* 7.13.2, citing Ennius *Annales* 271–2 Vahlen (252–3 Skutsch), but Erasmus quotes more than is found in Cicero, presumably supplementing it from the fuller quotation in Aulus Gellius *Noctes Atticae* 20.10 (see n13).
15 See below, *Adagia* v ii 38 Like a Latin flute-player (622 below).
16 Cicero *Pro L. Murena* 11.25–12.26
17 Varro *De lingua Latina* 6.64 (not book 2)

16 *Digest* (see n1). Added in *1533*

liar to a particular profession. For example, the old jurists used a word *Herciscere* 'To apportion an inheritance,' hence an action *herciscundae familiae* 'for apportioning an estate.' The word used here for 'estate,' *familia*, embraces the whole heritable property and heritable chattels. This kind of action finds its origin in the Twelve Tables, from which the following citation is given in the *Codex*: 'If the co-heirs desire to relinquish ownership in common, they shall institute action.'[1] If the phrase is used metaphorically of some other kind of division, it becomes a saying. An example is: 'When Guillaume Budé and Leonardo de Portis were in dispute over which of them first discovered the *as*,[2] Janus Lascaris was appointed arbiter *herciscundae gloriae* "in the apportioning of the glory."'[3] In the present century, quite a few monks have not hesitated to 'apportion' amongst themselves what was previously common property, and that without reference to any legal process.

17 Lapides flere
Make stones weep

A really heart-rending situation is said, in the words of an exaggerated but common turn of speech, to be piteous enough 'To wring tears out of a stone.' In that same work, *On the Making of an Orator*, Cicero writes:

> No, if you were upholding the will, you would make it appear that the validity of every will ever made hung on that particular case; if you were supporting a soldier's claim, your oratory would, as so often, rouse his father from the dead, set him before our eyes, you would embrace the son, commend him

* * * * *

1 Not in *Codex Justinianus* but Gaius, in *Digest* 10.2.1, *Familiae erciscundae*. See *Adagia* IV ix 1n (419 above). The phrase does not actually occur in what has survived of the Twelve Tables (see *Adagia* IV x 37 n2, 506 above).

2 Both Budé (1468–1540) and de Portis (circa 1464–1545) wrote books on ancient coinage, weights and measures. (Budé called his *De asse*, the *as* being an ancient Roman coin. It was one of his major works.) The works were so similar that charges of plagiarism arose. Erasmus subtly fails to give Budé pride of place. See CEBR 1:212–17; 3:115.

3 The phrase 'arbiter in the apportioning' is reminiscent of Cicero *Pro A. Caecina* 7.19.

17 Cicero (see n1). Otto 910. Added in *1533*

to the court with tears, make the very stones, God bless us, weep and wail, so that that old formula, 'As tongue hath uttered,' would seem to come, not from the Twelve Tables which you revere more than a whole library of books, but from some magic incantation.[1]

Our Lord used a similar hyperbole once or twice, when He said to the Pharisees that 'if these were silent, the stones would shout out'; and to the Jews, priding themselves on their ancestry, that 'God is able from these stones to raise up children to Abraham.'[2] Though in the mouth of Christ perhaps no statement is to be seen as a hyperbole, as He can bring about whatever is His will. In Cicero's words, the 'magic incantation' is an allusion to another saying, for anything that stirs us deeply is 'More effective than any spell,' as I recorded earlier.[3]

18 Amentatae hastae
Thonged spears

Cicero uses the term 'Thonged spears' of weapons supplied ready for use in battle. The *amentum* is a thong attached to the spear, into which the thrower inserts his hand. The phrase can be used metaphorically of a saying or form of words supplied by someone else. The passage in question comes from the book I have been citing hitherto: 'But on a point of law where experts disagree, it is not difficult for the orator to find some authority to support whatever side he is supporting. From that authority he will take his "thonged spears," which he will then hurl with all the muscle and force of the orator.'[1] Cicero again, in *Brutus*, speaking of Titus Accius of Pisaurum: 'He spoke for the other side when I was defending Aulus Cluentius. He was a careful and reasonably eloquent speaker, and equipped moreover with the precepts of Hermagoras. Even if these precepts do not supply much in the way of rich ornamentation, they do offer appropriate and ready-made

* * * * *

1 Cicero *De oratore* 1.57.245 (For the Twelve Tables see *Adagia* IV x 37 n2, 506 above.) The words are addressed to the distinguished orator L. Licinius Crassus (see *Adagia* v ii 19–21, 612–14 below).
2 Luke 19:40, Matt 3:9, Luke 3:8
3 *Adagia* IV viii 19 (366 above)

18 Cicero (see nn1–2). Added in *1533*
1 Cicero *De oratore* 1.57.242

arguments for all the different types of law-suits, rather like the thonged spears supplied to skirmishers.'[2] Again in *Topica*, speaking of jurisconsults, he says, 'They lend support and can be consulted, and when scrupulous advocates have recourse to their wisdom, they supply them with weapons.'[3] Quintilian has something on the same subject in book twelve, chapter three: 'Nor am I ignorant of the way we usually do things, or forgetful of those who sit, as it were, by the boxes of weapons and supply those in action; and I am well aware that Greek practice was the same, hence their name *pragmatici* for attorneys, that is, "dealing with the practical side"'[4] So a weapon ready for hurling, devised by another but delivered by you, can well be called 'a thonged spear.' This is like something I wrote about earlier, about a shoe made by one person and worn by another. Just such a weapon and just such a shoe was Lysias' speech, which Socrates certainly judged to be a very nice specimen, but said did not suit himself.[5]

19 **Discum quam philosophum audire malunt**
They would rather hear the discus than a philosopher

People are generally more inclined to frivolous pleasures than to worthwhile pursuits. Cicero put this neatly in the second book of his *Making of an Orator*: 'They would rather hear the discus than a philosopher.' There was an outdoor form of exercise in which a bronze disc was hurled into the air from ground level, being made by strength and skill to land within a certain area. The places where this sport was played, which were called gymnasia, were also used for philosophical lectures. But when the signal for the discus sounded, everyone abandoned the philosopher. Crassus is speaking in the passage in question:

> Gymnasia were invented centuries before the philosophers started jabbering away in them, and even today when philosophers have taken possession of every gymnasium, the audience prefers the sound of the discus to the philoso-

* * * * *

2 Cicero *Brutus* 78.271
3 Cicero *Topica* 17.65
4 Quintilian 12.3.4
5 See *Adagia* IV viii 31 (374–5 above), citing the story of Lysias and Socrates as told in Cicero *De oratore* 1.54.231.

19 Cicero (see n1). Added in *1533*

pher. As soon as the discus clinks, they abandon the philosopher right in the middle of his exposition of serious and important subjects and go and oil themselves for exercise. And so they put frivolous enjoyment before serious benefit, as the philosophers at least judge it.[1]

This can be jokingly transferred to a dish of food, the clink of which many would rather hear than the voice of a philosopher.

20 Conchas legere
Gathering sea-shells

Gathering shells and 'navels' on the sea-shore is a sign of being on holiday. It is usually done by children, but can be taken over by people who are normally busy with other things but allow less serious pursuits to intervene occasionally for the sake of relaxation.[1] The orator Crassus, in book two of Cicero's the *Making of an Orator*, speaking of Laelius and Scipio, says:

> I hesitate to say this of men of such standing, but Scaevola vouches for the story that they used to gather shells and 'navels' at Caieta and by the Lucrine Lake, and indulge in every kind of lightheartedness and prank.[2]

By 'navels,' I think he means either shells or pebbles shaped like a navel or the plant which is called 'Venus' navel' according to Dioscorides.[3] The incredible variety seen in sea-shells shows nature at her most sportive. See Pliny, book nine, chapter thirty-three, where he writes:

> So many different colours, so many different shapes – flat and concave, long and crescent-shaped, circular, semi-circular, humped, smooth, grooved,

* * * * *

1 Cicero *De oratore* 2.5.21

20 The impetus for this came from Brassicanus no 43, which contains the references to Cicero *De oratore* 2 and Valerius Maximus (see nn2 and 6). Erasmus adds a long disquisition on sea-shells from Pliny. For Brassicanus see *Adagia* IV iii 86 n2 (52 above). Added in 1533
1 Cf *Adagia* IV viii 39 Play in order to be serious (381 above).
2 Cicero *De oratore* 2.6.22. For the distinguished Romans Scipio Aemilianus and Gaius Laelius see *Adagia* IV ix 16 n7 (429 above).
3 Dioscorides *De materia medica* 4.92

toothed, striated, the body whorled like a murex, the margins tapering to a point, spreading outwards or folded inwards. Some with little streaks of colour, some fringed, crinkly, with undulations like tubes or combs or semi-circular tiles, or patterned like a net, thin and oblong or square, thick, elongated, wavy, joined with a small hinge or all along one side, open like a cupped hand or curved in like a horn . . .'[4]

In the underground habitation close to Cumae in Italy, popularly believed to have been the Sibyl's cave, though it was most likely the lair of robbers and pirates, visitors can observe the walls covered with all kinds of shells in the manner of a mosaic.[5] Valerius Maximus in book eight chapter eight tells the same story about Scipio and Laelius as Cicero does.[6]

21 Liber non est qui non aliquando nihil agit
A man is not free unless he sometimes does nothing

People entirely at leisure, free from all usual business, were said 'to do nothing.' Cicero, in the same work, makes Crassus say to Scaevola:

> Well then, I said, when will you carry out your public duties? Serve your friends? See to your own affairs? When for that matter will you do nothing? Then I added, 'I don't think a man is free if he can't do nothing sometimes.'

He then goes on to explain what 'doing nothing' means. 'I stick to my opinion, Catulus, and when I come here what I find so delightful is precisely this doing nothing, being totally idle.'[1]

Being idle means not only not doing something specific, but being at leisure. It is a good thing to do nothing sometimes, so that we can do other things properly. I showed earlier that people who waste their time are also said 'to do nothing.'[2]

* * * * *

4 Pliny *Naturalis historia* 9.102–3
5 Erasmus visited the Sibyl's cave in the spring of 1509 when he was in Italy with his pupil Alexander Stuart. See *Adagia* IV viii 14 n13 (363 above).
6 Valerius Maximus 8.8.1

21 Cicero (see n1). Added in 1533. See *Adagia* IV viii 39 Play in order to be serious (381 above).
1 Cicero *De oratore* 2.6.24
2 *Adagia* III vi 66 To achieve nothing

22 In herba luxuries
Rank growth

When crops put on too much growth, country men say they 'grow rank,' and call the unseasonal luxuriance 'rankness.' They deal with it by putting in horses or sheep to graze it down. Virgil: 'He grazes down the excessive growth while the blade is young.'[1] In the book cited above, Cicero writes:

> If our friend Sulpicius would do this, his style would be much more compact. As it is, it displays a certain rankness of growth, which, as farmers say when crops run to leaf, needs to be grazed down, in his case by the exercise of the eraser.[2]

23 Lacinia tenere
Hold by the hem

Those who have only a slight grasp of something are said to 'Hold it by the hem.' The opposite is 'To be gripped by the middle.'[1] Cicero, in book three of the *Making of an Orator*, writes, 'The other type, which is concerned with particular times, places, things, they do grasp, but only by the hem.'[2] Without doubt, Cicero drew this metaphor from popular speech, for we find the same saying today among our own countrymen, when someone is extending a half-hearted invitation.

Related to this is 'To tear the cloak.'[3] In Terence, Mida takes hold of Geta's cloak and jerks him back.[4] Cicero seems to be thinking here of Plautus' line in the *Comedy of Asses*: 'They're both in tears, and she's hanging on to the hem of his cloak.'[5]

* * * * *

22 Virgil and Cicero (see nn1 and 2). Added in *1533*
  1 Virgil *Georgics* 1.112
  2 Cicero *De oratore* 2.23.96

23 See Brassicanus no 56, which has the references to Cicero *De oratore* and Plautus *Asinaria* (see nn2 and 5). For Brassicanus see *Adagia* IV iii 86 n2 (52 above). Otto 1321n. Suringar 103. Added in *1533*
  1 *Adagia* I iv 96
  2 Cicero *De oratore* 3.28.110
  3 *Adagia* I i 99 (meaning 'to invite with urgency')
  4 Terence *Phormio* 863
  5 Plautus *Asinaria* 587

24 Surculum defringere
Break off a twig

In the same passage, Cicero uses a similar type of expression, 'Break off a
twig,' meaning that someone does not have a thorough grasp of a whole
discipline, but merely extracts the snippet that will do for present purposes.
The Jurisconsults often quote some sentence or excerpt from the theologians.
The passage in Cicero runs as follows:

> Thus they say so far, and they use this classification in determining the type of
> case, but in so doing they seem not to be claiming back some lost possession
> by legal process or in court, but staking a claim to it by breaking off a twig
> from the civil law.[1]

25 Mendacium utile
An advantageous lie

In Juvenal's *Satires*, the rich man says, 'Who cares about reputation if the
money's safe?'[1] And Dorio in Terence is not ashamed of his breach of faith
so long as it makes money.[2] More honourable is Orestes' remark in Sophocles' *Electra*: 'No word I deem can evil be that brings advantage.'[3] They had
agreed to pretend that he was dead, and these words show that he thinks
his being thought dead will not hurt the living, but will forward the course
of action on which they had decided. They had come with the intention of
avenging Agamemnon's death, and that they achieved.

* * * * *

24 Taken from Brassicanus no 55 (see *Adagia* IV iii 86 n2, 52 above), quoting Cicero
(see n1). Added in *1533*
1 Cicero *De oratore* 3.28.110. This section immediately precedes that treated
above (v ii 23 n2). Erasmus' text presents several inferior readings.

25 Erasmus now embarks on a series of 12 examples (*Adagia* v ii 25–36) taken
from Sophocles' *Electra* (see n3). Added in *1533*
1 Juvenal 1.48
2 Terence *Phormio* 525–6, quoted in *Adagia* III vii 14 Profit before shame
3 Sophocles *Electra* 61: Δοκῶ μὲν οὐδὲν ῥῆμα σὺν κέρδει κακόν, quoted in *Adagia*
III vii 13 Profit smells good whatever it comes from; it is cited in Athenaeus
3.122C.

26 Equi generosi senectus
A noble horse when old

῞Ιππου γῆρας, A horse's old age. I have already spoken of those who after a
distinguished career are rejected because they have grown old.[1] But Sophocles in the same play testifies to the old age of a noble horse in the following
lines:

> As a noble horse, though now advanced in years,
> When dangers threaten, still his wonted spirit shows
> And pricks his ears, even so do you encourage me
> And stand yourself beside me in the foremost line.[2]

Orestes says these words to his aged tutor whose support and counsel
helped him to kill Clytemnestra and Aegisthus.

27 Cunctatio noxia
Hesitation is fatal

In the same play, Electra says the following about Orestes, who is delaying
his return: 'Always proposing but never doing, / He has destroyed my
present and my absent hopes.'[1] The proverb lies in the use of the figure
'present and absent,' meaning 'all.'

28 In arduis contanter agendum
Go cautiously in difficult enterprises

When Electra complains about her brother, saying, 'He says, but does nothing of what he says,' the Chorus replies, 'He who embarks on a mighty

* * * * *

26 Sophocles (see n2). Added in 1533
 1 *Adagia* II i 32 A horse's old age. See Appendix 3.29.
 2 Sophocles *Electra* 25–8

27 Sophocles (see n1); see the end of the next adage for the heading. Added in
  1533
 1 Sophocles *Electra* 305–6

28 Sophocles (see n1). Added in 1533

deed must needs go cautiously.'¹ This means that one must not make hasty decisions in difficult and dangerous enterprises. To this Electra replies, 'It was not by caution that I saved his life.'² She means that hesitation can be fatal when danger is upon us.

29 **E paucis verbis ingens bonum aut malum**
A few words can be the source of great good or great evil

In the same play Electra says to her sister Chrysothemis:

Oftimes indeed have trivial words
Cast down mortal men or set them up.¹

She means that great mistakes can arise from a few words misunderstood, and also a misapprehension can be rectified from a few words understood aright. I have spoken elsewhere of the serious consequences that can follow on some trivial matter.²

30 **Uni cum duobus non est pugnandum**
One should not take on two

In the same play, Chrysothemis replies to her sister Electra and the Chorus who are both urging her to a particular course of action: 'I will do it. / "It is not reasonable for one against two to strive."'¹ This is related to 'Not even Hercules can take on two.'² And there is also a reference to the idea in Catullus' *Epithalamium*: 'Do not fight against the two.'³

* * * * *

1 Sophocles *Electra* 319–20: Φιλεῖ γὰρ ὀκνεῖν πρᾶγμ᾽ ἀνὴρ πράσσων μέγα.
2 Sophocles *Electra* 321

29 Sophocles (see n1). Added in *1533*
1 Sophocles *Electra* 415–16: Πολλὰ τοι σμικροὶ λόγοι / Ἔσφηλαν ἤδη καὶ κατώρθωσαν βροτούς.
2 *Adagia* III i 18 Words are the lightest of things

30 Sophocles (see n1). Added in *1533*
1 Sophocles *Electra* 466–7: Τὸ γὰρ δίκαιον οὐκ ἔχει λόγον / Δυοῖν ἐρίζειν.
2 *Adagia* I v 39
3 Catullus 62.64

31 Mala malis eveniunt
Evil grows out of evil

When Clytemnestra upbraids her daughter Electra for speaking ill of her
as a murderess who had killed her own husband, she gets this answer:
'From wicked deeds other wicked deeds are learned.'[1] This means that if
the daughter spoke disrespectfully of her mother, she herself was to blame
because she had taught her children to hate their mother by killing her
husband and plotting her son's death. A few lines later, Electra spells it out
more clearly: 'Actions generate the words to suit them.'[2] Everyone knows
Socrates' dictum 'A man should strive to be in reality what he wants to be
thought to be.'[3] Reputation has its roots in action, good from good acts, evil
from evil. A man who is discredited because of his own discreditable acts
has no right to be angry with those who speak ill of him, but only with
himself for supplying people with material to use against him. Nor should
he seek vengeance on his detractors, but rather endeavour by good deeds
to wipe out the evil repute he has earned.[4]

32 Numinis ira inevitabilis
The wrath of God cannot be escaped

In Homer, Jupiter is threatening his wife and says that his hands are 'not
to be resisted,'[1] because they harm whom they will and cannot be harmed
by anyone in return.[2] A similar idea is expressed by Orestes' tutor in the
same play: 'But whensoever a god does harm, / No one, however strong he
be, ever can escape.[3]

* * * * *

31 Sophocles (see n1). Added in 1533
 1 Sophocles *Electra* 621: Αἰσχροῖς γὰρ αἰσχρὰ πράγματ' ἐκδιδάσκεται.
 2 Sophocles *Electra* 625
 3 See *Adagia* IV i 92 Take care to be what you are said to be; Xenophon *Memorabilia*
   2.39; Cicero *De officiis* 2.12.43.
 4 See *Adagia* v i 48 Make up for failings with noble deeds (568 above).

32 Sophocles (see n3). Added in 1533
 1 Homer *Iliad* 1.567
 2 See *Adagia* v i 95 No one can injure God (595 above).
 3 Sophocles *Electra* 696–7: Ὅταν δέ τις θεῶν / Βλάπτῃ, δύναιτ' ἂν οὐδ' ἂν ἰσχύων
   φυγεῖν. See *Adagia* II vi 11.

Men usually find something or other to blame for their calamities, but in reality most of the misfortunes that occur are so beyond expectation that they seem to be visited upon us by the gods. Human foresight is powerless in the face of Heaven's decree.

33 Quo terrarum raperis
Where on earth are you off to?

Those who are not paying attention to the matter in hand are said to be 'away from home.'[1] Those who are far away from the truth are said to be 'in another country.' When her sister tells her that Orestes, who was reported dead, is alive, Electra replies, 'You do not know where on earth your thoughts are rushing you, / Or where in mind you roam.'[2] It is the metaphor that makes this proverbial. In the same way, one can say of someone who does not stick to the point, 'Where's he off to now?'[3] or 'What compass point is he being blown to?' This last is derived from sailing.

34 Bene natis turpe est male vivere
Shame it is for those well-born shamefully to live

Some persons are of the opinion that because they come of noble ancestry, this very fact entitles them to behave disgracefully. In reality, the distinction of the family functions like a torch,[1] with the result that the errors of those of noble birth earn more notoriety than those of humble origins. Electra expresses this sentiment in the following line from the same play: 'Shame it is for those well-born shamefully to live.'[2] But when she speaks of 'living shamefully' here, Electra does not mean doing things that are morally wrong, but living in servitude when one is free born. This agrees with 'When you are not the man you were, why wish to go on living?'[3]

* * * * *

33 Sophocles (see n2). Added in *1533*
 1 See *Adagia* II vii 84 Though present he is far away.
 2 Sophocles *Electra* 922: Οὐκ οἶσθ' ὅποι γῆς οὐδ' ὅποι γνώμης φέρῃ.
 3 Virgil *Eclogues* 3.19, though here it is used literally

34 Sophocles (see n2). Added in *1533*
 1 See Juvenal 8.138–40.
 2 Sophocles *Electra* 989: Ζῆν αἰσχρὸν αἰσχρῶς τοῖς καλῶς πεφυκόσι.
 3 *Adagia* I viii 45

35 Mortui non dolent
The dead have no pain

In the same play, Electra announces that she will seek an end to her sorrows by taking her life. She says, 'I do not see the dead enduring pain.'[1] It is in this belief that Pliny expresses the view that the greatest gift given by the gods to man is that each individual has the power in his own hands of choosing when to quit life.[2] Socrates said something better. He teaches that it is wrong for the soul to desert its post in the body without the express command of God, the commander-in-chief.[3]

36 Omnibus modis nocens
Harming in every way

In the same play, when Orestes asks how Clytemnestra is hurting her, whether by physical violence or other types of harm, Electra replies, 'By violence and by harm and every kind of ill.'[1] This phrase will therefore fit a man who destroys in every possible way, by poison, by violence, words, deeds.

37 A capite arcessere; a fonte ducere
Fetch from the fountain-head; draw from the source

Anything derived from the ultimate authority is said to be 'Fetched from the fountain-head.' In book two of the *Making of an Orator*, Cicero says, 'Persons of our maturity and experience will fetch what we want from the

*　*　*　*　*

35 Sophocles (see n1). Added in 1533
   1 Sophocles *Electra* 1170: Τοὺς γὰρ θανόντας οὐχ ὁρῶ λυπουμένους.
   2 Pliny *Naturalis historia* 2.27
   3 Plato *Phaedo* 62A–C. See also Cicero *De senectute* 20.73, where the same thought is attributed to Pythagoras.

36 Sophocles (see n1). Added in 1533
   1 Sophocles *Electra* 1196: Καὶ χερσὶ καὶ λύμαισι καὶ πᾶσιν κακοῖς.

37 For *Adagia* v ii 37–46 Erasmus returns to Cicero's works, mainly the rhetorical ones, as sources. See v ii 8n (601 above). Cicero (see nn1–4). Added in 1533

fountain-head and see whence flows all this material.'[1] Again, in the first
chapter of book one of *On the Laws*, we have: 'You are leading our enquiry
pretty far back, brother, right to the fountain-head.' And then: 'So do you
want us to trace the origin of justice right back to the source?'[2] He uses
'fountain-head' in the first two instances, 'source' in this last one. Again in
the *Topics*: 'When the argument is based on *genus*, it will not be necessary
to take that right back to the fountain-head.'[3] In the *Tusculan Disputations*,
somewhere or other, he uses 'Fetch from the fountain-head' in the sense of
'take right back to the beginning.'[4]

38 Latini tibicinis more
Like a Latin flute-player

There is a proverb to be found in the words I quoted earlier from Cicero's speech in defence of Lucius Murena. He says there that the legal expert, after instructing the plaintiff, crosses over 'Like a Latin flute-
player' to the defendant, to fit him up with the proper form of words.[1]
It is not all that clear how the simile originated, though it seems a reasonable conjecture that it started with those inhabitants of Latium in distant times who used to put on plays in the villages and towns, employing only one flute-player. The actors used to speak and move in time with
the music, being too inexperienced otherwise to preserve the rhythm of
the verse. After this flute-player had led one actor through his part, he
then had to cross over to the other actor when it was his turn to speak,
and by the notes of the flute guide him likewise through the measures of
the verse, and then go back to the first. These rural characters were incapable of acting out plays or mimes correctly without a flute-player to lead
them.[2] This suggestion is supported by a passage in Cicero's *Orator*, the

* * * * *

1 Cicero *De oratore* 2.27.117, already used in *Adagia* v ii 9 (602 above)
2 Cicero *De legibus* 1.6.18, 20
3 Cicero *Topica* 9.39
4 Cicero *De finibus* 5.6.17 (not the *Tusculan Disputations*)

38 Cicero (see n1). Added in *1533*
1 Cicero *Pro L. Murena* 12.26. See *Adagia* v ii 15 To lose one's action (605 above).
2 See possibly Livy 7.2 and Ovid *Ars Amatoria* 111–12.

work addressed to Brutus, where he is talking about verse so constructed
that it could pass for prose. He says there, 'We have something like this
in Latin poetry too, like the lines from Thyestes: "Whoever can you be,
coming in slow old age ..." Without the support of the flute-player, this
is very like prose.'[3] The earlier quotation is in the adage 'To lose one's
action.'[4]

39 In quadrum redigere
To square up

I quoted Aristotle in an earlier adage to the effect that a man whose spirit
is unalterable is 'A four-square man,' because a square is no different,
whichever side it is viewed from.[1] Anything appropriate and fitting is
said to 'square.' Cicero used the phrase 'to square up' in a metaphorical
way in the *Orator*, when he was speaking of well-arranged, rhythmical
diction:

> Once this periodic style, whether we call it *circumscriptio, comprehensio, contin-*
> *uatio,* or *ambitus*,[2] had come into being, nobody who counted for anything[3]
> composed a speech which was intended purely for enjoyment, away from the
> lawcourts and the confrontations of political life, without 'squaring up' prac-
> tically every sentence and giving it rhythmical shape.[4]

The metaphor is derived from stonemasons. I am well aware that I
have cited this phrase before, but I wanted to treat it more extensively, as
I only touched on it there.[5]

* * * * *

3 Cicero *Orator* 55.184, citing Ennius 348 Vahlen
4 See n1.

39 Cicero (see n4). Added in *1533*
1 *Adagia* IV viii 35 (378 above)
2 These are terms coined by Cicero as possible Latin equivalents of the Greek
  rhetorical technical term περίοδος 'periodic sentence.'
3 See *Adagia* V ii 44 (626 below).
4 Cicero *Orator* 61.208
5 See n1.

40 Ἀπάλαιστοι
Untrained

Clumsy men and clumsy movements devoid of technique Cicero tells us in
the same work were called by the Greeks ἀπάλαιστοι 'unfamiliar with the
palaestra or wrestling-ground.' Those who trained in the wrestling-ground
carried over a certain gracefulness of movement to other activities. As he
says in the *Orator*, the work dedicated to Brutus, 'Not that everything is
contained in philosophy, but it helps, just as physical exercises help the
actor.'¹ Examples are the roles of the Cyclops and Silenus.² What Cicero
says is: 'The style of people who do not give their sentences a rhythmical
closure seems to me like the movements of those whom the Greeks call
ἀπάλαιστοι "unfamiliar with the wrestling-ground."'³ In his book *On the
Best Style of Speaking*, Cicero uses the words 'stroll about like a man with a
disciplined body' for 'proceed with graceful and harmonious movement.'
He says:

> These faults were avoided by practically everyone who counted as an Attic
> speaker or employed the Attic style. But though they may be judged to be
> 'sound and unblemished,'⁴ insofar as this was their aim, this only qualifies
> them for strolling about in the exercise-ground *palaestrice* 'like men with dis-
> ciplined bodies,' not for aiming at an Olympic crown.⁵

The words 'aim at an Olympic crown' are themselves proverbial,
meaning 'aspire to great and solid praise via a hard struggle,' that is, to

* * * * *

40 Brassicanus no 44 (Ἀπάλαιστροι); see *Adagia* IV iii 86 n2 (52 above). Erasmus'
text reads ἀπάλαιστοι 'not thrown in wrestling' rather than ἀπάλαιστροι 'not
trained in the palaestra.' The two words were easily confused, but the second
is the one required by the context and Erasmus clearly understands the word
in that sense. He quotes the text of Cicero *Orator* (see n3) as found in the Basel
1528 edition. This applies also to *sani et sacri* 'sound and unblemished' (see
n4). This phrase appears in more recent texts as *sani et sicci* 'sound and spare.'
1 Cicero *Orator* 4.14
2 Presumably these rôles required athleticism. See *Adagia* v ii 42 (625 below).
3 Cicero *Orator* 68.229
4 On the phrase 'sound and unblemished' see introductory note.
5 Cicero *De optimo genere oratorum* 3.8

be successful in serious and weighty cases. Those who give private lectures under porticos for entertainment are 'taking a stroll in the exercise-ground'; those who conduct important cases in the public eye go out into the heat and dust, and face great danger in the hope of winning great praise.

41 Cadere in cursu
Fall in the race

'Fall in the race.' Cicero used these words to mean to fail to achieve some desired recognition, just as if someone seeking a degree in theology were to die before attaining the dignity of that title. In his book about famous orators, Cicero says, speaking of Galba, 'Our fathers' generation thought highly of him, and favoured him for the sake of his father's memory, but he fell in the race. Manilius' bill caused his downfall, in spite of the fact that he spoke in his own defence, because of the ill-will occasioned by the whole business of supposed conspiracy with Jugurtha.'[1]

We use a related figure when we speak of 'calling someone out of the race,'[2] when we make him abandon something on which he has started and do something else. And people are said to be 'in the race'[3] when they are making supreme efforts to achieve some goal. The metaphor is derived from competitive running and horse-racing.

42 Titius
The 'Titius'

Dancing with loose and sloppy movements was called 'dancing the Titius.' There was a dance of this sort which got its name from a bad orator called Titius. See Cicero, in the work I cited above: 'After these came Sextus Titius, a man with a fluent tongue and a sharp enough mind, but so sloppy and languid in movement that a dance was created called "the Titius." So you must beware of anything in delivery or manner of speaking that people will

* * * * *

41 Cicero (see n1). Added in 1533
  1 Cicero Brutus 33.127; on Jugurtha see Adagia IV viii 29 n3 (373 above).
  2 Cicero Topica 1 1
  3 As at Cicero Ad familiares 10.15.2; Ovid Fasti 6.362

42 Cicero (see n1). Added in 1533

laugh at when it is mimicked.'[1] Quintilian cites this passage from Cicero in book eleven, in the chapter on delivery.[2] Similar phrases are 'dance the Cyclops,' as in Horace: 'He asked him to dance "the Cyclops." '[3] Also, 'dance the cordax like Silenus.'[4]

43 Ut Phidiae signum
Like a statue by Phidias

Things that are universally acclaimed at first sight are said to please 'Like a statue by Phidias.' Some statues are not immediately attractive, but we grow to like them if we look at them closely and often. Cicero, in the same book: 'When Quintus Hortensius was still a very young man, his ability was no sooner seen than approved, like a statue by Phidias. He made his first appearance in the courts in the consulship of Lucius Crassus and Quintus Scaevola, in the presence of these very same consuls, and won the plaudits not only of everyone else present, but of the two consuls also, who knew more about the subject than anyone else. He was nineteen years old at the time.'[1] I imagine Cicero was thinking of the statue of Jove at Olympia, made by the famous Athenian sculptor Phidias, as Pliny tells us in book thirty-four, chapter eight and book thirty-six chapter five.[2]

44 In numerum pervenire
Begin to count for something

Those whom people are beginning to think well of are said to 'Begin to

* * * * *

1 Cicero *Brutus* 62.225
2 Quintilian 11.3.128
3 Horace *Satires* 1.5.63; see also *Epistles* 2.2.125.
4 The cordax was an indecent and vulgar dance employed in Bacchic rites. Silenus was the old, drunken and debauched companion of Bacchus. See Lucian *Saltatio* 22.

43 Cicero (see n1). Added in *1533*
1 Cicero *Brutus* 64.228–9
2 Pliny *Naturalis historia* 34.49; 36.18. On Erasmus' references to chapters in Pliny see *Adagia* IV iii 3 n3 (5–6 above).

44 Cicero (see nn1, 3, 4). Added in *1533*

count for something,' just as those who have already acquired some reputation are said to 'count for something.'[1] Those who are totally disregarded
'count for nothing.'[2] Cicero, in the same book: 'By such activities, though of
very humble birth, he achieved office, influence, and wealth, and in spite of
knowing no theory and having no real ability, he came to count for something in the ranks of pleaders.'[3] A little later, speaking of Gaius Sicinius, he
says: 'By following these rules and coming well-prepared to his cases, as he
was not short of words, he was able by means of these same resources and
the rhetorical theory which he had acquired, to come to count for something
in the ranks of pleaders.'[4]

45 E naevo cognoscere
To know by his birth-mark

'To know someone by his birth-mark' means to judge a person's whole
nature from some small characteristic, just as we say 'To know a lion by
his claws,'[1] and as Protogenes recognized Apelles from the line.[2] Cicero,
in the book about famous orators, writes, 'As you appear to want to know
me not from some birth-mark or cradle-token, but from my whole person, I will include some topics which might seem less essential.'[3] This
second metaphor is derived from the practice of adding cradle-tokens to
infants who are rejected or exposed, by which they can be recognized
later if ever the occasion arises.[4] Or else the parents note some birth-
mark on the body. Bankers often add some such sign to their contract
notes.

* * * * *

1 Cicero *De oratore* 3.9.33
2 Cicero *De oratore* 3.56.213
3 Cicero *Brutus* 69.243
4 Cicero *Brutus* 76.263

45 Cicero (see n3). Added in *1533*
1 *Adagia* I ix 34
2 For the story, see *Adagia* I iv 12 I haven't done a stroke today.
3 Cicero *Brutus* 90.313
4 In a number of ancient plays, the plot is resolved by the recognition of the
  long-lost child, as in Plautus *Cistellaria* and *Rudens*, Terence *Andria*.

46 **Ne pudeat artem**
Declare your occupation without shame

There was once a line of verse in common use: 'Be not ashamed to declare your occupation.' Many people are quite happy to live by some degrading but gainful occupation, but are ashamed to name it. Money-lenders prefer to be called financiers. Cicero cites this verse in the work I have already quoted. He says, 'Either it's that popular verse that says you shouldn't "be ashamed to declare your occupation," which won't let me conceal my pleasure in the subject; or else it's your enthusiasm that has extorted this volume from me . . .'[1]

47 Δωριάζειν
Follow Dorian fashion

Δωριάζειν, Follow Dorian fashion. Said of people who went about with their bodies uncovered in a rather indecent manner. The saying derived from the girls in the Peloponnese who normally wore neither girdle nor tunic, only an outer garment open at both sides through which part of their naked bodies could be seen. In Sparta the girls actually went totally naked on some days.[1] Juvenal complains vehemently about the see-through garments of the Romans.[2]

48 **Aetoli**
Aetolians

Αἰτωλιταί, Sons of Aetolians, a humorous proverbial name for people who were brazen and demanding like the Aetolians. The joke depends on the

* * * * *

46 Cicero (see n1). The 1533 edition of *Adagia* ended with this adage. The remaining miscellaneous five adages were added for the 1536 edition. Otto 168
  1 Cicero *Orator* 43.147

47 The material is taken from the *Suda* Δ 1458. See also the scholiast to Euripides *Hecuba* 934, citing PMG Anacreon fragment 54. Added in *1536*
  1 See Erasmus *Apophthegmata* I 'Sayings of Spartans' Lycurgus 268 (LB IV 126E).
  2 Juvenal 2.66, 76; 11.188

48 Stephanus of Byzantium (see n1). Added in *1536*

name: people who expected *donations* were said to speak *Dorian* fashion, and the *Aetolians* were so called, it seems, 'because αἰτεῖν ὅλον "they demanded the lot."' This is mentioned by Stephanus.[1]

49 Χαρωνῖται
Dead man's men

This was the joke nickname which the population of Rome gave to people who produced a defence for what they had done wrong out of a dead man's papers. It started with Mark Antony. At his funeral oration over Caesar's body, he displayed Caesar's clothes and incited the people against his assassins. He then laid hold of Caesar's papers, containing his enactments, and wrote into them whatever he fancied. He pretended to be doing whatever he did on their authority, awarding magistracies, recalling from exile, releasing from prison. All the people who benefited from this justified themselves by pointing to the dead man's papers, and so people mockingly called them 'Dead man's men,' as Plutarch tells us in his *Life of Mark Antony*.[1] This same nickname can be applied to those who use the same underhand ploy on wills.

50 Oculis ferre, etc.
Carry in one's eyes, etc.

We have the proverbial phrases 'Carry in our eyes' and 'Carry in our bosom,' meaning 'to love and cherish someone dearly.' These are metaphors transferred from mothers, who love their children tenderly and keep their eyes fixed on them to see that no harm befalls them, and carry them about cradled in their arms. Cicero uses both metaphors frequently.[1] There is something similar in book 10 of Plato's *Republic*: ἐπὶ ταῖς κεφαλαῖς περιφέρειν

* * * * *

1 Stephanus of Byzantium sub Αἰτωλία. For Aetolians see also Aristophanes *Knights* 79, and the *Suda* AI 1377, 1379. The word 'Dorian' is here supposed to be connected with δῶρον 'gift.'

49 Plutarch (see n1). Added in *1536*
1 Plutarch *Antony* 15.4. See also Cicero *Philippics* 5.4.11.

50 Cicero (see n1). Otto 1265. Added in *1536*
1 As at Cicero *Ad Quintum fratrem* 3.1.9; 2.11.1; *Ad familiares* 14.4.3

'to carry round on their heads.' 'On account of this wisdom they are so loved that their followers all but carry them round on their heads.'²

51 Iapeto antiquior
Older than Iapetus

Ἰαπέτου ἀρχαιότερος, Older than Iapetus. This is how Jupiter in Lucian addresses Cupid, when Cupid tries to make his youth an excuse: 'So you're a child, are you? You, Eros, older than Iapetus!'¹

* * * * *

2 Plato *Republic* 10.600D, already used in *Adagia* IV vi 98 To carry on our head (with a slightly different Latin version, 278 above)

51 Lucian (see n1). Added in 1536
1 Lucian *Dialogus deorum* 6.1; see also Hesiod *Theogony* 116–36. where Eros, that is, Cupid, is begotten before the Titan Iapetus. The Titans were a generation of gods preceding the Olympians headed by Zeus. Iapetus may be the same in origin as Noah's son Japheth.

WORKS FREQUENTLY CITED

This list provides bibliographical information for works referred to in short-title form in this volume.

Allen	*Opus epistolarum Desiderii Erasmi Roterodami* ed P.S. Allen, H.M. Allen, and H.W. Garrod (Oxford 1906–58) 11 vols and index
Apostolius	See CPG 2
·Appendix	See CPG 1
ASD	*Opera omnia Desiderii Erasmi Roterodami* (Amsterdam 1969–)
Baiter-Sauppe	*Oratores Attici* ed J.G. Baiter and H. Sauppe (Zurich 1839, 1850) 2 vols
Brassicanus	I.A. Brassicanus *Proverbiorum symmicta. Quibus adiecta sunt Pythagorae symbola xviii* (Vienna 1529)
Buecheler	*Petronii Saturae. Adiectae sunt Varronis et Senecae Saturae similesque reliquiae* ed F. Buecheler (Berlin 1963, 8th ed)
Bühler 1	*Zenobii Athoi proverbia. Volumen primum. Prolegomena* ed W. Bühler (Göttingen 1987)
Bühler 4	*Zenobii Athoi proverbia. Volumen quartum (libri secundi 1–40 complexum)* ed W. Bühler (Göttingen 1982)
CCSL	*Corpus Christianorum. Series Latina* (Turnhout 1954–)
CEBR	*Contemporaries of Erasmus. A Biographical Register of the Renaissance and Reformation* ed P.G. Bietenholz and T.B. Deutscher (Toronto 1985–7) 3 vols
Collectanea	Desiderius Erasmus *Adagiorum Collectanea* (Paris 1500). The numbers cited agree with the numeration of adages in the revised edition of 1506/7.
CPG	*Corpus paroemiographorum Graecorum* ed E.L. Leutsch and F.G. Schneidewin. 1: Zenobius. Diogenianus. Plutarchus (= Laurentianus 1). Gregorius Cyprianus cum Appendice proverbiorum (Hildesheim 1961); 2: Diogenianus (Epitome). Gregorius Cyprianus. Macarius. Aesopus. Apostolius et Arsenius. Mantissa proverbiorum (Hildesheim 1961); 3:

Supplementum: Crusius *Analecta*. Jungblut (= Laurentianus 2–5) (Hildesheim 1991)

CRF   *Comicorum Romanorum fragmenta* ed O. Ribbeck (Leipzig 1898, 3rd ed)

CSEL   *Corpus scriptorum ecclesiasticorum Latinorum* (Vienna 1866–)

CWE   *Collected Works of Erasmus* (Toronto 1974–)

DBI   *Dizionario biografico degli Italiani* (Rome 1960–)

Diels-Kranz   *Die Fragmente der Vorsokratiker* ed H. Diels and W. Kranz (Berlin 1951–2) 3 vols

Dindorf   Harpocration *Lexicon in decem oratores Atticos* ed W. Dindorf (Oxford 1853; repr Groningen 1969) 2 vols

Diogenianus   See CPG 1

ERSY   Erasmus of Rotterdam Society Yearbook

Estienne   Henricus Stephanus *Animadversiones in Erasmicas quorundam adagiorum expositiones* in Desiderius Erasmus *Adagiorum Chiliades* (Geneva 1558). Printed as footnotes in LB II

FGrHist   *Die Fragmente der griechischen Historiker* ed F. Jacoby (Berlin/Leiden 1923–) 14 vols

FHG   *Fragmenta historicorum Graecorum* ed C. Müller (Paris 1841–70)

Funaioli   *Grammaticae Romanae fragmenta* ed G. Funaioli (Leipzig 1907)

Gaisford   *Joannis Stobaei Florilegium ad manuscriptorum fidem emendavit et supplevit Thomas Gaisford* (Oxford 1822) 4 vols

Gow   *Theocritus* ed and comm A.S.F. Gow (Cambridge 1965) 2 vols

Harpocration   See Dindorf

Hesychius   *Lexicon*. Two editions are used: ed Kurt Latte (2 vols, Copenhagen 1953 and 1965), incomplete, for entries beginning A–O; ed M. Schmidt (Jena 1863; repr Amsterdam 1965), for entries from Π–Ω.

Jensen	*Hyperidis orationes sex cum ceterarum fragmentis* ed C. Jensen (Leipzig 1917)
Jordan	*Marcus Porcius Cato. Praeter librum de re rustica quae extant* ed H. Jordan (Leipzig 1860)
Kaibel	*Comicorum Graecorum fragmenta* ed G. Kaibel (Berlin 1899)
Kock	*Comicorum Atticorum fragmenta* ed T. Kock (Leipzig 1880–8) 3 vols
Körte-Thierfelder	*Menandri quae supersunt ... Pars II, addenda adiecit Andreas Thierfelder* ed Alfredus Körte (Leipzig 1959)
Krenkel	*Lucilius: Satiren* ed W. Krenkel (Leiden 1970) 2 vols
LB	*Desiderii Erasmi Roterodami opera omnia* ed J. Leclerc (Leiden 1703–6) 10 vols
LSJ	H.G. Liddell, R. Scott, and H.S. Jones *A Greek-English Lexicon* (Oxford 1940)
Macarius	See CPG 2
Malcovati	*Oratorum Romanorum fragmenta liberae rei publicae* ed H. Malcovati (Rome 1955)
Marx	*C. Lucilii carminum reliquiae* ed F. Marx (Leipzig 1904–5) 2 vols
Miscellanea	A. Politianus *Miscellaneorum centuria prima* (Florence 1489)
Nauck	*Tragicorum Graecorum fragmenta* ed A. Nauck (Leipzig 1889, 2nd ed)
NCE	*New Catholic Encyclopaedia* (New York 1967–79)
OCT	Oxford Classical Text
Otto	A. Otto *Die Sprichwörter und sprichwörtlichen Redensarten der Römer* (Leipzig 1890). Cited by proverb number
Otto *Nachträge*	A. Otto *Die Sprichwörter und sprichwörtlichen Redensarten der Römer. Nachträge* ed R. Häussler (Darmstadt 1968)
PCG	*Poetae comici Graeci* ed R. Kassel and C. Austin (Berlin and New York 1983–)

PG	*Patrologiae cursus completus ... series Graeca* ed J.-P. Migne (Paris 1857–86; repr Turnhout) 162 vols
Phillips	Margaret Mann Phillips *The Adages of Erasmus* (Cambridge 1964)
PL	*Patrologiae cursus completus ... series Latina* ed J.-P. Migne (Paris 1844–5, 1862–5; repr Turnhout) 217 vols and 4 vols indexes
PMG	*Poetae melici Graeci* ed D.L. Page (Oxford 1962)
PPF	*Poetarum philosophorum fragmenta* ed H. Diehl (Berlin 1901)
Rose	*Aristotelis qui ferebantur librorum fragmenta* ed V. Rose (Stuttgart 1967)
Spengel	*Rhetores Graeci* ed L. Spengel (Leipzig 1864) 3 vols
Skutsch	Otto Skutsch *The Annals of Quintus Ennius* (Oxford 1985)
Stangl	*Ciceronis orationum scholiastae* ed T. Stangl (Hildesheim 1964)
Suringar	W.H.D. Suringar *Erasmus over Nederlandsche spreekwoorden en spreekswoordlijke uitdrukkingen van zijnen tijd* (Utrecht 1873). Cited by proverb number
SVF	*Stoicorum veterum fragmenta* ed J. von Arnim (Leipzig 1902–23) 3 vols
Tilley	M.P. Tilley *A Dictionary of the Proverbs in England in the Sixteenth and Seventeenth Centuries* (Ann Arbor 1959)
TRF	*Tragicorum Romanorum fragmenta* ed O. Ribbeck (Leipzig 1897, 3rd ed)
TrGF	*Tragicorum Graecorum fragmenta* ed B. Snell, R. Kannicht, and S.L. Radt (Göttingen 1971–85) 4 vols
Vahlen	*Ennianae poesis reliquiae* ed J. Vahlen (Amsterdam 1963, 2nd ed)
Wachsmuth	*Sillographorum Graecorum reliquiae* ed C. Wachsmuth (Leipzig 1885)
Wehrli	Fritz Wehrli *Die Schule des Aristoteles* (Basel 1967–9)

West   *Iambi et elegi Graeci ante Alexandrum cantati* ed M.L. West
                        (Oxford 1998, 2nd ed) 2 vols

Wesseling (2001)   Ari Wesseling 'Additional notes to Erasmus' *Opera omnia*
                        II,8: Adagiorum chilias Quarta (pars altera – necnon
                        Adagiorum pars ultima (Amsterdam, 1997)' *Humanistica
                        Lovaniensia* 50 (2001) 455–8

Wesseling 'Dutch   Ari Wesseling 'Dutch proverbs and ancient sources in
   Proverbs'   Erasmus's *Praise of Folly*' *Renaissance Quarterly* 47 (1994)
                        351–78

Zenobius   *'Collectio proverbiorum Tarrhaei, et Didymi, item eorum, quae
   (Aldus)   apud Sudam aliosque habentur per ordinem literarum'* in
                        Habentur hoc volumine haec, videlicet: Vita et Fabellae Aesopi
                        ... published by Aldus (Venice 1505)

Zenobius   Ζηνοβίου ἐπιτομὴ τῶν Ταρραίου καὶ Διδύμου παροιμιῶν in E.
   (Athous)   Miller, *Mélanges de littérature grecque* (Paris 1839) 341–84
                        (index in Crusius *Analecta*)

TABLE OF ADAGES

This book

was designed by

V A L   C O O K E

based on the series design by

A L L A N   F L E M I N G

and was printed by

University

of Toronto

Press